D1539754

Multiprotocol Network
Design and Troubleshooting

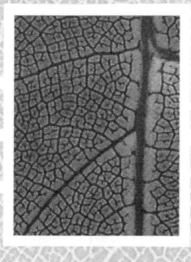

Multiprotocol Network Design and Troubleshooting

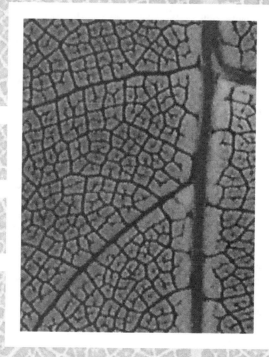

Chris Brenton

San Francisco • Paris • Düsseldorf • Soest

Associate Publisher: Guy Hart-Davis
Acquisitions Manager: Kristine Plachy
Acquisitions & Developmental Editor: Guy Hart-Davis
Editor: Alison Moncrieff
Technical Editor: Joe Prest
Book Designer: Patrick Dintino
Graphic Illustrator: Inbar Berman
Electronic Publishing Specialist: Nathan Johanson
Production Coordinators: Robin Kibby, Alexa Riggs, Anton Reut
Proofreaders: Katherine Cooley, Charles Mathews, Duncan Watson, Eryn L. Osterhaus
Indexer: Ted Laux
Cover Designer: Archer Design
Cover Illustrator/Photographer: The Image Bank

Screen reproductions produced with Collage Complete.
Collage Complete is a trademark of Inner Media Inc.

SYBEX, Network Press, and the Network Press logo are registered trademarks of SYBEX Inc.

TRADEMARKS: SYBEX has attempted throughout this book to distinguish proprietary trademarks from descriptive terms by following the capitalization style used by the manufacturer.

The author and publisher have made their best efforts to prepare this book, and the content is based upon final release software whenever possible. Portions of the manuscript may be based upon pre-release versions supplied by software manufacturer(s). The author and the publisher make no representation or warranties of any kind with regard to the completeness or accuracy of the contents herein and accept no liability of any kind including but not limited to performance, merchantability, fitness for any particular purpose, or any losses or damages of any kind caused or alleged to be caused directly or indirectly from this book.

Copyright ©1997 SYBEX Inc., 1151 Marina Village Parkway, Alameda, CA 94501. World rights reserved. No part of this publication may be stored in a retrieval system, transmitted, or reproduced in any way, including but not limited to photocopy, photograph, magnetic or other record, without the prior agreement and written permission of the publisher.

Library of Congress Card Number: 97-67760
ISBN: 0-7821-2082-2

Manufactured in the United States of America

10 9 8 7 6 5 4 3 2 1

In memory of Andie Zajaceskowski Sr., a jack of all trades.

Acknowledgments

I would like to give an *honest* thank you to all the people at Sybex for pulling this book together. I am particular grateful to Guy Hart-Davis, for having the insight to see what this book could be when I could not even perceive how to best describe it myself, and Alison Moncrieff, who is definitely one of the most patient, understanding, and articulate people I know.

Everyone has influences in their lives. If it where not for mine, I would most certainly be doing something else for a living that I absolutely hate. I would like to thank Darcie Callahan, Kendal Dowd, Al Follen Sr., Gene Garceau, Cheryl "The Evil Queen" Gordon, Sal LaRiccia, Vinnie Mistretta, Anne O'Flaherty, Morgan Stern, and last but certainly not least, Bill Suarez. All these people are wise beyond their years. I would also like to thank Sean Tangney, who has not only been an influence (sometimes good, sometimes bad), but who's help over the last few months made it possible for me to find the time to focus on this book. Thank you, one and all.

I would like to thank my Technical Editor Joe Prest, whose diligent behind the scenes work helped to insure that I was able to sound like I knew what I was talking about. I would also like to thank Deb Tuttle, who helped to insure that other people could actually understand what I was talking about. I would not be half as happy with this book if it where not for the technical input and influences of both of these people. Thanks as well to Tom Kusleika for help with the data collection and Chris Tuttle for the transcription work.

I would also like to thank my parents, Albert and Carolee. It was their love, nurturing, and support that showed me that anything that can be perceived is attainable, you just have to believe in yourself. I could not have picked two better people to grow up around, or learn from.

Finally, I would like to thank my wonderful wife Andrea for supporting me and editing this book even though it made her feel like a "computer widow." Besides being a wife, a companion, and a fellow geek, you are also my best friend. This book is dedicated to you as we are part of the same heart and soul. It would not have been possible without you.

Contents at a Glance

Table of Contents

Introduction

If you go into your local bookstore, you'll find many books that discuss IntranetWare, Windows NT Server, Unix, and Lotus Notes in great detail. Both the NOS manufacturers and third-party organizations (schools and publishers) have created tons of reading material and training classes that focus on setting up and administering each of these systems. But you'll find that these books pay very little attention to how these systems communicate on a shared network. For example, the Novell manuals or Certified Novell Engineer (CNE) training classes will tell you how to get your NetWare or IntranetWare server communicating on the network, and even what protocols are supported. But they do not go into any detail about how efficient each protocol is or the best way to have their server coexist with servers from other vendors while creating the least amount of traffic. Likewise, NT books concentrate on NT and pay scant attention to integrating NT into complex environments. This pattern continues with each of the NOSes covered in this book.

There are also very few single "all-in-one reference" books to aid a LAN administrator with the diversity of chores they may deal with on a daily basis. If you need to know how long your Ethernet segment can be, what command will show you the IP address on your Unix system, how to add a new network card to your NetWare server, and how to check which protocols are running on your NT server, chances are you'll be flipping through three or four different reference manuals.

This is where this book fits in. My goal is to help you reclaim the wild frontier that your network infrastructure has become. Instead of focusing on the NOS your network is running or the applications your end users are using, I'll show you how to assess the impact these applications may have on the overall network and reduce the number of protocols required to provide connectivity.

What This Book Covers

After introducing the multiprotocol environment in Chapter 1, we will look at transmission media in Chapter 2; here we will discuss what options are available when trying to get our data from point A to point B. We'll look at copper and fiber cables, and explore what other alternatives are available when connecting our network. When appropriate, I'll provide specifications for each media to describe their intended applications. I'll give rules for both individual lengths of cables as well as overall network size when segments are connected by a repeater (*repeated segments*).

Then in Chapter 3 we will look at topology, the set of rules for connecting transmission media. The topologies include Ethernet, Fiber Distributed Data Interface (FDDI), and Asynchronous Transfer Mode (ATM). We will look at these and many other local area network (LAN) configurations; I'll also cover wide area network (WAN) communications such as leased line, Integrated Service Digital Network (ISDN), and T1s.

From there, Chapter 4 gets into network hardware. Want to know what a repeater is or how to use VLANs? This is the place to look. I've covered every piece of networking hardware you're likely to need to support. Do you need to know if you should switch or route your network? We also look at some example networks to see when is it more appropriate to use a specific piece of hardware in trying to control network traffic.

Once our foundation is complete, we will look at how protocols communicate in Chapter 5. We'll look at how systems find each other on the network and how they make sure you reach the service you are looking for. A Web browser is capable of accessing Web pages, as well as transferring files via the File Transfer Protocol (FTP). How does the remote system know which of these you're trying to do? How does a firewall work and how does it figure out if it's even okay for my users to be running a Web browser? I'll answer these questions and more during our discussion on protocols.

From here, Chapter 6 gets into the ins and outs of each specific protocol: IP, IPX, AppleTalk, NetBIOS, and NetBEUI. Because these protocols can be found on 99.9% of the networks at large, I'll cover in great detail how each one works. Which protocol can transfer a file faster? Which takes the least number of packets? Which protocols cause problems under what circumstances, and how can you choose the best protocol for your situation? Which protocols are likely to require the greatest amount of resources from each of your desktop systems? I'll focus on providing you with a clear understanding of what the performance implications are when using each protocol.

Once we've covered communications, Chapters 7 through 10 cover each of the popular NOSes: Novell's IntranetWare and NetWare, Microsoft's NT 4.0, Unix, and IBM/Lotus Notes 4.x. While I'll cover the most current version of each operating system, many of the tools and features discussed are available on earlier product versions as well. Lotus Notes is not a true NOS (it simply runs on top of one of the other mentioned NOSes) but it does have a number of unique connectivity issues that you need to know if you're implementing it on your network.

In Chapter 11, we will look at desktop systems and how to get them to communicate with each of our NOSes. Getting a desktop system to communicate efficiently can be difficult at best. We will explore what options are available when tuning a workstation to communicate efficiently. When applicable, we'll also look at what desktop tools are available as we try to optimize multiprotocol communications.

Chapter 12 looks at what connectivity options are available as you try and integrate your systems. There are a number of tricks to perform to cut down on the amount of network and desktop overhead needed when access to multiple services is required. Need to have a Unix system log in to a NetWare server using IPX? Or how about letting desktop systems log into a Unix machine as if it were a NetWare server? Did you know you can also make both of these systems look like NT servers to your desktop systems if you need to? By fooling your clients into thinking a server is actually a different operating system, you can cut down on the number of protocols required when accessing these systems. We'll look at what options are available when server *spoofing* is required and give a few examples of when it may come in handy.

From here, Chapter 13 looks at what tools are available commercially for troubleshooting and documenting our network. Want to be able to measure the length of a cable without crawling into the ceiling with a yardstick? Need to be able to monitor traffic patterns on your network? I'll show you the wide variety of tools available to perform these and other tasks. We'll talk about cable testers and network analyzers in general as well as get into some specific models in order to get a better feel for what benefits they provide.

You say you're on a tight budget? You say your boss would just as soon chew off their right hand as use it to sign a PO for network diagnostic equipment? Cheer up—all is not lost. You may have some tools sitting right under your nose that you're not even aware of. Chapter 14 looks at how to extract information from both your network servers and other hardware in order to document and troubleshoot your network.

Finally, in Chapter 15, we'll go through some real-life troubleshooting problems. These are actual predicaments that can interrupt even a healthy network from time to time. I'll present the problems in mystery format—the way you'll encounter them in your work. I'll show you a situation along with a number of clues so that you can try and deduce the root cause. Later on, I'll give you the answers to these problems, along with the process used in determining the actual cause.

Who Should Read This Book

As we cover each NOS, we will remain focused on how they communicate on the network. This is not a super manual that covers all aspects of each system—it's a book targeted at getting the NOSes communicating effectively over the network. Want to know how a router filters traffic or collects network statistics from a NetWare server? Want to know what a firewall is or mount a remote file system with Unix? This is the place to look. Do you need to know how to set up a user account on each of the previously mentioned systems? If so, then this book may not be what you're looking for. As mentioned earlier, there are many wonderful books that cover the file and application maintenance of each of these systems. I've listed suggested reading for additional information in Appendix A.

This book covers a lot of ground. I've included detailed descriptions for those of you somewhat new to the field as well as charts and points of reference that even the most seasoned of us forget from time to time.

Please feel free to e-mail questions or comments to me at **cbrenton@sover.net**.

Conventions Used in This Book

We have used the following conventions in this book to make it easier for you to follow along:

- Text in **boldface** is either information you key in or the name of a particular command.

- *Italics* call attention to new terms or identify variables.

This is a note. It offers useful information or gives cross-references about the topic at hand.

This is a tip. It gives hints, shortcuts, or bits of advice to help you accomplish your task with ease.

This is a warning. It alerts you to common pitfalls or problems you might encounter as you do your work.

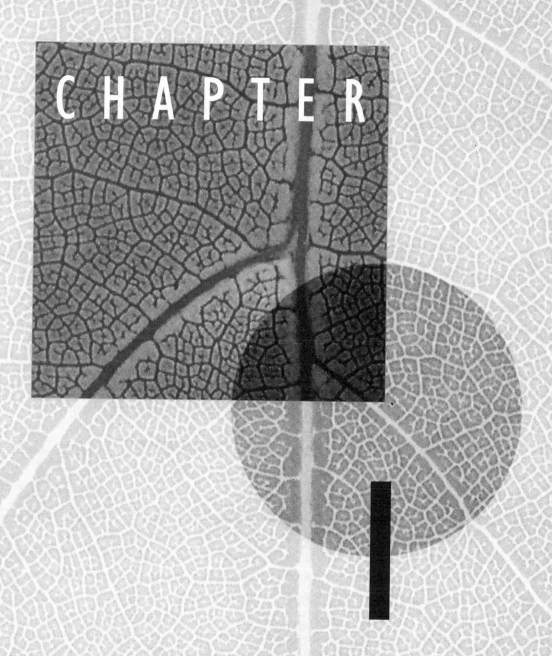

CHAPTER

1

Introduction to Multiprotocol
Networking

Multiprotocol networking. To a network administrator the very phrase is synonymous with gray hair, long work hours, and a diet that consists of caffeine and junk food from vending machines. In most environments, this predicament has not been constructed by design, but rather spawned as networking requirements grow unchecked.

In this chapter, I'll start by discussing how multiprotocol environments typically evolve and what challenges they present to the network administrator. I'll then outline the approach that this book takes to designing, implementing, and troubleshooting multiprotocol environments.

What Is a Multiprotocol Environment?

A protocol is the means by which information is communicated on a network. It is a set of rules that describe the etiquette to be used when one computer must find, greet, and transfer information to another. As an analogy, think of two people getting together for a business meeting. Proper etiquette states that both parties should be punctual, exchange verbal greetings, shake hands, and perhaps exchange some pleasantries prior to discussing the matter at hand. There is an understanding that some specific language (such as English) will be used when conveying all information. It is also expected that when one individual makes a statement, the other provides some form of recognition that the information has been heard and understood.

These rules may be thought of as the protocol of a business meeting, and they provide a similar function to the protocols used on a network. Both ensure that the parties involved are ready to receive data and that all transmissions have been received and interpreted correctly. Internetwork Packet Exchange (IPX), Internet Protocol (IP), Network Basic Input/Out System (NetBIOS), and NetBIOS Extended User Interface (NetBEUI) are the most widely used network protocols. Each defines a different set of rules to be followed when computers must relay information.

A multiprotocol environment is a network that includes a variety of different computer systems that each speak a different language when communicating. Imagine a large corporation that is in the process of establishing field offices in other countries. If each office communicates using only the local language, it will be difficult at best to relay information between offices. Establishing offices in other countries may require employees at the corporate site to learn diverse language skills just to continue doing their jobs.

A similar situation has developed in the networking world. Long ago the keyboards and monitors located on users' desks were referred to as "dumb terminals" because they were exactly that. The user had only the basic tools required (keyboard and monitor) to exchange information with a mainframe system that was required to deal with all computations and data storage. Like our corporation before it tried to establish the field offices, communication was not an issue. This was because the only computer these dumb terminals were required to communicate with was the mainframe itself.

Today's desktop systems have more in common with those old mainframes than they do with their predecessors, the dumb terminals. While both provide interfacing tools, the desktop system includes the mainframe's capacity to compute and store data. Each desktop system is not only required to do its own processing, but it has been thrust into the role of translator as multiprotocol networks have evolved.

As new systems require new protocols to be added to the network, the responsibility of communicating with them usually falls on the user's desktop system. While gateways (devices that translate from one protocol to another) can be used, they are not capable of translating between all protocols. Also, gateways tend to be difficult to configure, and they slow down communications considerably between systems. These days it's not uncommon to find a desktop computer using three or four different protocols in order to provide connectivity to all a corporation's systems. While this configuration will work, it is not always the best option. Running multiple protocols will invariably increase the amount of traffic to be carried by the network, as well as increase administration requirements. It also places a larger load on the desktop system, because each additional protocol requires memory and processor time in order to function. The problem may very well be that the person responsible for the network (usually referred to as a network administrator) may not even realize that there are alternatives to running multiple protocols. The network may be running multiple protocols not by design but because the network administrator lacks the knowledge or time to implement a single-protocol solution.

There may be times when a multiprotocol solution does make sense. For example, if you are dealing with a very small network (five to fifteen nodes) or need to provide the additional connectivity for only a few users, then it may be more appropriate simply to add the second protocol and live with the small amount of additional overhead. The point is that a modern network configuration is flexible. Gone are the days when each unique system will communicate using only one protocol. Network administrators have a number of tools available to help optimize network communications.

Where Do Multiprotocol Networks Come From?

In this section, I'll discuss two examples of how a multiprotocol network can evolve. The first is a simple network that grows insidiously into a multiprotocol monster. The second shows the challenges faced when two dissimilar networks need to be connected.

Step 1: From Simple Beginnings

Usually a multiprotocol network starts out innocently enough as a simple peer-to-peer network. A few users may decide that their lives would be easier if they could access each other's files and printers. They proceed to install network cards in their systems and connect them with some network cable. They buy some simple networking software—or use Windows built-in networking—and the company's first network is born. Each system becomes both a workstation and a server as it continues to allow the user to get their job done, but offers the added benefit of allowing other network users to access the local drives and printer. The company now has a peer-to-peer network.

As the network begins to grow, a number of undesirable situations begin to develop. The first is lost resources. Is the latest budget on Jim's or Lisa's computer? Who has the time card template? On which system are the expense reports? Without a central storage area, employees may become baffled quickly as to where to find certain resources.

Second, if the operating systems being used were not originally designed to offer remote file services (such as DOS or Windows 3.1), users will find that their systems grind to a crawl whenever someone else is accessing their files. There is nothing worse than putting in a late night in order to finish up a report that's due in the morning, only to have your system become as responsive as frozen maple syrup (because someone's running your system's copy of Doom).

Third, administration starts to become a real pain. As more users join "the network club," the existing users may be required to maintain account and file access rights to their own systems. This means that each network user is required to have sufficient time and computer knowledge to maintain appropriate access to their system. (This includes the guy who refuses to give up his typewriter because he thinks computers are just a passing fad.)

Step 2: The Server-Based Network

Problems are compounded as the network continues to grow. Eventually users begin to revolt. The company decides to purchase a dedicated NetWare server. A server will provide a single system for users to store their files and access remote printers. Because the network files are now centralized, revision control becomes much easier. Accessing other users' systems becomes a thing of the past.

Because the NetWare server wants to use the IPX protocol by default, workstations are configured to use this protocol when communicating with the server. The company's server-based network is now up and running.

Step 3: Birth of the Network Administrator

The server-based network creates a new problem. Even though it is only one system, someone has to be responsible for making sure it stays running and that users can log in. If the company is large enough to justify the cost, it may hire a single person to maintain the network and support the end users. If not, the company will assign the task to a person within the organization, and they will maintain the network along with doing their regular duties. Unfortunately, the main selection criterion for this assignment is that the employee be seated close to the new server. Too bad this same person doesn't drive past the bank on the way home—they could have been made chief financial officer instead.

So, we now have a single person responsible for all aspects of the network. These aspects include: creating and removing user accounts; maintaining the health of the server; setting up new PCs; training end users on applications; troubleshooting password, printing, and file-access problems; performing server backups; and running network cables. In short, if a task is remotely connected with using a computer, the network administrator is responsible for ensuring that it is functioning properly.

Step 4: The Protocols Snowball

The network configuration may run smoothly for quite some time. As additional users are added to the network, our LAN Administrator continues to keep up with the increasing demands of the position.

Then one day it happens. Someone is reading a trade magazine that sings the benefits of using IBM/Lotus Notes. Management decides that the company will simply implode if it does not deploy Lotus Notes on every desktop as soon as possible. Because the article also stated that Lotus Notes runs best on OS/2, the company purchases a second server. Our network administrator, who has been struggling to keep up with the numerous requests of their end users, is now thrown face first into learning this new system so that they can get it online and working. Because the default protocol for Lotus Notes is NetBIOS, the network administrator configures all workstations to handle NetBIOS as well as IPX.

A little later someone else is reading an article that chants the Internet mantra. They read how wonderful the Internet has become for sharing information and offering support to clients and potential customers. They decide that the company is in dire need of a full-time connection to the Internet. Because the Internet communicates using IP, the network administrator again reconfigures the company's workstations to handle IP as well as IPX and NetBIOS.

With all these protocol stacks running, our network administrator finds that most desktop systems do not have enough free memory left to run most of the company's corporate applications. The company decides to upgrade all users to run Windows 95 on the desktop. This requires a faster processor and more physical memory than most of the users have in their desktop systems. Our administrator finds that they not only need to roll out a new desktop platform, but also will be required to retrofit a large portion of the computer hardware.

Then the company owner decides he does not like the e-mail interface provided by Lotus Notes. He hears from a golf buddy that Exchange is the best mail package around. He decides, of course, that his company requires "the best mail package around" and sends down an edict to install Exchange as the corporate mail system. Exchange only runs on NT, so another server must be purchased. Because Exchange uses Named Pipes as its default protocol, all the company's workstations need to be configured with this protocol as well.

Meanwhile the crew down in Engineering are finding they miss the good old days when they could share files between their desktop systems. They really hate the fascist attitude the LAN administrator has toward security on the server and cannot understand why everyone is not simply given access to all file areas. They decide to turn on local file sharing on their Windows 95 systems. Unbeknownst to our poor LAN administrator, the NetBEUI protocol has just been added to the network.

From the moment we added that second protocol, NetBIOS, our example reached multiprotocol status. From there it snowballed. With all the changes taking place, our network administrator never had the opportunity to perform any type of long-term impact study on how all these protocols may affect network performance. They did not even have time to investigate whether they actually needed to run all these protocols (defaults are not always a good thing). This type of system growth usually stems from the "squeaky wheel syndrome." Because the average network job usually includes help-desk duties in the job description, it becomes easy to get lost in day-to-day requests and lose focus on maintaining the network infrastructure.

Even if the number of end users has remained constant since the time that first NetWare server was installed, the workload required to manage all these new systems has easily tripled. The constant number of end users can make it difficult, if not impossible, for our LAN administrator to justify the hiring of additional personnel to support the network. All too often the debate over whether additional resources are required rests solely on the raw number of end users, not on the complexity of the network infrastructure itself.

Would it be any surprise if our LAN administrator ran away to Vermont to take up beekeeping? The bee stings might actually be a comfort after running that multiprotocol environment!

While this example network may seem a bit far-fetched, I've seen quite a few networks that have proliferated this way. Only the names have been changed.

Network Consolidation

Our second example of how a multiprotocol network can evolve is a bit more straightforward. In the age of corporate mergers and business partnerships it is not uncommon for two networks to be consolidated or connected for the purpose of exchanging information. While these networks have developed independent of one another, they may now be required to combine into a single functional unit.

Problems arise when it is discovered that company A uses NetWare for all of its file and print services while company B uses NT. It may also be discovered that each company uses a different protocol when communicating with these network operating systems (NOSes). Because time is always a factor in these situations, our network personnel may be under the gun to provide full connectivity as soon as possible.

We now have two separate network staffs that are charged with providing connectivity to a network operating system (NOS) with which they are unfamiliar. Even if these two staffs are combined, each member may only be acquainted with providing connectivity to their specific NOS. Because both networks were originally homogeneous (utilizing only one NOS), none of the staff members may be versed in configuring both operating systems to communicate using a common protocol.

The most obvious solution (although not necessarily the best) may be simply to add the second protocol to everyone's desktop system. In doing this, we again create a multiprotocol network and add an additional load to each desktop system.

The Main Network Operating Environments

So far in this chapter, I've mentioned a number of different NOSes. In this section, I'll touch briefly on the salient features of each.

Unix

Unix is by far the oldest of these four NOSes. It grew as a simple project out of Bell Labs in the 1960s and is arguably the most powerful and versatile of all NOSes. It has both a command line and a graphical user interface, as well as the ability to support multiple inbound networking services, such as file and printer sharing.

Unfortunately, Unix's versatility has also been its largest hindrance. While DOS includes fewer than 100 maintenance commands, some Unix systems ship with 500 or more. This has unfortunately earned Unix the label of being complex to administer. While it is true that a certain sort of mind-set may be required to administer a Unix system, this does not necessarily mean that the system is complex. Additional tools are added to enhance the flexibility of the system—not every one of these tools is required every day. As an example, the **more** command exists on both DOS and Unix. Both utilities can be used when viewing large text files so that the information does not scroll off the top of the screen. The user can move through the file a full screen at a time by pressing any key. Unix, however, includes another command called **less** that not only includes all the functionality of **more**, but also activates the page up, page down, and arrow keys. This allows the user to move through a file in both directions, as well as line by line. Unix also includes two other commands called **head** and **tail** for viewing only the beginning or end of a file, respectively. So while DOS has only a single command for text file viewing, Unix supplies four. You are not, however, required to know all four to view a text file.

To add to the confusion, every Unix vendor ships a slightly different flavor of Unix. A seasoned user of Sun's flavor of Unix (Solaris) would find HP's version (HP-UX) similar but would still need some time to become familiar with the system. Still, Unix has enjoyed a wide deployment. The system's flexibility and native IP support has lead to it play a major role in providing Internet services.

NetWare/IntranetWare

Novell's NOS, NetWare, is the next oldest, having been around for approximately 15 years. NetWare has been the mainstay of many networks, providing extremely efficient file and printing services. It is not uncommon to see hundreds of users sharing the same NetWare server while still receiving extremely good performance.

If more than one NetWare server is required, user account and password information can be shared using NetWare's Novell Directory Services (NDS). This is a powerful tool that allows a LAN administrator to centrally manage user information. NDS is a considerable improvement from NetWare's bindery-based account system, which required separate user information to be maintained on each individual server. The LAN administrator is not required to maintain account information for each individual server.

The most recent evolution of the operating system, referred to as IntranetWare, includes IP tools that allow it to support Web and FTP access.

NT Server

NT Server was first released in 1993 and is the youngest of the NOSes covered in this book. With NT Server all administration is done through a graphical user interface that has remained consistent with the interfaces used on Microsoft's desktop systems. If you are familiar with the interface for Windows 3.1x or Windows 95, you already know your way around NT Server. Version 4.x of NT Server can also be configured to use either the Windows 95 interface or the legacy 3.1x. This ease of use has led to a quick acceptance of NT Server among administrators.

While NT's ability to provide shared file access is probably better suited for use in small network environments, its ability to provide access to networked applications has sparked the interest of administrators of even the largest networks. NT now ships with Internet tools as well, and has found its way into many roles that were originally dominated by the Unix environment. NT Server's combination of simple administration along with its wide acceptance by software developers has made it a major networking player.

Lotus Notes

Released in late 1989, Lotus Notes spent many of its earlier years as an enigma. While it won Best New Product of the Year, no one was sure exactly how to leverage the features it provided to make it a commercially acceptable environment.

Lotus Notes was created long before the term "groupware" was even conceived. The short description of Lotus Notes is that it is a *shared client-server database application*. "Client-server" refers to the fact that some of the processor time required for operating and maintaining a database is supplied by the server and some is supplied by the client. For example, if I need to clean up a database file, I do not need to perform this function from my client. I can simply use my client to create the request and submit it to the server, which will carry out the task. This frees up my desktop system to perform other functions. As a shared database system, Lotus Notes provides storage and retrieval services for corporate information. This can be as simple as a client address book or as complex as a full accounting/inventory system.

Along with some powerful database functionality, Lotus Notes also includes its own e-mail system. The latest release has a completely redesigned interface that makes the e-mail system a lot more user-friendly than earlier revisions. Also added is the ability to allow users to access e-mail and databases through a Web browser interface. This is a powerful feature that makes incorporating database searches extremely easy to integrate into a corporate Web server.

Lotus Notes is not a true NOS. While it does allow network users to access shared resources, it requires some form of underlying NOS in order to function. Lotus Notes supports OS/2, Unix, NetWare, and NT. Lotus Notes has taken heat for many years because the network communications it created were not exactly efficient. Administrators found that Lotus Notes created a lot of network traffic that would reduce the amount of available bandwidth when desktop systems needed to communicate with other systems. The later versions of Lotus Notes have taken great steps to remedy this.

Pulling It All Together

Each of these NOSes has been developed in its own little world. Until recently, very little attention has been paid to getting them to interoperate or communicate using a common set of protocols.

Cleaning up an established multiprotocol environment can be a daunting task. If you are charged with keeping a complex network running smoothly, take a good look through the rest of this book before you go out and invest in that first beehive.

In Chapter 2 we will start with the basics. We'll analyze the electrical characteristics of a communication session and discuss the physical aspects of the media used to carry communication signals.

CHAPTER

2

Transmission Media

The foundation of any network is the transmission media or circuitry used to interconnect and carry network signals between computer systems. Transmission media provide the path for one computer to transfer information to another. The most commonly used transmission media are:

- copper cable, which carries electrical signals

- fiber optic cable, which carries light

- the atmosphere, which can transmit light or radio waves

In this chapter, we will review each of these media and describe the guidelines for their use. As each medium has its own strengths and weaknesses, we will outline when it is more appropriate to choose one medium over another.

At the end of the chapter, I'll run you through three examples of how to choose the appropriate transmission medium or media for a given situation.

Transmission Basics

Regardless of the medium used for transmitting information, we need some method of transmitting information from one system to another. These transmissions can take two forms—analog or digital.

Analog and Digital Transmissions

An *analog* transmission is a signal that can vary in either power level (known as *amplitude*) or in the number of times this power level changes in a fixed time period (known as *frequency*). An analog transmission can have nearly an infinite number of permissible values over a given range. For example, think of how we communicate verbally. Our voice boxes vibrate the air at different frequencies and amplitudes. These vibrations are received by the eardrum and interpreted into words. Subtle changes in tone or volume can dramatically change the meaning of what we say. Figure 2.1 shows an example of an analog transmission.

Note the amplitude each time the waveform peaks. Each of the three amplitude levels could be used to convey different information (like alphanumeric characters). This makes for a very efficient way to communicate because each wave cycle can be used to convey additional information. In a perfect world, this might be the ideal way to communicate.

Frequency is measured in cycles per second or hertz (Hz). If Figure 2.1 were measured over a period of one second, it would be identified as a frequency of three cycles per second or 3 Hz.

The problem with analog transmissions is that they are very susceptible to *noise* or interference. Noise is the addition of unwanted signal information. Think of having a conversation in a room crowded with lots of people conversing. With all of this background noise going on, it is difficult to distinguish between your discussion and the others taking place within the room. This can result in a number of data retransmissions signaled by phrases such as "What?" and "What did you say?" These retransmissions slow down the rate of information transfer.

Figure 2.2 shows an example of an analog signal in a noisy circuit. Note that it is now more difficult to determine the precise amplitude of

FIGURE 2.1

An example of an analog
transmission plotted
over time

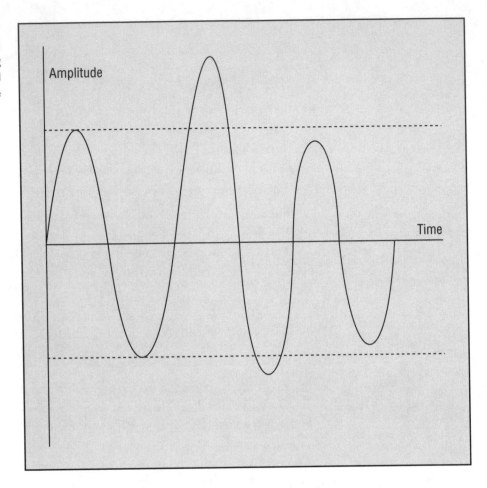

each waveform. This can result in incorrect information being transmitted or in requests for the correct information to be resent.

To the rescue come digital transmissions. Digital communications are based on the binary system, in that only two pieces of information are ever transmitted, a 1 or a 0. In an electrical circuit, a zero is usually represented by a voltage of zero volts and a one is represented by five volts. This is radically different from analog transmissions, which can have an infinite number of possible values. These ones and zeros are then strung together in certain patterns to convey information. For example, the binary equivalent of the letter A is 01000001.

F I G U R E 2.2

An analog transmission
on a noisy circuit

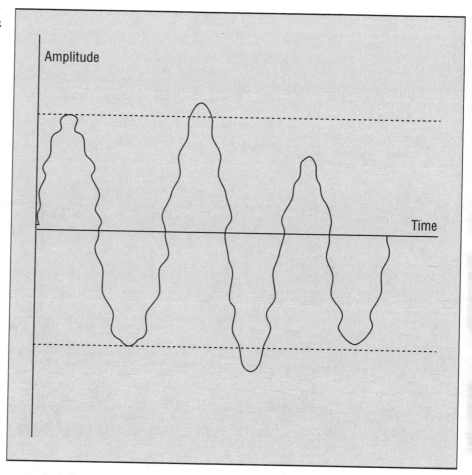

F I G U R E 2.2

An analog transmission on a noisy circuit

Each individual signal or digital pulse is referred to as a *bit*. When eight bits are strung together (like our binary equivalent of A) it is referred to as a *byte*. The byte is considered to be the base unit when dealing with digital communications. Each byte is expected to relay one complete piece of information (such as the letter A).

Digital communication is analogous to Morse code or the early telegraph system: Certain patterns of pulses are used to represent different letters of the alphabet.

If you examine Figure 2.3, you'll note that our waveform has changed shape. It is no longer a free flowing series of arcs but follows a rigid and predictable format.

FIGURE 2.3

A digital transmission plotted over time

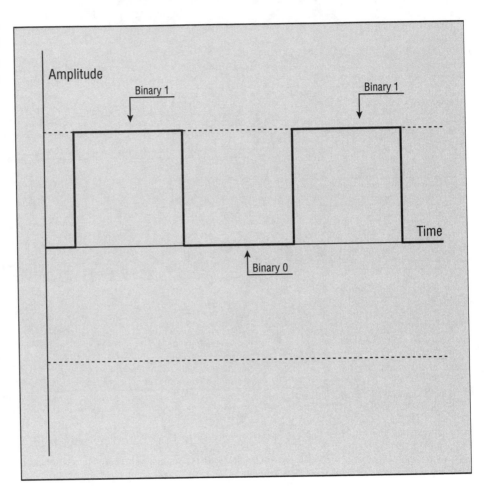

Because this waveform is so predictable and the variation between acceptable values is so great, it is now much easier to determine what is being transmitted. As is shown in Figure 2.4, even when there is noise in the circuit, you can still see which part of the signal is a binary 1 and which is a 0.

FIGURE 2.4

A digital transmission on a
noisy circuit

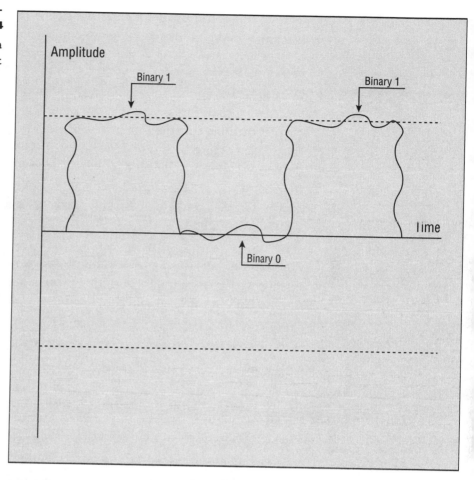

This simple format that allows digital communications to be so noise resistant can also be its biggest drawback. The information for the ASCII character A can be transmitted with a single analog wave or vibration, but transmitting the binary or digital equivalent requires eight separate waves or vibrations (to transmit 01000001). Despite this inherent drawback, it is usually much more efficient to use digital communication whenever possible. Analog circuits require a larger amount of overhead in order to detect and correct noisy transmissions. As we will discuss in the next chapter when we cover wide area network

(WAN) options, you can get greater bandwidth by simply converting a circuit from analog to digital communications.

> *Overhead* is the amount of additional information that must be transmitted on a circuit to ensure that the receiving system gets the correct data and that the data is free of errors. Typically, when a circuit requires more overhead, less bandwidth is available to transmit the actual data. This is like the packaging used when something is shipped to you in a box. You didn't want hundreds of little Styrofoam acorns, but they're there in the box taking up space to ensure your item is delivered safely.

Another big plus for digital communications is that computers process information in digital format. If you use analog communications to transfer information from one computer to another, you need some form of converter (such as a modem or a codex) at each end of the circuit to translate the information from digital to analog and then back to digital again.

Sources of Noise

So where does noise come from? Noise can be broken down into two categories, *electromagnetic interference* (or EMI) and *radio frequency interference* (or RFI).

Electromagnetic Interference (EMI)

EMI is produced by circuits that use an alternating signal like analog or digital communications (referred to as an *alternating current* or an *AC circuit*). EMI is not produced by circuits that contain a consistent power level (referred to as a *direct current* or a *DC circuit*).

For example, if you could slice one of the wires coming from a car battery and watch the electrons moving down the wire (kids: don't try this at home), you would see a steady stream of power moving evenly and uniformly down the cable. The power level would never change—it would stay at a constant 12 volts. A battery is an example of a DC circuit because the power level remains stable.

Now, let's say you could slice the wire to a household lamp and try the same experiment (kids: *definitely* do not try this at home!). You would now see that, depending on the point in time when you measured the voltage on the wire, it would read anywhere between -120 volts and +120 volts. The voltage level of the circuit is constantly changing. Plotted over time, the voltage level would resemble the analog signal shown earlier in Figure 2.1.

If you watched the flow of electrons in the AC wire, you would notice something very interesting. As the voltage changes and the current flows down the wire, the electrons tend to ride predominantly on the surface of the wire. The center point of the wire shows almost no electron movement at all. If you increased the frequency of the power cycle, more and more of the electrons would travel on the surface of the wire instead of at the core. This effect is somewhat similar to what happens to a water-skier—the faster the boat travels, the closer to the top of the water the skier rides.

As the frequency of the power cycle increases, energy begins to radiate at a 90-degree angle to the flow of current. As water will ripple out when a rock breaks its surface, so too will energy move out from the center core of the wire. This radiation is in a direct relationship with the signal on the wire, such that if the voltage level or the frequency is increased, the amount of energy radiated will also increase (see Figure 2.5).

This energy has magnetic properties to it and is the basis of how electromagnets and transformers operate. The downside to all of this is that the electromagnetic radiation can introduce an electrical signal into another wire if one is nearby. This interference either adds to or subtracts from the existing signal and is considered to be noise. EMI is the most common type of interference encountered on LANs and can be produced by everything from fluorescent lights to network cables to heavy machinery. EMI also causes signal loss. Any energy that is dissipated as EMI is energy that can no longer be used to carry the signal down the wire.

FIGURE 2.5

A conductor carrying an
AC signal radiating EMI

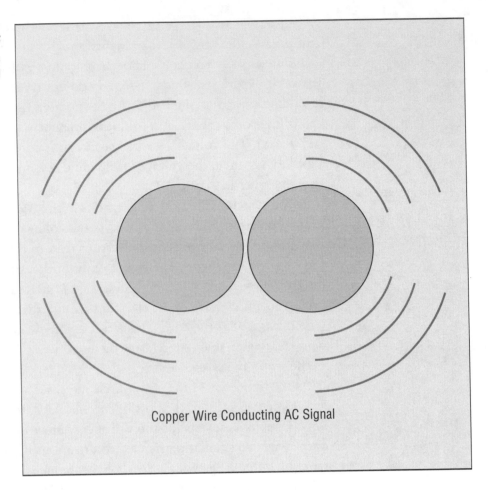

Copper Wire Conducting AC Signal

Radio Frequency Interference (RFI)

Radio Frequency Interference (RFI) can be produced when two conflicting signals have similar properties. The waveforms can join
together, changing the frequency or amplitude of the resulting signal.
This is why geographically close radio stations do not transmit on
adjacent frequencies. If they did, a radio might not be able to receive
the weaker of the two stations.

The most common source of RFI in networking is caused by a condition known as *reflection*. Reflection occurs when a signal is reflected back upon itself by some component along its connection path. For example, thinnet cabling (which I'll describe in greater detail later in this chapter) requires the use of a terminator at each end of the cable. The terminator's job is to *terminate* or absorb any electrical signal that reaches the end of the cable. If the terminator is faulty, it may not be able to fully absorb all of the signal. The portion of the signal which is not absorbed will be reflected back up the thinnet cable. This will distort any other signals that are currently being transmitted onto the wire.

Communication Synchronization

Another important property in communications is letting the receiving system know when to expect data transmissions. If the beginning of a transmission cannot be determined, a receiving system may mistake the beginning of a transmission for the middle, or vice versa. This is true for both analog and digital communications.

One way to achieve proper signal timing is to have the systems synchronize their communications so that each transmits data at a predetermined time. For example, the two systems may agree to take turns transmitting for one second each and then pass control over to the other system (similar to a human conversation). While this type of negotiation is simple and straightforward, it has a number of inherent flaws. First, if a station has nothing to say, its time slice will be wasted, while the second station sits by idle and waiting to transmit additional information. Also, if the stations' clocks are slightly different, the two systems will eventually fall out of sync and smother each other's communication. Finally, consider what happens when further stations are plugged into the same circuit and have something to say: The time slices could be renegotiated, but this will severely diminish the amount of data that could be transmitted on this circuit in a timely fashion.

To resolve these issues, communications use a *preamble*—a defined series of communication pulses that tell all receiving stations "Get ready, I've got something to say." The preamble ensures that all stations are able to "sync up" and receive the data in the same time measure that it was sent. This is just like a band's lead singer or drummer calling out the beat to lead in to the start of a song, to make sure all band members start the first note at exactly the same time and are in sync with each other. Because a station sends a preamble only when it needs to transmit data, dead air time is eliminated by leaving the circuit open for systems that need it. Also, if the data transmission bursts are kept fairly small, it resolves the issue of systems falling out of sync due to time variations, because the stations can resync their times during each data delivery.

Media Choices for Analog and Digital Transmissions

So which transmission media will work with either analog or digital communications? The short answer is that all media are capable of carrying either analog or digital signals. The circuit design determines which type of communication is most appropriate.

For example, copper wire was originally used for telegraphs, which were a type of digital communication. This was because the telegraph used an electromagnet that interpreted the electrical signals as a series of long and short audible clicks.

Now, change the circuit by trading the telegraph hardware for two telephones, and that same copper wire can be used for telephone communications, which are a type of analog signal. Information is transferred by a nearly infinite number of frequency and amplitude changes.

So how does one go about choosing which transmission media is most appropriate for their networking application? Typically, a number of different factors play a role in this choice.

Don't worry about the terminology or specifics of the following issues just yet. They're simply meant to get you looking at the big picture as we explore the technology in greater detail later in the book.

User and Application Bandwidth Demands

If you have a small number of users who will only need to share a printer and maybe exchange a few spreadsheet files, a medium that supports relatively slow communications—for example, CAT 3 copper cable—may be sufficient. But if you have a large number of users that will be sharing large graphic files or compiling common source code, stick with a medium that will support faster transmission rates (for example, fiber-optic cable).

Future Growth

Future growth is always one of the toughest variables to determine. For example, CAT 3 cable is all the small office mentioned in the previous section needs—for now. But if this small office has the potential to grow to hundreds of users, it may be wiser to start wiring with CAT 5 cable from day one, so you do not need to go back and rewire your network later when the office needs greater bandwidth.

Preparing for Future Growth

One of the most difficult and time-consuming tasks an administrator can undertake is to rewire a network. When in doubt, overestimate growth and bandwidth demands. For example, the cost of installing CAT 5 instead of CAT 3 is minimal. The cost of removing that CAT 3 cable in order to update to CAT 5 later is far more expensive than doing it right the first time (remember to factor in such things as labor and downtime).

If you are debating CAT 5 versus fiber, consider pulling the fiber cable at the same time as the CAT 5 but leaving it unused until needed.

Unfortunately there is no real rule of thumb for determining network growth. This can only be determined by evaluating your company's needs and intended expansion.

Distances between Computer Systems

All forms of transmission media have some form of distance limitation. This is why most larger networks incorporate a mixture of media types. Typically, for short runs, copper is sufficient, while longer distances may require fiber or satellite communications.

Geographic Environment

Location can quickly limit the number of available options. If the distance between the systems you're connecting is a matter of miles rather than meters, your choices will be limited to satellite or leased line ommunications.

Required Fault Tolerance

Fault tolerance is the ability of a network to remain functional despite a critical failure (such as a cable failure). While fault tolerance is more a function of the overlying topology or circuit design, keep it in mind when choosing media, as some topologies only support certain types of media. For example, the dual-ring design of the FDDI topology only supports fiber-optic cable.

Environment

Locations that contain devices that produce EMI or RFI noise will require transmission media that are not susceptible to this type of interference. For example, if the network will be used in a machine shop environment, media such as shielded coax or fiber would be better choices than twisted-pair cable because of their superior resistance to EMI interference.

Cost

As with most things in life, the media a company implements usually comes down to what it can ultimately afford. Typically, the better the media, the higher the cost. When justifying a media choice, work in such factors as lost productivity due to network slowdowns or full-blown outages. Also weigh the cost of upgrading at a later date. The cost of superior transmission media and connection hardware can suddenly look much more reasonable when you factor in circumstances such as downtime and additional administration. It's always cheaper to do it right the first time.

Now let's take a closer look at available media options.

There really is no consistent formula to determine which transmission medium is more cost effective, beyond estimating the footage required for each.

Thinnet Cable

Thinnet cable is somewhat of an enigma. While it has the potential to support high data transfer rates, it is currently not supported by any technology faster than 10 Mbps. Its tough outer sheathing makes the inner cabling difficult to damage, and yet its physical topology allows any single failure to bring down an entire network. Finally, while thinnet cable is very easy to install, it can be extremely difficult to troubleshoot when a problem occurs.

Cable Properties

Thinnet coaxial is cable that consists of a copper center core encased in a dialetric material. This dialetric is then encased in a braided shielding that in turn is covered in a protective plastic skin. The term *thinnet* comes from the fact that the overall wire diameter is .18" thick. The cable is termed *coaxial* because the cable uses two conductors that center around the same axis (the copper wire and the braided shielding). Figure 2.6 illustrates thinnet cable.

F I G U R E   2.6

A stripped back thinnet
cable and one with
connectors

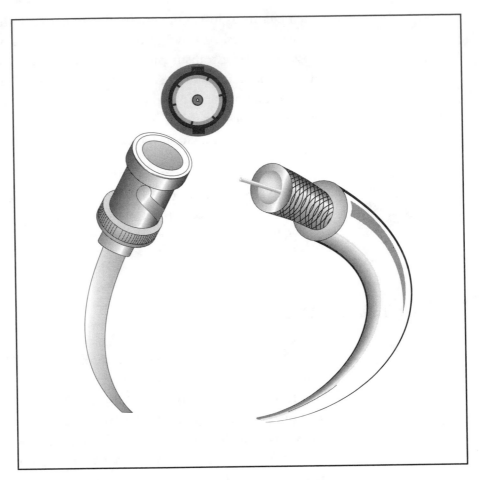

The center copper core carries the electrical signal along the media. This is the conductor on which the AC signal travels from station to station.

The dialetric is typically a ceramic/plastic mix that helps to reduce the amount of EMI produced by the copper core during data transmission. The dialetric resists the creation of the EMI waves, thus reducing noise and signal loss.

The braided cable serves two functions, one as a conductor, the other as a shield. All electrical circuits need a complete path to transmit energy. The braided cable acts as the return path or *ground* of the circuit. The braided cable's job is to maintain a voltage of zero volts. If this seems odd, think of the properties of an AC signal. The waveform is in a constant state of flux, changing from one voltage level to another. Without some form of reference, it is impossible to determine what is the actual voltage level on the circuit at any given time.

This is similar to driving down the road and passing a car traveling in the opposite direction. If you use a radar gun to measure the speed of the other car and find it reads 100 miles per hour, you really have no idea how fast the other car is traveling because the radar gun assumes you're stationary, which you are not. Without a reference, this measurement is meaningless. You also need to know how quickly you're moving to modify the radar gun's measurement. For example, if you are traveling at 55 mph, you can calculate that the other car must be moving at 45 mph (100 – 55 = 45). If you're traveling at 120 mph, you would know that the other car is actually backing up at 20 mph (100 – 120 = –20).

By keeping the braided cable at zero volts, we now have a known factor or reference to measure the copper core against and thus accurately determine the amplitude level of our signal.

The other function of the braided cable is to provide protection against EMI and RFI noise. Because the braided cable is kept at zero volts, it can shunt any interference received by the cable and keep it from affecting the signal on the copper core.

The outer coating is simply a tough skin to protect the cable from physical abuse. This coating (referred to as a *jacket*) is made from PVC or Plenum. PVC is the same material used for plumbing, only much thinner. Plenum is a similar material, but it is much more fire resistant.

Connector Types

Coax cable connectors are usually referred to as BNC (short for Bayonet Neill–Concelman) connectors. These connectors use a set pin with interlocking ring design so they may be connected and disconnected easily and without tools (see Figure 2.7).

The wiring design of a thinnet network is referred to as a bus topology and resembles a series type of connection: A single cable snakes from system to system, connecting them all in a row. Wherever a station is connected to the circuit the cable is split and a BNC T-connector is installed.

FIGURE 2.7

Examples of thinnet
connectors

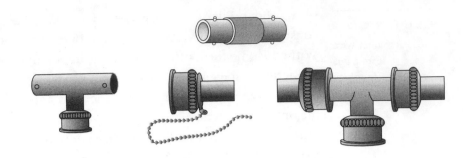

The T-connector contains two couplers for connecting the two pieces of cable and one coupler designed to connect a computer's network interface card (NIC). The end of the circuit is capped off with a terminator that shunts all electrical signals to ground to ensure that the signal is not reflected back down the wire. A reflected signal can introduce RFI noise into the circuit. A good terminator should measure 50 Ohms on a multimeter +/- 1 Ohm.

Figure 2.8 shows thinnet wire used to form a bus topology.

Note that in the above example one end of the thinnet circuit is grounded. Thinnet terminators come in two types, regular terminators and terminators with short beaded chains attached. The latter should be used on one end (and only one end) of the circuit. This beaded chain should be attached to a known ground, such as one of the screws in a metal computer chassis. This ensures that the voltage on the braided cabling remains at zero and that noise can be shunted effectively.

Advantages

Thinnet cable has the following advantages:

■ resistance to noise

■ tough shielding

■ relatively low cost

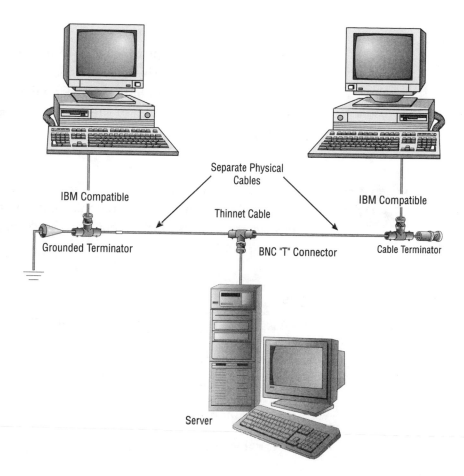

Example of thinnet wire
used to form a bus
topology

Resistance to Noise

Because of its braided shielding, thinnet cable is highly resistant
(although not impervious) to electromagnetic interference and radio frequency interference. This can make it a good fit for manufacturing or
other noisy environments.

Tough Shielding

Because of its tough outer skin and braided shielding, thinnet can be
more resistant to physical and environmental abuse than other cable
options like twisted-pair.

Cost

Thinnet is relatively inexpensive. At \$.15 to \$.50 a foot (without connectors), it is more expensive than twisted-pair cable but far less expensive than fiber. The cost of hardware that will use thinnet (NIC cards, repeaters, etc.) is on par with twisted-pair cable and substantially less than fiber.

If the cable is to be run in ceiling or wall areas, check your local building codes. While PVC coated thinnet is dramatically cheaper than Plenum, the latter is usually required to conform to fire and safety codes.

Disadvantages

Thinnet cable has the following disadvantages:

- bulky design

- poor scalability

- low fault resistance

- topology support is limited to 10 Mb Ethernet

Bulky Design

Because of its thick sheathing and large connectors, thinnet can be a real bear to wire. It is not nearly as flexible as twisted-pair cable; this can make it difficult to route through tight areas.

Scalability

Because each station is connected in a series fashion, thinnet does not lend itself to attaching and removing stations on the fly. If you need to add a station to a segment of cable that does not have an existing T-connector, you need to shut down the network and splice the cable to add one. Needless to say, shutting down the network is completely unacceptable during working hours in most networking environments.

The other problem with scalability is the old "Where does that cable go again?" syndrome. With twisted-pair, all cables are typically wired back to a central location. This makes determining a wire path pretty straightforward. Because thinnet is run from station to station, it can be difficult to keep track of where individual wire runs go as additional stations are added to the network. These runs may not follow straight lines between users but rather snake in and out of different office areas as connections are required. Unfortunately, these wire runs may go undocumented because the urgency is placed on getting the users connected to the network, not in planning the installation in case of future failure. This can make ensuring that your cable lengths remain within specification difficult at best and troubleshooting a problem a real nightmare.

Fault Resistance

Thinnet scores low in fault resistance, because the series connectivity comes back to haunt it. Because everyone is connected to the same logical segment of cable, a failure at any point in that cabling can cause the entire segment to go down. This could be due to anything from a faulty connector to a user who incorrectly disconnects their system from the network. Because a failure can affect a group of users, it becomes much more difficult to isolate the specific failure area.

One of my worst days was spent troubleshooting a segment failure that was being caused intermittently by someone running over a thinnet cable with their chair. As the user moved their chair in and out, it would either cause or fix the failure. Unfortunately this user had impeccable timing, as they were doing this while I was swapping out connectors at some other point on the cable. Needless to say, just as I would think the problem was resolved, the user would again trigger the failure mode. As I would again being to swap out additional suspect connectors and cables, they would move their chair, thus causing the cable to function properly again. While thinnet cable is quite rugged, you should still take appropriate steps to ensure it does not become damaged.

Topology Support

Thinnet is currently supported by 10 Mb Ethernet only. There is currently no specification to utilize thinnet cabling at 100 Mbps operation. While there is talk of incorporating thinnet under the 1 Gb Ethernet umbrella, these specifications will not be formalized until the summer of 1998. Even then, the adoption is questionable, because the number of thinnet installations has fallen off dramatically. Due to the significant drawbacks listed above, network administrators have started to look to other media for their connectivity needs.

Appropriate Applications

These are the appropriate applications for thinnet cable:

- areas of light to medium EMI and RFI interference, such as machine shop or manufacturing environments

- connection of non-workstation hardware like hubs and servers where 10 Mbps throughput is sufficient

- very small networks (such as home networks)

- medium-length cable runs where twisted-pair specifications would be exceeded, such as between multiple floors of a building

Cable Specifications

Table 2.1 shows the specifications for thinnet.

TABLE 2.1 Thinnet Cable Specifications	Item	Specifications
	Transmission source	electrical
	Topologies supported	10 Mb Ethernet
	Maximum cable length	600 ft (185 M)

TABLE 2.1 (cont.) Thinnet Cable Specifications	Item	Specifications
	Minimum cable length	1.5 ft (.5 M)
	Maximum number of stations	30 per cable segment
	Maximum number of segments	Dependent on topology; 10 Mb Ethernet is five repeated segments with only three populated by stations.
	Maximum overall segment length	Dependent on topology; 10 Mb Ethernet is 3000 ft. (925 M).

A repeated segment is when two lengths of cable are connected by an amplification device. A populated segment is a cable run that consists of end-user workstations or servers. A non-populated segment is a cable run that consists of only the two repeaters. Non-populated segments are used to connect populated segments that are separated geographically.

Twisted-Pair Cable

Used for both voice and data lines, twisted-pair cable can span a reasonable distance without a repeater, is somewhat resistant to outside noise and is relatively easy to work with. Twisted-pair cable enjoys a wide acceptance, because it is supported by nearly all LAN topologies. Combine this with a fairly robust wiring scheme, and it is easy to see why twisted-pair cable has become the cabling of choice for most organizations.

Cable Properties

Twisted-pair cable consists of four pairs (eight individual wires) of 24-gauge wire. This wire can be single- or multi-stranded. Each wire is covered by a uniquely color-coded plastic sheath which allows the wires to be distinguished from one another. Each wire pair is twisted together to provide a small amount of insulation from outside interference (thus the name twisted-pair). All of the wires are then encapsulated in a plastic sheath. Figure 2.9 shows a twisted-pair cable.

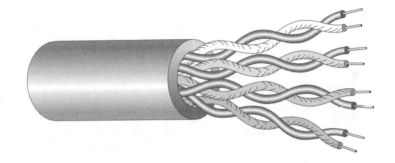

FIGURE 2.9

A stripped back twisted-pair cable

If you will be running strictly 10 Mb Ethernet, only two of the four pairs are actually required. This is similar to how most modern homes are wired, with four pairs of twisted cable—only two of the pairs are actually used, with the second set available for adding an additional phone line. I know of a few savvy individuals who have taken advantage of this setup to wire up an Ethernet network in their home using their existing phone cabling. For business applications, however, it is usually good practice to keep the phone and data lines separate and wire all four pairs for data use. If bandwidth limitations require the network to be pushed up to a faster speed later, you may need to put those additional wire pairs into use.

ANSI/EIA (American National Standards Institute/Electronic Industries Association) standard 568 calls out a number of categories (the singular is commonly referred to as *CAT*) to specify the fastest data transfer rates that can be supported by a particular cable construction.

These specifications cover everything from the material of the cables themselves to the types of connectors and junction blocks the cables use. These categories are:

Category	Description
CAT 1 & 2:	voice and low-speed data (like modem connections)
CAT 3:	voice and data rates up to 10 Mbps
CAT 4:	voice and data rates up to 16 Mbps
CAT 5:	voice and data rates up to 100 Mbps

CAT 5 is currently under consideration to be incorporated into the 1 Gb Ethernet specification. It is expected to be approved for short distance wiring only. While the mainstay of 1 Gb Ethernet is expected to run on fiber, the goal is to leverage the CAT 5 wiring most organizations currently use for connections out to the desktop.

The two most popular specifications are CAT 3 and CAT 5. While the two cables may look physically identical, CAT 3 has a lower specification that can cause errors if pushed to a faster transmission rate.

Always certify your cables with a tester that will check them at the transmission speed you will be using. I've seen quite a few wire runs that test fine at 10 Mbps but fall apart when the transmission rate is pushed to 100 Mbps.

You should examine every link in the chain while trying to maintain a certain category of wiring. I know more than one organization that has ended up in a bind by investing heavily in CAT 5 cabling only to cut corners later and purchase CAT 3 punch-down blocks (a punch-down block is a device used for organizing wires at central locations such as wiring closets or server rooms). Your network is only as good as its weakest link.

Twisted-pair networks are commonly wired in a *star* topology, as shown in Figure 2.10. In a small environment, all systems will connect back to a central device known as a *hub* or a *switch*. These devices can then be linked together to form larger networks. This linkage makes for a very robust environment, as the failure of one cable will typically affect only one system (unless of course that one system happens to be your server, in which case your entire environment is affected as its resources become unreachable).

F I G U R E 2.10

An example of twisted-pair cable being used in a star LAN topology

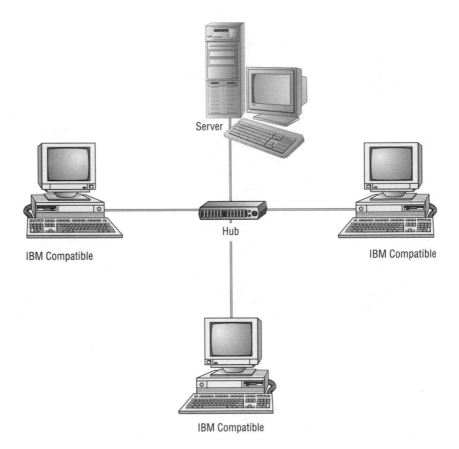

Server

Hub

IBM Compatible

IBM Compatible

IBM Compatible

Linking devices together also makes fault isolation far easier than dealing with thinnet's series type of connection. Because each office drop is its own circuit, a single user cannot bring down the whole network by incorrectly disconnecting their system.

We'll cover punch-down blocks, along with hubs and switches, in Chapter 4.

Full Duplex Support

One interesting property of twisted-pair cable is its ability to support full duplex communications. Most network communications take place in a half duplex mode. This means that while any one system is transmitting data, every other system must be in a listening mode. This is like Citizen Band (CB) radio communications—whenever one person is communicating, they, in effect, "own" the channel. If another individual tries to transmit at the same time, the two signals will interfere with each other. In order for a conversation to take place, everyone must communicate in an orderly fashion by taking turns. Only one person can be transmitting at any given time.

Full duplex allows communications to take place in both directions simultaneously. A telephone conversation is an example of full duplex communication. Both parties are allowed to send information at the same time (though the louder person's information usually comes through clearer). The catch to full duplex is that only two systems can be attached to any one logical segment. Still, full duplex can double the amount of data a system can process. With full duplex, a server with a 10 Mb Ethernet connection would have the potential to process 20 Mbps of information (transmitting 10 Mbps and receiving 10 Mbps). I'll cover this in greater detail later on.

Two quick notes here: First, while full duplex communications are possible with other cable types, they involve running two sets of cables rather than the one set that twisted-pair cable requires. Second, full duplex is topology dependent—some topologies (for example, 100VG-ANYLAN) do not support full duplex communications.

Connector Types

Connector types commonly used for twisted-pair cabling are RJ-11 and RJ-45 connectors, shown in Figure 2.11. These connectors are crimp-ons; each requires a different size crimping tool. RJ-11 is the smaller six-pin jack that is commonly used for telephone connections. RJ-45 is the larger of the two, has eight pins, and is the one most commonly used for data connections.

FIGURE 2.11

Twisted-pair cables with RJ-11 and RJ-45 connectors

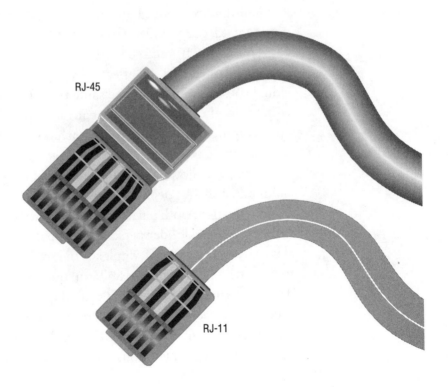

RJ-45

RJ-11

As mentioned before, each of the individual wires is encased in a color-coded sheath for easy identification. Unfortunately, the sequence in which these color codes get attached to a connector is not as standard as the rest of this cable's specifications. To date, there are at least five or more standards in use. The most common standard, AT&T 258A, is used by most cable installation companies, but you'll also run into the EIA Preferred Commercial Building Specification and the IEEE's 10Base-T specification from time to time.

If you view a twisted-pair connector from the bottom (i.e., the opposite side from the connector catch) and have the end that the cable plugs into facing down, the pins are numbered 1–8 from left to right, as shown in Figure 2.12.

F I G U R E 2.12

Pins 1 through 8 of a twisted-pair connector (from the bottom)

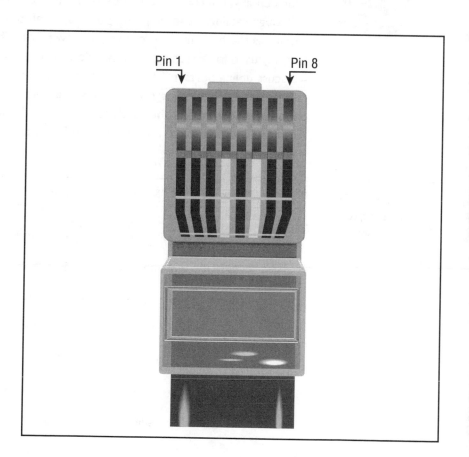

Which color coding should you use? (The color codes are listed in Table 2.2.) If you're given a choice, stay clear of the IEEE specification. If a different topology is required later, you may find yourself retrofitting or repulling cables. Neither the AT&T specification nor the EIA specification has an electrical advantage, but the AT&T specification is more widely used and supported. More important, though, is to remain consistent with the color codes currently in place if your building contains existing wiring.

Incidentally, the color codes shown in Table 2.2 are for straight-through cabling. At some point, you may need to create a *cross cable* that has the transmit and receive pairs switched. These cables are commonly used for attaching hubs that do not have an uplink port. (We discuss uplink ports in Chapter 4.) If you need to create a cross cable, the color codes for pins 1 & 3 and 2 & 6 should be swapped on one end (and one end only) of the patch cable. It's good practice to label cross cables as such to avoid mistaking them for straight-through cables

Pin #	Ethernet Usage	AT&T	EIA	IEE
1	+ output	white/orange	white/green	white/orange
2	- output	orange/white	green/white	orange/white
3	+ input	white/green	white/orange	white/green
4		blue/white	blue/white	not used
5		white/blue	white/blue	not used
6	- input	green/white	orange/white	green/white
7		white/brown	white/brown	not used
8		brown/white	brown/white	not used

TABLE 2.2
Pin numbers and color codes for an RJ-45 connector

Advantages

Twisted-pair cable has the following advantages:

- wide deployment
- industry acceptance
- ease of installation
- fault tolerance
- substantial bandwidth
- low cost

Wide Deployment

Twisted-pair cable is by far the most popular transmission medium. Your building may well already be wired for twisted-pair cable. If so, you can save a lot of time and money by utilizing the existing wiring.

NOTE Always have your cabling certified prior to use by a professional cable installer or by using a cable tester (we'll cover cable testers in Chapter 13).

Industry Acceptance

Because of its popularity, twisted-pair cable has been incorporated into more LAN topology specifications than any other transmission medium. Standardizing on twisted-pair cable ensures that you will have an upgrade path to faster topologies.

Easy Installation

Of the three cable media covered in this book, twisted-pair cable is by far the easiest to install. Its flexible design makes it easy to route through tight areas. The crimp connector design means that connectors can be installed with inexpensive tools (though, as always, you will need to test all cables before using them).

Fault Tolerance

The star configuration used by most topologies specifies that only two systems are ever connected to each cable. This means that a single cable fault usually only affects a single system, making troubleshooting straightforward.

Bandwidth

As I mentioned earlier, twisted-pair cable is the only cable medium to allow upgrading from half duplex to full duplex communications without the need to rewire (although you may have to replace network hardware). If you're stuck with legacy CAT 3 cabling, moving your servers to full duplex communications may be just the thing to squeeze a little more bandwidth out of your existing wiring.

Low Cost

Twisted-pair cable is the cheapest network cable on the market. Four-pair CAT 3 cable runs between $.01 and $.15 a foot. CAT 5 typically runs between $.15 and $.40 a foot, without connectors. As with thinnet, check local building and safety codes to see if the more expensive Plenum sheathing is required over the cheaper PVC.

Disadvantages

Twisted-pair cable has two main disadvantages: length and noise resistance.

Length

Twisted-pair cable is limited to 325 feet under most topologies. For most networking environments, this length limitation won't be a problem, but for a large facility, you may need to set up multiple wiring closets. Also, because twisted-pair cable requires a separate connection to each desktop system, it may require far more wire than thinnet cable would. This can make the cost comparison between the two a bit deceiving.

Noise Resistance

Twisted-pair cable is more susceptible to electromagnetic and radio frequency interference than thinnet or fiber. I've seen some strange network problems resolved by simply moving ceiling cables away from fluorescent lighting. If you're pulling twisted-pair cable, make sure the runs are as far away as possible from all noise sources. A few feet is usually sufficient, depending on the strength of the noise source. Items to be avoided are:

- fluorescent lights

- power transformers

- devices with motors

- devices that transmit a signal, like radio station antennas

Appropriate Applications

These are the appropriate applications for twisted-pair cable:

- areas of little to no EMI or RFI noise such as a standard office building

- relatively short cable runs

- connections out to users' desktops

- server connections that don't require 100% fault tolerance

Cable Specifications

Table 2.3 shows the specifications for twisted-pair cable.

	Item	Specification
T A B L E 2.3 Twisted-Pair Cable Specifications	Transmission source	electrical
	Topologies Supported	10 Mb, 100 Mb and 1 Gb Ethernet, FDDI, ATM
	Maximum cable length	325 feet (100 M)
	Minimum cable length	none
	Maximum number of stations	2 per cable, 1024 per logical segment
	Maximum number of segments	Dependent on topology: 10 Mb Ethernet is 5 repeated segments with only three populated. 100Tx and 100T4 is only two repeated segments. 100VG-ANYLAN is five repeated segments, all of which may be populated. 1 Gb Ethernet is still under examination, possibly two repeated segments.
	Maximum overall segment length	Dependent on topology: 10 Mb Ethernet and 100V-ANYAN is 3000 ft. (925 M). 100Tx and 100T4 are 650 ft. (200 M). 1 Gb Ethernet is currently 165 ft. (50 M). This may increase to 650 ft. (100 M).

Fiber-Optic Cable

Fiber is believed to be the medium of the 21st Century. While attaching connectors to fiber optic cable is currently a difficult chore, fiber's ability to support extremely high data rates makes it worth the additional effort. Today fiber is found mostly on high-speed network backbones, but expect to see it work its way out to the desktop over the next ten years as bandwidth requirements increase and the process for adding connectors becomes easier.

Cable Properties

Fiber-optic cable consists of a cylindrical glass thread center core, 62.5 microns in diameter, wrapped in cladding that protects the center core and reflects the light back into the glass conductor. This is then encapsulated in a tough kevlar jacket.

The whole thing is then sheathed in PVC or Plenum. The diameter of this outer sheath is 125 microns. The diameter measurements are why this cabling is sometimes referred to as 62.5/125 cable. While the glass core is breakable, the kevlar jacket helps fiber optic cable stand up to a fair amount of abuse. Figure 2.13 shows a fiber optic cable.

Kevlar is the same material that bulletproof vests are made of—talk about a bulletproof network!

Unlike twisted-pair cable and thinnet cable, fiber uses a light source for data transmission. This light source is typically a light emitting diode (LED) that produces a signal in the visible infrared range. On the other end of the cable is another diode that receives the LED signals. The light transmissions can take one of two forms, single mode or multimode.

Never look into the beam of an active fiber-optic cable. The light intensity is strong enough to cause permanent blindness. If you must visually inspect a cable, first make sure that it is completely disconnected from the network. Just because a cable is dark for a moment does not mean it is inactive. The risk of blindness or visual "dead spots" is high enough to not make it worth it unless you know the cable is completely disconnected.

Single mode fiber consists of an LED that produces a single frequency of light. This single frequency is pulsed in a digital format to transmit data from one end of the cable to another. The benefit of single mode fiber over multi-mode is that it is faster and will travel longer distances

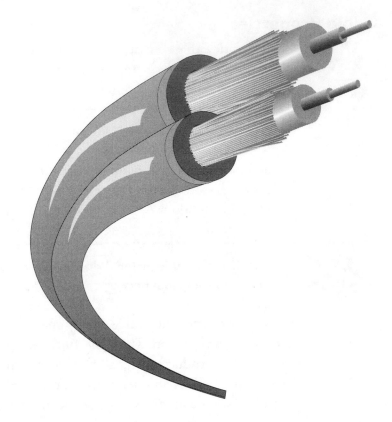

(in the hundreds-of-miles range). The drawbacks are that the hardware is extremely expensive and installation can be tedious at best. Unless your company name ends with the word "Telephone," single mode fiber would be overkill for any application, so I'll focus on multimode fiber.

Multimode transmissions consist of multiple light frequencies. Because the light range does not need to be quite so precise as it does with single mode, the hardware costs for multimode are dramatically less than for single mode. The drawback of multimode fiber is *light dispersion*, the tendency of light rays to spread out as they travel. You'll see light dispersion if you shine a flashlight against a nearby wall: the light pattern on the wall will have a larger diameter than the flashlight lens. If you hold two flashlights together and shine them both against the wall, you'll get a fuzzy area in the middle where it's difficult to determine which light source is responsible for which portion of the illumination. The further away from the wall you move, the larger this fuzzy area gets. This is, in effect, what limits the distance on multimode fiber (that is if you can call 1.2 miles a distance limitation for a single cable run). As the length of the cable increases, it becomes more difficult for the diode on the receiving end to distinguish between the different light frequencies.

Because multimode transmissions are light-based instead of electrical, fiber benefits from being completely immune to all types of EMI and RFI noise. Multimode transmission makes an extremely good candidate for high-noise environments. Fluorescent lights, transformers, and heavy machinery have no effect on these signal transmissions.

Fiber is also capable of handling extremely high bandwidths. As twisted-pair cable and other transmission media struggle to break the 100 Mbps barrier, fiber is already enjoying throughputs of 655 Mbps with ATM and even 1 Gbps under the new Ethernet specifications. If you remember that twisted-pair cable started out at 1 Mbps and has currently grown by a factor of 100, it's safe to say that we have not even begun to scratch the surface of what fiber-optic cable will handle.

The secret lies in its transmission properties. If you remember the discussion on transmission basics earlier in this chapter, you'll recall how EMI radiates out from an electrical cable whenever the voltage or frequency changes. Another property of EMI is that as the voltage level drops, the EMI field collapses and will actually put some of the energy back into the circuit. The result is that instead of the circuit immediately returning to zero volts, it slowly declines in voltage. The same is true during power up. EMI will resist the increase in voltage, causing the power to ramp up instead of immediately hitting full signal strength.

This transmission is like driving your car. If you step on the gas, you do not immediately jump to 65 mph but rather slowly increase in velocity until this speed is reached. This is because friction (like EMI in an electrical circuit) is resisting your change in speed. It takes you less time to move from a standing stop to 30 mph than it does to get to 70 mph.

Taking in to account the EMI forces, our nice clean digital signal actually looks more like Figure 2.14.

FIGURE 2.14

EMI effect on a digital electrical signal

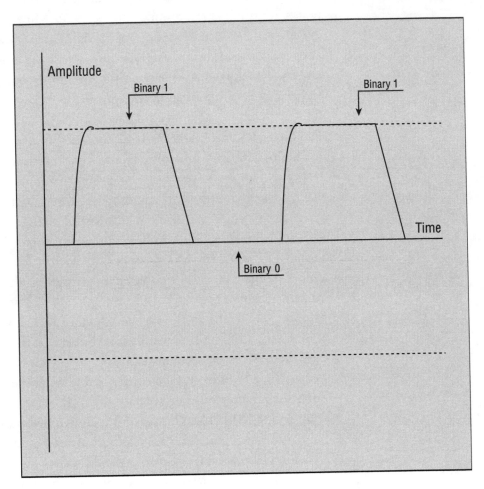

This delay is referred to as *switching time* and limits just how quickly information can be pushed down the wire. If the signal changes are faster than a circuit's switching time, the circuit will not have the opportunity to finish changing voltage levels before the next transmission is sent. To return to the car analogy, you can go from zero to 30 mph and back to zero faster than you can go from zero to 70 mph and back to zero. Slower speeds are easier to achieve.

Because light does not produce EMI, it does not suffer this shortcoming of electrical circuits. As the light pulses on and off, it has no real resistance to these changes in state. This allows the light to be pulsated very quickly, supporting very large data transfer rates (the more the light pulses in a given time period, the more information can be transferred). The limiting factor is the switching time of the sending and receiving diodes, which are, alas, electrical devices.

One minor inconvenience of fiber circuits is that all communications can take place in one direction only. The send and receive diodes are specific to their tasks and cannot accept data in the opposite direction. So fiber-optic cables are usually run in pairs, one cable to carry the data in each direction. Connections are usually labeled as Tx (for "transmit") and Rx (for "receive"). When connecting systems together, ensure the connections run from Tx on one system to Rx on the other. Because two channels are used, fiber connections are usually full duplex in nature. The exceptions to this are 100VG-ANYLAN, ATM, and FDDI.

Wiring topology for fiber networks can be configured as a bus (similar to thinnet) when only two stations are used, a star (similar to twisted-pair cable), or as a ring. Think of a bus topology twisted around into a circle and you get the idea of how a ring topology is laid out. The circuit follows a complete path with stations tapping in around the circumference. In a ring topology, the Tx port of a station is connected to the Rx port of its downstream neighbor (a fancy way of saying the next station along the ring). This station then has its Tx port connected to the next downstream neighbor. This continues until the circuit loops back to the original station. Figure 2.15 shows fiber-optic cable creating a ring topology.

FIGURE 2.15

Fiber-optic cable used to create a ring topology

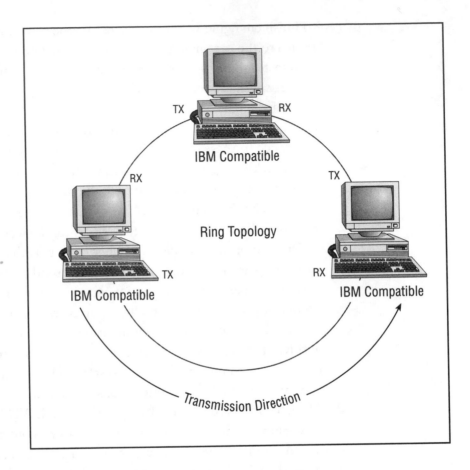

Fiber is supported by a number of different communication protocols. The existence of fiber-optic cable does not automatically mean you are running FDDI (or even operating at 100 Mbps, for that matter). I've run into a number of Network Administrators who have assumed their backbone was operating at 100 Mbps because they were using fiber, only to find out it was a normal 10 Mb Ethernet circuit. When in doubt, check the specifications on your hardware and be very specific when purchasing from your vendor.

Connector Types

There are a number of different connector types used with fiber. The most popular are SMA and FDDI connectors. Plan on buying all of your cabling with the connectors pre-installed or having a qualified professional install the connectors for you. Attaching fiber connectors is a precision art that must be done in a near clean-room type of environment, because a single spec of dust can destroy the transmission characteristics of a fiber optic cable. This will become less of an issue over time as the tools to both connect and test fiber optic cables become cheaper and more readily available. While dirt and dust will always be a problem, determining if a connector has been attached properly will be much easier. Figure 2.16 shows common fiber-optic cable connectors.

FDDI connectors are only used when connecting systems to an FDDI ring. SMA connectors make up a majority of the other connection requirements.

Advantages

Fiber-optic cable has the following advantages:

- resistance to noise
- it is difficult to tap
- high bandwidth
- wide industry acceptance

Resistance to Noise

Because fiber uses light as its transmission source, it is impervious to EMI and RFI noise.

FIGURE 2.16

Common fiber-optic cable connectors include FDDI and SMA.

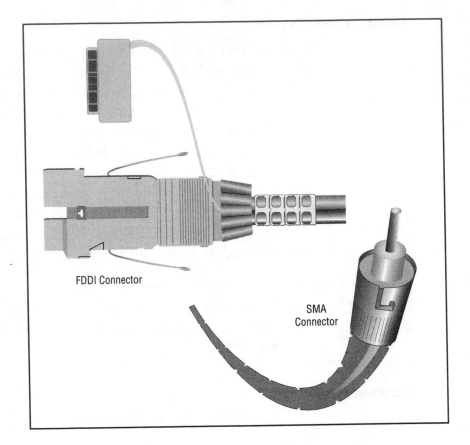

FDDI Connector

SMA
Connector

Security

Because light sources do not generate EMI fields, it is impossible to capture information traveling on the fiber optic cable without breaking the circuit.

Bandwidth

Fiber has the ability to transfer data at extremely high rates. It is faster than any other type of cabling.

Industry Acceptance

Because of its high bandwidth potential, fiber is guaranteed a place in all upcoming LAN topology specifications. Standardizing on fiber ensures that you will have an upgrade path to faster topologies later.

Disadvantages

Fiber-optic cable has two main disadvantages: difficult installation, and cost.

Installation

Fiber-optic cable is light and flexible, which makes it easy to route in tight areas, but the difficulty in adding connectors makes it cumbersome to work with. Fiber-optic cable is sold pre-connected in standard lengths, but if the standard length is one foot shy of what you need, you could be looking at custom length cables, which tend to be expensive.

It's a good idea always to overestimate your requirements for cable runs. Very rarely can you run your cables in a straight line from point A to point B. There are almost always obstacles that you will need to route your cables around. Never install a cable so that it is taut. Tension between the cable and the connector can lead to premature failure.

Cost

Fiber is the most expensive of the three cable media. Much of the expense comes from the work required to install the connectors: While a three-foot cable will run in the neighborhood of $50–$60, a ten-foot cable will usually be only a few dollars more ($60–$70).

Appropriate Applications

These are the appropriate applications for fiber:

- areas of medium to high EMI or RFI noise, such as machine shops or power plants

- extremely long cable runs, for example, in high-rise office buildings

- environments with sensitive data or where security is an issue, such as financial, military, or government contractor facilities

- high-speed backbone connectivity

- server connections where 100% fault tolerance is required (Fiber is required to support FDDI's dual ring design. We will discuss this in greater detail in Chapter 3.)

Cable Specifications

Table 2.4 shows the specifications for fiber-optic cable.

TABLE 2.4 Fiber-optic Cable Specifications	Item	Specification
	Transmission source	Infrared LED
	Topologies Supported	10 Mb, 100 Mb and 1 Gb Ethernet, FDDI, ATM
	Maximum cable length	1.2 miles (2 KM)
	Minimum cable length	None
	Maximum number of stations	Dependent on topology: Ethernet, 1,024 per logical segment; FDDI, 500 stations

TABLE 2.4 (cont.) Fiber-optic Cable Specifications	Item	Specification
	Maximum number of segments	Dependent on topology: 10 Mb Ethernet, five repeated segments with only three being populated; 100Tx, two repeated segments; 100T4, two repeated segments; 100VG-ANYLAN, five repeated segments, all of which may be populated; FDDI, dependent on configuration; 1 Gig Ethernet, still under examination, possibly two repeated segments
	Maximum overall segment length	Dependent on topology. 10 Mb Ethernet, 3000ft. (925 M); 100VG-ANYLAN, 3000 ft (925 M); 100Tx, 650ft. (100 M); 100T4: 650 ft. (100 M); FDDI, maximum ring size of 3,280 ft. (1 KM) ; 1 Gig Ethernet, under development, it may be 3,280 ft (1 KM)

The Atmosphere

The atmosphere is what is referred to as an *unbound* medium—a circuit with no formal boundaries. It has no constraints to force a signal to flow within a certain path. Coax, twisted-pair cable, and fiber-optic cable are all examples of *bounded* media as they restrain the signal to within the wire. An unbounded transmission is free to travel anywhere.

The atmosphere is capable of transmitting a variety of signal types. The most commonly used are light and radio waves. Each of these transmission types has its own set of strengths and weaknesses that makes it most appropriate for only specific applications.

Light Transmissions

Light transmissions use lasers. These devices operate in a very similar fashion to a fiber cable circuit, except without the glass media. Because laser transmissions are directional, they require a clear line of sight and precise alignment between the devices. This helps to enhance system security, but it limits the light transmissions' effective distance. They are also sensitive to environmental conditions—a heavy mist or snowfall can interfere with their transmission properties. Still, the use of light as a transmission medium makes high bandwidths easy to achieve.

Advantages

Light transmissions have the following advantages:

- They require no FCC approval.

- They have the potential for high bandwidth (10 Mbps or more).

- They require no cabling between systems.

Disadvantages

Light transmissions have the following disadvantages:

- They provide short effective distances.

- They are sensitive to environmental changes.

- Maintaining alignment between devices can be a nuisance.

Appropriate Applications

Light transmissions are especially useful in campus networks where running network cables between buildings is impossible due to zoning or physical obstructions.

Radio Waves

Radio waves used for networking purposes are typically transmitted in the 1–20 GHz range and are referred to as *microwave* signals. These signals can be fixed-frequency or spread-spectrum in nature.

A *fixed-frequency* signal is a single frequency used as a *carrier wave* for the information you wish to transmit. A radio station is a good example of a single frequency transmission. When you tune in to a station's carrier wave frequency on your FM dial, you can hear the signal that is riding on it.

A carrier wave is a signal that is used to carry other information. This information is superimposed onto the signal (much the same way as noise) and the resultant wave is transmitted out into the atmosphere. This signal is then received by a device called a "demodulator" (in effect, your car radio is a demodulator that can be set for different frequencies) which removes the carrier signal and passes along the remaining information. A carrier wave is used to boost a signal's power and extend the receiving range of the signal.

A *spread-spectrum* signal is identical to a fixed frequency except multiple frequencies are transmitted. The reason for this is the reduction of interference through noise. Spread spectrum is a technology that came out of wartime, when an enemy would transmit on an identical frequency and jam a fixed-frequency signal. Because spread spectrum uses multiple frequencies, it is much more difficult to interfere.

There are two methods that can be used to transmit both fixed-frequency and spread-spectrum signals. These are referred to as terrestrial and space-based transmissions.

Terrestrial Transmissions

Terrestrial transmissions are radio signals that are completely land-based in nature. The sending stations are typically transmission towers located on the top of mountains or tall buildings. The range of these systems is usually line-of-sight, although an unobstructed view is not required. Depending on the signal strength, 50 miles is about the maximum range achievable with a terrestrial satellite system. Local TV and radio stations are good examples of industries that rely on terrestrial-based broadcasts. Their signals can only be received locally.

Advantages

Terrestrial transmissions have the following advantages:

- They require no FCC approval on spread-spectrum signals under 1 watt.

- They are less affected by environmental changes than laser transmissions.

- They have a longer range than laser transmissions.

- Their long-term costs can be cheaper than using a local exchange carrier.

Disadvantages

Terrestrial transmissions have the following disadvantages:

- They require FCC approval for most configurations.

- Security is a concern, as the signal can be easily snooped.

Appropriate Applications

There are two main applications for terrestrial transmissions:

- metropolitan area networks (MANs)

- small mobile networks

Space-Based Transmissions

Space-based transmissions are signals that originate from a land-based system but are then bounced off one or more satellites that orbit the Earth in the upper atmosphere. The greatest benefit of space-based communications is range. Signals can be received from almost every corner of the world. The space-based satellites can be tuned to increase or decrease the effective broadcast area.

Unless you're charged with managing the backbone of a Fortune 500 company, or you're in the broadcasting business, space-based transmissions are probably overkill.

Advantages

Space-based transmissions have the following advantages:

- Transmission distances are greater than with any other technology.

- They are less affected by environmental changes.

- They are capable of supporting a fully portable network.

Disadvantages

Space-based transmissions have two main disadvantages:

- They are expensive to set up and maintain.

- They require FCC and foreign licensing prior to installation.

Appropriate Applications

The most appropriate application for a space-based transmission is as a backbone of a very large organization.

Network Design Examples

Let's look at three separate network examples and try to determine which medium or media would be the best fit for their network wiring. Because we have not yet discussed topology or network operating systems, we will not factor these in as part of our discussion—we will only be focusing on the criteria covered in this chapter.

A Small Field Office

Let's assume we have been charged with networking a small remote office that consists of four salespeople. The office space is a single room and is not expected to grow over the next five years. Most sales activity takes place back at the corporate office. These individuals are located here in this office space as a convenience to some of the organization's larger customers. This group's bandwidth requirements are minimal.

There are three key points to pull out of this description:

■ small number of users (four)

■ no expected growth

■ minimal bandwidth requirements

Based on these factors, our best choice would probably be thinnet wiring. Wiring would be laid out as a bus topology. Because all of our users are located in a single room, keeping track of which computer is directly connected to which other computer should not be a problem. The benefit would be an easy and inexpensive installation.

A Medium-Size Network

In our next example, we need to develop the wiring scheme for a 250-user network. There are multiple servers providing a central storage area for all files. Bandwidth demands are high, as many users are graphic artists who are rendering large images across the network.

The key points of this description are:

- 250 users

- high bandwidth demands

Clearly, thinnet would not be a good choice in this situation. Its susceptibility to causing a major network outage has the potential of affecting too many users. Also, its ability to support no more than a 10 Mbps throughput rate makes it a poor choice.

Due to the bandwidth demands, we need to attack this network as two separate halves. The first portion is the user connectivity. While each user needs to push large amounts of information, it is doubtful that they will need more than the 100 Mbps supported by twisted-pair cable. In fact, depending upon the performance level of their computers, even 10 Mbps may be sufficient. Each user could be connected to the network using CAT 5 twisted-pair cable in a star topology.

The server portion of the equation has a much higher bandwidth requirement. Because we have many end users that will be attempting to transfer information with only a few servers, these servers will require "fatter pipes" in order to keep up with the data rate. The server may need to communicate with the network at 100 Mbps or possibly even 1 Gbps. With this in mind, fiber optic cables may be our best choice.

For now, do not worry about the technology required to connect systems running at different speeds, or even connecting dissimilar cabling types.

We cover the hardware required to accomplish these tasks in Chapter 4.

A Campus Network

Finally, we are required to design the wiring for a multi-building organization. Each building is 16 stories high. Users on each floor require network access. While each building will contain its own data center, users will still need access to networking resources in the other building.

The twist is that the buildings are 300 yards apart and separated by a set of railroad tracks. The railroad company that owns the tracks will not grant permission to dig underneath them for the purpose of running cable. The local exchange carrier (telephone) will allow you to use their poles for cable routing, but only at a high monthly service rate.

Our key points are:

- There are two 16-story buildings.

- Each building has a data center but connectivity is required between each building.

- Options for cabling between buildings are expensive due to obstructions.

Again, let's break our network up into manageable groups. We have three separate areas to focus on:

- connecting the end users

- connecting the floors of each building together

- connectivity between the two buildings

As in our last example, our users on each floor could be connected via twisted-pair cabling in a star topology. While no bandwidth requirements were given, it may be best to wire CAT 5 cabling just in case a high level of throughput is required now or sometime in the future.

Our next problem is providing connectivity between the different floors of each building. While no precise distances were given, it is probably safe to assume that there is a distance of 200 ft. to 300 ft. between the first floor and the 16th floor. This could be connected as well with twisted-pair cable, as it is below our maximum length of 325 ft. To be safe we could even add a repeater, which would extend our maximum distance to 650 ft.

What's also missing from this description, however, is what space is available for running the cabling between floors. It is not uncommon for the network wiring to be run alongside the power cables that provide electricity to the upper levels. In fact, it may also be possible that some of the rooms the network backbone passes through will contain large transformer units.

With this in mind, we may be better off connecting our floors using fiber optic cable. Its resistance to electromagnetic fields will leave it completely unaffected in these environments.

Our final problem is how to connect our two buildings. Our choices here will depend upon the annual climate and how well outages can be tolerated.

If the prevailing weather is temperate and brief outages due to inclement weather can be tolerated, using lasers may be the best option. The laser hardware could be set up on each roof and aligned to provide network connectivity between the two buildings.

If the climate tends to be a bit more hostile, with frequent bouts of fog and snow, or if connectivity between the two buildings must be operational at all times, then terrestrial radio transmissions may be the way to go. While more expensive than the laser solution, radio is a much more robust option.

Summary

There are a number of choices available when selecting a transmission medium. Each has its own inherent strengths and weaknesses and is most appropriate for only certain applications. There is no single "killer medium" yet that can combine low cost, high noise resistance, easy installation, long cable runs, and high bandwidth. It's important to analyze your environment and choose media wisely. Out of all the pieces that go into making up a network, transmission media are the most difficult to try and upgrade later.

In the next chapter, we'll discuss topology and learn how to connect these media into a functional network.

CHAPTER

3

Network Topology

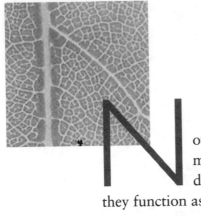

ow that we have a good understanding of which transmission media are available for carrying our data, we will discuss how these media should be configured so that they function as a network.

Topology Basics

The *topology* of a network is the set of rules for physically connecting and communicating on a given network medium. When you decide on a particular topology for connecting your network systems, you will need to follow a number of specifications that tell you how the systems need to be wired together, what type of connectors to use, and even how these systems must speak to each other on the wire.

Topology is broken down into two categories, physical and logical.

Physical Topology

Physical topology refers to how the transmission media is wired together. I touched on physical topology in the last chapter while discussing media, but here's a quick review. The three types of physical topology are *bus*, *star*, and *ring*.

Bus Topology

The bus topology is the common configuration for Thinnet wiring. Systems attached to the bus are connected in a series type of connection. All systems are connected via a single long cable run and tap in via T connectors. A bus topology can also be used to directly connect two systems. Figure 3.1 shows an example of bus topology.

F I G U R E 3.1

An example of bus topology

All Systems connect to the same logical cable length

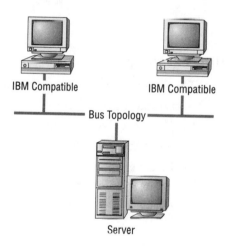

Server

Star Topology

The star topology is the common configuration of twisted-pair wiring. Each system is connected to a central device, such as a hub or a switch. Only two stations are ever connected to each physical wire run and branch out from the central device like a starburst. These hubs and switches can be linked together to form larger networks. Figure 3.2 shows an example of star topology.

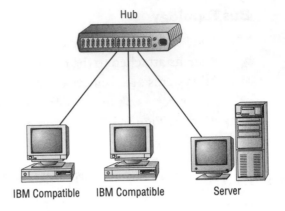

FIGURE 3.2

An example of star
topology

Ring Topology

The ring configuration is the common configuration for fiber cable. The output data port (Tx for "transmit") is connected to the input data port (Rx for "receive") of the next station along the ring. This continues until the last station connects its output data port to the input data port of the first system, forming a complete ring. Figure 3.3 is an example of ring topology. Systems are connected in a similar fashion to the bus topology, except with the two ends of the bus tied together.

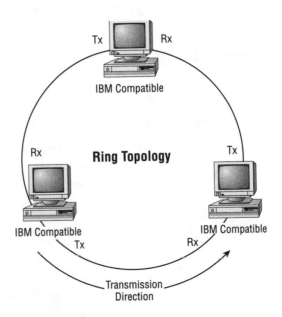

FIGURE 3.3

An example of ring
topology

The transmission media is separate from the physical topology. The examples I've just given are what you will commonly run into in the field, but they are not hard and fast rules. For example, even though fiber is commonly used in a ring topology, you can use it in a star or even a bus topology. We'll cover this in greater detail later in the chapter.

As mentioned in Chapter 2, each of these physical topologies has its own inherent strengths and weaknesses. In order to determine which physical topology best fits your environment, you must first decide on which logical topology you will use.

Logical Topology

A *logical topology* describes the communication rules each station should use when communicating on a network. For example, the specifications of the logical topology describe how each station should determine if it's okay to transmit data, and what a station should do if it tries to transmit data at the same time as another station. The logical topology's job is to ensure that information gets transferred as quickly and as error free as possible. Think of a discussion group moderator and you'll get the idea. The moderator ensures that each person in the group gets a turn to speak. They also ensure that if two individuals try to speak at the same time, one gets priority and the other waits their turn.

So how are physical and logical topologies related? Any given logical topology will operate on only specific physical topologies. For example, the Ethernet specification will operate on a bus or a star physical topology but will not work on a ring; FDDI will function on a ring or a star topology but not on a bus. Once you have determined which logical topology you will use, you can then go about selecting your physical topology.

Logical topologies are defined by the Institute of Electrical and Electronics Engineers (IEEE). The IEEE is a not-for-profit organization that consists of an assembly of companies and private individuals within the networking industry. The members of the IEEE work together to define specifications, preventing any single company from claiming ownership of the technology and helping to ensure that products from multiple vendors will interoperate successfully in a network.

The most common network specifications are:

Specification	Defines
IEEE 802.3	10 Mb Ethernet
IEEE 802.3u	100 Mb Ethernet
IEEE 802.3x	Full Duplex Ethernet
IEEE 802.3z	1 Gb Ethernet
IEEE 802.5	Token Ring
IEEE 802.11	Wireless LANs
IEEE 802.12	100VG-AnyLAN
IEEE 802.14	Cable Modem

Note that 802.3z is still under development, and its final spec is not due until 1998.

> These network specifications should not be confused with the *frame types* (802.2, 802.3, and so on) that have been specified by Novell for transmitting data on a NetWare network. These frame types are all based on the IEEE 802.3 standard. We will cover frame types in more detail in the NetWare section of the book.

Now let's explore the rules involved in each of our logical topologies. The logical topology of a large network can contain multiple paths to the same destination. This is usually done for *redundancy* (if one link dies, another can be used) or for *load balancing* (spreading the load over multiple links).

When data is transmitted onto a network, it is broken up into smaller pieces referred to as frames (I'll talk more about frames when I cover

Ethernet later in this chapter). Each frame is stamped with a *sequence number* to identify the order in which the data was split up. By looking at these sequence numbers, a station receiving these frames knows in what order to place them to reassemble the data correctly.

Connection Types

Every logical topology uses one of three methods for creating the connections between end stations. These are referred to as *circuit switching*, *message switching*, and *packet switching*.

Circuit Switching

Circuit switching means that when data needs to be transferred from one node to another, a dedicated connection is created between the two systems. Bandwidth is dedicated to this communication session and remains available until the connection is no longer required. A regular phone call uses circuit switching. When you place a call, a connection is set up between your phone and the phone you are calling. This connection remains in effect until you finish your call and hang up. Figure 3.4 illustrates a circuit-switched network. The best route is selected and bandwidth is dedicated to this communication session, remaining in place until no longer needed. All data follows the same path.

FIGURE 3.4

An example of a circuit-switched network

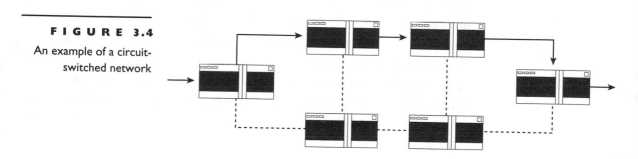

Circuit-switched networks are useful for delivering information that must be received in the order it was sent—for example, applications such as real-time audio and video cannot tolerate the delays incurred in reassembling the data in the correct order. While circuit switching ensures that data is delivered as quickly as possible by dedicating a connection to the task, it can also be wasteful compared to other types of connections because the circuit will remain active even if the end stations are not currently transmitting.

Examples of circuit-switched networks include:

■ Asynchronous Transfer Mode (ATM)

■ analog dial-up line (public telephone network)

■ ISDN

■ leased line

■ T1

Message Switching

Message switching means that a *store-and-forward* type of connection is set up between connectivity devices along the message path. The first device creates a connection to the next and transmits the entire message. Once this is complete, the connection is torn down, and the second device repeats the process if required.

The delivery of e-mail is a good example of message switching. As you type in your e-mail message, your computer queues the information until you are done. When you hit the Send button, your system delivers your message in its entirety to your local post office, which again queues the message. Your post office then contacts the post office of the person to whom you have addressed the message. Again, the message is delivered in its entirety and queued by the receiving system. Finally the remote post office delivers your message to its intended recipient using the same process.

Figure 3.5 illustrates a message-switched network. While all the data still follows the same path, only one portion of the network is dedicated to delivering this data at any given time.

FIGURE 3.5

An example of a message switched network

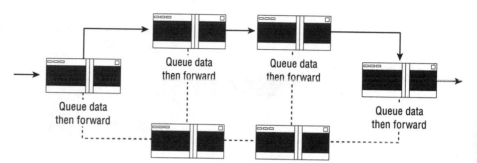

None of the logical topologies covered in this book utilize message switching for the delivery of data.

Message switching increases the memory and processing requirements on interim hardware in order to store the information prior to delivery.

Packet Switching

The final method for connecting end stations is *packet switching*. This method is by far the most widely used in current networking topologies. Within a packet-switched network, each individual frame can follow a different path to its final destination. Because each frame may follow a different path, frames may or may not be received in the same order they were transmitted, so the receiving station uses the sequence numbers on the frames to reassemble the data in the correct order.

Note the operative phrase "can follow a different path." As you'll see later in the chapter, there are other factors besides the logical topology that play a part in determining whether this feature is exploited. For now, it is enough to realize that in a packet-switched network all the data may not follow the same path.

Figure 3.6 illustrates a packet-switched network. Data is allowed to follow any path to its destination. Packet switching does not require that any bandwidth be reserved for this transmission.

FIGURE 3.6

An example of a packet-switched network

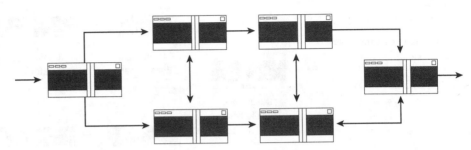

Packet-switched networks are useful for transmitting regular network data. This includes storing files, printing, or cruising the Web. In short, all the activities you would normally associate with network usage will run fine in a packet-switched network. While packet switching is a poor choice for the delivery of live audio and video, it is extremely efficient for delivering information that is not time sensitive, because it does not require dedicating bandwidth to the delivery of information. Other nodes are capable of sharing the available bandwidth as required.

Examples of packet-switched networks include:

- all Ethernet topologies

- 100VG-ANYLAN

- FDDI

- Frame Relay and X.25

Ethernet Networks

Ethernet is by far the most popular networking topology. Its ability to support a wide range of cable types, low-cost hardware, and plug-and-play connectivity has caused it to find its way into more corporate (as well as home) networks than any other topology.

Ethernet's communication rules are called *Carrier Sense Multiple Access with Collision Detection* (CSMA/CD). This is a mouthful, but it's simple enough to interpret when you break it down:

- **Carrier Sense** means that all Ethernet stations are required to listen to the wire if they are not currently transmitting. By "listen," I mean that the station should be constantly monitoring the network to see if any other stations are currently sending data. By monitoring the transmissions of other stations, a station can tell if the network is open or in use. This way, the station does not just blindly transfer information and interfere with other stations; also, being in a constant listening mode means that the station is ready for when another station wants to send it data.

- **Multiple Access** simply means that more than two stations can be connected to the same network, and that all stations are allowed to transmit whenever the network is free. As we discussed in Chapter 2, it is far more efficient to allow stations to transmit only when they need to than it is to assign each system a time block in which it is allowed to transmit. Multiple access also scales much easier as you add more stations to the network.

- **Collision Detection** answers the question "What happens if two systems think the circuit is free and try to transmit data at the same time?" When two stations transmit simultaneously, a *collision* takes place. A collision is similar to RFI interference, and the resulting transmission becomes mangled and useless for carrying data. As a station transmits data, it watches for this type of condition; if it detects such a condition, the workstation assumes that a collision has taken place. All stations involved in the collision (all stations that were currently transmitting) will signal to the network that a collision has taken place. This causes all stations to back off, wait for a random period of time, and then retransmit.

Each station is responsible for determining its own random waiting period before retransmission. This helps to ensure that each station is waiting for a different period of time so that another collision does not take place. In the unlikely event that a second collision does occur, each station is required to double its waiting period before trying again. When two or more collisions take place, it is referred to as a *multiple collision*.

A *multiple collision* occurs when more then one collision takes place at the same time. While collisions are a normal part of Ethernet communications and are expected to happen from time to time, multiple collisions can be a sign that there is a problem with the network (for example, that there is a bad network card or that the network is carrying too much traffic).

If you were to chart CSMA/CD, it would look something like Figure 3.7.

An integral part of Ethernet communications is that each system is constantly monitoring the transmissions of all the other stations on the wire. It is possible to configure a workstation to read all of this information it receives. This is commonly referred to as a *promiscuous mode* system. Operating in promiscuous mode is what allows most network analyzers to function and can be leveraged by a network administrator to monitor a network from one central station so that errors and network statistics can be gathered.

Unfortunately, the existence of promiscuous mode also means that a not-so-honest person may be able to eavesdrop on the communications of their coworkers. This fact has increased the popularity of security and encryption products.

F I G U R E 3.7

Flowchart of Ethernet communication rules

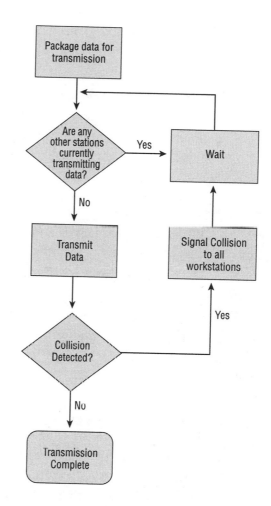

So how does a station determine if it should read or ignore the data being transmitted? To answer this, we must examine the concept of the Ethernet frame.

Ethernet Frames

An Ethernet frame is a set of digital pulses transmitted onto the transmission media in order to convey information. An Ethernet frame can be anywhere from 64 to 1,518 bytes (a byte being eight digital pulses or bits) in size and is organized into four sections, the *preamble*, the *header*, *data*, and the *frame check sequence* (FCS).

Preamble

I introduced the concept of the preamble in Chapter 2. A preamble is a defined series of communication pulses that tells all receiving stations, "get ready—I've got something to say." The standard preamble is eight bytes long.

 NOTE Because the preamble is considered part of the communication process and not part of the actual information being transferred, it is not usually included when measuring a frame's size.

Header

A header always contains information regarding who sent the frame and where they are trying to send it. It may also contain other information, such as how many bytes the frame contains; this is referred to as the *length field* and is used for error correction. If the receiving station measures the frame to be a different size than indicated in the length field, it asks the transmitting system to send a new frame. If the length field is not used, the header may instead contain a *type field* that describes what type of Ethernet frame it is.

The header size is always 14 bytes.

Data

The data section of the frame contains the actual data the station needs to transmit. It can be anywhere from 46 to 1,500 bytes in size. If a station has more than 1,500 bytes of information to transfer, it will break up the information over multiple frames and identify the proper order by using sequence numbers. Sequence numbers identify the order in which the destination system should reassemble the data. If the frame does not have 46 bytes' worth of information to convey, the station pads the end of this section by filling it in with 1 (remember that digital connections use binary numbers). Depending on the frame type, this section may also contain additional information describing what protocol or method of communication the systems are using.

We will cover protocols in Chapters 5 and 6.

Frame Check Sequence (FCS)

The frame check sequence is used to ensure that the data received is actually the data sent. The transmitting system processes the frame check sequence portion of the frame through an algorithm called a *cyclic redundancy check* or CRC. This CRC takes the values of the above fields and creates a 4-byte number. When the destination system receives the frame, it runs the same CRC and compares it to the value within this field. If the destination system finds a match, it assumes the frame is free from errors and processes the information. If the comparison fails, the destination station assumes that something happened to the frame in its travels and requests that another copy of the frame be sent by the transmitting system.

The Frame Header Section

Now that we have a better understanding of what an Ethernet frame is, let's take a closer look at the header section. The header information is what is ultimately responsible for identifying who sent the data and where they wanted it to go.

The header contains two fields to identify the source and destination of the transmission. These are the node addresses of both the source and destination systems. This number is also referred to as the *media access control* (MAC) address. The *node address* is a unique number that serializes the network devices (like network cards or networking hardware) and is a unique identifier that distinguishes it from any other networking device in the world. No two networking devices should ever be assigned the same number. Think of this number as being the equivalent of a telephone number. Every home with a telephone has a unique phone number so that the phone company knows where to direct the call. In this same fashion, a system will use the destination systems MAC address to send the frame to the proper system.

The MAC address has nothing to do with Apple's computers and is always capitalized. It is the number used by all that systems attached to the network (PCs and Macs included) to uniquely identify themselves.

This 6-byte, 12-digit hexadecimal number is broken up into two parts. The first half of the address is the manufacturer's identifier. A manufacturer is assigned a range of MAC addresses to use when serializing their devices. Some of the more predominant MAC addresses are:

First Six Bytes of MAC Address	Manufacturer
00000C	Cisco
0000A2	Bay Networks
0080D3	Shiva
00AA00	Intel
02608C	3Com
080009	Hewlett-Packard
080020	Sun
08005A	IBM

The first six bytes of the MAC address can be a good troubleshooting aid. If you are investigating a problem, try to determine the source MAC address. Knowing who made the device may put you a little closer to determining which system is causing the problem. For example, if the first six bytes are 0000A2, you know you need to focus your attention on any Bay Networks device on your network.

The second half of the MAC address is the serial number the manufacturer has assigned to the device. Figure 3.8 shows some examples of decoded addresses. The first denotes all digits that constitute the full address. The second assumes that the leading 0 is always implied and ignores them.

FIGURE 3.8

Two forms of formatting are commonly used when writing a MAC address.

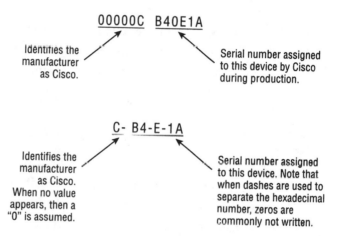

Two Examples of the Same Node Address

00000C B40E1A

Identifies the manufacturer as Cisco.

Serial number assigned to this device by Cisco during production.

C- B4-E-1A

Identifies the manufacturer as Cisco. When no value appears, then a "0" is assumed.

Serial number assigned to this device. Note that when dashes are used to separate the hexadecimal number, zeros are commonly not written.

One address worthy of note is FF-FF-FF-FF-FF-FF. This is referred to as a *broadcast address*. A broadcast address is special in that it means all systems receiving this packet should read the included data. If a system sees a frame that has been sent to the broadcast address, it will read the frame and process the data if it can.

You should never encounter a frame that has a broadcast address in the source node field.

How do we find out what the destination node address is in order to send data to a system? After all, network cards do not ship with phone books. This is done with a special frame referred to as an *address resolution protocol* frame or ARP frame. ARP functions differently depending on which protocol you're using (for example, IPX, IP, NetBEUI). I will describe ARP in greater detail later in the book when we discuss networking protocols. For now, it is simply worth noting that on an Ethernet network, systems have a method of automatically discovering each other. No initial setup is required by the network administrator.

A quick point about Ethernet frame size. We mentioned that each frame contains a 14-byte header and a 4-byte FCS. These field lengths are fixed and never change. The sum of the two is 18 bytes. The data field, however, is allowed to vary from 46 to 1,500 bytes. This is where our minimum and maximum frame sizes come from.

```
46 + 18 = 64 bytes (minimum frame size)

1,500 + 18 = 1,518 bytes (maximum frame size)
```

Speaking of protocols, note that we already have the capability of transferring information on our Ethernet network and yet we've made no mention of them. The reasons for this will become clearer when we discuss the Open Systems Interconnect (OSI) model. For now, remember that every system on our Ethernet segment sees every packet and needs to look at that packet to see if it is addressed to it or not. If I am using a PC that only speaks IPX to a NetWare server, and somewhere on my network are two Apple computers speaking AppleTalk, my system still sees those frames and needs to look at every one of them to determine if it needs to read the data within the frame or not. The fact that my system speaks a different protocol makes no difference—the CSMA/CD communication rules of Ethernet require every computer on the segment to look at every packet.

That a computer must dedicate some CPU time to analyzing frames on a network may seem a minor point, but it isn't—if the network is busy, a workstation can appear to respond sluggishly, even though it is not intentionally transmitting or receiving network data.

Ethernet communications fall into a number of different categories. While most use identical means of communication, they differ in their rate of data transmission. Let's take a look at each category now.

Local Area Network (LAN) Topologies

Local area network (LAN) topologies are network configurations that are confined to a small area such as a single floor or a building. LAN topologies are focused on delivering data to many systems within a small geographical area.

10 Mb Ethernet

10 Mb Ethernet is the oldest member of the Ethernet family. Developed in the late 1970s by Xerox, it later evolved into the IEEE specification 802.3 (pronounced *eight oh two dot three*). Its flexibility, high transmission rate (at the time anyway), and nonproprietary nature quickly made it the networking topology of choice for many network administrators.

10 Mb stands for the transmission speed of 10 megabits per second. This means that 10 Mb Ethernet is capable of transferring 10,000,000 bits (or 1,250,000 bytes) from one network station to another in a one-second period of time. This is under ideal conditions, however, and your mileage may vary. Note that 10 Mb does not translate into a 10-megabyte (MB) transfer rate but rather 1.25 megabytes per second (MBps). This confusion arises from the fact that some people refer to this topology as *10 Meg Ethernet*, which makes it sound as though the phrase refers to 10MB instead of 10 Mb.

The CSMA/CD nature of Ethernet means that most networks will begin to show a degradation in performance at 40–50% (4,000,000 to 5,000,000 bits per second) of maximum throughput. By the time

90% utilization is reached, response time is usually so slow that applications begin to time out.

The percentage of maximum throughput is referred to as the *utilization rate*. For example, if you were to take a measurement and note that 7,500,000 bits of data were passing by on the network, you could refer to this as a 75% utilization rate (7,500,000/10,000,000 x 100).

High utilization can be a bad thing. Every station needs to monitor the network for traffic prior to transmitting. The more traffic on the network, the longer a station has to wait before it is allowed to transmit its frame. This can make network response appear to be sluggish. Also, because more stations are trying to get their information out, there is an increased chance of collision. While collisions are a normal part of Ethernet transmissions, they slow down the transfer of information even more.

Another common measurement of throughput is *frame rate* or the number of frames that pass from one station to another in a one-second period of time (frames per second, or *fps*). The relationship between frame rate and utilization is directly related to the size of the frames.

As I mentioned earlier, a legal Ethernet frame can be anywhere from 64 to 1,518 bytes in length. This means that a 10 Mb Ethernet segment that is experiencing 100% utilization of 1,518 byte frames would have a frame rate of approximately 813fps. Written out mathematically it would look something like this:

```
(10,000,000/8)/(1,518+8+12) = 813 fps
```

- The (10,000,000/8) portion converts the maximum transfer rate in bits to bytes. This way the unit of measure is consistent throughout the formula, because our frame size is in bytes as well.

- 1,518 is the size of the frame as stated in our example.

- We add 8 to this because of the preamble. As mentioned earlier in this chapter, the preamble is technically not considered part of the frame, but it does use up bandwidth on our media.

■ The 12 is due to station listening time. As mentioned earlier, CSMA/CD requires each station to monitor the network for other transmitting stations before sending data.

The preamble and the listening time would be considered overhead on this circuit. It represents 20 bytes worth of bandwidth that is lost every time a packet is transmitted. A breakdown of maximum fps based on frame size would be as follows:

Frame Size in Bytes	Number of Frames at 100% Utilization
64	14,881
256	4,529
512	2,350
1,024	1,193
1,518	813

This breakdown brings up an interesting question—which is more efficient, many small frames or fewer larger ones? As you saw earlier, transmitting Ethernet frames carries with it a certain amount of overhead due to listening time and the preamble. If we multiply the size of the data field (frame size minus the header and FCS) by the number of frames transmitted, we can get a rough idea of what our potential throughput of raw data would be:

Data Field Size Times Frame Rate	Bytes of Data per Second
46 x 14,881	684,526
238 x 4,529	1,077,902
494 x 2,370	1,170,780
1,006 x 1,193	1,200,158
1500 x 813	1,219,500

As you can see, the frame size can make a dramatic difference in the amount of information the network is capable of transferring. Using the largest possible frame size, we can move 1.2 megabytes per second of data along the network. At the smallest frame size, this transfer rate is cut almost in half to 685 kilobytes per second (Kbps).

Some of the factors that go into controlling a network's average frame size are protocol selection and regulating the amount of broadcast traffic (broadcast frames tend to be small in size).

So which is a better measuring stick of network health, frame rate or utilization? While both are important, utilization is the meter that tells you how much of your bandwidth is currently in use, and the percentage of bandwidth in use dictates whether a network responds quickly to requests or appears to slow down application speed. The key is the frame size. I've seen networks running at 1,100 fps that appear to crawl while others sustain 3,000 or more fps with no noticeable performance degradation. When utilization levels consistently range from 30% to 50%, it may be time to look at load balancing the network, with more efficient protocols, or faster topologies like 100 Mb Ethernet.

Appropriate Applications

10 Mb Ethernet is appropriate for the following applications:

- **Small office environments:** If your environment is, say, a small law office or accounting firm, then 10 Mb Ethernet may be all you need. The average workstation bus is only capable of processing data at a rate of 1.5 Mbps to 5.0 Mbps, so in light-traffic environments the network is definitely not the *performance gate*.

The performance gate of a system is that portion of the configuration that supports the lowest level of throughput. For example, if I have two computers that can process data at 20 Mb, and they are connected by a network that supports only 10 Mb communications, the network would be the performance gate because it is capable of processing the least amount of data.

- **Workstation connections:** If you have a large environment (100 or more nodes), 10 Mb Ethernet may still be sufficient for workstation connection. There are devices available that allow you to run your servers on one topology (such as 100 Mb Ethernet) and your workstations on another. This type of configuration is usually sufficient when you are dealing with simple word processing and spreadsheet files but there are more nodes doing it. If you have a few workstations with higher data transfer needs (such as graphics development), they can be placed on the faster topology as well.

Topology Rules

Table 3.1 summarizes the topology rules for 10 Mb Ethernet.

T A B L E 3.1 Topology Rules for 10 Mb Ethernet	Item	Rules
	Maximum cable lengths	Thinnet: 600 ft Twisted pair: 325 ft Fiber: 3,000 ft
	Minimum cable lengths	Thinnet: 1.5 ft
	Maximum number of stations per cable	Thinnet: 30 Twisted pair: 2 Fiber: 2
	Maximum number of stations per logical network	1,024
	Maximum number of segments	5 segments, only three of which are populated
	Maximum overall length of logical network	3,000 ft

100 Mb Ethernet

100 Mb Ethernet is the natural progression from 10 Mb Ethernet. Communication is still CSMA/CD, only faster. The time between digital pulses is condensed and the time a system is required to wait and listen is

shorter. The result is a tenfold increase in throughput. Because 100 Mb Ethernet is an extension of 10 Mb Ethernet, the IEEE simply extended the original Ethernet specification and dubbed this topology IEEE 802.3u. The "u" is used for revision control and indicates that this specification has simply been appended to the original 802.3 specification.

There are currently two implementations of 100 Mb Ethernet: 100Tx and 100T4. 100Tx is the older of the two and by far the more widely used. 100T4 has the additional benefit of working with CAT 3 twisted-pair cabling, while 100Tx requires CAT 5.

WARNING   100Tx and 100T4 are not directly compatible. For example, you cannot use 100T4 network cards with a 100Tx hub and expect them to work. When purchasing hardware for a 100 Mb Ethernet network, make sure you know what you're getting.

The improvements that 100 Mb Ethernet offers do not come without a price, however. The shorter transmission times mean that the overall cable lengths for 100 Mb Ethernet must be shorter than for 10 Mb Ethernet.

In the last chapter, we discussed switching time—the delay experienced when an electrical circuit tries to change state from one voltage level to another. A similar phenomenon to this is *propagation delay*. Propagation delay is the period of time it takes for a signal change to travel from one end of a cable to the other.

As an analogy, think of a very long and skinny fish tank. If I start to quickly fill the tank from one end, the water will eventually work its way through the tank and will attempt to remain level. The side of the tank that I'm filling from, however, will always contain just a little more water because the forces of gravity and friction will be resisting the water's movement to seek its own level. At any given time, there will be a delay between the time when the side I'm filling reaches a certain level and the time when the opposite end reaches that same level. This is, in effect, propagation delay. Figure 3.9 is an example of propagation delay. As station A transmits its data, there will be a brief delay before the electrical signal reaches station B and then station C. This is because the wire is resisting the change in voltage of the signal.

FIGURE 3.9

An example of
propagation delay

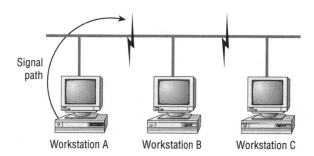

Signal
path

Workstation A   Workstation B   Workstation C

As an example, let's say I have a very long length of cable similar to that in Figure 3.9. Let's also assume that workstation A sends a digital pulse onto the network cable as it begins to transmit an Ethernet frame to workstation B. Using our fish tank analogy, the forces resisting this change in voltage level would be the resistance in the wire and electromagnetic radiation. Therefore, there would be a difference in voltage level at each end of the wire as the signal moves down the network cable.

Now, let's also assume that workstation C needs to transmit data to workstation B, but it is currently in a listening mode. If the cable length is long enough, the propagation delay (measured in seconds) from one end of the cable to the other could be longer than the time it takes a station to completely transmit a frame. This means that station A may be able to complete the transmission of a frame before the first digital pulse of that frame reaches station C.

The result would be a collision resulting in both frames becoming unusable. While collisions are normal in an Ethernet network, this situation has a unique spin. Workstation A (and possibly workstation C as well) completed frame transmission before the collision took place. As far as workstation A is concerned, it was not involved in the collision and does not need to retransmit the data! Depending on the upper level protocol used on the network, the data would either be lost or workstation A would eventually time out from waiting for a receipt acknowledgment from workstation B and would retransmit the data. But this time-out is typically far longer than the time it would normally take to retransmit after a collision.

Propagation delay is not as much of an issue with fiber cable, because the delays are almost unmeasurable for your average network cable run. This is why the speed of light is used for measuring extremely long distances like the separation of celestial bodies.

So propagation delay is the reason why maintaining specified cable lengths is so important and why cable lengths must be shorter under 100 Mb Ethernet. The shorter transmission times when sending frames mean that a smaller propagation delay can be tolerated.

Appropriate Applications

The appropriate applications for 100 Mb Ethernet are as follows:

- **High end workstations:** If your environment includes end users who process large graphic files or compile code over the network, 100 Mb Ethernet may be just the trick to improve performance. These stations usually have a high performance bus that allows them to process data at a rate of 10 Mbps to 20 Mbps. While these types of data rates would overwhelm 10 Mb Ethernet, 100 Mb gives a bit more breathing room. The additional bandwidth may be just the thing to improve network response time. A word of caution, however: Some of the newer desktop machines utilize the same bus technology as server-class machines. A busy 100 Mb segment can easily move the performance gate from the network to the server itself. The result is that the server is unable to keep up with the rate of file requests and responds by crashing or losing data. You will need to ensure that your server is up to the task of servicing a 100 Mb network. RAID level 5 (RAID is short for *redundant array of inexpensive disks*) and other *go fast* technologies go a long way towards ensuring that a server will remain stable at these higher data rates.

■ **Backbones and server connections:** As I mentioned in the section on 10 Mb Ethernet, a larger environment (100 or more nodes) may benefit from your leaving the user community at 10 Mb while upgrading the servers to 100 Mb. Busy, non-populated segments that connect office floors or departments could benefit from the performance increase as well.

Topology Rules

Table 3.2 shows the topology rules for 100 Mb Ethernet.

T A B L E 3.2 Topology Rules for 100 Mb Ethernet	Item	Rules
	Maximum cable lengths	Twisted pair: 325 ft Fiber: 650 ft
	Minimum cable lengths	None
	Maximum number of stations per cable	Twisted pair: 2 Fiber: 2
	Maximum number of stations per logical network	1,024
	Maximum number of segments	2
	Maximum overall length of logical network	650 ft

I Gb Ethernet

Network transmission speeds are definitely on the rise. It was not until June of 1995 that the IEEE gave their full blessing to the final specification of 100 Mb Ethernet. By July of 1996, they were back in committee appointing a task force to create specifications for 1 Gb Ethernet. This task force has been dubbed 802.3z, as the specification is expected to simply be a natural progression from the original Ethernet standards. This new specification has received phenomenal support, with more than 80 organizations having joined the Gigabit Ethernet Alliance as of this writing. While a final specification is not due till the summer of 1998, some vendors have already begun shipping 1 Gb Ethernet products. Truly, the need for speed has taken hold in full force.

The 1 Gb Ethernet specification is meant to be direct competition for asynchronous transfer mode (ATM) on LANs. ATM, which has been in development for a number of years, currently has the potential of supporting data rates up to 622 Mb. Lack of agreement between vendors has delayed approval of final specifications for ATM, so it appears that 1 Gb Ethernet may become a fully recognized topology before ATM does.

Even though 1 Gb Ethernet appears to be following in the footsteps of its predecessors, there is one change of focus. While 10 Mb and 100 Mb Ethernet have been implemented mostly on twisted-pair cabling, 1 Gb Ethernet is made to run over fiber. Concessions will be made to leverage existing twisted-pair cable runs from wiring closets out to the desktop, but the majority of the cabling will need to be fiber. At this writing, it appears that 1 Gb Ethernet over CAT 5 twisted-pair will be limited to approximately 80 feet. Any lengths over that distance will require fiber cable.

The reasoning is twofold:

- First, the current specification has adopted the communication properties of Fiber Channel, which was developed for fiber-optic cable.

- Second, propagation delay is a factor. 1 Gb Ethernet represents a 100X increase in transmission speed over 10 Mb Ethernet. This means that only a minimal amount of propagation delay can be tolerated. Fiber is a perfect mate for this technology, as its propagation delay is very close to zero.

Appropriate Applications

About the only good fit for 1 Gb Ethernet would be a server or backbone connection when the desktop systems are already running at 100 Mb. My earlier cautions about ensuring that servers are up to handling this high rate of data apply even more with 1 Gbps transmission speeds. Only a top-of-the-line server specifically designed for this rate of data processing can ever hope to keep up in a busy environment.

Topology Rules

These rules are somewhat speculative. Because a final specification has not yet been drafted, it is based on early publishing notes from the 802.3z Task Force.

Table 3.3 shows the topology rules for Gigabit Ethernet.

T A B L E 3.3 Topology Rules for Gigabit Ethernet	Item	Rules
	Maximum cable lengths	Fiber: 1,640 ft Twisted-pair: currently 82 ft, possibly increasing to 325 ft later
	Minimum cable lengths	None
	Maximum number of stations per cable	Twisted-pair: 2 Fiber: 2
	Maximum number of stations per logical network	Still under development, should be 1,024
	Maximum number of segments	Still under development, should be 1 or 2
	Maximum overall length of logical network	Will be media dependent

This concludes our discussion of purely Ethernet-based topologies. Next, we will explore what other options besides CSMA/CD are available for constructing a network topology.

100VG-ANYLAN

100VG-ANYLAN was developed by Hewlett-Packard in parallel to the development of 100Tx. The *VG* portion of the name stands for *voice grade*, implying that the technology can be utilized on voice grade wiring (100VG supports CAT 3 twisted-pair cabling).

While HP worked hard to have its specification considered as the successor to 10 Mb Ethernet, it has a few additional features that prompted the IEEE to give it a specification all its own. The specification 802.12 was incorporated to cover 100VG, while 100Tx was incorporated as 802.3u, thus becoming the successor to the Ethernet legacy.

Demand Priority

As far as communications go, 100VG does away with CSMA/CD. Instead, it utilizes a feature called *demand priority*. Demand priority is an attempt to take some of the best features of Ethernet and ATM and mix them together. It's designed to have the ease of setup that Ethernet enjoys along with the *quality of service* supported by ATM.

Quality of service is the ability to allocate bandwidth to support real-time audio and video. While normal network data is robust enough to deal with short delays and frames received out of order, real-time audio and video is not. Quality of service ensures that these less tolerant applications receive the bandwidth required to function properly when it is needed.

In a true Ethernet environment, a hub is a dumb multi-port amplifier. When a frame is received on a specific port, it is immediately amplified and transmitted on all other ports of the hub. The hub does not care if it receives a proper frame or a noisy signal; it simply boosts the voltage level and passes it along. The first frame it receives is the one amplified and sent along its merry way.

In a 100VG environment, a hub is an intelligent device; it is a central control unit with functionality that echoes back to the old days of the mainframe. While the 100VG hub still amplifies network signals the same way an Ethernet hub does, it determines which frames get transmitted first by scanning its ports in order. Workstations are allowed to set a priority level to their data—either normal or high. As the hub scans its ports, it gives a larger slice of the bandwidth pie to this high-priority data. High-priority data is considered to be data that cannot tolerate delays—for example, real time audio and video. If a video conference does not receive all the bandwidth it requires to immediately send information back and forth, the images received may be choppy or the audio may be unrecognizable. Demand priority attempts to allocate the bandwidth these applications require to function smoothly.

In Favor of 100VG

There are some strong arguments for 100VG technology over regular Ethernet. First, 100VG does make some concessions for quality of service. While 100VG is capable of allotting additional bandwidth to applications like video conferencing, Ethernet would handle these frames like any other data on the wire.

Second, bandwidth becomes a bit more predictable on a 100VG network. Because the hub systematically scans its ports to look for pending transmissions, it is a bit easier to predict what the available bandwidth is for each workstation.

For example, on an Ethernet network, the amount of bandwidth available to any given station depends on how much information the other stations are trying to send. If the other stations are transmitting many large files, it is harder for our station to find a moment of free network time to transmit its frame. If the other stations only need to transmit occasionally, there are more windows of opportunity for frame transmission.

Because 100VG scans each of the ports and will accept one frame transmission at a time, every station has an equal opportunity to transmit their information.

100VG Drawbacks

Unfortunately, at this writing, 100VG has more drawbacks than benefits. The first drawback is performance. Even though it was designed from the ground up to support high utilization rates, 100VG has slightly less usable bandwidth than 100Tx networks with no priority data. This is mostly due to the overhead involved in port scanning. 100VG stations must wait until the hub tells them that it is okay to transmit. Even then, if the data is a normal priority, the hub will only accept one data frame before moving on to the next port. Ethernet does not have this problem, as any station can transmit when it is ready, provided the circuit is free.

Another drawback of 100VG is that the wiring has no allowances for supporting full-duplex communications. Full duplex allows a station to effectively double the amount of available bandwidth. This allows a network using 100Tx to reach nearly a 200 Mb data transfer rate. 100VG does not have this ability.

Third, 100VG has also suffered from poor vendor support. While everyone seems to be shipping 100Tx products, there are very few 100VG vendors besides HP. This syndrome is similar to what happened to IBM's Token Ring topology. With limited product sources, some potential end users went with Ethernet because there was a much larger vendor base to choose from. Limited vendor support also helps to drive up the cost, which makes the technology even less appealing.

Probably the biggest drawback of 100VG is how demand priority determines if a station needs to send normal or high-priority data. Hewlett-Packard originally hoped that application developers would support the technology. Software that needed to send time-sensitive data could send a request to the hub requesting a high-priority channel. When this type of support was not developed (it requires that the software be written specifically for 100VG networks), hardware vendors started adding the support to their network card drivers. The problem is that it is very easy for any savvy end user to enable this feature, setting all their network communications to high priority. The result is that this one user can suck up nearly all available bandwidth and bring a network to its knees.

CAT 3 Operation

As I mentioned a little earlier, 100VG has another interesting feature: the ability to operate over CAT 3 cabling. As you may remember from Chapter 2, CAT 3 cabling is only rated for 10 Mb operation. 100VG circumvents this limitation by transmitting and receiving over all four wire pairs. Each pair sustains a 30 Mb transmission rate, with approximately 5 Mb going to communication overhead. The result is (30–5) x 4 or 100 Mbps worth of throughput.

Despite all its drawbacks, 100VG does bring some interesting technology to the table. Using multiple wire pairs to transmit data goes a long way towards extending the life of twisted-pair cabling. Don't be surprised if you see this functionality utilized in other topologies down the road. Also, demand priority is a wonderful first pass at providing quality of service on a topology other than ATM. It is rumored that Hewlett-Packard may extend 802.12 to include transmission rates of up to 1 Gbps. It's possible that if the 100VG specifications are revised, improvements may be made to some of the current inadequacies of demand priority. While it is somewhat of a dead end technology, 100VG-ANYLAN deserves some credit for the innovations it has produced.

Appropriate Applications

Given 100VG's advantages and disadvantages, its most appropriate application at present is in leveraging old network wiring. If you find yourself administering a network made up of CAT 3 wiring, and it is unlikely that funding will be made available to upgrade the cabling to CAT 5, 100VG-ANYLAN may be a good fit. Keep in mind that you must have all four pairs of cable available. Some installations have split their cabling so that two pairs are used for networking and two pairs are used for the phone system.

If your network meets all of the above criteria, 100VG may be just the thing to breathe new life into your network.

Topology Rules

Table 3.4 shows the topology rules for 100VG-ANYLAN.

	Item	Rules
T A B L E 3.4 Topology Rules for 100VG-ANYLAN	Maximum cable lengths	CAT 3 twisted-pair: 325ft CAT 5 twisted-pair: 700ft Fiber: 1,640 ft
	Minimum cable lengths	None
	Maximum number of stations per cable	Twisted-pair: 2 Fiber: 2
	Maximum number of stations per logical network	1,024
	Maximum number of segments	5
	Maximum overall length of logical network	Twisted-pair: 4,200 ft Fiber: 1.2 miles

FDDI

Fiber Distributed Data Interface (FDDI) was the first of the popular networking topologies to reach 100 Mb throughput. For a number of years, if you needed 100 Mb performance, FDDI was the only way to go. While other topologies have caught up in raw throughput, FDDI has benefits in network stability and fault tolerance that still make it a good choice. While the transmission media of choice for FDDI is fiber, the specification also makes concessions for running CAT 5 out to the desktop.

FDDI supports two physical topologies, ring and star. Ring is far more widely implemented than star because it allows the use of FDDI's fault tolerant features. FDDI's ring topology is similar to IBM's legacy Token Ring topology, but with an additional ring that has been added for redundancy. This second ring is normally dormant and is only used if a failure occurs in the primary ring.

Figure 3.10 shows FDDI networks with star and ring physical topologies. As a ring, FDDI can recover from a cable failure by activating the secondary ring. This redundancy is lost when FDDI is implemented in a star topology.

FIGURE 3.10

An example of an FDDI network, including star and ring physical topologies

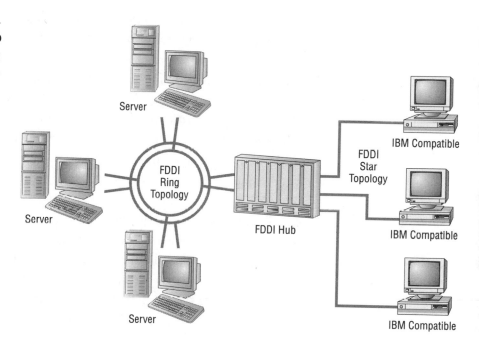

FDDI has also borrowed Token Ring's method of data transmission. A single frame referred to as a token is passed around the ring from station to station. When a station has data to transmit, it grabs the token and transmits a frame of data in its place. This frame then travels around the ring until it is received by the destination node it was addressed to. The destination station then makes a copy of the frame and continues to forward it along the ring, setting the Frame Copied Indicator (FCI) bit.

When the station that originally transmitted the frame receives the frame back and sees that the FCI bit has been set, it assumes the transmission has been successful. It then removes the frame from the ring and transmits the token in its place. The next station wishing to transmit data will then grab the token and repeat the process.

Token communications have some inherent advantages over Ethernet. The first is the ability to support a larger frame size of 4,096 bytes. If you remember our discussion about frame size versus network utilization, you will remember that the larger the average frame size, the more data can be transmitted in a given period of time due to reduced overhead.

Token passing is also a bit more orderly than Ethernet's CSMA/CD method of communication. It tends to perform better as higher utilization levels are achieved. This makes it an ideal choice when you are expecting to move very large data files over the network.

You'll remember from our discussion on fiber media that fiber stations get their output data port (Tx) connected to the input data port (Rx) of their downstream neighbor. This continues around the ring until the last station connects its Tx port to the Rx port of the first station.

This still applies to FDDI topology as well, except that an FDDI station will have a second set of transmit-and-receive ports for the second ring. On the second ring, the Rx port of a station connects to the Tx port of their down stream neighbor. This dual set of transmit-and-receive ports makes these stations *dual-attach stations* (DAS). To avoid confusion these ports are grouped by destination and labeled A and B. This yields two sets to deal with instead of four individual wires. When connecting DAS systems, you attach connection A to connection B of its downstream neighbor. This simplifies wiring and avoids cross-connecting the rings.

Figure 3.11 illustrates FDDI dual-attach stations. Note that each node connects to both rings in case of a failure.

The reason that stations are connected in this fashion is to guard against cable or hardware failure. Let's assume that we have a cable failure between two of the routers shown in Figure 3.11. When this

FIGURE 3.11

An example of FDDI dual-
attach stations

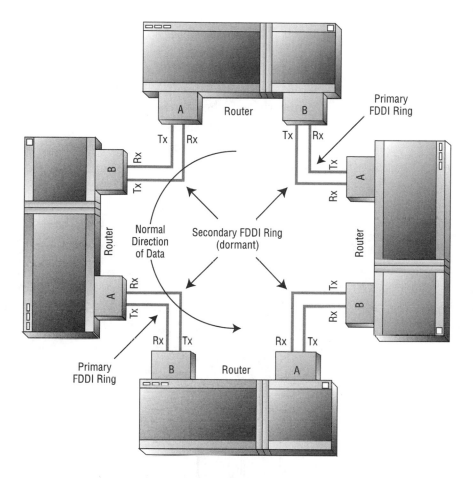

cable failure occurs, the system immediately downstream from the failure will quickly realize it is no longer receiving data. It then begins to send out a special maintenance packet called a *beacon*. A beacon is the method used by token stations to let other systems around the ring know it has detected a problem. A beacon frame is a system's way of saying "Hey, I think there is a problem between me and my upstream neighbor because I am no longer receiving data from him." The station then initializes its connection on the secondary ring so that it sends and receives data on connector A.

The beacon packet continues to be forwarded until it reaches the beaconing system's upstream neighbor. This upstream neighbor then initializes its connection to the secondary ring by sending and receiving on connector B. This in effect isolates the problem area and returns normal connectivity. When the beaconing station begins to receive its own beacons, it ceases transmission, and ring operation returns to normal. The final transmission path resembles the network shown in Figure 3.12. By using beacon frames, the systems on the network can determine the failure area and isolate it by activating the secondary ring.

FIGURE 3.12

How FDDI DAS stations recover from a cable failure

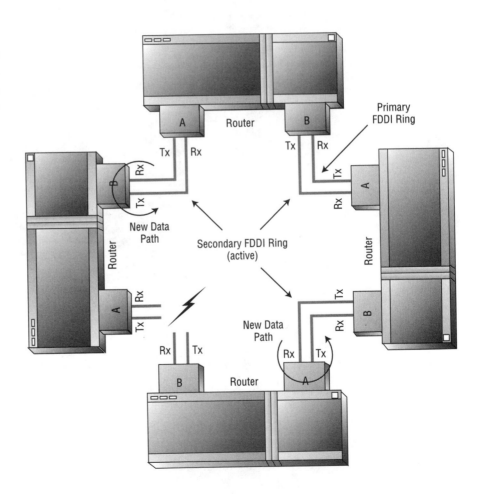

If this had in fact been a hardware failure caused by a fault in the upstream neighbor and that system was unable to initialize the secondary ring, the faulty system's upstream neighbor would have detected this and stepped in to close the ring. This would isolate the problem hardware while allowing the rest of the network to continue to function.

The DAS stations continue to monitor the faulty links until it appears that connectivity has been restored. If the link passes an integrity test, the primary ring returns to full operation, and the secondary ring again goes dormant. This type of network fault tolerance can be deemed critical in environments where connectivity must be maintained seven days a week, 24 hours a day (referred to as 7 by 24 operation). This functionality is what still makes FDDI the most fault tolerant networking topology available today for LANs.

One drawback of this dual ring design is that distance specifications are half of what is usually supported by fiber cable. This is because when a ring fails, the effective ring size can double (because the effective ring size is the primary ring size plus the secondary ring size). However, given the exceptional distance specification of fiber cable, this is rarely a problem.

FDDI also supports a star topology for connecting systems that do not require this level of fault tolerance. Devices called Dual Attach Concentrators (DAC) are connected to the ring topology, providing multiple single attach station (SAS) connections. SAS connections are typically used for end user workstations. These stations are usually not deemed critical and can endure short periods of downtime due to cable or hardware failures. While DAS and DAC connections must be made with fiber, SAS connections can be fiber or CAT 5 twisted pair. Figure 3.13 shows a network using a mixture of DAS, DAC, and SAS connections. The ring topology is deployed in the area requiring fault tolerance (server connections) while the less critical workstations are connected as a star.

FIGURE 3.13

FDDI DAC connecting
SAS systems to the ring

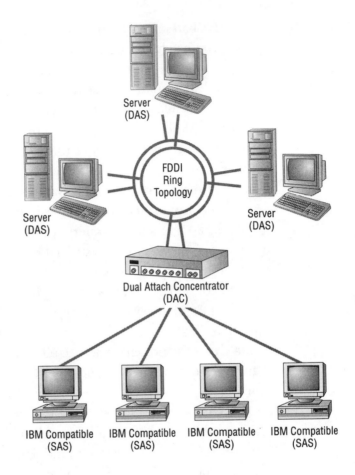

Appropriate Applications

The most appropriate applications for FDDI are servers and backbones. Because of its high level of fault tolerance, FDDI is a wonderful fit for server rooms and connecting workgroup clusters. And its resilience to cable and hardware failures makes for a stable environment.

FDDI has been around for a while, so finding hardware vendors and support is not very difficult. Because it is a more efficient topology than Ethernet, it can keep up when connected to multiple 100Tx segments.

Topology Rules

Table 3.5 shows the topology rules for FDDI.

TABLE 3.5 Topology Rules for FDDI	Item	Rules
	Maximum cable lengths	CAT 5 twisted-pair: 325 ft Fiber: 1.2 miles
	Minimum cable lengths	None
	Maximum number of stations per cable	Ring topology: 500 Star: 2
	Maximum number of stations per logical network	500
	Maximum number of segments	Gated by performance
	Maximum overall length of logical network	62 miles

ATM

Asynchronous Transfer Mode (ATM) is probably the most elusive and least understood of all network topologies. ATM was conceived in 1983 by AT&T Bell Labs, but it took nearly 10 years before an official forum was created to try and mature this technology into a production-quality topology. It then took the ATM forum another four years (until June 1995) just to release its first specification for ATM LAN emulation (LANE). In November 1996, the much anticipated LANE 2.0 was released, only to be found lacking much needed features such as scalability and multiprotocol support. To add insult to injury, some LANE 1-compliant hardware was incapable of supporting LANE 2. Pioneers of this new technology found themselves replacing some very expensive hardware just to stay current.

With this kind of a track history, why has ATM captured so much attention? Because ATM has the potential of providing high data rates, quality of service, and blurring the lines between local and wide area networks.

ATM represents a significant change in network design. To start, ATM does not vary its frame size like Ethernet or token-based topologies. Instead, ATM uses a fixed packet size of 48 bytes (referred to as a *cell*) for all communications. This fixed size allows for a more predictable traffic rate than networks with variable-length packets. By regulating the number of packets that flow between connections, ATM can accurately predict and closely control bandwidth utilization. The drawback to this fixed packet size, of course, is increased overhead. As we found in our discussion of 10 Mb Ethernet, smaller packets mean a less efficient data transfer and more network bottlenecks. An ATM cell is roughly 3% the size of a full Ethernet frame and 1% the size of a token ring or FDDI frame.

To quantify this loss in performance, when 155 Mb ATM is deployed on a LAN to handle normal network traffic (file access and printing, for example), it provides less throughput than 100 Mb Ethernet. While some of this loss is due to protocol translation (described below), a good portion of it is due to the smaller frame size.

Another significant difference is how ATM stations communicate with each other. While other topologies rely on upper-layer protocols like IPX and IP to route information between logical networks, ATM uses permanent virtual connections (PVCs) and switched virtual connections (SVCs) between communicating stations. Virtual connections (VCs) are logical communication channels between end stations—logical because this circuit is created along shared media that may also contain other virtual connections providing a circuit between other end stations. While the circuits must share available bandwidth along the media, communications are kept separate from each other through the use of connection identifiers. This is the complete opposite of Ethernet, where every station shares a single circuit along the media and is required to listen to packet transmissions between other stations. Figure 3.14 shows an example of virtual circuit and virtual path switching.

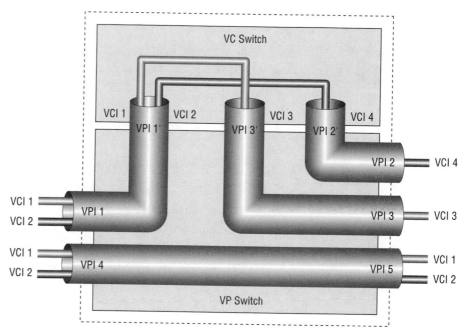

F I G U R E   3.14

Virtual Circuit and Virtual
Path Switching

ATM is an end station centric topology. This means that a connection or VC circuit must be established between the source and destination stations before data transfer. Again, this is in contrast to other topologies like Ethernet, which simply transmit the data onto the wire and rely on networking hardware to route the information to its destination network. With ATM connectivity, devices on the network called ATM switches maintain tables with the identifications of all end stations. When a station needs to transmit data, it issues a maintenance packet called a virtual path identifier (VPI) that propagates out into the network, setting up a virtual connection between the two systems. The purpose of the VPI is to create a circuit-switched connection between the two systems and to ensure that each portion of the path along the way has enough available bandwidth to carry the signal. Once this circuit is complete, data transmission can begin.

We'll discuss routing information between logical networks in greater detail when we discuss the upper-layer protocols in Chapters 4, 5, and 6.

A big plus to this type of connectivity is quality of service. If the bandwidth demands of the application can be identified before setting up the virtual connection, the VPI can reserve the required bandwidth and only pick routes that can support the required transmission rate. In effect, this is a form of automatic load balancing of the network.

This type of connectivity is nearly identical to the connectivity of the public telephone network (PTN). When you dial a phone number, a signal similar to a VPI goes out over the network, setting up a connection between your phone and the phone at the number you just dialed. This is accomplished in that brief period of time between when you dial the number and when you hear that first ring. If there is a problem in a direct line connection between you and the destination number (for example, if there is a broken connection or if there is currently heavy usage), the network will switch you to an alternate circuit path that is free. When the circuit is complete, your call goes through, and the phone rings on the other end. When your call is complete, the circuit is torn down and the bandwidth is made available to other users.

Because ATM functions in a similar fashion to the PTN, it is an ideal candidate for large networks. ATM is able to leverage the largest existing network in the world (PTN) by integrating, without translation or modification. A connection can be made from LAN to WAN to LAN using strictly ATM. The PTN becomes a seamless extension of the local network, as no translation is required.

Let's say we have two Ethernet LANs connected by a frame relay WAN. Let's also assume we wish to send a frame of data from one Ethernet network to the other. With this configuration, our network will require additional hardware at both ends of the WAN to translate between the two topologies. Our fame will undergo translation as it enters the WAN, and then again when it leaves it to be transmitted onto the other Ethernet segment. If we replace this configuration with ATM, no translation is required because ATM can be supported on both the LAN and the WAN.

ATM Drawbacks

Currently there are some problems with ATM. To start, ATM wants to handle all of the end-to-end connections. This is the same type of functionality provided by existing upper-layer protocols like IPX and IP. Methods for incorporating these existing protocols with ATM have met with a number of delays. For example, LANE 2 was supposed to include changes to the frame header to support multiple protocols, but this feature was dropped from the specification by the time it was released. Such configuration problems are not an issue in an ATM-only environment, but they can make incorporating ATM functionality into an existing network infrastructure difficult at best.

Another issue with ATM is the node maps maintained by ATM switches. These node maps are what allow VPIs to create paths from one end station to another. There is currently no auto-discovery method for creating these tables in PVC circuits; these tables must be maintained manually. This can make maintaining a network with many nodes a real nightmare. While SVCs do not have this limitation, there is no guarantee that the circuit will be able to allocate the full bandwidth required by the end station if a WAN connection is required. If you have ever tried to make a phone call during peak hours and received a busy circuit signal, you have experienced this phenomenon. If the connection is not permanent, there is no guarantee it will be there 100% of the time. In some environments (such as money transfers or credit checks), this type of unpredictability can be unacceptable.

As if all of this were not confusing enough, a number of ATM vendors have grown weary of waiting for specification drafts to add functionality to their networking hardware. To compensate, they have developed proprietary implementations of this functionality that may or may not work with equipment from other vendors. In effect, you could end up locked into a single vendor for all your ATM needs. This has created a real "buyer beware" environment for those purchasing network components. As an example, when LANE 2.0 was released, some ATM vendors were able to provide the additional functionality it supported with a simple software upgrade to existing hardware; other vendors, however, were unable to provide this level of support, and customers found themselves in the position of needing to replace some very expensive hardware to gain the additional functionality.

Appropriate Applications

ATM specifications are still in a state of flux. While the technology shows great promise, it is difficult to recommend it for any application at the time of this writing. There are still a number of bugs that need to be shaken out of this technology. With the recent hype over 1 Gb Ethernet, it is questionable if ATM will receive the resources and attention it so desperately needs to be molded into a stable production topology.

Most network managers have decided to err on the side of caution by letting others ride out ATM's bumpy road ahead and adopting a wait-and-see policy. ATM's greatest benefits will be in backbone implementations, which is the last place a seasoned network person wants to introduce a metamorphosing technology.

Wide Area Network (WAN) Topologies

Wide area network (WAN) topologies are network configurations that are designed to carry data over a great distance. Unlike LANs, which are designed to deliver data between many systems, WAN topologies are usually point-to-point. *Point-to-point* means that the technology was developed to support only two nodes sending and receiving data. It is expected that if multiple nodes need access to the WAN, a LAN will be placed behind it to accommodate this functionality.

Figure 3.15 displays this type of connectivity. The only devices communicating directly on the WAN are the two routers. The routers provide connectivity from one single point to another. Any other devices that need to use the WAN, must communicate through the two routers.

FIGURE 3.15

There are only two devices (routers) that are directly communicating on the WAN.

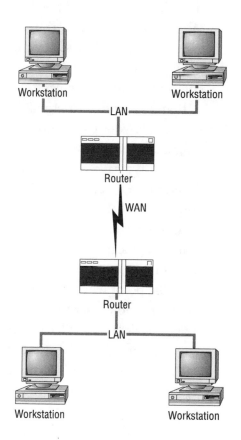

We will get into what the best ways are to connect LANs and WANs when we discuss networking hardware.

Local Exchange Carriers

In the last chapter, we discussed means for setting up private networks and transmitting data over wide geographical areas. But sometimes it is more cost effective to take advantage of the services provided by a local exchange carrier. Most local exchange carriers can provide WAN connectivity from 56K to 45 Mb. If your bandwidth demands are minimal (less than 10 Mb) and the distance between nodes is great, leasing services from your local carrier may make more sense than setting up a private network. While the raw long-term costs can seem to be higher, they can easily be offset by not being required to maintain the WAN communication equipment.

If an exchange carrier will be handling your WAN needs, you first need to get your data onto the carrier's network. This is done by running a connection between you and the closest local exchange carrier facility—typically one of the baby Bells created by the AT&T split-up in 1984, or an independent. The local exchange carrier will take care of connecting their facility to yours. Somewhere within your facility is a point referred to as the *demarc* (demarcation point). This is the point to which the local carrier guarantees service. You want to make sure that this point is as close to your networking hardware as possible, as it identifies the point where the local exchange carrier's responsibility ends. If the connection is active up to the demarc, but you're still having connectivity problems, most local exchange carriers will be of little help.

For example, if your demarc is in the same room as your servers and network hardware, it's a straightforward process to isolate a connectivity problem (it's either the WAN link or the hardware). If your demarc is in another building or 20 floors away, you have an additional length of cable to add into the equation. To compound the problem, you may find that no one wishes to take ownership of a problem caused by that cable. Does it belong to the exchange carrier? The building owner? Your organization? By locating the demarc in the same room as your network hardware, you remove this gray area.

If you are establishing a WAN that connects to a local geographical location, all that may be required is to have the same local exchange carrier wire up to the other site. If the connection is required to span a large distance, however, you will probably need to involve a long-distance carrier. Long-distance carriers like AT&T, Sprint, and MCI connect to the local carrier at a location called the *point of presence* (POP). A POP is simply telephone-speak for the point where the networks for the local exchange carrier and the long distance carrier meet. Most towns will have at least one POP. Major cities will have quite a few.

FIGURE 3.16

Responsibilities of both local exchange and long distance carriers

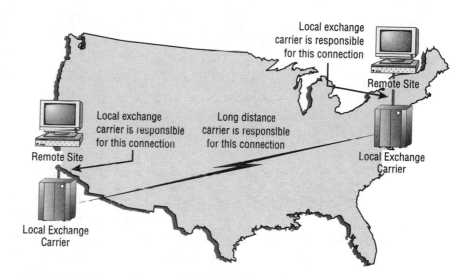

If all this sounds a bit complex—well, it can be. But most long distance carriers have revamped their service departments and are willing to take care of the setup for you. They will take care of contacting all local exchange carriers involved, and schedule the wiring and testing for you.

Dial-Up Analog

Dial-up analog connections use the same PTN to create end-to-end connections that your telephone uses. The largest data communication use of this network is by using a modem (short for *modulator/demodulator*) to dial up the phone number you wish to contact.

Unfortunately, the public telephone network was originally designed to carry voice, which does not require a large amount of bandwidth. This is why modem connections are in the kilobit range instead of the megabit range. Because it was easier to service voice with an analog connection, the telephone network was originally designed to be analog, not digital. These analog lines are referred to as *plain old telephone service* (POTS).

A modem takes the digital signals from a computer and converts them to analog. This analog signal is then transmitted over the dial-up line to the POP, where it is converted back to a digital signal. Even though analog is still used to connect to people's homes, most of the connections between POPs have been upgraded to digital.

So our modem's signal has been returned to a digital format. It travels over the backbone to the destination POP where it is again translated into an analog signal. The analog signal travels down the POTS on the other side to the receiving modem.

Analog transmission rates peak around 9600 bps. Despite this limitation, modem vendors have been able to push raw throughput to 28.8k and even 56k bits per second (Kbps) by leveraging technologies such as *frequency shifting* or *phase shifting*. Include data compression, and this rate can be as high as 115 Kbps. 115 Kbps is not the true transfer rate—it is the effective rate through the use of compression. For example, a 33.6K modem may be able to achieve a throughput rate of 115 Kpbs through the use of compression, but the raw transfer rate is still 33.6 Kbps.

Frequency shifting and phase shifting involve using more than one carrier wave to transmit a signal. *Compression* involves removing redundant characters from the data prior to transmission.

Limiting the speed of a modem is the noise created when the signal is translated between the digital and analog formats. The faster a connection, the more susceptible it becomes to errors from noise interference.

Modem manufacturers must walk the line between making modem transfer data as fast as possible, but not so fast that noise begins to generate errors. 56K modems get around this noise problem by eliminating some of these translations, and thus reducing the amount of noise generated on the circuit.

56K modems function under the principle that converting information from digital to analog creates more noise than translating it from analog to digital. In order for a 56K modem to work properly, the signal cannot go through any digital-to-analog conversions once it leaves the modem. The theory is that if the destination system has a digital connection to their local POP, no digital-to-analog conversions are required (besides the modem itself).

For example, let's assume you are using a 56K modem to call your Internet Service Provider (ISP). This ISP maintains a T1 digital connection to their local POP for dial-in access. This connection leads directly into their network, which is also digital.

When the signal leaves your modem, it is converted from digital to analog. The signal then travels down the POTS to the POP, where it is converted back to a digital signal. This signal then travels down a digital backbone to the ISP's POP. Up until now, the functionality has been identical to a regular modem connection. Once the signal leaves the ISP's POP, however, it does not need to be converted. Because the ISP maintains a digital connection, the signal can remain digital from your POP all the way into the ISP's network. This eliminates the need to perform any digital-to-analog conversions once the signal has left the modem.

There are a few caveats with this type of connection. First, you cannot put two 56K modems on each end and expect a 56K connection. Doing so would require the use of POTS on each end, which need to perform a digital to analog conversion by the destination POP. Special hardware is required on the receiving end to accommodate a digital connection to the POP (such as the T1 mentioned above).

When two 56K modems are connected via POTS, the connection speed drops to the highest level the two modems can negotiate, usually between 22K and 33.6K.

The second issue is that this connection speed assumes that near-perfect phone conditions and wiring exist, which is rarely the case. Even if the receiving station is outfitted for a digital connection, expect a 56K modem to connect between 45K to 53K.

In a business environment, dial-up analog is good for load-balancing; you can also use it as a backup connection to some other WAN topology. Many WAN devices include circuitry to switch over to a secondary means of connection if the primary means of connection fails. For example, a company may rely on a frame relay circuit to connect a remote office site, but have an analog dial-up connection configured in case the frame relay fails.

Dial-up connections may also be required when users need remote access to the local network. The user dials in to some form of remote connectivity device and receives access to network resources, typically either via remote node or via remote control.

Remote Control

A *remote control* dial-in connection involves dedicating a computer with a modem as the host and running remote-control software such as Symantec's pcANYWHERE on it. Note that usually one dedicated computer is required for each concurrent connection to be supported. The user also runs a version of the remote-control software and dials in to the host computer. When the user authenticates (usually by entering a user name and password), they gain control of the host located on the network. The user can now run applications located on that host and access network resources.

In remote control, the remote client becomes the equivalent of a dumb terminal. All processing, disk activity, and network access is provided by the host system. This means that special steps must be taken to print and copy files to the remote client. If you are in a remote session and simply click the Print button, it will be the host system that prints, not the remote client.

The benefit to this type of connection is speed. The only information that travels the analog line is screen update information. Response time is much faster than remote node (described below). The downside to this type of connectivity is that a single computer must be dedicated to each concurrent connection. All required software must be loaded on the machine or available over the network. Special considerations must be taken with programs such as e-mail that expect the same user to always be using the same client. Also, two licensed copies of the remote-control software may be required—one for the host and one for the client.

Remote Node

A *remote node* connection allows the user to dial in to the network and have their computer attach to the network as if they were physically located in the offices. Examples of remote-node devices are Shiva's LAN-Rover and Netmodems or Microsoft's remote access server (RAS). The remote user dials in to the modem pool and is authenticated by the device. Once this is complete, the user is able to access network resources the same way they normally do.

The benefit to this type of connection is flexibility and cost. If you dial in to a remote control system and need access to a Unix system, but the host only supports IPX, you're out of luck. With a remote node connection, you simply have to make sure that the computer dialing in supports IP. The cost factor comes into play in that a remote node connection does not require a fully configured PC loaded with software on the network end.

NOTE Most remote node devices will allow you to still use network-based remote control devices if you later wish to locate hosts on your network or wish to provide both types of connectivity.

The downside to remote node connections is speed. If you think a 10 Mb network is slow, response time can absolutely crawl when squeezed through a 28.8 Kb connection. It is not uncommon for it to take five minutes or more just to log in to a NetWare server. Clearly if remote node is to be used effectively, preparation is required. Plan on running as many applications as possible from the remote system and only use the dial-up connection to transfer needed data files.

Creating Hunt Groups for Modem Pools

Whether you are using remote control or remote node, modem pools can be made easier to use by creating *hunt groups*. A hunt group allows you to assign a single dial-in number that can scan multiple phone lines looking for a connection that is free. For example, let's say you have four telephone numbers—555-1212, 555-1313, 555-1414, and 555-1515—each connected to a modem providing remote connectivity to your network. Normally your remote users would have to remember all four separate numbers in case the first one they try is busy. With a hunt group, you could point the 555-1212 number at each of the three remaining numbers, so that if 1212 is busy, the call is directed to 1313. If this line is free, the number will ring, and the user will connect without even knowing their call was redirected. If 1313 is also busy, the connection will be hunted to 1414 and so on. This will continue until the last number is reached (1515 in this example). If all the numbers were in use, the user would then receive a busy signal.

I've seen this work quite well, except for one flaw. Sometimes when a user abnormally disconnects (for example, if they break the connection by shutting off their modem), the modem on the network side can become hung and drop off of auto-answer. If auto-answer becomes disabled, the modem will not answer the phone when it rings. Because the hunt group only looks for a free line, it will direct users to this modem, and they will not be able to connect.

Given the above hunt group, let's assume that 1313 drops off of auto-answer. The first user to call in is directed to 1212, and connects to the network. The next user calls in and is hunted to 1313 because 1212 is busy. 1313 then proceeds to ring off the hook because the modem is no longer answering the phone. When this user gets tired of listening to the phone ring and the next user calls in, they are hunted to 1313 and receive the same response. Even though I have only one functionally challenged modem, I have only one operational phone line. 1414 and 1515 are not used unless someone happens to call in while someone is sitting listening to 1313 ring without answer. What makes this problem even more dramatic is that it appears to be intermittent. Some users will be able to connect while others cannot (depending on whether the first line is free).

To troubleshoot a hung modem in a hunt group, you must start at the end of your hunt group (1515) and work backward until you find the modem that will not pick up. Usually you need to *power cycle* the modem—switch it off and then back on—to clear the problem.

Some remote access devices that use internal modems provide the capability to dial in on a free line and reboot the device remotely, power-cycling the modems. This is a last resort because rebooting the device will disconnect anyone who is currently dialed in.

I've seen hunt groups set up as described here but with the additional criterion that all numbers also hunt to the first (for example, calling 1313, 1314, or 1515 causes 1212 to ring first). This can be a very bad thing; if you have a bad modem line, you have no easy way to isolate it.

Hunt groups can be set up through your local telephone company. Simply contact your customer representative, and they'll point you in the right direction. Hunt group charges vary but are usually pretty reasonable.

Use Regular Analog Lines for Remote Access

When setting up remote network access, use straight analog lines. Many businesses will try to run their modem pool through their PBX in order to save on phone costs. The problem is that most PBXs are made to support voice, not data, and fall apart at connection speeds above 9600 baud. A good indication that this is occurring is if users have problems establishing connections or if the connection is frequently dropped while in use.

If the line requires you to dial a 9 or an 8 to call outside of your office, it may be connected through your PBX. When in doubt, consult your company's phone technician—unless of course you happen to wear that hat as well!

Dial-up analog can be an effective solution for creating remote connectivity. The cost breakpoint occurs when you are using dial-up analog to connect the same two locations for more than four or five hours a day. At this point, it may be more cost effective to use some other form of WAN connectivity that creates a permanent connection and bills on a flat-rate basis.

Appropriate Applications

The following are appropriate applications for dial-up analog:

- home access to the Internet
- home access to the corporate network
- corporate access to the Internet when only a few users need access
- backup connectivity for other WAN services

ISDN

Integrated services digital network (ISDN) is the digital alternative to the analog PTN. There are two levels of service available, basic rate ISDN (BRI) and primary rate ISDN (PRI).

Basic rate ISDN is two 64 Kb channels referred to as B channels (*bearer* channels) and one 16 Kb channel referred to as a D channel (*data* channel). The two B channels are used for transmitting data. The D channel is used for overhead in maintain the connection. Primary rate ISDN includes 23 B channels and 1 D channel and has the effective throughput of a T1 connection (1.544 Mb).

An ISDN line uses separate phone numbers for each channel the same way an analog dial-up connection does for each line. For example, a BRI connection would have two separate phone numbers, one for each B channel. Because the two channels are completely separate, ISDN can load-balance a connection by using the second line only when required or by leaving it open for other communications.

For example, let's say you're using your ISDN connection to cruise the Internet. You're buzzing around from Web page to Web page. At this point, you're most likely only have one B channel active for an effective throughput rate of 64 Kb. You then run across a site that has every Dilbert comic for the last three years located in a single 450-meg zip file. Interested in cubicle art, you click on the link and start downloading the file. At some predetermined point in the communication, the second B channel will kick in, increasing the transfer rate to 128 Kb. This effectively cuts the time it would take to download the file by nearly half. When the large file transfer is complete, the second B channel drops and your effective throughput rate returns to 64 Kb.

As mentioned, this second channel can also be used for completely separate communications as well, both inbound and outbound. While cruising the Web on the first B channel, you could also be carrying on a telephone conversation or sending (or receiving) a fax on the second B channel.

Because ISDN uses digital transmissions, it is typically a more stable connection than analog. Connectivity is provided by an ISDN card that fits in your PC or by a piece of hardware you can connect to your network. The network version allows anyone on the network to open an ISDN connection through the device. Connection times are near instantaneous. This is a good thing, as a connection can easily be established before a network connection can time out. The delays imposed in setting up an analog modem connection makes this type of connectivity impractical if not impossible. In effect ISDN can serve up *bandwidth on demand*, leaving the connection closed when not in use.

Unfortunately this has led to some abuses of ISDN. Small companies have been sucked in by the glamour of ISDN hoping that a pay-as-you-go structure would be more economical than a full-time connection, only to get burned when they receive the phone bill.

As mentioned, ISDN is capable of doing load balancing by bringing up the second B channel when needed. This is usually configured as a balance between time and current throughput. We want the second line to kick in under heavy traffic loads, but not so quickly that it responds to small files and is used for a few seconds and then not at all. Conversely we do not want it to kick it in too late, because it would then do very little to improve file transfer time.

At the other end of the transmission we want to tear that second connection down as quickly as possible when it is no longer needed. We do not want to tear it down too quickly, however, as the user may have a number of files to transfer, which would cause the line to just be immediately brought back up again.

The above is somewhat true for the initial B channel as well. Initialization is easy, you bring up the channel when it is needed. The question is, when do you tear it down? In the Web example above, if you tear the connection down too quickly, you will end up bringing the link back up every time the user clicks on a new link.

Here's the kicker. ISDN costs anywhere from two to four times what you would pay for an analog line. This varies with your local exchange carrier, but should get you in the ball park of what ISDN will cost. Like an analog call, the first minute of an ISDN call is typically far more expensive than the minutes that follow. The result is if you are tearing down and bringing up lines continuously, you could end up paying as much as $1 or more per minute. I know of a few companies that have been shocked to receive a first-month phone bill over $4,500. This is over twice what they would have paid for a T1 sporting 1.544 Mb bandwidth!

Also, if you are using ISDN for Internet connectivity, keep in mind that the connection can only be established from your end. While this is not a problem if you are connecting from a single system and rely on your provider for services such as mail, it can cause problems if you are trying to connect your company's network to the Internet. Services such as mail and domain name services (DNS) need to be able to create connections bi-directionally. If someone on the Internet needs to send your company mail, your mail systems needs to be constantly accessible. Because ISDN connections are constantly brought up and torn down, your mail system may or may not be accessible. This can cause mail to be delayed or, even worse, undeliverable.

If your ISP offers ISDN network connections, make sure they can host your Web server, reply to any DNS requests for you, and can queue your mail until your connection is brought back up online. You should also make sure that their method of transferring your mail to your local site is supported by your mail gateway. For example, some ISPs expect your mail system to use the **finger** command to trigger mail delivery. This command is supported by very few mail gateways.

This type of one-way connectivity can also cause problems if you are using ISDN to connect to a remote office. Keep in mind that you must specifically design the circuit so that it may be initiated from either side (possibly by using two dial-up numbers). Otherwise, your home office may not be able to contact the remote network unless the connection has already been initiated by the remote office.

Another misconception is that a firewall or some other form of network protection is not required with an ISDN connection to the Internet. In fact, when an ISDN connection is active, a network is just as susceptible to attack as if it is linked to the Internet with a full-time connection.

Because ISDN is digital, it is not directly compatible with devices such as analog phones and faxes. These devices must be replaced with their digital counterparts or run through a coder/decoder (codec). A codec converts the analog signal from these devices to digital.

Appropriate Applications

These are the most appropriate applications for ISDN:

- home access to the Internet

- home access to the corporate network

- corporate access to the Internet when only a few users need access

- backup connectivity for other WAN services

- connectivity of remote office sites

Leased Lines

Leased lines are dedicated analog or digital circuits that are paid for on a flat-rate basis. This means that whether you use the circuit or not, you are paying a fixed monthly fee. Leased lines are point-to-point connections—they are used to connect one geographical location to another. You cannot dial a phone number and point them to a new destination.

There are two common way leased lines are deployed:

- The leased line constitutes the entire length of the connection between the two geographic locations.

- The leased line is used for the connection from each location to its local exchange carrier. Connectivity between the two exchange carriers is then provided by some other technology like frame relay (discussed later in this chapter).

Analog leased lines are conditioned to facilitate a lower error rate than would normally be achieved with a dial-up line. Conditioning helps to remove noise from the circuit which allows the connection to be used with less overhead for error correction. Digital leased lines are also referred to as *digital data service lines* and are available with bandwidths up to 56K. With analog leased lines a modem can still be used. Digital data service lines require a channel service unit/data service unit, or CSU/DSU (I will talk about these when we cover network hardware in Chapter 4). They also require some form of data terminating equipment (DTE)—typically, a router—to regulate traffic flow across the line. The DTE connects to the CSU/DSU via an RS232 serial connector, or possibly an RS449 connector for 56K connections. Digital data services are full duplexed, meaning that data transmissions are bi-directional, flowing in both directions at the same time.

Analog leased lines are used very little today. They were popular back in the mainframe days when they were used for connecting dumb terminal users at remote sites. Digital leased lines are usually sufficient for connecting small companies to the Internet or providing connectivity for remote offices.

NOTE A leased line is not expandable. To provide more bandwidth, you have to replace the line with a T1 (discussed in the next section).

Appropriate Applications

The following are appropriate applications for leased lines:

- connecting remote sites to the corporate office when bandwidth requirements are small

- Internet connectivity for small offices

- carrying voice or data

T1

A T1 is a full-duplex signal over two-pair wire cabling. This wire pair terminates in a receptacle that resembles the square phone jacks used in older homes. T1s are used for dedicated point-to-point connections in the same way that leased lines are. Bandwidth on a T1 is available in increments from 64 Kb up to 1.544 Mb.

T1s use time division to break the two wire pairs up into 24 separate channels. *Time division* is the allotment of available bandwidth based on time increments. In the case of a T1 circuit, each channel is allowed to transmit for 5.2 microseconds (µs). This is the amount of time a T1 requires to transmit 8 bits (or 1 byte) of information. At the end of 5.2 µs, the channel must stop transmitting and relinquish control of the circuit to the next channel. If the channel has additional information to transmit, it must wait 119.8 µs—the amount of time it takes to cycle through the other 23 channels so that it is again that channel's turn to transmit.

To determine the available bandwidth on each channel, we must first determine the *sample rate*. The sample rate is the number of times each channel is allowed to transmit in a one-second period of time. Because each channel is allowed to transmit for 5.2 µs before releasing control to the next channel, we can determine the number of transmission per second by using the following calculation:

```
1 (second) /.0000052 (transmit time per channel) =
192,398 transmissions per second
```

This is the total number of transmissions possible in a one-second period of time along a T1 line. These 192,398 transmissions are then broken up equally over the 24 channels:

```
192,398 (transmissions) / 24 (the number of channels) =
8,000
```

Each of the 24 channels is allowed to transmit 8,000 times per second. This is our sample rate—the number of times per second that each channel is sampled or checked to see if it needs to transmit data.

To determine the available bandwidth per channel, we multiply the sample rate by the amount of data we can transmit each sample period:

```
8 bits x 8000 samples per second = 64 Kbps
```

The short answer to all this number-crunching is that each of the 24 channels on a T1 line is capable of moving 64 Kb worth of data per second.

With 24 active channels, the full bandwidth available on a T1 is:

```
64 Kbps x 24 = 1.536 Mbps
```

You'll notice that there is 8 Kbps unaccounted for from the 1.544 Mbps bandwidth stated in the first paragraph (1544 Kbps - 1536 Kbps = 8 Kbps). This 8 Kbps is overhead that goes towards managing the connections. So while a T1 is able to move 1.544 Mb of information per second, only 1.536 Mb of this can be actual data.

The nice thing about this setup is that an exchange carrier will lease you individual channels of this T1 based on your bandwidth requirements. This is called a *fractional T1*. If you only need 512 Kb, then you only need to lease eight channels. In the long term, this can save a considerable amount of money over leasing a full T1. This can be an ideal solution for a company that only needs 64 or 128 Kb now, but may want to upgrade to a larger pipe later. By initially connecting via a fractional T1 instead of a leased line, you will not need to rewire—you can simply turn on additional channels.

These 24 channels can also be broken up and dedicated to different services. For example, three channels can be dedicated to data with one channel being dedicated to voice. In this way, a single connection can provide connectivity for multiple services. By combining these services over a single T1, an organization can achieve a lower communication cost than if separate wiring was used for each.

The cost of a T1 is based on bandwidth requirements and the distance to your local exchange carrier. The typical cost for a T1 can be anywhere from $500 to $1500 per month. Consult your local exchange carrier for their price structure.

Appropriate Applications

The following are appropriate applications for T1 lines:

- connecting remote sites to the corporate office when a large amount of bandwidth is required

- Internet connectivity for all but the largest offices

- carrying multiple voice and data lines to reduce cost

Frame Relay/X.25

Frame relay and X.25 are packet-switched technologies. Because data on a packet-switched network is capable of following any available circuit path, such networks are represented by clouds in graphical presentations such as Figure 3.17.

Both topologies must be configured as *permanent virtual circuits* (PVCs), meaning that all data entering the cloud at point A is automatically forwarded to point B. These end points are defined at the time the service is leased.

Note that the packet-switched network is a shared medium. Your exchange carrier uses the same network for all PVCs they lease out. In effect, you are sharing available bandwidth with every one of their clients. While this does not provide the truly private connection supplied by a leased line, it does help to keep down the costs of available bandwidth.

Frame relay supports data transmission rates of 56K to 1.544 Mb. Frame relay is identical to and built upon the original X.25 specification, except that X.25 is analog and frame relay is digital. As a digital transmission, frame relay requires less overhead for error correction and thus supports higher bandwidths than X.25 (X.25 only supports

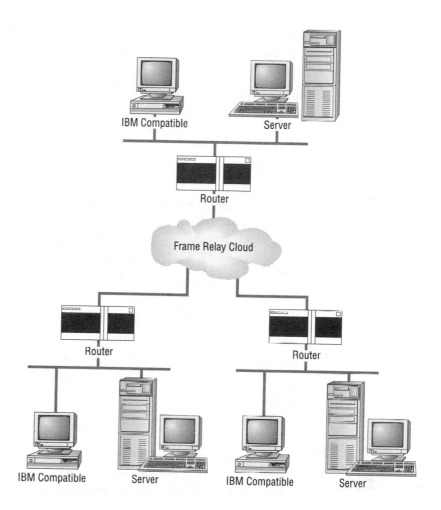

FIGURE 3.17

A WAN frame relay cloud
connecting three
networks

56 Kb). These topologies are excellent examples of how more usable
bandwidth can be achieved by simply switching from analog to digital
communications.

When ordering frame relay, the amount of bandwidth you purchase
is based on a *committed information rate* (CIR). The CIR is the minimum amount of bandwidth your exchange carrier will guarantee available at any given time. Many carriers will allow you to burst above that
rate depending on how much traffic is currently being passed through
the cloud.

For example, let's say that you order a frame relay circuit with a CIR of 128 Kb. If traffic is light within the frame relay cloud, you may be able to achieve momentary burst rates of 150 Kb to 190 Kb. Because frame relay has become popular, however, it has become more difficult to find windows where these higher transfer rates are available.

While many warn that the Internet may be headed for a meltdown, frame relay may already be experiencing a meltdown of its own. As a packet-switched network, each PVC connection shares available bandwidth with other PVCs. It is not uncommon during peak utilization hours for a connection's effective throughput to fall below the CIR rate. If your bandwidth demands cannot endure momentary lapses, go for a higher CIR rate or stick with leased line.

X.25 is a mature technology with connectivity world wide. Frame relay is a bit newer and, as such, not as widely deployed. Most implementations should be able to utilize the benefits of frame relay. If you're running a truly global network, however, you may be stuck with X.25 in some areas.

To connect to a frame relay or X.25 network, you must have a leased line or T1 wired between your organization and your local exchange carrier. From there, the circuit enters the cloud instead of following a dedicated path.

Appropriate Applications

The following are appropriate applications for frame relay and X.25:

- connecting remote sites to the corporate office when only data connectivity is required

- carrying data that is not time sensitive (not voice or video)

SONET

SONET, or *synchronous optical network*, is available in bandwidths from 64 Kb to 2.4 Gbps. SONET uses time division (the same as a T1) over fiber and is being billed as the next-generation replacement to the T1. SONET has some additional benefits that certainly make this replacement a possibility.

The first benefit that SONET offers is direct support of the ATM topology. If ATM technology should ever take off on the LAN, SONET will be poised to extend the boundaries of ATM LAN networks by providing transparent support over the WAN. This, in effect, helps to blur the lines between LAN and WAN by utilizing similar communication rules across the entire transmission domain. If ATM has been deployed on the LAN, SONET is the ideal medium to utilize ATM over the WAN as well. This removes the usual requirement of translating between LAN and WAN topologies.

SONET is also in a much better position to support global networks. One drawback of the T1 is that it is deployed in North America only. Most countries follow Conference and European Posts and Telecommunications Standards, which specify an E1 carrier that is not directly compatible with a T1 carrier. SONET is a much closer match to the European optical WAN specification called Synchronous Digital Hierarchy. When you're implementing a large global network, you can encounter many problems between the services offered by U.S. and European carriers. SONET is an approach to try and close some of these gaps.

SONET supports private virtual channels and will transmit ATM as well as ISDN natively; this removes the translation requirement between LAN and WAN topologies.

Appropriate Applications

The following are appropriate applications for SONET:

- connecting large metropolitan networks together

- Internet connectivity for large global companies

- network backbones for Internet service providers

- carrying voice and data via ATM from LAN to WAN to LAN

Summary

In this chapter, we took our transmission media and looked at how they are wired together to form physical and logical topologies. It is important to analyze your environment and choose your topology wisely. Most sites are best suited to a mixture of topologies but again you need to look at your specific requirements.

In the next chapter, we'll look at the hardware used to extend the specifications of our transmission media and the hardware used to connect different topologies.

CHAPTER

4

Networking Hardware

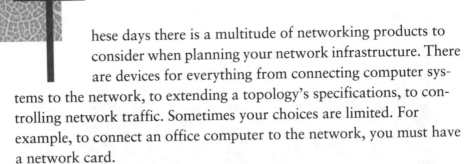

hese days there is a multitude of networking products to consider when planning your network infrastructure. There are devices for everything from connecting computer systems to the network, to extending a topology's specifications, to controlling network traffic. Sometimes your choices are limited. For example, to connect an office computer to the network, you must have a network card.

Some products, however, require extensive planning prior to selection. For example, should you buy a bridge, a switch, or a router to control network traffic? Not knowing the right answer to this question could lead to a purchase based on your hardware vendor's recommendations. This recommendation may or may not be the best choice, as the vendor may not understand your environment as well as you think. None of these devices are one-size-fits-all. If a consultant is willing to give you design recommendations based on a five-minute phone call, then find another consultant. Each device has been designed with a specific purpose in mind. The trick is to ensure that this purpose is a correct match for the way you use your network.

In this chapter we will define some of the common hardware used in building a network. The only mandatory hardware is a network card (for connecting each computer to the network cable), and, if you will be running twisted-pair cable or Fiber Distributed Data Interface (FDDI) in a star topology, you will require a hub. From here, simply add cables and computers until you have a fully functional network.

The rest of the devices outlined in this chapter are used for providing additional functionality. For example, you do not need to use punch-down panels, but they can greatly simplify wire management of a large network. You do not need to use repeaters or switches, but they can be effective means of extending the distances your network will cover or controlling traffic.

As we discuss these devices, I will cover the pros and cons of each and give examples of its intended use.

Punch-Down Panels

Use a *punch-down panel* to connect hardware located in wiring closets or server rooms to the cabling that runs out to the users' workstations. A punch-down panel is a panel the width of a network rack (a rack with a 19"-wide frame used to hold networking equipment) and contains female RJ-45, RJ-11 (for twisted-pair), or SMA (for fiber) connectors in the front and *punch-down blocks* in the back. Panels with RJ-11 connectors are typically used for phone connections, while RJ-45 is used with networking. Check the ANSI/EIA category standards (listed in Chapter 2) to see what level of bandwidth a particular punch-down panel supports. While CAT 3 is sufficient for phone use, you will usually want CAT 5 for any panels used to support network communications.

Punching Down the Wire

The punch-down blocks on a twisted-pair panel (CAT 3 or CAT 5) for data use a set of eight bare metal teeth which consist of two blades each. The separation between the two blades is such that a single wire from a standard twisted-pair cable can be pushed in between them and the cable insulation will be cut back, allowing the blades to make an electrical connection with the conductor.

NOTE The act of connecting a cable is referred to as *punching down the wire.* While fiber does not use metal teeth (it's a standard buffed and polished fiber connection), the term is still used for consistency.

Punch-down panels are extremely useful for keeping your wiring organized. Typically these panels are wall or rack mounted. The punched-down wire will lead back to a wall connector in an office area or to another central wiring point. This allows you to plug a cable into the front connector on the panel and either connect the *drop* to a device (like a hub) within the room or route it to another drop area.

A drop is a wire run from one geographical location to another.

Using punch-down panels is greatly preferred over simply putting a connector on the wiring room side of the drop cable, as it increases the flexibility of the wiring plan. A cable with a connector on the end cannot be as easily rerouted to another drop area and it cannot be lengthened if you need to move equipment around the room.

You cannot extend a twisted-pair cable by splicing in more wire with the old twist and tape method. Don't even think about it. Spliced cable is too susceptible to signal loss and outside noise. If you need a longer cable, you must replace the entire length.

Things to Consider

Consider the following items when deciding to use a punch-down panel:

- Use a punch-down panel that supports your wiring specification. For example, do not use a CAT 3 punch-down panel with CAT 5 cable. The result is a network that only meets CAT 3 specification.

- Choose the location of your punch-down panel wisely. Once it's in place it can be a real bear to move.

- Ensure that wherever you locate the punch-down panel there is some means of supporting the weight of all the cables that will be running to it (both in the front and in the back). It always helps to think big and plan on having two or three times as many wires as you think you will ever need. While you may initially be wiring only a few drops, this number can grow quickly. Wire runs that hang or droop prior to being punched down will cause stress on the punch-down block. It's not uncommon for wires to pull themselves loose in these situations. Use a wiring ladder or fasteners to carry the weight of the wires.

- Label your network drops on the front of the panel. Someday you will have a problem that can only be resolved by tracing the cables. If drops are not labeled you're in for a long night. A label can simply be some form of unique alphanumeric identifier that indicates where the cable drop goes. Make sure you label the wall plate on the other end with this same identifier.

Labeling Schemes

I've run across many labeling schemes and found one in particular that seemed to be pretty efficient. The label identifies the punch-down location of the user's network drop. It has six characters but can be modified for smaller environments. Wire drops are labeled as follows:

- with a number indicating to which floor the drop connects

- with a letter indicating to which wire or server room the drop connects

- with a number indicating to which rack the drop connects

- with a letter indicating to which patch panel on the rack the drop connects

- with a number indicating to which connector on the panel the drop connects

Let's say a user calls the help desk line and states that they cannot connect to the network. After questioning them you feel that their system may be okay, but you want to check their network connection.

You ask them to read the label on their network wall plate and they reply, "4A3B23." You now know you need to go to the 4th floor, Room A. Within the room this user's network drop is wired to the 3rd rack on the patch panel labeled B. Their connection would be number 23 on that panel. For smaller environments you could simply drop the floor and room identifiers. Figure 4.1 shows a set of patch panels mounted in a standard network rack.

FIGURE 4.1

A set of patch panels mounted in a standard network rack

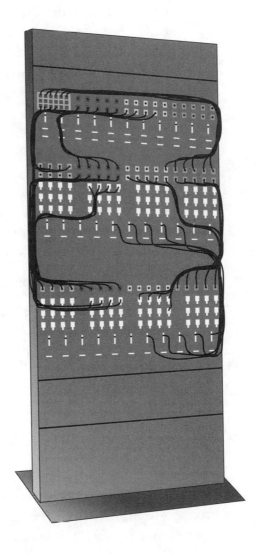

Most of the other numbering systems I've seen require you to look up the user's location in some form of matrix and cross reference this information to find the drop's location. This can be a pain if the user catches you in the hall or in some other location where you cannot quickly access this information

Network Interface Card

A network interface card (NIC) is used to connect a computer to the network. It includes two interfaces—one to connect to the network and one to connect to the computer itself. The NIC is the brains of the network connection, containing its own processor chip to help take some of the load off the computer's central processing unit (CPU). The more efficient the NIC card's circuitry, the less of a load it will place on the system. While this is not a big deal on a workstation, it can kill a server if it contains multiple NICs. When choosing a server network card, make sure you stick with a vendor who is known to produce high-performance cards.

There are a number of different varieties of NIC cards. The first thing to look at is how the card interfaces with the computer. There are three types of NIC card interfaces:

- attaching to an external port on the computer such as the parallel port

- installed internally in a Peripheral Component Interconnect Mezzanine/Computer Interface Adapter (PCIM/CIA) slot, now known simply as a PC slot

- installed internally within the system connecting directly to the computer bus

External Port Connection

An external port interface is probably the easiest to use but yields the poorest performance. An external port is typically an oval-shaped device that fits in the palm of your hand. On one side is a male 25-pin connector that attaches directly to the parallel port of the computer. This is why these network cards are commonly referred to as *parallel port* network cards.

On the other side is a 10BT, a coaxial connector, or both for connecting to the network. Most of these devices also require power and need to be plugged into an AC outlet or the PS/2 port of the computer. The software drivers used are identical to your standard network card drivers except they direct all network traffic through the parallel port. If you use one of these cards you lose the use of the parallel port for local printing (although you can still print to a network printer). Figure 4.2 shows a parallel port network adaptor card.

The benefit of a parallel port connection is ease of use. It was originally intended to connect laptop systems which did not have a bus or PC slot available. If you have an older laptop this may be your only means of connecting it to a network.

The downside to external ports is that their performance is poor. Because everything runs through the parallel port, these network cards saturate at about 1,300 frames per second (fps). Still, this may be ample for someone who is looking to simply share a few files or print. The other drawback is that supported topologies are usually limited to 10 Mb Ethernet. Don't expect to see expanded support for these devices, due to their poor performance and the popularity of PC cards. One final thing to be sure of is that the parallel port supports bi-directional communications. A standard parallel port only supports one-way (outbound) communications—as it was designed to send data to a printer without expecting a reply back. While bi-directional parallel ports are pretty common these days, the older systems that could benefit most from this type of network connection are the ones that were outfitted with the standard ports.

A parallel port network adapter card. The knobs on each side of the unit attach it securely to the parallel port.

PC Card Connection

PC card connections are pretty common these days and are typically used for connecting a laptop to a network. These cards are about the size of a credit card and only three or four times thicker. The card slides into a PC card slot on the computer and usually has some type of special cable that allows the card to connect to standard network wiring.

The upside to PC cards is increased performance. The average user will not notice a performance difference between a PC slot network card and one that plugs directly into the bus. A PC card is the preferred method of connecting a laptop to a network when possible.

One major drawback of PC cards is configuration. If you're using a plug-and-play computer and operating system, then set-up is usually pretty easy (it's almost plug-and-play). If you are using a non plug-and-play operating system like DOS, then the configuration can be a real nightmare for even a seasoned PC support specialist. Most such systems require about a half dozen drivers to be loaded prior to loading the network drivers. Even if you are successful in configuring the system and are able to log in to the network, there is no guarantee you will still have enough conventional memory left on your system to actually run any of your programs. Figure 4.3 shows a PCIM/CIA or PC card network adapter. Note the special cable used to connect this card to a standard RJ-45 connector.

FIGURE 4.3

A PCIM/CIA or PC card
network adapter

Internal Network Card Connection

Internal network cards are by far the most popular variety of connection. They are internal cards that plug directly into the computer's bus through installation to a free expansion slot in the back of the system, as shown in Figure 4.4. The circuit board plug at the bottom of the card plugs into the expansion slot of the computer.

FIGURE 4.4

A standard internal network card

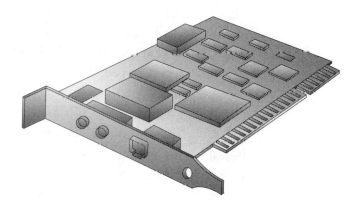

Make sure you use a card that supports the computer's bus type!

Internal network cards support the largest diversity of network topologies. There are vendors making internal network cards for every topology we cover in this book. One important consideration is to determine what kind of bus your computer uses. The most common are:

ISA (Industry Standard Architecture) Developed in 1979 for the IBM XT and implemented in all PC compatible systems to date, ISA is the slowest bus architecture available for the PC, typically running at only 8 megahertz (MHz). This is fine, however, for a low-end workstation connecting to a 10 Mbps network to do simple file and printer sharing. The average ISA NIC can push a 10 Mb network to about a 35% utilization rate if it is tuned properly. While there are 100 Mbps ISA cards available, their performance is pretty dismal. The bus is just too slow to take advantage of the additional bandwidth that 100 Mbps provides. This is definitely not the bus to use in a server!

EISA (Extended Industry Standard Architecture) Developed in 1987 to provide 32-bit throughput using the standard ISA architecture, this is the next generation to the ISA bus. Because EISA can easily keep up with wire speed traffic (100% utilization) on a 10 Mb network, it makes a good fit for server class machines. When the bandwidth jumps to 100 Mb, however, they have trouble keeping up. While there are some decent 100 Mb cards available, they are best limited to workstation use only at these speeds. Keep in mind that your server needs to process information from multiple network clients. Therefore it is always a good idea to maintain it as the fastest system on the network.

Micro Channel Developed in 1987 to provide a proprietary 32-bit alternative to ISA, this was IBM's next generation to the ISA bus. Performance is on par with EISA but the fact that it is only supported by IBM makes for a minimal number of card options.

NU-Bus Developed by Texas Instruments in 1984, this architecture relies on one proprietary processor slot, the Processor Direct Slot. This is legacy bus architecture used by Apple for the Macintosh computers. Most new Macs include PCI bus slots as well.

VESA Bus The Video Electronics Standards Association standard is an enhanced EISA design that provides a dedicated 32-bit line directly from the Vesa slot to the processor. This is known as local bus technology and is ten times faster than ISA.

S-Bus This is SUN's bus architecture for the SPARC station.

PCI (Peripheral Component Interconnect) Developed by Intel, this is now the bus architecture of choice and certainly the fastest of the bunch. To top it off, it is also cheaper to implement than all of the buses listed above with the exception of ISA. Most newer PC systems will contain a minimum of two PCI slots with the rest being made up of some other architecture. PCI has not only found its way into PC compatibles but into Macs as well. All 100 Mbps and faster cards should use a free PCI slot when possible. If the server's PCI slots are at a premium, you may want to check out some of the multi-port cards that have hit the market. These are specifically designed for servers that need to connect to more than one network segment. Each card contains two or four RJ-45 connections.

In the old days workstations used ISA NICs and servers used EISA. Because the server had the faster bus, it was in a better position to handle data requests from multiple clients. The result was a built-in *check valve* to control the flow of network traffic. Life was good and traffic flowed smoothly.

PCI has brought an interesting spin to network design. Because it is so inexpensive, it is also widely implemented, finding its way into both server and workstation class machines. This means that many of the new workstations are able to crank out data just as fast as the server (maybe even more so if the server has not been upgraded to PCI over the last few years). The result is that the server's NIC card is pushed into saturation, receiving more traffic than it can handle. While this is rare on 10 Mbps networks it can be quite common when speeds are pushed up to 100 Mbps. PCI is currently the fastest thing around, but it still has trouble with a 100 Mbps or more network pushed to full speed. This needs to be taken under careful consideration when you are planning network upgrades. I've seen servers that have run stable for months roll over and play dead when upgraded to 100 Mbps pipes, because the bus has become saturated from the increase in traffic it receives.

Topology and Wiring Support

The final consideration in choosing a network card is to ensure it supports the topology and the wiring you are using. If your topology is 100VG-ANYLAN, then you need a 100VG card. A 100 Mb Ethernet card will not work. Many vendors are now shipping cards that support multiple topologies. If you are currently running 10 Mb Ethernet but have your eye on 100 Mb Ethernet for the future you can purchase 10/100 cards that support both topologies. The card will work in your current environment and be ready for when you upgrade later. Most of these include an auto sensing feature which will detect what network speed you are running at. This is a great feature in that when the upgrade does take place, you will not have to configure any of the workstations; simply power cycle them and they will connect at the faster speed.

Also ensure the NIC's connector is correct for your cabling. If you are using Thinnet, the card should have a BNC connector, for twisted pair, an RJ-45. While media converters are available to connect dissimilar media types, it is always a good idea to limit the number of connectors used. An excessive number of connectors can introduce noise or signal loss to the circuit. Many vendors have had multi-port cards (referred to as *combo cards*) available for a number of years, and these will connect to a variety of media types. They contain an RJ-45, a BNC, and an AUI (Attachment Unit Interface) connector. An AUI connector is a type of generic connection that requires that a transceiver be used to connect to your cabling. A transceiver is a type of media converter that allows you to attach the network card to any type of cabling that your topology allows. Figure 4.5 shows two transceivers.

FIGURE 4.5

A transceiver—these devices connect a generic networking port called an AUI to any type of cable media supported by the device.

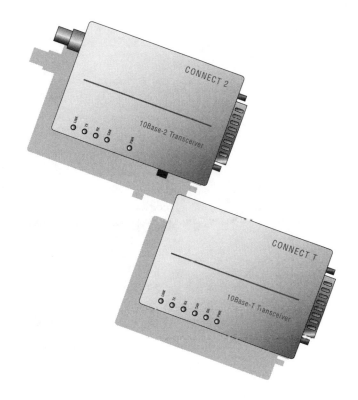

Media Converters

Media converters are devices used to connect two dissimilar cable types. They are usually palm-size boxes with mating connectors on either end. Converts are available to connect together twisted pair, coax, and fiber in any possible combination. Depending on the application, they may or may not require an external power source.

While it is not always practical to upgrade all network devices when a media change occurs, media converters can be lifesavers in a pinch.

When using a media converter you must pay close attention to the maximum distances of your cables. Keep the combined distance to the smallest specification of the two cables to avoid difficulty. For example,

Saved by a Media Converter

I was upgrading an operations center from thinnet to twisted-pair. The center contained a good mixture of Banyan Vines, NetWare, SUN, and Lotus Notes systems. In the process of the upgrade we discovered that a NetWare 2.2 and two Banyan 4.0 servers did not have combo cards like we thought. The network cards were of an unknown vendor and contained only a BNC connector. All three systems were scheduled to be replaced over the next few months but were currently critical to the company's day-to-day operations. Rather than scheduling additional downtime to replace the network cards and taking the chance that these dinosaurs might never come back up again, we installed a media converter instead.

The systems were connected together with a short run of thinnet cable. We terminated and grounded one end and on the other installed a media converter. The media converter was then connected to a twisted-pair cable which in turn connected to our brand new switch (more on switches later).

The result? The systems were back online and functional and we avoided dedicating another Sunday or more to the project.

given the above situation you would want to keep your cable distance to 325 feet, because this is the requirement for twisted-pair cabling. A converter introduces *latency*, so it is a good idea to stay well below the maximum.

Latency is the delay incurred on a circuit when the signal must undergo processing.

The act of amplifying the signal takes a small amount of time, which can be measured as the time from when the repeater receives the signal to when it transmits it on its other port. If too much latency is added to a network, connections may time out prematurely. We'll discuss this further when we cover troubleshooting later in the book.

Repeaters

Repeaters are simple two-port signal amplifiers. They are used in a bus topology to extend the maximum distance that can be spanned on a cable run. The strength of the signal is boosted as it travels down the wire. A repeater will receive a digital signal on one of its ports, amplify it, and transmit it out the other side.

A repeater is like a typical home stereo amplifier. The amp takes the signal it receives from the CD, tape deck, etc., and amplifies the signal and sends it on its way to the speakers. If the signal is a brand new Alanis Morisett CD, it simply boosts the signal and sends it on its way. If it's an old Grateful Dead concert tape that is inaudible from the amount of background hiss, it happily boosts this signal as well and sends it on its way.

Repeaters function similar to stereo amplifiers. They simply boost whatever they receive and send it on its way. Unfortunately the signal they receive could be a good frame of data, a bad frame of data, or even background noise. A repeater does not discern data quality; it simply looks at each of the individual digital pulses and amplifies them.

Why Use a Repeater?

A repeater is a cheap, effective way of extending your cable lengths. For example, the maximum allowable distance for thinnet cable is 600 feet. By using a repeater, this distance can be extended to 1,200 feet. By using multiple repeaters this distance can continue to be extended until the maximum overall length specification of the topology is reached. For example 10 Mb Ethernet is 3000 feet, so no more than five thinnet repeaters could be used.

A repeater does not follow Ethernet's CSMA/CD rules of listening before transmitting. If another station is partially through a frame transmission, a repeater will blindly transmit as well, causing a collision. This is why the overall maximum topology length must still be adhered to with a repeater. Stations at either end still need to be able to monitor the entire length of the network correctly, prior to transmission.

Choosing a Repeater

When choosing a repeater, ensure that it has transmit and jam lights for each of its ports. These lights are LED indicators that monitor the repeater's operation. The transmit lights let you know when traffic is detected on each of the ports. The jam lights let you know if a collision or a cable problem occurs along an individual length of cable. If a jam light blinks quickly, then two frames have collided. If the light turns on solid, then you probably have a failure somewhere along the length of cable. These indicators can be invaluable troubleshooting tools when you are trying to diagnose a connectivity problem. Figure 4.6 shows a common network repeater. The front indicator lights quickly verify the operation of the device.

FIGURE 4.6

A common network repeater

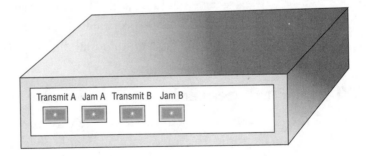

Hubs

Hubs are probably the most common piece of network hardware after network interface cards. Physically, they are boxes of varying sizes that have multiple female RJ-45 connectors. Each connector is designed to accept one twisted-pair cable outfitted with a male RJ-45 connector. This twisted-pair cable is then used to connect a single server or workstation to the hub.

Hubs are essentially multi-port repeaters that support twisted-pair cables in a star typology. Each node communicates with the hub, which in turn amplifies the signal and transmits it on its remaining ports. As with a repeater, hubs work at the electrical level. Because hubs have no way to determine if a frame is good or bad, they should be looked at, when you design your network typology, as functionally identical to repeaters.

Chassis Hubs

Hubs come in two categories, chassis and stackable. A chassis hub is a large box (typically one or two feet tall and the width of a network rack) that is made to mount into a network rack. The chassis has slots similar to (but not the same as) the expansion card slots in the back of a standard PC. These are usually designed so that a card can slide directly in from the front without disassembling the device. On the front of the card are multiple RJ-45 connectors. The number of stations a hub can supported depends on the port density of each card and how many cards are installed. Cards typically support anywhere from four to 24 connections. The number of cards supported by the chassis varies from model to model. Typically, one slot is lost to some form of management card that is used to configure and monitor the remaining cards. Besides hub cards, a chassis hub may also support cards that supply bridge, switch, or even routing functionality.

The appeal of a chassis hub is that it is compact. There are chassis hubs that will support 200 or more connections. If you have a large number of users to support but do not have a lot of room for networking equipment, a chassis hub may be your best bet. Also alluring is the chassis hub's ability to monitor all these ports through a single point of management. A chassis hub management card will usually allow you to monitor every port, allowing you to determine which ones are in use.

Unfortunately, chassis hubs also have many drawbacks, the first of which is a single point of failure. If you support 150 users through a single chassis hub and it goes down, your entire network is offline. Another drawback is that many of the denser hub cards do away with the RJ-45 connectors and use a single proprietary connector with separate twisted-pair cables attached to it. This is the only way to fit 24 or more connections onto a single card; this increases the number of connections a single card can handle, but it can make it difficult to trace wires. While you will be able to determine which card the drop connects to, you may be hard pressed to determine which of the card's ports it is using. Also, if one cable is just a wee bit too short, you cannot just replace it with a standard twisted-pair patch cord. You will need to replace the entire assembly with a longer proprietary unit, if one is even available. These longer units are proprietary in that they do not use connectors commonly deployed with network wiring, so they must be specially made and are not considered an off-the-shelf item like a standard twisted-pair patch cord, which is available from most computer stores and mail order catalogs.

Another major drawback of chassis hubs is the lack of indicator lights. LEDs that indicate port status are removed in order to connect more users. Link status and transmit indicators for each port on a hub are convenient visual aids in trying to diagnose a problem. The link status light will come on when a system is connected and correctly wired to the hub port. The transmit light will flash whenever that station sends data. While most chassis hubs have the ability to monitor a port's health through some form of management software, the loss of visual indicators can greatly inhibit the troubleshooting process.

Chassis hubs are also not very flexible. If I fill a 200-port chassis hub, I may end up with so much traffic on my network that end users constantly complain about poor network performance. While most vendors will sell you an optional card to segment the chassis into multiple *virtual hubs,* you can usually only create three or four of them. Again, with 200 users I would still have 50 or more people contending for bandwidth. In a busy environment this can still be grossly inadequate. While the argument can be made to refrain from putting so many users on a single chassis hub, doing so would limit a chassis hub's greatest appeal, which is that it supports many users within a small enclosure.

As if all this was not enough, chassis hubs also tend to cost more than their stackable counterpart. With management and segmentation modules the per-port cost can easily be two to three times or more than what you would pay for the equivalent number of ports using stackable hubs.

Stackable Hubs

Stackable hubs are slim line boxes which usually contain between six and 24 ports. Most have link and transmit lights to help monitor the health of each port. Stackables are so named because, as your port requirements grow, you can simply buy another hub and stack it on top of the first. Stackables can also be rack mounted or flush mounted to a wall.

Stackables have a lot going for them, which has made them the hub of choice. The first is cost. If you have a small network, purchase a cheap six-port hub and you're off and networking. As your needs grow you can purchase larger hubs or link smaller ones together.

One of the nice things about stackables is that, if you are using more than one, you do not have a central point of failure. If a hub fails, you can simply move your important users (your boss, his boss, the secretary that brings you cookies every day, and so on) to the hub that is still functioning until a replacement can be found. Note that you can usually mix and match stackable hubs from different vendors, so in a real pinch you may be able to run down to your local computer store and purchase a replacement.

The mix-and-match nature of stackable hubs is in contrast to chassis hubs, which are proprietary, meaning replacements can usually only be purchased through the manufacturer or one of their *value added resellers*.

Managed Stackable Hubs

Stackables come in two varieties, managed and unmanaged. A managed hub (sometimes referred to as an intelligent hub) runs some form of software that allows you to communicate with the device (either over the network or from a directly attached terminal) and check operating parameters like port status (up or down). This communication is useful if you have an extremely large environment and it is impractical to walk over to the hub and check the indicator lights.

NOTE This capacity to check operating parameters is identical to what you get with a chassis hub. Some vendors are even including backbone connectors that allow you to connect multiple hubs together and manage them as if they were one device.

It is also possible to have an intelligent hub send out alerts to a management station, however this may not be as useful as it sounds because these alerts are limited to when the hub has been rebooted or if a port goes down. Personally I would be less concerned with rebooting and more concerned with it going offline initially. Unfortunately, an offline hub has no way of sending an alert. Also, a port will technically go down every time a user shuts off their workstation. Clearly, intelligent hubs are not quite as clever as their name implies. Their useful application is tailored to very specific environments. Unless you know that you will definitely use additional functionality, they may not be worth the additional cost.

Unmanaged Stackable Hubs

An unmanaged hub does not have any type of management or monitoring software. The only indication of their status is the supplied LEDs. I have seen hubs that have locked up, and even though they appear operational at first glance they will not transmit any data. In such a case, the online LED will be lit as will be the link lights for each of the attached stations. If you watch the transmit lights, however, you will see no activity. It is clearly important to only use hubs with indicator lights. One other LED to look for is a collision indicator. Because a hub is a dumb amplifier, it only needs a single collision light for all of its ports. A collision light can be an early warning signal that something is not right with the network. If this light is turned on solid, it's time to break out a network analyzer and find out what is going on.

Backbone Connection

Stackable hubs have two different methods of being connected together—through a backbone connection (if one is supplied) or through an uplink port. A backbone connection is a separate connector designed to be attached to hubs; it is usually implemented as a BNC connector in 10 Mbps hubs and connects the hubs with a short run of thinnet cable.

Some vendors use a proprietary cable to connect their hubs together for management purposes. In this case, these cables will supply the required network connection between the hubs as well.

Uplink Port Connection

An uplink port is a special port that reverses the transmit-and-receive pair of a twisted-pair cable. An uplink port can look like any other hub port, so you should be careful not to use it inadvertently. An uplink port is required because if you directly wire two hubs together the wire pairs will be connected transmit-to-transmit and receive-to-receive; wired this way the hubs will be unable to communicate with each other. Some uplink ports will have a switch next to them to allow you to select their mode of operation. If you have a small network and do not need to connect your hub to another, you can usually throw the switch and use it to connect an extra workstation. Note that only one hub needs to be uplinked. If you use the uplink port on both sides, the hubs will still be unable to communicate.

If you need to connect two hubs together and neither one has an uplink port, you can connect them together with a cross cable. A cross cable is a twisted-pair wire that has the transmit-and-receive pairs switched at one end; this provides the same functionality as an uplink port. Make sure cross cables are labeled as such so they are not confused with regular cables.

The hub can have its RJ-45 connectors on either the front or the back of the unit. Select a unit that fits your wiring scheme. For example, if the hub will be rack mounted it may make more sense to purchase a hub with the connectors in the back. This cuts down on cable clutter, giving the front of the rack a cleaner look.

Figure 4.7 shows three stackable hubs of various port densities. Note the lack of front indicator lights.

FIGURE 4.7

Three stackable hubs of various port densities

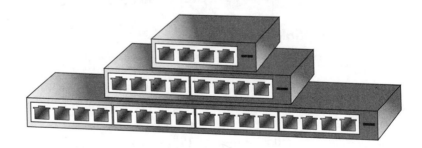

Bridges

A bridge looks a lot like a repeater; it is a small box with two network connectors that attach to two separate portions of the network. A bridge incorporates the functionality of a repeater (signal amplification), but it actually looks at the frames of data, which is a great benefit. A common bridge is nearly identical to a repeater except for the indicator lights, as shown in Figure 4.8. A *forward* light flashes whenever the bridge needs to pass traffic from one collision domain to another.

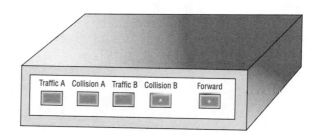

In our discussion of Ethernet in the last chapter we introduced the concept of a data frame and described the information contained within the frame header. Bridges put this header information to use by monitoring the source and destination MAC address on each frame of data. By monitoring the source address the bridge will learn where all the network systems are located. It will construct a table listing which MAC addresses are directly accessible by each of its ports. It will then use that information to play traffic cop and regulate the flow of data on the network. Let's look at an example.

A Bridge Example

Given the network in Figure 4.9, Betty needs to send data to the server Thoth. Because everyone on the network is required to monitor the network, Betty first listens for the transmissions of other stations. If the wire is free, Betty will then transmit a frame of data. Our bridge is also watching for traffic and will look at the source address in the header of Betty's frame. Because it is unsure of which port the system with MAC address 00C08BBE0052 (Thoth) is connected to, it amplifies the signal and retransmits it out port B. Note that up until now the bridge functionality is very similar to that of a repeater. The bridge does a little extra, however; it has learned that Betty is attached to port A and creates a table entry with her MAC address.

F I G U R E 4.9

Betty transmits data to the server Thoth by putting Thoth's MAC address into the destination field of the frame.

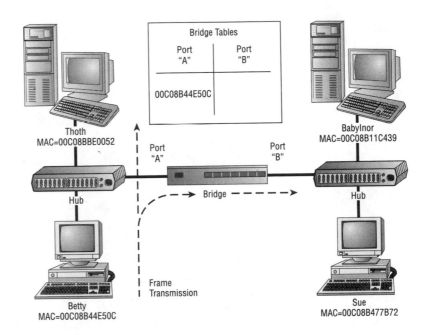

When Thoth replies to Betty's request, as shown in Figure 4.10, the bridge will look at the destination address in the frame of data again. This time, however, it finds a match in its table, noting that Betty is also attached to port A. Because it knows Betty can receive this information directly, it drops the frame and blocks it from being transmitted out of port B. It will also make a new table entry for Thoth, recording the MAC address as being off of port A.

The benefit is that, for as long as the bridge remembers each station's MAC address, all communications between Betty and Thoth will be isolated from Sue and Babylnor. Traffic isolation is a powerful feature because it means that systems on both sides of the bridge can be carrying on conversations at the same time, effectively doubling the available bandwidth. The bridge ensures that communications on both sides stay

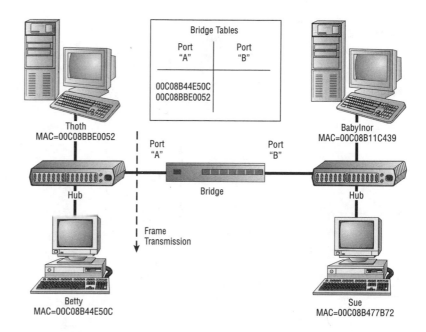

FIGURE 4.10

Thoth's reply to Betty's
message

isolated, as if they were not even connected together. Because stations cannot see transmissions on the other side of the bridge, they assume the network is free and send their data.

Each system only needs to contend for bandwidth with systems on its own segment. This means that there is no way for a station to have a collision outside of its segment. Thus, these segments are referred to as *collision domains*, as shown in Figure 4.11. Note that one port on each side of the bridge is part of each collision domain. This is because each of its ports will contend for bandwidth with the systems it is directly connected to. Because the bridge isolates traffic within each collision domain, there is no way for separated systems to collide their signals. The effect is a doubling of potential bandwidth.

So what happens when traffic needs to traverse the bridge? As stated before, when a bridge is unsure of the location of a system it will always pass the packet along just in case. Once the bridge learns that the system is in fact located off of its other port, it will continue to pass the frame along as required.

FIGURE 4.11

Two separate collision
domains

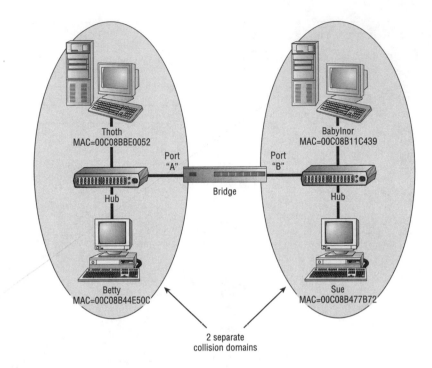

This example is specific to two stations carrying on a data exchange. As we mentioned in our discussion on Ethernet frames there is a special destination address referred to as a broadcast address. Broadcasts contain information required by multiple stations on the network. Broadcast frames are typically used by upper-layer protocols like IPX and IP to relay network and server information. For this reason a bridge will always pass a broadcast frame.

Balancing Traffic Segmentation and Bridge Latency

There is an old bridging rule which states that 80% of your traffic should be directly connected with only 20% or less being bridged. This rule is a general guideline to ensure that you keep a good balance between traffic segmentation and *bridge latency*. A bridge will introduce a bit more latency than a repeater or a hub; this is because it actually needs to look at the frame information and respond, depending on the destination MAC address. In short, if your users frequently access a particular server, do not put a bridge in between them and that server.

Bridge latency refers to the theory that a full 100% utilization is never achievable through the device because the signal is being delayed en route. While this is a true statement, the amount of delay is rarely noticeable. From the testing I've performed, it appears that your average bridge is able to keep up with a 90% utilization level. While the 10% loss may seem quite large, remember that an Ethernet network starts to degrade in performance by the time it reaches 50% utilization. At 90%, performance feels downright dismal. So, to the average end user the bridge should show no noticeable performance hit if they need to access systems on the other side of it. In fact, if the bridge is implemented properly it should improve performance because it would regulate traffic flow and hopefully bring the utilization level down to a more reasonable level.

Bridges reset the maximum spans for a topology. The maximum span for an Ethernet network is 3000 ft. If I attach a bridge to the end of it I could add another 3000 ft. to my overall network length; this is because a bridge listens to the network prior to transmitting just like any other intelligent network device. Hubs and repeaters do not do this because they function at the electrical level only.

Protocol Independence

Bridges are protocol independent. This means that it does not matter if you're running AppleTalk, IPX, IP, NetBEUI or any other 802.3-compliant means of communicating. All a bridge cares about is the source and destination MAC address present in any valid Ethernet frame. Protocol independence can come in handy if you're using a protocol that receives limited hardware support like Banyan Vine's VinesIP. Note that many of these protocols operate by having the administrator assign a network address for them to use. Because bridges do not look at the upper layer protocol, this number would be the same on both sides of the bridge.

We'll talk a little more about protocols and network addresses when we cover routers.

Some bridges can analyze the frame check sequence (FCS) located in the trailer of the frame. As mentioned before, the FCS contains the cyclic redundancy check (CRC), which is an algorithm used to determine if the frame is intact or has become damaged during transmission. If FCS checking is enabled, the bridge will perform its own CRC check on the frame and compare the value to what is contained in the FCS field of each frame before forwarding the frame along. If a frame is found to fail the CRC comparison, then the bridge contacts the transmitting system and asks it to send a new copy of the frame.

If you commonly have a lot of CRC errors on your network, this check feature may be useful as it keeps the frame from being passed to the destination system, which would then find the CRC failure and need to request a new frame itself. By letting the bridge do it, you cut down on the bandwidth used by the bad frame and the resulting request to only a single collision domain.

If you do not see a lot of error, you may want to keep this feature disabled, as it does require some additional overhead on the bridge. If you do see a lot of errors (if, say, 1% of your traffic is bad CRC frames), enable this feature. Then set out to determine their cause and eliminate it.

Excessive CRC failures are usually caused by a bad network interface card.

The Spanning Tree Protocol

Bridges are capable of communicating with each other via a set of rules called the Spanning Tree protocol. The spanning tree protocol is used to configure default paths dynamically when two or more bridges are connected in parallel to each other.

Bridge Looping Causes Problems

Spanning Tree protocol helps to avoid a situation called *bridge looping*. To get an idea of how bridge looping works, let's look at an example.

Given a network layout similar to our last example, you decide to add a second bridge for redundancy. This way, if someone spills coffee on the first bridge and it quickly dies in a shower of sparks, the second bridge can continue to provide connectivity between the two collision domains. The configuration would look something like Figure 4.12.

FIGURE 4.12

Two bridges connected in parallel to each other create a redundant link between the two collision domains.

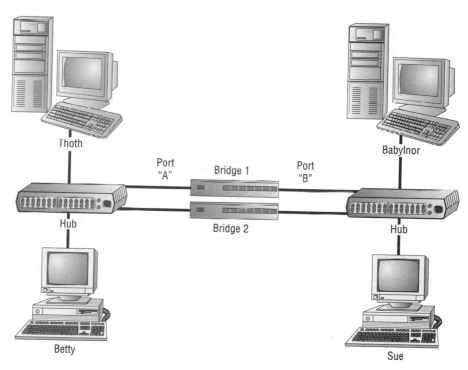

If both bridges are active, a curious behavior occurs. Given a situation where Betty sends a frame of data to Thoth, both bridges would detect the frame and be unsure where Thoth is located, so they would both transmit the data to the other segment and make an entry for Betty in their tables, placing her off of port A. When both bridges detect the frame and transmit the data to the other segment, two separate copies of the frame have been transmitted onto the other collision domain (off of port B).

As each bridge detects the frame sent by the other on the port B collision domain, it assumes that this is a new attempt by Betty to send Thoth a frame of data. Because both bridges would still be unsure where Thoth is located, they would pass the frame back to the collision domain off of port A. Each bridge will also assume that Betty has now moved to the other collision domain and would incorrectly list the system as being off of port B.

We have a couple of problems at this point. First, we have three identical frames (one from Betty and one from each of the bridges) floating around off of port A when there should only be one. Instead of improving our traffic pattern, the bridges have tripled our frame rate on this segment. Also, because Betty is now incorrectly listed as being off of port B, any data transmitted to Betty by Babylnor and Sue would be blocked by both bridges because they now incorrectly assume that Betty is on the same local segment as Babylnor and Sue. The result is that Betty is unable to receive any data sent to her from stations off of port B because neither bridge will forward the information.

At this point the entire situation repeats itself. Both bridges detect the frame transmission of the other off of port A. They retransmit the frame onto the segment attached to port B and move the entry for Betty's MAC address back to port A again. At this point, Betty is able to receive data across the bridge, but only until the tables are incorrectly reset again.

This looping effect is referred to as *counting to infinity*. The bridges will continue to pass the frame back and forth until the end of time or until the bridge's power plug is pulled, whichever comes first. This happens because the bridge has no way of identifying duplicate frames. When the frame is analyzed, the bridge only looks at the source and destination MAC addresses. Performing some form of a check to determine if it has seen a particular frame before is beyond the scope of a bridge's functionality; it would also severely degrade a bridge's performance, causing it to become a bottleneck on the network.

Now, take this situation with Betty's system and multiply it by a network full of systems. It's easy to see how two misconfigured bridges could easily bring an entire network to its knees.

Eliminating Bridging Loops with the Spanning Tree Protocol

To the rescue comes the Spanning Tree protocol. This protocol allows bridges to communicate with each other and learn where they are in relation to one another. If a bridge is configured to use the Spanning Tree protocol, it will transmit a maintenance frame on startup called a Bridge Protocol Data Unit (BPDU). This frame contains an ID number for the bridge and is transmitted on all the bridge's ports. This ID number is a combination of a number preset by the network administrator and the device's MAC address.

If the Spanning Tree protocol is used in the above example, both bridges would transmit BPDUs from each of their ports. Each bridge would receive a BPDU from the other bridge on both of its ports and realize that the two devices are hooked up in parallel. They would then compare their BPDUs to see which bridge has the lowest ID number. The bridge with the lower ID number would become active, while the other would enter a standby mode. The second bridge would remain in standby mode until it detects that the first bridge is no longer passing packets. If the first bridge drops offline, the second bridge would step in to supply connectivity. Because there is only one active path for the frames to follow, bridge looping is eliminated.

A bridge's ID is prefixed by a number that you can assign. If you prefer to use one bridge over another for performance reasons you can assign a lower number (like 01) to it to ensure that it initiates as the active bridge.

About the only drawback of the Spanning Tree protocol is that the switchover occurs so quickly that you will probably never know the bridge has failed unless you are monitoring the devices.

Use a Bridge to Segment Traffic

Let's look at three sample networks and determine which environment would benefit the most by the use of bridging. Note that we're focusing on the network infrastructure, not on the actual operating systems or the functionality of the protocols being used. As you read each example, see if (and why) you think bridging would be a good idea before reading on.

Example 1

Our first example is a group of 25 engineers using SGI Unix workstations. Each engineer uses their machine to write code and create images for computer games. As part of the software development process the engineers need to exchange file information with each other. They are not broken up into defined work groups, as all development is a collaborative effort. Each engineer may need to share files with any one of the other engineers at any given time. The data transfers between systems can also be quite intensive, as large graphic files are used and source code is compiled over the network. Figure 4.13 depicts our first example.

Example 2

Our second example is a small advertising firm with approximately 50 employees. They have three servers—one NetWare, one Mac and one Unix. 15 of the 50 use Mac workstations to do graphic design work that involves moving some average-size image files. All files are stored on the Mac server using Apple's native AppleTalk protocol. The remaining 35 users perform mostly administrative tasks and connect with the NetWare system via the IPX protocol for file and print services. All users run IP as well to connect to the Unix system for mail and Internet access. Figure 4.14 depicts our second example.

FIGURE 4.13

Our first example
network with 25 (eight
shown here) engineers
who need to share file
information between
their systems

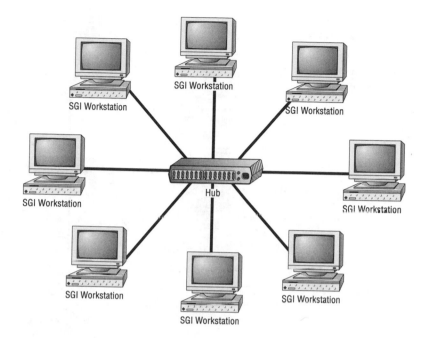

Example 3

Our last example includes 100 users with three NT servers. 50 of the users use one of the servers for file and print services. The remaining 50 use the second server for the same. The third system runs the company's mail program and needs to be accessed by everyone. NetBEUI is used to access all servers. Figure 4.15 shows our third example.

In all three examples the users are complaining about slow network response time. As always, cost is a factor and any hardware purchases will need to be justified.

While the task of redesigning each of the above mentioned networks may seem a bit overwhelming, think of what we have learned about a bridge's functionality and try to apply its traffic isolation features to each of the above examples. Move systems around as required, if you think it will help improve performance.

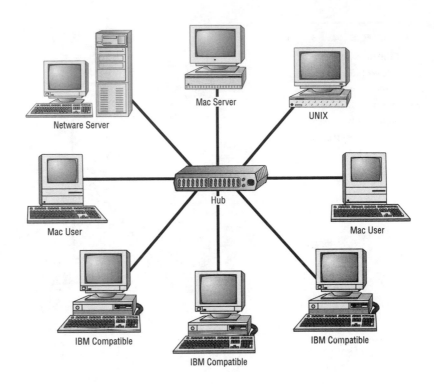

Feel free to stop for a moment before reading on. A large part of being a successful network engineer is having good problem solving skills and learning to be analytical. Learning the theory of how network systems work is the easy part. Applying it on a daily basis is the real challenge.

Our first example is clearly not a good choice for implementing a bridge. Because everyone shares files with everyone else, there is no way to maintain our "directly connect 80% and bridge no more than 20%" rule. Bridging would be of very little use in this environment.

Our second example shows a bit more potential. Users are somewhat broken up into work groups as administration mostly uses the NetWare server and graphic design mostly accesses the Mac server. We may very well be able to meet our 80% / 20% rule in this environment. If we were to separate these work groups with bridges, putting the Unix

FIGURE 4.15

Our third example
network with users neatly
broken up by work group
and everyone needing
access to mail

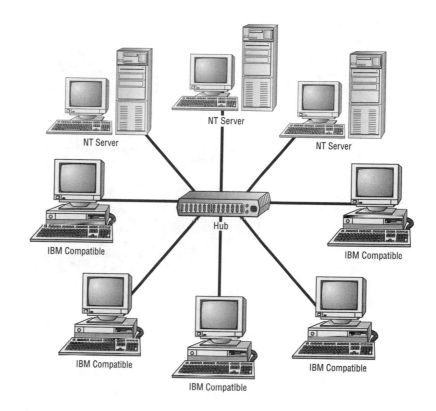

system in the middle, as shown in Figure 4.16, we may be able to isolate
enough traffic to improve network performance.

The only caveat to this is that we have three different protocols in
use. As mentioned previously, protocols make use of the broadcast
address to relay information concerning servers and networks. Also, as
we discussed in the section on Ethernet, all stations are required to process a frame which contains a broadcast address in the MAC destination field, whether it is currently using the protocol that sent it or not.
Of course, if it is not, the frame is discarded because the information
has no relevance. However, it still takes time and CPU cycles for the
system to determine it did not actually need this information.

Clearly, if we could isolate the protocols from the stations that do
not need to see them, we may well be able to increase overall performance even more. Because bridging is protocol-stupid and cannot provide this functionality, we may be better off waiting to see if another

FIGURE 4.16

A potential network design for our advertising firm

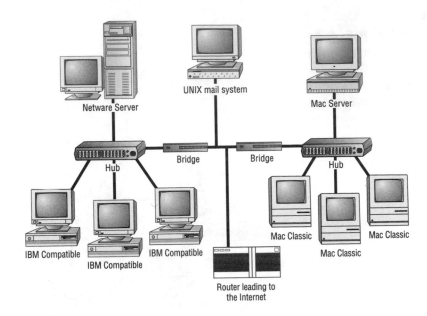

technology would be a better fit. Unfortunately, we cannot simply disconnect them from each other because they still need to share the Unix system for mail and have access to the Internet.

Our third example looks like a good fit. It has a similar layout to the last example but without the multiple protocols to worry about. Users are broken up into two distinct work groups but have a common need to share mail. If we install two bridges, as shown in Figure 4.17, we set up three distinct collision domains. This isolates the work groups from each other and even isolates file and print traffic from the mail server. Overall, bridging looks like a good fit for improving performance on this network.

Monitoring Traffic in a Bridged Environment

While bridges have many benefits, they do have one minor drawback. If you are trying to monitor your network's health with some form of network analyzer, a bridge will block you from ever seeing a full picture.

FIGURE 4.17

A bridging design for our
third network example

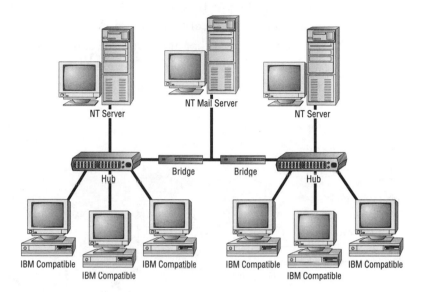

An analyzer relies on being able to detect each frame in order to collect statistics. When you use a bridge, your view is limited to the collision domain you are connected to. If you have a single bridge installed and want to monitor all traffic on your network you will need to purchase a second analyzer and keep one hooked up to each collision domain.

Switches

Switches are the marriage of hub and bridge technology. They resemble stackable hubs in appearance, having multiple RJ-45 connectors for connecting network systems. Instead of being a dumb amplifier like a hub, however, switches function as though they have a little miniature bridge built into each port. A switch will keep track of the MAC addresses attached to each of its ports and direct traffic destined for a certain address only to the port to which it is attached.

Figure 4.18 shows a switched environment in which the device will learn the position of each station once a single frame transmission occurs (identical to a bridge). Assuming that this has already happened, we now find that at exactly the same instant station 1 needs to send data to server 1, station 2 needs to send data to server 2 and station 3 needs to send data to server 3.

FIGURE 4.18

A switch installation showing three workstations and three servers that need to communicate

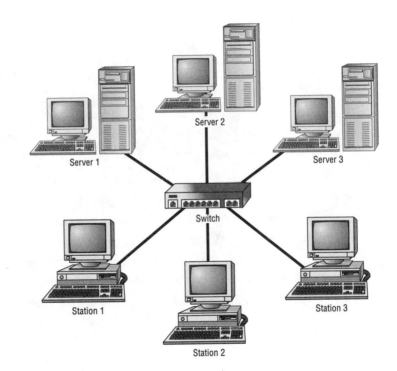

There are some interesting things about this situation. The first is that each wire run involves only the switch and the station attached to it. This means that each collision domain is limited to only these two devices, because each port of the switch is acting like a bridge. The only traffic seen by the workstations and servers is frame traffic specifically sent to them or the broadcast address. The result is that all three stations will see very little network traffic and will be able to transmit immediately. This is a powerful feature that goes a long way towards increasing potential bandwidth. Given our example, if this is a 10 Mb topology, the effective throughput has just increased by a factor of three. This is because all three sets of systems are able to carry on their conversation simultaneously as the switch isolates them from each other. While it is still technically 10 Mb Ethernet, potential throughput has increased to 30 Mbps.

Because each collision domain is limited to only two devices (the switch and the system attached), we could completely eliminate the chance of any collisions if we can come up with some way to keep these two systems from stepping on each other's transmissions.

Full Duplex Operation

This is where full duplex operation comes into play. Full duplex under Ethernet calls for the wire pair that signals frame collisions on the network to be used by one of the systems for data transmission. Because the goal is to have no collisions, this wire pair will not be required to provide this service. This leaves the data pair open for the other device to use for unrestricted transmission. The result is that each system has its own *personal* wires to transmit on without having to worry about pesky collisions. A system can continually transmit 10 Mbps on one wire pair while receiving 10 Mbps on the other. Applying this to our above mentioned network, our potential throughput has just jumped from 30 Mbps to 60 Mbps! Our topology has not changed—we are achieving these bandwidth potentials using standard 10 Mb Ethernet hardware.

Note the operative word "potential." It would be an extremely rare situation for these six systems to transmit this much data simultaneously. Still, having exclusive wire access is a great way to ensure that a system can transmit whenever it needs to. If applied only to servers, full duplex operation gives these systems a bit of an edge in keeping up with requests from multiple clients. The result is a governing effect allocating more bandwidth to the server than the workstations. This will help the server keep up with the additional frames it will see now that each workstation has its own 10 Mbps pipe.

Some network cards have a feature that allows them to *auto-detect* when full duplex operation may be used. This feature should be disabled and the card should be specifically configured for the correct mode of operation (full or half duplex). I have seen situations where the first two computers booted on the network will assume they have exclusive access to a collision domain and switch to full duplex mode. They will not realize they are connected through a shared hub. This works fine until the rest of the network's systems begin to power up. The result is that one station will be attempting to transmit data on the collision pair; this causes the entire network to crawl to a halt, as each system assumes multiple collisions are taking place. This can be a difficult problem to diagnose. The only clue is that the collision light will be lit up like a Christmas tree.

Cut Through Mode

Switches have two modes of operation—cut through and store-and-forward. In cut through mode the switch receives only the first 14 bytes of the frame (just the header) and will immediately begin to make a decision as to where the frame should be sent. In cut through mode a switch has the ability to begin transmitting the frame on the destination port before it receives it in its entirety; this results in extremely fast switching times with a minimal amount of latency added to the circuit. The greatest benefits of cut through mode are in quiet or full duplex environments where it is unlikely the switch will need to pause prior to transmission.

The benefits of cut through mode diminish as traffic levels increase. If utilization is high, it is unlikely that the switch will ever be able to transmit the frame onto a collision domain prior to receiving it in its entirety anyway. In these cases store-and-forward mode can be just as effective.

Store-and-Forward Mode

Store-and-forward mode requires the switch to read the entire frame into memory prior to transmission. While reading the entire frame adds a bit of a delay, the store-and-forward mode definitely has its advantages. Like a bridge, a switch in store-and-forward mode has the ability to check the FCS field for CRC errors; this ensures that bad frames are not propagated across the network. Another cool feature is that store-and-forward mode gives the switch the ability to support multiple topologies. A server could be connected to a 100 Mbps port while all the workstations are connected to 10 Mbps ports, allowing the server to keep up with data requests easily from multiple workstations and speeding overall network performance.

Store-and-forward switching is always used with mixed topologies because it ensures that the switch has the entire frame available prior to attempting a transmission. Because, in cut through mode, a switch can begin transmitting a frame prior to receiving it in its entirety, problems may arise in a mixed speed situation. Let's say a frame is received on a 10 Mbps port and it is addressed to a system on the 100 Mbps port. In cut through mode the switch would immediately begin delivery on the faster segment. This can be a problem because there is the potential for the switch to transmit all the frame information it has received on the faster segment and then have to pause and wait for the delivery of the rest of the frame information. Obviously, this would cause communication problems on the faster segment.

Avoiding Switch Overload

Take care to not overload the switch with excessive traffic. Let's look at an extreme example of how switch overload can occur.

Assume you have an old 286 server running NetWare 2.15. Because the system has continued to function it has been pretty much ignored over the years. Your users are a different story, however, complaining about how slow the system is and claiming they require dual processor

Pentium machines with PCI buses and every go-fast computer part you can think of (insert a Tim Allen grunt here).

You decide to upgrade your network infrastructure by replacing your old hub with a brand new switch. You swap in the new device, connect all systems but the server in full duplex mode (the server has an old card that does not support this feature) and wait for your users to begin working. A curious thing occurs—network performance actually gets worse! Why did this happen? To answer this, let's look at what was probably going on prior to the switch installation.

On a repeated network (remember that your hub is just a multi-port repeater) all systems are in direct communication with each other. When a server receives more frames of data than it is able to process, it will trigger a collision warning. This is the server's way of fooling other systems into thinking there is a network problem and that they should back off and wait before trying to transmit again. This gives the server time to process the frames it has already received before it transmits additional information. Because the workstations know they have not yet been able to transmit, they queue the information until the collisions stop and the wire is free again. The nice thing about this situation is that it is self regulating. Granted, network performance can be a bit sluggish, but it helps to keep any one system from becoming overloaded (although this can still occur).

Now, let's drop our switch back in and see what happen. In full duplex mode each workstation assumes it has full bandwidth available and will transmit information whenever it needs to. Because each workstation never has to contend for bandwidth, it is capable of sending more information in a period of time than before the switch was installed. The switch then attempts to deliver these frames of data to the server.

As the server begins to become overloaded it sends out the same collision signals, causing the switch to back off from transmitting. As the switch waits for the server to catch up and stop sending collision warnings, it begins to queue up packets sent by the workstations. If the server is not able to catch up eventually with the frames stored in the switch's queue (a very likely situation given our example), the frames will eventually fill up the switch's memory pool. Once this occurs, any new frames transmitted to the switch have nowhere to be stored and subsequently are ignored. In short, the switch is throwing away information because it has nowhere to store it. So why does the switch not send out a collision signal like the server did to slow the rate of traffic from the workstations? Because it cannot; the workstations are connected in full duplex mode, which means the collision wire pair is being used for data transmission.

To make matters even worse, the workstations will eventually time out waiting for a reply to the frames the switch threw away; this causes them to transmit the same information again, compounding the bottleneck.

This is a good example of why it is important to maintain a balance on your network and ensure you know the impact of any hardware you install. While this example may seem a bit extreme, it is not too far off from a real-life network situation I had to diagnose.

Some switches handle queued frames better than others. There are even some high-end switches that could handle the above example without dropping a single frame.

It is a good idea to try and verify a vendor's performance claims through some impartial review prior to purchasing any equipment.

VLAN Technology

Switching introduces a new technology referred to as *the virtual local area network* (VLAN). Software running on the switch allows you to set up connectivity parameters for connected systems by workgroup instead of by geographical location. The switch's administrator is allowed to organize port transmissions logically so that connectivity is grouped according to each user's requirements. The "virtual" part of it is that these workgroups can span over multiple physical network segments. By assigning all switch ports that connect to PCs used by accounting personnel to the same workgroup, a virtual *accounting network* can be created.

Let's take a look at a more detailed example of how this works.

A VLAN Example

Say we have two groups of users who work exclusively with each other and a particular server. We could create two VLANs, isolating the traffic so that all communications remain within the group. While a switch will do this anyway for point-to-point communications, the addition of the VLANs will block broadcast traffic as well. This isolation will help to reduce unnecessary traffic even further. The added bonus is security, as users from one VLAN will be unable to try and connect to the server in the other VLAN. This extra security may be useful in a secure environment.

There may be a problem with this setup, however. What if the two servers are running NetWare 4.11 and need to exchange NDS information with each other? The solution is to add a third VLAN that includes only the servers. VLANs are allowed to overlap as circumstances require. This overlap allows server broadcasts to reach all members of the workgroup as well as the other server. Workstations located in the other workgroup would not see these broadcasts and thus be safeguarded from this additional traffic. Our network would look something like Figure 4.19.

While the true benefits of VLANs may not be apparent immediately, let's increase the scale of our network and watch what happens. Figure 4.20 shows an organization that occupies a number of floors in a building. If each department is confined to each floor, then our network design may be fine as is.

Unfortunately this is rarely the case and work groups can find themselves spread out over a wide geographical area. If the marketing server is located on the first floor, then any marketing personnel located on a different floor will find themselves traversing the backbone on a regular basis. Let's assume this situation is true for other departments as well.

F I G U R E 4.19

VLAN implementation in a small networking environment

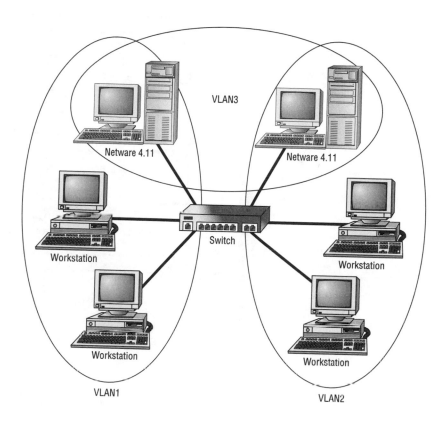

A *backbone* is a network segment used to connect other segments that contain end users. It usually runs a faster topology than the populated segments in order to keep up with the larger bandwidth demands it may experience.

Because our workgroups are not organized geographically, network broadcasts must be propagated to every corner of the network, as valid users could be located anywhere; this can make for a very busy network.

Now let's create some virtual networks and see what happens. If I use VLANs to segment our network, traffic can be confined to each individual workgroup, even though they are spread throughout the building. This confinement would give us better traffic isolation, and

F I G U R E 4.20

A large network using
switches to connect to
the backbone

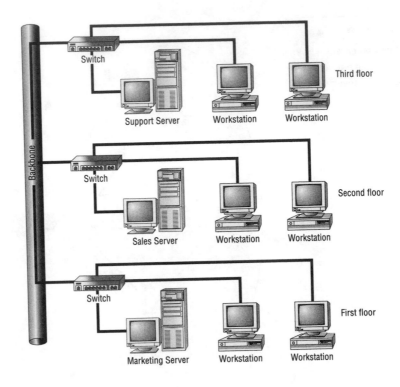

thus, better network performance. Figure 4.21 shows how these users
could be grouped.

While we may be able to wire each user physically to the floor where
their server is located, this could be impractical. Ignoring the fact that
this kind of wiring could create a spaghetti nightmare, what happens
when a user moves down the hall? Then you would have to rewire their
new office space to connect to their server location and you might also
have to rewire their old office if a user from another department moves
in. With a VLAN, this type of relocation would mean a simple configuration change through the switch's management software.

F I G U R E 4.21

A large network using
VLANs to better isolate
network traffic

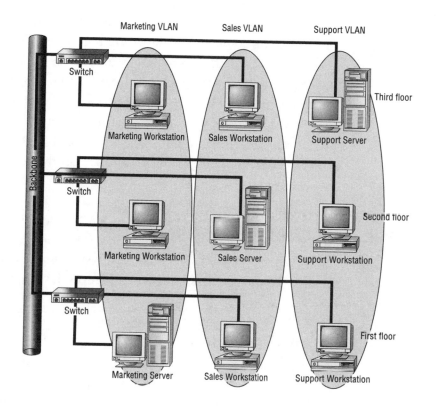

VLAN Drawbacks

VLANs do have a few drawbacks. The first is that the above noted scalability is usually vendor specific. There are a number of different ways virtual LANs are created. You may find that some vendor implementations will not work with others. While this discrepancy should correct itself over the next few years, you will need to be conscious of this limitation for now.

Also, segmentation is very specific. Each user is completely isolated to working only within their workgroup. While this was acceptable in the above examples, what if all users need to share access to multiple servers or require access to the Internet? In these situations, VLAN usefulness can begin to fall apart. As with any technology, make sure you know exactly how you plan to use it and that it does in fact support this use before you make any hardware purchases. To take poetic liberty with an old carpenter's saying, research twice and purchase once.

One final drawback of VLANs is that they can be very high maintenance. If you have a large network with each user connected to a single switch port, it will take some time to get all the ports configured correctly and it will require you to make changes whenever a user is moved. Plan on gaining an intimate knowledge of the administration software.

When to Deploy Switching

When is it a good idea to deploy switching? Let's revisit our three example networks, shown in Figures 4.13–4.15, to see where it makes sense.

With 25 Engineers

Our group of 25 engineers would be a great fit for switching technology. Let's say we gave each engineer their own port connection. When they share files with another engineer, the traffic generated would stay isolated from the remaining systems. If each system is outfitted with a 100 Mbps card, the potential bandwidth would be in the 1.2 Gbps range. In fact, because we have only one system per port, we could utilize full duplex connections and increase the potential bandwidth to the 2.4 Gbps range.

Increasing the potential bandwidth to the 2.4 Gbps range could yield up to a 2400% improvement in available bandwidth. Not bad for replacing a single piece of hardware!

With Multiple Servers and Protocols

There are two potential network layouts for our second network example. The first is to use VLANs and segregate traffic by workgroup.

Each virtual LAN would include the users and their server. The Unix system and the Internet connection would be overlapped by both VLANs, as shared access is required for both. Our network design may appear similar to Figure 4.22.

FIGURE 4.22

A potential network design for our advertising firm's network using VLANs

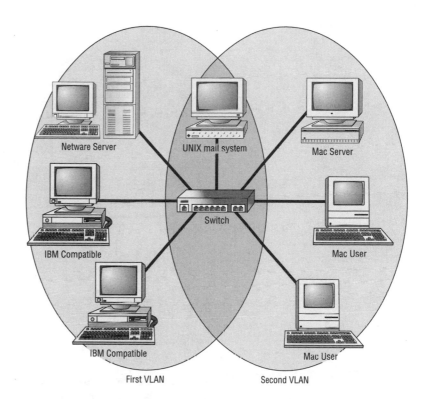

While this design would yield an increase in network performance, it does have a few minor drawbacks. The first is that switches with VLAN support are expensive, running between $200 to $400 per port. This cost could be considered excessive by an organization this small. The fact that bandwidth requirements would not be considered excessive would make this cost outlay even more difficult to justify. Also, networks this small generally have poor network support. Even if they do staff a LAN administrator they are usually focused on supporting the end users. The added task of supporting VLAN tables may be beyond their skill set.

Our second option would be to use the switch as the network backbone with hubs cascaded off of it to support small user groups. Servers could receive a dedicated connection and be connected in full duplex mode. Our potential design appears in Figure 4.23.

FIGURE 4.23

Another potential design
for our advertising
network

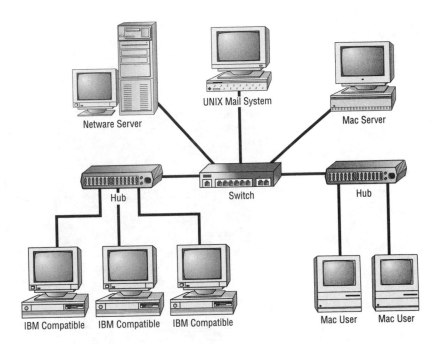

This option may be more desirable because it can be supported by a switch with a minimal number of ports and thus reduce the cost. It also reduces the maintenance requirements, as we did not need to create any VLANs.

This option would not be able to help with our protocol broadcast issue.

With Three NT Servers

Our final example network would benefit in much the same way. If we gave each of the three NT servers their own port and cascaded hubs off of the switch for the user community, we would strike the best balance between cost and performance. A switch would cost a bit more than the bridge solution we discussed earlier, but it would allow for greater flexibility. When bridging the network, each collision domain consisted of 50 users each. There was no easy way to segment the users even further. With a switch, we could simply cascade an additional hub off of a free hub port and migrate some of the users over to it. Because only a single protocol is in use, we are not concerned with isolating broadcast frames as we were in the last example.

Routers

A router is a multi-port device that makes decisions on how to handle a frame, based on protocol and network address. To truly understand what this means we must first look at what a protocol is and how it works.

Up until now we've been happily communicating using the media access control address assigned to our networking devices. Our systems have used this number to contact other systems and transmit information as required.

The problem with this scheme is that it does not scale very well. For example, what if I have 2,000 systems that need to communicate with each other? Even by employing switching and virtual networking I will eventually reach a point where network performance will degrade and no more systems can be added. This is where protocols come in.

Protocols

A protocol is a set of communication rules that provide the means for networking systems to be grouped by geographical area and common wiring. To indicate they are part of a specific group, each of these systems is assigned an identical protocol network address.

Network Addresses are kind of like zip codes. Let's assume someone mails a letter and the front of the envelope simply reads: Amber Apple, 7 Spring Road. If this is a very small town, this letter will probably get through (as if you used a MAC address on a LAN).

If the letter was mailed in a city like Boston or New York, however, the post office where it lands would have no clue where to send it (although they would probably get a good laugh). Without a zip code they may not even attempt delivery. The zip code provides a way to specify the general area where this letter needs to be delivered. The postal worker processing the letter is not required to know where exactly Spring Road is located. They simply look at the zip code and forward the letter to the post office responsible for this code. It is up to the local post office to know where Spring Road is located and use this information to ensure that the letter reaches its destination address.

Protocol network addresses operate in a similar fashion. A protocol-aware device will add the network address of the device it wishes to reach to the data field of a frame. It will also record its own network address in case the remote system needs to send a reply.

This is where a router comes in. A router will maintain a table of all known networks. It will use these tables to help forward information to its final destination. Let's walk through an example to see how a routed network operates.

A Routed Network Example

Let's assume we have a network similar to that shown in Figure 4.24 and that system B needs to transmit information to system F.

System B will begin by comparing its network address to that of system F. If there is a match it will assume the system is local and attempt to deliver the information directly. If the network addresses are different (as they are in our example) it will broadcast a *route request* query to see if any other systems on its network segment (network 1) know how to get to the destination system's network (network 3). A

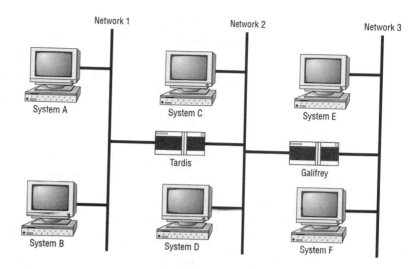

FIGURE 4.24

An example of a routed
network

route request is essentially a request for directions. It's a networked
system's way of asking, "How do I get there from here?"

Because Tardis is a router it maintains tables of all known networks.
Tardis knows it can get to network 3 by delivering information to Galifrey. Tardis would then send this information to system B as a reply to
its routing request. Because this is the only reply system B receives to its
route request, it assumes that Tardis is the only route. System B would
then add the delivery information for system F (its network and MAC
addresses) to the data and create a frame using Tardis's MAC address
as the destination. It does this because Tardis indicated that it knew the
way to network 3 in its reply. System B is sending the frame to Tardis
because it assumes that Tardis will take care of forwarding it to the destination network.

Once Tardis receives the frame it performs a CRC check to ensure
the integrity of the data. If the frame checks out, it will then completely
strip off the header and trailer. It would then create a new frame around
the data by creating a new CRC, adding its MAC address to the source
address field, and putting Galifrey's MAC address in the destination
field.

While all this stripping and recreating seems like a lot of work, it is a necessary part of this type of communication. Remember that routers are placed at the borders of a network segment. The CRC check is performed to ensure that bad frames are not propagated throughout the network. The header information is stripped away because it is only applicable on network 1. When Tardis goes to transmit the frame on network 2, the original source and destination MAC addresses have no meaning. This is why it must replace these values with ones that are valid for network 2. Because the majority (12 of the 14 bytes) of the header needs to be replaced anyway, it is easier to simply strip it completely away and create it from scratch. As for stripping off the trailer, once the source and destination MAC addresses change, the original CRC value is no longer valid. This is why the router must strip it off and create a new one. By the way, a data field that contains protocol information is referred to as a *packet*. While this term is sometimes used interchangeably with the term *frame*, it in fact only describes a portion of it.

So Tardis has created a new frame around the packet and is ready to transmit it. Tardis looks at the destination and has no idea who system F is but it does know it can get to network 3 by delivering the frame to Galifrey. It then transmits the frame out onto network 2. Galifrey then receives the frame and processes it in a similar fashion to Tardis. It checks the CRC and strips off the header and trailer.

At this point, however, Galifrey realizes that it has a local connection to system F because they are both connected to network 3. It builds a new frame around the packet and, instead of needing to reference a table, it simply delivers the frame directly.

Protocol Specificity

In order for a router to provide this type of functionality, it needs to understand the rules for the protocol being used. This means that a router is protocol specific. Unlike a bridge, which will handle any valid topology traffic you throw at it, a router has to be specifically designed to support both the topology and the protocol being used. For example, if your network contains Banyan Vines systems, make sure that your router supports VinesIP.

WARNING All of this functionality comes at a cost. Routers are typically poor performers when compared to bridges and switches. This is due to the overhead involved with removing and recreating the frame. While a router can be a valuable tool, it should be used wisely.

Routers can be a powerful tool for controlling the flow of traffic on your network. If you have a network segment that is using IPX and IP but only IP is approved for use on the company backbone, simply enable IP support only on your router. Any IPX traffic the router receives will be ignored.

A wonderful feature of routers is their ability to block broadcasts. As mentioned earlier, broadcasts are frames that contain all Fs for the destination MAC address. Because any point on the other side of the router is a new network, these frames are blocked.

NOTE There is a counterpart to this called an *all networks broadcast* that contains all Fs in both the network and MAC address fields. Fortunately these frames are far less common than regular network broadcasts.

Most routers also have the ability to filter out certain traffic. For example, let's say your company enters a partnership with another organization. You need to access services on this new network but do not want to allow them to access your servers. To accomplish this, simply install a router between the two networks and configure it to filter out any network information that would normally be propagated from your network to theirs. Without this information they have no way of accessing servers on your network.

Protocol Address Conventions

Different protocols use different address conventions. While we will cover this in greater detail in the section on protocols, they are:

- **IP** four blocks of numbers ranging from 1–255 separated by periods such as 10.254.11.105

- **IPX** an eight digit hexadecimal number such as BA5EBA11

- **AppleTalk** any combination of alphanumeric characters such as Manufacturing

NetBEUI and NetBIOS do not have network addresses and are referred to as non-routable protocols. While it is still possible to get them across a router, it is not by design. Without a network address to evaluate, a router cannot determine where to send the frame.

Many network servers have the ability to accept multiple network cards and function as routers. The level of support varies from providing just connectivity to providing advanced features like full-blown filter tables. In either case a hardware router should always outperform its server-based counterpart. A hardware router is dedicated to this type of functionality. A server-based solution needs to share CPU and bandwidth with all the other processes running on the system.

Now let's revisit our three network examples to see if any of them could benefit from the addition of routing.

With 25 Engineers

Our first example is clearly a no go. Due to the unpredictable nature of traffic flow, a router would be of very little use.

With Multiple Servers and Protocols

Our second network shows more promise. It has two of the main ingredients that make routing an interesting choice, multiple protocols and the need for traffic isolation. If we were to configure our network as shown in Figure 4.25, we would have the following:

- the ability to isolate IPX and AppleTalk traffic by simply not passing them across the router

- the ability to support IP traffic throughout the network while still isolating each workgroup from the traffic generated by the other

- the ability to add a second line of defense between our internal systems and the Internet

Routing holds some interesting possibilities in this configuration.

FIGURE 4.25

Our accounting network is segmented with a router.

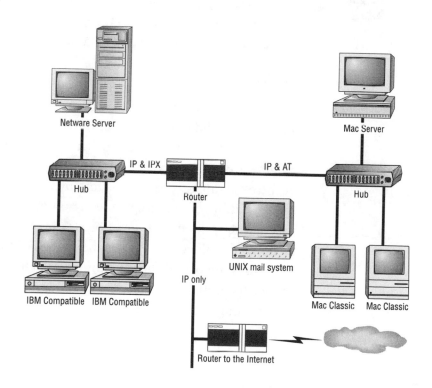

With Three NT Servers

As for our third example, we could configure it in a similar fashion to the second. Each workgroup could be located off of a router port along with its NT server. The mail system could be installed off of a third port to isolate users communicating to it from the other workgroup. This configuration would provide the traffic isolation we need as well as continued shared access to the mail server. This may, however, be over-kill, because we're only dealing with one protocol, NetBEUI.

WARNING   This configuration may even be a bad idea because NetBEUI is a non-routable protocol. It can require a large amount of overhead in order to propagate it across the router. We could very well end up with a network that performs worse than when we started.

Variations

You may have noticed that two of the three examples had multiple answers. We did not even get into the possibilities of mixing and matching different technologies! This is because we are trying to make a judgment based on a very limited amount of information. While some of these examples appear to be toss-ups in terms of which technology is the best fit, if you dig deep enough you may find some little tidbit that will tip the scales in one direction or the other. For example, we never mentioned if all employees use the network at the same time or if they are broken up over different daily shifts. This could dramatically change the traffic patterns and, thus, our network requirements. Do not take anything for granted.

Switch Routers

Switch routers are fairly new to the networking world. These devices provide all the functionality of a switch and include some of the benefits of a router when VLANs are implemented.

Consider Everything

I had an experience a few years back that really drove home how important it is to consider all factors. I was working as a LAN administrator for a company that made network print servers. As part of my long-winded job description, I used to help out with second line tech support. If service engineers got in over their head, they would conference me in to give them a hand.

One day an engineer called me and asked if I could give him a hand with a customer. He had spent the last hour and a half on the phone with her and was unable to get the print server working. He was confused because this was a small single NetWare server environment. There was nothing out of the ordinary with the environment from what he could tell.

I listened in as he walked her through setting up a print queue and print server in Pconsole. Usually once this is complete you can simply plug in the device and it works. At the end of the process he asked her to try a test print. She stated that the print server still didn't work. Frustrated but still willing to give it another shot, he sent her back into Pconsole to delete the last configuration and create it from scratch. As they were creating the print server entry yet again, I realized that I was not hearing the usual background noises of someone wrestling with a phone or using a speakerphone. On a hunch I spoke up and asked her to read to me what was on the screen.

"C-colon-backslash-D-O-S."

The engineer spoke up and said, "You mean you are not in Pconsole?"

To which the client replied, "What's that? You mean you expect me to type all this stuff?"

Never assume!

As discussed, switches are protocol-stupid. When a VLAN is created it restricts all communications to within itself. There is no way to tell a VLAN to react differently depending on protocol. Segmentation is done by port selection or by analyzing the system's MAC address.

When a Switch Router is Useful

Let's assume we have a network of 75 users. These users are broken down into groups of 25, each with its own NetWare server. The users communicate only with their own server and use the IPX protocol. So far we have a good application for a regular switch. We could create three VLANs and segregate traffic as we did in earlier examples.

Now let's throw in a twist and assume that all the workstations are providing file sharing via IP to all other workstations on the network. With a regular switch, our VLANs would immediately become useless. This is because every workstation requires the ability to communicate with every other workstation on the network, and our switch VLANs would block this connectivity.

This is where a switch router comes in handy. In this situation a switch router could be configured to restrict IPX traffic to the VLANs we defined while allowing IP traffic to flow freely throughout the network. The switch router provides an additional level of fine tuning when isolating traffic on the network.

Because switch routing is a new technology, its features and design advantages are still under development. As people become more familiar with switch routers, expect to see additional features added and new applications discovered.

Switch routers are still quite expensive and will need to come down in price before they become widely implemented.

Translational Gateways

Translational gateways are used to convert communication of one protocol into another. This functionality can be extremely useful if you need to provide connectivity to some foreign network or server and do not wish to support an additional protocol on your network.

For example, let's assume you're administering a very large network which currently supports only the IPX protocol. Your company decides it needs to connect all of its users to the Internet, which uses the IP protocol. Instead of dealing with the additional administration and overhead of adding another protocol to your network you could opt to install a translational gateway instead. Users would transmit their information destined for the Internet to the gateway via the IPX protocol. The gateway would then repackage the information into IP packets and forward them along to the Internet. When a reply returns, the gateway translates the packets from IP back into IPX and forwards them along to the internal workstation.

Drawbacks

Translational gateways are not the magic solutions they appear to be, however. Workstation applications used for Internet connectivity (like Web browsers and FTP software) require that a small program be running in the background to fool them into thinking a real IP stack is running. Unfortunately, not all programs are fooled by this software, and this limits the number of applications from which you can choose. Most translational gateways will ship with a small suite of Internet applications that are approved for use with their product.

Performance can be a bit poor as well. It takes time for the translational gateway to repackage and pass along data. This can make connectivity to Internet resources appear to be extremely sluggish. If your users attempt to access resources on a busy site, they may experience connection time-outs making the resource unreachable.

One misconception is that translational gateways provide firewall services. While it is true that translational gateways make inbound connections difficult to create, they do not yield the same level of security provided by a true firewall.

When a workstation is accessing services out on the Internet, the gateway expects that these services will need to reply with requested data. The gateway will leave a small inbound hole open to the workstation, so the requested data can be received. It is possible that an unscrupulous user out on the Internet could exploit this hole and use it to send commands to the receiving workstation. The security with this connection lies in that it is extremely difficult to find this hole and capitalize on it during normal gateway operations. This security method is referred to as *security through obscurity*. It relies on the difficulty of obtaining certain information to keep the connection secure. It does not explicitly protect the system from attack if this information becomes known.

Internet connectivity is not the only application of a translational gateway. The most common gateway is used to connect workstations to mini and mainframe systems. A good example is IBM's SAA gateway for NetWare. This software runs on a Novell server and translates IPX/SPX traffic to SAA, which is the protocol used by their AS400 systems.

Firewalls

Entire books can and have been dedicated to the discussion of firewall technology. While we obviously cannot cover firewalls at that level of detail, it will be helpful to have a basic understanding of their functionality.

Firewalls are similar to other network devices in that their purpose is to control the flow of traffic. Unlike other network devices, however, a firewall must control this traffic, taking into account that not all the frames it sees are what they appear to be.

As an example, a bridge filters traffic based on the destination MAC address. If a station is incorrectly labeling the MAC address and the bridge inadvertently passes the packet along, the bridge is not looked at as being faulty or inadequate. It is expected that the station will follow certain network rules, and, if it does not, then it is the station that is at fault, not the bridge.

A firewall, however, must assume that a station may try to fool it in order to sneak information past it. It cannot use communication rules as a crutch but rather should expect that the rules will not be followed. This places a lot of pressure on the firewall design, as it must plan for every contingency.

A firewall operates under a specific set of filter rules. These rules indicate what type of traffic should be allowed to pass and what traffic should be blocked. When evaluating these rules, a firewall will typically look at the following frame information:

- source network address

- destination network address

- type of service being requested

- protocol being used

- type of data frame (Is this a request for data or a reply?)

Packet Filtering

There are three ways to firewall—*packet filtering*, *proxy*, and *stateful inspection*. Packet filters are the simplest of the three and they are not considered a true firewalling method by some security experts. Packet filters typically look at some or all of the above listed criteria and use this information to determine if a packet should be passed or blocked. While packet filters afford some protection, they are still fallible to a number of attacks. An experienced network engineer would be able to come up with a few ways to circumvent the security provided by a packet filter. If properly configured, packet filters are usually sufficient for protecting small environments that do not have any internal systems offering IP services such as a web or FTP. Most routers are capable of providing packet filtering functionality. If you absolutely must ensure the integrity of your internal systems, however, then one of the two other methods should be used.

Proxy

A proxy is a representative of, or surrogate replacement for, some other networked device. As the name implies, a proxy firewall acts as a delegate for all communications. When an internal system needs to send data to the Internet, it first sends it to the proxy. The proxy will then repackage the frame and replace the network address of the original system with its own. This ensures that all communications on the insecure side of the firewall only take place with the firewall itself. This means that the network address of the system that initially transmitted the frame is hidden and does not have to be made known. When the destination system receives the packet, it believes that the frame originated from the proxy.

If the insecure system needs to respond to the frame it will reply to the source network address, which points to the proxy firewall. The proxy would then receive the frame, analyze it, and forward it along to the original system. By acting as a mediator the proxy ensures that the insecure system never has direct access to the internal system.

Stateful Inspection

The final type of firewall is stateful inspection. A stateful inspection firewall monitors and records all outbound traffic and uses this information in addition to the filtering rules to determine what traffic will be let back in.

For example, we mentioned that when a system connects to a resource, concessions must be made to allow replies to data requests back in. Also mentioned was that this opens up a potential hole through which a slippery hacker may worm their way in. Stateful inspection helps to plug this hole by recording who the data request was originally sent to. A stateful inspection firewall will monitor inbound traffic, only letting in information that originates from the system to which the data request was sent.

Note that the above discussions focus on servers providing IP services. Other protocols and services can be firewalled as follows:

Firewalling Other Protocols

NetWare server running IPX: Filter out the server name and internal network address.

AppleTalk Devices: Filter out the zone names and network addresses.

NT running NetBEUI: Dependent on transport. If IPX is used, block type 20 packets. If IP is used, block ports 137 through 139.

Notes running IP: Block access to service port 1352.

Do not worry about how to implement the above filters for now. This will become clearer when we discuss protocols in Chapter 6. The point is that you can block just about any service if you need to.

Modem

While most people are familiar with modems, they are worth a brief mention here. The modem is a device used for converting a digital signal into an analog transmission that is capable of traversing plain old telephone lines (POTS).

There are two separate measurement terms used when describing modems, bit and baud. A bit is simply a single digital pulse or transmission. With POTS communications these pulses are in the form of tones.

The term bit is used to referred to the amount of digital information the device is capable of converting into an analog signal, such as 28800 bits per second (bps).

So why is the bit rate so low compared to a LAN? When POTS was first conceived it was designed to carry voice communications only. Because the average human voice will only produce sounds between 300 and 3300 cycles per second, this was all the bandwidth that was supported. Modems are required to operate within these constraints. They do not have the benefit of being designed from the ground up to relay digital information. This is sort of like trying to fit a round peg into a square hole. It will fit, provided you whack it with a hammer a few times.

A baud refers to an individual signal event along the POTS line. This can be any change in frequency, amplitude or phase of the analog signal being transmitted. Baud and byte are not directly comparable. The baud rate usually lags behind the bit rate in value as modem manufacturers attempt to squeeze every bit of bandwidth they can out of the phone lines.

The modem industry can appear at times to be a little bit like Scotty from Star Trek. With each new release of modem speeds a claim is made that we've reached the maximum bit rate for POTS lines and "She can't take any more, Captain!" This has been occurring since the 9600 bps modems where released. At the time of this writing, 56000 bps modems are just hitting the market.

The reason for this is simple—technology is still evolving. Just as computers that used to take up entire rooms will now fit in your shirt pocket, so too have communication engineers continued to find new ways to push larger quantities of information through this same tiny pipe.

Codex

A codex is the opposite of a modem. Short for coder/decoder, a codex is used for converting an analog signal into a digital transmission. Physically, they are small boxes, or computer expansion cards, with multiple RJ-11 connectors. If it is an external unit, a connector is also provided to connect a digital device such as a computer.

With the popularity of ISDN comes a problem—what do we do with all the analog devices we have for communicating over a dial-up network. A codex is a type of converter that allows you to plug a standard telephone, fax, or even a modem into one side and communicate digitally with an ISDN line on the other. While there are digital equivalents to the standard phone and fax, these devices are new to the market and still quite expensive. In fact, a single digital phone can cost as much as a codex providing multiple analog connections. Of course, the drawback of using a converter is lost bandwidth. An analog phone run through a codex is incapable of leveraging the additional available bandwidth. Then again, if you are using the phone for voice communications, do you really need the additional bandwidth?

CSU/DSU

A CSU/DSU is a device that combines the functionality of a channel service unit (CSU) and a data service unit (DSU). These devices are used to connect a LAN to a WAN, and they take care of all the translation required to convert a data stream between these two methods of communication. Figure 4.26 shows a 56K leased-line DSU. The indicator lights on the front of the unit let you monitor its operational status.

FIGURE 4.26
A 56K leased-line DSU

FIGURE 4.26
A 56K leased-line DSU

DSU

A DSU provides all the handshaking and error correction required to maintain a connection across a wide area link. In this aspect it is similar to a modem or codex in functionality. The DSU will accept a serial data stream from a device on the LAN and translate this into a useable data stream for the digital WAN network. For example, if the WAN link is a T1 connection, the DSU would break the information up into a time division format acceptable for use on this circuit. It would also take care of converting any inbound data streams from the WAN back to a serial communication.

CSU

A CSU is similar to a DSU except it does not have the ability to provide handshaking or error correction. It is strictly an interface between the LAN and the WAN and relies on some other device to provide handshaking and error correction.

The network device of choice to combine with a CSU is a router. While it is possible to use a bridge or a switch with these devices, a router is more appropriate as it is better able to isolate traffic and keep unwanted packets from traversing the WAN. Because bandwidth is at a premium over a wide area link, the more unnecessary traffic that can be kept off it the better. The combination of a CSU with a router has become so common that there is currently a trend to incorporate the functionality of the CSU directly into the router itself.

CSU/DSUs differ in the type of wide area links and amount of bandwidth they will support. If you currently have a digital leased line and you're thinking of upgrading to a full T1, expect to replace this hardware.

Workstation

A workstation is simply a regular desktop system outfitted with a network card. The system will contain a central processor unit (CPU), memory, and usually a hard drive. The hardware allows the system to run programs across the network or off of the local drive as required. Except for the network card, these systems can be identical to the computers purchased for home use.

Common operating systems are Microsoft's disk operating system (DOS), Windows, Apple's System 7 (used on the MAC), or Unix. If the operating system does not have built-in network support then additional software that allows the system to communicate on the network will be required. Most network operating system software will ship with all the software required to allow a workstation to communicate with it.

In a commercial environment, a workstation would usually be configured with all the user's required applications loaded on the local drive. By having the user's word processor, spreadsheet program, and so on loaded on the hard drive it reduces traffic by not requiring that these applications be loaded across the network. Due to the number of features added over the years, desktop applications have become quite large.

As an example, just the main executable file for Microsoft Excel (excel.exe) has a file size of 4.7 MB. This means that for a single workstation to load this one file (not including all the required support files) over a 10 Mbps network would require 4 to 10 seconds (depending on frame size). Not only does this greatly increase the amount of time it will take to load the application, but this large data request will reduce the amount of bandwidth available to other stations while the data transfer is taking place. While this will probably not be an issue if it is only one workstation, consider what the effect may be if you have 10–15 accountants who are frequently popping in and out of Excel in the course of the day.

Data files created by these programs are then saved out to a network server so that they can be protected by a nightly backup system. Each user is typically given a directory area on the server to save their files as required.

If users are not saving work files on their local system then recovery from system crashes becomes much easier. Most administrators will create what is referred to as a *workstation image*. This image is simply a copy of a fully configured workstation including all corporate applications. If a user's system crashes, it is a simple matter of using this image to create a new system quickly. A workstation image is also useful when configuring new hardware before releasing it to the end user community. Let's see how this can work.

Your company has a standard workstation configuration that includes DOS, Windows 3.11, Microsoft Office, cc:Mail, and Novell's software for connecting to a NetWare server. Each user has these software packages loaded on their system, as a minimum. To create a workstation image you would simply take a single workstation and load each of the above applications. Each piece of software would be installed using the packages installation routine (usually a matter of running *setup* or *install*). Up to this point the process is identical to how you may custom configure a system, except that information specific to an individual user is omitted (such as their NetWare or cc:Mail login name).

Once you have loaded all the necessary applications, simply copy all files and directories up to a local server. Now, whenever a new workstation must be configured, simply boot and format the workstation with a floppy disk and copy this directory structure to the workstation's local drive. The new workstation will contain all the applications required by the end user. Because you are simply copying files and no longer running setup programs, the amount of time it takes to create a usable workstation is greatly reduced. Also, because the file copy does not require user interaction, it is possible to configure many workstations simultaneously. I've seen people configure 20–30 workstations an hour using this method.

If your corporate workstations are running a more advanced operating system such as Windows 95 or NT, then a simple directory copy may not suffice. In these cases look to third party administration software which can create this image for you. The additional benefit of these programs is that they will compress the image as it is stored so that it uses up less space on your server.

Because workstations make up the largest portion of your network, it is a good idea to have a solid handle on their administration. Reducing the amount of time spent supporting end user problems will greatly increase the amount of time you can dedicate to maintaining your network infrastructure.

From Boot Prom to Thin Clients

Thin clients are a good example of dusting off an old idea and packaging it with a new face. A thin client is simply a computer without any drives. The hype over these systems has been mostly due to the promises of reduced support. Without any local drives, the system cannot be used to store information locally. This prevents users from customizing their setup or potentially making changes to their configuration that could make their operating system unstable.

In the early days of networking, NIC card vendors would outfit their network cards with a chip called a *boot prom*. A boot prom allows a workstation to receive all the information it required to boot up off of a local server. The benefit of this was that the workstation did not require its own hard drive or even a floppy. When the system was powered up the boot prom would seek out the local server and pull the operating system and all supporting files it needed over the network.

This configuration made a lot of sense at the time. Applications were relatively small, so that being required to load all software off of the server did not greatly effect network traffic. Also, hard drives were extremely expensive at the time. The average rate of a megabyte of hard drive storage was $8 to $10 (compared to $ 0.18 today). Finally, except for the missing floppy drive, this configuration was completely invisible to the end user. The system would still boot up using DOS, and all the applications they had grown to know and love could be used.

Drawbacks

Unfortunately, at the time of this writing thin clients probably have more drawbacks than benefits. One feature not shared with their predecessors is that these systems tend to be proprietary. A special server must be used when working with these systems. If you want to use SUN's thin clients, then you must purchase a SUN server. Want to use IBM clients? Then you will need to purchase an IBM server. The systems will not interoperate with each other.

The same goes for the operating system as well. Programs such as Lotus 123, WordPerfect, and Access do not run on these system. The hope is that third parties will create comparable products for these operating systems in order to fill in the missing gaps. Unfortunately, this software has been slow in coming. If your users have been spoiled by Windows 95's highly customizable interface, Unix's wide berth of tools, or even the many available features of applications like Word, then running a thin client will feel like a step into the stone age. The applications available for these platforms usually contain only the most rudimentary of features.

Probably the largest drawback of this configuration is that it creates a central point of failure. If a server that supports a number of thin clients drops off line, then all users relying on that server are dead in the water. While a workstation user would be free to continue running their local programs during a server failure, a thin client has no means of accessing the software it requires to keep its user productive. Thus, the financial impact that can be caused by a major server outage while using thin clients can easily offset the cost of providing support under a workstation–server configuration for many years.

Server

A server, simply put, is a networked computer that offers up some kind of service to other computers on the network. These systems are typically identical to your average workstation except they may contain more memory, a faster processor, and larger hard drives. For software, they need to run some form of network operating system (NOS) that provides connectivity for many users. While a workstation only needs to interface with one user at a time, a server may be expected to take care of multiple users and offer up multiple services.

Server Types

The three types of servers are:

- **file server** provide a common area for users to share and use files

- **print server** provide a common printer that networked users can access

- **Application Server** provide a software program for common user access.

File Server

A file server is the most common type of server. Disk space is allocated on a networked system that users can access to store and retrieve files. Permissions can be set such that the user may have exclusive access to these files or the files may be sharable with other networked users. Security is provided by requiring the user to enter a user name and password prior to file access. If the user passes this security check they are allowed access to their files.

How this file system appears varies depending on the workstation. If the user is running DOS, the file system on the server would appear as additional drive letters. The user is not required to know anything about the network beyond, if I save to the F drive, "I'm saving to the server."

On a Unix workstation the server's file system would appear as a simple extension to one of the workstation's directories. For example, the command **cd /mount/mars/home** may bring you to your home directory on the remote server MARS. The act of adding this remote file system to a workstation is referred to as *mounting* the directory.

A MAC system mounts file systems as well, except that it appears as an icon on the desktop. Clicking this icon opens the remote file system. While this is not quite as *invisible* to the end user as a Unix mount, it is sufficient to provide access to the remote file system.

Windows based systems use two methods for incorporating remote file systems. The first is identical to a DOS system allocating drive letters that point to remote file areas located on the server. The second is by using a *share*, referred to as a universal naming convention or UNC. A UNC is a pointer that can be retrieved on the fly that specifies a remote file system location. For example, a shared file area may have a UNC of \\talsin\share. The benefit of this type of connection is that you are not limited by the quantity of letters in the alphabet. If I start mapping network drives in a DOS environment at F I will have 21 pointers available to remote file areas (F–Z). While this may sound like a lot it can be used up quickly in an environment with many file servers. If I use UNC's instead of drive mappings I can use as many pointers as I require.

Print Server

A print server provides a central point for network users to share a printing device. When a user needs to print, the output is directed to a central holding area called a queue. This can be done by using *network aware* applications that can communicate directly with a network print queue or by using redirection software that captures all information sent to a printer port. While your application thinks it's printing to a printer directly attached to the system, the redirector diverts the print job to the network queue.

A network print queue is a holding area for print jobs. The queue is typically located on a file server and is used to stage the print jobs prior to printing. Because a computer can transmit data faster than the typical printer is capable of putting this information to paper, a staging area is required in case someone tries to print while the printer is servicing another user. If this occurs the second print job will be retained in the print queue until the first job is completed.

The print server provides the processing power required to poll the queue and determine if there is a job that needs to be printed. If one is found, the print server takes care of feeding the print job to the printer.

The final type of server is an application server. An application server is software that runs on a NOS and provides direct connectivity to a software program. Application servers usually require that a portion of the software be running on both the client and the server at the same time. For example, a backup server would be a type of application server that provides system backup services to clients on the network. A backup server would require that software be running on the NOS to collect the remote file information and write it to tape. It may also require that a portion of its software be running on the workstation so that the server may access the file system to back it up.

Lotus Notes is also a kind of application server. It is a database system that includes a server portion, which maintains the data files and security access to the server. It also includes a workstation portion referred to as a *client*, which is used to access and manipulate information stored in the remote Lotus Notes server.

Application Servers

Application servers are sometimes confused with file servers that hold software programs that users can run from their network drive. For example, if Microsoft Word is located on the server and is accessed by multiple network users, it would not be considered an application server. This is because the server simply provides disk space to store the program. It does not provide any of the processing power required to execute the program. When you run Word from the network all necessary processing power is provided by your local workstation.

An application server usually employs some form of client server technology to connect the *front end* running on the client with the actual application running on the server. Lotus Notes is a good example of an application server as it is a database being processed by a server which can be accessed from a network client.

Workstation or Server?

With the increased deployment of 32-bit Windows operating systems, as well as the long established use of Unix machines, the definition of which systems should be considered *servers* has become blurred. It is more common these days to find a computer that is doing double duty as both a workstation and a server.

Back in the old DOS/NetWare days there was a distinct line between workstations and servers. Because DOS was designed to be a single user only interface it was never very good at providing services to network users. It was a workstation in the full sense of the word in that it provided an interface for only a single user to do their work. The NetWare server, because it provided both file and printer sharing, was considered to be the network server. In this configuration security was pretty straightforward. Guard the NetWare system and you can sleep well knowing your network is secure.

Blurring the Lines between a Workstation and a Server

With the release of Windows 95 and NT it is not uncommon for that same user's workstation to not only be accessing a NetWare server but also be offering up file, print, and even application services of its own. While this multi-user environment has been available for many years in

Unix (it was designed from the beginning to support multi-user environments) and even Mac systems, it was not quite as extensive a problem as it is now for two reasons.

The first is magnitude, these systems never achieved the same level of acceptance as their DOS counterpart. While parents purchased Macs for their small children and Unix found its way into universities, research, and programming organizations, it was DOS that embodied the largest portion of the business community.

The second reason is that networks have become larger and more accessible from remote locations. With the growth of the Internet and remote network access, many LANs are no longer isolated when the doors are locked at night.

These days multi-use environments can make for some administrative nightmares. While you may do an extensive job of locking down your network and systems that are considered servers in the conventional sense, it does not help if one of your users running NT has a modem attached and decides to enable the remote access server (RAS) and hand out the number to their friends so they can access the Internet. While this may sound far fetched, I've seen this happen and seen people lose their jobs over it.

In short, just about any system these days is capable of fitting into the classification of being a server. Part of the job of a Network Administrator is to identify these systems and ensure that they meet the security policies set forth by their organization. What's that? Your company does not have any network security policies? As network administrator it may very well be your job to develop these policies as well.

Summary

You should now have a good idea of what hardware is available for designing your network. We've even covered some of the basics as to how they are used. Along with the previous chapters, this completes the foundation pieces of our networking infrastructure. We will continue to explore how these pieces are best fit together in the next chapters when we begin talking about protocols.

CHAPTER

5

The OSI Model and Protocol Communications

Before jumping into the esoteric, let's review some of the major points we've covered so far:

- All communications are either analog or digital in nature.

- Because of its resistance to interference, digital communications are the method of choice when transmitting information.

- Digital communications consist of pulses referred to as bits. A collection of 8 bits is referred to as a byte, which represents one piece of information to be transferred.

- A topology defines how systems will be connected in order to communicate these bytes.

- Bytes are organized into logical frames when moving data along a specific topology.

- Most WAN topologies are designed to communicate point-to-point between two systems only.

- Most LAN topologies rely on shared media to allow multiple systems to communicate.

- When shared media is used, all systems see every frame transmitted.

- Devices such as bridges and switches can be used to regulate the flow of data by segmenting the network and restraining traffic to specific areas.

A Protocol's Job

The points just mentioned constitute the baseline that all network communications have in common. How this baseline is implemented, however, is dependent on which protocol is used. For example, we learned that when a system wants to transfer information to another system it does so by creating a frame with the target system's MAC address in the destination field of the frame header. This method of communication is part of our topology's communication rules. This transmission raises the following questions:

- Should the transmitting system simply assume the frame was received in one piece?

- Should the destination system reply, saying, "I received your frame, thanks!"?

- If a reply should be sent, does each frame require its own acknowledgment or is it okay to send just one for a group of frames?

- What if the destination system is not on the same local network?

- If the destination system is running e-mail, transferring a file, and browsing HTML Web pages on the source system, how does it discern which data goes to which application?

This is where a protocol comes in. A protocol's job is to answer each of the above questions as well as any others that may pop up in the course of the communication. When we talk about IP, IPX, AppleTalk, or NetBEUI we are talking about protocols. So why are the specifications that characterize a protocol not simply defined by the topology? For the answer to this question we need to go back a few years to what was taking place in the 70s besides bell bottoms and disco.

A Little Background

Back in 1974, IBM released the System Network Architecture (SNA). This was the method used to communicate with its main frame systems of the time. The specification defined everything from the method of communication to what type of connectors to use. Life was simple for a network administrator, provided you didn't mind buying everything from IBM and their systems were capable of providing all the services your organization required.

In 1976, DEC released their Digital Network Architecture (DNA). Again, this described every facet of communicating with a DEC system, specifying every wire and byte to be used. Again, life was simple, provided that DEC could provide everything your organization required.

These systems are what is referred to as *proprietary*. The original vendor was typically the sole supplier of parts, updates, and software. While they made sure that their systems were able to communicate together, they unfortunately did a pretty good job of ensuring that they could not interconnect with a system from another vendor. If your organization wanted to use a DEC machine for manufacturing and inventory control but liked the looks of the IBM system for corporate functions, you would be hard pressed to communicate any information between the two systems.

Proprietary systems where the fad of the time. A vendor would sit in their own little bubble and define every aspect of the network. Besides the two companies mentioned above, there were many others that specified all facets of their systems' communications that have since gone the path of the Pet Rock.

A good analogy for proprietary systems is organized religion. Most organized religions are proprietary in that they have their own set of beliefs or specifications. Like vendors of the 70s, each has its own way of doing things which it believes to be most correct and can be a bit intolerant of other practices. A person who tries to incorporate the beliefs of two separate religious systems may be shunned by both. Shunning was pretty common in the computer industry as well as each vendor fought to maintain market share from their true believers. The term "religious war" is still used quite frequently when describing the discussions between two proponents of a specific product or operating system.

The OSI Model

In 1977, the International Organization of Standards developed the Open Systems Interconnection Reference Model (OSI model) to help improve communications between different vendors' systems. This organization was a committee representing many different organizations whose goal was not to favor a specific method of communication but rather to develop a set of guidelines that would allow vendors to ensure that their products would interoperate.

The OSI was setting out to simplify communications between systems. There are many events that need to take place in order to ensure that data first reaches the correct system and is then passed along to the correct application in a useable format. A set of rules was required to break down the communication process into a simple set of building blocks.

An analogy to this would be the process used for building a house. While the final product may seem a complex piece of work, it is much easier to deal with when it is broken down into manageable sections.

A good house starts with a foundation. There are rules that define how wide the wall of the foundation should be as well as how far below the frost line it needs to sit. After that, the house is framed off or *packaged*. Again, there are rules to define how thick the lumber needs to be as well as how long each piece of framing can span without support.

Once the house is framed, there is a defined process for putting on a roof, adding walls, and even connecting the electrical system and plumbing. By breaking this complicated process down into small, manageable sections, the process of building a house becomes easier. This breakdown also makes it easier to define who is responsible for which section. For example, when the electrical contractor shows up at the job site, they expect to be running wires and adding electrical outlets. They do not expect to show up and shingle the roof.

The entire structure becomes an interwoven tapestry with each piece relying on the others. For example, the frame of our house requires a solid foundation. Without it, the frame will eventually buckle and fall. The frame may also require that load-bearing walls be placed in certain areas of the house in order to ensure that the frame does not fall in on itself.

The OSI model strives to set up these same types of definitions and dependencies. Each portion of the communication process is broken out into separate building blocks. This makes it easier to determine what each portion of the communication process is required to do. It also helps to define how each piece will be connected together.

The OSI model is a set of seven layers. Each layer describes how its portion of the communication process should function, as well as how it will interface with the layers directly above it, below it, and adjacent to it on other systems. This model allows a vendor to create a product that operates on a certain level and be sure it will operate in the widest range of applications. If the vendor's product follows a specific layer's guidelines, it should be able to communicate with products created by other vendors that operate at adjacent layers.

To return to our house analogy for just a moment, let's assume we have a lumber yard that supplies main support beams used in house construction. So long as they follow the guidelines for thickness and material, they can expect their beams to function correctly in any house that has a proper foundation structure.

Figure 5.1 is a representation of the OSI model in all its glory. Let's look at the layers one at a time to determine what functionality is expected of each.

FIGURE 5.1

The OSI Model

OSI Layer Model

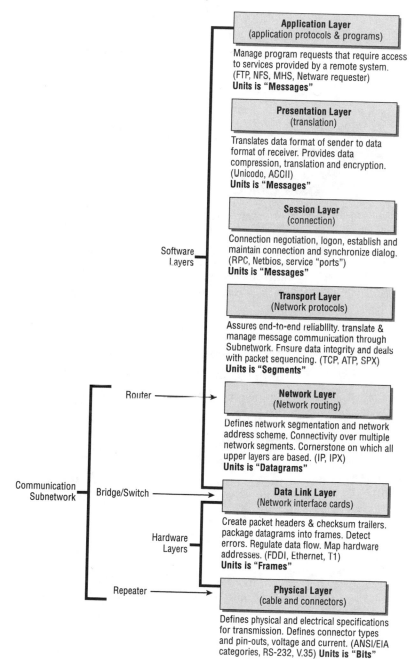

Physical Layer

The physical layer describes the specifications of our transmission media, connectors, and signal pulses. A repeater, or a hub, is a physical layer device because it is frame-stupid and simply amplifies the electrical signal on the wire and passes it along.

Effectively, everything covered in Chapter 2 is a discussion of physical layer functionality.

Data Link Layer

The data link layer describes the specifications for topology and communication between local systems. Ethernet is a good example of a data link layer specification, as it works with multiple physical layer specifications (twisted-pair cable, fiber) and multiple network layer specifications (IPX, IP). The data link layer is the "door between worlds," as it connects the physical aspects of network (cables and digital pulses) with the abstract world of software and data streams. Bridges and switches are considered to be data link devices because they are frame-aware. Both use information specific in the frame header to regulate traffic. Topics in Chapter 3 deal with functionality at this level.

Network Layer

The network layer describes how systems on different network segments find each other; it also defines network addresses. A network address is a name or number assigned to a group of physically connected systems.

The network address is assigned by the network administrator and should not be confused with the MAC address assigned to each network card. The purpose of a network address is to facilitate data delivery over long distances. Its functionality is similar to the zip code used when mailing a regular letter.

IP, IPX, and AppleTalk's Datagram Delivery Protocol (DDP) are all examples of network layer functionality. Service and application availability are based on functionality prescribed at this level.

This chapter covers network layer functionality later in more detail.

Transport Layer

The transport layer deals with the actual manipulation of your data and prepares it for delivery through the network. If your data is too large for a single frame, the transport layer breaks it up into smaller pieces and assigns sequence numbers. Sequence numbers allow the transport layer on the other receiving system to reassemble the data into its original content. While the data link layer performs a CRC check on all frames, the transport layer can act as a backup check to ensure that all the data was received and that it is usable. Examples of transport layer functionality would be IP's Transmission Control Protocol (TCP), User Datagram Protocol (UDP), IPX's Sequence Packet Exchange (SPX), and AppleTalk's AppleTalk Transaction Protocol (ATP).

Session Layer

The session layer deals with establishing and maintaining a connection between two or more systems. It is responsible for ensuring that a query for a specific type of service is made correctly. For example, if you try to access a system with your Web browser, the session layers on both systems work together to ensure you receive HTML pages and not e-mail. If a system is running multiple network applications, it is up to the session layer to keep these communications orderly and ensure that incoming data is directed to the correct application.

Presentation Layer

The presentation layer ensures that data is received in a format that is usable to applications running on the system. For example, if you are communicating over the Internet using encrypted communications, it would be the responsibility of the presentation layer to encrypt and decrypt this information. Most Web browsers support this kind of functionality for performing financial transactions over the Internet. Data and language translation is also done at this level.

Novell's Unicode, which ensures that multiple users of a specific server can view information in the language of their choice, would be considered a presentation layer function.

Application Layer

The label "application layer" is a bit misleading as it does not describe the actual "program" that a user may be running on their system. Rather, this is the layer that is responsible for determining when access to network resources is required. For example, Microsoft Word does not function at the application layer of the OSI model. If the user tries to retrieve a document from their home directory on a server, however, it is the application layer network software that is responsible for delivering their request to the remote system.

In geek lingo, the layers are numbered in the order described above. If I were to state that bridges function at layer 2 of the OSI model, you would interpret this to mean that bridges work within the guidelines provided by the data link layer of the OSI model.

How the OSI Model Works

Let's look at an example to see how these layers work together. Assume you're using your word processor program and trying to retrieve a file called resume.txt from your home directory on a remote server. The networking software running on your system reacts similarly to the process discussed in the following sections.

Formulating a File Request

The application layer detects that you are requesting information from a remote file system. It formulates a request to the system that `resume.txt` should be read from disk. Once this request has been created, the application layer passes the request off to the presentation layer for further processing.

The presentation layer determines if it needs to encrypt this request or perform any type of data translation. Once this has been determined and completed, it would then add any information it needs to pass along to the presentation layer on the remote system and forward the packet down to the session layer.

The session layer checks which application was requesting the information and verifies what service was being requested from the remote system (file access). The session layer adds information to the request to ensure that the remote system knows how to handle this request. Then it passes all this information along to the transport layer.

The transport layer ensures that it has a reliable connection to the remote system and begins the process of breaking down all the above information so that it can be packaged up into frames. If more than one frame is required, the information is split up and each block of information is assigned a sequence number. These sequenced chunks of information are passed one at a time down to the network layer.

The network layer receives the blocks of information from the above layer and adds the network address for both this and the remote system. This is done to each block before it is passed down to the data link layer.

At the data link layer the blocks are packaged up into individual frames. Note that all the information added by each of the above layers (as well as the actual file request) must be fit into the 46 to 1,500 byte data field of the frame. The data link layer then adds a frame header which consists of the source and destination MAC addresses and uses this information along with the contents of the data field to create a CRC trailer. The data link layer is then responsible for transmitting the frame according to the topology rules in use on the network. Depending on the topology, this could mean listening for a quiet moment on the network, waiting for a token, or waiting for a specific time division before transmitting the frame. As the data link layer transmits the frame, it passes it along to the physical layer (our network cables).

FIGURE 5.2

The location of each layer's information within our frame

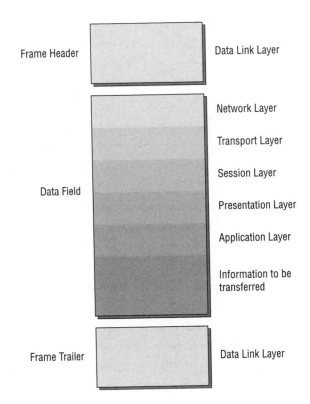

Frame Header — Data Link Layer

Network Layer

Transport Layer

Session Layer

Data Field — Presentation Layer

Application Layer

Information to be transferred

Frame Trailer — Data Link Layer

As the amount of required layer information increases, the amount of available space within the data field decreases. This leaves us with less room to transmit the core information of our request. By optimizing the amount of space that each layer requires, we can move our information using fewer frames. Less frames directly translates into a greater amount of available bandwidth for other transmissions. The physical layer does not add any information to our frame.

The physical layer is responsible for carrying the information from the source system to its destination. Because the physical layer has no knowledge of frames, it is simply passing along the digital signal pulses transmitted by the data link layer. The physical layer is the medium by which a connection is made between the two systems; it is responsible for carrying the signal to the data link layer on the remote system.

Our workstation has successfully formulated our data request (send me a copy of `resume.txt`) and transmitted it to the remote system. At this point, the remote system follows a similar process, but in reverse.

Receiving Data on the Remote System

The data link layer on the remote system reads in the transmitted frame. It notes that the MAC address in the destination field of the header is its own and recognizes that it needs to process this request. It performs a CRC check on the frame and compares the results to the value stored in the frame trailer. If it is a match, it strips off the header and trailer and passes the data field up to the networking layer. If the value does not match, it sends a request to the source system asking that another frame be sent.

The network layer on the remote system analyzes the information recorded by the network layer on the source system. It will note the network address of the source system and record this information in a table. This way, if this system needs to send a reply, the network layer already has this information and will not need to discover it through some other means. Once complete, the network layer removes information related to this level and passes the remainder up to the transport layer.

The transport layer receives the information and analyzes the information recorded by the transport layer on the source system. If it finds that packet sequencing was used, it will queue any information it receives until all the data has been received. If any of the data is missing, the transport layer uses the sequence information to formulate a reply to the remote system, requesting that this piece of data be resent. Once all the data has been received, the transport layer strips out any transport information and passes the full request up to the session layer.

The session layer receives the information and verifies that it is from a valid connection and that the station requesting data has already passed the security check for the service it is requesting (login and password for file access). If the check is positive, the session layer strips out any session information and passes the request up to presentation layer.

The presentation layer receives the frame and analyzes the information recorded by the presentation layer on the source system. It will then perform any translation or decryption required. Once the presentation layer has completed what translation or decryption was required, it will strip out the presentation layer information and pass the request up to the application layer.

The application layer ensures that the correct process running on the system receives the request for data. Because this is a file request, it is passed to whichever process is responsible for access to the file system.

This process reads the requested file and passes the information back to the application layer. At this point, the entire process of passing the information through each of the layers repeats. If you're amazed that the requested file is retrievable in anything less than a standard coffee break, then you have a pretty good idea of the magnitude of what is taking place just to request a simple file.

Each layer needs to communicate with the layers adjacent to it as well as with its counterpart on the remote system. While this all seems a bit complex, it's actually a good way to ensure that resources remain flexible and will interoperate with other products and technologies. For example, Ethernet is so adaptable to different topologies because it strictly adheres to the functionality outlined in layer 2 (data link) of the OSI model. This allows it to function seamlessly with a number of popular protocols like IP and IPX, which are designed to operate at layer 3 (network). In contrast, ATM specifies not only layer 2 functionality but also layer 3 and above. The fact that it does not follow the OSI model has contributed to its slow deployment and low acceptance, because it is difficult to incorporate it into existing network infrastructures.

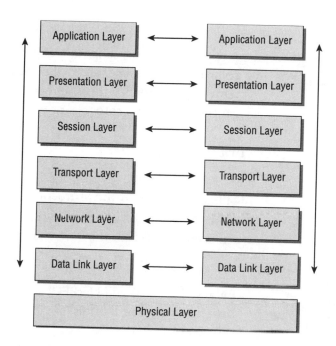

FIGURE 5.3

The OSI model in action

 The OSI model is simply a guideline—it is not a specification like Ethernet or the IP protocol. In this, it holds true to its original purpose of not favoring any specific way of providing network communications.

More on the Network Layer

In earlier chapters, we discussed the first two layers of the OSI model (physical in Chapter 2 and data link in Chapter 3). Let's continue along that path by analyzing what goes on at the network layer.

As mentioned earlier, the network layer is used for delivery of information between *logical networks*.

A logical network is simply a group of systems which are assigned a common network address by the network administrator. These systems may be grouped together because they share a common geographical area, protocols, or wiring.

Network Addresses

The terminology used for *network addresses* is different, depending on the protocol in use. If the protocol in use is IPX, the logical network is simply referred to as a network address. With IP it is a *subnet*, and when using AppleTalk it is referred to as a *zone*.

Because NetBIOS and NetBEUI are non-routable protocols, they have no counterpart at this level. They do not use network numbers and do not have the ability to propagate information between logical network segments. A non-routable protocol is a set of communication rules that expect all systems to be connected locally. They have no direct method of traveling between logical networks. A NetBIOS frame is incapable of crossing a router without some form of help.

Routers

Routers are used to connect logical networks, which is why they are sometimes incorrectly referred to in the IP world as *gateways*. Figure 5.4 shows the effect of adding a router to a network. Protocols on either side of the device must use a unique logical network address. Information destined for a nonlocal system must be routed to the logical network on which the system resides. The act of traversing a router from one logical network to another is referred to as a *hop*. When a protocol hops a router, it must use a unique logical network address on both sides.

So how do systems on one logical network segment find out what other logical segments exist on the network? Routers use a special type

FIGURE 5.4

The effects of adding a
router to the network

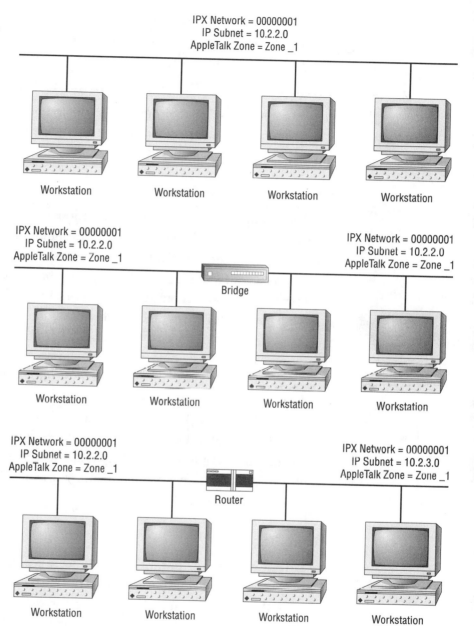

of maintenance frame called the router information protocol (RIP) to relay information about known networks. Routers use these frames to create a blueprint of the network known as a *routing table*.

> Routing tables tell the router which logical networks are available to deliver information to and which routers are capable of forwarding information to that network.

The Traceroute Command

One example of how routing information is relayed is illustrated in Figure 5.5, which shows the output of running the **Traceroute** command (renamed Tracert on Windows 95 systems). The **Traceroute** command is an IP protocol tool for documenting the subnets that must be traversed as a packet travels from one logical network to another. The lefthand column indicates the number of networks, so we must travel over 12 subnets to reach www.sun.com. If I subtract 1 from this, I get my hop count because 12 subnets would require 11 routers to separate them. The next three columns measure the link speed for three consecutive tries. This is the amount of time it took our frame to travel from one router to the next. An asterisk (*) indicates that the attempt was not replied to in a reasonable amount of time. Links that display high numbers of * for results are indications of a slow topology (such as a 28.8 dial-up connection) or heavy traffic. The final column identifies the name of the router we had to hop as well as its IP address.

Routing Tables

Do not confuse the output of the **Traceroute** command with an actual routing table. The output is simply the path my data followed to get from Point A to Point B (Point B being www.sun.com). As an analogy, think of a routing table being like a road map. A road map shows all the streets in a local city or town in much the same way a router table keeps track of all the local networks. Now, think of the directions you

may give a friend to get to your house based on this map (follow Oak
street to Pine and then take a left on Elm). These directions are synonymous with the output of the **Traceroute** command. It does not show
you the entire map, just how to get to a specific location.

Without having some method for each of these routers to communicate and let each other know who is connected where, this type of communication would be impossible.

FIGURE 5.5

Output from running the
traceroute command

```
C:\>tracert www.sun.com

Tracing route to www.sun.com [192.9.9.100]
over a maximum of 30 hops:

  1    *          *          *        Request timed out.
  2   197 ms    193 ms    195 ms    gis-gate.gis.net [206.42.64.1]
  3   204 ms    212 ms    204 ms    agis-gis.boston1.agis.net [206.185.153.25]
  4   209 ms    205 ms    207 ms    a2-0.1022.washington1.agis.net [206.185.153.210

  5   229 ms    222 ms    278 ms    maeeast-1.bbnplanet.net [192.41.177.1]
  6   258 ms    332 ms    252 ms    collegepk-br2.bbnplanet.net [4.0.1.17]
  7   364 ms    372 ms    360 ms    collegepk-br1.bbnplanet.net [128.167.253.5]
  8   290 ms    252 ms    256 ms    chicago2-br1.bbnplanet.net [4.0.1.5]
  9   317 ms    300 ms    307 ms    paloalto-br1.bbnplanet.net [4.0.1.1]
 10   329 ms    333 ms    305 ms    paloalto-cr5.bbnplanet.net [131.119.0.205]
 11   315 ms    285 ms    312 ms    sun2.bbnplanet.net [131.119.28.98]
 12   308 ms    306 ms    309 ms    www.sun.com [192.9.9.100]

Trace complete.

C:\>
```

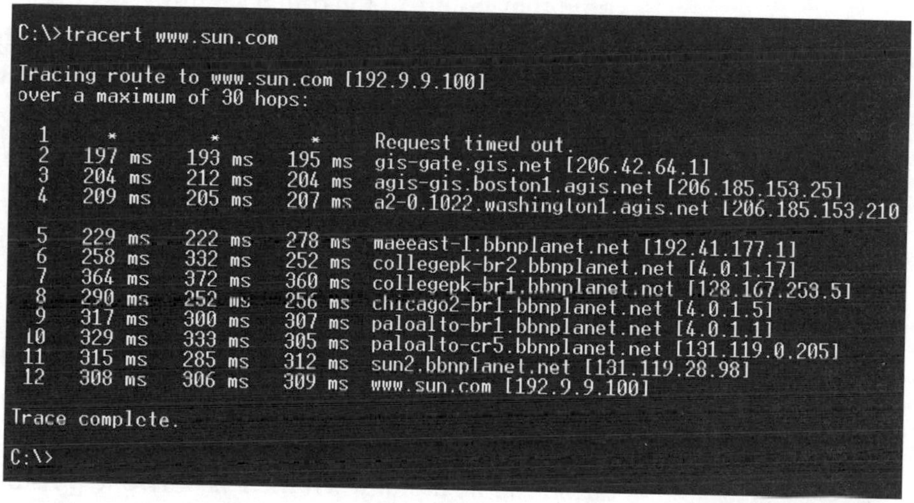

There are three different methods used when routing information
from one network to another—static, distance vector, and link state.
While each protocol has its own ways of providing routing functionality, each implementation can be broken down into one of these three
categories.

Static Routing

Static routing is the simplest method of getting information from one
system to another. Used mostly in IP networks, a static route defines a
specific router to be the point leading to a specific network. Static
routing does not use RIP, but relies on a configuration file that directs

all traffic bound for a specific network to a particular router. This of course assumes that you can predefine all the logical networks you will wish to communicate with. When this is not feasible (for example, when communicating on the Internet), a single router may be designated as a default to receive all traffic destined for networks that have not been predefined. When static routing is used, most systems receive an entry for the default router only.

For example, let's assume I configure my system to have a default route that points to the router Galifrey. As my system passes information through the network layer it analyzes the logical network of the destination system. If the system is located on the same logical network, the data link layer adds the MAC address of that system and transmits the frame onto the wire. If the system is located on some other logical network, the data link layer uses the MAC address for Galifrey and transmits the frame to it. Galifrey is then responsible for ensuring that the frame makes it to its final destination.

The benefits to this type of routing are simplicity and low overhead. My workstation is not required to know or care about which other logical networks may be available and how to get to them. It has only two options to worry about—deliver locally or deliver to Galifrey. This limitation can be useful when there is only one possible route to a final destination. For example, most organizations have only one Internet connection. Setting up a static route that points all IP traffic to the router which borders this connection may be the easiest way to ensure that all frames are delivered properly. Because all my routing information is configured at startup, my routers do not need to share route information with other routers. Each system is only concerned with forwarding information to its next default route. I do not need to have any RIP frames propagated through my network because the location to which each router will forward information has been preset.

This routing has a few obvious drawbacks, however. What happens if I have multiple routers connecting to my logical network segment and the traffic actually needs to traverse one of the other routers? As shown in Figure 5.6, the frame would still be delivered to Galifrey, who must then process the frame and pass it along to Tardis. Not only have I required Galifrey to process a frame that it did not need to see, but I have doubled my network traffic (one frame to Galifrey, one frame to Tardis). If this is an occasional occurrence, then it would probably not be a problem. However, a regular, large amount of traffic destined for the network on the other side of Tardis could overload Galifrey. In the latter situation, a single default route is definitely not recommended. Use a more detailed static table or a routing method capable of advertising route information.

FIGURE 5.6

When static routing is used, the default router must deliver all nonlocal frames.

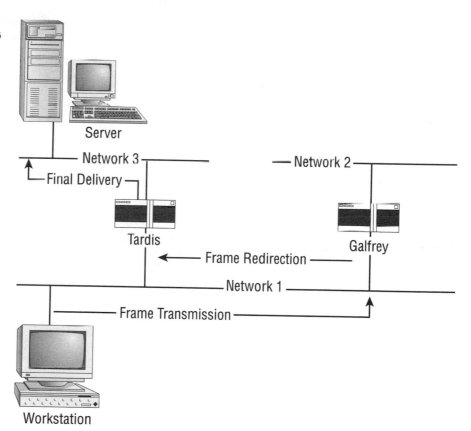

With static routing, the default router must process frames to all non-local stations even if the traffic must pass through a different, locally attached router.

Another problem with static routing is that it nullifies any attempts to add redundant routes. Redundant routes help to ensure that remote networks remain reachable when a single hardware device fails. For example, in Figure 5.7 I have two routers hooked up in parallel. The theory is that if one router dies then the other can continue to pass traffic to the remote network.

If I have set up Hermes as the default router and it drops offline, Bridgett will not be able to step in automatically. Because my systems are configured to send all nonlocal traffic to Hermes by default, they will not know that Bridgett is capable of supplying the same connectivity as Hermes. They will continue to attempt delivery to Hermes and eventually fail with a "Remote host unreachable" error. In order to let them know Bridgett supplied the same connectivity as Hermes, I would have to reconfigure each system by changing the default route to point at Bridgett instead of Hermes. Because manual intervention is needed to recover from a network failure, using static routes neutralizes any type of benefit provided by having redundant routes.

While static routing is easy to use, it does suffer from some major drawbacks that severely limit its application. When redundant paths are provided or even when multiple routers are used on the same logical network, you should use a routing method that is capable of exchanging RIP packets. RIP allows routing tables to be developed on the fly which can compensate for hardware failures. Both distance vector and link state routing use RIP frames to ensure that routing tables stay up to date.

FIGURE 5.7

Two parallel routers,
Hermes and Bridgett

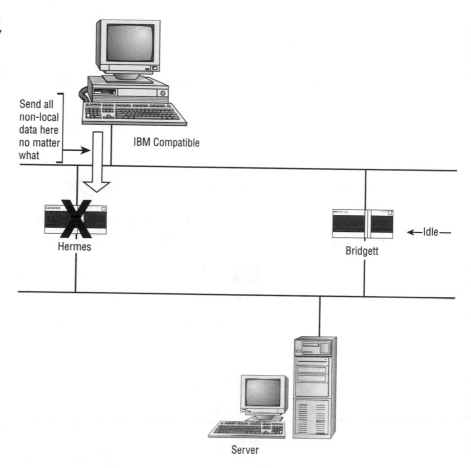

FIGURE 5.7

Two parallel routers,
Hermes and Bridgett

Distance Vector Routing

Distance vector is the oldest and most popular form of creating routing tables. In fact, when someone says, "I'm using RIP to create my routing tables," they are probably referring to distance vector. Distance vector routing was the only dynamic routing option available for so long that people sometimes directly associate it with RIP.

Distance vector routers build their tables based on secondhand information. A router will look at the tables being advertised by other routers and simply add 1 to the advertised hop values to create its own table. With distance vector, every router will broadcast their routing table once per minute.

Propagating Network Information with Distance Vector   Figure 5.8 shows how propagation of network information works with distance vector.

FIGURE 5.8

A routed network about to build its routing tables dynamically

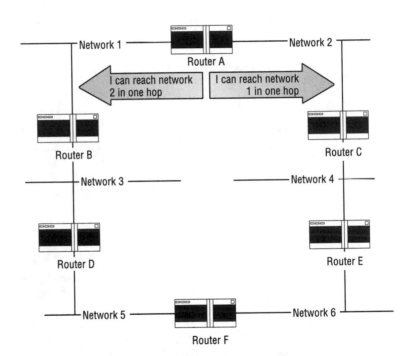

Router A has just come online. Because the two attached networks (1 and 2) have been programmed into it, it immediately adds these to its routing table, assigning a hop value of 1 to each. The hop value is 1 instead of zero because this information is relative to other attached networks, not the router. For example, if the router is advertising the route to network 1 on network 2, then 1 hop is appropriate because any system sending information to network 1 from network 2 would have to travel 1 hop (the router itself) to get there. A router usually does not advertise routing information about a directly attached network on that network itself. This means that the router should not transmit a

RIP frame stating, "I can reach network 1 in 1 hop," on network 1 itself.

So our router sends out two RIP packets, one on each network, to let any other devices know about the connectivity it can provide. When routers B and C receive these packets, they reply with RIP packets of their own. Remember that the network was already up and running. This means that all the other routers have already had an opportunity to build their tables. From these other RIP packets, router A collects the following information shown in Table 5.1.

	Router	Network	Hops To Get There
TABLE 5.1 Router-to-network hop counts	B	3	1
	B	5	2
	B	6	3
	B	4	4
	B	2	5
	C	4	1
	C	6	2
	C	5	3
	C	3	4
	C	1	5

Router A then analyzes this information, picking the lowest hop count to each network in order to build its own routing table. Routes that require a larger hop count are not discarded, but are retained in case of a link failure and an alternate route is required. These higher hop values are simply ignored during the normal operation of the router. Once complete, the table appears similar to Table 5.2.

	Network	Hops To Get There	Next Router
TABLE 5.2 Router A's routing table	1	1	direct connection
	2	1	direct connection
	3	2	B
	4	2	C
	5	3	B
	6	3	C

All we've done is pick the lowest hop count to each network and add 1 to the advertised value. Once the table is complete, router A again broadcasts two RIP packets, incorporating this new information.

Now that routers B and C have noted that there is a new router on the network, they must reevaluate their routing tables as well. Prior to router A coming online, the table for router B was similar to Table 5.3.

	Network	Hops To Get There	Next Router
TABLE 5.3 Routers B's routing table	1	1	direct connection
	2	5	D
	3	1	direct connection
	4	4	D
	5	2	D
	6	3	D

Now that router A is online, router B modifies its table to reflect the information shown in Table 5.4.

	Network	Hops To Get There	Next Router
TABLE 5.4 Router B's routing table changed to reflect that router A is online	1	1	direct connection
	2	2	A
	3	1	direct connection
	4	3	A
	5	2	D
	6	3	D

It takes us two RIPs on the same logical network to get to this point. The first time router A sent a RIP to router B it only knew about Network 2, shown in Figure 5.8. It was not until router C sent a reply RIP that router A realized that it had a path to networks 4, 6, 5 and 3 (in that order) through router C. This required it to send a second RIP frame to router B, incorporating this new information. The entire table above would be broadcasted with only the direct common network information being removed (network 1). This means that, while router A was updating router B with the information, it learned from router C it was also relaying back the route information originally sent to by that router (router B). The only difference is that router A has increased each hop count reported by router B by 1. Because the hop value is larger than what router B currently has in its tables, it simply ignores this information.

Router C goes through a similar process adjusting its table according to the information it receives from router A. Again, it requires two RIP frames on the same logical network to yield a complete view of our entire network so that router C can complete the changes to its tables.

These changes begin to propagate down through our network. Router B updates router D when A first comes online and then again when it completes its tables. This activity continues until all the routers have an accurate view of our new network layout. The amount of time that is required for all our routers to complete their table changes is known as the time to convergence. The convergence time is important, as our routing table is in a state of flux until all our routers become stabilized with their new tables.

WARNING Keep in mind that in a large network convergence time can be quite long, as RIP updates are only sent once per minute.

Distance Vector Routing Problems   It's also important to note that this table has been almost completely built on secondhand information. Any route that a router reports with a hop count greater than 1 is based upon what it has learned from another router. When router B tells router A that it can reach network 5 in 2 hops or network 6 in 3, it is fully trusting the accuracy of the information it has received from router D. For those who have played the telephone game (where each person in a line tries to relay an identical message to the next) when they were younger, you quickly realize that secondhand information is not always as accurate as it appears to be.

Figure 5.9 shows a pretty simple network layout. It consists of four logical networks separated by three routers. Once the point of convergence is reached, each router will have created a routing table as shown in the diagram.

Now, let's assume that router C dies a fiery death and drops offline. This will make network 4 unreachable by all other network segments. Once router B realizes that router C is offline, it will review the RIP information it has received in the past, looking for an alternate route. This is where distance vector routing starts to break down. Because router A has been advertising that it can get to network 4 in 3 hops,

FIGURE 5.9

Given the diagrammed network, each router would construct their routing table.

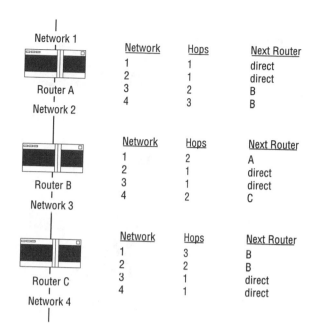

Network	Hops	Next Router
1	1	direct
2	1	direct
3	2	B
4	3	B

Network	Hops	Next Router
1	2	A
2	1	direct
3	1	direct
4	2	C

Network	Hops	Next Router
1	3	B
2	2	B
3	1	direct
4	1	direct

router B simply adds 1 to this value and assumes it can now reach network 4 through router A. Relying on secondhand information causes problems because, of course, router B can't reach network 4 through router A, now that router C is offline.

As shown in Figure 5.10, router B would now begin to advertise that it can now reach network 4 in 4 hops. Remember that RIP frames do not identify *how* a router will get to a remote network, only that it *can* and how many hops it will take to get there. Without this information, router B has no idea that router A is basing its route information on the tables it originally received from router B.

So router A would receive a RIP update from router B and realize that it has increased the hop count to network 4 from 2 to 4. Router A would then adjust its table accordingly and begin to advertise that it will now take 5 hops to reach network 4. It would again RIP and router B would again increase the hop count to network 4 by 1.

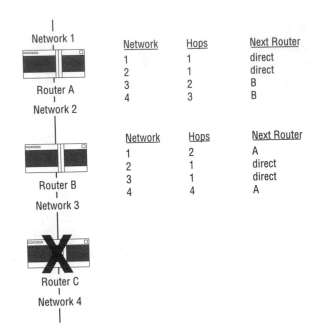

FIGURE 5.10

Router B incorrectly believes that it can now reach network 4 through router A and updates its tables accordingly.

Network	Hops	Next Router
1	1	direct
2	1	direct
3	2	B
4	3	B

Network	Hops	Next Router
1	2	A
2	1	direct
3	1	direct
4	4	A

This phenomena is called *count to infinity* because both routers would continue to increase their hop counts forever. It is because of counting to infinity that distance vector routing limits the maximum hop count to 15. Any route that is 16 or more hops away is considered unreachable and is subsequently removed from the routing table. This allows our two routers to figure out in a reasonable amount of time that network 4 can no longer be reached.

Reasonable is a subjective term however. Remember that RIP updates are only sent out once per minute. This means that it may be a minute or more before our routers buy a clue and realize that network 4 is gone. With a technology that measures frame transmissions in the microsecond range, a minute or more is plenty of time to wreak havoc on our communications. For example, let's look at what is taking place on network 2 while our routers are trying to converge.

Once router C has dropped offline, router B assumes that it has an alternate route to network 4 through router A. Any packets it receives are checked for errors and passed along to router A. When router A receives the frame, it performs an error check again. It then references its tables and realizes it needs to forward the frame to router B in order to reach network 4. Router B would again receive the frame and send it back to router A.

This is what is referred to as a *routing loop*. Each router plays hot potato with the frame, assuming the other is responsible for its delivery passing it back and forth. While this is only one frame, imagine the amount of bandwidth lost if there is a considerable amount of traffic destined for network 4. With all these frames looping between the two routers, it leaves very little bandwidth available on network 2 for any other systems that may need to transmit information.

Fortunately, the network layer has a method of eliminating this problem as well. As each router handles the frame, it is required to increment a hop counter within the frame by 1. The hop counter is responsible for recording how many routers the information has crossed. As with RIP frames, this counter has a maximum value of 15. As the information is handled for the 16th time, the router realizes that the information is undeliverable and simply drops it.

While this 16-hop limitation is not a problem for the average corporate network, it can be a severe limitation in larger networks. For example, if you look back at Figure 5.5, you'll remember that we needed to hop 11 routers in order to reach Sun Microsystems' Web server. This is very close to our 15-hop maximum with distance vector. If RIP was used through out the Internet, many resources would be unreachable from certain areas of the Internet.

It was the combination of all the above mentioned limitations that spawned the development of link state routing.

Link State Routing

Link state routers function in a similar fashion to distance vector but with a few notable exceptions. Most importantly, link state routers use only firsthand information when developing their routing tables. Not only does this help to eliminate routing errors but it drops our time to convergence to nearly zero. Let's assume that our network from Figure 5.8 has been upgraded to using a link state routing protocol. Now, let's bring router A online and watch what happens.

Propagating Network information with Link State   As Router A powers up, it sends out a type of RIP packet referred to as a *hello*. The hello packet is simply an introduction that states, "Greetings! I am a new router on this network, is there anybody out there?" This packet is transmitted on both of its ports and will be responded to by routers B and C.

Once router A receives a reply from routers B and C, it creates a link state protocol (LSP) frame and transmits it to routers B and C. An LSP frame is a routing maintenance frame which contains the following information:

- the router's name or identification

- the networks it is attached to

- the hop count or cost of getting to each network

- any other routers on each network that responded to its hello frame

Routers B and C would then make a copy of this frame and forward the information along through the network. Each router receiving the frame would then copy it and pass it along. With link state routing, each router maintains a copy of every other router's LSP frame. This way the router can use this information to diagram the network and build routing tables. Because each LSP frame contains only the route information that is local to each router that sent it, this network map is created strictly from firsthand information. A router will simply fit the LSP puzzle pieces together until their network picture is complete.

Router A would then make a LSP frame request from either router B or C. Because each router has a copy of all LSP frames, either router is capable of supplying a copy from every router on the network. This avoids the necessity of router A requesting this information from each router individually and saves bandwidth. Once an LSP network is up and running, updates are only transmitted every two hours or whenever a change takes place (such as a router going offline). This makes it an effective solution for networks that utilize *bandwidth on demand* WAN connections such as analog dial-up or ISDN. While a distance vector network would require the link to be brought up once per minute in order to transfer route information, link state would only need to bring this link up once every two hours.

Even in a non-WAN environment, link state is a great way to save bandwidth. The RIP packets sent by a distance vector router have a broadcast address in the destination MAC field. This means that once per minute every station is required to analyze every RIP packet whether it needs the information or not. If the information is not required by the station, it will be dropped once it reaches the network layer. However, this still means that my station is required to perform a CRC check, strip off the frame, and pass along the data field.

If you get the impression that the author has a vendetta against broadcast traffic, then proceed to Go and collect $200. While broadcasts do have their place, they are the banditos of networking, robbing precious CPU time from all systems they encounter. Some broadcasts are necessary, such as our example above, when learning what networks are available for access. As you will see a little later on, however, some protocols have based all their communications around broadcasting frames instead of taking advantage of direct delivery. Not only does this type of connectivity not scale well, it can lend itself to dismal network performance.

Convergence Time with Link State   So our distance vector network is up and running. Note that routers B and C were not required to recompute their routing tables. They simply added the new piece from router A and continued to pass traffic. This is why convergence time is nearly zero. The only change required of each router is that they add the new piece to their tables. Unlike distance vector, updates were not required in order to normalize the routing table. Router B did not need a second packet from router A, telling it what networks where available through router C. Router B simply added router A's LSP information to its existing table, and was already aware of the links.

Load Balancing   This brings us to an interesting point. What if someone on network 3 needs to send information to a system on network 2. Obviously, it would simply pass the information to router B because it is reporting that it is only 2 hops away from network 2. This is in contrast to router D, which would require 4 hops.

Now, let's say that network 1 is a 300 bps analog dial-up connection (hey, it still works) while networks 2–6 are 1 Gb Ethernet. What would happen then? Unfortunately, with most routing protocols it would still attempt to deliver the information through router B. Because hop count is typically used as the sole means of selecting the best route, the link speed would not be taken into consideration. Thus the route with the lowest hop count gets the frame.

This is where load balancing comes in. Load balancing introduces the concepts of link speed and segment congestion to determine which route is best. A routing protocol that takes this information into consideration along with hop count is much better suited to make an informed decision about where to route traffic. The combination of link response time and hop count is referred to as *cost*. What's nice about load balancing is that it is dynamic. If a router notes that the cost along a certain path is increasing, it can divert traffic to a different path to avoid an overload. The cost of a certain path can (and does) change with traffic load. The more information passing along a specific logical network segment, the higher the cost associated with using that link. Conversely, the faster the topology in use by a logical network segment, the lower the cost. For example, a 100 Mb Ethernet segment would have a lower cost value than an identical link operating at 10 Mbps. Figure 5.11 shows a server performing load balancing over two network cards. Note that the outbound traffic count is nearly identical on both cards. The addition of a second card helps to ensure that the server is able to keep up with networks that experience a high frame rate.

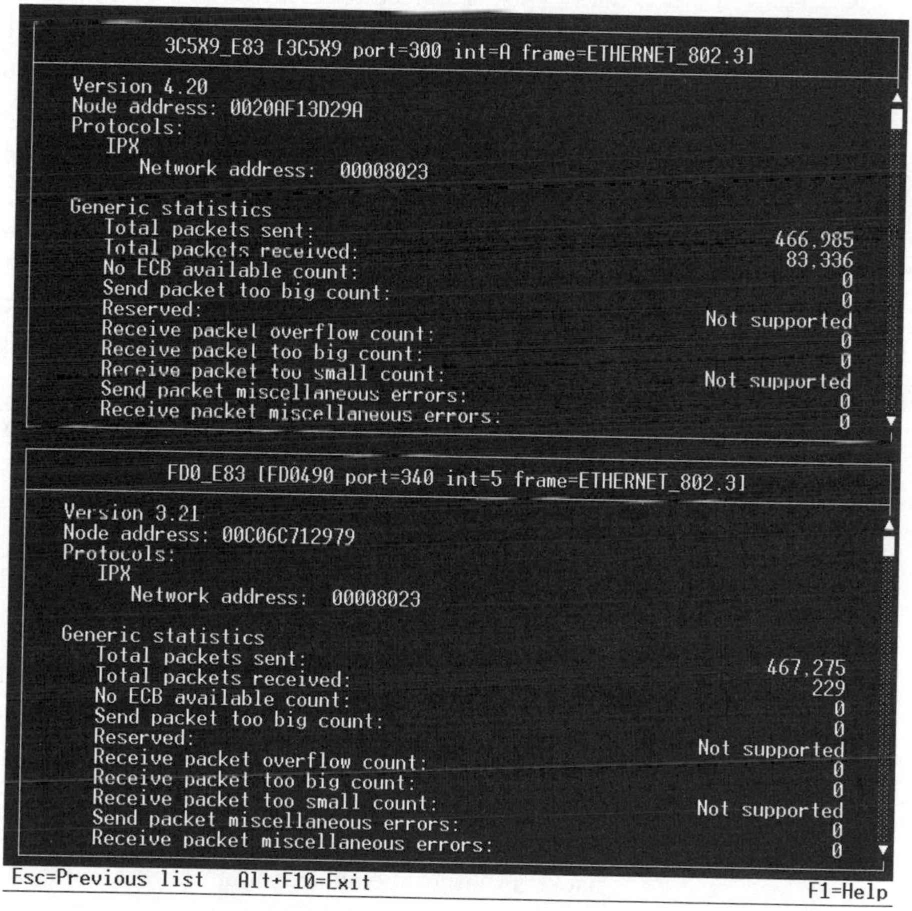

FIGURE 5.11

A NetWare server performing load balancing over two network cards

```
      3C5X9_E83 [3C5X9 port=300 int=A frame=ETHERNET_802.3]

    Version 4.20
    Node address: 0020AF13D29A
    Protocols:
       IPX
          Network address:   00008023

    Generic statistics
       Total packets sent:
       Total packets received:                          466,985
       No ECB available count:                           83,336
       Send packet too big count:                             0
       Reserved:                                              0
       Receive packet overflow count:             Not supported
       Receive packet too big count:                         0
       Receive packet too small count:                       0
       Send packet miscellaneous errors:          Not supported
       Receive packet miscellaneous errors:                  0
                                                             0

      FD0_E83 [FD0490 port=340 int=5 frame=ETHERNET_802.3]

    Version 3.21
    Node address: 00C06C712979
    Protocols:
       IPX
          Network address:   00008023

    Generic statistics
       Total packets sent:
       Total packets received:                          467,275
       No ECB available count:                              229
       Send packet too big count:                             0
       Reserved:                                              0
       Receive packet overflow count:             Not supported
       Receive packet too big count:                         0
       Receive packet too small count:                       0
       Send packet miscellaneous errors:          Not supported
       Receive packet miscellaneous errors:                  0
                                                             0

Esc=Previous list   Alt+F10=Exit                          F1=Help
```

Because link state routing has such a low convergence time, it is much better suited to do load balancing than distance vector. It is possible, however, to do load balancing using either one. Load balancing is implementation specific. This means that it is the actual design of the routing protocol itself that determines whether load balancing is possible, not the fact that it may be distance vector or link state.

Typically, however, most routing protocols that are capable of performing load balancing operate as link state as well. This is because the need to balance network traffic was not as much of an issue until network speeds started to rise. Because the latest release of routing protocols are link state, the ability to perform load balancing was built into them. As an example, NetWare supports two routing protocols, IPX RIP and Novell's link state protocol (NLSP). RIP has been around since NetWare was released. Because it predates the need for load balancing it does not support it. NLSP, however, is a fairly new protocol and supports the use of cost when making routing decisions.

Recovering from a Router Failure in a Link State Environment

Finally, let's revisit Figure 5.9 to look at how link state routing reacts when a router goes offline. Again, for the purpose of this example let's assume that our routing protocol has been upgraded from distance vector to link state. Let's also assume that our routing tables have been created and that traffic is passing normally.

If router C is shutdown normally, it transmits a maintenance frame (known as a dying gasp) to router B informing it that it is about to go offline. Router B then deletes the copy of router C's LSP frame that it has been maintaining and forwards this information along to router A. Both routers now have a valid copy of the new network layout and realize that network 4 is no longer reachable. If router C is not brought down gracefully and again dies a fiery death, there would be a short delay before router B realizes that router C is no longer acknowledging packets that are being sent to it. At this point, router B realizes that router C is offline. It then deletes router C's LSP frame from its table and forwards the change along to router A. Again, both systems have a valid copy of the new network layout. Because we are dealing with strictly firsthand information, there are no pesky count-to-infinity problems as we experienced with distance vector. Our router tables are accurate and our network is functioning with a minimal amount of updating. This allows link state to traverse a larger number of network segments. The maximum is 127 hops, but it can be less, depending on the implementation.

Connectionless and Connection-Oriented Communications

So we are now able to get our information from point A to point B, regardless of whether the systems are located on the same logical network. This raises the question, "Once we get there, how do we carry on a proper conversation?" This is where the transport layer comes in.

The transport layer is where we begin to set down the rules of communication etiquette. It's not enough that we can get this information from one system to another; we also have to ensure that both systems are operating at the same level of decorum.

As an analogy, let's say you pull up to the finest restaurant in the city in your GMC Pacer and proceed to the front door donning your best set of leather chaps, Harley jacket, and bandanna. Once inside, you greet the maitre d' by stating, "Yo wimp, gimme a table and some grub, NOW!" Surprisingly, you're escorted out of the restaurant at gun point. What went wrong? Why, improper etiquette was used of course. Everyone knows the correct term is not "grub" but "escargot."

The above verbal breakdown, as well as those in network communications, can be avoided by ensuring that all parties involved are communicating at the same level of etiquette. The two forms of communication etiquette are referred to as connectionless and connection-oriented communications.

A connection-oriented communication exchanges control information referred to as a *handshake* prior to transmitting data. The transport layer uses the handshake to ensure that the destination system is ready to receive information. A connection-oriented exchange will also ensure that data is transmitted and received in its original order. Modems are heavy users of connection-oriented communications, as they need to negotiate a connection speed prior to sending any information. In networking this functionality is accomplished through the use of a transport layer field referred to as a *flag* in the IP and AT world, or as the connection control field under IPX. Only connection-oriented communications use these fields. When IP is the underlying routing protocol, TCP is used to create connection-oriented communications. IPX uses SPX and AppleTalk uses ATP to provide this functionality. As a communication session is started, the application layer (not necessarily the program you are using) will specify if it needs to use a connection-oriented protocol. Telnet is just such an application. When a Telnet session is started, the application layer will request TCP as its transport service in order to better ensure reliability of the connection. Let's look at how this session is established to see how a handshake works.

At your workstation, you type in **telnet thor.foobar.com** to establish a remote connection to that system. As the request is passed down through the transport layer, TCP is selected to connect the two systems so that a connection-oriented communication can be established. The transport layer sets the synchronization (SYN) flag to 1 and leaves all other flags at 0. IP uses multiple flag fields and uses the binary system to set values. This means that the only possible values of an IP flag are 1 and 0. IPX and AT use a hexadecimal value, as their frames only contain one flag field. This allows the one field to contain more than two values.

By setting SYN=1 and all other fields to 0, we let the system on the other end (`thor.foobar.com`) know that we wish to establish a new communication session with the system. This request would then be passed down the remaining layers, across the wire to the remote system, and then up through its OSI layers.

If the service is available (more on services in a moment), the request is sent back down the stack until it reaches the transport layer. The transport layer would then set the SYN flag to 1, as did the originating system, but it will also set the acknowledgment (ACK) flag to 1. This lets the originating system know that its transmission was received and that it's okay to send data. The request is then passed down the stack and over the wire back to the original system.

The original system would then set the SYN flag to 0 and the ACK flag to 1, and transfer this frame back to Thor. This lets Thor know, "I'm acknowledging your acknowledgment and I'm about to send data." At this point, data would be transferred with each system being required to transmit an acknowledgment for each packet they receive. Figure 5.12 is a Telnet session from the system Loki to the system Thor. Each line represents a different frame that has been transmitted from one system to the other. Source and destination systems are identified as is some summary information about the frame. Note that the first three frames are identified as TCP frames, not Telnet, and that they perform the handshaking described above. Once TCP establishes the connection-oriented connection, then Telnet can step in to transfer the data required. The TCP frames that appear later in the conversation are for acknowledgment purposes. As stated, with a connection-oriented protocol every frame must be acknowledged. If the frame was a request for information, the reply can be in the form of delivering the requested information. If a frame is sent that does not require a reply, however, the destination system is still required to acknowledge that the frame was received.

If you're still a bit fuzzy on handshaking and connection-oriented communications, let's look at an analogy. Let's say you call a friend to inform them you'll be having a network Quake party on Saturday night and that they should come by with their laptop. You follow these steps:

- You dial your friend's phone number. (SYN=1, ACK=0)

- Your friend answers the phone and says, "Hello." (SYN=1, ACK=1)

- You reply by saying, "Hi Fred, this is Dave." (SYN=0, ACK=1)

FIGURE 5.12

An example of a
connection-oriented
communication

No.	Siz	Source	Destination	Layer	Summary
1	64	LOKI.FOOBAR.COM	THOR.FOOBAR.COM	tcp	Port:1042 ---> TELNET SYN
2	64	THOR.FOOBAR.COM	LOKI.FOOBAR.COM	tcp	Port:TELNET ---> 1042 ACK SYN
3	64	LOKI.FOOBAR.COM	THOR.FOOBAR.COM	tcp	Port:1042 ---> TELNET ACK
4	82	LOKI.FOOBAR.COM	THOR.FOOBAR.COM	telnt	Cmd=Do; Code=Suppress Go Ahead; Cmd=Will; Code=Termin
5	64	THOR.FOOBAR.COM	LOKI.FOOBAR.COM	tcp	Port:TELNET ---> 1042 ACK
6	70	THOR.FOOBAR.COM	LOKI.FOOBAR.COM	telnt	Cmd=Do; Code=Terminal Type; Cmd=Do; Code=Terminal Spe
7	64	THOR.FOOBAR.COM	LOKI.FOOBAR.COM	telnt	Cmd=Won't; Code=; Cmd=Will; Code=Terminal Type;
8	73	THOR.FOOBAR.COM	LOKI.FOOBAR.COM	telnt	Cmd=Will; Code=Suppress Go Ahead; Cmd=Do; Code=; Cmd=
9	64	THOR.FOOBAR.COM	LOKI.FOOBAR.COM	tcp	Port:TELNET ---> 1042 ACK
10	67	LOKI.FOOBAR.COM	THOR.FOOBAR.COM	telnt	Cmd=Subnegotiation Begin; Code=; Data=..P....
11	76	LOKI.FOOBAR.COM	THOR.FOOBAR.COM	telnt	Cmd=Subnegotiation Begin; Code=Terminal Speed; Data= .....
12	64	LOKI.FOOBAR.COM	THOR.FOOBAR.COM	tcp	Port:1042 ---> TELNET ACK
13	64	THOR.FOOBAR.COM	LOKI.FOOBAR.COM	tcp	Port:TELNET ---> 1042 ACK
14	92	LOKI.FOOBAR.COM	THOR.FOOBAR.COM	telnt	Cmd=Subnegotiation Begin; Code=Terminal Speed; Data= .38
15	64	THOR.FOOBAR.COM	LOKI.FOOBAR.COM	telnt	Cmd=Do; Code=Echo;
16	64	LOKI.FOOBAR.COM	THOR.FOOBAR.COM	telnt	Cmd=Won't; Code=Echo;
17	129	THOR.FOOBAR.COM	LOKI.FOOBAR.COM	telnt	Cmd=Will; Code=Echo; Data=..Red Hat Linux release 4.1 (Var
18	64	LOKI.FOOBAR.COM	THOR.FOOBAR.COM	telnt	Cmd=Do; Code=Echo;
19	64	LOKI.FOOBAR.COM	THOR.FOOBAR.COM	tcp	Port:TELNET ---> 1042 ACK
20	65	THOR.FOOBAR.COM	LOKI.FOOBAR.COM	telnt	Data=login:
21	64	LOKI.FOOBAR.COM	THOR.FOOBAR.COM	tcp	Port:1042 ---> TELNET ACK

You would then proceed to transfer your data about your upcoming party. Every time you pause, your friend would either transfer back information (yes, I'm free Saturday night) or send some form of acknowledgment (ACK) to let you know they have not yet hung up.

When the conversation is complete, you would both tear down the connection by stating goodbye, which is a handshake to let each other know that the conversation is complete and that it's okay to hang up the phone.

The purpose of connection-oriented communications is simple. They provide a reliable communication session when the underlying layers may be considered less than stable. By ensuring reliable connectivity at the transport layer, it helps to speed up communication when data becomes lost. This is because the data does not have to be passed all the way up to the application layer before a retransmission frame is created and sent. While this is important in modem communications, where a small amount of noise or a crossed line can kill a communication session, it is not as useful with network based communication. TCP and SPX originate from the days when the physical and data link layer could not always be relied on to successfully transmit information. These days, this is less of a concern as reliability has increased dramatically from the earlier years of networking.

A connectionless protocol does not require an initial handshake or that acknowledgments be sent for every packet. When a connectionless transport is used, it makes its best effort to deliver the data, but relies on the stability of the underlying layers as well as application layer acknowledgments to ensure that the data is delivered reliably. IP's User Datagram Protocol (UDP) and IPX's NetWare Core Protocol (NCP) are examples of connectionless transports. Both protocols rely on connectionless communications to transfer routing and server information as well. While AppleTalk does not utilize any connectionless communications for creating data sessions, it does use it when advertising servers with its Name Binding Protocol (NBP).

As an example of connectionless communications, check out the Network File System (NFS) session in Figure 5.13. NFS is a service that allows file sharing over IP. It uses UDP as its underlying transport protocol. Note that all data acknowledgments are in the form of a request for additional information. The destination system (Thor) assumes that the last packet was received if the source system (Loki) requests additional information. Conversely, if Loki does not receive a reply from Thor for information it has requested, NFS takes care of requesting the information again. So long as we have a stable connection that does not require a large number of retransmissions, this is a very efficient method of communicating, as it does not generate unnecessary acknowledgments.

FIGURE 5.13

NFS uses UDP to create a connectionless session.

No.	Size	Source	Destination	Layer	Summary
1	198	LOKI.FOOBAR.COM	THOR.FOOBAR.COM	nfs	Call Lookup ???/games.tar.gz
2	174	THOR.FOOBAR.COM	LOKI.FOOBAR.COM	nfs	Reply Lookup for games.tar.gz
3	182	LOKI.FOOBAR.COM	THOR.FOOBAR.COM	nfs	Call Get File Attributes for games.tar.gz
4	142	THOR.FOOBAR.COM	LOKI.FOOBAR.COM	nfs	Reply Get File Attributes
5	194	LOKI.FOOBAR.COM	THOR.FOOBAR.COM	nfs	Call Read From File games.tar.gz; Offset 0; 1024 bytes
6	1,170	THOR.FOOBAR.COM	LOKI.FOOBAR.COM	nfs	Reply Read From File; 1024 bytes
7	194	LOKI.FOOBAR.COM	THOR.FOOBAR.COM	nfs	Call Read From File games.tar.gz; Offset 1024; 1024 bytes
8	1,170	THOR.FOOBAR.COM	LOKI.FOOBAR.COM	nfs	Reply Read From File; 1024 bytes
9	194	LOKI.FOOBAR.COM	THOR.FOOBAR.COM	nfs	Call Read From File games.tar.gz; Offset 2048; 1024 bytes
10	1,170	THOR.FOOBAR.COM	LOKI.FOOBAR.COM	nfs	Reply Read From File; 1024 bytes
11	194	LOKI.FOOBAR.COM	THOR.FOOBAR.COM	nfs	Call Read From File games.tar.gz; Offset 3072; 1024 bytes
12	1,170	THOR.FOOBAR.COM	LOKI.FOOBAR.COM	nfs	Reply Read From File; 1024 bytes
13	194	LOKI.FOOBAR.COM	THOR.FOOBAR.COM	nfs	Call Read From File games.tar.gz; Offset 4096; 1024 bytes
14	1,170	THOR.FOOBAR.COM	LOKI.FOOBAR.COM	nfs	Reply Read From File; 1024 bytes
15	194	LOKI.FOOBAR.COM	THOR.FOOBAR.COM	nfs	Call Read From File games.tar.gz; Offset 5120; 1024 bytes
16	1,170	THOR.FOOBAR.COM	LOKI.FOOBAR.COM	nfs	Reply Read From File; 1024 bytes
17	194	LOKI.FOOBAR.COM	THOR.FOOBAR.COM	nfs	Call Read From File games.tar.gz; Offset 6144; 1024 bytes
18	1,170	THOR.FOOBAR.COM	LOKI.FOOBAR.COM	nfs	Reply Read From File; 1024 bytes
19	194	LOKI.FOOBAR.COM	THOR.FOOBAR.COM	nfs	Call Read From File games.tar.gz; Offset 7168; 1024 bytes
20	1,170	THOR.FOOBAR.COM	LOKI.FOOBAR.COM	nfs	Reply Read From File; 1024 bytes
21	194	LOKI.FOOBAR.COM	THOR.FOOBAR.COM	nfs	Call Read From File games.tar.gz; Offset 8192; 1024 bytes
22	1,170	THOR.FOOBAR.COM	LOKI.FOOBAR.COM	nfs	Reply Read From File; 1024 bytes
23	194	LOKI.FOOBAR.COM	THOR.FOOBAR.COM	nfs	Call Read From File games.tar.gz; Offset 9216; 1024 bytes

Let's look at another analogy to see how this type of communication differs from the connection-oriented one described earlier. Again, let's say you call a friend to inform them you'll be having a network Quake party on Saturday night and that they should come by with their laptop. You call their number but this time get their answering machine. You leave a detailed message indicating when the party will take place and what they are required to bring. Unlike the first analogy, you are now relying on:

- your ability to dial the correct phone number as you did not reach this person to confirm that this number was in fact theirs

- the fact that the phone company did not drop your phone connection in the middle of you leaving your friend the message (answering machines do not ACK unless of course you talk until the beep and it cuts you off)

- The answering machine properly recorded the message and did not eat the tape.

- Your friend's cat does not mistake the tape for a ball of yarn

- The power did not go out hiding the fact that your friend has a new message to listen to.

- Your friend has the ability to retrieve this message between now and the date of the party.

As you can see, you have no real confirmation that your friend will actually receive the message. You are counting on none of the above events taking place so that your friend will receive the message in a timely manner. If you wanted to ensure the reliability of this data transmission, you could send an application layer acknowledgment request in the form of, "Please RSVP by Thursday." If you do not get a response by then, you could try transmitting the data again.

The benefit of a connectionless protocol is that it allows for a bit more freedom when determining how nitpicky the systems must be to ensure proper data delivery. As we will find in our discussion on IPX, this can be leveraged so that many frames of useful information can be sent before an acknowledgment of their receipt is required.

So which is a better transport to use? Unfortunately, the answer to this is, "Whichever one is specified by your application layer." If Telnet wants TCP, you cannot force it to use UDP.

When a network program is initially coded, it is up to the programmers involved to choose which transport they will support. A majority of applications today use a connection-oriented transport. There are a couple of reasons that this has occurred.

The first is the conditions at the time of development. Telnet has been around for so long that TCP was the appropriate transport at the time of development. Networking was still a very unstable animal back then. Trying to switch over to UDP now is possible but would cause a complete mess as some systems are upgraded before others.

The other driving force is a misunderstanding as to when a connection-oriented protocol is required. A programmer who is faced with using a *reliable* or *unreliable* transport for moving their data will usually choose the former without regard to how inefficient this may make the communication session. They simply look at the term "unreliable" and shy away.

Some applications do require a connection-oriented session even today. An example would be a network-based video conference program. Lost frames must be recovered immediately, and the data must be received in the order it was sent to ensure that the resulting image does not appear choppy or as if the person on the other end is moving in slow motion replay. This information is considered to be time sensitive, as the information must be displayed as quickly as it is received in order to avoid delays.

Data transmissions that are not time-sensitive in nature, such as e-mail or file transfers are usually better left to a connectionless protocol. Because networks today are much more reliable, the number of times a retransmission is required is minimal. This means that this functionality can easily be provided by some upper layer. Also, receiving the data in its original order should not be a concern. The transport layer has the ability to sequence data so that packets received out of order can be queued and assembled properly. While this may cause a brief delay before information is passed along to upper layers, this time is easily compensated for by streamlining communications and requiring fewer ACKs to maintain the data stream.

One technology that has made good use of the flag field of connection-oriented communications is firewalls. A firewall will use the information in the flag field to determine if a connection is inbound or outbound and based on its rule table, either accept or deny the connection.

For example, let's say our firewall rules allow internal users access to the Internet but blocks external users from accessing internal systems. This is a pretty common security policy. The question is how do we accomplish this?

We cannot simply block all inbound traffic because this would prohibit our internal users from ever receiving a reply to their data requests. We need some method of allowing replies back in while denying external systems from being able to establish connections with internal systems. The secret to this is our TCP flags.

Remember that a TCP-based session needs to handshake prior to sending data. If we block all inbound frames that have the SYN field set to 1 and all other fields set to 0, we can prevent any external user from establishing a connection with our internal system. Because these settings are only used during the initial handshake and do not appear in any other part of the transmission, it is an effective way of blocking external users. If external users cannot connect to an internal system, they cannot transmit or pull data from it.

Most firewalls will deny all UDP connections—UDP does not have a flag field, and most firewalls have no effective way of determining if the data is a connection request or a reply. This is what has made *stateful inspection* firewalls so popular, as they monitor and remember all connection sessions. With stateful inspection you can create a filter rule that accepts UDP packets from an external host only when that host has been previously queried for information using UDP. This ensures that only UDP replies are allowed back in past the firewall. While a packet filter or proxy firewall can only effectively work with TCP connections, a stateful inspection firewall can safely pass UDP as well.

Network Services

We can now find our remote system and ensure that both systems are using the same level of communications. The question now is how to tell the server what we want. While computers are powerful tools—capable of processing many requests per second—they still have a problem with the phrase, "You know what I mean?" This is why we require a method of letting a system know exactly what we want from it. It would be a real bummer to connect to a slick new Web site only to have the server start spewing e-mail or routing information at you because it had no idea what you were looking for.

To make sure the computer knows what we want from it, we need to look to the session layer.

You may remember from our discussion of the session layer at the beginning of this chapter that it is responsible for ensuring that requests for service are formulated properly.

A service is a process or application which runs on a server and provides some benefit to a network user. E-mail is a good example of a value-added service. A system may queue your mail messages until you connect to the system with a mail client in order to read them. File and print sharing are two more common examples of network services.

Services are accessed by connecting to a specific port or socket. Think of ports as virtual mail slots on the system and you'll get the idea. A separate mail slot (port number) is designated for each service or application running on the system. When a user wishes to access a service, the session layer is responsible for ensuring that the request reaches the correct mail slot or port number.

On a Unix system IP port number are mapped to services in a file called (oddly enough) `services`. An abbreviated output is listed below in Table 5.5. Note that the first column identifies the service by name while the second column identifies the port and transport to be used. The third column is a brief description of the functionality provided by the service. This is only a brief listing of IP services. More information can be found in request for comment (RFC) 1700. Note that these port numbers are not Unix specific; any operating system using smtp will connect to port 25.

T A B L E 5.5 An abbreviated listing of IP output services	**Service**	**Port/Transport**	**Functionality**
	ftp-data	20/tcp	#Used to transfer actual file information
	ftp	21/tcp	#Used to transfer session commands
	telnet	23/tcp	#Creates a remote session
	smtp	25/tcp	#e-mail delivery
	whois	43/tcp	#Internic domain name lookup
	domain	53/tcp	#Domain name queries
	domain	53/udp	#DNS zone transfers
	bootps	67/udp	# bootp server
	bootpc	68/udp	# bootp client
	pop-3	110/tcp	# PostOffice V.3
	nntp	119/tcp	# Network News Transfer
	ntp	123/tcp	# Network Time Protocol
	ntp	123/udp	# Network Time Protocol

	Service	Port/Transport	Functionality
T A B L E 5.5 *(cont.)* An abbreviated listing of IP output services	netbios-ns	137/tcp	#nbns
	netbios-ns	137/udp	#nbns
	netbios-dgm	138/tcp	#nbdgm
	netbios-dgm	138/udp	#nbdgm
	netbios-ssn	139/tcp	#nbssn
	snmp	161/udp	#Simple Network Management protocol
	snmp-trap	162/udp	#Simple Network Management protocol

So according to the above file, any TCP request received on port 23 is assumed to be a Telnet session and is passed up to the application that handles remote access. If the requested port is 25, it is assumed that mail services are required and the session is passed up to the mail program.

The above file is used by a process called the Internet Demon (inetd). Inetd monitors each of the listed ports on a Unix system and is responsible for *waking up* the application that provides services to that port. This is an efficient means of managing the system for ports that are accessed infrequently. The process is active and using system resources (memory, CPU time, and so on) only when the service is actually needed. When the service is shut down, the process returns to a sleep mode waiting for inetd to call on it again.

Applications that receive heavy use should be left running in a constant listening mode—this is typically more efficient. For example, Web server access usually uses port 80. Note that it is not listed in the services file above as a process to be handled by inetd. This is because a Web server may be called upon to service many requests in the course of a day. It is more efficient to leave the process running all the time than to bother inetd every time you receive a page request.

All of the above mentioned port numbers are referred to as *well known ports*. Well known ports are defacto standards used to ensure that everyone is capable of accessing services on other machines without needing to guess which port number is used by the service. For example, there is nothing stopping you from setting up a Web server on port 573, provided that the port is not in use by some other services. The problem is that most users will expect the service to be available on port 80 and may be unable to find it. Sometimes, however, switching ports may be done on purpose—we will look at that in just a minute.

NOTE Defacto standard means that it is a standard by popularity; it is not a rule or law.

Ports 0-1023 are defined by the Internet Assigned Numbers Authority (IANA) for most well known services. While ports have been assigned up to 7200, it is the ports below 1024 that make up the bulk of Internet communications. These assignments are not hard fast rules but rather guides to ensure that everyone offers public services on the same port. For example, if you want to access Microsoft's Web page, you can assume they are offering the service on port 80 because this is the well-known port for that service.

When a system requests information, it not only specifies the port it wishes to access but also specifies which port should be used when returning the requested information. Port numbers for this task are selected from 1024 to 65535 and are referred to as *upper port numbers*.

To illustrate how this works let's revisit our Telnet session in Figure 5.12. When Loki attempts to set up a Telnet session with Thor, it will do so by accessing port 23 on that system (port 23 is the well-known service port for Telnet). If we look at frame number 2, we see that Thor is sending the acknowledgment (ACK) back on port 1042. This is because the session information in the original frame that Loki sent Thor specified a source port of 1042 and a destination port of 23. The destination port identified where the frame was going (port 23 on Thor) while the source port identified which port should be used when sending replies (port 1042 on Loki). Port 23 is our well known service port, while port 1042 is our upper port number used for the reply.

Upper reply ports are assigned on the fly. It is nearly impossible to predict which upper port a system will request information to be received on, as the ports are assigned based on availability. It is for this reason that most packet filters used for firewalling purposes are set up to leave ports above 1023 open all the time.

This leads to one of the reasons why a port other than a well known port may be used to offer a service. A savvy end user who realizes that a packet filter will block access to the Web server running on their system may assign the service to some upper port number like 8001. Because the connection will be made above port 1023, it may not be blocked. The result is that despite your corporate policy banning internal Web sites and a packet filter to help enforce it, this user can successfully advertise their Web site provided they supply the port number (8001) along with the universal resource locator (URL). The URL would look similar to the following:

```
http://thor.foobar.com:8001
```

The :8001 tells your Web browser to access the server using port 8001 instead of 80. Because most packet filters have poor logging facilities, the network administrator responsible for enforcing the above policy of "no internal Web sites" would probably never realize it exists unless they stumble across it.

The next time your boss accuses you of wasting time by cruising the Web correct him by stating, "I am performing a security audit by attempting to purse links to renegade internal sites which do not conform to our corporate security policy. This activity is required due to inefficiencies in our firewalling mechanism." If they do not fire you on the spot, quickly submit a PO for a new firewall while the event is clear in their mind.

Speaking of switching port numbers, try to identify the session in Figure 5.14. While the session is identified as a Simple Mail Transfer

Protocol (SMTP), it is actually a Telnet session redirected to port 25 (the well know port for SMTP). We've fooled the analyzer recording this session into thinking that we simply have one mail system transferring mail to another. Most firewalls will be duped in the same fashion because they use the destination port to identify the session in progress—they do not look at the actual applications involved. This type of activity is usually analogous to someone spoofing or faking a mail message. Once I've connected to the remote mail system I'm free to pretend the message came from anywhere. Unless the routing information in the mail header is checked (most user friendly mail programs simply discard this information), the actual origin of this information cannot be traced.

FIGURE 5.14

While this looks like a normal transfer of mail, it is actually someone spoofing a mail message to the destination system.

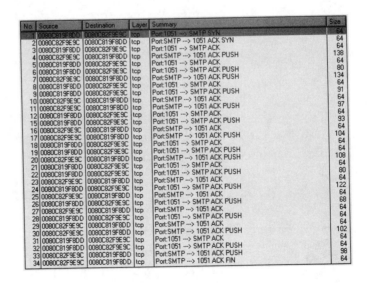

No.	Source	Destination	Layer	Summary	Size
1	0080C819F8DD	0080C82F9E9C	tcp	Port:1051 ---> SMTP SYN	64
2	0080C82F9E9C	0080C819F8DD	tcp	Port:SMTP ---> 1051 ACK SYN	64
3	0080C819F8DD	0080C82F9E9C	tcp	Port:1051 ---> SMTP ACK	64
4	0080C82F9E9C	0080C819F8DD	tcp	Port:SMTP ---> 1051 ACK PUSH	138
5	0080C819F8DD	0080C82F9E9C	tcp	Port:1051 ---> SMTP ACK	64
6	0080C819F8DD	0080C82F9E9C	tcp	Port:1051 ---> SMTP ACK PUSH	80
7	0080C82F9E9C	0080C819F8DD	tcp	Port:SMTP ---> 1051 ACK PUSH	134
8	0080C819F8DD	0080C82F9E9C	tcp	Port:1051 ---> SMTP ACK	64
9	0080C819F8DD	0080C82F9E9C	tcp	Port:1051 ---> SMTP ACK PUSH	91
10	0080C82F9E9C	0080C819F8DD	tcp	Port:SMTP ---> 1051 ACK	64
11	0080C82F9E9C	0080C819F8DD	tcp	Port:SMTP ---> 1051 ACK PUSH	97
12	0080C819F8DD	0080C82F9E9C	tcp	Port:1051 ---> SMTP ACK	64
15	0080C819F8DD	0080C82F9E9C	tcp	Port:1051 ---> SMTP ACK PUSH	93
16	0080C82F9E9C	0080C819F8DD	tcp	Port:SMTP ---> 1051 ACK	64
17	0080C82F9E9C	0080C819F8DD	tcp	Port:SMTP ---> 1051 ACK PUSH	104
18	0080C819F8DD	0080C82F9E9C	tcp	Port:1051 ---> SMTP ACK	64
19	0080C819F8DD	0080C82F9E9C	tcp	Port:1051 ---> SMTP ACK PUSH	64
20	0080C82F9E9C	0080C819F8DD	tcp	Port:SMTP ---> 1051 ACK PUSH	108
21	0080C819F8DD	0080C82F9E9C	tcp	Port:1051 ---> SMTP ACK	64
22	0080C819F8DD	0080C82F9E9C	tcp	Port:1051 ---> SMTP ACK PUSH	80
23	0080C82F9E9C	0080C819F8DD	tcp	Port:SMTP ---> 1051 ACK	64
24	0080C819F8DD	0080C82F9E9C	tcp	Port:1051 ---> SMTP ACK PUSH	122
25	0080C82F9E9C	0080C819F8DD	tcp	Port:SMTP ---> 1051 ACK	64
26	0080C82F9E9C	0080C819F8DD	tcp	Port:1051 ---> SMTP ACK PUSH	68
27	0080C82F9E9C	0080C819F8DD	tcp	Port:1051 ---> SMTP ACK	64
28	0080C819F8DD	0080C82F9E9C	tcp	Port:1051 ---> SMTP ACK PUSH	64
29	0080C82F9E9C	0080C819F8DD	tcp	Port:SMTP ---> 1051 ACK	64
30	0080C82F9E9C	0080C819F8DD	tcp	Port:SMTP ---> 1051 ACK PUSH	102
31	0080C819F8DD	0080C82F9E9C	tcp	Port:1051 ---> SMTP ACK	64
32	0080C819F8DD	0080C82F9E9C	tcp	Port:1051 ---> SMTP ACK PUSH	64
33	0080C82F9E9C	0080C819F8DD	tcp	Port:SMTP ---> 1051 ACK PUSH	98
34	0080C82F9E9C	0080C819F8DD	tcp	Port:SMTP ---> 1051 ACK FIN	64

Figure 5.15 shows the final output of this *spoofing* session. Without the header information, I may actually believe this message came from bgates@microsoft.com. The fact that the message was never touched by a mail system within the Microsoft domain indicates that it is a phony. I've used this example in the past while instructing Internet and security classes. Do not believe everything you read, especially if it comes from the Internet!

F I G U R E 5.15

The output from our
spoofed mail message

```
From bgates@microsoft.com  Wed Feb  5 16:42:21 1997
Return-Path: <bgates@microsoft.com>
Received: from loki.foobar.com (loki.foobar.com [10.2.2.20])
        by thor.foobar.com (8.8.4/8.8.4) with SMTP
      id QAA00887 for cbrenton@thor.foobar.com; Wed, 5 Feb 1997 16:41:04 -0500
Date: Wed, 5 Feb 1997 16:41:04 -0500
From: bgates@microsoft.com (Bill Gates)
Message-Id: <199702052141.QAA00887@thor.foobar.com>
Subject: Quake Party
Status: R

The party sounds cool! I'll bring the P5's and the cheeze wiz!

Later...
```

This type of redirection can also have its benefits. Let's assume that you already have a corporate Web server running on your system. Let's also assume that you pick up a product like Software.com's Post.Office. This product allows users to administer their Post Office Protocol (POP) e-mail accounts using a friendly Web browser interface. The problem here is that port 80 is already in use by the company Web server. To resolve this conflict, simply set Post.Office to use some port number for the Web browser interface other than 80, and let your users know the correct URL to use when accessing this system. Using multiple port numbers allows you to have two separate Web servers running on the same system without conflict.

Port numbers are also used to distinctly identify similar sessions between systems. For example, let's build on Figure 5.12. We already have one Telnet session running from Loki to Thor. What happens if four or five more sessions are created? All sessions have the following information in common:

Source IP address: 10.2.2.20 (loki.foobar.com)

Destination IP address: 10.2.2.10 (thor.foobar.com)

Destination port: 23 (well know port for Telnet)

The source ports remain distinctive in order to identify each individual session. Our first connection has already specified a source port of 1042 for its connection. Each sequential Telnet session that is established after that would be assigned some other upper port number to uniquely identify it. The actual numbers assigned would be based upon what was not currently being used by the source system. For example ports 1118, 1398, 4023, and 6025 may be used as source ports for the next four sessions. The actual reply port number does not really matter, only that it can uniquely identify that specific session between the two systems. If we were to monitor a number of concurrent sessions taking place, the transaction would look similar to Figure 5.16. Now we see multiple reply ports in use to identify each session.

FIGURE 5.16

Multiple Telnet session in progress between Loki and Thor

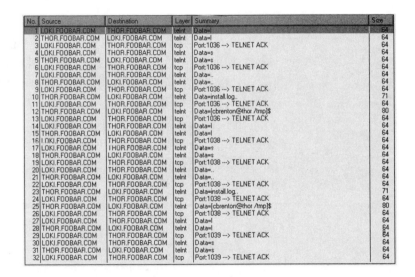

No.	Source	Destination	Layer	Summary	Size
1	LOKI.FOOBAR.COM	THOR.FOOBAR.COM	telnt	Data=l	64
2	THOR.FOOBAR.COM	LOKI.FOOBAR.COM	telnt	Data=l	64
3	LOKI.FOOBAR.COM	THOR.FOOBAR.COM	tcp	Port:1036 ---> TELNET ACK	64
4	LOKI.FOOBAR.COM	THOR.FOOBAR.COM	telnt	Data=s	64
5	THOR.FOOBAR.COM	LOKI.FOOBAR.COM	telnt	Data=s	64
6	LOKI.FOOBAR.COM	THOR.FOOBAR.COM	tcp	Port:1036 ---> TELNET ACK	64
7	LOKI.FOOBAR.COM	THOR.FOOBAR.COM	telnt	Data=.	64
8	THOR.FOOBAR.COM	LOKI.FOOBAR.COM	telnt	Data=.	64
9	LOKI.FOOBAR.COM	THOR.FOOBAR.COM	tcp	Port:1036 ---> TELNET ACK	64
10	THOR.FOOBAR.COM	LOKI.FOOBAR.COM	telnt	Data=install.log.	71
11	LOKI.FOOBAR.COM	THOR.FOOBAR.COM	tcp	Port:1036 ---> TELNET ACK	64
12	THOR.FOOBAR.COM	LOKI.FOOBAR.COM	telnt	Data=[cbrenton@thor /tmp]$	80
13	LOKI.FOOBAR.COM	THOR.FOOBAR.COM	tcp	Port:1036 ---> TELNET ACK	64
14	LOKI.FOOBAR.COM	THOR.FOOBAR.COM	telnt	Data=l	64
15	THOR.FOOBAR.COM	LOKI.FOOBAR.COM	telnt	Data=l	64
16	LOKI.FOOBAR.COM	THOR.FOOBAR.COM	tcp	Port:1038 ---> TELNET ACK	64
17	LOKI.FOOBAR.COM	THOR.FOOBAR.COM	telnt	Data=s	64
18	THOR.FOOBAR.COM	LOKI.FOOBAR.COM	telnt	Data=s	64
19	LOKI.FOOBAR.COM	THOR.FOOBAR.COM	tcp	Port:1038 ---> TELNET ACK	64
20	LOKI.FOOBAR.COM	THOR.FOOBAR.COM	telnt	Data=.	64
21	THOR.FOOBAR.COM	LOKI.FOOBAR.COM	telnt	Data=.	64
22	LOKI.FOOBAR.COM	THOR.FOOBAR.COM	tcp	Port:1038 ---> TELNET ACK	64
23	THOR.FOOBAR.COM	LOKI.FOOBAR.COM	telnt	Data=install.log.	71
24	LOKI.FOOBAR.COM	THOR.FOOBAR.COM	tcp	Port:1038 ---> TELNET ACK	64
25	THOR.FOOBAR.COM	LOKI.FOOBAR.COM	telnt	Data=[cbrenton@thor /tmp]$	80
26	LOKI.FOOBAR.COM	THOR.FOOBAR.COM	tcp	Port:1038 ---> TELNET ACK	64
27	LOKI.FOOBAR.COM	THOR.FOOBAR.COM	telnt	Data=l	64
28	THOR.FOOBAR.COM	LOKI.FOOBAR.COM	telnt	Data=l	64
29	LOKI.FOOBAR.COM	THOR.FOOBAR.COM	tcp	Port:1039 ---> TELNET ACK	64
30	LOKI.FOOBAR.COM	THOR.FOOBAR.COM	telnt	Data=s	64
31	THOR.FOOBAR.COM	LOKI.FOOBAR.COM	telnt	Data=s	64
32	LOKI.FOOBAR.COM	THOR.FOOBAR.COM	tcp	Port:1039 ---> TELNET ACK	64

IP is not the only protocol to make use of ports. AppleTalk and IPX also use ports, only they are referred to as *sockets*. Unlike IP and AT, which use decimal numbers to identify different ports, IPX uses hexadecimal numbers. The functionality of well known and upper ports are the same as IP with these two protocols. The major difference is that there are not nearly as many different services defined. We will get into this in more detail when we cover each protocol individually.

Upper Layer Communications

Once we get above the session layer our communications become pretty specific to the program in use. The responsibilities of the presentation and application layers are more a function of the type of service requested than they are the underlying protocol in use. Data translation and encryption are considered *portable* features.

Portable means that these features can be applied easily to different services without regard for the underlying protocol. It does not matter if I'm using IP or IPX to transfer my data; the ability to leverage these features will depend on the application in use.

For example, IBM/Lotus Notes has the ability to encrypt mail messages prior to transmission. This activity is performed at the presentation layer of the program. It does not matter if I'm connecting to my mail system via TCP, SPX, or a modem. The encryption functionality is available with all three protocols because the functionality is made available by the program itself. It is not dependent on the underlying protocol.

Summary

This concludes our general discussion of protocols and should help answer some questions about how two systems communicate. We've covered a lot of the terminology used in describing each portion of a transmission; this will come in handy during the next chapter when we cover each protocol in greater detail. Don't worry if you're still a bit fuzzy on how this all fits together. We'll continue to build upon our OSI foundation when we specify the particular nuances of each individual protocol. There will be many more examples of communication sessions, so just stick with it. There is a lot of information here to process.

CHAPTER

6

Protocols

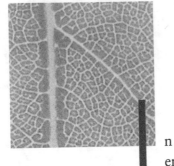

n the last chapter we discussed protocol communications generally. We looked at the methods that can be used for discovering different networks as well as the processes used for accessing different services. It's now time to get specific and look at how each protocol implements these communication properties.

The Internet Protocol Suite (IP)

T he IP protocol suite has become a network administrator's tool kit. When dissimilar systems are used, administrators tend to turn to IP for providing connectivity. IP has its roots in the Unix operating system. It was this NOS that first leveraged the flexibility and diversity of services that IP can offer. This was a perfect match as both were designed to provide a plethora of services.

The IP protocol suite's versatility does not come without a price, however—it requires a higher level of administrator expertise and management in order to ensure it is implemented correctly.

Figure 6.1 outlines where different portions of the IP suite match up to the OSI model. This really is not an exact match as the IP protocol predates the development of this model. As we continue through this chapter we will continue to refer back to the OSI model in order to provide a quick reference to how each of the pieces in our communication puzzle fit together. If you do not recognize all the pieces outlined in the diagram, do not worry; we will cover them later in this chapter.

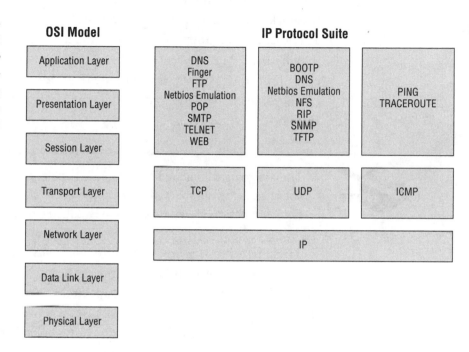

FIGURE 6.1

The portions of the IP protocol suite and how they relate to the functionality outlined on the OSI model

IP Address Conventions

As mentioned, IP logical network segments are referred to as *subnets*. A proper subnet address is made up of four blocks of numbers separated by periods. Each of these number blocks is referred to as a byte. Values for each of these bytes can range from 0-254. When writing a subnet, trailing 0's are used to imply that an entire network segment is being referred to. For example, when I write 192.168.175.0 it is assumed that I am referring to the entire IP subnet whose address is 192.168.175. If I write 10.0.0.0 it is assumed that I am referring to the entire IP subnet whose address is 10.

When writing an IP address for a server or workstation (referred to as an IP host), the 0 field is replaced with a number to uniquely identify that system on the IP subnet. Values for these number can range from 1-254. For example, given the IP subnet 192.168.175.0, the first system on this network may receive the address 192.168.175.1, the next may receive 192.1168.175.2 and so on. In our subnet 10 example, the first IP host may be 10.1.1.1, the next may be 10.1.1.2 and so on. On an IP subnet, every host must be assigned a unique IP address. If not, communications can become crossed and information can be delivered to the wrong system.

The assigning of unique IP addresses is analogous to the assigning of social security numbers. If two people are assigned the same number, tax information would be extremely difficult to straighten out.

These IP addresses are referred to as *unicast* addresses, as they are designed for point-to-point communications. When unicast addresses are used, only a single system is expected to receive and process the data. There are other types of addresses referred to as *broadcasts* and *multicasts* which we will cover later in this chapter.

Standard Subnet Masks

So our IP address contains two parts—one that refers to the network segment and one that refers to the host. We now have a small problem. By simply looking at an IP host address, it can be difficult to determine which part of the address refers to the network and which portion refers to the host. For example, if I say that my IP address is 10.73 .201.5, the combinations shown in Table 6.1 are possible.

This is why a subnet mask is used. A subnet mask listed along with an address allows us to identify which portion of the host address identifies

	Network Portion of the Address	Host Portion of the Address
T A B L E 6.1 Possible combinations for the 10.73.201.5 address	10	73.201.5
	10.73	201.5
	10.73.201	5

the network, and which portion identifies the host. The subnet mask follows the same format as an IP host address consisting of four blocks of numbers separated by periods. In a standard subnet mask (we will talk about non-standard subnetting in a moment) the only values used are 255 and 0. A 255 denotes the network portion of the address while a 0 denotes the host portion. Some systems (such as a NetWare server) require the subnet mask to be entered in a hexadecimal format. In these cases we must convert our decimal value to its hexadecimal equivalent. A decimal 255 directly converts to a hexadecimal value of FF.

NOTE Because decimal value is most prevalent, it will be used for all examples in this book. The reader should be aware, however, that sometimes a hexadecimal value will be required.

Table 6.2 shows each possible subnet mask and the effect it would have on the above host address.

	Decimal Subnet Mask	Hexadecimal Subnet Mask	Network Portion	Host Portion
T A B L E 6.2 Decimal and hexadecimal values for the 10.73.201.5 address	255.0.0.0	FF.0.0.0	10	73.201.5
	255.255.0.0	FF.FF.0.0	10.73	201.5
	255.255.255.0	FF.FF.FF.0	10.73.201	5

Clearly if we are going to identify an IP host properly, we must know both the IP address and subnet mask. It is important that a consistent subnet is used on all IP hosts to ensure that routing conflicts are not encountered. An IP host with an incorrect subnet mask may not be able to determine which other systems occupy the same logical network. Figure 6.2 shows a transmission decision table.

Transmission Decision Table

FIGURE 6.2

In order for a network device to transmit information, it needs to know if the receiving device is on the same logical subnet or not.

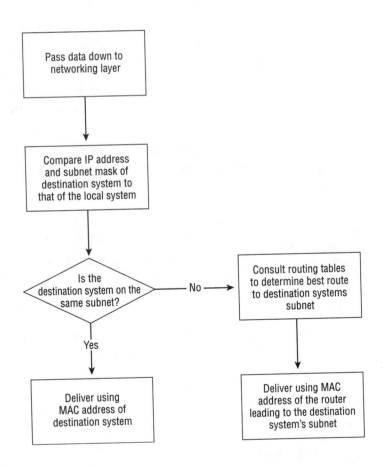

So why is subnetting even used? Because every network has different requirements for the number of hosts that must be supported on any given network. By adjusting the subnet mask, I can increase or decrease the number of hosts supported on any given subnet by using up a portion of the network space. Table 6.3 shows how the maximum numbers of networks and subnet hosts change as the subnet mask is adjusted. The quantities reflect the segmentation of a single address. For example, 10.0.0.0, 11.0.0.0, 12.0.0.0, and so on.

TABLE 6.3

Change in maximum numbers of networks and subnet hosts

Subnet Mask	Maximum Number of Networks	Maximum Number of Hosts
255.0.0.0	1	16,387,064
255.255.0.0	254	64,516
255.255.255.0	64,516	254

If I decide to use the address range of 10.0.0.0 for my IP addresses, I can use the subnet mask to customize the number of available hosts based upon my network requirements. If I have a small number of subnets with a large quantity of hosts on each, I may want to use a subnet mask of 255.255.0.0. This would support 254 subnets (10.1.1.0 – 10.254.0.0) with a maximum of 64,516 hosts on each.

If I'm responsible for a large number of subnets that each have a small number of hosts, I may want to use a subnet mask of 255.255.255.0. This would support 64,516 subnets (10.1.1.0 – 10.254.254.0) with a maximum of 254 hosts on each. The choice is mine to make—however, keep in mind that you should always plan for growth. The chore of changing the subnet mask on 250 or more hosts simply because you ran out of address space is a time consuming one at best.

WARNING Technically, zero is considered a legal value when addressing an IP host. In other words, 10.0.0.113 is considered a valid IP address. It has been my experience, however, that networking devices from many vendors have difficulty dealing with host addresses that contain the character 0. While some systems will interpret 0 to be part of the network address, others will mistake it for a broadcast. I strongly recommend that you do not use 0 in your address ranges.

Registered IP Addresses

While you can select any random IP range to assign to your network, you may want to plan ahead for Internet connectivity and use a set of registered IP addresses. The *Internic* is the authority responsible for assigning and registering IP addresses when an organization wishes to communicate on the Internet. The Internic tracks which organizations are assigned which IP addresses to ensure that there are no conflicts. If two organizations inadvertently try to use the same subnet numbers, routing errors will occur. If you assign random IP addresses to your network and later wish to connect to the Internet, you may find yourself reconfiguring your address range.

Prior to being connected through your Internet service provider, you will be required to fill out a number of forms documenting your current network configuration as well as the amount of network growth expected over the next five years. Based on this information, the Internic will assign one or more IP subnet numbers to your organization.

The Internic has broken up the available IP subnets into different classes—A, B, and C. The class determines the size of your organization's address space. Table 6.4 defines these classes.

	Address Class	Address Range	Assumed Subnet Mask	Available Networks
TABLE 6.4 Class definitions	A	1.0.0.0 - 126.0.0.0	255.0.0.0	64,516
	B	128.0.0.0 - 191.0.0.0	255.255.0.0	254
	C	192.0.0.0 - 223.0.0.0	255.255.255.0	1

For example, let's assume I'm bringing a major telecommunications company onto the Internet for the first time. My company has an extremely large worldwide network. Given the size of my network, the Internic may see fit to assign me a class A address. Let's say they assign me the address 10.0.0.0. This gives me control of the range of values between 10.1.1.0 and 10.254.254.254.

While the subnet mask 255.0.0.0 is assumed, I am actually free to break this range up any way I see fit. A class A subnet mask will only support a single logical subnet. If I have more than one logical subnet I will need to change my subnet mask to accommodate the additional networks. Also, I may not be required to support up to 16,387,064 hosts on a single subnet. (If I do have that many hosts on a single subnet I have much bigger problems than just assigning IP addresses!)

For example, I could choose to use a class B subnet mask of 255.255.0.0 to subnet the range given to me by the Internic. This would support 254 subnets allowing me to use the values 10.1.0.0 – 10.254.0.0 for my subnet range. Each subnet would be capable of supporting 64,516 hosts.

In Figure 6.3 the subnet portion of the address changes whenever a router is crossed. Any given logical subnet is the area confined within our routers.

I could also choose to use a class C subnet mask of 255.255.255.0. This would support up to 64,516 subnets allowing me to use the values 10.1.1.0 – 10.254.254.0 for my subnet range. Each subnet could have a maximum of 254 hosts. Figure 6.4 shows our network renumber for a class C subnet mask.

When a class B subnet is assigned, my choices are similar but somewhat more limited. Let's assume that our telecommunications company is really not quite so large. Perhaps it services only a specific continent or country. In this case, the Internic may assign a class B address instead. For our example, let's say they assign the address 172.25.0.0 to this organization.

Given this class B address we can choose to use a class B subnet mask of 255.255.0.0 which would yield a single logical network with 64,516 hosts. If I need to support more than one logical subnet, I could opt to use a class C subnet mask of 255.255.255.0. This would support 254 networks with 254 hosts on each.

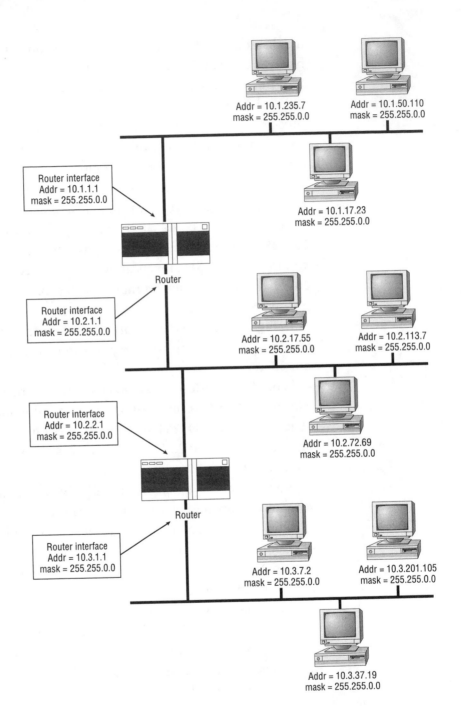

FIGURE 6.3

A small section of what our telecommunications network may look like if a class B address is used

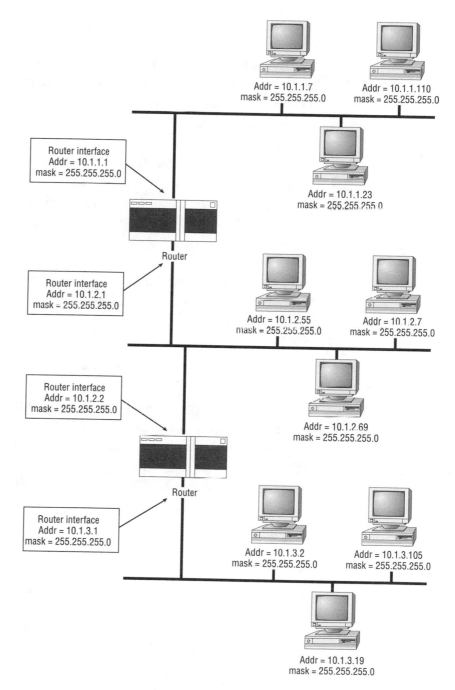

F I G U R E 6.4

Our network renumbered
for a class C subnet mask

Finally, let's assume we are registering a small company with only 75 computers. In this case the Internic may issue a class C address such as 192.168.10.0. With this address I can only support a single network with up to 254 hosts. If this network is actually made up of two logical subnets I may have to request a second address from the Internic. This address may be sequential (as in 192.168.11.0) or could end up being in a completely different address range.

You may note that the class C address range stops at 223.0.0.0 instead of 254.0.0.0. This range of addresses is reserved for a special purpose that we will cover in the next section.

Special addresses

There are some special IP addresses that are not assigned by the Internic for regular use. Each of these addresses are defined here.

127.0.0.1

Referred to as a *loop back address*, 127.0.0.1 is a test address automatically assigned to every IP host regardless of the operating system it is load on. This address is useful when ensuring that the IP protocol stack is loaded and functioning properly. If a system is not communicating with other network systems, I can try to *ping* the address 127.0.0.1. If this is successful, I know that my IP stack is functioning properly and that the problem may be related to my network card or cabling. If the attempt is unsuccessful, I know that my problem is software related and that the protocol stack is at fault.

Broadcast Address

In the above examples we noted that 255 was not a valid IP host address value. This is because the address is reserved for network broadcasts. If I send information to the address 10.1.1.255, I am effectively sending information to every host on the network 10.1.1.0. Broadcasts are useful when a system needs to convey information but is unsure of the destination system's address. For example, when a router sends a RIP packet, it will address it to the broadcast address to ensure that all routers located on the network segment will receive the information.

A simple broadcast is local to the subnet and is not propagated by any routers.

There is a special type of broadcast referred to as an *all network broadcast* that always has the destination address of 255.255.255.255. This type of broadcast is propagated by routers as it is addressed to all networks. The number of routers the information is capable of crossing depends on the routing protocol in use. Each router will increment the hop count by one. When the maximum number of hops is reached, the information is discarded.

If you have a WAN connection to other sites or are connected to the Internet, be very careful when using all network broadcasts. As mentioned previously, a broadcast packet must be analyzed by every network device to determine if it actually needs to process the data. An all network broadcast requires every device on the entire network to allocate processing time to analyze the packet.

Multicast Addresses

There is a fourth address type, not mentioned above, referred to as the class D or multicast address range. This class includes IP addresses in the range of 224.0.0.0 - 254.0.0.0. Multicast is a special type of information delivery that is designed to let one IP host efficiently deliver information to multiple recipients on remote networks. It is based upon configuring the routers on the network with address mapping tables. These tables tell the router which other systems to forward information to, based upon the transmission of a specific host. When a multicast host transmits, routers on the local subnet pick up the transmission and search their mapping tables for a match to its IP address. If a match is found, the router will forward the information to all the destination hosts listed in the table. Let's take a look at an example to see how this works.

Let's say we are designing a network for a large commercial television organization. This organization would like to develop a special service for delivering time sensitive news to all of its affiliates. The organization would like to have the following criteria worked into the design:

- All information should be transmittable from a single system.

- There are well over 3,000 nodes that will require the delivery of the news feeds.

- The delivery should be as quick as possible as the information is timely and is updated frequently.

- A minimal amount of bandwidth should be used because most links are frame relay operating at only 56Kbp/s.

Figure 6.5 shows a small portion of how our network may appear. (This figure represents only a small portion of the network as there are over 3,000 end stations.)

Let's review the two other types of communications to see the effect they would have on this network.

Unicast   Unicast is our regular point-to-point communication. It would require our transmitting host to establish an individual communication session with each recipient host. This immediately causes two problems. The first is traffic. If our transmitting host is required to set up a communication session with 3,000 receiving hosts (including transmissions and acknowledgments), the amount of traffic generated would quickly saturate the network. The second problem is time. It will take our transmitting host a certain amount of time to run through all 3,000 hosts when delivering information. If there are frequent news updates, it is possible that the delivery time may make it difficult for the transmitting host to keep up.

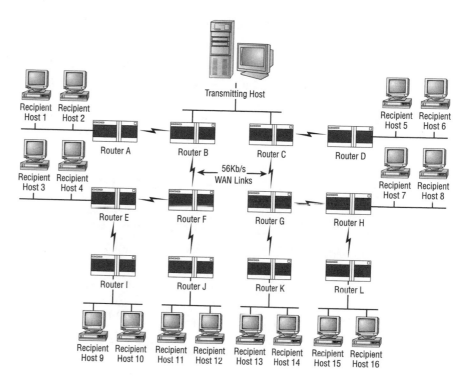

FIGURE 6.5

Our commercial television
station's wide area
network

Broadcast Broadcasts are delivered either to all hosts located on the same local subnet, or to all hosts on the entire network. Again, we have two problems. The first is performance. Given our network design we would need to use all network broadcasts. This would produce dismal network performance because the network would be saturated with broadcasts. The second problem is security. Because our broadcasts will be propagated to all networks indiscriminately, there is the potential that our news information could find itself on networks where it does not belong.

Given the above descriptions, multicasting would be our most efficient means of transmitting our news feeds along this network. Let's apply some multicast tables to our routers to see how this would work.

According to Table 6.5, when Router B receives a packet from the address 224.10.10.5, it knows to forward the information to Routers A and F. When Router A receives the packet, it looks up the source address in its table which tells it to forward the information to hosts one and two. This type of propagation continues down through the network until all the hosts have received the information.

Router	Source Address	Forward To
A	224.10.10.5	Hosts 1 & 2
B	224.10.10.5	Routers A & F
C	224.10.10.5	Routers D & G
D	224.10.10.5	Hosts 5 & 6
E	224.10.10.5	Hosts 3 & 4
F	224.10.10.5	Routers E & J
G	224.10.10.5	Routers H & K
H	224.10.10.5	Hosts 7 & 8
I	224.10.10.5	Hosts 9 & 10
J	224.10.10.5	Hosts 11 & 12
K	224.10.10.5	Hosts 13 & 14
L	224.10.10.5	Hosts 15 & 16

T A B L E 6.5

A Network routing table

There are a couple of points worth noting with this type of communication. First, our single source host is able to communicate efficiently with a large number of recipients. It is only required to transmit the data once, the tables on the routers take care of propagating the information as required. This spreads out the overhead required to communicate with each of our 3,000 recipient systems.

A second benefit to this type of communication is that we are creating very little traffic along our WAN links. For example Router B is only required to generate a single communication session along each of its 56 Kb connections. If a retransmission is required, the request can go back to the previous router in the chain. The request is not required to return all the way back to the source system. Again, this cuts down on the amount of traffic along our slow links.

Because of the one-shot data transmission and light network traffic, we can deliver information in a timely manner. No single network device is required to communicate with all systems on the network. This overhead is spread out over multiple routers and network connections. This means that our source system is immediately free to transmit new information as required.

There are some drawbacks to this type of communication, however, that make it applicable in only specific situations. First, in order for multicasting to work properly our routers must be preconfigured so they know what information needs to be forwarded where. If the destination is dynamic or random it will be nearly impossible to keep up with the table changes.

Finally, multicast communication is in a single direction only. The destination systems are not able to relay information back up to the source system. This means that software such as Web browsers or FTP clients will not work.

Reserved Address Range

There are certain IP addresses that the Internic has reserved for general use; their use does not need Internic approval. While these addresses may be used freely by any organization, they are not allowed to be used for Internet communications. They will never be assigned to an organization by the Internic, and therefore, may be used by anyone for internal use only. Table 6.6 shows which IP address ranges are considered reserved.

	Starting Address	Ending Address
TABLE 6.6 Reserved IPS address ranges	10.0.0.0	10.254.254.0
	172.16.0.0	172.31.254.0
	192.168.0.0	192.168.254.0

The use of reserved addresses has come about as a result of the depletion of registered addresses. As more and more organizations connect to the Internet, the pool of *legal* IP addresses available for Internet connectivity has shrunk dramatically. Reserved addresses are available for use when an IP subnet does not need Internet connectivity or when a translational gateway will be used.

A translational gateway is a network device capable of changing packets from one IP address to another. For example, a large network that requires a class A address could use the reserved address range of 10.0.0.0 when assigning IP addresses to internal hosts. When Internet access is required, a translational gateway could then intercept these communications and map these addresses to a legal class C subnet address. If multiple class A addresses are mapped to a single class C host address, port number are used by the gateway to keep the communication sessions orderly. This allows a large number of hosts to be easily supported by a small legal address range. Because the gateway must sit between the internal network and the Internet, its functionality has been incorporated into many of the top firewalling products.

Nonstandard Subnetting

All of our IP examples up until now have used standard subnet masks. By standard, we mean that the mask has had two possible values, 0 or 255. While this is fine in most situations, sometimes a little more control over our address range is required.

For example, let's say that you administer a very busy 80-node network and as part of traffic control you have created two separate subnets with a router in between. Let's also assume that your organization has decided to connect to the Internet but does not want to use address translation because of performance concerns. You want every internal host to receive a valid IP address. You find an Internet service provider (ISP), and file all the required paperwork with the Internic in order to get connected. Our example network is shown in Figure 6.6. Due to traffic concerns, the network is split into two separate subnets with a single router. The IP address information reflects what was in place prior to connecting to the Internet.

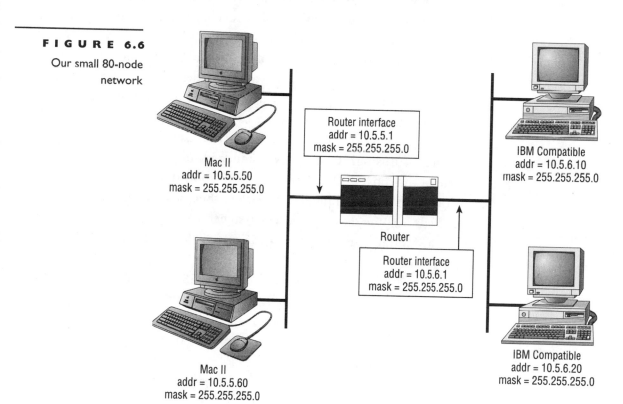

FIGURE 6.6

Our small 80-node network

Router interface
addr = 10.5.5.1
mask = 255.255.255.0

Mac II
addr = 10.5.5.50
mask = 255.255.255.0

IBM Compatible
addr = 10.5.6.10
mask = 255.255.255.0

Router

Router interface
addr = 10.5.6.1
mask = 255.255.255.0

Mac II
addr = 10.5.5.60
mask = 255.255.255.0

IBM Compatible
addr = 10.5.6.20
mask = 255.255.255.0

You find, however, that because your network is considered quite small, your ISP is only willing to give you one valid class C address. This leaves you with four options:

- Find another ISP that will give you two valid addresses.

- Only allow one of your subnets to have Internet access.

- Combine your two logical subnets into one and live with the performance degradation.

- Apply a nonstandard subnet mask.

A nonstandard subnet mask lets you take a single network address and break it up into multiple subnets. This is done by using some other value for the mask's bytes besides 0 or 255. A value of 255 designates that the corresponding section of the IP address should be considered part of the network address. A value of 0 denotes that the number is unique to one specific host. By using some value in between 0 and 255 for the final byte in the mask, we can set a portion of it aside as being part of the network address and a portion as belonging to the host. Sound confusing? It can be. Nonstandard subnetting is considered to be one of the most difficult theories to grasp in IP networking. Let's continue with our example to help clarify the above statements.

Let's assume that the address assigned to us is `192.168.50.0`. If we use a standard subnet mask of `255.255.255.0`, we can configure a single subnet with 254 hosts.

If we change our subnet mask to `255.255.255.128`, we have effectively split our network in half. Each of our two new networks can use roughly half the host addresses available between 1 and 254. Table 6.7 shows our new configuration. Figure 6.7 shows this configuration applied to our network.

A couple of changes are worth noting here. Because of our nonstandard subnet mask, 127 is now considered to be the broadcast address for our first subnet. Also, 128 is now considered a valid

	Network	Subnet Mask	First Host Address	Last Host Address	Broadcast Address
TABLE 6.7 The network split in half	192.168.50.0	255.255.255.128	192.168.50.1	192.168.50.126	192.168.50.127
	192.168.50.128	255.255.255.128	192.168.50.129	192.168.50.254	192.168.50.255

FIGURE 6.7

Our network example with a nonstandard subnet mask applied

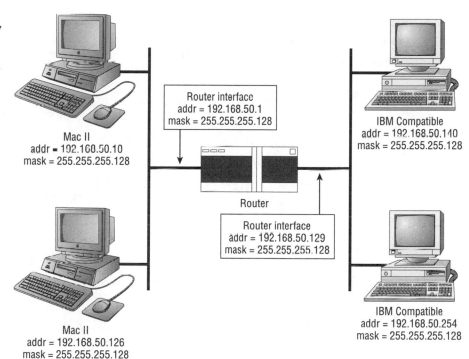

Router interface
addr = 192.168.50.1
mask = 255.255.255.128

Router interface
addr = 192.168.50.129
mask = 255.255.255.128

Router

Mac II
addr = 192.168.50.10
mask = 255.255.255.128

Mac II
addr = 192.168.50.126
mask = 255.255.255.128

IBM Compatible
addr = 192.168.50.140
mask = 255.255.255.128

IBM Compatible
addr = 192.168.50.254
mask = 255.255.255.128

network address number just like 0. This reinforces our earlier comment that an IP address is really meaningless unless you know the subnet mask as well. With a standard subnet, 127 and 128 would signify specific hosts. Here they indicate a broadcast address and our entire second network respectively.

Table 6.8 depicts some potential nonstandard subnet masks as well as their effect on an IP address range. Masks that create more than four subnets have been abbreviated in the interest of saving space. Only the first three subnets and the last are defined here. Given this information, it should be a simple matter for the reader to calculate the values for the subnets not listed. All address values are for the final byte in an IP address because this is the only value which changes.

T A B L E 6.8

Some potential nonstandard subnet masks

Mask	# of Subnets	Hosts per Subnet	Available Host Address Ranges	Network Address Value	Broadcast Address Value
255.255.255.0	1	254	1 - 254	0	255
255.255.255.128	2	126	1 - 126	0	127
			129 - 254	128	255
255.255.255.192	4	62	1 - 62	0	63
			65 - 126	64	127
			129 - 190	128	191
			193 - 254	192	255
255.255.255.224	8	30	1 - 30	0	31
			33 - 62	32	63
			65 - 94	64	95
			225 - 254	224	255
255.255.255.240	16	14	1-14	0	15
			17 - 30	16	31
			33 - 46	32	47
			241 - 254	240	255
255.255.255.248	32	6	1-6	0	7
			9 - 14	8	15
			17 - 22	16	23
			249 - 254	248	255

	Mask	# of Subnets	Hosts per Subnet	Available Host Address Ranges	Network Address Value	Broadcast Address Value
TABLE 6.8 (cont.) Some potential nonstandard subnet masks	255.255.255.252	64	2	1 - 2	0	3
				5 - 6	4	7
				9 - 10	8	11
				253 - 254	252	255
	255.255.255.254	128	0	0	0	0

Our first table entry is our standard class C subnet mask. This creates only one logical subnet. Our final nonstandard mask, 255.255.255.254, creates 128 subnets but none are able to support any hosts. This means our largest useful subnet mask is 255.255.255.252. Because only two hosts are supported, this mask is typically used on WAN links where the only devices that are on the segment are the routers at both ends of the link.

It is also possible to mix and match different subnet masks within the same IP address range. For example, let's say that I have a single subnet with approximately 100 hosts and four other subnets with 20 hosts on each. This gives me a total of five subnets to address. Our closest match in the above table is 255.255.255.224 which will yield eight subnets. The problem is that this mask is only capable of supporting 30 hosts per subnet.

The answer is to use a 255.255.255.128 subnet for half my address range, and 255.255.255.224 for the other half. This will allow me to break up my range into a total of five subnets. The mask of 255.255.255.128 could be used to reserve the first half of our available host addresses for the 100 host segment. The remaining half of our address range could be broken up using a mask of 255.255.255.224 to create four additional segments supporting 30 hosts each.

Table 6.9 shows how the address range would be broken down using these masks. Let's assume that the class C address I'm subnetting is 192.168.200.0.

	Mask	# of Subnets	Hosts per Subnet	Available Host Address Ranges	Network Address Value
TABLE 6.9 Address Range Breakdown	255.255.255.128	192.168.200.0	192.168.200.1	192.168.200.126	192.168.200.127
	255.255.255.224	192.168.200.128	192.168.200.129	192.168.200.158	192.168.200.159
	255.255.255.224	192.168.200.160	192.168.200.161	192.168.200.190	192.168.200.191
	255.255.255.224	192.168.200.192	192.168.200.193	192.168.200.222	192.168.200.223
	255.255.255.224	192.168.200.224	192.168.200.225	192.168.200.254	192.168.200.255

Figure 6.8 shows this address scheme applied to a network. By mixing our subnet masks we can achieve the most efficient use of a single address range.

Lost Address Space

As the last table shows, each time we further subnet our address the number of supportable hosts decreases. For example, while a class C subnet will support 254 hosts, a nonstandard subnet mask of 255.255.255.248 will only support 192 (32 subnets of 6 hosts each). This is because each time we further divide our address, we lose two potential host numbers—one to identify the network address, and one to identify the broadcast address.

Also, the request for comments (RFCs), which define how the IP protocol will operate, require that the first and last subnet created by a nonstandard subnet mask be ignored. Therefore, while a mask of 255.255.255.248 will create 32 subnets, only 30 of them are really legal. This drops the number of supported hosts to 180 (30 legal subnets with 6 hosts each).

F I G U R E 6.8

A mixture of subnet masks being used to support multiple subnets with a varying number of hosts.

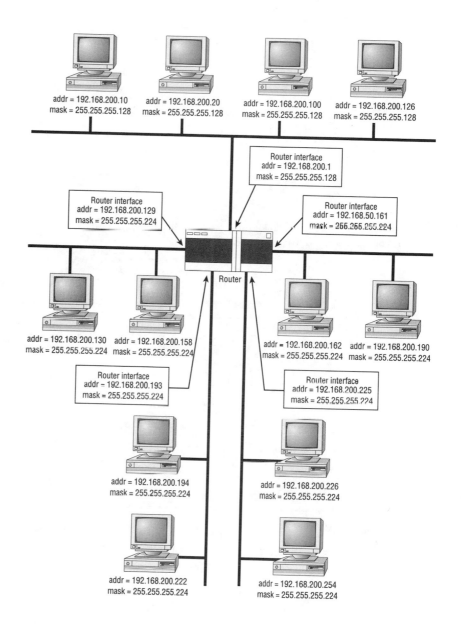

With this in mind, our network in Figure 6.7 would actually be considered illegal. In order to bring it into full compliance we would need to use a mask of 255.255.255.192, which will create four subnets. This will allow us to ignore the first and last subnets while still having two subnets available for our network. Our revised network appears in Figure 6.9.

FIGURE 6.9

Due to the requirement that the first and last subnet range created by a nonstandard subnet mask must be ignored, we must further divide our network address.

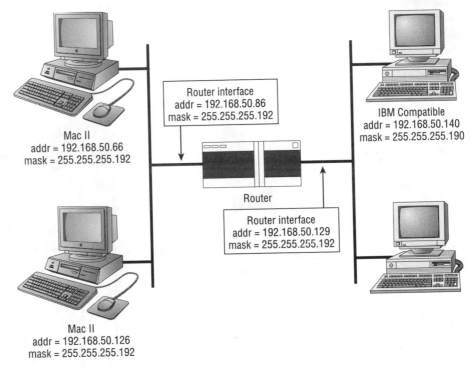

Router interface
addr = 192.168.50.86
mask = 255.255.255.192

IBM Compatible
addr = 192.168.50.140
mask = 255.255.255.190

Mac II
addr = 192.168.50.66
mask = 255.255.255.192

Router

Router interface
addr = 192.168.50.129
mask = 255.255.255.192

Mac II
addr = 192.168.50.126
mask = 255.255.255.192

Figure 6.8 would be considered illegal as well, because we are using the entire address range—we do not have the luxury of ignoring the first and last subnet.

In an age where IP addresses are at a premium, many have questioned the practice of ignoring the first and last subnet range created by a nonstandard mask. The activity started when nonstandard subnetting was just starting to be used. Many network devices would assume that a last byte value of 0 or 255 would apply to all local hosts. This would occur in part because the subnet mask was not being referenced properly. In fact some vendors would specifically configure their IP stack to not accept outer range values. NetWare 3.1*x* is a good example.

Today, these limitations are rarely experienced. Most (if not all) modern network operating systems will accept and communicate within these outer address ranges. While doing so means that your network does not fully meet RFC specifications, it does have the benefit of providing additional address space.

WARNING   Using the first and last subnet ranges should only be a last resort. While all of your internal systems may be up to date and quite happy communicating with these subnets, sooner or later you will run across an old system (on the Internet perhaps) that considers these addresses invalid and will not communicate with them.

Address Discovery

IP uses the Address Resolution Protocol (ARP) when it needs to perform the delivery of data. All local delivery is performed using the destination system's media access control (MAC) number. ARP is used by a transmitting system to map the destination system's IP address to its MAC address.

For example, let's say you are using your favorite Web browser, and enter the URL:

```
http://www.sun.com
```

Your system will first use Domain Name Services (DNS) (see the description of DNS later in this section) to map the host www.sun.com to an IP address. Your system would then compare this IP address to its own to see if the system is located on the same subnet or not. At this point one of two things will happen:

- If the system is local, your computer will ARP (send an Address Resolution Protocol frame) for the destination system's MAC address.

- If the system is on another subnet, your computer will ARP for the MAC address of the local router.

ARP is simply a local broadcast frame that states, "If you are using this IP address, please reply." The frame contains the IP address for which it needs to find a MAC address. The Ethernet portion of the frame header will contain your system's MAC address in the source field and a broadcast address of FFFFFFFFFFFF in the destination field.

When the system using the IP address replies, saying, "I'm here," the frame it sends you will contain the system's MAC address in the Ethernet source field. Now your system can associate the IP address with a MAC address and perform a local delivery. Your system will also cache this information in its *ARP table*. This way if you need to send this system more information, your system already knows the local address.

ARP can also be used to avoid IP address conflicts. Most modern network operating systems now ARP during startup to ensure that there are no address conflicts with other systems. Before assuming it can use a specific IP address, the machine will ARP for the address on the local subnet. If it does not receive a reply, it assumes the address is free to use. If it does receive a reply, it will display an error message and disable IP networking. This process helps to ensure that no two machines try to share the same IP address.

Routing with IP

IP supports both static and dynamic routing between subnets. These may be used exclusively, or in combination on any given network. When dynamic routing is used, both distance vector and link state options are available. We covered the differences between these routing methods in Chapter 5. Let's now take a look at how each method is implemented when communicating with IP.

Static Routing

Static routing is when the path from one subnet to another is programmed into a networking device. This is done by defining the router that a data stream must pass through when traveling to a remote subnet. The entry may be manually entered by an administrator or the device may be configured to reset the static path during startup. With the exception of NetWare, this is normally performed with the **route** command. While the **route** command varies slightly from platform to platform, the common syntax is as follows:

```
route switch subnet mask subnet mask router
```

Valid switches are **add, delete, change** and **print**. Here is an example:

```
route add 10.3.3.0 mask 255.255.255.0 10.2.50.5
```

The above command line would add an entry to a systems routing table that states "when communicating with any system on the subnet 10.3.3.0, forward all packets through the router located at 10.2.50.5." The command assumes that the router located at 10.2.50.5 is on the local subnet and will know how to reach the network 10.3.3.0. While the **mask** switch is optional, the **route** command will assign a subnet mask based on the class of the IP subnet address if the mask switch is not used. In the above example **route** would have assigned a class A mask of 255.0.0.0 (because 10.3.3.0 falls between 1.0.0.0 and 126.0.0.0), which would be incorrect. Figure 6.10 shows the above example applied to a workstation. In the figure, our first entry is a default route—any subnet that does not have a route entry will be reached through the router at this address. The entry we added appears four lines down. The "interface" column lists the IP address that the workstation is using.

When **route** is used with the **delete** switch, an existing entry may be removed from the local routing table. The following would delete the routing entry created with the above **add** command:

```
route delete 10.3.3.0 mask 255.255.255.0 10.2.50.5
```

The switch **change** is used to modify the routing table entry so that a different router is used. For example:

route change 10.3.3.0 mask 255.255.255.0 10.2.50.10

would change the border router used when communicating with system on the subnet 10.3.3.0 from 10.2.50.5 to 10.2.50.10.

Finally, the print switch displays all matching router entries. For example:

route print 10.3.3.0

will produce a list of routers used when communicating with that subnet. Given our above example, the only entry would be 10.2.50.5.

The **route** command also allows for the definition of what is referred to as a *default route*. A default route tells a system to forward all traffic bound for any remote subnet to a specific router. Depending on the operating system, the command would appear similar to one of the following:

route add 0.0.0.0 10.2.50.1
route add default 10.2.50.1

The **route** command and its switches, as with other IP tools, are platform specific commands. They are not considered to be an IP protocol command per se. There is nothing in the IP protocol suite that defines the command **route**, only how static routing should be implemented.

The developers of the NOS can choose to ignore the command or give it a different name.

For example, NetWare does not use the command **route,** but rather uses additional switches with the **bind** command to provide the same functionality. Another example would be Microsoft's **tracert** command which provides the same functionality as Unix's **traceroute** command, but the name was shortened to meet DOS's *eight.three* file naming criteria.

Usually, however, the command names for IP tools used on Unix are adopted on other NOSes to maintain consistency. For example, the command **ping** was first used on Unix. A command with the same name has been developed for nearly every platform that supports IP which uses the same name (**ping**) and provides nearly the same functionality.

Static routing is the most common configuration used for workstation configurations. It frees up the local system from having to maintain dynamic tables and relies on the network routers to keep track of the best routes. Static routing generates the least amount of traffic for it does not require that routing updates be propagated throughout the network. It also requires the greatest amount of administration, because each system must be configured manually with its own routing table.

Static routing is supported by all network operating systems that support IP.

Dynamic Routing

Dynamic routing allows a network to learn which subnets are available and how to reach them. This is particularly useful when more than one path is available between subnets. The ability of a network to deal with routing changes is highly dependent on the routing protocol in use.

Routing Information Protocol (RIP)   RIP was first developed in 1980 by Xerox for use with their Xerox Network System (XNS) protocol. It saw its first use with IP in 1982 when it was adapted and shipped with BSD Unix. After 1982, different Unix vendors began shipping slightly different versions of RIP which caused incompatibility problems. This was all tied together in 1988 with the release of RFC

1058 which defined a common structure for RIP. While RIP is the oldest IP routing protocol, it is still widely used today.

RIP is a distance vector protocol which gives it a slow convergence time and makes it prone to routing errors. It can route information for no more than 16 hops and bases its routing decisions strictly on hop count. It cannot intelligently load balance traffic by using such variables as link speed and traffic load.

RIP is also one of the easiest routing protocols to use and configure. Simply enable RIP and the protocol will propagate route information through the use of RIP broadcasts. While it is a somewhat noisy protocol, sending routing updates every 60 seconds, this amount of traffic is usually negligible on a small network.

RIP is best suited for small networks (10-15 subnets or less) or in networking environments where redundant routes are not used. In larger environments RIP can cause broadcast storms as each router attempts to propagate its table information throughout the network. When redundant routes are available, RIP cannot make use of the multiple paths for load balancing. Secondary routes are only used when the primary route fails. In each of these situations it is better to use one of the link state protocols described below.

RIP is supported by all flavors of Unix and NetWare 3.1*x* and 4.*x*. Windows NT has added support for RIP as of version 4.0.

Exterior Gateway Protocol (EGP)   EGP is another distance vector protocol that was developed in the mid-1980's as the Internet began to grow beyond the bounds of what could be easily supported by RIP. EGP introduced the concept of *autonomous systems* (AS) as a way to reduce the amount of routing information propagated between networks.

An AS is a collection of subnets which are all administrated by the same group or organization. Typically this would be an entire domain but can be divided even further for larger networks. By "domains" we are referring to the domain names issued by the Internic, not a Microsoft NT domain.

EGP reduces the amount of information propagated by advertising *reachability* information only. Instead of advertising hop information, an EGP router will simply list all the networks it is responsible for within its autonomous system. In Figure 6.11 we see three AS groups connected by a backbone. Each EGP router transmits reachability information only along the backbone. This tells the other EGP routers, "If you need to send information to one of these subnets, forward the frame to me, and I'll take care of delivery." This reduces the amount of information that must be propagated along the backbone. Because a single router is responsible for delivery to any given subnet, hop counts do not need to be calculated during a failure. Either the subnet is reachable or it is not. This limitation on the information being sent helps to eliminate convergence problems along the backbone.

Inside each AS another routing protocol such as RIP can be used to ensure delivery and provide secondary routing paths as required. EGP simply eliminates the need to send this RIP information along the backbone.

The biggest drawback of EGP is that it relies on a hierarchical design with all traffic passing through a single point. Not only does this create a single point of failure but it eliminates the ability to perform load balancing through alternate links. EGP routers also need to be configured to reflect which subnets they are responsible for.

NOTE   While EGP was extremely useful in its prime, the explosive growth of the Internet has dated it. Use of EGP has been on the decline due to some of the more advanced link state protocols that are now available.

EGP is typically supported only by hardware routing devices. Because EGP is an external routing protocol, most vendors have not seen a need to include it with their NOSes.

Open Shortest Path First (OSPF)   OSPF was the first protocol to integrate both internal and external autonomous system updates into a

FIGURE 6.11

EGP used to propagate
information between
autonomous systems

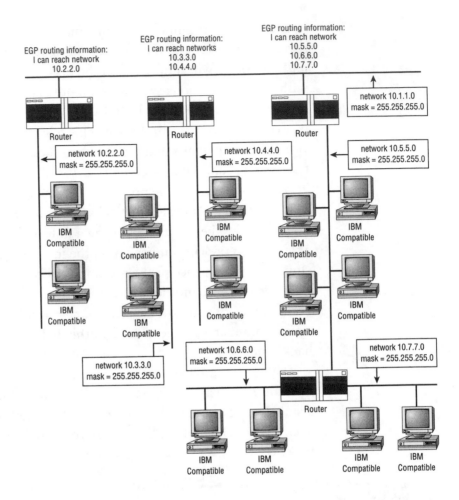

single IP routing protocol. Like EGP, it can be configured to exchange
only reachability information along a network backbone. Unlike EGP,
however, it can also be configured to provide full routing table information within each autonomous system. This eliminates the need to run two
separate routing protocols, one for inside the AS and one for outside.

OSPF also brings authentication to the table, requiring routers to
supply a password in order to participate in routing updates. This helps
to ensure that a rogue system cannot propagate information that can
either corrupt the current routing table or breach network security.

As a link state protocol, internal AS routing decisions are based upon such metrics as link speed and traffic load. It is not limited to using only hop count information when selecting the best route. Its ability to support load balancing as well as a hierarchical network structure has lead to OSPF's wide acceptance.

OSPF is supported by NetWare 4.1 and many flavors of Unix. Windows NT has not yet added support to OSPF or any other link state routing protocol.

Border Gateway Protocol (BGP)   BGP is designed to be used both inside and between autonomous systems. The brainchild of Cisco Systems, BGP is the routing protocol which glues most of the Internet's backbone together. BGP comes in two flavors, Internal Border Gateway Protocol (IBGP) and External Border Gateway Protocol (EBGP). IBGP is used when two routers that are part of the same autonomous system need to exchange information. EBGP is used between routers of different autonomous systems.

On a BGP network, each autonomous system is assigned a unique group number. Each router must be configured with a table defining its neighbors' IP addresses and autonomous system group numbers. A router will assume that any neighbor that has the same group number is part of the same autonomous system and thus responsible for the same group of subnets. This allows for the use of multiple paths and provides a greater degree of flexibility over EGP or OSPF in backbone areas. Neighboring routers communicate using unicast TCP connections instead of simply broadcasting table information.

As a link state protocol, BGP can leverage these multiple paths by providing load balancing based on link speed, Internetwork delay, and available bandwidth. This allows for the most efficient use of network resources when multiple paths are available along a backbone connection.

There are no network operating systems which support BGP at the time of this writing. Like EGP, it has been implemented on hardware routing devices only.

Transport Layer Services

IP's transport layer services were described in great detail in Chapter 5, so I will add only a simple review here.

Transmission Control Protocol (TCP)

TCP is IP's connection-oriented transport. It is used when an application wants the transport layer to ensure that all packets have been received by the destination system correctly. In a TCP transmission, the receiving system is required to acknowledge every packet it receives.

User Datagram Protocol (UDP)

UDP is IP's connectionless oriented transport. UDP is used when an application is capable of ensuring that all packets have been received by the destination system. If a packet is missed, it is the application, not UDP, which is responsible for first realizing that a packet was missed and then retransmitting the data. Due to its reduced overhead, UDP has the potential to transmit more information with fewer packets than TCP.

IP Application Services

There is a large number of application services that are designed to use IP as a transport. Some are designed to aid the end user in transferring information while others have been created to support the functionality of IP itself. A description of some of the most common services are listed below. Included is the transport used for data delivery and the well known port number assigned to the service.

Boot Protocol (bootp) and Dynamic Host Configuration Protocol (DHCP)

There are three methods of assigning IP addresses to host systems. They are:

Manual—Manually configure an IP host to use a specific address.

Automatic—Have a server automatically assign a specific address to a host during startup.

Dynamic—Have a server dynamically assign free addresses from a pool to hosts during startup.

Manual is the most time consuming but the most fault tolerant. It requires that each IP host be configured with all the information the system requires to communicate using IP. Manual is the most appropriate method to use for systems that need to maintain the same IP address or systems that need to be accessible even when the IP address server may be down. Web servers, mail servers, and any other servers which are providing IP services are usually manually configured for IP communications.

Bootp supports automatic address assignment. A table is maintained on the bootp server which lists each host's MAC number. Each entry also contains the IP address to be used by the system. When the bootp server receives a request for an IP address, it references its table and looks for the sending systems MAC number. It then returns the appropriate IP address for that system. While this makes management a little simpler because all administration can be performed from a central system, the process is still time consuming because each MAC address must be recorded. It also does nothing to free up IP address space that may not be in use.

DHCP supports both automatic and dynamic IP address assignments. When addresses are dynamically assigned, IP addresses are issued by the server to host systems from a pool of available numbers. The benefit of a dynamic assignment over an automatic is that only the hosts that require an IP address have one assigned. Once complete, the IP addresses can be returned to the pool to be issued to another host. The amount of time a host retains a specific IP address is referred to as the *lease period*. A short lease period ensures that only systems that require an IP address have one assigned. When IP is only occasionally used, a small pool of addresses can be used to support a large number of hosts.

The other benefit of DHCP is that the server can send more than just address information. The remote host can also be configured with its host name, default router, domain name, local DNS server, etc. This allows an administrator to remotely configure IP services to a large number of hosts with a minimal amount of work. A single DHCP server is capable of servicing multiple subnets.

The only drawbacks with DHCP are increased broadcast traffic (clients send an all networks broadcast when they need an address) and address space stability if the DHCP server is shut down. On many systems the tables that track who has been assigned which addresses are saved in memory only. When the system goes down this table is lost. When the system is restarted it's possible that IP addresses may be assigned to systems that were already leased to another system prior to the shutdown. If this occurs you may need to renew the lease on all systems or wait until the lease time expires.

Both bootp and DHCP use UDP as their communication transport. Clients transmit address requests from a source port of 68 to a destination port of 67.

Domain Name Services (DNS)

DNS is responsible for mapping host names to IP addresses and vice versa. It is the service which allows you to connect to Novell's Web server by entering www.novell.com instead of having to remember the system's IP address. All IP routing is done with addresses, not names. While IP systems do not use names when transferring information, names are easier for people to remember. It is for this reason that DNS was developed to make reaching remote systems that much easier. DNS allows a person to enter an easy-to-remember name while allowing the computer to translate this into the address information it needs to route the requested data.

DNS follows a hierarchical, distributed structure. No single DNS server is responsible for keeping track of every host name on the Internet. Each system is responsible for only a portion of the framework.

Figure 6.12 is an example of how DNS is structured. Visually it resembles a number of trees strapped to a pole and hanging upside down. The *pole* is not meant to represent the backbone of the Internet, it simply indicates that there is DNS connectivity between the different domains. The systems located just below the pole are referred to as the *root name servers*. Each root name server is responsible for one or more top level domains. The top level domains are the `.com`, `.edu`, `.org`, `.mil`, or `.gov` found at the end of a domain name. Every domain that ends in `.com` is said to be part of the same top level domain.

FIGURE 6.12

A visual representation of the hierarchical structure of DNS

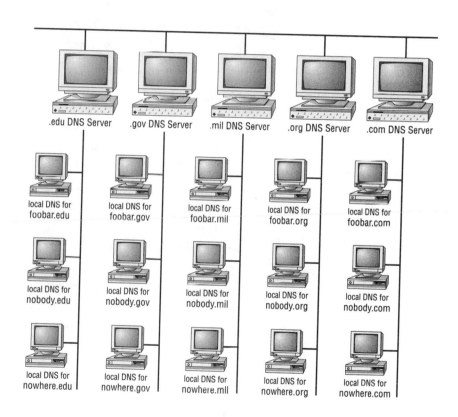

The root name servers are responsible for keeping track of the DNS servers for each subdomain within a top level domain. They do not know about individual systems within each subdomain, only the DNS servers that are responsible for them.

Each subdomain DNS server is responsible for tracking the IP addresses for all the hosts within its domain.

Let's walk through an example to see how it works. Assume you're part of the `foobar.com` domain. Also assume that you're running a Web browser and have entered the following URL:

`http://www.sun.com`

Your system will first check its DNS cache (if it has one) to see if it knows the IP address for `www.sun.com`. If it does not, it forms a DNS query (a DNS query is simply a request for IP information) and asks one of the DNS servers within the `foobar.com` domain for the address. Let's assume the system it queries is `ns.foobar.com`.

If `ns.foobar.com` does not have this information cached, it also forms a DNS query and forwards the request to the root name server responsible for the top level domain `.com` because this is where the Sun domain is located.

The root name server will consult its tables and form a reply similar to the following: "I do not know the IP address for `www.sun.com`. I do, however, know that `ns.sun.com` is responsible for all the hosts within the `sun.com` domain. Its IP address is `10.5.5.1`. Please forward your query to that system."

`ns.foobar.com` now knows that if it needs to find a system with the `sun.com` domain, it needs to ask `ns.sun.com`. It caches this information and forwards the request to `ns.sun.com`.

`ns.sun.com` will then in turn consult its tables and look up the IP address for `www.sun.com`. It would then forward this information to `ns.foobar.com`. `ns.foobar.com` will then cache this information and forward the answer to your system. Your system would now use this IP address information to reach the remote Web server.

If it appears that there is a whole lot of querying going on, then you have a good understanding of the process. The additional traffic is highly preferable, however, to the amount of overhead that would be required to allow a single system to maintain the DNS information for every system on the Internet.

As you may have noticed, DNS makes effective use of caching information during queries. This helps to reduce traffic when looking up popular sites. For example if someone else within foobar.com now attempts to reach `www.sun.com`, the IP address for this system has been cached by `ns.foobar.com`. `ns.foobar.com` is now able to answer this query directly.

The amount of time that `ns.foobar.com` remembers this information is determined by the time to live (TTL) set for this address. The TTL is set by the administrator responsible for managing the remote name server (in this case ns.sun.com). If `www.sun.com` is a stable system, this value may be set at a high value such as 30 days. If it is expected that the IP address for `www.sun.com` is likely to change frequently, the TTL may be set to a lower value such as a few hours.

Let's look at an example to see why this is important. Let's say the mail relay for `foobar.com` is run from the system `mail.foobar.com`. Assume that a high TTL value of 30 days has been set in order to reduce the number of DNS queries entering the network from the Internet. Also assume that our network has changed ISPs and we have been assigned a new set of IP numbers to use when communicating with the Internet.

The network is readdressed, and the changeover takes place. Immediately users begin to receive phone calls from people saying that mail sent to their address is being returned with a delivery failure notice. The failure is intermittent—some mail gets through while other messages fail.

What went wrong? Since the TTL value has been set for 30 days, remote DNS servers will remember the old IP address until the TTL expires. If someone sent mail to the `foobar.com` domain the day before the changeover, it may be 30 days before their DNS server creates another query and realizes that the IP address has changed! Unfortunately the domains most likely affected by this change are the ones you exchange mail with the most. There are two ways to resolve this failure:

1. Ignore it and hide under your desk. Once the TTL expires mail delivery will return to normal.

2. Contact the DNS administrator for each domain you exchange mail with and ask them to reset their DNS cache. This will force the remote system to again look up the address the next time a mail message must be sent. This option is not only embarrassing but may be impossible when dealing with large domains such as AOL or CompuServe.

Avoiding this type of failure takes some fundamental planning. Simply turn down the TTL value to an extremely short period of time (like one hour) at least 30 days prior to the changeover. This forces remote systems to cache the information for only a brief amount of time. Once the changeover is complete, the TTL can be adjusted back up to 30 days to help reduce traffic. 30 days is a good TTL value for systems that are not expected to change their host name or address.

DNS uses TCP and UDP transports when communicating. Both use a destination port of 53.

File Transfer Protocol (FTP)

FTP is used to transfer file information from one system to another. FTP uses TCP as its transport and utilizes ports 20 and 21 for communication. Port 21 is used to transfer session information (username, password, commands) while port 20 is referred to as the *data port* and is used to transfer the actual file.

Figure 6.13 shows an FTP command session between two systems (Loki is connecting to Thor). Note the three-packet TCP exchange which was described in Chapter 5 at the beginning of the session. All communications are using port 21 which is simply referred to as the FTP port. Port 1038 is the random upper port used by Loki when receiving replies.

FIGURE 6.13

An FTP command session
between two systems

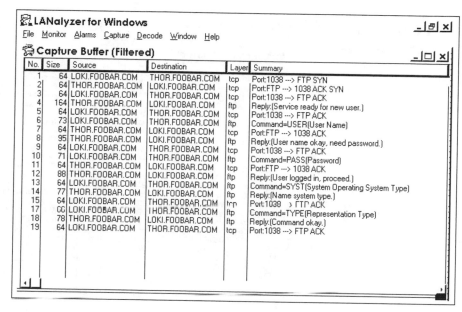

Figure 6.14 shows a capture of Loki initiating a file transfer from Thor. Lines 7, 8, and 9 show the TCP three-packet handshake we discussed in Chapter 5. We also discussed that connections are made from a random upper port number on the originating system to a well known service port on the destination system.

This is where things get a bit weird. Loki and Thor are still communicating on ports 1038 and 21, as indicated in Figure 6.13. Figure 6.14 is a second separate session running parallel to the one shown in Figure 6.13; it has been initiated in order to transfer the data. FTP uses two separate sessions, one to transfer commands and the other to transfer data. Note that Loki has connected to the well known port of 20 on Thor.

This type of configuration can be a problem when firewalls or packet filters are used. The two systems must be able to initiate a communication session using both ports in order to transfer data. Proxy firewalls are usually configured with a specific application just for dealing with FTP's special requirements.

FIGURE 6.14

An FTP data session

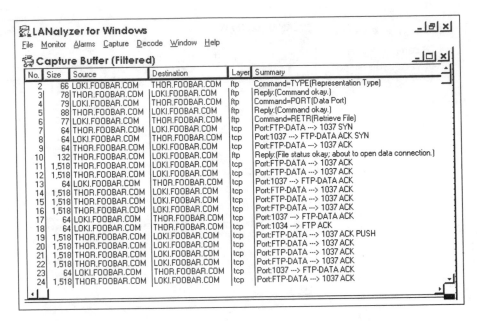

 FTP uses the TCP transport for all communications. Commands are sent over port 21 while data uses port 20.

Gopher

Gopher is a powerful, yet simple, file retrieval tool. Its functionality lies somewhere between FTP and a Web browser. Gopher has a very simple menu interface that can be used to browse directories and retrieve files.

Like Web servers, gopher servers can be linked together. This allows a user to search transparently for file information across multiple systems. Like a Web browser, a gopher client can distinguish between different file types and respond appropriately. For example, if the file being retrieved is text, the gopher client will display it to the screen. If it is a binary file, it will transfer it to the local system in a similar fashion to FTP.

Gopher does not support the more advanced features of HTTP such as displaying graphics or playing sounds or video. This is why gopher clients are very rarely used. When the typical user accesses gopher services, it is through a Web browser interface when file searching capability is required.

Gopher uses TCP as a transport for all communications. Gopher requests are sent to a destination port of 70.

Hypertext Transfer Protocol (HTTP)

HTTP is used in communications between Web browsers and Web servers. It differs from most services in that it does not create and maintain a single session while a user is retrieving information from a server. Every request for information, whether it is text, graphics, or sound, creates a separate session which is terminated once that request is completed. A Web page with lots of graphics needs to have multiple simultaneous connections created in order to be loaded onto a browser.

Since version 1.0, HTTP has included Multimedia Internet Mail Extensions (MIME) to support the negotiation of data types. This has helped HTTP to become a truly cross platform service, because it allows the Web browser to inform the server as to what type of file formats it can support. It also allows the server to alert the Web browser as to what type of data it is about to receive. This allows the browser to select the correct platform-specific viewing or playing software for the data it is about to receive.

HTTP uses the TCP transport and a destination port of 80 when communicating.

Internet Message Access Protocol, Version 4 (IMAP4)

IMAP is designed to be the next evolutionary step from the Post Office Protocol (see below for a description of POP). While it has the same features as POP, it includes many more which allow it to scale easier in a work group environment.

Like POP-3, the user has the option to either leave their messages up on the server and view them remotely (referred to as "online mail") or download the messages to the local system and reading them off-line (referred to as "off-line mail"). IMAP, however, supports a third connection mode referred to as "disconnected."

In online mode, all messages are stored on the IMAP server. While it can be time consuming to start up a POP mail client in online mode if many messages are involved, IMAP avoids this problem through the use of flags.

When connecting to a POP server, a POP client will simply authenticate and begin to download messages. All messages on the server are considered to be new and unread. This means that the user's entire inbox must be transferred before messages can be viewed or read. When an IMAP client connects to an IMAP server, however, it authenticates and checks the flag status on existing messages. Flagging allows a message to be marked as seen, deleted, or answered. This means that an IMAP client can be configured to collect only messages that have not been seen and avoid the transfer of the entire mailbox.

In offline mode, connection time can be reduced through the use of *previewing*. Previewing allows the user to scan the header information of all new messages without actually transferring them to their local system. This way if the user is looking to remotely retrieve only a specific message, they can choose which messages to receive and which messages to leave on the server as unread. It also allows the user to delete messages based upon the header information or file size without having to transfer them to the local system first. This can be a real time-saver if you usually retrieve your mail remotely and receive a lot of unsolicited advertisements.

IMAP includes a third connection mode not supported by POP, referred to as *disconnected* (someone *certainly* had a twisted sense of humor when they called it that—you can just see the poor technical writers and support people pulling their hair out over this one. "I disconnected my computer just like the instructions said, so how come I can't see my mail?"). When a remote IMAP client is operating in disconnected mode, it retrieves only a copy of all new messages. The originals are left up on the IMAP server. The next time the client connects to the system, the server is synchronized with any changes made to the cached information. This mode has a few major benefits:

- Connection time is minimized, reducing network traffic or dial-in time.

- Messages are centrally located so they can be backed up easily.

- Because all messages are server-based, mail can be retrieved from multiple clients and/or multiple computers.

The last benefit is extremely useful in an environment where people do not always work from the same computer. For example, an engineer who works from home a few days a week can easily keep their mail synchronized between their home and work computers. When working in offline mode as most POP clients do, mail retrieved by the engineer's work system would not be viewable on their home system. An IMAP client does not have this limitation.

Another improvement over POP is that IMAP supports the writing of messages to the server. This allows a user to have server-based folders as well as local ones. These folders can be synchronized in disconnect mode as well.

Group folders are also supported. This allows mail users to have *bulletin board* areas where messages can be posted and viewed by multiple people. This functionality is similar to news under NNTP (see below for a description of NNTP and news). Group folders provide an excellent means of sharing information. For example, the human resources department could set up a group folder for corporate policy information, reducing the need to create printed manuals.

If you are using IMAP, or if your current e-mail system supports group folders, create one entitled computer support or something similar. In it you can post messages providing support for some of your most common support calls. This can help reduce the number of support calls received and provide the user with written directions about how to work through their problem. You can even add screen captures which can make resolving the problem much easier than walking through it over the phone would.

IMAP has been designed to integrate with the Application Configuration Access Protocol (ACAP). ACAP is an independent service which allows a client to access configuration information and preferences from a central location. Support for ACAP enhances the portability of IMAP even further.

For example, our engineer who works from home a few days a week could also store their personal address book and configuration information on the server. If they are at work and add a new name and e-mail address to their address book, that name would be available when using their home system as well. This would not be true with POP as each client would have a separate address book saved on each local system. Any configuration changes would take effect on both systems as well.

ACAP also provides mail administrators some control to setup corporate standards for users when accessing mail. For example, the administrator can set up a global address book which would be accessible by everyone.

IMAP uses TCP as a transport with a destination port of 143.

Network File System (NFS)

NFS provides access to remote file systems. The user is able to access the remote file system as if the files are located on the local system. NFS provides file access only, which means that other functionality such as processor time or printing must be provided by the local system.

NFS requires configuration changes on both the server and the client. On the server, the file system to be shared must first be exported. This is done by defining which files are to be made sharable. This can be a single directory or an entire disk. Also, define who has access to this file system.

On the client side, the system must be configured to "mount" the remote file system. On a Unix machine this is done by creating an entry in the system's /etc/fstab file, indicating the name of the remote system, the file system to be mounted, and where it should be placed on the local system. In the Unix world this is typically a directory structure located under a directory. In the DOS world the remote file system may be assigned a unique drive letter. DOS and Windows 95 require third party software in order to use NFS.

While a convenient way to share files, NFS suffers from a number of functional deficiencies. File transfer times are comparatively slow when compared to FTP or when using NetWare's NCP protocol. NFS has no file locking capability to ensure that more than one user does not attempt to write to a file. As if this was not bad enough, NFS makes no assurances that the information has been received intact. I've seen situations where entire directories have been copied to a remote system using NFS and have become corrupted in transit. Because NFS does not check data integrity, the errors where not found until the files where processed.

NFS uses the UDP transport and communicates using port 2049.

Network News Transfer Protocol (NNTP)

NNTP is used in the delivery of *news*. News is very similar in functionality to e-mail, except messages are delivered to *news groups*, not end users. Each of these news groups is a storage area for messages that follow a common thread or subject. Instead of a mail client, a news client is used to read messages that have been posted to different subject areas.

For example, let's say you are having trouble configuring networking on your NetWare server. You could check out the messages that have been posted to `comp.os.netware.connectivity` to see if anyone else has had the same problem and has found a way to resolve it. There are literally tens of thousands of news groups on a wide range of subject matters. The author's personal favorites are:

```
comp.protocols
```

```
alt.clueless
```

```
alt.barney.dinosaur.die.die.die
```

In order to read news postings, you must have access to a news server. News servers exchange messages by relaying any new messages they receive to other servers. The process is a bit slow as it can take three to five days for a new message to be circulated to every news server.

News is very resource intensive. It's not uncommon for a news server to receive several gigabits of information per week. The processes required to send, receive, and clean up old messages can eat up a lot of CPU time as well.

News has dwindled in appeal over the last few years due to an activity known as *spamming*. Spamming is the activity of posting unsolicited or off-subject postings. For example, at the time of this writing the `comp.os.NetWare.connectivity` news group contains 383 messages. Of these 11% are advertisements for get rich quick schemes, 8% are ads for computer-related hardware or services, 6% are postings describing the sender's opinion on someone or something using many superlatives, and another 23% are NetWare related but have nothing to do with connectivity. This means that slightly more than half the postings are actually on-topic. For some groups the percentages are even worse.

NNTP uses TCP as a transport and port 119 for all communications.

NetBIOS over IP

NetBIOS over IP is not a service per se, but it does add session layer support to enable the encapsulation of NetBIOS or NetBEUI traffic within an IP packet. This is required when using Windows NT or Samba, which use NetBIOS for file sharing. If IP is the only protocol bound to an NT server, it is still using NetBIOS for file sharing via encapsulation.

Samba is a suite of programs which allow Unix file systems and printers to be accessed as shares. In effect, this makes the Unix system appear to be an NT server. Clients can be other Unix systems (running the Samba client) or Windows 95 and NT systems. The Windows clients do not require any additional software because they use the same configuration as when they are communicating with an NT server.

The source code for Samba is available as freeware on the Internet. Over 15 different flavors of Unix are supported.

We will discuss the functionality of NetBIOS and NetBEUI later in this chapter.

When NetBIOS is encapsulated within IP, both TCP and UDP are used as a transport. All communications are conducted on ports 137 through 139.

Post Office Protocol (POP)

The post office protocol is used when retrieving mail from a Unix shell account. It allows a user to read their mail without creating a Telnet connection to the system.

When a Unix user receives an e-mail message, it is typically stored in the /var/spool/mail directory. Normally this message could be retrieved remotely by Telnetting to the system and running the **mail** command. While a useful utility, **mail** does not have much of a user interface. To the inexperienced user the commands can appear to be cryptic and hard to remember.

POP allows a user to connect to the system and retrieve their mail using their user name and password. POP does not provide shell access, it simply retrieves any mail messages the user may have pending on the system.

There are a variety of mail clients available that support POP (POP-3 being the latest version) so the user has a good amount of freedom to choose the e-mail client they like the best.

When using POP-3, the user has the option to either leave their messages up on the POP server and view them remotely (*online mail*) or download the messages to the local system and read them offline (*offline mail*). Leaving the messages on the server allows the system administrator to centrally back up everyone's mail when they back up the server. The drawback, however, is that if the user never deletes their messages (I've seen mailboxes with over 12,000 messages), the load time for the client can be excruciatingly long. Because a copy of all messages is left up on the server, they must be downloaded every time the client connects.

The benefit of using the POP client in offline mode is that local folders can be created to organize old messages. Because messages are stored locally, the load time when many messages are involved is relatively short. This can provide a dramatic improvement in speed when the POP server is accessed over a dial-up connection. Note that only local folders can be used. POP-3 does not support the use of global or shared folders. The downside to offline mode is that each local system must be backed up to ensure recovery in the event of a drive failure. Most POP clients operate in offline mode.

One of POP-3's biggest drawbacks is that it does not support the automatic creation of global address books. Only personal address books can be used. For example, if your organization is using a POP-3 mail system, you have no way of automatically viewing the addresses of other users on the system. This leaves you with two options:

- Manually discover the other addresses through some other means and add them to your personal address book.

- Require that the system administrator generate a list of e-mail addresses on the system and e-mail this list to all users. The users can then use the file to update their personal address book.

Neither one of these options is particularly appealing, so POP is best suited for the home Internet user who does not have a need for sharable address books or folders. For business use, the IMAP4 protocol described above is more appropriate.

When a message is delivered by a POP 3 client, the client either forwards the message back to the POP server, or on to a central mail relay. Which is performed depends on how the POP client is configured. In either case the POP client uses Simple Mail Transfer Protocol (SMTP) when delivering new messages or replies. It is this forwarding system, not the POP client, that is ultimately responsible for the delivery of the message.

By using a forwarding mail relay, the POP client can disconnect from the network before the message is delivered to its final destination. While most SMTP messages are delivered very quickly (in less than 1 second), a busy mail system can take 10 minutes or more to accept a message. Using a forwarding system helps to reduce the amount of time a remote POP client is required to remain dialed in.

If the mail relay encounters a problem (such as a typo in the recipient's e-mail address) and the message cannot be delivered, the POP client will receive a delivery failure notice the next time it connects to the POP server.

POP uses TCP as a transport and communicates using a destination port of 110.

Simple Mail Transfer Protocol (SMTP)

SMTP is used to transfer mail messages between systems. SMTP uses a message switched type of connection as each mail message is processed in its entirety before the session between two systems is terminated. If more than one message must be transferred, a separate session must be established for each mail message.

SMTP is capable of transferring ASCI text only. It does not have the ability to support rich text or transfer binary files and attachments. When these types of transfers are required, an external program is needed to first translate the attachment into an ASCII format.

The original programs used to provide this functionality were uuencode and uudecode. A binary file would first be processed by uuencode to translate it into an ASCII format. The file could then be attached to a mail message and sent to its intended recipient. Once received, the file would be processed through uudecode to return it to its original binary format.

Uuencode/uudecode has been replaced by the use of MIME. While MIME performs the same translational duties, it also compresses the resulting ASCII information. The result is smaller attachments which produce faster message transfers with reduced overhead. Apple computers use an application called Binhex which has the same functionality as MIME. MIME is now supported by most Unix and PC mail systems.

Uuencode/uudecode, Binhex, and MIME are not compatible. If you can exchange text messages with a remote mail system but attachments end up unusable, then you are probably using different translation formats. Many modern mail gateways provide support for both uuencode/uudecode and MIME to eliminate these types of communication problems. Some even include support for Binhex.

SMTP uses the TCP transport and destination port 25 when creating a communication session.

Simple Network Management Protocol (SNMP)

SNMP is used both to monitor and control network devices. The monitoring or controlling station is referred to as the *SNMP management station*. The network devices to be controlled are required to run *SNMP agents*. The agents and the management station work together to give the network administrator a central point of control over the network.

The SNMP agent provides the link into the networking device. The device can be a manageable hub, a router, or even a server. The agent uses both static and dynamic information when reporting to the management station.

The static information is data stored within the device in order to identify it uniquely. For example, the administrator may choose to store the device's physical location and serial number as part of the SNMP static information. This makes it easier to identify which device you're working with from the SNMP management station.

The dynamic information is data that pertains to the current state of the device. For example, port status on a hub would be considered dynamic information as the port may be enabled or disabled, depending on whether it is functioning properly.

The SNMP management station is the central console used to control all network devices that have SNMP agents. The management station first learns about a network device through the use of a Management Information Base (MIB). The MIB is a piece of software supplied by the network device vendor, usually on floppy disk. When the MIB is added to the management station, the MIB teaches it about the network device. This helps to ensure that SNMP management stations created by one vendor will operate properly with network devices produced by another.

Information is usually collected by the SNMP management station through polling. The SNMP management station will issue queries at predetermined intervals in order to check the status of each network device. SNMP only supports two commands for collecting information, **get**, and **getnext**. **get** allows the management station to retrieve information on a specific operating parameter. For example, the management station may query a router to report on the current status of one of its ports. **getnext** is used when a complete status will be collected from a device. Instead of forcing the SNMP management station to issue a series of specific **get** commands, **getnext** can be used to sequentially retrieve each piece of information a device is capable of reporting on.

SNMP also allows for the controlling of a network devices through the command **set**. **set** can be used to alter some of the operational parameters on a network device. For example, if our above **get** command reported that port two on the router was disabled, we could issue a **set** command to the router to enable the port.

SNMP typically does not offer the same range of control as a network device's management utility. For example, while we may be able to turn ports on and off on our router, we would probably be unable to initialize IP networking and assign an IP address to the port. How much control is available through SNMP is limited by which commands are included in the vendor's MIB as well as the command structure of SNMP itself. The operative word in SNMP is "simple." SNMP provides only a minimal amount of control over network devices.

While most reporting is done by having the SNMP management station poll network devices, SNMP does allow network devices to report critical events immediately back to the management station. These messages are referred to as *traps*. Traps are sent when an event occurs that is important enough to not wait until the device is polled again. For example, our router may send a trap to the SNMP management console if it has just been power cycled. Because this event will have a grave impact on network connectivity, it is reported to the SNMP management station immediately instead of waiting until the device is again polled.

SNMP uses the UDP transport and destination ports 161 and 162 when communicating.

Telnet

Telnet is used when a remote communication session is required with some other system on the network. Its functionality is similar to a main frame terminal or remote control session. The local system becomes little more than a dumb terminal providing system updates only. The remote system supplies the file system and all processing time required when running programs.

Telnet uses the TCP transport and destination port 23 when creating a communication session.

WHOIS

whois is a utility used to gathering information about a specific domain. The utility usually connects to the system rs.internic.net and displays administrative contact information as well as the root servers for a domain.

This is useful when you wish to find out what organization is using a particular domain name. For example, typing the command:

whois sun.com

will produce the following information regarding the domain:

```
Sun Microsystems Inc. (SUN)SUN.COM   192.9.9.1
Sun Microsystems, Inc. (SUN-DOM)   SUN.COM
```

If we performed a further search by entering the command:
whois sun-dom
the following additional information would be produced:

```
Sun Microsystems, Inc. (SUN-DOM)
2550 Garcia Avenue
Mountain View, CA 94043

Domain Name: SUN.COM
```

Administrative Contact, Technical Contact, Zone Contact:
Lowe, Fredrick (FL59) Fred.Lowe@SUN.COM
408-276-4199

Record last updated on 21-Nov-96.
Record created on 19-Mar-86.
Database last updated on 16-Jun-97 05:26:09 EDT.

Domain servers in listed order:

NS.SUN.COM192.9.9.3
VGR.ARL.MIL128.63.2.6, 128.63.16.6, 128.63.4.4

The InterNIC Registration Services Host contains ONLY
Internet Information

(Networks, ASN's, Domains, and POC's).

Please use the whois server at nic.ddn.mil for MILNET
Information.

whois can be an extremely powerful troubleshooting tool for we now
know who is responsible for maintaining the domain, how to contact
them, and which systems are considered to be primary name servers.
We could then use a DNS tool such as **nslookup** to find the IP addresses
of Sun's mail systems or even their web server.

whois uses the TCP transport and destination port 43 when creating
a communication session.

Internetwork Packet Exchange (IPX)

In 1986 Novell released NetWare 2.0 and with it the IPX protocol. Based upon Xerox's Xerox Network System (XNS) protocol, IPX is highly optimized and designed to provide efficient network communications. With the release of such enhancements as Large Internet Protocol (LIP) and burst mode, IPX has arguably become the most effective protocol in use today. Figure 6.15 is a graphic representation as to how the pieces of the IPX protocol suite match up to the OSI model.

FIGURE 6.15

The IPX protocol suite as it compares to the OSI model

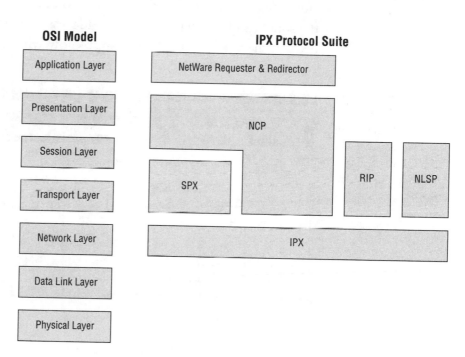

IPX Network Addressing

If IP addressing has left you a bit confused, than you'll love the simplicity of IPX. IPX uses an 8-bit hexadecimal network address which means that any value from 0-9 and A-F are valid. The only exceptions are 00000000 and FFFFFFFF. The former because it is a null value and the latter because it is considered an all networks broadcast address.

Devices on the network which will be performing routing services (this includes NetWare servers even if they have only one NIC) must be configured manually with their network address. All other devices are capable of auto-configuring their network address during startup.

Figure 6.16 shows the initial packet sent by an IPX workstation in order to discover the local network address. In this case the workstation SAPs but some client software (such as Microsoft's) may RIP instead. In either case the handshake is similar. If you look closely, you'll see that the source and destination network address is set to zero. This is because the workstation does not yet know where it is located.

FIGURE 6.16

A Windows 95 workstation with Client32 attempting to discover what IPX network segment it is on

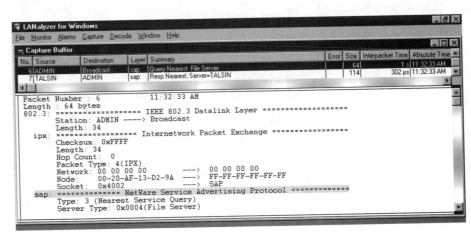

Figure 6.17 shows the server's response to the client. Note that the address values are now filled in. Our workstation will record the value in the destination network address field and use it during all future communications.

Figure 6.18 shows the very next packet sent by the Admin workstation. Note that the address field is filled in and our workstation now knows the local network address (00008023) and will use it during all

FIGURE 6.17

The server Talsin's
response to the SAP
packet

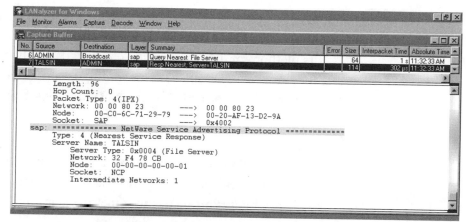

FIGURE 6.18

The Admin workstation
has now learned the
address for the local
network.

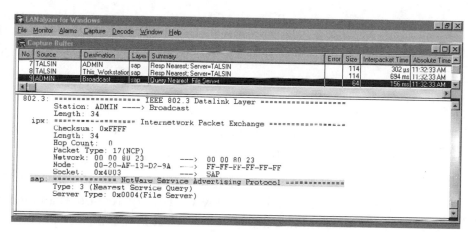

future communications. With a simple exchange of only two frames our workstation is now ready to properly communicate on the network.

You may remember from our discussion of IP that each station requires a unique network address to avoid communication conflicts. The same is true with IPX. Our Admin workstation will simply append its MAC address to the end of the local network number. Its full address will become 00008023:0020AF13D29A. Because every network device is required to have a unique MAC number, there should be no possibility of this address conflicting with another system.

IPX Routing

IPX supports static, distance vector, and link state routing. Unlike IP with its plethora of dynamic routing choices, IPX only has one routing protocol for each. Distance vector routing is supported with RIP and link state routing is provided by the NetWare Link State Protocol (NLSP).

RIP

As with RIP under the IP protocol suite, RIP under IPX is based upon the distance vector routing information protocol developed for XNS. This is why it is prone to the same problems and limitations as its IP counterpart. In summary, these are:

- Routing tables are built on second hand information.

- Time to convergence is long, due to slow propagation.

- During convergence the routing table is susceptible to errors and loops.

- Maximum hop count is 15, in order to counteract the count-to-infinity problem.

All 3.*x* and 4.*x* versions of NetWare support IPX RIP. It is also supported by Windows NT (as of version 4) and many Unix systems—Linux, SUN, and SCO being the most popular.

NLSP

NetWare's link state protocol is a vast improvement over RIP. As with most LSP protocols it sports the following features:

- Only first hand information is used to build routing tables.

- Minimal convergence time means a reduced chance of routing errors.

- Less network traffic is required to keep routing tables up to date.

- Most communications are unicast, not broadcast based.

- Traffic load balancing is based upon utilization and link speed.

- Maximum hop count is 64.

NetWare NLSP routers retain backwards compatibility by transmitting RIP as well as NLSP packets on segments where RIP-only devices are detected. Without this type of backwards compatibility a RIP device would see the server during its initialization and add it to its routing table. It would then remove the entry three minutes later as NLSP routing information is not broadcast once per minute, but rather every two hours or when a change takes place. This would cause the RIP-only device to assume that the NLSP system is no longer available.

NetWare servers will perform load balancing when two or more NIC cards are attached to the same logical segment and NLSP is used (see Figure 5.11). Load balancing is when the quantity of traffic sent over two or more paths is equalized. This can be an excellent performance enhancing feature because it nearly doubles the communication speed of the server. Take care that the disk subsystem does not become overloaded now that the server is able to receive more read and write requests per second.

When load balancing is performed, traffic is switched between the cards on a per-message basis, not per packet. In other words, if the server transfers a file to a workstation that requires six frames, and two cards are performing load balancing, all six frames will travel through the same network interface card. It will not send three over one and three over another. The very next file request by that same workstation may very well use the second card, depending on the current load.

While this limitation may appear to greatly diminish the effectiveness of load balancing, it actually does not. Remember that a busy server is required to process many read and write requests per second. The server will have many opportunities to simultaneously send two separate replies, one to each card.

NetWare is the only NOS which supports NLSP. It is, however, supported by many router hardware vendors.

Transport Layer Services

IPX uses three separate transports when sending and receiving data. They are IPX, Sequence Packet Exchange (SPX and SPX II), and NetWare Core Protocol (NCP). Each has its own responsibilities when conducting IPX communications.

IPX

IPX is the foundation of the IPX protocol suite. All communications take place on top of IPX. Each frame contains a 30-byte section following the frame header which contains all the information required to route and identify the frame.

IPX is a connectionless protocol meaning that it does not require a handshake prior to data transmission. It also does not require packet acknowledgments. This means that it has no way to guarantee the final delivery of data. Also, IPX does not guarantee sequential delivery which means that packets can be received in any order.

Sound like a pretty poor protocol? Actually, it is quite the opposite. IPX is specifically designed to do only one thing well—route information. It does not concern itself with things like acknowledgments and packet sequencing, but rather leaves this to the upper layers to deal with. By leaving the scope of IPX fairly loose, the door is left open to optimize communications.

For example, burst mode, which we will discuss later in this section, allows for the sending of multiple frames before an acknowledgment is sent. If IPX had been designed to require an acknowledgment after each frame, burst mode would not be possible without a ground up revamping of the entire protocol suite. This would of course lead to backwards compatibility problems because it would be difficult to keep the new and old specifications compatible.

Because IPX is a loose specification and acknowledgments are handled at a higher communication layer, IPX did not need to change when burst mode was introduced. This allowed older systems to continue to function as they always did while the newer software was deployed on the same network.

The only drawback to this type of design is that acknowledgments need to be passed further up the stack in order to be verified. Because this means that additional communication layers become involved during a retransmission of a frame, the system uses more resources and takes longer to send a replacement. Figure 6.19 shows why this occurs. If a protocol requires an acknowledgment of successful frames at the network layer, as in Protocol A, it can respond with a replacement frame quickly using a minimal amount of CPU time. If acknowledgments are handled at a higher layer, as in Protocol B, the replacement frame requires more processing than it did with Protocol A because it needs to be handled by additional layers.

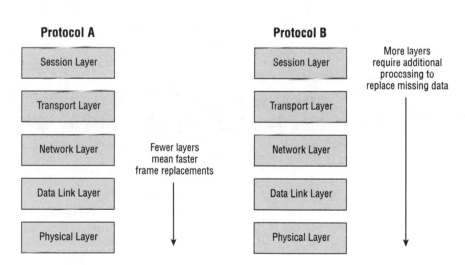

FIGURE 6.19

Protocol A requires less processing than Protocol B.

How much of an effect this has depends on the stability of the network. If errors are few and far between, the ratio of retransmissions to the amount of data that is moved becomes negligible. Modern day networks can be very stable when designed and installed properly.

IPX supports both unicast and broadcast frames. Multicast is not supported at this time. A *raw* (no other transport is used) IPX packet will have an IPX type field value of zero or four.

Note that this field is different than the type field used by some frame headers. The IPX type field is located in the data portion of the frame, not in the frame header.

SPX

SPX is the connection-oriented portion of the IPX protocol suite. SPX does not replace IPX, but rather communicates just above it. All SPX frames still include a IPX header section. As shown in Figure 6.20, the SPX header follows the IPX header within the data portion of a frame. SPX packets are identified by an IPX packet type value of five. Note that we have an Ethernet section (identified as 802.3), an IPX section, an SPX section, and then Data. Because our Ethernet frame has a fixed header length which includes the information required for local delivery, the IPX and SPX fields are stored in the data section of the frame.

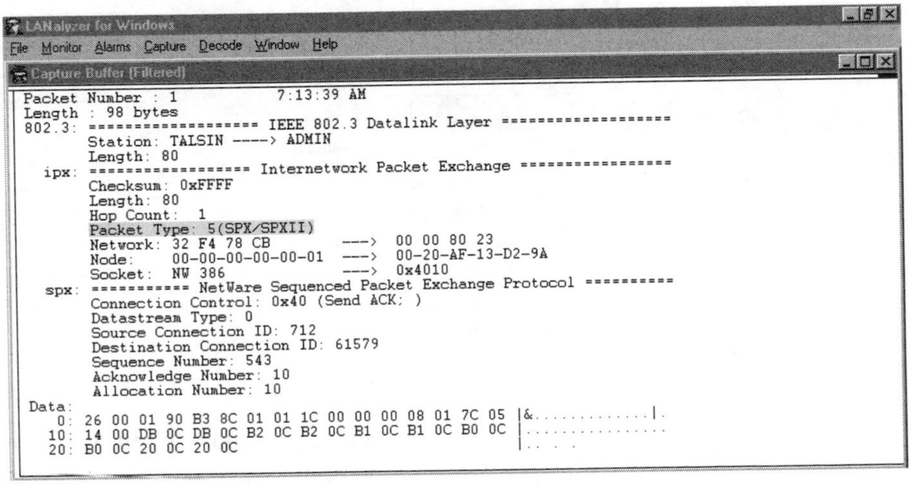

FIGURE 6.20

A packet decode of an SPX frame

```
LANalyzer for Windows                                                  _ |8|X
File  Monitor  Alarms  Capture  Decode  Window  Help
Capture Buffer (Filtered)                                              _ |□|X
Packet Number : 1                    7:13:39 AM
Length : 98 bytes
802.3: =================== IEEE 802.3 Datalink Layer ===================
       Station: TALSIN ----> ADMIN
       Length: 80
  ipx: =================== Internetwork Packet Exchange ===============
       Checksum: 0xFFFF
       Length: 80
       Hop Count: 1
       Packet Type: 5(SPX/SPXII)
       Network: 32 F4 78 CB       ---> 00 00 80 23
       Node:    00-00-00-00-00-01 ---> 00-20-AF-13-D2-9A
       Socket:  NW 386            ---> 0x4010
  spx: ========== NetWare Sequenced Packet Exchange Protocol ==========
       Connection Control: 0x40 (Send ACK: )
       Datastream Type: 0
       Source Connection ID: 712
       Destination Connection ID: 61579
       Sequence Number: 543
       Acknowledge Number: 10
       Allocation Number: 10
 Data:
    0: 26 00 01 90 B3 8C 01 01 1C 00 00 00 08 01 7C 05 |&.............|.
   10: 14 00 DB 0C DB 0C B2 0C B2 0C B1 0C B1 0C B0 0C |..............
   20: B0 0C 20 0C 20 0C                               |.. . ..
```

SPX communications handshake prior to the data transmission and require an acknowledgment for each frame of data sent. SPX sequences transmitted frames (note the sequence number in the SPX section of Figure 6.20) and ensures that they are received in the proper order. Because of its connection-oriented nature, SPX supports unicast communications only.

Figure 6.21 shows an SPX session in progress. This is an Rconsole connection between a workstation and a server. Rconsole is a NetWare utility that allows a remote control session to be setup from the workstation to the server. All information that is shown on the server's monitor is also displayed through the Rconsole session window. In our example, the session has been idle long enough for the server's screen blanker to be activated. The screen blanker is simply a blank screen with an ASCII character snake moving randomly around the screen. The busier the server's CPU, the longer the tail is on the snake.

FIGURE 6.21

An SPX session in progress

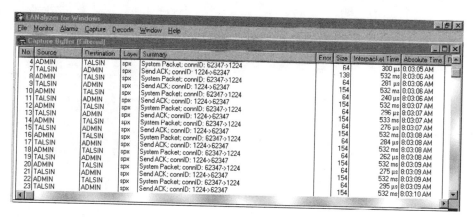

Have a look at the "ping pong" effect between data transmission and acknowledgments (ACK). We are transmitting four frames per second just watching the snake move around the screen! To avoid unnecessary traffic, Rconsole sessions should be shut down when not in use.

There are actually two separate versions of SPX—SPX and SPX II. The above descriptions apply to both specifications. The original SPX has been available since NetWare version 2.0. SPX II was introduced with NetWare 4.0.

SPX I

The original SPX protocol uses 12 bytes within the data field and has a maximum frame size of 576 bytes. If you refer to Figure 6.22, you'll see that this only leaves 516 bytes free to carry actual data. Combine this with SPX's requirement for an acknowledgment after each frame transmission, and we have a horribly inefficient means of communication.

F I G U R E 6.22

Only 516 bytes are available to carry data.

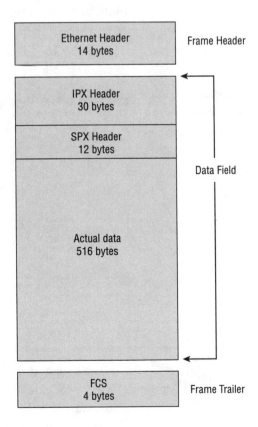

Total Frame = 576 bytes

Ethernet Header
14 bytes — Frame Header

IPX Header
30 bytes

SPX Header
12 bytes

Actual data
516 bytes — Data Field

FCS
4 bytes — Frame Trailer

So why all the overhead and the smaller packet size? The overhead is used to ensure proper delivery of every single frame. SPX was not designed for everyday communications, it is reserved for those special situations when a stable connection is preferable to speed. For example, when the above described Rconsole session is created, stability while controling the server is far more important than speed. SPX was spawned in the days of Thinnet and Thicknet wiring as well as 1200 BPS modems with minimal error correction. This is why it is so uptight about ensuring that all the data is received in one piece. In the old days, the physical layer of networks was not as stable as it is today. In situations where the stability of the circuit between the two communicating systems is questionable, SPX is the best method available to ensure that the data is sent in one piece.

As for its puny frame size, prior to 1992 IPX would negotiate a frame size of 576 bytes if the server and client were not on the same logical network. By fixing the SPX frame at 576 bytes, this negotiation was not required. This was fixed when Novell released LIP which is described later in this section.

Because of the above noted issues, SPX should be avoided in stable network environments whenever possible. Its small frame size (size *does* matter in networking) and connection-oriented nature can generate an excessive number of frames in medium to large environments. The following is a list of common software known to use SPX:

- Rconsole

- Pserver

- Lotus Notes when IPX is selected as the transport

- SAA Gateway when IPX is selected as the transport

- many client/server database programs

In many cases the administrator has a choice in not using SPX. For example, Notes can be run over IP as well and operates much more efficiently. Sometimes, however, SPX may be the only transport supported by the software. Rconsole is a good example of a program which only runs over SPX. If SPX must be used, an administrator's only recourse is to limit its effects on the rest of the network.

SPX II

SPX II fixed many of the problems with SPX while still maintaining a connection-oriented session. The packet size was increased to support the maximum allowable frame size per the topology in use. In the case of Ethernet, this means that a frame could be as large as 1,518 bytes.

SPX II also assumes that the physical layer connecting the two systems is a bit more stable than it used to be. With this in mind, SPX II supports a method of communication known as *windowing*. With SPX, a frame must be acknowledged before the next one can be sent. SPX II allows for multiple frames to be outstanding without receiving an acknowledgment. While the windows size is negotiated using the allocation number field within the SPX II header, the window size is not allowed to exceed 10 outstanding packets at any given time.

SPX II will use the sequence numbers and negative acknowledgments (NAK) to recover lost frames during a communication session. When a frame is lost the receiving system will send a NAK to the transmitting system identifying the sequence number of the missing frame. This allows the transmitting system to resend just the missing piece of information.

SPX II is a big improvement in communication efficiency over SPX. Some backup software vendors have developed *push agents* which allow their software to leverage SPX II during server-to-server backups. Cheyenne's ARCServe and Seagate's Backup Exec are two popular examples.

NCP

The NetWare Core Protocol is appropriately named, as it is the transport responsible for a majority of IPX communications. NCP defines the structure of requests and responses as they apply to most NetWare communications. The packet type field with the IPX header section has a value of 17 when NCP is used. The NCP header follows the IPX header, as well as the SPX header if one is required.

NCP uses a type field to identify the purpose of the information contained within the data field of the frame. Because a NetWare environment uses black and white definitions of a "client" and a "server" (for example, you cannot sit at the server console and access files located on a logged in client), the type field is labeled according to what kind of system originated the information. If the frame originates from a client, the field is referred to as *request type*. If the frame originates from a server, the field is called *reply type*. The most common NCP communication types are listed in Tables 6.10 and 6.11.

TABLE 6.10 Client Request Types	Type Value	Description
	1111	Used prior to authentication to request a server connection.
	2222	Manipulation or information request. Most commonly used during directory listings, path searches, file and directory creation or deletion, or when trustee right information is required or must be set.
	5555	Destroy connection. Most commonly used when the server that replies to the initial "Get nearest server" request is not the server the client wishes to authenticate with. This removes the client's connection and frees it up for another client. Connections identified as being "not logged in" are clients that have not yet sent a type 5555 request.

	Type Value	Description
T A B L E 6.11 Server Reply Types	3333	Information reply. A type 3333 reply is always preceded by a client sending a type 2222 request.
	9999	Request pending, no ECB time out. A type 9999 reply is a server's way of saying "She can't take any more speed, Captain! The emergency bypass control of the matter, anti-matter integrator is going to fuse!" When a server replies with a type 9999 NCP frame, it is telling the client that its buffer for accepting inbound requests is currently full. It needs to process the pending requests before it can accept any more from the client.

There is a single NCP type that is used by both the client and the server. A NCP type 7777 is used during all packet burst communications. This includes requests, acknowledgments and actual data transfers.

In addition to NCP types, other fields are used to further identify the purpose of a frame. All NCP frames include a *function code* and *subfunction code* field as well. Novell has specified a number of codes to provide more granularity in identifying a frame's purpose beyond that provided by the NCP type field.

For example, Figure 6.23 shows a decode of the NCP portion of a frame. The request type is 2222, so we know it is a client requesting manipulation or information regarding a file or directory. If we look at the value of the data field it is identified as *temp*. The question is, "What is temp and what do we want to do with it?"

This is where our function code and subfunction code fields come in handy. Novell has defined a request type of 2222, with a function code of 87 and a subfunction code of 1 as being a request to open or create a file or directory.

So now we know we need to open or create a file or directory named temp. While a bit closer, we are still lost as to the precise action our workstation is requesting of the server. While all NCP frames contain a function code and a subfunction code, other fields are used only as required.

F I G U R E 6.23

A decode of the NCP
portion of a frame

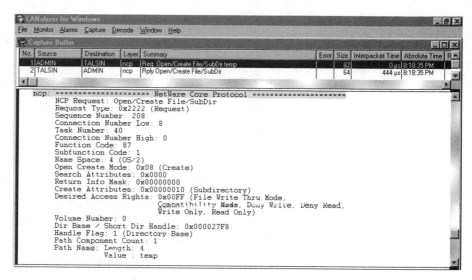

This particular frame has an open create mode field which identifies whether we want to open or create the value in the data field (`temp`). A value of 8 tells us we wish to create it. There is also a Create Attributes field which identifies with a value of 10 that `temp` is a directory.

Through the use of these five fields, we now know that `temp` is a directory we wish to create at our current location. While cryptic for the average network geek to read, control fields are an efficient, space-saving means of relaying information. In most situations only the type, function, and subfunction fields are required. When this is true, only eight bytes of frame space are needed to identify the requested service. Novell has categorized over 350 services using these three fields.

Large Internet Protocol (LIP)   LIP was added to the functionality of NCP back in 1992. Prior to that time, a client would limit the size of its frames to 576 bytes when it detected a router between itself and the server. LIP allows a client to communicate with the server using the maximum allowable frame size (1,518 bytes for Ethernet), even when the hop count field indicates there are one or more routers in between.

Burst Mode   Burst mode is arguably the single biggest improvement Novell has made to the NCP transport. In short, burst mode allows a system using NCP to send multiple frames of data without having to acknowledge the receipt of each one. It also allows the communicating systems to adjust the wait time between frame transmissions, known as the *interpacket gap.*

Figure 6.24 shows burst mode in action. Frame number 112 is the client Admin requesting 28,720 bytes of file information from the server Talsin. Frame numbers 113 through 133 is Talsin replying with the requested file information. Note that the only required acknowledgment is when Admin requests another 29,084 bytes in frame number 134. What would normally require 42 frames to transfer (between data transfers and acknowledgments), is completed in just 22 frames. This is approximately a 50% reduction in network traffic!

F I G U R E 6.24

A NCP client and server communicating in burst mode. Note that an acknowledgment is not required until all the requested file information is transferred.

No.	Source	Destination	Layer	Summary	Error	Size	Interpacket Time	Absolute Time	R
112	ADMIN	TALSIN	ncp	Req Burst Read 28720 bytes		108	5 ms	7:46:36 AM	
113	TALSIN	ADMIN	ncp	Burst Packet; 1428 bytes		1,512	2 ms	7:46:36 AM	
114	TALSIN	ADMIN	ncp	Burst Packet; 628 bytes		712	1 ms	7:46:36 AM	
115	TALSIN	ADMIN	ncp	Burst Packet; 1428 bytes		1,512	936 µs	7:46:36 AM	
116	TALSIN	ADMIN	ncp	Burst Packet; 1428 bytes		1,512	1 ms	7:46:36 AM	
117	TALSIN	ADMIN	ncp	Burst Packet; 1428 bytes		1,512	1 ms	7:46:36 AM	
118	TALSIN	ADMIN	ncp	Burst Packet; 1428 bytes		1,512	1 ms	7:46:36 AM	
119	TALSIN	ADMIN	ncp	Burst Packet; 1428 bytes		1,512	1 ms	7:46:36 AM	
120	TALSIN	ADMIN	ncp	Burst Packet; 1428 bytes		1,512	1 ms	7:46:36 AM	
121	TALSIN	ADMIN	ncp	Burst Packet; 1428 bytes		1,512	1 ms	7:46:36 AM	
122	TALSIN	ADMIN	ncp	Burst Packet; 1428 bytes		1,512	1 ms	7:46:36 AM	
123	TALSIN	ADMIN	ncp	Burst Packet; 1428 bytes		1,512	1 ms	7:46:36 AM	
124	TALSIN	ADMIN	ncp	Burst Packet; 1428 bytes		1,512	1 ms	7:46:36 AM	
125	TALSIN	ADMIN	ncp	Burst Packet; 1428 bytes		1,512	2 ms	7:46:36 AM	
126	TALSIN	ADMIN	ncp	Burst Packet; 1428 bytes		1,512	1 ms	7:46:36 AM	
127	TALSIN	ADMIN	ncp	Burst Packet; 1428 bytes		1,512	1 ms	7:46:36 AM	
128	TALSIN	ADMIN	ncp	Burst Packet; 1428 bytes		1,512	1 ms	7:46:36 AM	
129	TALSIN	ADMIN	ncp	Burst Packet; 1428 bytes		1,512	1 ms	7:46:36 AM	
130	TALSIN	ADMIN	ncp	Burst Packet; 1428 bytes		1,512	1 ms	7:46:36 AM	
131	TALSIN	ADMIN	ncp	Burst Packet; 1428 bytes		1,512	1 ms	7:46:36 AM	
132	TALSIN	ADMIN	ncp	Burst Packet; 968 bytes		1,052	1 ms	7:46:36 AM	
133	TALSIN	ADMIN	ncp	Burst Packet; 968 bytes		108	702 µs	7:46:36 AM	
134	ADMIN	TALSIN	ncp	Req Burst Read 29084 bytes					

When a client and a server are both capable of burst mode communications, they will negotiate how many packets to transfer between acknowledgments (burst packet count), and how long to wait between transmissions (interpacket gap). During the course of their communication these values will be adjusted as required. For example, in Figure 6.24

we observed that our server was able to successfully transfer 28,720 bytes to our client in burst mode. When our client requested additional file information in frame number 134, it pushed the envelope a bit and requested 29,084 bytes. This would continue until an error occurs or the maximum burst mode size is reached.

Figure 6.25 shows what happens when a burst mode session is not successful. In frame number 185 the client Admin is notifying the server Talsin that it missed 4,284 bytes worth of information. Frame numbers 186 through 189 is the server replying with the requested information. Note that these four frames total exactly 4,284 bytes.

FIGURE 6.25

A burst mode communication recovering from a transmission error. Only the missing data needs to be retransmitted.

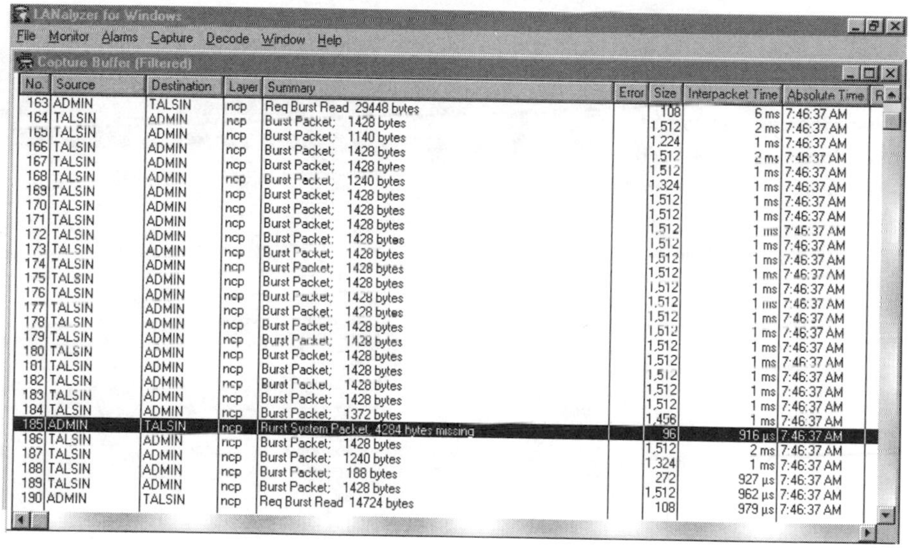

What is extremely interesting (if you are a wire geek that is) is Admin's next request for data in frame number 190. The client is only requesting 14,724 bytes of information. This is exactly half the amount of file information it requested in frame number 163. Because an error was encountered, the client has decided to back off on the number of burst packet in order to avoid future problems. If this transfer is successful, it may again negotiate a slightly larger number of burst packets until it finds the maximum number of frames that can be transferred without error.

This intelligent tuning allows the two systems to optimize their communication based upon the current network conditions. The healthier the network, the more information can be transferred between acknowledgments and the less time each system is required to wait between transmissions.

So just how fast can you go? Figure 6.26 shows burst mode pushed just about to its limits. A write request of 65,024 has been requested by the client with an interpacket gap of 2 ms. This is a 10 MB Ethernet segment. A faster pipe may be able to produce a slightly lower gap time.

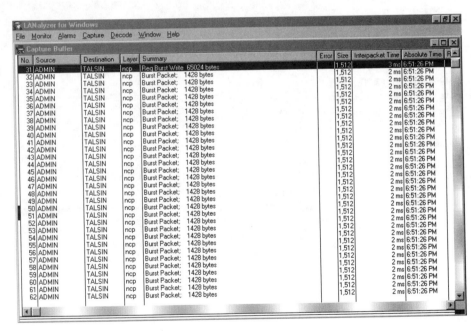

F I G U R E   6.26

Burst mode pushed to the max. 45 burst packets will be transmitted before an acknowledgment is required.

So how does this translate into actual improvements in network performance? Table 6.12 tells the story. The identical network and computer configurations where used in each example. The only change was configurations where used in each example. The only change was whether burst mode was turned on or off. The data in question is a 5 MB .zip file. This test is prejudiced towards measuring the raw transfer rate of a file, your mileage may vary. No animals were harmed while performing this test.

TABLE 6.12
Network performance when burst mode is enabled and disabled

Connection Mode	File Transfer Time	Number of Frames Required
burst mode enabled	6 seconds	3,946
burst mode disabled	12 seconds	7,790

As you can see, burst mode can have a dramatic effect on the time and number of frames it takes to transfer a file. Because regular network usage is a mixture of file transfers as well as other activities, the net effect of enabling burst mode on a network is usually quite a bit less than an improvement by a factor of two. Still, it's hard to beat free bandwidth.

IPX Application Layer Services

IPX uses the term *sockets* instead of ports to identify application layer services. While not nearly as diverse as IP, there are a few commonly used socket numbers worth noting. These services are listed in Table 6.13. IPX socket numbers are identified in a hex format.

SAP frames are used to advertise what services are available from each IPX system on the network. The NetWare **display servers** command will list each server on the network, once for each service it provides. This is why some NetWare servers may appear multiple times within a server list. Table 6.14 lists the most common services available on an IPX network. SAP types are identified in hex format.

TABLE 6.13

A few commonly used
socket numbers

Socket	Service	Description
0451	NCP	NetWare Core Protocol
0452	SAP	Service Advertising Protocol
0453	RIP	Routing Information Protocol
0455	NetBIOS	NetBIOS over IPX
0456	Diag. Packet	Server diagnostic packet
0457	Serial # check	License serial number check between servers
2000	Quake	default for multi-player updates
4000-8000	reply	upper reply socket randomly assigned by client
5100	Descent	default for multi-player updates
869C	Id games	default for DOOM2, Heretic, etc.

TABLE 6.14

The most common
services available on an
IPX network

SAP Type	Service
0004	File Server
0047	Print Server
0278	NDS Server
026B	Time Sync Server

Network Basic Input/Output System (NetBIOS)

Developed by IBM for their PC Network LAN, NetBIOS was created to be an application program interface (API). NetBIOS is designed to be a *front end* for carrying out inter-application communications. NetBIOS defines the interface to the network protocol, not the protocol itself. At the time of development it was assumed that the application accessing NetBIOS would assume responsibility for defining the rules required for transmitting the information.

F I G U R E   6.27

NetBIOS as it compares
to the OSI model

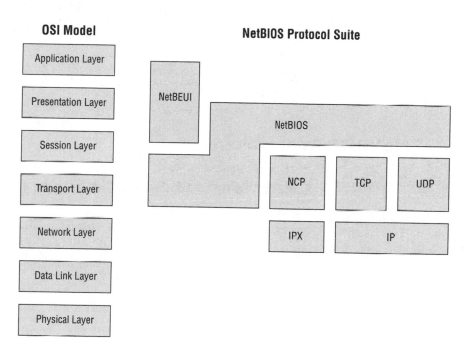

Figure 6.27 is a graphic representation of NetBIOS and some of its related components, as they compare to the OSI model. NetBIOS provides transport and session layer services only. It does not provide networking services, which means that NetBIOS is a non-routable

protocol. If a network is broken up by one or more routers, NetBIOS does not have the ability to reach nodes located on remote segments.

NetBIOS has a very loose specification for the presentation and application layers. There is no standard structure or format specified. This has led to NetBIOS being paired with other protocols such as NetBEUI which can provide a precise specification. It has also led to incompatibility problems for vendors were left to create proprietary implementations. Artisoft's LANtastic is a good example of a system which communicates using a proprietary NetBIOS implementation and is unable to communicate with other NetBIOS systems.

NetBIOS is designed to allow all nodes on a network to communicate on an equal basis. This is also known as *peer-to-peer networking*. All NetBIOS systems are able to both share local files as well as access shared file on remote systems. This model is the exact opposite of that discussed under IPX and NCP.

NetBIOS Addressing

Each machine on a NetBIOS network receives a unique name. This name can be up to 16 characters long but must not start with an asterisk (*). NetBIOS uses this name to discover a system's media access control number. Once the MAC address is known, all local transmissions will take place using this address. A system's NetBIOS name is very similar to a system's host name under IP. In a mixed protocol environment, these two names are usually kept the same.

When a NetBIOS system first initializes on a network, it is required to register its NetBIOS name. How the registration process takes place depends upon the node type of the system.

Node Types

NetBIOS identifies four different node types. The node types are categorized based upon how they resolve names on the network.

The four types of nodes are:

- b-nodes, which use broadcast communications to resolve names.

- p-nodes, which use point-to-point communications with a name server to resolve names.

- m-nodes, which first function as b-nodes and then, if necessary, function as p-nodes to resolve names.

- h-nodes, which first function as p-nodes and then, if necessary, function as b-nodes to resolve names.

A *b-node* system uses broadcasts for name registration and resolution. Figure 6.28 is a b-node system named Fenrus which is in the process of powering up. When NetBIOS is initialized, the system broadcasts the name it wishes to use.

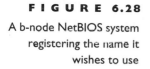

FIGURE 6.28

A b-node NetBIOS system registering the name it wishes to use

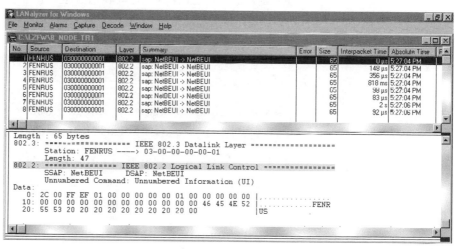

If no response is received, the station assumes the name is not in use and will begin identifying itself as Fenrus. If the name is in use by another system, the station will receive a name challenge. A name challenge lets the broadcasting system know that the name is already in use. Names are

registered on a first come, first served basis. Because NetBIOS names must be unique, a system should back off and never register a NetBIOS name for which it has received a challenge.

WARNING   It is possible to force a workstation into registering a name even after it has received a challenge. This should never be done in a production environment as it will affect connectivity to the system which originally registered the name.

A b-node system will also broadcast when it is performing a discovery. A discovery is performed when one system wishes to connect to another but does not know its network address. The system will broadcast a discovery message asking the destination system to reply with its address. Once a b-node system finds the address of the system it wishes to contact, it will begin communicating in a unicast mode.

Returning to Figure 6.28, note the destination broadcast address. This is not the typical broadcast address of FFFFFFFFFFFF that we normally see. 030000000001 is a special broadcast address used only by NetBIOS systems operating in broadcast mode. There are two major benefits to this mode of operation:

1. Non-NetBIOS systems are not required to process this broadcast. It will be viewed as a unicast frame to some other system.

2. The only systems that will interpret this frame as a broadcast are the ones that need to process it anyway. All b-node systems need to be involved in each name registration and discovery message.

So while b-node communications are broadcast based, they are not as bad as the typical network broadcast. Still, if we can remove our workstations from the registration and discovery process, it will free up bandwidth and CPU cycles to perform other functions.

When *p-nodes* are used, a central system referred to as a NetBIOS Name Server (NBNS) tracks the registration of NetBIOS names. A p-node system does not need to broadcast during startup. It simply sends a unicast query to the NBNS to find out if the name it wishes to register is already in use.

Likewise, when the system needs to discover another system, it will again contact the NBNS with a unicast query. This communication method eliminates the need for network broadcasts during registration and discovery and prevents all systems from being involved in each of these queries.

The drawback to using p-nodes is that each system needs to be pre-configured with the network address of the NBNS. It also relies on the NBNS being online and functional to support all NetBIOS communications. If the NBNS goes down, discovery is no longer possible. Another problem with the NBNS crashing is that it could lose all p-node table information regarding systems that had been registered prior to the crash. If this occurs, a second system could conceivably register a name that is already in use.

Note that b-node and p-node systems are not compatible. A b-node system will not register or discover through a NBNS, and a p-node system will ignore any NetBIOS broadcasts it receives from a b-node system. To get around some of the problems with both p-node and b-node systems, *m-node* and *h-node* systems provide a mixture of the functionality supported by each.

An m-node system will broadcast when performing registration and discovery. If the discovery should happen to fail, the m-node will then act like a p-node and query the local NBNS. While adding a bit of versatility, this does not really address many of the problems noted with b-node and p-node operation.

An h-node system will first register and discover through a NBNS in the same manner that a p-node does. If either of these two processes fail, it will drop back to b-node and use broadcasts to perform registration and discovery.

This mode of operation offers the best of both worlds. The h-node will first communicate using unicast transmissions. This helps to limit the number of broadcasts being transmitted on our network. If this should fail (for example, if the NBNS is offline), the system is able to recover by communicating in broadcast mode.

When Microsoft's DHCP services is used, the node operation of Windows systems can be configured as desired. Operating as a b-node is the default for Microsoft Windows systems as well as SAMBA. When NetBIOS is run over IP and Windows Internet Name Service (WINS) is used, the Microsoft Windows default changes to h-node. WINS is Microsoft's implementation of a NBNS. We will discuss WINS further, as we get into the dilemma of trying to pass NetBIOS traffic over a router.

Routing with NetBIOS

When routers must be crossed, NetBIOS needs to be run on top of IPX or IP. Only when a NetBIOS packet is encapsulated within an IPX or IP packet can it traverse routers. This inadequacy can severely limit NetBIOS's ability to scale in larger networks. NetBIOS was originally designed to operate on single segment LANs with 200 or less nodes.

NetBIOS over IPX

IPX supports the encapsulation of NetBIOS messages. When a NetBIOS message is contained within an IPX packet, the type field is set to a hexadecimal value of 14 and uses a socket of 0455. When NetBIOS is encapsulated within IPX and it is passed across a router, it is commonly referred to as *type 20 propagation*. This is because the type field value of 14 converts to a decimal value of 20.

Figure 6.29 is a NetBIOS name claim (registration) encapsulated with an IPX packet. The NetBIOS header follows the IPX header within the data portion of the frame. Our IPX header has not only identified our IPX network number (8023), but it has correctly flagged the packet type as being NetBIOS (Packet Type 20).

Our IPX header has also converted our NetBIOS broadcast to a standard network broadcast. This means that our NetBIOS message will now have to be processed by every system on the local network.

FIGURE 6.29

A NetBIOS message
encapsulated within an
IPX packet

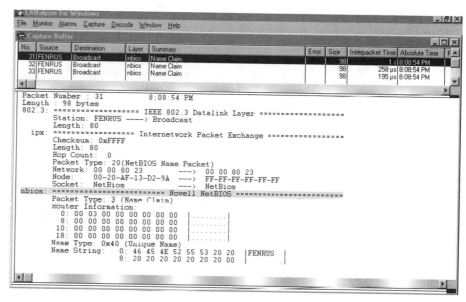

Now that our NetBIOS message is contained with an IPX packet, it is capable of traversing a maximum of eight hops. Many routers will require the additional step of enabling type 20 propagation on each port that must pass this frame. Once the frame has passed the router, it will be handled in a similar manner as an all network broadcast.

NetBIOS over IP

IP also supports the encapsulation of NetBIOS messages. UDP is used to support broadcast messages, while TCP takes care of unicast transmissions. Ports 137 through 139 are used for all communications. The NetBIOS header information immediately follows the TCP or UDP header within the frame.

With IP as the underlying transport, p-node systems can be supported for communications across a router. A good example of this type of functionality is Microsoft's WINS.

Figure 6.30 shows an example of a WINS implementation. Each WINS server acts as a NBNS for each of the p-node systems on its local subnet by maintaining a table of each system's NetBIOS name. In addition, it stores each system's IP address.

FIGURE 6.30

Our example network with three WINS servers, one located on each subnet

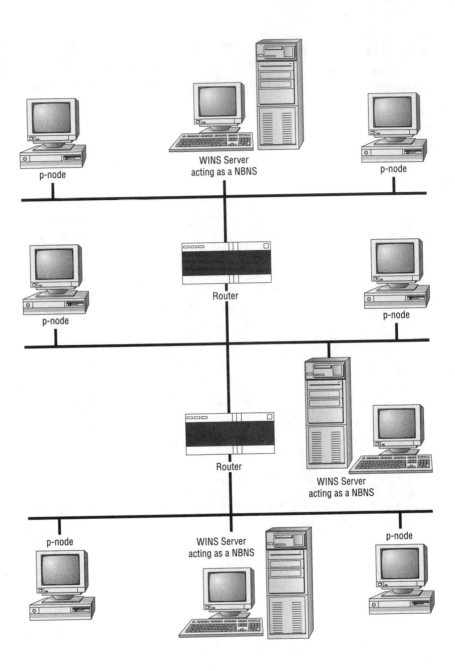

Each WINS server periodically updates the other WINS servers with a copy of its table. The result is a dynamic listing mapping NetBIOS names to IP addresses for every system on the network. A copy of the table is then stored on each of the three WINS systems.

When a p-node system needs the address of another NetBIOS system, it sends a discovery packet to its local WINS server. If the system in question happens to be located on a remote subnet, the WINS server returns the remote system's IP address. This allows the remote system to be discovered without propagating broadcast frames throughout the network. When h-nodes are used, the functionality is identical.

When NetBIOS is run over IP, a NetBIOS scope can be used to group systems together. A NetBIOS scope is a group of computers along which a registered NetBIOS name is known. A system's NetBIOS name must be unique within a specific scope. WINS server will propagate name information within a specific scope. A scope identifier is a unique character string by which the scope is known.

The scope identifier is very similar in functionality to the domain name used with DNS under IP. If the scope identifier is set to the same name as the IP domain name (for example, foobar.com), than the NetBIOS and IP fully qualified domain names will be identical.

As with DNS, this feature can also be used to increase the available name space. For example, a large company could use two scopes, one called corp.foobar.com and the other eng.foobar.com. This would double the available name space, because two systems would be allowed to share the same name provided they are part of two separate scopes.

NetBIOS over IP is outlined in great detail in request for comments (RFC's) 1001 and 1002. 1001 provides an overview of this functionality while 1002 has been written in greater detail.

Session and Transport Layer Support

NetBIOS supports three types of communication services: name, datagram, and session. The name services have been explained in detail. This service is used when a NetBIOS system needs to register or discover a name.

Datagram is NetBIOS's connection-less service for data delivery. While it is arguably faster than session, it provides no error correction and no guarantee of final delivery. If the receiving system is offline or busy, any data sent is lost. Datagram supports both unicast and broadcast based communications.

Datagram supports the following four API calls:

Send—Send message using unicast communications

Send Broadcast—Send message using broadcast communications

Receive—Receive unicast message

Receive Broadcast—Receive broadcast message

Session is NetBIOS's connection oriented data delivery service. It handshakes prior to transmitting data but provides no flow control. Session provides error correction but can only guarantee delivery on the first 64 kb of a message. All session communications are unicast in nature.

Session supports the following API calls:

Call—Initialize a session with a listening system

Listen—Accept sessions attempting a call

Hangup—Normal session termination

Send—Transmit one message up to 131,071 bytes in length

Receive—Receive message

Session Status—Report on all current sessions

NetBIOS Extended User Interface (NetBEUI)

Designed for LANManager in 1985 by IBM, NetBEUI formalizes the transport framework left a bit vague by NetBIOS. NetBEUI specifies how the upper layer software should send and receive messages when NetBIOS is the transport.

Like NetBIOS, NetBEUI is not routable. It is optimized for the same single segment networks with 200 nodes or less. The current version of NetBEUI is 3.0, which has fixed the problems encountered by earlier versions in the following ways:

- 254 sessions limit over a single NIC can be exceeded

- better memory optimization

- self tuning to optimizing local communications

- slightly better WAN performance

Except for a few missing API calls, NetBEUI 3.0 is fully compatible with NetBIOS 3.0.

Despite its limitations, NetBEUI has been implemented on a number of platforms. It is supported by all of Microsoft's Windows operating systems, LANManager, WARP, and Pathworks.

When installing NetBEUI on an NT system with multiple protocols, set NetBEUI first. This will cause NT to use raw NetBEUI for all local communications. Encapsulation will only be used when communicating with remote networks.

AppleTalk

AppleTalk was developed by Apple Computers in 1984 as a means of connecting their MAC and Apple II computers on an Ethernet network. AppleTalk should not be confused with LocalTalk, which was also developed by Apple but was a data link layer protocol designed to run on a proprietary bus topology (in other words not Ethernet). These are two separate protocols. While AppleTalk includes support for various flavors of Unix, DEC VAX, and even DOS systems, it is primarily used to provide connectivity for the MAC.

In 1989 Apple produced AppleTalk Phase II which is the current revision in use today. Phase II offered solutions to a number of problems with Phase I, most notably:

■ Increased the number of supported hosts beyond 254 per network segment.

■ Allowed for more than one Zone Name to be used per network.

■ Improved coexistence when other protocols are used on the same network.

■ Included support for ring topologies.

Figure 6.31 is a graphic representation of the AppleTalk protocol suite and how it compares to the OSI model.

Address Space

AppleTalk Phase II supports the use of extended network numbers. Numbers can range from 1 through 65,279. Network addresses are assigned in ranges, so a starting and stopping value must be specified. AppleTalk hosts are dynamically assigned a node address within the specified range. Valid node addresses are 1 through 254. Table 6.15 shows some potential numbering schemes.

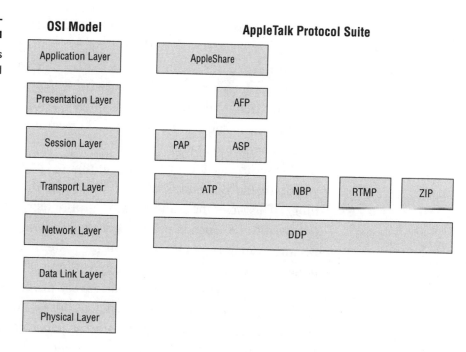

F I G U R E 6.31

AppleTalk as it compares
to the OSI model

T A B L E 6.15

Potential numbering
schemes

Network Range	First Node Addresses	Last Node Address	Number of hosts supported
1 - 1	1.1	1.254	254
200 - 201	200.1	201.254	508
65100 - 65200	65100.1	65200.254	50,800

AppleTalk, unlike IP, does not use address classes or subnet masks. This gives the administrator the freedom to adjust the network range values as required for their growing network. If you need to support an additional 254 hosts, simply increase the network range. AppleTalk nodes will automatically (after rebooting) take advantage of the additional address space.

There are two categories of AppleTalk nodes, seeding and non-seeding. Seed systems have their network range pre-configured and are responsible for advertising this network range to other systems.

Non-seed systems have their network range set to 0–0 which tells them to discover the real network range during startup. Once the network range is known, the system will attempt to register a valid node address within the range.

This setup has a few major advantages. The first is that only one system (usually a router) needs to be configured with the network range. This saves the administrator a lot of legwork as each system does not need to be touched prior to communicating on the network. Because a majority of the users on the system can learn their address dynamically, administration is minimized.

AppleTalk has shortened the discovery process by allowing a non-seed host to remember their last node address. When the system initializes, it first ensures that the network range has not changed. If it has not (which is usually the case), it tries to use its old node address. If it receives a challenge from another node using this address it will then go back through the discovery process to find a free address.

The big drawback to AppleTalk addressing is that it does not accept changes very easily. If a network address range is changed, other systems on the network will challenge this new address stating that the old range is the correct one. It is for this reason that *all* AppleTalk devices (hosts, servers, printers, and so on) must be shut down while the change takes place. Once the devices power up they will accept the new address range and all will be happy.

Needless to say this does not bode well for large environments. If you have 1,000 or more AppleTalk hosts it may be nearly impossible to shut down every system. I was once in a situation where we needed to make AppleTalk network changes on a 250 node network. The changes had to be completed by the end of the weekend.

While we thought we had powered down every AppleTalk device within the building, it became apparent that we had not. Our new network ranges were not being accepted. A walk through the building confirmed that there were some inaccessible areas which probably had AppleTalk devices.

We did, however, have access to all the hub closets and quickly identified which hub ports were still active. The solution? We unplugged every connection which still had a link light. This disconnected the remaining AppleTalk systems from the network which allowed us to successfully make our changes. On Monday morning when we again had access to these locked areas, we simply shut down the remaining systems and reconnected them back into the network.

Local Frame Delivery

Just like the other protocols we have discussed, AppleTalk uses a network card's MAC address when delivering frames to systems located on the same network range. AppleTalk uses the AppleTalk Address Resolution Protocol (AARP) to discover these addresses.

AARP functions in the same fashion as IP's ARP protocol. AARP will send out a network broadcast containing the node address of the system it needs to send information to. When the system replies the value in the Ethernet source address field can now be used for local delivery.

AARP will cache this information in its Address Mapping Table (AMT). The AMT serves the same purpose as IP's ARP cache, mapping MAC addresses to node addresses. This allows the system to reference the table instead of issuing another AARP when it again needs to send this system data.

Zone Names

Zone names allow for the assignment of a useful name to a specified network range. Zone assignments are made as part of the seeding systems configuration. Every AppleTalk network range must be assigned at least one zone name which is known as the primary zone. Secondary zones may be assigned to the network range as required.

Through the use of zones, resources can be logically grouped for easier access. For example, let's assume that we have a large network with many remote sites. The office located in Boston, MA could be assigned the primary zone name of Boston. If a user is looking for a network resource (server, printer, etc.) located at the Boston office, they can logically assume that they need to look in the Boston zone.

Secondary zones could also be assigned to provide even greater resolution. For example, let's assume we create secondary zones under Boston called HR, Sales and Dilbert. If a Human Resources person needs to print a document, they can probably assume that the closest printer to their location is located in the HR zone. Sales people's resources could be located in the Sales zone and upper management would keep their resources in the Dilbert zone (don't worry, they probably wouldn't get it anyway).

The Zone Information Protocol (ZIP) is used when a network address need to be mapped to a zone name. The Name Binding Protocol (NBP) is used when a zone name must be mapped to a network address. It is also used to translate host names into node addresses.

Network Layer Services

Network layer services are provided by the Datagram Delivery Protocol (DDP). DDP is similar to IPX in that it is the foundation on which all AppleTalk communications travel. The DDP header appears at the front of the data portion of the frame.

DDP is a connection-less protocol which performs no handshaking and requires no acknowledgments. Like IPX, it is happy to deliver information, but it makes no guarantee that it will arrive at its final destination. These responsibilities are left to the upper layers.

DDP does not support packet sequencing. As such, it can make no guarantee that frames will be delivered in order. Again, this is left to the upper layer protocols.

AppleTalk Routing

AppleTalk support static and only a single dynamic routing protocol. The Routing Table Maintenance Protocol (RTMP), is a distance vector protocol used to maintain the network address tables. Figure 6.32 is a packet decode of an RTMP frame.

FIGURE 6.32

A router using RTMP to broadcast its known routes

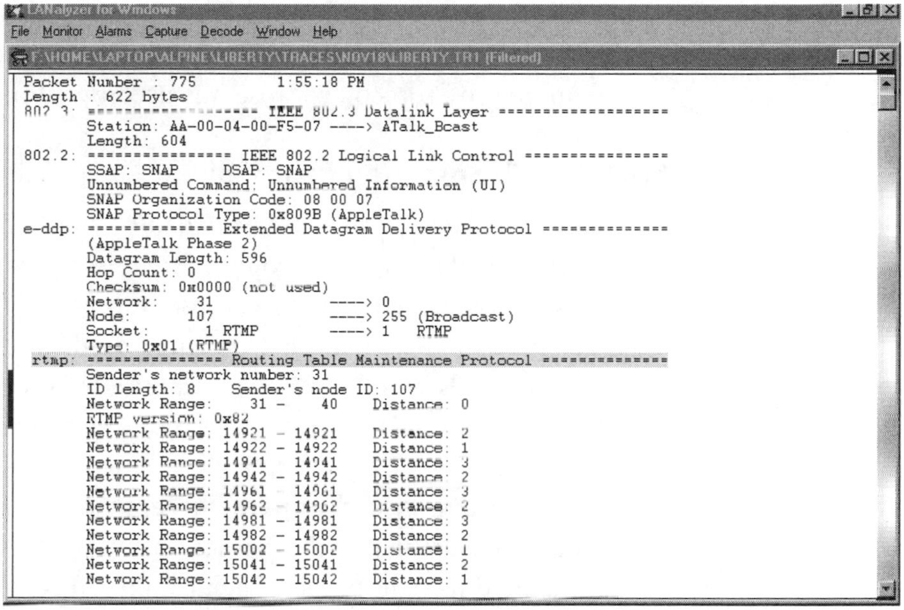

```
LANalyzer for Windows
File  Monitor  Alarms  Capture  Decode  Window  Help
F:\HOME\LAPTOP\ALPINE\LIBERTY\TRACES\NOV18\LIBERTY.TR1 [Filtered]
Packet Number : 775           1:55:18 PM
Length : 622 bytes
802.3: ================== IEEE 802.3 Datalink Layer ==================
       Station: AA-00-04-00-F5-07 ----> ATalk_Bcast
       Length: 604
802.2: ================= IEEE 802.2 Logical Link Control =============
       SSAP: SNAP      DSAP: SNAP
       Unnumbered Command: Unnumbered Information (UI)
       SNAP Organization Code: 08 00 07
       SNAP Protocol Type: 0x809B (AppleTalk)
e-ddp: ============== Extended Datagram Delivery Protocol ============
       (AppleTalk Phase 2)
       Datagram Length: 596
       Hop Count: 0
       Checksum: 0x0000 (not used)
       Network:     31          ----> 0
       Node:        107         ----> 255 (Broadcast)
       Socket:      1 RTMP      ----> 1   RTMP
       Type: 0x01 (RTMP)
rtmp:  =============== Routing Table Maintenance Protocol ============
       Sender's network number: 31
       ID length: 8    Sender's node ID: 107
       Network Range:  31 -  40      Distance: 0
       RTMP version: 0x82
       Network Range: 14921 - 14921   Distance: 2
       Network Range: 14922 - 14922   Distance: 1
       Network Range: 14941 - 14941   Distance: 3
       Network Range: 14942 - 14942   Distance: 2
       Network Range: 14961 - 14961   Distance: 3
       Network Range: 14962 - 14962   Distance: 2
       Network Range: 14981 - 14981   Distance: 3
       Network Range: 14982 - 14982   Distance: 2
       Network Range: 15002 - 15002   Distance: 1
       Network Range: 15041 - 15041   Distance: 2
       Network Range: 15042 - 15042   Distance: 1
```

Note in Figure 6.32 the RTMP information listed at the bottom. It contains the telltale signs of a router handing out secondhand information and thus using a distance vector protocol. If this was a link state routing protocol, we would not require a distance value, since link state routers only report first hand information.

As a distance vector routing protocol, RTMP is susceptible to all the previously mentioned problems encountered when using secondhand routing information. The only difference is that RTMP broadcast routing updates every 30 seconds instead once per minute. While this gives it a faster convergence time, it also makes it twice as noisy as most distance vector routing protocols.

At the time of this writing, Apple has not announced any plans to update AppleTalk to include link state routing.

Transport and Session Layer Services

AppleTalk uses a number of different protocols to maintain transport and session communications. The most important is the AppleTalk Transaction Protocol, because it is used by all file and print sharing.

AppleTalk Transaction Protocol

Transport layer services are provided by the AppleTalk Transaction Protocol (ATP). ATP is a connection-oriented protocol which supports packet sequencing. ATP differs from most transport protocols in that it is transaction based, not byte stream based. A transaction consists of a request by client followed by a response by a server. Requests and responses are tracked through the use of a transaction ID number, as shown in Figure 6.33.

ATP also takes care of packet fragmentation and reassemble. In order to ensure that each transaction can be tracked properly, messages are limited to eight frames. Each frame can contain no more than 578 bytes of data. This means the maximum frame size with header information is limited to 625 bytes.

AppleTalk Session Protocol

The AppleTalk Session Protocol (ASP) is a client of ATP and works with it to provide connectivity for file share access. As a session layer protocol, it is responsible for negotiating a connection when a client wishes to access files on a server. This is not to say that it takes care of authentication. It is simply responsible for establishing the connection between the two systems. The upper layers are actually responsible for the authentication process.

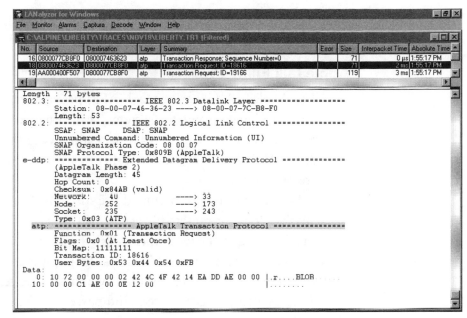

F I G U R E   6.33

Packet decode of an ATP
frame

ASP is also responsible for maintaining the connection once it is
established. It makes sure that queries and command sets are in an
acceptable format for the upper layer service. ASP is also responsible for
properly terminating a connection when the session is complete.

Printer Access Protocol

The Printer Access Protocol (PAP) performs identical services to ASP
except that it is responsible for printer access. It takes care of sessions
between printers located directly in the network as well as printers that
are being shared by host systems.

Upper Layer Services

AppleTalk supports two upper layer services. The AppleTalk Filing
Protocol which takes care of file requests on both clients and servers,

and AppleShare, which provides remote file and printer services to network clients.

AppleTalk Filing Protocol

The AppleTalk Filing Protocol (AFP) provides transparent access to both local and remote file systems. It is designed to make dealing with remote file systems just as easy as dealing with the files on the local drive. AFP also takes care of authentication when remote file systems are requested.

When a file access command is issued, AFP determines if the request involves local or remote file access. If the access is local, the request is passed along to the local operating system (usually System 7). If remote file access is requested, AFP passes the request down through ASP and across the network to the server. AFP on the server accepts the request (if authentication is accepted) and passes it along to AppleShare.

If the remote file system is not compatible (System 7 uses a special file system which requires a fork file and a data file for each piece of information), AFP takes care of translating the two file formats if it can. AFP then takes care of returning the information to the requesting client.

AppleShare

AppleShare is the roof that sits on top of the AppleTalk protocol suite. It is the application that coordinates file and printer access through the lower layers. AppleShare has three major components—AppleShare File Server, AppleShare Print Server, and AppleShare PC.

AppleShare File Server works with AFP to allow users to remotely access and save their files. AppleShare is responsible for registering users and mapping them to their appropriate volumes and directories.

AppleShare Print Server works with NBP and PAP to allow users to remotely access printers. When a printer is selected, NBP is used to find the remote printer's node address and PAP is used to send it data. AppleShare is responsible for spooling the print job prior to sending it to the printer. AppleShare uses the postscript command set when communicating with a printer.

AppleShare PC allows a network client using a DOS based file system to access and exchange files with a Macintosh server. AppleShare takes care of all the conversion requirements between the two dissimilar file systems.

Summary

This completes our discussion of the major protocol suites. Hopefully at this point your eyes are not too bloodshot; there is a lot of information to digest in this chapter. For those who prefer a more hands-on approach, feel free to refer back to this section as we discuss protocol configuration on each operating system. This may help to reinforce any portions of this chapter that did not quite sink in.

We will now look at each of the most popular network operating systems. We'll start by taking a look at what each operating system has to offer and then go straight into getting them to communicate on a network. The first NOS we will look at is Novell's IntranetWare.

CHAPTER

7

IntranetWare

Released in 1983, Novell's NetWare has been the mainstay for a majority of networks in providing file and print services. As of version 4.11, a number of IP applications are included with the product which are designed to facilitate the construction of an internal Internet, known as an *intranet*. An intranet provides many of the connectivity options usually associated with the Internet (HTTP, FTP, and so on), except access to these resources are usually restricted to internal personnel only. With the addition of these features, the product was renamed IntranetWare.

IntranetWare Features

While this book focuses on networking, I am also including a description of the features and applications included with IntranetWare. This section has been added to give you a brief overview of the connectivity options available through IntranetWare.

IntranetWare Setup

The IntranetWare setup utility now supports hardware auto-detection. The installation program has the ability to go out and discover the configuration of the server on which the software is being installed. This is a real time-saver for the novice administrator who may not be familiar with the model numbers of each piece of hardware installed in their server.

Protocol configuration has also been enhanced. If the server is attached to a network during configuration, the installation program will detect which protocols are in use along with their appropriate network and zone numbers.

The biggest weakness of the IntranetWare installation is that it does not automatically include all the server's features. There are separate procedures for installing the online help, FTP server, and multiprotocol router. While the CD case is clearly marked as to how to install these products, it would be nice if they were directly integrated into the installation process.

IntranetWare now includes a stripped down version of the DSMigrate utility. DSMigrate is a Windows based utility which simplifies the upgrade process from NetWare 3.1x to IntranetWare.

DSMigrate has the ability to read the old bindery databases used by NetWare 3.1x to track user logon and group information. It can also read the file system trustee rights which define who has access to which directories. Once it has learned this account information from the older server, DSMigrate can manipulate it into the hierarchical structure of NetWare Directory Services (NDS is described in greater detail later in this chapter) which is used by IntranetWare.

All of this is done offline so that if an NDS tree already exists, it is not affected during the development process. Once you have completed your additions, it is a simple matter to *set* these changes by incorporating them into an existing tree, or by creating a new one from scratch. Once the account information has been moved, the NetWare file manager takes care of moving the file information from the old server onto the new one.

The only real drawback with this process is that password information is not migrated. This means that after a migration, users will either have no password or one that has been chosen by the administrator. This makes the migration process a bit less transparent to the end user community.

NetWare Core OS

The core of IntranetWare is a 32-bit, multithreaded kernel. Symmetrical multiprocessor support is now included with the core OS. This means that multiple processors are supported right out of the box. Additional software and licensing is no longer required as it was in earlier versions.

The kernel is designed to be modular. This means that applications and support drivers can be loaded and unloaded on the fly. It also means that a majority of the changes can be made without rebooting the system. Need to change an IP address? This can be done with two commands at the command prompt and take effect immediately. This can be a lifesaver for environments that cannot afford to reboot a server every time a change has been made.

IntranetWare is designed to run completely within the physical memory installed on the server. IntranetWare does not use swap space or virtual memory. This means that the total memory available to the system is that which is physically installed on the server. IntranetWare cannot partition a portion of the disk as alternate memory, as most network operating systems can.

By using only physical memory, system response time is dramatically reduced. Accessing information from disk takes approximately 100 times longer than accessing the same information from memory. This fact is what made disk caching software so popular and why this software has such a dramatic effect on system performance.

Memory never goes to waste on an IntranetWare server. Any memory that remains after the core OS, supporting applications, and drivers have been loaded goes to caching frequently-accessed files. The more available memory there is, the more files can be cached. This means that when a user requests a commonly used file, the server can access the information from the faster memory instead of the disk. When additional memory is required by the operating system, it takes it from the file caching pool.

So by running applications only within physical memory, the core OS is able to access them more quickly. The limitation is that programs must be written efficiently so they use as small a portion of memory as possible. This is why the IntranetWare server still uses an archaic prompt and ASCII menus instead of a full graphical user interface.

Novell has also improved recovery from critical system errors, known as *abnormal ends* or ABENDs. In previous versions of Net-Ware, an ABEND would cause a server to stop all processing. The only forms of recovery were restarting the server through the online debugger or by hitting the power switch.

IntranetWare now has the ability to isolate or reset the offending process. This allows the server to continue running so that it can be reset during non-work hours. Figure 7.1 shows a typical error message. Note that the server continues to function after the error and the command prompt is returned.

F I G U R E 7.1

An IntranetWare server recovering from an ABEND

```
Abend: Page Fault Processor Exception (Error code 00000000)
    OS version: Novell NetWare 4.11  August 22, 1996
    Running Process: Server 05 Process
    Stack: 3F 58 23 F1 5C 18 02 F8 D8 3A E2 01 40 64 B4 01
           00 00 00 00 00 17 03 FB 73 73 73 73 0C CC 65 F0
           00 30 00 00 A0 46 03 00 78 56 34 12 46 72 65 65

Additional Information:
    The CPU encountered a problem executing code in IPXRTR.NLM.  The
    problem may be in that module or in data passed to that module
    by a process owned by SERVER.NLM.

The running process will be returned to a safe state.

 5-14-97  11:23:26 am:      SERVER-4.11-4631
    WARNING! Server TALSIN experienced a critical error.  The offending
    process was suspended or recovered.  However, services hosted by this
    server may have been effected.

TALSIN <1>:
```

IntranetWare also has the ability to restart the server after a predetermined period of time if an ABEND occurs. It is also possible to select what kind of an ABEND causes a server restart. For example, the server can be set to simply recover from application ABENDs but to perform a system restart if the failure mode is hardware related.

IntranetWare also includes a *garbage collection* setting. While this will not stop by your cubicle and empty your trash, it can recover server memory from unloaded processes.

With earlier versions of NetWare, if a poorly coded application was unloaded from memory, it may not return all the memory it was using to the free memory pool. This can be a problem if the application is loaded and unloaded a number of times because the amount of available memory would slowly become unusable. The garbage collection process scans for these memory areas that are no longer in use. When they are found, the pointers are deleted and the space is returned to the free memory pool so that it can be used by other applications.

New features have been added to ensure that applications do not tie up the processor(s) for an excessive amount of time. IntranetWare includes a Relinquish Control Alert setting that produces an error message when an application refuses to play fair and share the available CPU cycles. There is also a CPU Hog Time Out setting which allows the system to automatically kill any process which is monopolizing all of the server's processor time.

File System

IntranetWare includes a high performance file system that supports DOS, Macintosh, Unix, OS/2, and Windows' long file names. The file allocation table has been enhanced so that it does not require a disk optimization utility for file fragmentation.

Long file name support used to be provided by the OS2.NAM driver. As of IntranetWare, this driver name has been change to LONG.NAM.

The system excels as a file server due to a number of features designed to enhance the system's performance. Along with the file caching mentioned above, there are settings that allow for the optimizing of file storage.

Disk Suballocation

IntranetWare includes disk sub-allocation. This feature allows the system to reduce the number of sectors required to store a specific file. This provides additional free space on the system for file storage.

Compression

File system compression is also supported. This reduces the amount of space needed to save a file to disk and extends the storage capacity of the system. For example, it is not uncommon to have a 500 MB hard disk store over 1 GB worth of information.

Compression is performed on a per file basis similar to Pkzip, rather than the per volume basis used by such utilities as Microsoft's Drive Space. This allows files to be selectively compressed, instead of simply compressing the entire file system. Where Novell's compression differs from Pkzip is that the compression is completely invisible to the end user. File extensions remain unchanged and the system automatically decompresses the file during access.

The administrator is allowed to tune compression by setting which files can be compressed and how long a file must go unaccessed before compression is performed. This allows the administrator to tune compression so that only infrequently used files are reduced in size. Compression slows down file access time slightly, so this setting helps to ensure that common files will not have to be decompressed during access.

An administrator can also tune what type of compression gains must be achievable before the system will compress a file. For example, the administrator may decide not to bother compressing any files which will not yield at least a 10% reduction in storage space. Again, this helps to improve file access time.

Data Migration

IntranetWare also supports file migration. Migration is the process of moving older files to a larger capacity, but slower, medium while still appearing to reside in their original directory. For example, let's say we have an accounting firm that processes financial and tax information for a number of clients. Information that is over three years old is rarely used but is still required to be online in case a client calls in with a question.

Data migration would allow the system administrator to move all client records over three years old from the server's hard drives to an optical jukebox. An optical jukebox is a storage device that has a capacity in the tens of GBs, but has a slower file access time equivalent to a CD-ROM drive. By moving these files to the jukebox, more hard drive space is made available for storing recent client files.

When migration is used, the directory where the file was originally located contains a "shortcut" to the file in its new location on the jukebox. To the end user, this shortcut is identical to the file itself and as far as they know the file is still located in its original directory. This allows them to continue accessing this older information in the same manner they always have. The difference is that file access is noticeably slower. Still, it beats having to have the administrator search through three year old backup tapes.

Account Administration

As mentioned, IntranetWare uses NetWare Directory Services (NDS) for tracking user access to network resources. NDS is hierarchical, meaning that all administration can be done from a central point and that access to network resources can be specified on a granular scale.

It is even possible to assign sub-administrators who only have supervisor type privileges for a small portion of the tree. This NDS scales extremely well because it allows a large organization to have administrators that can only manage the resources for their specific group, while allowing full management rights to the people responsible for the entire network.

Network access is also centralized. When a user logs in to the network they are authenticating to the entire NDS tree, not just a specific server or portion of the tree. This means that they automatically receive access to all network resources that have been assigned to them, even if a resource exists on a remote portion of the tree (such as a printer in a remote field office).

NDS is not just for assigning user access rights. NDS can be used to create an online phone book of all network users. This information can include the person's full name, e-mail address, phone extension, department, and so on. It is even possible to extend the available fields (known as the scheme) to include additional information.

For example, when the IntranetWare Web server is installed, the scheme is extended to include a graphic file for each user. If the Web server is configured to allowing browsing of the NDS account information, a photo of each user can be included. This creates an online company directory that not only provides a mailing address and phone number for each user, but also a picture for identification.

Novell's Application Launcher

Also included with IntranetWare is Novell's Application Launcher (NAL). NAL extends NDS to record information for network applications. Network programs become their own objects with the NDS tree. The benefit of associating users with application objects instead of simply giving them access to the application's directory is fault tolerance. If the program is located on multiple servers, and one of those servers go offline, NAL will ensure that all users attempting to access the program will be pointed to the servers that are still in operation.

NAL also allows for the creation of standard desktops. Administrators can assign program groups to individual users or to groups of users. When a user logs in, they are presented with a program group which contains all the software they have access to. This information is associated with the user's logon ID, not their computer. This means that if the user walks down the hall and logs in, they will be presented with the same program group.

When ManageWise (Novell's network management product) is used, NAL can include setup scripts for local software installation. For example, if a company decides to upgrade the version of the word processing software they are using, NAL and ManageWise can work together to add a *setup* icon to each user's program group. The user simply runs the setup script which automatically installs and configures the new software.

NAL supports Windows 3.1*x*, Windows 95, and Windows NT workstation.

Security

NetWare (and thus IntranetWare) is the only distributed network operating system to receive C2 certification as a trusted network from the National Computer Security Center (NCSC). While NT is also C2 certified, at the time of this writing it is not approved as a trusted network. It is only certified as a stand-alone workstation with no removable media or network connection.

At the time of this writing, IntranetWare is also being evaluated for Electronic Data's E2 rating. E2 is the European counterpart to C2. The specifications of each are very similar.

Inherent Rights Mask

As mentioned above, file system access can be tuned down to the file level. Normally, file access rights trickle down through directories. This means that if a user is given read access to directories at a certain level, they will also have read access to any subsequent sub-directories. IntranetWare provides an *inherent rights mask* that allows these rights to be masked out as they attempt to trickle down. This allows the system administrator to assign the precise rights required at any level.

Packet Signature

IntranetWare also has a packet signature option. There is a type of system attack that has been around for a number of years known as *connection jumping*. Connection jumping is when someone on the network sends information to a server and pretends that the data is actually coming from an administrator that is currently logged in. This allows the attacker to send commands to the server which the server will accept, thinking they are coming from the system administrator.

Packet signature is useful in deterring these types of attacks because it requires both the server and the workstation to "sign" each frame prior to transmission. The signature is determined dynamically and changes from frame to frame. The server will only accept commands from a station that is properly signing frames.

In practice, if an attacker sends commands to the server pretending to be the administrator, the server will reject and log all frames received without a valid signature. Because the correct signature is changing constantly, it is extremely difficult for an attacker to determine what to use for a signature. This feature helps to protect an administrator's connection during daily maintenance. The feature can also be enabled for all users.

Auditcon

IntranetWare also includes *Auditcon*, Novell's system auditing utility. Auditcon allows the system administrator, or someone they designate, to monitor server events. Events range from user logons to password changes to specific file access, and over 70 events can be monitored. The benefit of Auditcon being a separate utility is that the administrator can designate a regular user to monitor events.

Auditcon is an excellent solution for large organizations where the person administrating the network is not the same person who is monitoring security. An auditor can be designated to monitor system events without being given any other type of administration privileges.

Tightening Server Security

IntranetWare includes a script called SECURE.NCF. When run during server startup, it automatically enables many of IntranetWare's security features, thus enhancing the security of the server.

Networking

IntranetWare includes support for IPX, IP, and AppleTalk. All three protocols can be used when accessing file and print services. IP support is via encapsulation. The client and server still create an IPX packet, however the packet is encased inside of an IP frame. This is similar to how NetBIOS is supported over IP. When IP is used for IntranetWare file and print services, UDP ports 43981 and 43982 are used for transferring data while port 396 (both TCP and UDP) are used for SAP and RIP broadcasts.

IntranetWare includes support for Ethernet, Token Ring, ATM, FDDI, PPP, X.25, ISDN, and Frame Relay. Monitoring and diagnostic consoles are provided for each of the WAN topologies to aid in their setup and maintenance.

IntranetWare also includes Novell's multiprotocol router. If a server has two or more network cards (either LAN or WAN), the server can act as a bridge or a router between the connected segments. Consoles are provided to both monitor traffic and configure filtering for each of the three supported protocols.

When acting as a router, the following routing protocols are supported:

- IPX—RIP, NLSP

- IP—RIP, EGP, OSPF

- AppleTalk—RTMP

Both a distance vector and a link state routing protocol is supported for both IPX and IP. AppleTalk only supports distance vector.

IntranetWare also includes an IPX to IP gateway. This allows a client communicating with IPX to access Internet and Intranet resources. The `Winsock.dll` file on the client's system must be replaced with one that supports IPX as a transport. Once complete, the gateway takes care of translating all packets into IP and delivering them to their intended destination.

The gateway can be configured to allow only certain users or certain groups access to IP resources. The gateway also logs each session so that the administrator can keep track of which sites are being visited. This can even be combined with the filtering portion of the multiprotocol router to block out certain sites.

There are two important benefits when using the IPX to IP gateway. First, all internal users can be hidden behind a single IP address. This means that an very large site can communicate using a single class C address or even just a portion of one. The second benefit is that the server automatically functions as a firewall. Because internal systems are not using IP to communicate, it is that much harder for a would-be attacker to reach these systems.

The downside is that a gateway does add a sizable delay to all communication sessions. Access to IP resources is noticeably slower than when a direct connection is established. This can cause problems if a slow WAN link is used. For example, if a server is configured to use both the gateway and a 28.8k PPP dial up connection, users may find that their software times out before a session can be established.

IP Applications

Most of IntranetWare's IP applications have been available for a number of years, but as separate add-on products. IntranetWare is the first release that includes them free of charge with the core OS.

Some applications are maintenance related in that their function is to aid client systems in accessing IP resources. DHCP and DNS are good examples.

The DHCP server is capable of dynamically assigning clients their IP address, domain and host name, default router, and the address of the DNS server. Bootp is also supported, however care should be take if both bootp and DNCP are to be serviced from the same server. Remember that a bootp client assumes it can keep the IP address assigned to it, while DHCP expects addresses to be returned upon the expiration of the lease period.

WARNING Bootp and DHCP can conflict with each other when run from the same server. If you need to service both types of clients, either statically assign addresses to one of them or divide the services over two separate servers.

The DNS server can act as a primary or secondary domain name server. This can be run on the same system as DHCP or from a separate server. The DNS server can also act as a Network Information Server (NIS). NIS is used by SUN SPARC systems to share host, group, and user information.

An FTP and Web server is also included. The FTP server can be configured to allow anonymous logons, or to only accept connections from certain IntranetWare users. When users connect to the FTP server, they simply use their regular password.

The Web server supports the Common Gateway Interface (CGI), Perl 5.0, Java, and NetBasic. NetBasic is an easy to use programming language that is similar in structure to regular Basic. The Web server also supports Secure Sockets Layer (SSL). SSL is a public/private key encryption system that allows for secure HTTP sessions. SSL is by far the most popular Web encryption system and is supported by major browsers such as Netscape.

Novell's Web server also supports multihoming. Multihoming provides the ability to support multiple domains on the same Web server. For example, let's say our company has two subdivisions, each with their own domain name. The first is foobar.com and the second is nowhere.com. Both wish to host their own Web site and have the server appear within their domain.

With multihoming, both Web servers could be housed on the same IntranetWare server under two separate directory trees. When a user enters the address www.foobar.com the server will automatically point them to the directory tree with foobar's files. If the user enters the address www.nowhere.com, they will be pointed to nowhere's files instead. The fact that these two Web sites are being hosted on the same server is completely transparent to the user.

IntranetWare ships with a slightly modified version of Netscape's Web browser.

Configuring IntranetWare for Network Access

There are two methods for providing connectivity to an Intranet-Ware server. The first is via the command line. This is the same method used to configure networking on NetWare 3.1x systems. These commands can be saved in the autoexec.ncf file so they are executed automatically on server startup. The second method is to use a graphical utility called Inetcfg. This utility walks the administrator through the configuration of the network interfaces and automatically generates the commands necessary to enable networking.

Regardless of which method you choose, you will still be required to select an appropriate frame type.

Frame Types

IntranetWare provides multiple frame formats in order to natively support each of the above mentioned protocols. For example, while IPX, IP, and AppleTalk will all communicate over an Ethernet topology, each requires that the Ethernet frame contain certain information fields. By selecting the correct frame format, you ensure connectivity with devices from other manufacturers. Table 7.1 is a quick reference list of the frame types supported by IntranetWare.

Here are a couple of qualifiers for the following table. The statement "No fields contained in the data portion of the frame" means that there are no Ethernet (OSI layer two) fields. Each protocol (OSI layer three)

	Topology	Frame Type	Protocols Supported	Distinguishing Fields
TABLE 7.1 Frame types supported by IntranetWare	Ethernet	802.3	IPX	Header includes length field. No fields contained in the data portion of the frame.
	Ethernet	802.2	IPX	Header includes length field. The data portion of the frame contains two service access point fields to identify the encapsulated protocol.
	Ethernet	Ethernet_SNAP	IPX, IP AT Phase II	Identical to 802.2 frame except that the data portion also includes a control, type, and organizational code field.
	Ethernet	Ethernet_II	IPX, IP AT Phase I	Header includes a type field to identify encapsulated protocol. No fields contained in the data portion of the frame.
	Token	Token_Ring	IPX	Similar to 802.2
	Token	Token_SNAP	IPX, IP, AT Phase II	Similar to Ethernet_SNAP

still stores header information within the data portion of the frame, as described in Chapter 6. The topology "Token" refers to all physical topologies that use a token passing method of communication. This includes FDDI, 100VG-ANYLAN, as well as the older Token Ring specification.

When selecting a frame type, ensure that it supports the protocol you wish to use for communication. Multiple protocols can be supported by a single or multiple frame types. For example, let's assume that my IntranetWare server needs to speak IPX, IP, and AppleTalk Phase II.

Let's also assume that the server is connected to an Ethernet network. I could choose to:

- support all three protocols through Ethernet SNAP

- support IPX with Ethernet 802.2, IP with Ethernet II and Apple-Talk with Ethernet SNAP

It is up to you to decide which configuration to use. Using a single frame type does reduce server overhead by a slight margin. If you are running a mixed NetWare environment, and you have 3.1x servers to support as well, you may want to use go with the second option. NetWare 3.1x does not support the use of a single frame for multiple protocols. Only a single protocol is allowed per frame type. The second option would allow you to remain consistent from server to server.

You must ensure that your clients are configured to use the same frame type as your IntranetWare server. For example, if the server is using an 802.2 frame for IPX (the default for IntranetWare) and your clients are configured to use 802.3 with IPX, the systems will be unable to communicate.

Configuring Networking from the Command Line

Enabling networking from the command line requires the execution of three steps. These are:

- load protocol support files (required for IP and AppleTalk only)

- load the network driver and select a frame type

- bind the appropriate protocol to the network driver

If you are using IP, the protocol support module needed is TCPIP.NLM. If you are using AppleTalk, the protocol support module is APPLETLK.NLM (note the missing letter "a"). IPX does not require an additional protocol support module. These support modules must be loaded prior to binding the protocol to the network driver.

Loading the Support Module

Table 7.2 identifies the switches supported by TCPIP.NLM.

	Switch	Description
TABLE 7.2 *Switches supported by* *TCPIP.NLM*	Forward=yes/no	Enable (y) or disable (n) the forwarding of IP traffic. If two or more network cards are installed in the server, this switch determines if it will act as a router and forward packets from one segment to another.
	RIP=yes/no	Enable (y) or disable (n) the processing of RIP packets. When this switch is set to "no" the server will not create or process RIP packets. This value should be "yes" if the server will be routing IP traffic between two network cards or "no" if it has a single card and will be acting as an end node.
	Trap=Address	Identify the host to receive SNMP trap messages. The address can be either an IP address or a host name (if the server is capable of resolving the name to an IP address). The default is to use the loop back address.

An example of a command for loading TCP/IP support would be:

```
load tcpip forward=yes rip=no trap=10.5.7.3
```

Reading from left to right, the server would interpret this command to mean "Load the support driver for the IP protocol. When it is loaded, allow the server to forward IP packets, thus acting as a router. Do not use RIP to advertise or learn routing information. If a critical error occurs, send a trap message to the SNMP management station located at IP address 10.5.7.3."

Table 7.3 identifies the switches supported by APPLETLK.NLM.

An example of a command for loading AppleTalk support would be:

```
load appletlk phase1=no checksum=no routing=yes zfiles=no
Internal_net_mode=yes net=10000-10000 zone={"Dilbert"}
```

TABLE 7.3	Switch	Description
Switches supported by *APPLETALK.NLM*	Phase1=yes/no	Defines whether AppleTalk networking will comply with Phase 1 (y) or Phase 2 (n) addressing rules. It is preferable to use Phase 2 when possible, as it supports extended addressing.
	Checksum=yes/no	Enable (y) or disable (n) the use of the DDP checksum field. The Datagram Delivery Protocol provides a checksum field in addition to the FCS field provided by the layer two topology for additional data verification. This is normally left off, as it adds additional overhead and provides very little additional insurance that the data is received intact.
	Routing=yes/no	Enable (y) or disable (n) AppleTalk routing. When enabled, the server can pass AppleTalk frames between multiple network cards. It also allows for an additional zone to be defined just for AppleTalk services provided by the server. When disabled, the server appears as an end node within the defined zone.
	Internal_net_mode=yes/no	Enable (y) or disable (n) the use of an internal AppleTalk network. If routing is disabled, this switch is not valid. If routing is enabled, it determines if the server will use its own zone and network number for the AppleTalk services it provides or if it will appear as an end node within the defined zone.
	Zfiles=yes/no	Define whether zone names will be defined in the file `atzones.cfg` (y), located in the sys:\system directory or if zones will be defined on the command line (n). The default is yes.
	Net=start addr-end addr	If `Internal_net_mode=yes`, then this command defines the network range for the internal AppleTalk network. Typically the start and end address are the same value because this provides 254 node addresses which is more than sufficient for a server (only two to five are ever used).

TABLE 7.3 (cont.) Switches supported by *APPLETALK.NLM*	**Switch**	**Description**
	Zone={"zone name"}	If zfiles=no and Internal_net_mode=yes, then this command defines the zone name to use on the internal network. All AppleTalk services provided by the server will appear in this zone. The zone name must appear within braces and quotes.

Reading from left to right, the server would interpret this command to mean "Load support for the AppleTalk protocol. When it is loaded, do not enable support for older Phase 1 networks. Do not use the checksum field within the AppleTalk header to perform additional CRC checking. Allow this system to act as an AppleTalk router using DDP to learn and propagate AppleTalk network information. Do not use the atzones.cfg file for Zone name information, all Zones will be specified on the command line. Allow this server to operate its own internal AppleTalk network which has a network address range of 10000–10000 and a Zone name of Dilbert."

If the server will be providing file services to AppleTalk workstations, you can customize the description of the server's volumes. If a Macintosh computer mounts the server's SYS volume, the icon created on their desktop is identified as server_name.SYS. All subsequent volumes however, are only identified with the volume name. This can make determining file locations difficult if your servers follow a naming convention such as vol1, "vol2. The Macintosh user has no way of knowing where the volume is located. You can edit the hidden text file sys:\system\volname.afp to add descriptions for the additional volumes. The syntax is: volume_name=aliases

Loading the LAN Driver

Next you need to load the network driver and select a frame type. Table 7.4 shows a list of valid switches to use when loading the driver.

TABLE 7.4	Switch	Description
Valid switches to use when loading the driver	Driver Name	The name of the driver supplied by the driver manufacturer for supporting IntranetWare with their NIC
	Port=addr	The input/output port address in use by the NIC
	Int=addr	The interrupt address used by the NIC
	Mem=addr	The memory address used by the NIC
	DMA=addr	The direct memory access channel used by the NIC
	slot=number	The slot number in which the NIC is installed
	Frame=	The frame type being associate with the NIC
	Name=	The name used to describe the NIC/frame type association
	Retries=number	The maximum number of times this card should retry a failed frame transmission. When the retry count is reached, the card assumes it cannot reach the destination system.
	Node=addr	The 12-byte node address to be used by this card. Every card has a node address assigned to it by the manufacturer. This switch allows that address to be overridden.

An example of a command for loading LAN driver support would be:

```
load 3c5x9 slot=3 frame=Ethernet_802.2 name=board1
retries=3
```

Reading from left to right, the server would interpret this command to mean, "Load LAN driver support for a 3COM Etherlink_III network card. The LAN card is located in expansion slot number 3. Load support for the 802.2 frame type and name this LAN driver/frame type combination board1. When this LAN card transmits a frame to which it does not receive a reply, it should retry the transmission three times."

Reading from left to right, this command is understood to mean "load the driver support for the 3c5x9 LAN card located in slot number three. Attach to this driver the Ethernet 802.2 frame type and name the combination *board1*."

The name identifies the combination of this frame type associated with this particular LAN card. If multiple frame types were associated with this card, each would receive a different name so that the combination can be easily identified.

To identify the network card, the slot the card is installed in may be used when the server has an EISA or PCI bus. If the network card is in an ISA slot, the DMA, PORT, INT, and MEM switches are used. Most ISA NIC cards do not require all four parameters, only two or three. Which parameters are required is specified by the manufacturer of the network card.

Binding Protocols to the LAN Card

The final command starts up networking on the card. Valid switches for all protocols are identified in Table 7.5.

	Switch	Description
T A B L E 7.5 Valid switches for all protocols	Protocol	Define the protocol to be bound to the NIC/frame combination.
	Board Name	Define the name of the board used to identify the NIC/frame combination.

Table 7.6 defines additional switches when IPX is the protocol being bound.

	Switch	Description
T A B L E 7.6 Additional switches for IPX	Net=addr	Define the attached network address. All IPX servers attached to the same segment and using the same frame type must also use the same network address.

An example of a command for binding the IPX protocol would be:

```
bind IPX to board1 net=ba5eba11
```

From left to right, the server would interpret this command to mean "Bind the IPX protocol to the LAN driver/frame type combination named "board1." The IPX network address for the attached network segment is "ba5eba11."

From left to right, this command reads "bind IPX to board1 ("board1" being the LAN card and frame type combination defined in the load statement). The IPX network attached to the card has a network address of ba5eba11".

Table 7.7 defines additional switches when AppleTalk is the protocol being bound.

T A B L E 7 . 7 Additional switches for AppleTalk	**Switch**	**Description**
	Net=addr-addr	If the protocol is AppleTalk, define the network address range to use on the attached segment. A value of "0-0" defines the interface as non-seeding. This means that some other device on the segment is acting as a seed router and that it is broadcasting the network address range. If any other value than "0-0" is used, it is assumed that this device is the seed router responsible for setting the network address range. Each network can only have one seed router.
	Zone={"zone name"}	Defines the zone name of the attached segment. If the server does not have an internal address, this is the zone in which the server will appear. Note that if zfiles=yes was defined during the loading of the AppleTalk support module, the system will retrieve the zone name from the file sys:\system\atzones.cfg.

An example of a command for binding the AppleTalk protocol would be:

```
bind appletlk to board1 net=100-101 zone={"Combat"}
```

From left to right, the server would interpret this command to mean "Bind the AppleTalk protocol to the LAN driver/frame type combination that has been named "board1." This interface will act as the seed router for this network segment and should assign a network address range of 100-101. The interface should also assign the default Zone name of Combat (without quotes) to this network segment.

Table 7.8 defines additional switches when IP is the protocol being bound.

	Switch	Description
TABLE 7.8 Additional switches for IP	ARP=yes/no	Enables (y) or disables (n) the use of ARP for resolving IP addresses to media access control numbers. If you disable ARP, the host portion of the IP address is mapped directly to the local hardware address. The default is yes.
	Addr=	Specify the IP address to be assigned to this interface.
	Mask=	Define the subnet mask for the specified IP address. If a mask is not specified, it is assigned based upon the class of the address assigned.
	Bcast=	Define the broadcast address for this interface. If not defined, the all network broadcast address is used.
	Gate=	Define the default router on the local subnet. If not defined, the server will only use the routers it learns about through RIP.
	Defroute=yes/no	When set to yes, the server announces itself as the default router through RIP. The default is no.
	Cost=	The cost value added to a packet that crosses the server. Cost can be used to control traffic patterns. The default value is 1.
	Poisonn=yes/no	Enable (y) or disable (n) the broadcasting of routing information back onto the subnet on which it was received. To prevent routing loops, routing information is normally not broadcast back onto the subnet from which it was received. This switch allows that functionality to be overridden. The default is no.

An example of a command for binding the IP protocol would be:

```
bind tcpip to board1 addr=10.5.5.100 mask=255.255.255.0
gate=10.5.5.1
```

Reading from left to right, the server would interpret this command to mean "Bind the IP protocol to the LAN driver/frame type combination named "board1." Assign an IP address to this interface of 10.5 .5.100, over riding the default subnet mask and setting it to 255.255 .255.0. The default router to use when transmitting non-local traffic is at IP address 10.5.5.1".

Enabling Networking during System Startup

Each of the above commands can be run from the server command line to immediately initialize networking. They can also be saved within the AUTOEXEC.NCF file so that networking is enabled during system startup. Figure 7.2 is a portion of a server's AUTOEXEC.NCF file.

FIGURE 7.2

A Server using the
AUTOEXEC.NCF file to
initialize networking

The second and third lines of the displayed portion of the file add support for IP and AppleTalk respectively. Note that AppleTalk has internal routing enabled but a zone name is not specified. This is because the switch "zfiles=yes/no" defaults to yes when it is not specified. Zones names will be retrieved from the file sys:\system\atzones.cfg rather than specified on the command line.

The three load commands are defining three separate frame types for use on our server. Note that we can tell this is an ISA LAN card because a port and interrupt value is specified. While this is fine for a test server, production servers should always use PCI network cards for optimal performance.

The three bind statements assign a protocol to be used with each NIC/frame combination. The board name allows us to specify which NIC/frame combination each protocol should be bound to. Note that the first bind statement has the word "TO" after the protocol while the other two do not. Either syntax is correct. Using the word "TO" makes the line easier for humans to read while leaving it out saves a bit of typing.

If the network card is initialized prior to the mounting of all network volumes, users may receive only some of their drive mappings if they attempt to log on while the server is starting up. To prevent this, move the "mount all" statement up in the autoexec.ncf file so that it is executed prior to initialization of the networking card.

Configuring Networking with *inetcfg.nlm*

The inetcfg utility was originally used to configure Novell's Multi-protocol router. As of NetWare version 4.0, it is the default method of configuring networking on Novell Servers. While you can use the autoexec.ncf file to configure networking on a NetWare 4.*x* server, if you later run inetcfg.nlm it will attempt to remove these commands.

inetcfg provides an ASCII graphical interface and is designed to greatly simplify the processes of configuring protocols on the server. Figure 7.3 is the opening screen for inetcfg. Note the context sensitive help displayed at the bottom of the screen. More help can be achieved by pressing the F1 key.

If this is the first time you are configuring networking, inetcfg will ask if you wish to import all networking commands located in the

FIGURE 7.3

The initial screen for
INETCFG

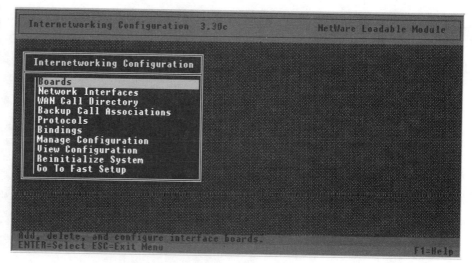

autoexec.ncf file. You should answer "yes," so that all networking commands are located in one area. The existing autoexec.ncf network commands will be commented out and the statement sys:\etc\initsys.ncf will be added. This makes a call to the script file initsys to initialize networking.

To configure networking, you will first define the LAN card under Boards, then select which protocols you wish to use under Protocols and finally define which protocols to enable on which cards under Bindings.

Boards

When the Board menu option is selected, the Configured Boards window will appear, listing all defined boards. If no boards are defined, the list will simply contain the value <Empty List>, as shown in Figure 7.4.

By pressing the Insert key, we can begin to configure our first board. This brings up a list of known LAN drivers in alphabetical order by driver name. If the driver you wish to install is not listed, you can press the Insert key again and define the path to where the driver is located. This will add the driver to the list. We can then select the driver and move on to configuration.

FIGURE 7.4

The Configured Boards
window

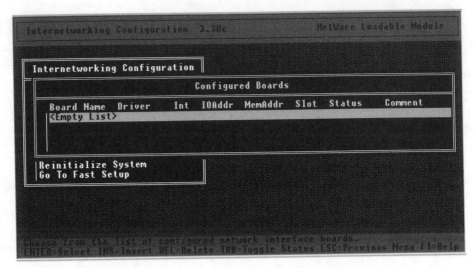

To scroll through the driver list quickly, begin typing the name of the
driver. The list is *hot keyed*. You can simply begin typing the driver
name and the selection bar will jump to the appropriate selection.
Hot keys are available on most configuration menus.

We are presented next with the Board Configuration window as
shown in Figure 7.5. First we are asked to name the board. This is not
the LAN card/frame name as discussed in the last section. This is simply
a unique name to be used when identifying this specific card. A name
that includes the type of card and which bus slot it is installed in helps
to simplify troubleshooting. Later, when we define bindings, we will
associate protocols and network numbers with these names. By naming
the cards with their slot number, we have an easy reference to which
network numbers are used by each card.

The next set of menu options is dependent on the driver we have
selected. Because this driver is for a 16-bit ISA card, the configuration
options reflect the setting used by this card. If this had been an EISA card,
Interrupt and I/O Base would have been replaced by Slot Number.

FIGURE 7.5

Once a LAN driver is
selected, it is configured in
the Board Configuration
window.

The values shown are the default factory setting for the card. By
pressing Enter on the settings for Interrupt, I/O Base, and Memory
Base, you receive a menu of available values. Scroll through the list to
select the desired value.

Not all available values may be listed. For example, you may have
configured a card to use interrupt 7, but this value may not be available
from this menu. If this occurs you will need to edit the driver configuration file associated with the LAN driver. This is a text file which has the
same name as the driver but has the file extension of .LDI. Simply edit
the file with a text editor to add the values you require. The following is
an example .LDI file for the driver FD0490:

```
;DrIvEr DeScRiPtIoN
VER:    1.00
SYN:    1.00
DR FD0490
{

        DES:    $DES
        HELP:   $HELP
        PAR:    1.00
```

```
FILE:    FD0490.LAN
OF:      MSM.NLM, ETHERTSM.NLM


PR INT REQ
{

          VAL:    2, 3, 4, 5, B, C
          DEF:    3

}


PR PORT REQ
{

          VAL:    300, 320, 340, 360
          DEF:    300
          RES:    20

}
```

The section entitled PR INT REQ defines our interrupt setting. VAL: defines which interrupts are available for selection, while DEF: defines the default value. To add a configuration value, simply follow the formatting and inset it into the proper section. For example, if we want interrupt seven to be available for selection, we would add 7, in between the values of 5 and B.

The next section entitled PR PORT REQ is similar except it applies to the port address. Edit this section in the same manner. The rest of the Board Configuration values are optional; you may complete them only if you require them. A brief description of each is listed in Table 7.9.

T A B L E 7.9	Menu Option	Description
Board Configuration options	Node	Override the 12-byte node address assigned to the card.
	Number of Retries	The number of times to retry a failed transmission. When the retry count is reached, the card will assume the destination system is unreachable.

T A B L E 7.9 (cont.) Board Configuration options	**Menu Option**	**Description**
	Comment	Allows you to add a brief description or comment for this card.
	Board Status	Whether this board will be enabled or disabled during startup. *Disable* is useful if you wish to define the required parameters for the card, but do not need to enable networking on it at this time. If you later need to use the card, its required configuration parameters will be known. **Force** automatically causes all frame types to be loaded for this driver. This command should not be required as frame types are selectively loaded when protocols are selected.

Once complete, press Escape and select Yes to save changes. There will now be an entry for the card on the Configured Boards list. Repeat the procedure for each network card installed in the server.

Network Interface

The Network Interface option is used for assigning network interfaces to board names. By default, LAN cards receive a single network interface and are not configurable through this menu option. For WAN Cards, the number of available interfaces is dependent on the type of card in use. Figure 7.6 shows the Network Interfaces list with WAN boards supporting DIALUP and an ISDN PRI. Note that even though LAN cards are listed as well, no configuration options are available. The ISDN card has 23 interfaces listed, one to support each PRI channel.

If we select the dial up board (which uses Novell's AIO driver), we are presented with a menu to select a medium. Because this is an *on demand* connection, our only option is PPP. Had this been a full-time connection, we would have received options for Frame Relay or X.25 as well. After selecting the medium, we are presented with the configuration window shown in Figure 7.7.

The PPP Network Configuration window displays general options as well as those that are specific to using a PPP connection. A brief description of each option is listed in Table 7.10.

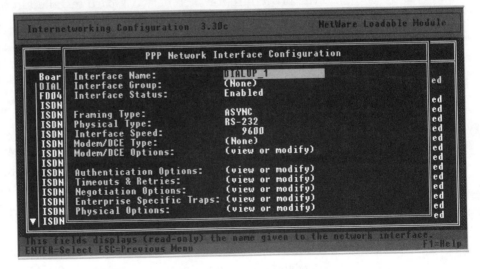

F I G U R E 7.6

The Network Interfaces
list for configuring WAN
cards

F I G U R E 7.7

The PPP Network
Interface Configuration
window

Once our configuration is complete, we can press Escape and select
Yes to save changes. Our dial-up connection will now appear in the
Network Interfaces list as being configured.

TABLE 7.10	Menu Option	Description
PPP Network Configuration options	Interface Name	Name given to this particular interface on the board.
	Interface Group	Allows us to associate this and other PPP interfaces with a group name. This allows WAN calls to be associated with a group instead of a specific interface. When a call is placed the first available interface within the group is used.
	Interface Status	Defines whether this interface is initialized during system startup.
	Framing Type	Defines whether this connection is synchronous or asynchronous. If the server's serial ports are used, this value must be asynchronous.
	Physical Type	Defines the type of serial connector. RS-232 is the default.
	Interface Speed	Specifies the clock rate of the serial interface. The interface speed is not set automatically depending on your modem selection. You must configure this option manually.
	Modem/DCE Type	Select the brand of modem attached to this interface.
	Modem/DCE Options	Allows you to define attention (AT) commands for use with the above specified modem.
	Authentication Options	Allows you to define security parameters for inbound PPP sessions.
	Timeouts & Retries	Allows you to customize communication recovery when transmission failures occur.
	Negotiation Options	Allows you to customize communication properties associated with PPP sessions on this interface.
	Enterprise Specific Traps	Allows you to set logging options for session diagnostics and monitoring.
	Physical Options	Allows you to customize communication options between the serial port and the modem.

WAN Call Directory

The WAN call directory allows us to associate WAN network interfaces with specific destinations. Let's walk through the configuration of our above PPP network interface so that we can connect to a local ISP and receive Internet access.

When the WAN call directory option is selected, we are presented with the Configured WAN Call Destinations list. At this point, the list is empty. Press the Insert key to configure our ISP connection.

We are prompted to name the destination. This is an alphanumeric name to describe this specific connect. For the sake of our example, we will name the destination *Internet*. We are then asked to select a wide area medium. Because this is a dial-up connection we select PPP. This brings us to the PPP Call Destination Configuration window, shown in Figure 7.8.

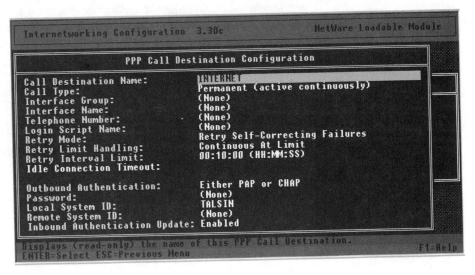

FIGURE 7.8

The PPP Call Destination Configuration window

Setting the Call Type We are first asked to define the call type. Our options are Permanent or On Demand. Permanent keeps the WAN connection up as long as the server is active. On Demand only brings up the connection if the server needs to route data over the WAN link. Because we are using an analog modem, we will probably want to configure a permanent connection.

It takes 30 seconds or so for a modem to listen for the carrier (a dial tone), dial the phone number, and authenticate on the remote system. This means that if the server waits until data is received before initializing the call, it will take 30 seconds before it can pass this data along the link. This is more than sufficient to time out an application wishing to send data across the link.

If ISDN is used, the connection can be made to be on demand because a much lower connection time is required. An ISDN circuit can begin passing data in as little as one second.

Hunting to Available Network Interfaces   We are then asked to assign this destination to an Interface Group. Pressing Enter in this field will bring up a menu of any interface groups defined while configuring the network interfaces. Defining a group allows us to hunt for an available network interface.

If a group is selected, the Interface Name field becomes grayed out. If we did not select a group, we can use this field to select a specific interface to use when placing the call.

Setting the Destination Options   The Telephone Number field allows us to configure the number to call when bringing up the WAN link. If you need to dial a 9 for an outside line, make sure it is specified here. A comma can be used to add a one second delay between numbers.

The Login Script Name field is used when the destination requires authentication prior to establishing a PPP connection. The sample script provided has the field to pass along a logon name and password during authentication. The sample script should be sufficient for most applications.

Retry Mode defines how the server should react when it encounters a problem. While all errors are logged to the call manager (utility that monitors WAN sessions), this mode defines what additional action should be taken.

The server can be told not to retry on failures, retry regardless of the failure mode or only retry on self-correcting failures. The self-correcting option allows the server to recover from the failures it can, and stop on the failures it cannot. For example, a busy signal would be considered a self correcting failure and the server would simply continue to try the number. If the modem cannot detect a carrier (no dial tone), the server has no hope of correcting this failure mode and will simply stop.

`Retry Limit Handling` and `Retry Interval Limit` work together to determine how long the system should spend trying to establish the PPP connection. If the retry limit is set for `Continuous at Limit`, the value in the retry interval field is how often the server will attempt to establish a connection. The server will retry the connection forever at the interval specified.

If retry limit is set for `Stop at Limit`, the server will retry the connection for the amount of time specified in the retry interval field. The frequency of the retry varies. The first retry will take place after eight seconds. The pause before each subsequent retry will increase exponentially until the retry interval value is reached.

`Idle Time Connection Timeout` defines how long the server should wait since the last packet of data crossed the WAN link before bringing the link down. This allows the link to be shutdown when not in use. If a permanent connection type has been selected, this option is grayed out.

`Outbound Authentication` allows you to choose the authentication method used to establish the link. Password Authentication Protocol (PAP) and Challenge Handshake Authentication Protocol (CHAP) are supported. The default of `PAP` or `CHAP` will try both methods. The method selected needs to match the authentication protocol in use by the destination system. The next field, `Password`, defines the outbound authentication password to use with PAP or CHAP. Authentication also uses the `Local System ID` to identify this system during authentication. For ISP authentication, this value should match the logon name specified in the sample script.

Remote System ID is used to define which remote systems are allowed to connect to this interface. If this field is left blank, the interface will only allow outbound calls to be established. Because we are configuring this interface for outbound use only, the Inbound Authentication Update field is not required.

Once our configuration is complete, we can press Escape and select *Yes* to save changes. If the authentication name and logon name do not match, you will receive an error message stating this is the case. The system will not change either value; you must go back into the configuration screen and change the appropriate value.

Backup Call Association

The backup call association allows us to define an alternate method of creating our WAN if the primary connection fails. When the server detects a failure in the primary connection (due to lost carrier or failed data transmissions), it can automatically enable a secondary connection for use in its place.

For example, let's say we have a Frame Relay WAN connection that is used to connect to a remote site in Boston. We have gone through the process of configuring the board and network interface for this connection. The link has been tested and found to be operational.

Let's also assume that we wish to configure a backup solution in case this Frame Relay link fails. This is where the backup call association options comes in. It allows us to define another interface for creating an alternate method of communication. If the Frame Relay link fails, this alternate solution will be brought up in its place.

A secondary board has been defined to create a dial-up PPP link if the Frame Relay connection fails. While PPP supports a much slower transmission speed than Frame Relay, it is usually sufficient to bridge the brief outages experienced on the primary link. It is also a far less expensive solution than using ISDN.

The configuration process for our secondary PPP link is similar to the ISP connection detailed above, except that the board is left disabled until it is needed. Once both interfaces are configured, we can associate them with each other.

Figure 7.9 shows the configuration window for backup association. The call destination for our Frame Relay link has been named BOSTON. This is the primary destination that will be monitored in case of failure. The backup destination, Boston_ALT, is our PPP call destination. This is the link that will be enabled if the primary link fails.

FIGURE 7.9

The Backup Association Configuration window

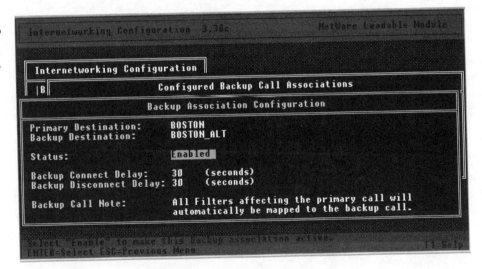

The Backup Connect Delay is the amount of time to wait after the failure of the primary link before bringing up the secondary. This value should be set high enough to give the primary link time to recover from a failure.

The Backup Disconnect Delay is the amount of time the primary link should be active before the secondary is brought down and the primary is again used for providing connectivity. This delay should be long enough to ensure that the primary link has returned and is stable.

Once our configuration is complete, we can press Escape and select Yes to save changes. Our backup link is now defined to step in when the primary link fails.

Protocols

Our next menu option allows us to configure which protocols will be used on the server. We will not yet define information specific to each interface, but rather the general information required by the server to use each of the protocols we wish to support. Figure 7.10 shows the initial Protocol Configuration window.

FIGURE 7.10

The Protocol
Configuration window

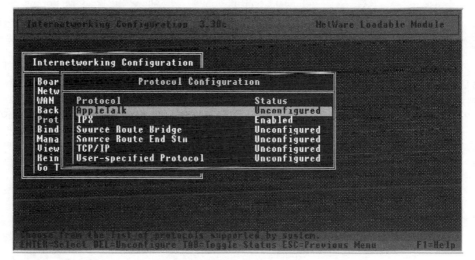

By default, IPX must always be enabled.

Configuring the IPX Protocol   Pressing Enter on the IPX menu option brings up the configuration menu for the IPX protocol. The available menu options are listed in Table 7.11.

	Menu Option	Description
T A B L E 7.11 Menu options for IPX configuration	Packet Forwarding	Enable or disable IPX router functionality on the server. This option must be enabled for the server to pass IPX traffic from one network interface to another.
	Routing Protocol	Select the IPX routing protocol. NLSP or RIP/SAP may be selected.
	Tunnel IPX through IP	This option is used to pass IPX traffic through an IP only link. The IPX packets are encapsulated within an IP frame prior to transmission.
	Tunnel Configuration	Allows the IP address of the server on the remote end of the tunnel to be defined. The remote server must be configured to support tunneling as well.
	Mobile IPX Support	Enables or disables the mobile IPX home router support used for remote LAN connectivity.
	Mobile IPX Configuration	Used to configure parameters for mobile communications.
	Filtering Support	When enabled, it tells the server to filter out RIP and SAP information as defined through the FILTCFG utility.
	IPX/SPX Parameters	Used to configure communication parameters and time outs.
	Expert Configuration Options	Allows for the configuration of advanced features.

When you press Enter on the Expert Configuration Options field, a sub menu of advanced configuration options appears. These options are defined in Table 7.12.

TABLE 7.12	Menu Option	Description
Advanced options for configuration	Get Nearest Server Requests	Defines whether the server should respond to get nearest server requests. Requests are accepted by default but should be disabled on test servers or servers with a low connection license.
	Override Nearest Server	Allows the server to respond to a get nearest server request with another server's name. This method is preferable to simply ignoring the request as it allows the workstation to find a server that much quicker.
	Nearest Server	Grayed out unless Override Nearest Server is enabled. This field contains the name to use when replying as another server.
	Advanced Packet Type 20 Flooding	When disabled, NetBIOS frames are indiscriminately propagated to all interfaces. When enabled, reverse path forwarding is used to ensure that the frame is not propagated to a network segment more than once.
	Hop count Limit	The maximum number of routers a packet can cross before it is discarded. This should be set to reflect the diameter of your network to reduce traffic load during convergence.
	Maximum Number of Path Splits	Used for load balancing. This value should reflect the number of network cards attached to the same logical network segment. This option is only available if NLSP was selected as the routing protocol on the previous screen.
	Load Balance NCP Packets	Used for load balancing. When enabled, frame transmissions to clients will be equally split on a per-session basis between each card connected to the same logical network segment. This option is only available if NLSP was selected as the routing protocol on the previous screen.

	Menu Option	Description
T A B L E 7.12 *(cont.)* Advanced options for configuration	LSP Size	Used by NLSP to tune convergence. The size should reflect the smallest frame size used on your network, minus the space used by the IPX header. The default value is sufficient for most networks. This option is only available if NLSP was selected as the routing protocol on the previous screen.
	NLSP Local Area Addresses	Allows you to define with which IPX networks this NLSP router should exchange information. If an update is received from an undefined network, it is ignored. The default is to accept information from all networks. This option is only available if NLSP was selected as the routing protocol on the previous screen.
	Override NLSP System ID	Disables NLSP's ability to dynamically assign a unique ID to this router. When enabled, the NLSP System Identification field becomes active, requiring you to manually assign an ID to this system. This option is only available if NLSP was selected as the routing protocol on the previous screen.
	NLSP Convergence Rate	Set the rate of convergence when network changes occur. Changing this value to fast improves recovery time but increases network traffic. Setting this field to manual allows you to manually configure the convergence parameters. This option is only available if NLSP was selected as the routing protocol on the previous screen.
	NLSP Convergence Rate Configuration	This sub menu contains read-only information unless manual was selected under convergence rate. The menu provides configuration parameters for NLSP timing. This option is only available if NLSP was selected as the routing protocol on the previous screen.

Once our configuration is complete, we can press Escape and select Yes to save changes. The IPX protocol is now configured. We are ready to assign IPX information that is specific to each interface.

Configuring the AppleTalk Protocol   Pressing Enter on the Apple-Talk menu option on the main Protocol Configuration screen brings up the configuration menu for the AppleTalk protocol. The available menu options are listed in Table 7.13.

TABLE 7.13 Menu options for AppleTalk	Menu Option	Description
	AppleTalk Status	When enabled, AppleTalk is initialized during system startup.
	Packet Forwarding	When enabled, the server acts as an AppleTalk router. When disabled, the server acts as an end-node.
	Type of Packet Forwarding	Defines if the AppleTalk network is Phase 2 and extended network numbers can be used or if Phase 1 numbering must be used for backwards compatibility. This option is only available if packet forwarding is enabled.
	DDP Checksum	The Datagram Delivery Protocol provides a checksum field in addition to the FCS field provided by the layer two topology for additional data verification. This is normally left off, as it adds additional overhead and provides very little additional insurance that the data is received intact.
	Tunnel AppleTalk through IP	This option is used to pass AppleTalk traffic through an IP only link. The AppleTalk packets are encapsulated within an IP frame prior to transmission. This option is only available if packet forwarding is enabled.
	AURP Configuration	Allows the IP address of the server on the remote end of the tunnel to be defined. The remote server must be configured to support tunneling as well. This option is only available if packet forwarding and tunnel AppleTalk through IP is enabled.
	Filtering Support	When enabled, it tells the server to filter out device and network address information as defined through the FILTCFG utility. This option is only available if packet forwarding is enabled.

	Menu Option	Description
T A B L E 7.13 *(cont.)* Menu options for AppleTalk	Internal Network	Enables the use of an internal network address and zone name. This option is only available if packet forwarding is enabled.
	Network number	Allows an internal network number to be defined if packet forwarding and internal network is enabled. A single address is specified instead of a start and end address because it is assumed the values are the same.
	Network Zone list	Assigns one or more zone names to the internal network number. This option is only available if packet forwarding and internal network is enabled.
	Static Routes for on Demand Calls	Enables or disables the use of static routing for WAN links. This option is only available if packet forwarding is enabled.
	Expert Configuration Options	When WAN links are used, this option allows for the definition of the remote hardware so that compatibility may be maintained. This option is only available if packet forwarding is enabled.

Once our configuration is complete, we can press Escape and select Yes to save changes. The AppleTalk protocol is now configured. We are ready to assign AppleTalk information that is specific to each interface.

Configuring the IP Protocol   Pressing Enter on the TCP/IP menu option on the main Protocol Configuration window brings up the configuration menu for the IP protocol. The available menu options are listed in Table 7.14.

Menu Option	**Description**
TCP/IP Status	When enabled, AppleTalk is initialized during system startup.
IP Packet Forwarding	When enabled, the server acts as an AppleTalk router. When disabled, the server acts as an end-node.
RIP	Enables or disables the use of RIP.
OSPF	Enables or disables the use of OSPF.
OSPF Configuration	When OSPF is enabled, this option allows the operational parameters for OSPF routing to be configured.
Static Routing	Enables or disables the use of static routing.
Static Routing Table	When static routing is enabled, this option allows routes to be configured. A static route can define the next hop when traveling to a network, or a specific IP host. A single default route entry may be created as well.
SNMP Management Table	Defines the hosts to receive SNMP trap messages.
IPX/IP Gateway	When selected, a sub menu appears with options to enable or disable the gateway, enable client logging, and enable the use of an access control list.
Filter Support	When enabled, it tells the server to filter out packets based upon source address, destination address, and port number as defined through the FILTCFG utility.
Expert Configuration Options	Allows for the advanced configuration of IP broadcast traffic.

T A B L E 7.14

Menu options for IP

Once our configuration is complete, we can press Escape and select Yes to save changes. The IP protocol is now configured. We are ready to assign IP information that is specific to each interface.

Bindings

The Bindings menu option allows us to configure protocol information that is specific to each interface. For example, if we enabled IP under protocols, this option allows us to assign IP addresses to each of our interfaces.

When the bindings option is selected, we are presented with the Protocol to Interface/Group Bindings list. To add protocol support, press the Insert key. This will bring up a list of protocols that where configured under the Protocol menu option. Highlight the protocol you wish to configure and press Enter.

The next menu will ask if you wish to bind the protocol to a specific network interface or to a WAN group that was defined under the Network Interface menu option. If you select an interface, the values you configure apply to that interface only. If you select a group, the values apply to whichever interface is selected to create the WAN connection defined under the WAN Call Directory menu option.

Depending on your selection, an appropriate list of choices will be presented. If you selected a network interface, you will see a list of interfaces that have not been assigned to a group. If you selected Group from the bind to menu, you will be presented with a list of valid group names.

Configuring a LAN interface to Use IPX   When you select to configure IPX on a LAN interface, the Binding IPX to a LAN Interface menu appears. The available options are defined in Table 7.15.

Once complete, press Escape and select Yes to save changes. The IPX protocol is now configured for this interface.

T A B L E 7.15 Menu options for IPX	**Menu Option**	**Description**
	IPX Network Number	Define a hexadecimal network address to assign to this interface.
	Frame Type	Select a frame type to use with the above assigned address. If multiple frames using IPX are required, you must create separate entries for each frame assigning each a unique network address.
	Expert Bind Options	Configure routing and SAP communication values for this interface. The default values are sufficient for most networks.

Configuring a LAN Interface to Use AppleTalk   When you select to configure AppleTalk on a LAN interface, the Binding NetWare AppleTalk to a LAN Interface menu appears. The available options are defined in Table 7.16.

T A B L E 7.16 Menu options for AppleTalk on a LAN interface	**Menu Option**	**Description**
	Network Range and Zone Configuration	Define if this interface will seed the network address and Zone names for this network segment (seed) or if it will learn this information from another router on the network (non-seed). This option is only available if packet forwarding was enabled under the protocol configuration.
	AppleTalk Network Type	Define if the attached network is an extended (Phase 2) or non-extended (Phase 1) network.
	Network Range	If packet forwarding was enabled under the protocol configuration and this interface is configured to seed, this field defines the network range to use on this interface.
	Zone List	If packet forwarding was enabled under the protocol configuration and this interface is configured to seed, this field defines the zone names to be assigned to the attached interface. Pressing the Insert key allows a new zone name to be defined.

TABLE 7.16 *(cont.)* Menu options for AppleTalk on a LAN interface	Menu Option	Description
	Provide Applications on this Interface	If no internal network address or zone is defined, this setting identifies if the AppleTalk server applications (such as file and print) appear within the zone and network address defined for this interface.
	Application Zone Name	Select which zone assigned to this interface server applications should be located in. This option is only available if `Provide Applications on this Interface` is set to Yes.

Once complete, press Escape and select Yes to save changes. The AppleTalk protocol is now configured for this interface.

Configuring a LAN interface to use IP   When you select to configure IP on a LAN interface, the Binding TCP/IP to a LAN Interface menu appears. The available options are defined in Table 7.17.

TABLE 7.17 Menu options for IP on a LAN interface	Menu Option	Description
	Local IP Address	Assign an IP address to this interface. If multiple addresses are required, then a separate binding must be completed for each.
	Subnet Mask	Assign a subnet mask for the attached network. The default value is based upon the class of the address assigned.
	RIP Bind Options	Activates a sub menu which allows the configuration of the interface cost, whether this interface advertises itself as a default route and timing updates for RIP traffic.
	OSPF Bind Options	Activates a sub menu which allows the configuration of the interface cost, the area address range, and timing updates for OSPF traffic.
	Expert TCP/IP Bind Options	Activates a sub menu which allows a frame type to be selected, the use of ARP to be enabled, and a broadcast address to be specified.

Once complete, press Escape and select Yes to save changes. The IP protocol is now configured for this interface.

Configuring a WAN Group to Use IP   The WAN group configuration is very similar to the LAN interface configuration. As an example, we will walk through the setup of a WAN group which will be bound to the IP protocol. When TCP/IP is selected from the list of configured protocols, we would then select to bind to each interface in a group rather than a specific interface.

Selecting to bind IP to a group activates the Binding TCP/IP to a WAN Interface configuration menu. The available options are defined in Table 7.18.

TABLE 7.18 Menu options for IP on a WAN	Menu Option	Description
	Interface Group	Identifies the WAN Group selected for configuration.
	WAN Network Mode	Identifies if one or more destinations will be used and if an IP address is required by the remote systems.
	Local IP Address	Assign an IP address to the WAN group. The interface that creates the WAN connection will use this as its IP address.
	Subnet Mask	Assign a subnet mask to the WAN link. The default value is based upon the class of the address assigned.
	WAN Call Destination	Define the entry created under the WAN Call Directory menu option to use with this configuration. This configuration defines the connection type as well as the phone number to be dialed.

All remaining configuration options (RIP, OSPF and Expert) are identical to their LAN counterparts. We can now press Escape and select Yes to save changes. The IP protocol is now configured for use with our WAN group. Figure 7.11 shows our completed set of bindings as they are displayed in the Protocol to Interface/Group Bindings list.

FIGURE 7.11

Our list of configured
interfaces and groups

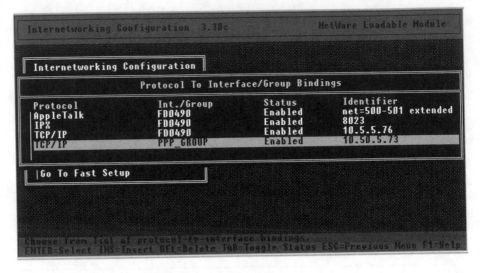

Manage Configuration

The Manage Configuration option allows us to define system management parameters. From here we can configure SNMP information, import or export our network configuration, and configure remote access to the server. Figure 7.12 shows the Manage Configuration window.

FConfigure SNMP Parameters   From this menu option we can configure SNMP access to this server from SNMP management stations. We can configure which communities (if any) have read and set access, as well as how traps are handled.

Configure SNMP Information   This menu allows us to configure how this server identifies itself to SNMP management stations. We can configure the name of the system, a brief description of its hardware, identify where the server is physically located as well as who to contact if the server is generating trap errors.

FIGURE 7.12

Configuration
management is
performed from the
Manage Configuration
window.

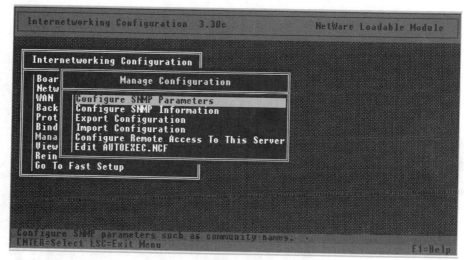

Export Configuration

Export Configuration   The export configuration option allows us to save our networking configuration to an external medium, usually a floppy disk. By default, all local interface information is saved. We can also selectively save X.25 profiles, WAN call destinations, and authentication files.

The purpose of the export file is disaster recovery. If the network configuration is changed or becomes corrupt, the exported file can be used to return our networking configuration to a known working state.

Import Configuration   The import configuration allows us to import the backup file created through the export menu option. All configuration information is restored. You can then go back through the other menu options and customize the configuration as required.

Configure Remote Access to this Server   The remote access menu allows us to define which methods can be used to remotely access the server beyond the normal logon process. These options should be enabled with care because most provide access to the server console.

Figure 7.13 shows the Configure Remote Access To This Server window.

FIGURE 7.13

The Configure Remote Access To This Server window

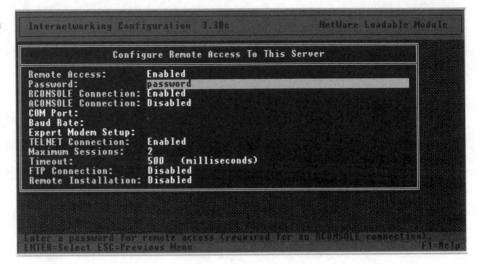

The remote access field enables or disables remote access to the server. When this field is disabled, all other fields are grayed out. The only console access is then from the console itself. Enabling this option allows for an alternate means of connecting to the server console.

The password field contains the value of the challenge string presented to the user when they attempt to remotely access the server. When remote access is enabled, this is the only form of authentication used. You are not prompted for a valid user logon, just the remote access password. This password should be guarded carefully because some methods of remote connection (such as Telnet and Remote Installation) are not logged.

The Rconsole field enables or disables the use of Rconsole as a remote means of console access. Rconsole uses SPX to provide *in-band* console access over the network. When a user connects using Rconsole, their network and MAC address are recorded in the System Error log and displayed on the server.

In-band means "over the network." You do not need a separate cable connection to support an in-band management session.

The `Aconsole` field enables or disables remote access to the console via a dial-up connection. When this option is enabled, the COM Port, BAUD Rate, and Modem Setup field become active as well. Aconsole allows out-of-band remote access to the server without requiring a network connection.

The `Telnet connection` field enables or disables Telnet and XWindows access to the server. IP must be enabled on the server and connectivity is provided in-band over the network. While this provides a convenient means of console access, care must be taken when enabling this option as sessions are not logged to the console or the System Error log.

When this option is enabled, the maximum sessions and timeout fields become active. These are used to limit the number of sessions and to set the timing on enabling the use of the Escape key (the Escape key character is used during connection negotiation and must be disabled until the session is established).

The `filtcfg` utility can be used to restrict Telnet access to the server from only certain IP addresses.

The `FTP Connection` field does not enable a fully functional FTP server. It simply allows single session FTP access. Authentication is through the remote password specified above. This option will rarely be needed and should be left off unless absolutely required.

The `Remote Installation` field enables or disables the ability to install software from a remote server. It is possible to access software located on other servers from the console prompt. Remote Installation allows NetWare Loadable Modules (NLM) to be loaded from remote systems.

Remote Installation can be a potential security breach and should only be enabled as required. If a potential attacker is able to gain console access, they may be able to load NLM software located on a remote system that they have already cracked. Remote Installation could aid them in gaining access to this server.

Of course the argument can be made that if the attacker has console access, they have sufficient access to simply load the support modules required for remote software installation. Even if this option is left disabled, they can enable it because they have access to the console. This only enforces the statement that the remote access password should be well safeguarded and changed often.

Edit autoexec.ncf   This menu option provides a convenient means of editing the startup file, autoexec.ncf. It allows you to view or change any modifications made by the inetcfg utility.

Once you have completed your changes to the Manage Configuration menu, simply press Escape to return to the main inetcfg window.

View Configuration

The View Configuration menu allows you to view all, or just a portion of, the networking changes you have made so far using the inetcfg utility. If you are an old salt who is used to configuring networking on the command line, this is a good place to review your changes to ensure they are correct. Figure 7.14 shows a small portion of the commands generated by the inetcfg utility. If any of our selections require support modules, they are automatically added to the network startup script. This file is read-only and cannot be edited. If you need to make changes, you must do it through the menu options described above.

The displayed networking commands are updated dynamically. The configuration files are not updated when you exit the inetcfg utility, but rather each time you finish configuring specific menu option.

Also from this menu you can review the log created by the console .nlm utility. console.nlm logs all messages that are displayed on the

FIGURE 7.14

A sample set of commands generated by *INETCFG*

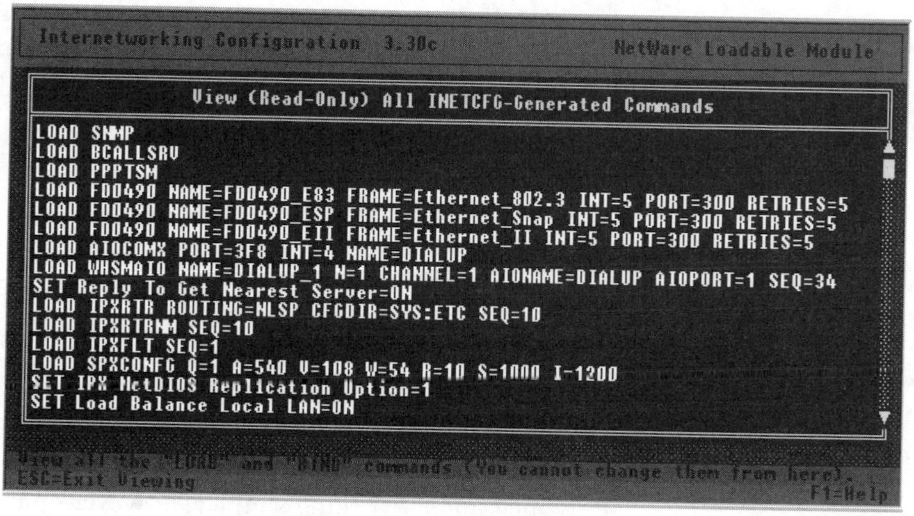

```
Internetworking Configuration  3.30c                    NetWare Loadable Module

                    View (Read-Only) All INETCFG-Generated Commands
LOAD SNMP
LOAD BCALLSRV
LOAD PPPTSM
LOAD FD0490 NAME=FD0490_E83 FRAME=Ethernet_802.3 INT=5 PORT=300 RETRIES=5
LOAD FD0490 NAME=FD0490_ESP FRAME=Ethernet_Snap INT=5 PORT=300 RETRIES=5
LOAD FD0490 NAME=FD0490_EII FRAME=Ethernet_II INT=5 PORT=300 RETRIES=5
LOAD AIOCOMX PORT=3F8 INT=4 NAME=DIALUP
LOAD WHSMAIO NAME=DIALUP_1 N=1 CHANNEL=1 AIONAME=DIALUP AIOPORT=1 SEQ=34
SET Reply To Get Nearest Server=ON
LOAD IPXRTR ROUTING=NLSP CFGDIR=SYS:ETC SEQ=10
LOAD IPXRTRNM SEQ=10
LOAD IPXFLT SEQ=1
LOAD SPXCONFG Q=1 A=540 V=108 W=54 R=10 S=1000 I=1200
SET IPX NetDIOS Replication Option=1
SET Load Balance Local LAN=ON

View all the "LOAD" and "BIND" commands (You cannot change them from here).
ESC=Exit Viewing                                                        F1=Help
```

console screen. It is typically used during system startup to record module information. This is helpful, as messages typically scroll past the screen at a faster rate than most people can read. The console log is a good place to troubleshoot connectivity problems if you think a LAN driver is not loading properly or a bind command is incorrect.

Reinitialize System

The Reinitialize System option restarts networking on the server, but it does not restart the server itself. This option should not be used during normal working hours as it may interrupt user connectivity to the server. When using this option, do so from the server console, not from a remote session. Once activated, Reinitialize System will cause you to lose your remote connection to the server.

If you've made a few minor changes and need them to take effect during working hours, enter the commands manually at the server command line. This will enable the new networking commands without effecting user connectivity.

For example, if your users connect to the server using IPX, you could enter the required commands manually to initialize IP connectivity without affecting any user connections. You can later (during off hours) reinitialize the server to insure that your saved changes are correct. While this method creates a little extra work, it allows your changes to take effect immediately without affecting normal server operation.

Go to Fast Setup

Fast Setup allows you to review the changes you have made with the above menu options and edit them as required. It also allows you to configure new boards and bindings. The option is prompt driven, and is designed to ease setup through a series of questions. This makes configuring network parameters easier if you are not familiar with the inetcfg utility.

By making networking simpler, however, many of the advanced options are not available. For example, you cannot configure Apple-Talk or access the expert options for any of the protocols. Still, if you have a small environment and your networking requirements are simple, the fast setup is a simplified method of getting your server up and running.

IntranetWare IP Applications

Describing the configuration and administration of all of IntranetWare's new IP applications are beyond the scope of this book. For setup and configuration of the new IP applications that have been added to IntranetWare, I refer you to Morgan Stern and Tom Rasmussen's book *Building Intranets on NT, NetWare, and Solaris* (Sybex 1997). It is an excellent reference on how to setup and administer these newly added features.

The Future of IntranetWare

At the time of this writing, Novell has produced an alpha release of the successor to IntranetWare, code named MOAB. MOAB builds upon the foundation created by IntranetWare and should include the following new features:

- Portable NCP—NCP will be broken off from IPX so that it is supported by other protocols. This will bring connectivity features of NCP to other protocols such as IP. This will create native support for other protocols, so that communications are no longer IPX dependent.

- Process Prioritization—Processes running on a server will be able to be prioritized by the system administrator. This is a similar functionality as to what is currently supported by Unix. The administrator can decide which server applications are deemed most important and give them a larger percentage of the available CPU cycles.

- Virtual Memory—The administrator will be allowed to set up a portion of disk space as virtual memory. Processes that are not currently active can be moved from physical memory to disk. This allows for the creation of larger applications than would normally be supported by the amount of physical memory installed in the server.

- Java Virtual Machine—MOAB will support network client machines through the use of Java applications. The network client is not required to save any applications locally. It can access all required applications from the server using a browser interface.

- IP Version 6—As registered address space becomes limited, work is being performed to expand the available address range through a new version of IP. While version 6 is not backwards compatible, MOAB will release support for this version for organizations that wish to begin testing.

Enhancements to file storage, replication, and printing services will also be included when the final version of MOAB is released.

Summary

This completes our discussion of configuring network communications on IntranetWare. You should now have a good understanding of how to provide connectivity to an IntranetWare server. You should also have a good understanding of the features and services provided by this NOS.

In Chapter 8, we will take a similar look at Microsoft's NT Server. We will look at its supported features as well as how to configure it for network communications.

Later, in Chapter 12, we'll revisit IntranetWare and look at options for optimizing network communications. In Chapter 14, we will again revisit this NOS to evaluate the network monitoring and connectivity tools it provides.

CHAPTER

8

Windows NT Server

Released in 1993, Windows NT Server was arguably the first NOS to focus on ease of use and administration. Its initial release used the same interface as the then popular Windows 3.1. For the administrator familiar with this desktop system, it was not a far stretch to set up and administer an NT system using this same interface.

The latest release of Windows NT Server, version 4.0, follows in its predecessor's footprints by utilizing the Windows 95 interface. If you are familiar with Windows 95, you'll feel right at home using NT. The NT Server interface is identical to Windows 95. The differences lie in the additional features supported by NT Server.

Windows NT Features

As mentioned in the last chapter, we will cover some of the features of Windows NT in order to give you a good feel for the operating system. As is apparent from its connectivity options, Windows NT is designed to appeal to a slightly different market group than IntranetWare or Unix.

Windows NT Setup

Unlike IntranetWare, NT Server provides a full GUI interface during most of the server configuration. Curiously, the setup runs in two passes.

The first copies some (but not all) of the files needed for installation to the hard drive. During the second pass, the installation is actually performed. While this is normally not a problem, you should ensure that you have an additional 100MB of free disk space over and above what the OS will require. These temporary files are cleaned up during the final stages of the install.

While NT supports hardware auto-detection, it does not support plug-and-play like Windows 95. This simply means that each hardware component must be preset with the interrupts and memory addresses it needs. For the seasoned administrator, this is usually not a problem.

The network configuration requires a bit more work than Intranet-Ware. NT Server does not detect which protocols are currently running on your network. It simply presents the administrator with the usual defaults for providing file and print services. This is usually not a problem because NT relies on NetBEUI for these services. Unlike IPX, NetBEUI has no network layer support, so entering the correct network address number is not a concern.

NT is also a bit lacking in the infrastructure department. While IntranetWare will detect which NDS trees are available on the network and walk the administrator through the process of grafting the server onto an existing tree, NT is unable to detect existing domains. The administrator must know which server and domains are available. While most administrators are aware of their network environment, it does simplify this step and prevent misspellings.

We will discuss domains in greater detail later in this Chapter.

To its credit, NT has fully integrated all available server options into its installation process, something that IntranetWare has yet to do. For example, the administrator help files must be installed separately under IntranetWare, but are part of the standard installation with NT Server. To be fair, however, the NT Server help files are not nearly as thorough or complete as IntranetWare's.

As for performing server migrations, NT Server provides an easy-to-use utility for environments upgrading from NetWare 2.2x or 3.1x. NetWare 4.x and IntranetWare are not supported. The utility first documents the existing server and all account information. This information can then be migrated from one platform to another over the network. The only things lost during the migration are trustee rights for file access; these must be re-created manually.

Curiously, there is no migration utility for upgrading from NT Server 3.x. The only supported upgrade method is to overwrite the existing server. This can be a pain because it does not allow for the complete upgrade of the server platform or for the ability to have the old server on standby in case there is a problem. Once a same server migration is started, the only way back is by restoring the old system from backup tape—not a happy alternative if the problem is found during working hours.

NT Server can support both Intel and RISC processors. This dramatically increases the number of platforms supported by this NOS. Not all NT applications will run if a RISC processor is used, however. If you are investigating the use of a RISC-based server, ensure that the platform will support all your required applications.

NT Core OS

The core OS of NT Server is 32-bit. While this creates some backwards compatibility problems with 16-bit applications, it ensures that the OS kernel remains stable. Unlike IntranetWare, NT is both multi-tasking and multi-threaded. This helps to prevent any single process from monopolizing all available CPU time.

NT Server uses the same Windows 32 application programming interface as NT workstation and Windows 95 (95 actually only supports a subset of Win32). This ensures a familiar programming environment which, in theory, allows a programmer to write a more stable application.

For example, a programmer who is familiar with writing Windows desktop applications will find programming for NT Server very similar as both use the Win32 interface. This is in contrast to the NetWare Loadable Module (NLM) technology used by an IntranetWare server. A programmer writing code for an IntranetWare server must be specifically aware of the NLM environment.

Because the server uses the same Win32 interface as a Windows workstation, most desktop applications are supported. This can be a real money saver for small environments that cannot afford to dedicate a system to server activities. Unlike IntranetWare, which requires you to dedicate a system as a server, NT Server can perform double duty as a user workstation as well.

Unfortunately it is also missing the remote control features of IntranetWare's Rconsole. While there are tools available from Microsoft's Web site and from their Resource Kits to manage some server functions remotely, you cannot remotely add or remove protocols, launch applications, or access the NT Server desktop from a remote location. Third party software is required to provide this functionality.

NT Server supports memory isolation of all applications running on the system. This is similar to Novell's core OS rings, except once an application has been found to be stable it can never be promoted to having direct access to the core OS. While increasing server stability, it does so at a cost of application execution speed.

Out of the box, NT Server provides support for up to four processors. With hardware support, this can be increased to 32. The benefit of additional processors is that more CPU time can be made available to applications running on the server.

NT Server supports the use of virtual memory. This allows the server to utilize more memory than what is physically installed in the system. The benefit is that applications are free to use more memory to add additional features. The drawback is that virtual memory is stored to disk, which has a slower access time than physical memory by a factor of 100. Again, this can be a real cost saver to a small environment which cannot afford to outfit a server with a lot of physical memory.

This is important as the minimum memory requirements are four times higher than that of IntranetWare. For a minimal server providing basic file, HTTP, and WINS services, plan on installing at least from 96MB to 128MB of physical memory.

Tracking down what applications are loaded into memory and which processes are using CPU time can also be a bit of a chore. To determine what is running, you must check the services dialog box, the device dialog box, and the task manager (both the application and processes tab). This check is in contrast to IntranetWare, which requires you to look in two places (the process monitor and the **modules** command) and Unix, which only requires one (the Process ID or **pid** command).

File System

NT Server supports two file systems, FAT and the NT file system (NTFS). While both support long file names, FAT is optimized for drives up to 500MB while NTFS is designed for drives of 500MB and larger. Neither format supports Macintosh files in their native format. NTFS is the preferred file system for storing applications and user files.

While file compression is supported under NTFS, there is no method to have the server automatically compress files at a preset time or selectively perform compression based upon compression gains like there is with IntranetWare. Files must be manually compressed through Explorer or can be processed through batch files.

If you are going to use NTFS drive partitions larger than 2048MB and you wish to use compression, use the command line **format** command to force the cluster size at 4KB when formatting the drive. NT Server does not support compression when clusters are larger than 4KB. After 2048MB, the cluster size increases to 8KB.

Unlike IntranetWare, NT Server does not support disk sub-allocation. The configured cluster size is the only size available for storing files. This means that you should carefully analyze what type of data will be stored on each of your NTFS drives. If your applications create large files (database, graphics, and so on), then a larger cluster size should be used to decrease the number of required reads when accessing a file. This will speed up file access.

If you will be storing small files (text, HTML, and so on) then use a small cluster size to avoid wasting disk space. When a file is written to disk, it is stored in one or more clusters. If the file does not completely fill a cluster, the remainder goes to waste. A small cluster size ensures that the minimal amount of disk space goes unused.

For example, If I have an 11K file that I write to a disk with 2KB clusters, the file is saved in six separate clusters with 1KB unused and going to waste. If I save the file to a disk with 16KB clusters, it only takes one cluster to save the file (and only one cluster needs to be read for file access) but I'm wasting 5KB worth of potential storage space.

This is why it is important to determine up front what type of files will be saved to the drive. Preplanning ensures that you strike a good balance between space conservation and disk access speed.

NT Server supports directory replication. This allows entire directories to be exported to other servers or even NT workstations. Any changes are updated immediately. This can be extremely useful when it is not practical to always use the server for access to these files.

For example, let's say we are using an NT Server to provide services to a number of programmers. The programmers use a common set of tools and code extensions while compiling their code. They do not wish to run their compile jobs over the network due to the amount of traffic this creates.

The solution would be to create a master copy of these files on the server and export them to each user's NT workstation. This allows them to store their tools locally so that their compile jobs do not have to be run over the network. Because the replication option will immediately export any changes, the programmers can be sure they are always using the latest tools.

Recovering deleted files is only supported under the FAT file system. NT provides no tools for recovering files deleted from an NTFS drive. Also missing is a defragment utility for NTFS. Applications such as Microsoft Exchange are constantly creating and deleting files; this tends to fragment the file system over time. If you are running a file intensive application, pick up a third party defragment utility. Without such a utility, you must back up the file system, delete and re-create the drive, and then restore your files to return them to an unfragmented state.

Account Administration

NT Server uses the Windows NT Directory services for user and group management. This is not, as the name implies, a fully hierarchical directory service like IntranetWare's NDS. It is a flat security structure based upon the use of domains. Domains can be extended to support NetWare 2.2x and 3.1x servers. At the time of this writing, 4.x is not supported.

A domain is a group of workstations and servers associated by a single security policy. A user can perform a single logon and gain access to every server within the domain. They do not need to perform separate logons for each server.

To try and emulate a hierarchical structure, domains can be configured to be trusting. When a domain *trusts* another domain, it allows users of that trusted domain to retain the same level of access they have in the trusted domain.

For example, domain A trusts domain B. This means that everyone that has domain user rights to domain B (trusted domain) will be allowed the same level of access to domain A (trusting domain).

While fine for a small environment, this model does not scale very well. For example, I cannot administer each domain for a single user manager. I must connect to each domain I wish to work with, one at a time.

The other problem is, what if I only want some of the users to have access to the other domain? With IntranetWare, I can simply create an aliases object in each container where I wish the user to have access. With NT Server, this is not possible.

Finally, I cannot check my trust relationships from a central location. I must go to each primary server in each domain to see what trust relationships have been set up. If it is a large environment, I may have to put pen to paper to ensure that I have not set up any trust loops that unintentionally give access to users who shouldn't have access. With IntranetWare, a simple scan of the NDS tree will identify who has access to what.

Domain information is stored on domain controllers. Each domain has a single Primary Domain Controller (PDC). The PDC contains the master record of all domain information. Any other NT Server can be set up as a Backup Domain Controller(BDC). The BDC receives updates from the PDC so that there is a backup copy of the domain information. When a user logs in, they can authenticate with either the PDC or any one of the BDCs.

This brings a bit of a server-centric dependency to the whole domain model. To ensure that changes stay synchronized, all user administration must be performed on the PDC. Any user information that is not specific to the domain must be manually updated out to the BDCs if they will be performing logon authentication.

For example, if the PDC contains a logon script to connect users to network resources, a copy of this logon script must be provided on each BDC. If the logon script on the PDC is changed, the change must be synchronized with each of the BDC servers. This is in contrast to NDS where the user logs on to a container instead of server—regardless of which system replies, the same logon script is available to them.

There is also no way to optimize network performance by specifying which users authenticate with which servers. For example, with NDS partitions of the NDS tree can be placed on only certain servers allowing authentication traffic to be better balanced. In an NT domain, the user authenticates with the first server that replies.

NT Server supports the use of policies to help enforce a standard desktop. Policies can be setup for users, groups or systems. There are 30 different policies that can be configured for a user or a group of users. These allow customization ranging from the selection of a standard wallpaper to the removal of the **run** command from the start menu.

NT policies are not like NAL under IntranetWare. Policies are more focused on customizing the look and feel of the interface, as well as removing available options. It does not include some of the higher level features that NAL does such as standard network program groups or software distribution and setup. Also, policies are only supported by NT while NAL includes support for Windows 3.1*x* and Windows 95. These features are typically utilized by only large organizations. A small network environment may not even use these features.

NT has *Administrative Wizards* for administrators who are new to the NT environment or are just unsure of how to perform certain operations. Figure 8.1 shows the main window for the Administrative Wizards.

FIGURE 8.1

The Administrative
Wizards main window

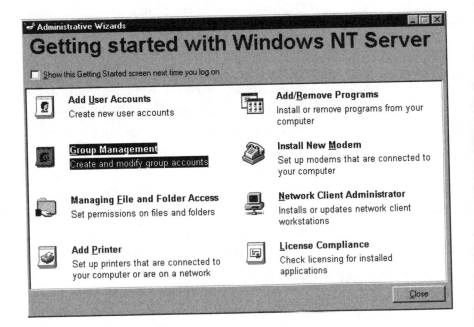

The Administrative Wizards are question-and-answer based, so the administrator is walked through all necessary configuration steps. Figure 8.2 is an example of one of the wizard windows for adding a new user. There are also wizards for administrating groups, printers, program licenses, and installing new modems or software.

FIGURE 8.2

A sample window from the administration wizard for adding user accounts

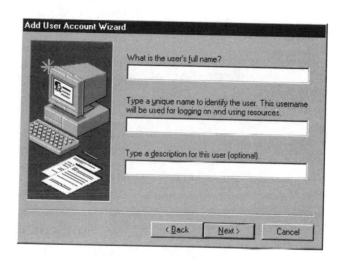

Security

Windows NT has been C2 certified by the National Computer Security Center (NCSC) for stand-alone use. It has not yet received approval as a trusted network. This means that to comply with the C2 approval, the NT system cannot have any means of remote connection (no NIC card or modem). Because this defeats the purpose of a server, you cannot run NT as a server and comply with its C2 certification.

Users are assigned their access rights based on association to pre-defined groups. When a user is part of a group, they receive all the access rights associated with that group. NT supplies eight local and three domain groups to which users can be associated for varying levels of access.

For example, there is a Backup Operator group which provides read access to the entire server for the purpose of performing backups. There is also a Print Operator group which allows its members to manage printers and print queues.

While this is fine for small environments with simple security requirements, it does not scale very well. For example, let's assume we have 15 NT Servers. 13 provide file and print services, one runs Lotus Notes, and the other runs a Web server. We wish to give the Notes administrator full, unrestricted access to the Notes server and the Web master the same level of access to the Web server. We want both of these users to have regular user rights on the remaining 13 servers.

Under the single domain model, this is not possible. As soon as we give them administrator access to their respective systems, they have the same level of access throughout the domain.

In order to work around this problem we would need to setup three separate domains. One for the 13 file and print servers, and one for each of the two remaining systems. If we later bring in a mail server under the same conditions, we are now looking at adding domain number four. Because in a typical small network the same person or group of people is responsible for all aspects of the network, the above mentioned problem is rarely an issue.

NT Server supports auditing of user activity and system events. Seven events can be monitored in all. While this number pales in comparison to IntranetWare's ability to monitor 70, it is usually sufficient for the auditing requirements of a smaller environment.

These seven events are not very customizable, however. For example, while we can monitor when people log on and log off of the server, we cannot specify a specific account to monitor (such as Administrator). Also, while we can log who accesses a file, we cannot specify which files to watch or even what type of access was performed (read, delete, copy, and so on).

NT Server allows trustee rights to be assigned to directories on NTFS drives. This regulates who is permitted to access the files and what they are allowed to do with them. For example, some users may be allowed to delete and change files while others have only read access.

There are a few drawbacks with this system. First, all users are given full access by default. It is up to the administrator to go back and restrict access to only those users who require it. Also, trustee rights cannot be assigned through the same utility where users and groups are created. This means the administrator must check in two separate areas to identify what type of access a user has to a server.

Networking

NT Server includes support for NetBEUI, IP, IPX, AppleTalk, and DLC. NetBEUI, IP, and AppleTalk can be used when accessing file and print services. IP support is via NetBEUI encapsulation.

NT Server includes support for Ethernet, Token Ring, ATM, FDDI, PPP, ISDN, and Frame Relay. Monitoring of all LAN topologies is performed through a single network monitoring tool. The network monitor is covered in Chapter 14.

When two or more networking cards are installed, NT Server has the ability to act as a router. For outbound connectivity (LAN to WAN), only full-time WAN links are supported. For inbound (WAN to LAN), both full-time and bandwidth-on-demand connections are supported.

Inbound dial-up connections are handled by the *remote access server* (RAS) component. RAS provides authentication based upon NT account information. Users can dial in via PPP or ISDN using the same logon name and password they use while on the LAN. The administrator has the ability to selectively grant rights on a user-by-user basis. Callback options are even available for enhanced security. Once authentication is complete, the user has access to all IP, IPX, and NetBEUI services on the network, not just the NT server itself. This is an extremely cost-effective feature for environments that cannot afford the additional cost of a modem pool.

RAS supports multilink channel aggregation. Channel aggregation allows a dial-in user to utilize more than one phone line for network access. For example, a user with two 28.8k modems can dial in on two separate lines to receive an effective throughput of 57.6k. At the time of this writing, only NT Workstation and Server can leverage this capability with anything but ISDN.

NT Server also supports the *point-to-point tunneling protocol* (PPTP). This service allows users to access the NT Server from any place out on the Internet, which means that an administrator is not required to run a modem pool to allow home users to access the internal network. Users can dial in to their regular ISP account and use the Internet as a transport when accessing the organization's network resources.

As a router, NT Server supports static routing under IP and distance vector for IP, IPX, and AppleTalk. Link state routing is not supported for any protocol. Because NT's primary focus is the small network environment, this is usually not a problem.

When IPX is used, NT has the ability to auto detect (during startup) which frame types and network numbers are being used. It will also perform a test ARP during startup to ensure that no other systems are using the server's IP address. These two features help to greatly simplify administration.

Unlike IntranetWare, NT Server does not support any packet filtering for IPX or AppleTalk, and does not support a full set of tools for IP. While it will filter IP based on port number, there are a number of drawbacks with this minimal configuration.

First, it will not selectively pass traffic based upon source and destination address. This makes it ineffective as a packet filter for Internet use. Also, filtering is performed on the NIC as the traffic comes into the server. You cannot filter traffic as it is exiting the server through the NIC.

For example, if you want to setup the NT Server as a Web server on one of its ports and hide what type of system the Web server is running on to minimize the chance of an attack, you have no way of shutting off the NetBIOS broadcast on that port that in effect says, "Hi, I'm an NT Server, come and get me!" This is the Internet equivalent of walking around with your money roll pinned to your sleeve. Once an attacker knows what you have, it's easier for them to figure out how to violate it.

The one extremely annoying peculiarity of NT networking is that any change, no matter how minor, requires a reboot of the machine to initialize the changes. Want to point to a new WINS server? The machine must be rebooted. Want to add a new protocol? Again, the machine must be rebooted. This is usually not a problem in small environments where server availability is only required from 8 AM to 5 PM. It can be completely unacceptable in a larger shop that requires server access 7×24 (7 days a week, 24 hours a day).

If you have just rebooted an NT server and receive the error message "The service database is currently locked," when working with the network configuration, have a cup of coffee and try again later. Being able to log on to an NT server does not mean it has finished initializing. How long the initialization process will take is dependent on how many services it is required to start.

IP Applications

NT Server ships with a full set of IP applications. About the only things missing are an IPX to IP gateway (or even a NetBEUI to IP gateway), and a decent set of packet filters or firewall (Microsoft does sell a proxy server as an add-on product). With this in mind it is better to keep an NT server inside the protection of a firewall.

NT Server includes the *Internet Information Server* (IIS). IIS installs servers for Web, FTP, and gopher services. The Web server sports an access speed that is nearly twice as fast as its predecessor which ran on NT version 3.51 (although the access speed is not quite up to par with IntranetWare or Unix). For Web development, CGI, WINCGI, Visual Basic, and Perl are supported. The Web server also supports *secure sockets layer* (SSL) for secure transactions (although support is for version 2.0, not 3.0 which is current). The Web server does not support multihoming.

Microsoft has also made an index server available for download, free of charge. The index server is capable of accepting advanced queries and searching text, HTML or Microsoft Office documents for instances of the search string. The index server is an easy way to add document retrieval to the list of features supported by your Web server.

NT Server also supports DNCP, IP printing, DNS, and WINS. When DNS is configured to refer to WINS for host information, the two are capable of exchanging information. When a NetBIOS-based system registers itself with the WINS server, that information is conveyed to the DNS server. This allows a system to be known by the same name under NetBIOS and IP. It also allows the administrator to keep the DNS host name table up to date with a minimal amount of administration.

Configuring NT Server for Network Access

All network connectivity is installed through the Network Properties window. This can be accessed by right-clicking the network neighborhood and selecting Properties or by starting the networking icon under the control panel.

System Identification

Figure 8.3 shows the Identification tab for the Network Properties window. This server is identified as using the NetBIOS name Talsin and belonging to the domain Brenton. Under the identification description it states, "You may change the name of this computer or the name of the domain that it manages." This lets you know that this machine is a PDC.

While NT servers can be promoted from a regular server to a BDC and from a BDC to a PDC, once a system has become a PDC the operating system must be reinstalled to make it anything else. This is in contrast to NDS on IntranetWare that allows you to promote or demote any server on the fly.

F I G U R E 8.3

The Identification tab for
our NT Server identifies
its NetBIOS name, the
domain, and that this
particular server is a PDC.

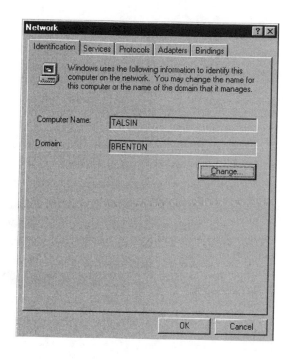

If you click the Change button, you are presented with the dialog box
shown in Figure 8.4. Because this system is already a PDC, we are not
allowed to make it a BDC or join another domain. Our only options are
to change the server's name or the name of the domain it is responsible
for. If we change our domain name, we will also be required to reconfigure our BDC servers.

F I G U R E 8.4

Because this system is
already a PDC, our only
options are to change its
name or change the
domain name.

Once our changes are complete, we can continue through the remaining tabs or reboot the server to initialize our changes.

Services

Our next option is to configure Network Services. Services are the applications we can make available to our clients using the protocols we will configure in the next step. For example, if we will be running IP on our network, we can install the IIS server to provide Web, FTP, and Gopher access to this system. Figure 8.5 is a sample Network Services tab with a number of supported services installed.

FIGURE 8.5

A sample Network Services tab—this is where you will install the network applications and connectivity options that you will make available to your clients.

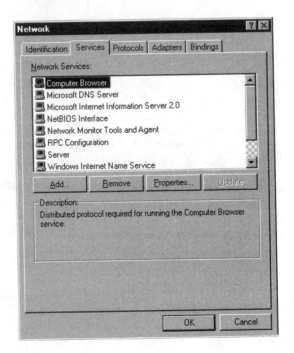

By clicking the Add or Remove buttons, you can selectively choose which services you wish to run on the server. The Properties button is only available for some services. For example, Figure 8.6 shows the configurable properties for the Server services. These options allow the server to be optimized, based upon your system requirements.

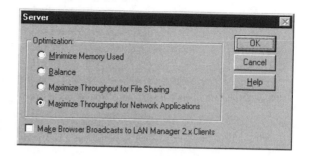

FIGURE 8.6

Server properties under the Services tab—these settings allow the server to be tuned based upon its intended use.

Pay close attention to your configuration when you are adding and removing services. NT does not always track the relationship between installed services and protocols. For example, if you remove IP as a protocol from the system, it will not automatically remove support for any IP applications (DNCP, DNS, and so on). In fact you may find yourself reinstalling the protocol just to remove the services. For example, let's assume you no longer require IP services on the system and remove IP from the list of protocols. Later, you realize that you forgot to remove the IIS server as well. When you attempt to remove it, NT will require you to reinstall IP prior to removing the IIS service.

Available Services

The following is a list of available services that come with NT Server and a brief description of each. Figure 8.7 shows the menu for adding additional services. The listed services are those that ship with NT Server. The Have Disk option can be used for adding services created by third party developers.

FIGURE 8.7

The menu for adding
additional services to the
NT Server

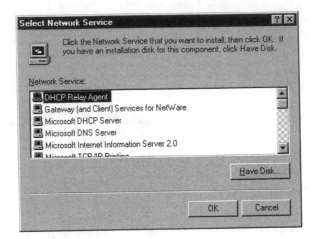

Computer Browser   When NetBIOS and NetBEUI are used, the computer browser creates and maintains a list of system names on the network. It also provides this list to applications running on the system such as the network neighborhood. The computer browser properties allow you to add additional domains to be checked for system names.

DHCP Relay Agent   When a DHCP client and server exist on two separate network segments, the DCHP relay agent acts as a proxy between the two systems.

The DHCP relay agent ensures that the client's DHCP requests are passed along to the segment where the DHCP server resides. In turn, it also ensures that the replies sent by the server make it back to the client. The benefit of a DHCP relay agent is that it removes the necessity of having a separate DHCP server on each logical network. The relay agent can be located on the same network segment as the client, or at the border between the client's and the DHCP server's network segments (acting as a router).

The DHCP relay agent requires the IP protocol to be installed. It also requires the IP address of at least one DHCP server.

Gateway (and Client) Services for NetWare   This service allows an NT server to access file and print services on a NetWare server. The client portion of the services allow the server to log on to the NetWare server in a similar fashion as any NetWare client. The logon script can be processed, and the NT server is allowed to map drive letters pointing to the file system on the NetWare server.

The gateway portion of the service allows users running only NetBEUI, to access files on the NetWare server through the NT server. The gateway has a separate authentication configuration from that used by the client. Once the gateway has authenticated and mapped drive letters to the NetWare server, it can make these drives available as shares.

The gateway allows the NT server to create share names for each of the drive letters mapped to the NetWare server. From the user's perspective, these shares appear to be located on the NT server, not the NetWare server. Figure 8.8 shows how this share may be configured. The NT server Loki logs on to the NetWare server Athena using IPX, just like any other client. As part of the logon process, Loki maps drive G to the apps directory on VOL1 of Athena.

The gateway allows Loki to then in turn share drive G as \\Loki\apps. The NT clients can then direct file requests to Loki using NetBEUI. Any requests received by Loki are translated to IPX and passed along to Athena. When a reply is received, Loki translates the response to NetBEUI and passes it along to the client. As far as Loki clients are concerned, the shared files reside on Loki.

While the gateway service is a good way to bridge the gap between NT and NetWare, the translation does reduce file access speed. The gateway is designed to be a migration aid or to provide occasional access to files on the NetWare server. When heavy NetWare file access (compiling code or database searches) is required, direct access should be used.

Once the gateway service is installed, a new button called Network Access Order appears at the bottom of the Services tab. Clicking this button produces the window shown in Figure 8.9. The Network Access Order dialog box allows you to configure the order in which the NT server attempts to find resources.

FIGURE 8.8

The NT client and gateway services for NetWare allow an NT server to share files located on a NetWare server.

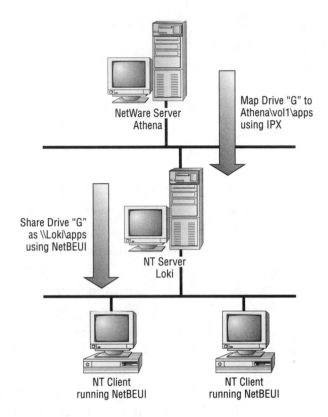

NetWare Server
Athena

Map Drive "G" to
Athena\vol1\apps
using IPX

Share Drive "G"
as \\Loki\apps
using NetBEUI

NT Server
Loki

NT Client
running NetBEUI

NT Client
running NetBEUI

With the configuration shown in Figure 8.9, the NT server will look for NetWare resources (IPX) before it will look for Windows resources (NetBEUI). For example, if you tell the NT server to search for a specific computer name, it will first attempt to access the resource via IPX. If name is not found, it then looks for the name using NetBEUI.

If the NT server will be authenticating during startup to all the NetWare servers it needs access to, change the network access order so that "Microsoft Windows Network" precedes the "NetWare or Compatible Network." This will allow the NT server to discover other Windows systems (such as Windows 95 machines with file sharing enabled) faster.

FIGURE 8.9

The Network Access
Order dialog box allows
you to select the order in
which the NT server
should search for
resources.

The NetWare client and gateway services require that the NwLink IPX/SPX compatible transport protocol be installed. The client portion creates an icon on the control panel (labeled GSNW) so that a preferred server or tree may be selected. There is a Enable Gateway check box in the Configure Gateway dialog box, shown in Figure 8.10, which allows for the gateway portion of the services to be enabled and configured. The Configure Gateway dialog box also accepts the account information required to connect with the NetWare server and to share information for each of the drives.

Microsoft DNCP Server   The DHCP server allows the NT server to automatically provide IP address information to network clients. When a client sends out a DHCP request, it can receive all information required to communicate on an IP network, including an IP address, subnet mask, domain name, and DNS server.

The DHCP server requires that the IP protocol be installed. When the DHCP server is installed, it automatically adds a menu option for the DHCP manager to the Administrative Tools menu.

F I G U R E 8.10

The Configure Gateway
dialog box allows you to
enable or disable the
NetWare gateway and
enter account
information.

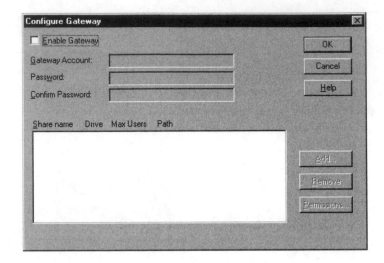

Microsoft DNS Server   The Microsoft DNS server allows the NT
server to respond to clients and other DNS servers with IP domain
name information. When the DNS server is configured to use WINS
resolution, host name information is provided by WINS, based upon
NetBIOS system names.

A DNS server normally requires that host name information be manually maintained in a set of text files. If a machine changes its IP address,
the DNS tables must be updated to reflect this change. If DHCP is used
to provide IP address information, DNS has no way of knowing which
host names will be assigned to which IP address.

By using WINS resolution, the DNS server can query the WINS
server for host information. The DNS server passes the query along to
WINS, which uses its NetBIOS table to match an IP address to a host
name. The WINS server then returns this information to the DNS server.
To a client querying a DNS server, the transaction is transparent. As
far as the client is concerned, the DNS server is solely responsible for
responding to the request. The two services do not need to be configured
on the same NT server.

The DNS server requires that the IP protocol be installed. When the DNS server is installed, it automatically adds a menu option for the DNS manager to the Administrative Tools menu.

Microsoft Internet Information Server (IIS) 2.0   The Microsoft Internet Information Server adds Web, FTP, and Gopher functionality to the NT server. Once installed, clients can access HTML pages, transfer files via FTP, and perform Gopher searches for files.

By default, the installation creates the directory InetPub, and places four directories inside of it. The first three are the root directories for each of the three servers. All files and directories for each of the three services are to be placed under their respective root directory.

The fourth directory is for scripts. Web applications developed with CGI, WINCGI, Visual Basic, or Perl can be stored in this directory. This directory also contains some sample scripts as well as a few development tools.

The IIS requires that IP be installed. During IIS installation, a menu folder called Microsoft Internet Server is created for the management tools required for these services.

Microsoft TCP/IP Printing   Microsoft's TCP/IP printing allows an NT Server to support Unix printing, referred to as a line printer daemon (lpd). TCP/IP printing allows the NT server to print to a print server that supports lpd, or to a Unix system that has a directly connected printer.

IP printing also allows the NT server to act as a printing gateway for Microsoft clients. The NT server connects to lpd via IP, and can advertise this printer as a shared resource on NetBEUI. Microsoft clients using only NetBEUI can send print jobs to this advertised share. The NT server then forwards these jobs on to the lpd printer.

Microsoft TCP/IP printing requires that the IP protocol be installed. During installation, it adds a new printer port type called LPR, as shown in Figure 8.11. LPR is Line Printer Remote which provides remote access to lpd printers.

FIGURE 8.11

Installing IP printing adds
an additional printer
port, called the LPR port,
through which an NT
server can access Unix
printers.

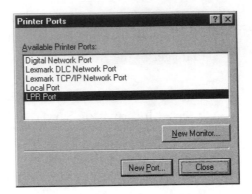

NetBIOS Interface   The NetBIOS interface provides backwards
compatibility with LAN MAN systems that do not use the NetBEUI
protocol for communications.

Network Monitor Agent   The network monitor agent allows the NT
server to be remotely accessed and monitored by systems running the
NT server Network Monitoring Tools.

Network Monitor Tools and Agent   The network monitoring tool
installs a network analyzer similar to Novell's LANAlyzer or Network
General's Sniffer. It allows the server to capture and decode network
frames for the purpose of analysis. Figure 8.12 shows a typical packet
capture with the network monitoring tool. The tool displays the source
and destination address of each system, as well as the protocol in use.

Network Monitor is a great tool for diagnosing problems or analyzing traffic patterns on the network. We will discuss this tool in
greater detail in Chapter 14 when we discuss network monitoring.

Remote Access Server (RAS)   The remote access server allows the
NT server to provide dial-in access to the server and other network
resources. Clients can dial-in to RAS and authenticate using their standard Microsoft user name and password.

FIGURE 8.12

The network monitoring tool can capture network traffic so that it can be decoded and analyzed.

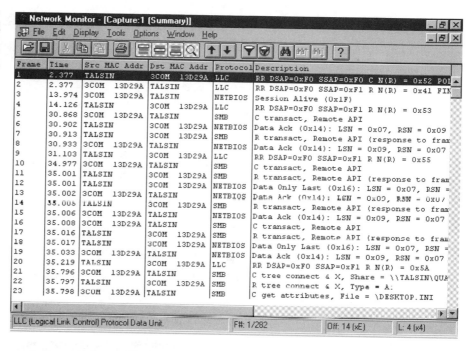

FIGURE 8.12

The network monitoring tool can capture network traffic so that it can be decoded and analyzed.

The Remote Access Setup dialog box, shown in Figure 8.13, allows you to select which modems are attached to the server to dedicate to RAS use. If you attempt to install RAS without any modems configured, it will warn you and offer to startup the modem configuration utility. This box also allows you to select which modems RAS should monitor for dial-in activity.

RAS allows you to select if dial-in users will be allowed to access just the RAS server, or if they will be allowed full network access. If network access is allowed, RAS lets you select which protocols are acceptable for dial-in access.

For example, if you wish to give dial-in users access to your NT and NetWare servers, but do not wish to give them access to the Internet, simply disable the IP protocol. The only drawback is that this is a global setting, it is not configurable on a user-by-user basis. If the network administrator wishes to enable IP services just for themselves for network

FIGURE 8.13

The Remote Access Setup
dialog box

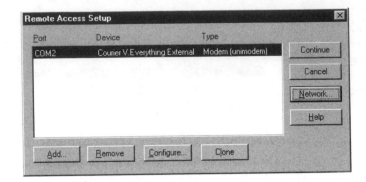

diagnostic purposes (for example to ensure that the Dilbert site and Subspace arena servers are still accessible), the administrator will need to find some other method of accessing the network remotely. Figure 8.14 shows the Network Configuration dialog box.

FIGURE 8.14

The Network
Configuration dialog box
allows the administrator
to select which protocols
are available during dial-in
access.

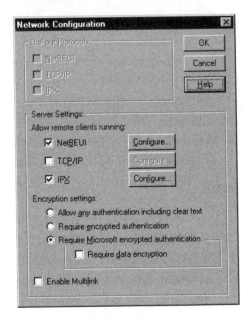

RAS requires that the NetBIOS interface service be installed. During RAS installation, a menu option for the Remote Access Manager is added to the Administrative Tools menu.

Remoteboot Service   The remoteboot service allows the NT server to boot DOS, Windows 3.1, and Windows 95 workstations remotely. Windows for workgroup clients are not supported. This allows the use of network clients that do not have any means of internal storage (no floppy or hard drive). The client's network card must have a *boot prom* installed in order to access its required initialization files on the NT Server. 3COM-, AMD-, Intel SMC-, and NE2000-compatible network cards are supported.

When a diskless client first powers up, the boot prom sends out a network broadcast requesting the systems startup files. When remoteboot is installed on the NT server, it allows the server to reply to these requests with the initialization files that the client requires.

The remoteboot manager allows the NT administrator to configure what type of startup information the client receives. The NT administrator first creates a workstation profile, which describes what type of network cards will be used in the workstation, as well as which operating system they will be running. Figure 8.15 shows the New Profile dialog box. Enter the operating system in the Description text box and select the type of network card to be used by the client. This combination can be given a profile name in the Profile Name text box for later use when the individual workstations are configured.

FIGURE 8.15

The New Profile
dialog box

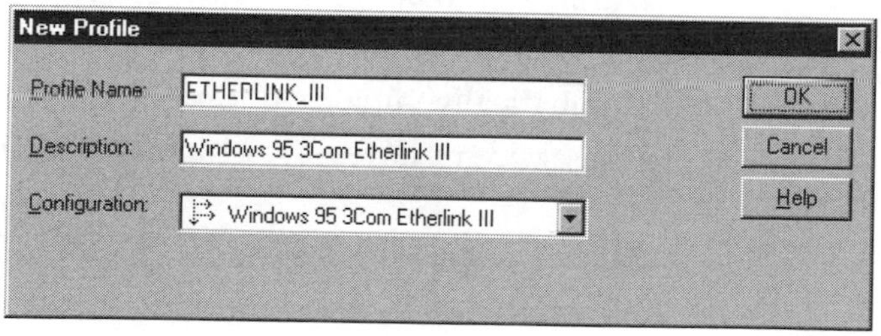

Once a profile is created, each individual workstation can be configured. Figure 8.16 shows the New Remoteboot Workstation dialog box. The Adapter ID field requires the MAC address for the workstation to be configured. This address is used by the workstation when it queries the server for its configuration information. The remoteboot service can provide the workstation with a unique system name, IP address (if DHCP is not used), and all the files required to initialize the operating system. These files are stored as system images on the NT server.

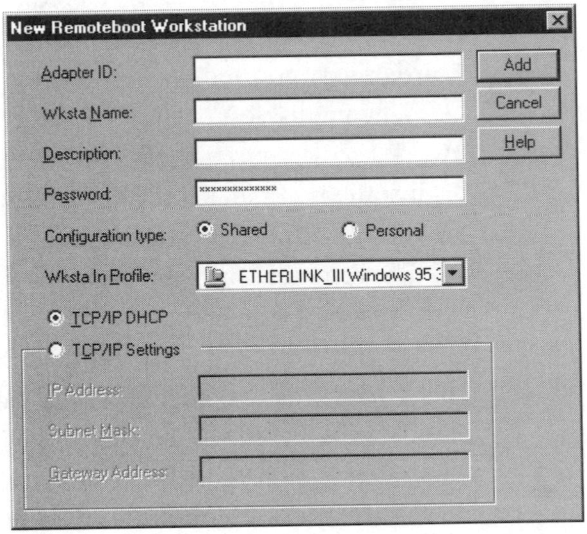

FIGURE 8.16

The New Remoteboot Workstation dialog box

The Remoteboot service requires that the DLC protocol be installed. During Remoteboot installation, a menu option for the Remoteboot Manager is added to the Administrative Tools menu. Remoteboot does not automatically initialize during system startup. It must be manually started as a service or have its startup changed from manual to automatic.

RIP for Internet Protocol   The RIP for Internet protocol service allows the NT server to use and propagate routing information broadcasts for the IP protocol. RIP is the only dynamic routing protocol supported for IP. NT server does not support any IP border gateway or link state routing protocols.

RIP for Internet protocol requires that the IP protocol be installed.

RIP for NwLink IPX/SPX Compatible Transport   The RIP for NwLink service allows the NT server to propagate routing information broadcasts for the IPX protocol. This service is typically enabled when the NT server will be acting as a router and needs to propagate IPX network information. NT server only supports RIP routing with the IPX protocol. Link state routing is not supported. If the NT server is to coexist on a network with IntranetWare servers, the IntranetWare servers must have Backwards Compatibility with RIP enabled.

There are no properties for NwLink RIP, only a dialog box which prompts you to enable or disable the forwarding of NetBIOS over IPX frames (referred to as type 20 propagation). RIP for NwLink requires that the NwLink IPX/SPX Compatible Transport protocol be installed.

RPC Configuration   The RPC configuration service enables NT Server support for Remote Procedure Call (RPC). RPC is used by some applications to exchange information at a peer-to-peer level.

RPC Support for Banyan   RPC support for Banyan allows RPC enabled applications running on an NT server, to exchange information with their counterpart applications operating on a Banyan Vines server.

SAP Agent   The SAP agent allows an NT server to propagate IPX *Service Advertising Protocol* (SAP) broadcasts. This service is typically used when the NT server will be acting as a router and needs to propagate IPX service information.

The SAP agent requires that the NwLink IPX/SPX Compatible Transport protocol be installed.

Server   The server service is what allows the NT server to offer up file and print services to network clients. This service is installed by default and allows clients to communicate to the server via NetBEUI. Without the server service, the NT system can only offer up application services.

The server service requires that the NetBEUI protocol be installed.

Services for Macintosh   Services for Macintosh installs all the required software components to allow Apple's Mac computers to exchange files on an NT server.

The Microsoft AppleTalk Protocol Properties dialog box allows the administrator to choose which zone the NT server will reside in. They can also configure if the NT will act as a soft seed and discover the local network addresses or if it will act as a router and seed the network. When acting as a seed, zone names can also be assigned and at least one zone name must be specified. Figure 8.17 shows the Routing tab of the Microsoft AppleTalk Protocol Properties dialog box.

FIGURE 8.17

When services for Macintosh are installed, the NT server can learn the network address range by acting as a soft seed, or it can define the network range by acting as the seed router.

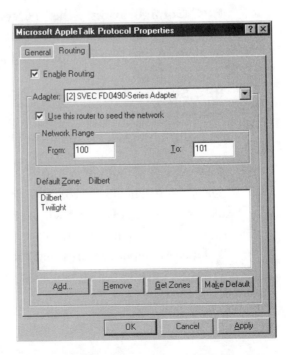

Services for Macintosh requires that at least one NT server drive be configured as an NTFS partition. Software translation along with NTFS's support for extended files is used to allow Mac system to save and retrieve file information. Because Services for Macintosh installs all required software, no additional protocol loading is required.

Simple TCP/IP Services Simple TCP/IP services installs support for some fun, but little used, IP applications such as Echo and Quote of the Day. The quote of the day can serve up such selections as, "We want a few mad people now. See where the sane ones have landed us!" by George Bernard Shaw (1856-1950).

The Simple TCP/IP services requires that the IP protocol be installed.

SNMP Service The SNMP service allows the NT server to be monitored by an SNMP management station. It also allows the performance monitor on the NT server to monitor IP statistics as well as statistic for IP applications (DNS, WINS, and so on).

When the SNMP service is installed, the NT server can send configuration and performance information to an SNMP management station such as Hewlett-Packard's HP Openview. This allows the status of the NT server, as well as other SNMP devices, to be monitored from a central location. Monitoring can be performed over the IP or IPX protocol.

The SNMP service also adds additional functionality to the NT performance monitor. For example, it allows you to monitor the number of IP packets with errors or the number of WINS queries the server has received. Both SNMP and the applicable service must be installed for these features to be added to performance monitor.

SNMP services requires that either the IP or IPX protocol be installed for station monitoring.

Windows Internet Name Service (WINS) As described in Chapter 6, a WINS server allows NetBIOS or NetBEUI systems to communicate across a router using IP encapsulation of NetBIOS. The WINS server acts as a NetBIOS Name Server (NBNS) for p-node and h-node systems located on the NT server's local subnet. WINS stores the system's NetBIOS name, as well as its IP address.

Each WINS server on the network periodically updates the other WINS servers with a copy of its table. The result is a dynamic list, mapping NetBIOS names to IP addresses for every system on the network. A copy of the list is then stored on each WINS server.

When a p-node system needs the address of another NetBIOS system, it sends a discovery packet to its local WINS server. If the system in question happens to be located on a remote subnet, the WINS server returns the remote system's IP address. This allows the remote system to be discovered without propagating broadcast frames throughout the network. When h-nodes are used, the functionality is identical.

WINS requires that the IP protocol be installed. During WINS installation, a menu option for the WINS Manager is added to the Administrative Tools menu.

Workstation   The workstation service is the counterpart to the "Server" service. It allows the NT server to access file and printer shares on other computers acting as a client.

The workstation service requires that the NetBEUI protocol be installed.

Once we have completed changes to our services we can continue through the remaining tabs or reboot the server to initialize our changes.

Protocols

Our next option is to configure network protocols. Protocols provide the means of communication required to support the applications we reviewed in the last section. For example, if we decided to install the DNS services, we must ensure that the IP protocol is installed and configured. Figure 8.18 shows a sample Protocol tab.

The Add and Remove buttons allow us to selectively choose which protocols we require. The Properties button allows us to configure any

F I G U R E 8.18

From the Protocols tab of
the Network window, we
can install all the protocols
required to support our
required services.

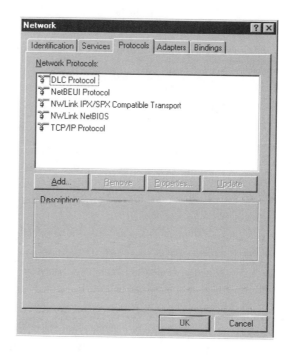

protocol parameters, if required. Figure 8.19 shows the list of available
protocols when the Add button is selected. The Have Disk button is
used to add third party protocol support.

F I G U R E 8.19

The Select Network
Protocol dialog box

Available Protocols

The following is a list of available protocols that come with NT Server and a brief description of each.

DLC Protocol The Data Link Control (DLC) protocol provides applications with hardware level communications (using MAC addresses). It provides local segment communications only. DLC is used by IBM mainframes, as well as print server companies such as HP.

When DLC is installed, it adds additional printer port drivers, as shown in Figure 8.20. The Hewlett–Packard Network Port, as well as the Lexmark DLC Network Port, are added during the installation of the DLC protocol. This adds print server support for each company's print server products. The DLC protocol has no configurable properties.

F I G U R E 8.20

The Printer Ports
dialog box

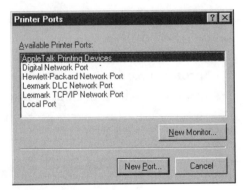

NetBEUI Protocol The NetBEUI protocol provides support for NT Server file and printer sharing. If Microsoft clients will be accessing the NT server for file and printer services, this protocol should be installed. NetBEUI has no configurable properties.

NwLink IPX/SPX Compatible Transport NwLink is Microsoft's implementation of the IPX protocol. This protocol is required if the NT server needs to communicate with a NetWare server (either as a client or as a gateway).

When NwLink is installed, the NT server can be assigned an internal IPX network number just like an IntranetWare server, or this field can be left blank. The internal IPX number is used when you wish to have the NT server transmit SAP frames and emulate a NetWare server. This functionality requires the SAP agent to be installed as well.

The NT server can also be configured to auto detect, or manually assign an IPX network address to each network card. Figure 8.21 shows the General tab of the NwLink IPX/SPX Properties window. When the Manual Frame Type Detection button is selected, you must specify which NetWare frame type and what IPX network number to use for the selected network card. If the NT server is the only IPX server or router on a particular network segment, the frame type and address should be configured manually.

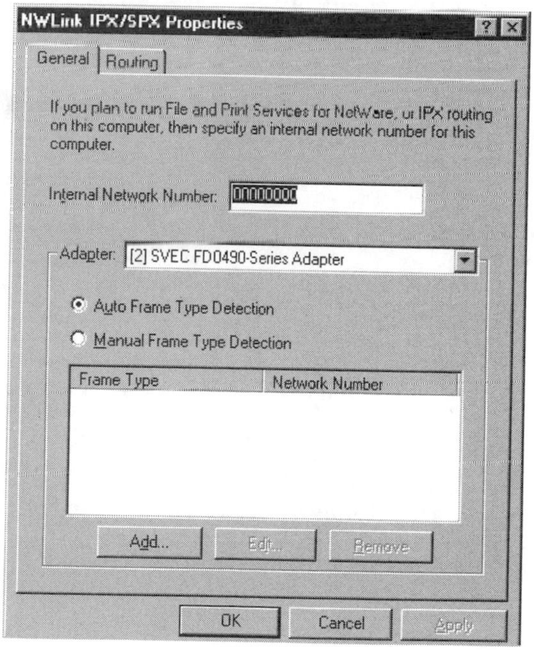

FIGURE 8.21

The General tab of the NwLink IPX/SPX Properties window

NwLink NetBIOS　NwLink NetBIOS is Microsoft's implementation of NetBIOS over IPX (referred to as Type 20 IPX packets). Enabling the NwLink NetBIOS protocol allows the NT server to exchange type 20 IPX packets with other network devices.

If the server is acting as a router, RIP for NwLink must have type 20 propagation enabled in order for an NT server to forward these packets from one network segment to another.

NwLink for NetBIOS has no configurable properties.

Point to Point Tunneling Protocol (PPTP)　The point-to-point tunneling protocol allows a user to access a RAS server over an insecure network such as the Internet. PPTP sets up a virtual private network (VPN) between the client and the RAS server.

The PPTP Configuration dialog box, shown in Figure 8.22, allows the administrator to configure how may VPN sessions may be set up to the server. Once this value is set, you will be prompted to install and configure the RAS server as well.

FIGURE 8.22

Configure how many VPN sessions will be supported by the server in the PPTP Configuration dialog box.

As part of the RAS server configuration, you can define the VPN sessions as potential ports for users to use when connecting to the RAS server. The Remote Access Setup dialog box is shown in Figure 8.23 with one VPN port available for network sessions.

In order to connect to the RAS server over a VPN, the client must have an additional WAN driver installed in their dial-up networking that supports PPTP. Windows NT (both Server and Workstation) ships

F I G U R E   8.23

Once you have defined
the number of available
VPN sessions, you can
assign them as available
connection ports for the
RAS server to monitor.

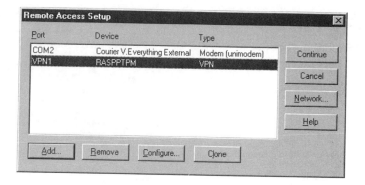

with a PPTP driver. At the time of this writing, a beta driver has been made available for Windows 95.

The client can then connect to their ISP as they would for regular network access. Once they have complete the authentication process with the ISP, they can use the PPTP driver to access the RAS server. The authentication process uses the same logon name and password that the user enters when they are on the network.

Once a session is established, the user is provided services based upon the RAS server configuration as described above. The user can be limited to accessing just the RAS server, or they can connect to other network resources. PPTP supports the tunneling of NetBEUI, IP, and IPX, so any resource using these protocols can be accessed.

When PPTP is used, the RAS server can be configured to only accept PPTP traffic by selecting the Enable PPTP Filtering button. This is a good security feature because it permits only PPTP traffic to access the server. Used in combination with a good firewall, this feature can help ensure that "undesirables" do not access your NT server from the Internet. If the NT server will be providing Web or FTP services to the Internet as well, leave PPTP filtering disabled. PPTP filtering is configured under the Advanced IP Addressing dialog box, as shown in Figure 8.24.

PPTP uses the Password Authentication Protocol (PAP) and Challenge Handshake Authentication Protocol (CHAP), as defined in Request For Comment (RFC) 1334, for performing session authentication. These

FIGURE 8.24

PPTP Filtering can be
enabled from the
Advanced IP Addressing
dialog box.

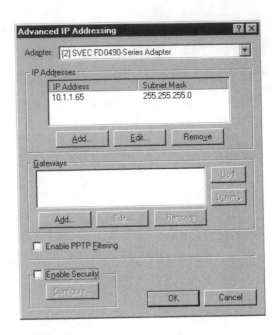

authentication methods were designed for the Point-to-Point Protocol (PPP) which is normally used over a dial-up link. With this in mind, security is not exactly *bullet proof*. PAP sends passwords as clear text and CHAP only occasionally verifies that the remote system is authentic.

Through RAS, PPTP supports bulk data encryption with a 40-bit session key that is negotiated once authentication is complete. This means that the encryption key is transmitted between the two systems during the remote session. While this is in no way as secure as a public-private encryption key scheme, it is certainly more secure than using Telnet or FTP to access network resources.

Streams   Streams provides encapsulation of other network protocols such as IPX or IP. By wrapping around the transport protocol, it can provide a common interface to applications as well as data link layer drivers. Streams is not a true protocol per se, as it relies on the encapsulated protocol to provide transport services.

Streams is primarily for the use of third party protocols. It acts as a common interface allowing developers to port other transports to NT. Streams has no configurable properties.

TCP/IP   TCP/IP adds support for the IP protocol. Figure 8.25 shows the Microsoft TCP/IP Properties window. This window allows the administrator to configure an IP address for each interface or receive the address automatically from a DHCP server. If this NT server will be running the DHCP service, IP addresses should be configured manually. If more than one IP address is required on a given interface, configure it in the Advanced Addressing dialog box (see Figure 8.24).

FIGURE 8.25

The IP Address tab of the Microsoft TCP/IP Properties window

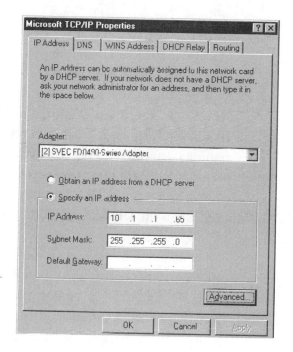

As you look at Figure 8.25, note that a default gateway has not been set. This server must have the RIP for Internet Protocol service installed

if it needs to communicate with unknown subnets. Know subnets can be configured with the ipconfig command line utility.

If the DNS tab is selected, an IP host name and domain can be set. The host name should match the server's NetBIOS machine name for consistency. The DNS servers this machine should use when resolving IP host names can also be configured in this dialog box. Multiple DNS servers can be specified for redundancy. If the first DNS server does not respond to queries, the system can redirect the query to the second DNS server listed.

When the WINS Address tab is selected, the IP address of the local WINS servers can be identified. The WINS server is the system to be referenced when the NT server needs to resolve a NetBIOS name to an address. The *scope ID* allows the server to be identified as part of a specific group of NetBIOS machines. The scope ID follows a similar hierarchical structure to DNS. Refer to the NetBIOS section of Chapter 6 for more information on scope IDs.

When the DHCP Relay tab is selected, the IP address for the DHCP server that is responsible for the local subnet can be entered. When an IP address is entered, the NT server will forward any Bootp or DHCP requests it receives to the DHCP server. It is expected that the DHCP server is not located on the local subnet as it would then be able to receive and reply to DHCP requests directly. This parameter is only used when the DHCP server is not located on the same network as the NT server.

The Routing tab allows IP routing to be enabled or disabled. This option is only needed when there are two or more network cards in the server. Selecting the check box allows the NT server to route IP packets from one network interface to another.

Once we have completed changes to our protocols, we can continue through the remaining tabs or reboot the server to initialize our changes.

Adapters

The Adapters tab in the Network window, shown in Figure 8.26, allows you to install and configure NICs in the NT server. From here we can add and remove network adapters. When a newer revision driver is required, simply select the appropriate card and press the Update button. You will be prompted to install the disk with the updated Microsoft NT driver.

F I G U R E 8.26

The Network
Adapters tab

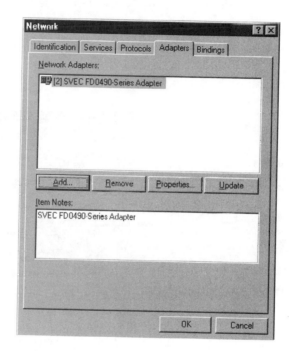

The Properties button allows us to configure operation parameters. If our network card requires an interrupt or an I/O port setting, you will be prompted for these values under Properties. Windows NT does not support plug-and-play, so all configuration parameters must be set manually if they cannot be detected.

Once we have completed changes to our Adapter tab we can move on to Bindings or reboot the server to initialize our changes.

Bindings

The Bindings tab allows you to configure in what order the NT server should utilize the installed protocols. This order should reflect the communication characteristics of your network. Separate orders can be defined for the NetBIOS interface, server connectivity, and workstation connectivity. The Network Monitor Tools and Agent object defines which protocols will be available for decoding. Figure 8.27 shows the Bindings tab.

FIGURE 8.27

The Bindings tab of the Network window

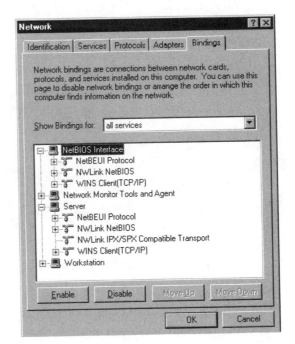

For example, let's assume my workstation bindings list the NetBEUI protocol and then WINS Client (TCP/IP). I launch Explorer, and tell it to search for the computer Phoenix which is not currently listed in my network neighborhood. Because of the workstation bindings order, the NT server will first attempt to find this system using NetBEUI. If this fails, it will then use WINS.

Set the protocol binding order to reflect which communication protocols your system will use the most. For example, if most of the resources you are likely to access are NetBEUI systems located on a remote network, set WINS at the top of the workstation binding order.

Saving Your changes

Once your network configuration is complete, select the OK button and reboot the system to initialize your changes. If you accidentally add the wrong protocol or service during the installation process, you may have to reboot the server anyway before the server will let you remove it. Once the reboot is complete and the service database is unlocked, you can remove the unneeded service or protocol. You will then have to reboot the system one last time to finalize the configuration.

NT Support for Large Environments

Microsoft has released NT Server Enterprise Edition, which is a beefed up version of NT Server designed to support the requirements of large network environments and mission-critical server applications. Along with the features described above, the enterprise edition includes:

- support for 8 CPU chips without specialized vendor hardware

- a smaller memory footprint than NT Server 4.0

- transaction tracking and message queuing

- server clustering so that applications may be executed over multiple systems

These features are designed to make NT Server more appealing to organizations that have relied on Unix for their application server needs.

Summary

You should now have a good understanding of how to configure NT Server for network communications. You should also be familiar with the applications and features provided by this NOS.

In Chapter 9 we will take a look at Unix, the granddaddy of NOSes. We will discuss why it has remained popular for so many years, as well as the features it can provide that no other NOS has been able to replicate.

CHAPTER

9

Unix

D

eveloped in 1969 at Bell Labs, Unix is by far the oldest distributed NOS in use today. Its creation is credited to Ken Thompson, who was working at that time for Bell Labs on the Multiplex Information Computing System (MULTICS) for a General Electric mainframe. Bell Labs eventually dropped the project, and with it went a very important piece of software, a game called Space Travel.

It is rumored that Ken set out to create a new operating system to which the game could be ported. MULTICS assembly code was rewritten for an available DEC PDP-7, and the new operating system was named UNICS (I'm sure the emasculation reference was not intentional).

Bell Labs eventually took interest in UNICS, as additional functionality beyond the game Space Travel was added,which gave the operating system some commercial applications. By 1972, it was named Unix and had an install base of 10 computers. In 1973, Ken and Dennis Richie rewrote the kernel in C which made the operating system much more portable.

In 1974, the IP protocol was developed and integrated into the Unix operating system. No longer were multiple terminals required to access a single Unix system. A shared media called Ethernet could be used to access the system. Unix had become a true NOS.

In the mid 70's Bell Labs started releasing Unix to universities. Because Ma Bell was still regulated at the time, they were not allowed to profit from Unix's sales. For this reason, only a minimal fee was charged for the Unix source code which helped to make it widely available.

Once Unix hit the universities, its development expanded from the injection of fresh blood. Students began improving the code and adding additional features. So dramatic were these changes at the University of California at Berkeley, that Berkeley began distributing their own flavor of Unix called the Berkeley Software distribution (BSD). The Unix version that continued to be developed by Bell Labs is known as System V(5).

In 1983, IP became the official protocol of the Internet. Around this same time, none other than Microsoft released the first PC-compatible version of Unix.

So Many Flavors, So Few Pages

While all Unix implementations are similar, each has its own particular feel. Commands and their uses are fairly consistent between different flavors. The difference is that each vendor may take liberties as to where they choose to store particular executables or startup scripts. Some versions may even include a few extra commands that others do not.

The latter is rarely a problem if you understand C code. Most Unix utilities are available as source code which can be compiled to run on your specific Unix platform. For example, if you would like to send and receive Internet mail but do not have a copy of Sendmail on your system, you can obtain the source files for free from a number of FTP sites on the Internet. Then you simply adjust the Make file to fit your operating system and run the source through your compiler.

A Make file is a plain text file that customizes the source code as it is compiled into an executable. Usually, modifying this file is a simple matter of uncommenting the lines that pertain to your implementation of Unix.

It is beyond the scope of this book to pay appropriate attention to every flavor of Unix. Entire books have been written on any given specific implementation. This is why we will focus on just a single flavor.

As mentioned above, most Unix applications are portable, so what we discuss for one particular version can usually be applied to any other.

I have chosen to focus on the Linux implementation of Unix for a number of reasons. The first is that it holds true to the roots of Unix in being a collaborative effort. Linux has been developed over the Internet on a mostly volunteer basis. The second is that it is free software and accessible to all who wish to use it.

Linux History

Linux was first developed in 1991 by Linus Torvalds, a Finnish student. He developed a minimal Unix operating system and posted a message to an Internet news group, asking if anyone would be interested in helping to develop it.

What followed shows the true power of the Internet as a method of collaboration. First tens, then hundreds of individuals began dedicating their free time to developing Linux. Now the number of volunteers has grown into the thousands. Individuals volunteer their time to perform such tasks as kernel debugging, quality control, and writing documentation.

The result is a production class operating system that rivals, and even arguably exceeds, commercial releases of Unix available today. Its stability and breadth of features has captured the attention of network administrators who have deployed Linux for file, print, and Web servers. Linux has even been recognized by InfoWorld magazine, who named it their desktop operating system of the year in 1996.

In April of 1997, Linux even made it onto the space shuttle to be used in monitoring hydroponics experiments. Who could have guessed that this small band of loosely knit hackers would create an operating system that would literally reach for the stars.

Linux is Copyleft Software

Linux is not shareware or public domain freeware. It has been copyrighted by Linus through the Free Software Foundation's GNU General Public License (GPL). This is sometimes referred to as *copyleft* as it does not prevent you from freely distributing the software.

The GPL states that you are allowed to distribute the Linux software, provided:

- You do not attempt to further restrict or copyright your modification.

- You make the source code available as part of the distribution.

In effect this means that you could create a 1,000-node network using only Linux and not pay a dime in software charges.

The GPL does allow a software manufacturer to recoup some of their costs if they distribute the software to the public market. For example, you could decide to go into production selling CD-ROM releases of Linux without having to pay a royalty charge. You would, however:

- not be able to restrict usage of the software. If an individual wishes to purchase a single copy to load on 1,000 machines, it is their right.

- have to make the source code available as part of the distribution.

All this has been done to ensure that Linux remains freely available to all who wish to use it.

Linux Features

As we discuss Linux, we will specifically look at a release developed by a company called Red Hat. There are many releases of Linux available. All provide the same core OS and are capable of running the same applications. The differences usually lie in the setup and configuration program, as well as in which applications are included.

Red Hat has made a name for itself by providing an extensive list of applications, as well as an easy to use installation program. While you can purchase a CD-ROM copy of their Linux bundle for a minimal fee, they have also made their distribution freely available over the Internet via FTP.

Unless you have a TI connection to the Internet, you will probably want to purchase a copy of Linux on CD-ROM. The NOS has many features and can literally take days to install over a slow link. Purchasing Linux on CD-ROM is extremely reasonable when compared to other NOSes. Once you have installed the base operating system from CD-ROM, you can use your Internet connection to retrieve free updates.

Linux Setup

No matter how you choose to install Red Hat Linux (CD-ROM, FTP, and so on), the installation processes are almost identical. If you purchase the CD-ROM, it is supplied with a single boot disk for initializing a minimal Linux kernel to perform the install. If you are installing over the Internet, you must first retrieve an image of the floppy from Red Hat's FTP site, and create a boot disk using *rawwrite*.

Rawwrite is a DOS based utility that allows you to create Unix floppy disks from image files.

Once you have a bootable floppy (which can also be used for disaster recovery), simply boot the system and follow the prompts. As shown in Figure 9.1, you will be asked if you wish to install Linux from CD-ROM, hard drive, FTP, an NT or SAMBA share, or NFS. If you select CD-ROM, you simply select if it is a IDE or SCSI unit, and the device is automatically configured. If you select SAMBA, FTP or NFS, you are walked through your network card configuration and will need to supply the name or IP address of a host where the installation files can be found.

FIGURE 9.1

Red Hat Linux allows you to decide which method of installation you would like to perform.

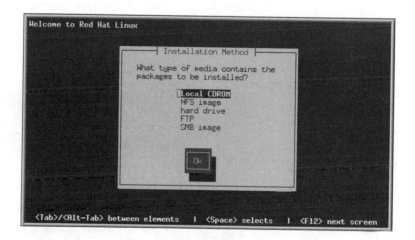

From here on, the setup process is identical for both methods. While the installation program is ASCII-based menus and not a true GUI, it is sufficient for installing the software.

One of the additional features of using the Red Hat installation is that it performs a dependency check for all selected software packages. Unix uses programs and libraries that can be accessed by multiple applications. The benefit of this is a reduction in the amount of required disk space. Instead of each application requiring a full set of support files, they can share one or more sets of common routines. This reduces the amount of required storage space and makes upgrades far easier.

The Red Hat installation will verify the dependencies of each program you have selected to install. If a required program or library is missing, you will be informed and offered the opportunity to include it as part of the installation. This can be extremely helpful if you are doing a selective install in order to save disk space.

The dependency check will verify that all required support programs are installed. If any are found to be missing, the user is notified, and Red Hat offers to include them as part of the installation. For example, Figure 9.2 shows two applications that require the installation of XFree86 in order to run.

Because XFree86 was not selected as one of the packages to install, the dependency check is warning that these two programs will not run without it.

FIGURE 9.2

Two applications that require the installation of Xfree86 in order to run

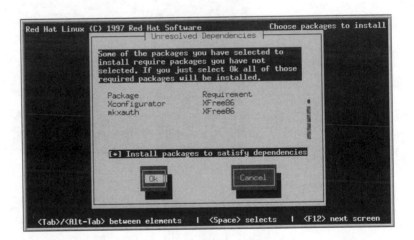

The rest of the setup walks the administrator through the required steps to get the system running and communicating on the network (such as creating user accounts and configuring IP networking). All selected network applications are setup to initialize during system startup (when applicable), but are not configured as part of the initial setup process.

For example, if the administrator chooses to install *bind*, Unix's DNS application, bind will be setup to initialize once its main configuration file, /etc/named.boot, has been created. The install process will not, however, walk the administrator through the procedure of creating named.boot, but rather will leave that to be accomplished once the installation is complete. For the novice Unix user, this can prove a bit frustrating as they may not even be aware that the named.boot file is required. Once the system is operational, however, there is extensive help available in text, HTML, and post script format.

A minimal install can be performed in about 40MB worth of disk space. A Linux system with only network-related tools (Web server, FTP, NFS, and so on) will require closer to 150MB. If you perform a full installation which also includes a client server relational database, desktop publishing tools, programming tools for six languages, games, and so on, and so on (there are over 800 software packages included), the installation will take closer to 500MB of space.

Core OS

Linux is a full preemptive multitasking, multithreaded, and multi-user, *Unix-like* environment. It is Unix-like because, while it includes extensions for system V and BSD, it utilizes a different software base.

Linux strives to meet the IEEE "Portable Operating System Interface for Computing Environments" (POSIX) specification. POSIX defines the Application Programming Interface (API) between C language applications and the underlying operating system. POSIX's purpose is to ensure that compliant applications developed for one POSIX environment can be easily ported to another.

Linux is certainly one of the most "equal opportunity" operating systems when it comes to hardware selection. There are versions of Linux that will run on PC, Mac, SUN, DEC Alpha, PowerPC, MIPS, and even Amiga and Atari hardware platforms. Linux is not run on top of the original operating system, but rather replaces it. When an Intel or SUN SPARC is used, symmetrical multiple processors are supported.

As mentioned, Linux is a work in progress by many volunteers. As such, the kernel is constantly under development. A standard has been created for identifying which kernels are considered *production* and which are considered *development*. When the character in the tenths place of the version number is even, the kernel is a stable release. If it is odd, it is considered work in progress. For example, 2.0, 2.4.5, and 3.6 would all be considered production. 2.1, 2.5.4, and 3.7 would all be considered development kernels.

Linux supports virtual memory. This means that like NT, Linux can execute programs larger than the available physical memory size. Unlike NT, however, Linux fully supports memory paging. Memory paging allows the system to selectively move portions of an executable to virtual memory, instead of the entire file. This allows infrequently accessed sections of the program's code to be placed in virtual memory while the heavier used sections are executed in faster physical memory. The result is quicker application speed and less delay from *memory shuffle*.

Like IntranetWare, Linux supports a unified memory pool. This means that free memory does not go to waste. If a portion of physical memory is not currently in use, the system allocates it for file caching. When an application needs additional memory, the memory is allocated from the file caching pool as required. Because cached files are read from physical memory instead of from disk, file caching can make a dramatic difference in file access time.

Linux also utilizes demand loading of executables. This means that only the required portion of an application's file is read into memory. For example, if the main executable for my Web server application is 2MB in size, but only 100KB of that code is required to monitor incoming connections, Linux will only use 100KB of memory until a connection is established. This can substantially reduce the memory requirements of a system that is required to run multiple processes.

While Linux supports memory protection between processes so that no single application can bring down the entire system, it also supports *shared copy on write* pages. This allows two applications to utilize the same memory space. If one of the applications attempts to write to the memory area, the required code is moved elsewhere. The benefits of shared copy on write is that it reduces system memory requirements which will increase performance by decreasing the number of required memory swaps.

Linux supports both a command-line interface (similar to DOS) as well as a graphical user interface called X-Windows (similar to Microsoft's Windows). The Red Hat installation even includes extensions for X-Windows to give it the same look and feel as a Windows 95 machine. X-Windows even supports remote connections which Microsoft's Windows does not. For example, think of using your Windows 95 or NT interface but to be actually working on, and controlling, a remote machine without the need of setting up shares.

Linux is a true multi-user system. All tasks that can be performed at the console, can also be performed through a remote connection (either dial-up or over the network). This is in contrast to NT Server, which provides no remote console ability or shared execution space, or IntranetWare that dedicates the server console only to administration of the operating system.

For example, let's assume we are working for a company called Foobar which employs over 1,000 people. Foobar has three separate network groups, one to manage servers, one to manage the routers and WAN links to remote offices, and a third to manage infrastructure hardware such as hubs and switches. Foobar decides to purchase an SNMP management system to control and monitor all their network hardware. We need to decide whether to run the management system on NT Server or Unix.

In a Unix environment, only one SNMP management station would be required. Each group could simply attach to this system through a separate Telnet or X-Windows session. From this session, they could manage the hardware their group is responsible for. Only one SNMP management license would be required, because it is all running from a single system.

Because NT Server does not support remote sessions, multiple SNMP management stations, and thus licenses, would be required. Each group would need direct access to the SNMP management system in order to view the network hardware they are responsible for.

Even if a remote console product such as pcANYWHERE was used, there would still be problems, as this does not provide separate sessions. Each group would end up controlling the same desktop and may require a different network view to work with their pertinent network hardware.

The result is that Unix's multi-session ability allows all three groups to retrieve the information they need from a single system. This reduces both hardware and licenses cost. In fact, if the Unix system being used is Linux, the supplied CMU SNMP tools can be used to create a custom SNMP management station.

Another useful feature of Linux is its ability to initiate background processes. When a command is followed by an ampersand (&), it is assigned a process ID (PID) and allocated as a background function. This frees up the workspace to continue working on something else. When the process is complete, a message is sent to the console session.

Figure 9.3 shows an example of this functionality. Our first command begins a search for files larger than 2MB. The command also states that the output should be redirected to the file largefile.txt which is to be created in the /home/cbrenton directory. The & at the end tells the system to run this command in the background. On the second line, the system informs us that it has assigned a PID of 552 to this command.

FIGURE 9.3

The ampersand (&) can be used to run commands or applications in the background.

```
[cbrenton@toby /usr]$ find . -size 2000k >/home/cbrenton/largefile.txt &
[1] 552
[cbrenton@toby /usr]$ ls
X11            dict          i486-linuxaout  libexec      sbin
X11R6          doc           include         local        share
X386           etc           info            man          src
bin            games         lib             openwin      tmp
[cbrenton@toby /usr]$
[1]+  Done                    find . -size 2000k >/home/cbrenton/largefile.txt
[cbrenton@toby /usr]$
```

The third line shows our command line being returned to us so that we are free to go off and perform other activities. In this case we have simply listed the contents of the current directory. The second to last line is the system letting us know that it has completed the background task.

While similar functionality can be achieved by simply opening multiple windows in a GUI environment, this feature allows us to perform multiple activities without the additional overhead of a GUI environment.

All running applications and processes can be monitored from a single command, **ps**. Figure 9.4 shows the output of the ps command. The first column identifies the process ID (PID) number assigned to the process. This is useful in case we need to manipulate it or shut it down. Because a process can be executed multiple times—for example, if accepting multiple FTP or mail connections—it cannot be identified just by name. The PID ensures that each process can be uniquely identified.

F I G U R E   9.4

Output of the **ps**
command

```
[cbrenton@toby cbrenton]$ ps -ax
  PID TTY STAT  TIME COMMAND
    1  ?   S    0:05 init [3]
    2  ?   SW   0:00 (bflushd)
    3  ?   SW<  0:00 (kswapd)
   21  ?   S    0:00 /sbin/kerneld
  101  ?   S    0:00 syslogd
  110  ?   S    0:00 klogd
  121  ?   S    0:00 crond
  144  ?   S    0:00 inetd
  320  ?   S    0:00 sendmail: accepting connections on port 25
  309  1   S    0:00 /bin/login -- root
  390  2   S    0:00 /sbin/mingetty tty2
  391  3   S    0:00 /sbin/mingetty tty3
  397  ?   S    0:00 update (bdflush)
  421  1   S    0:00 -bash
  655  ?   S    0:00 in.telnetd
  801  6   S    0:00 /sbin/mingetty tty6
  803  5   S    0:00 /sbin/mingetty tty5
  804  4   S    0:00 /sbin/mingetty tty4
  851  1   R    0:03 find . -size 2000
  132  ?   S    0:00 portmap
  715  p1  S    0:00 login -h 10.1.1.150 -p
  721  p1  S    0:00 -bash
  855  p1  R    0:00 ps -ax
[cbrenton@toby cbrenton]$
```

The second column identifies which terminal session created the process. A question mark (?) usually indicates that the process was started during system initialization or that the process does not require a terminal session (such as transferring e-mail). A number identifies which server console session is using the process. If the number is preceded by a **p**, it indicates a remote connection.

For example, we have three processes listed with a TTY of 1. PID 389 shows us that the root user is logged on and using the first local console. PID 421 identifies the environment shell that root is using (bash), and PID 851 shows that root is currently running the **find** command.

We also have three processes identified with a TTY of p1. PID 715 identifies that this is a remote user coming from the IP address 10.1.1.150. PID 721 identifies that this user is also using the bash shell, and 855 identifies that they are running the **ps-ax** command.

The STAT column shows the current status of each process. If it is identified as an S, the process is sleeping and is not currently performing any work. An R indicates that the process is in a running state.

The TIME column identifies how much of the CPU clock time is being utilized by this process. It is a percentage based upon the number of cycles used since the process was initiated. A higher number means that the process is extremely busy.

Finally, the COMMAND column identifies the name of the process being identified. The **ps** command provides a lot of useful information regarding the state of our processes and who is responsible for them. Other **ps** switches would even allow you to monitor memory utilization of each process. This gives us a single command to monitor all core server activities.

This single command management is in contrast to other operating systems that separate processes into separate categories and require different procedures to manage them. For example, in an NT environment, you would use task manager to monitor and stop any process that was started through the GUI interface. If the application was started as a service, however, you will need to administer it from the service manager. If you need to monitor the memory or process usage of a running services, you will then need to use a third utility called Performance Monitor.

Unix (and Linux) have been developed to provide 7X24 availability. I have personally worked with Unix machines that have been operational for over two years without a crash or being rebooted. This is largely why Unix has been accepted into environments where system availability is considered critical.

Linux will also coexist with other operating systems on the same machine. For example, you can use the Linux boot manager (LILO) to start a machine such as Linux, NetWare, or Windows 95. Linux can even read files created in another operating system, as described below.

File System

Linux provides a POSIX compliant file system that accepts file names up to 254 characters. Names are case sensitive, so `Myfile.txt` and `myfile.txt` would be considered two separate files. It is a high performance file system which helps to reduce the amount of file fragmentation. A file defragmentation utility is provided for systems that have files created and deleted frequently.

Linux supplies some unique tools for maintaining the file system. The first is a revision control utility, which can be used to monitor and track file changes. This can be used to maintain older copies of files. If required, a file or a set of files can be rolled back to a certain date or revision.

As with NT Server, file system replication is also supported. This helps to maintain an identical set of files over multiple systems.

Linux will also natively support a wide range of file systems. Figure 9.5 shows the output of the **fdisk** command, which lists the file systems supported by Linux. This is not remote support but support for drives that are local to the system. For example, you can read a floppy disk created by a DOS or OS/2 file system. You could also mount a volume created by NetWare. This functionality can be invaluable in a mixed system environment or when the machine can be multi-booted between different operating systems.

FIGURE 9.5

A list of Linux supported file systems

```
Command (m for help):
  0   Empty              9   AIX bootable   75   PC/IX          b7   BSDI fs
  1   DOS 12-bit FAT     a   OS/2 Boot Manag 80  Old MINIX      b8   BSDI swap
  2   XENIX root        40   Venix 80286    81   Linux/MINIX    c7   Syrinx
  3   XENIX usr         51   Novell?        82   Linux swap     db   CP/M
  4   DOS 16-bit <32M   52   Microport      83   Linux native   e1   DOS access
  5   Extended          63   GNU HURD       93   Amoeba         e3   DOS R/0
  6   DOS 16-bit >=32   64   Novell Netware 94   Amoeba BBT     f2   DOS secondary
  7   OS/2 HPFS         65   Novell Netware a5   BSD/386        ff   BBT
  8   AIX

Command (m for help):
```

Unfortunately, Linux does not support online file or disk compression, nor can it read other files systems that use it (such as DOS or Windows 95).

Unix uses *mount points* instead of drive letters when additional disks are added. A mount point is simply a point in the directory structure when the storage of the additional disk has been added. This provides a cleaner feel to the file structure and helps to consolidate information.

For example, let's assume I have two drives that I wish to use for creating a Unix machine. I wish to dedicate the first drive to the operating system, while utilizing the second drive for my user's home directories.

Instead of installing the OS on C and putting the user's home directories on D, I would simply assign the second drive for storage of all files under the /home directory. This would store all files on the primary drive except for those located under the home directory.

There are a few benefits to this. First, it allows the addition of extra drives to be transparent. If I am looking for a file and have no idea where it is located, I can simply go to the root and perform a single search. I am not required to repeat the search for each additional drive because they have been woven into the fabric of the directory structure.

Using mount points also helps to reduce system wide failures due to a crashed drive. For example, if my second disk was to fail, I would lose only the user's home directories, not the entire system. This is in contrast to NetWare which requires you to span the entire volume structure over both disks. If one of those drives fails, none of the files on the volume can be accessed.

Account Administration

Linux has the ability to be self sufficient when it administrates users and groups, or to be centrally managed through Network Information Services (NIS), formally known as Yellow Pages (YP).

NIS is a flat database system designed to share user and group information across multiple systems. A collection of systems sharing NIS information are referred to as a *domain*. To give a user access to the domain, an administrator simply needs to add their account to the master NIS server. The master then takes care of propagating this information out to the other NIS systems on the network.

NIS shares the same drawbacks as NT's domain structure because neither are hierarchical. Because Unix provides many additional services over NT, this problem is compounded. As we will cover under security, file permissions under Unix can be a bit loose. This combined with NIS can provide some additional loop holes for a potential attacker to wiggle through.

All versions of Linux provide command line tools for administrating user's and groups. Red Hat Linux also provides a GUI utility. While the GUI can be a bit slower if multiple accounts need to be configured, it provides a simple interface for the novice Unix administrator. Figure 9.6 shows Red Hat's GUI interface for managing users and groups. This interface also tells you which accounts have passwords and which ones do not. The application runs under X-Windows.

FIGURE 9.6

The Red Hat user and group manager can be used to add and delete accounts.

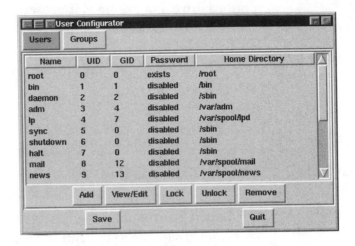

Security

Most Unix administrators have a love/hate relationship when it comes to implementing security on a Unix system. Unix's flexibility allows it to be configured as an extremely secure system, or incorrectly configured to give attackers a wide open door. Think of Unix as a finely tuned ACE Cobra. In the hands of a professional driver, the car is capable of amazing speed. In the hands of a novice, it will most likely end up being a bow tie on the first oak tree.

Linux Security Tools

Linux provides the administrator with some wonderful tools for safeguarding their system. Cracker is a program that allows the administrator to verify the integrity of users' passwords. Passwords can be checked against known words to ensure that they cannot be easily broken.

TCP Wrapper is a program that allows an administrator to monitor and control the access of services to a machine. For example, a computer could be configured to allow Telnet access from a specific network or host and reject connections from other sources. There is even a verification program to check the configuration of the wrapper and suggest appropriate changes.

Linux supports shadow passwords. Shadow passwords allow the encrypted password information to be stored in a separate location than the user information. This helps to keep the encrypted passwords away from prying eyes.

As with most things in life, these features are only useful if they are actually implemented. TCP Wrapper cannot help to protect your system if you do not configure system access appropriately and check the logs for suspect connection attempts.

Some of these tools can even be used against the administrator if they are not carefully guarded. For example, Cracker can be used to break passwords as easily as it can be used to verify them. It is a wise system administrator who checks their system with these tools instead of letting an attacker do it for them.

To be fair, there are applications similar to Cracker for NetWare and NT, they're just not as widely publicized.

If Unix has one major security weakness, it is its file permission settings. Permissions are set by three distinctive classes—owner, group, and nobody. I can set specific permissions for when I access a file, when anyone in my group accesses a file, or when anyone else on the system accesses a file.

For example, let's assume I have a file called serverpasswords.txt in my home directory (bad idea I know, but this is only an example). Let's also assume that I am part of a group called Admin. I can set permissions on this file so that I can read and write to it, members of the Admin group have read-only access, and everyone else on the system has no access.

There are a few problems with this setup. First of all, even though "everyone else" has no access, they can still see that the file exists. This may prompt them to take further steps to try and access the file now that they know it is there.

Another problem is that permissions are too general. I cannot say, "Give read and write access of this file to Sean and Deb from the Admin group, but give all other members read-only access." Unix was spawned out of a much simpler time when complicated file access was not required. In fact, for many years the focus was on making system access easier, not more difficult.

To its credit, Unix has one security feature that is still missing on all other operating systems, the ability for a regular user to assume the privileges of the root users. The **su** command allows a user to assume the privileges of the root level account. This is an extremely useful tool as it allows high-level access to the system to be strictly monitored and controlled.

The system can be configured so that a root logon is not possible except from the server console. This way, users connecting to the system remotely must use their regular user name and password. Once connected they can assume the privileges of root. These connections can be logged to see who is accessing the root account and when. The system can be configured to only give certain users the ability to access root.

Why all these restrictions? Think of it this way—if I have a group of 10 NetWare or NT administrators, how many of them have been granted administrator equivalent logons? Half? All 10 maybe? If something becomes broken by an administrator level account, how do you determine who may have caused the problem?

Because in a Unix environment each user would be required to access root from their own account, there will be a log entry tracking this event.

Networking

Linux may very well be the undisputed king of networking. It provides connectivity through more protocols and offers more services than any other network operating system.

OSI Layer Two Support

At OSI layer two, Linux supports Ethernet, Token Ring, FDDI, ATM, Frame Relay, T1 cards, PPP, SLIP, ISDN, and spread spectrum wireless LANs. It can even support dumb terminals. Clearly, whatever kind of connectivity you're using, Linux can support it.

Linux is frequently found hanging out at the borders of LANs and WANs. It is an extremely popular product for providing a link to an ISP, as well as running the connectivity services at the ISP itself. In fact, there is an entire how-to manual dedicated to describing how to use Linux to provide ISP services.

If you will be using a dial-up connection to create your link to your ISP, then PPP load balancing may come in handy. Linux's PPP load balancing allows you to create your Internet connection with more than one dial-up line. This is true for POTS and ISDN connectivity. The only real drawback is that the additional lines are not "on demand." There is no method of monitoring traffic to see if the second line is required for providing greater bandwidth.

As for networking protocols, Linux supports IP, NetBEUI, IPX, AppleTalk, and even DECNET. Again, whatever type of connectivity you may require is probably already supported.

IP Networking Support

Unix was the original platform for the IP protocol, so it should be no surprise that Linux has embraced this protocol by supporting every available feature.

Linux provides support for some of the higher level IP methods of connectivity. Along with the typical unicast and broadcast communications, Linux also supports multicasting, IP encapsulation in IP, mobile IP, IP masquerading, a transparent proxy, and even firewalling.

While encapsulating IP packets within IP packets may seem like a strange thing to do, it can actually be quite useful. Some amateur radio communications are now taking place across the Internet. IP encapsulation of IP provides the transport needed to move these transmissions. It also provides the baseline for mobile IP, which allows a system to use a fixed IP address and communicate from any point on the Internet. Along with autorouting, this provides a means for a mobile user to connect to the Internet from any location and appear to be communicating from their home base network.

When Linux is used as a router, IP masquerading allows many IP addresses to be hidden behind a single address. For example, let's assume we have the network diagrammed in Figure 9.7. If the Linux system is using IP masquerading, all internal traffic that goes out to the Internet will appear to be originating from the Linux machine's external interface. This allows our internal network to communicate using a reserved address range which improves security since a reserved address cannot be easily reached from the Internet. It also means that the external interface of the Linux system is the only legal address we need to communicate. All passing traffic can be logged so that activity can be monitored.

When IP masquerading is combined with the transparent proxy, a powerful combination is formed for protecting your internal network. The transparent proxy allows the Linux system to redirect requests for certain services to an internal machine.

For example, let's assume that the Mac II in Figure 9.7 is running a HTTP server. Using a transparent proxy, we could advertise the IP

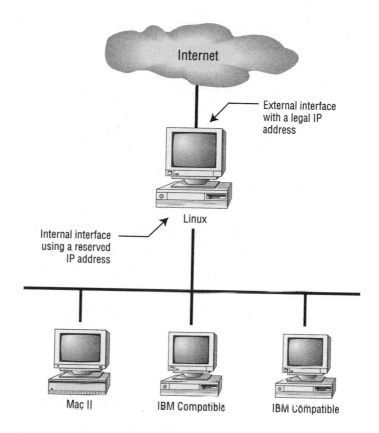

FIGURE 9.7

IP masquerading allows us to hide an entire network behind a single, legal IP address.

address of the external interface of the Linux machine as the address of our HTTP server. When an Internet user attempts to connect to this address, the Linux machine transparently passes the request on to the Mac II. As the reply is returned, the Linux machine again rewrites the IP header so that it appears that the reply originated from the Linux machine.

The benefits here are twofold—first, while the Linux machine could easily house any IP services we wish to offer, this allows the load to be balanced over multiple machines. We could be using a separate computer for mail, HTTP, and FTP services, but the transparent proxy would make it appear to Internet users that all these services share the same IP address. The side benefit of this is that we have hidden the real

IP address of these machines, making it more difficult to launch a direct attack against them.

Firewalling can be added to the mix to make our Internet connection even more secure. Linux ships with a packet filter firewall that is integrated directly with the kernel. The benefit of direct integration over a separate application is that if the firewall is broken by a would be attacker, it is extremely likely that the kernel will break as well, causing all processing to stop. This in effect shuts down the connection, not allowing any traffic to pass.

If you feel more comfortable with a proxy type firewall instead of a packet filter, Trusted Information Systems (TIS) have provided a proxy tool kit as free software for Linux and other Unix platforms. While not as comprehensive as their commercial product, it has been used successfully to protect many internal networks and is one of the most popular firewalling methods available.

IPX Networking

Linux includes a set of NCP tools which allows it to both emulate and connect to a NetWare server. In emulation mode, the system advertises itself as a $3.1x$ network server. Users can log on to the system and print or map drives as they would any NetWare server. The only catch is that Linux does not supply the files typically found in a NetWare public and login directory. These files must be copied over from a NetWare server. Also, Linux is unable to be integrated into an NDS tree. Despite these drawbacks, the ability to emulate a NetWare server and provide connectivity to IPX-only workstations can be a valuable feature.

The NCP tools also allow a Linux user to connect to a NetWare server. This is useful for transferring files or providing additional storage on the NetWare system. The client NCP tools provide functionality similar to NFS. NetWare volumes can be mounted anywhere with the Linux directory structure. The only two drawbacks are that Linux will not process a logon script and it requires a bindery or bindery emulation to connect to a NetWare server.

NetBEUI Networking

Linux can also emulate or connect to an NT server via NetBEUI or Net-BIOS over IP. Linux ships with SAMBA, a set of tools that allows the Linux system to advertise shares (both file and printers) just like an NT server. It also includes client tools so that a Linux user may log on to an NT server.

As with IntranetWare, the only drawback of using Samba is that it does not allow a Linux system to join a domain and share account information with other NT servers.

AppleTalk Networking

Linux's AppleTalk support allows it to function only in server mode. Linux can offer print or file services to Macintosh machines including the saving of files in their native fork format. When routing, Linux can act as a seed or a soft seed router.

Network Routing

Routing support is a bit weaker when Linux is compared to Intranet-Ware. Distance vector routing is supported for all protocols except Net-BEUI (which is non-routable). The only link state routing protocol supported is IP's OSPF.

IP Applications

Linux includes many IP applications. I will list a few of the more popular ones here to give you a feel for what is included. If there is a service you require that is not on the list, chances are someone has already ported it to Linux. You can check one of the many Linux archives to see if it exists.

bootp Server   Linux provides a bootp server for providing bootp and DHCP services to network clients. DHCP and bootp clients can be serviced independently or in a mixed environment. There is also a bootp client so that the Linux system may remotely access its IP address information if a server already exists.

DNS Server   Red Hat Linux ships with the latest version of Bind. Bind is the original, and still the most popular utility used to exchange domain name information on the Internet. A Bind server can be configured to provide primary, secondary, or caching only domain name services.

Finger Server   Finger is one of those services that is extremely useful but receives very little attention. Linux provides both client and server Finger services, which allow you to Finger an account by name and see if the person is online.

Besides account information, Finger can also be used to supply information. For example, Finger the addresses:

- `smiley@goldendome.net`

- `coke@ucc.gu.uwa.edu.au`

The first returns a random ASCII character smiley face. The mohawk smiley `-:-)` is a bit bizarre, but it certainly beats the standard smiley `:)`.

The second returns an inventory of the local Coke machine. It lets you know what flavors are available, as well as how many cans of each.

While this is fun for the entertainment value, Finger can also provide useful business services as well. For example, some sites that have dial-up network access to their ISP can use Finger to let the ISP's mail server know that you're back online. When the mail server is Fingered, it begins to transfer any mail messages sent to your organization while your connection was inactive.

FTP Server   Linux provides FTP services including the ability to service anonymous FTP requests. A directory structure is setup under `/home/ftp` for anonymous file access. Directories set up under this structure can allow anonymous users to receive read-only or read-write access to files.

The administrator can optionally disable the ability to connect to the server with the root user account; this is done as a security precaution. Red Hat Linux has this functionality enabled by default.

Gopher Server   While not as widely used since the introduction of HTTP, Linux still provides a Gopher server for searching documents. HTTP has replaced Gopher, as it can provide the user with a graphical interface when searching for documents. Still, Gopher is a quick way to perform keyword searches when your are rummaging through a large number of files looking for a specific piece of information.

HTTP Server   Linux ships with Apache to provide Web server access. Apache is one of the more popular Unix Web servers and supports advanced features such as Java scripting and multihoming. Multihoming is the ability to host multiple domain names on the same Web server. Apache looks at the destination Web server address and directs the query to the appropriate directory structure for that domain.

Linux also provides both graphic and text only Web browsers for accessing HTTP services. Red Hat Linux ships with a set of help files formatted for Web browser viewing.

IMAP and POP-3 Servers   Linux supports remote mail retrieval using both POP-3 and IMAP. POP-3 is the older standard and is supported by most remote mail clients. IMAP has more features than POP-3 but is just starting to become popular. With Linux as your mail server, you can use POP-3 today, and later migrate to IMAP as clients become available for your specific platform.

Internet Relay Chat (IRC)   Linux provides both a client and a server for communicating using Internet Relay Chat. When an IRC client connects to an IRC server, the client can select from any of the available *channels* on which they wish to communicate. Once a channel is selected, the IRC client user can relay text messages in realtime to other IRC client users. Communications can be private between two users or part of a large group.

Mail Server   Red Hat Linux always ships with the latest version of Sendmail to provide connectivity for SMTP messages. Sendmail is the most widely used mail program on the Internet. Linux also provides at least a half dozen local mail clients for users to send, receive, and read their mail. The user simply Telnets to the Linux system and runs their mail utility of choice.

News Server   Linux provides the InterNetNews daemon (INND) for news server connectivity. When a Linux news server is provided with an appropriate feed, remote users can connect to the server to read and post news articles. If no feed is available, the server can be used for Intranet discussion groups.

NFS Server   Linux can use NFS either to export portions of the server's file system to NFS clients, or act as an NFS client itself and mount remote file systems. Functionality is similar to NetWare, where you would map a drive letter to a section of the remote file system or NT Server where you would map to a share. The remote NFS file system can be mounted to any point in Linux's file system.

SNMP Manager   Linux ships with tools for creating an SNMP management station. SNMP allows the management station to both monitor and control SNMP devices on the network. Linux can both provide information to other SNMP management stations or house the management station itself.

Talk   Linux also supports *talk*, which is similar to IRC. Talk does not require a server, as a connection is established directly between two users. You establish a connection by typing:

```
talk user@host.domain
```

The recipient has the ability to accept or reject the connection. Once a connection is established, the screen is split so that each user may be typing a message at the same time.

Time Server   Linux can use the network time protocol (NTP) to both send and receive time synchronization updates. Typically, one system on the network is set up as a time reference server. This server syncs its time with one of the many available time servers out on the Internet. Other systems on the network then check with the reference time server to ensure that their system time remains accurate.

Telnet Server   Linux can accept Telnet requests to provide remote console access to the server. Clients connecting to the system through telnet have the same abilities as if they were sitting in front of the server console.

The administrator can optionally disable the ability to connect to the server with the root user account. This is done as a security precaution. Red Hat Linux has this functionality enabled by default.

Configuring Network Access

Most network administration on Red Hat Linux can be done from either the command line or through a graphical utility in X-Windows. Because the command line uses less overhead, it is usually faster for the experienced user. If you are new to Linux, you may find the GUI utilities a bit easier to use.

There are two basic steps to configuring network support on Linux. The first is adding driver and protocol support to the kernel. This is referred to as *making the kernel* because you will use a utility called **make** to compile the kernel, in effect turning the kernel into an executable C program (take a deep breath, it's not as tough as it sounds). If you are using Red Hat Linux, this may not be required. The default kernel provides support for many popular networking cards and the more popular protocols and topologies are already enabled.

Once you have customized your kernel, you will then need to start your required services. Again, Red Hat Linux ships with the more popular services enabled. You may, however, wish to disable the ones you have installed but do not plan to use just yet.

To Make or Not to Make...

The Red Hat Linux installation adds support for a single network card. If the system will be acting as a server, this is probably all you will ever need. If you need to add support for another card, however, it may be time to rebuild the kernel.

Even if you do not need to add a second network card, there are other reasons why you may wish to customize the modules used by the kernel:

- enable support for other required features

- disable support for unneeded features

- tune memory utilization

- because it's cool...

The stock Linux kernel is configured using the lowest common denominators. While this allows it to run on the widest range of systems, it is probably not optimized for your specific configuration. For example, the kernel is configured to support a 386 that requires math coprocessor emulation. If you are running a 486, Pentium, or higher, you can optimize the system's performance and save memory by changing these settings.

There are five commands used in making the kernel. They are:

- **make config**, or **make menuconfig**, or **make xconfig**

- **make dep**

- **make clean**

- **make zImage**

- **make zlilo**

Only one of the three commands in the first bullet needs to be used. The differences are explained below. **make clean** is no longer a required command, but it will not hurt to run it. All five commands should be executed from the /usr/src/linux directory.

Configuring the Kernel

Always back up your kernel before you start. That way if something embarrassing happens you can always fall back to your original configuration. The kernel file is /vmlinuz. Simply copy (do not move!) the file to /vmlinuz.old. There are three command choices when it comes to selecting the configuration parameters of the kernel. They are:

- **make config**

- **makc menuconfig**

- **make xconfig**

make config is the oldest and the most familiar command to administrators who are old salts with Linux. The **make config** interface is completely command line driven. While not very pretty, the user is provided with default setting that should be fine if left alone. If you do not understand a prompt, do not change it. You can access on line help by typing a question mark in the prompt answer field. The biggest drawback is that you pretty much have to walk through each and every prompt. With the menu utilities, you can jump in and just change what you need to. Figure 9.8 shows the typical output when a **make config** is performed.

Typing **make menuconfig** enables the ASCII character interface shown in Figure 9.9. Using the arrow keys, you can navigate between menu options. Selecting **y** while an option is highlighted enables support, pressing **n** disables support. Some menu items allow you to select **m** for modular support. This allows the driver to be loaded or unloaded as required while the system is running. Pressing **h** brings up a helpful description of the command.

make xconfig is intended to be run from a shell within X-Windows. It is similar to **menuconfig**, but it's a lot prettier. It is also a bit easier to navigate around. Figure 9.10 shows the network section of the xconfig utility.

F I G U R E 9.8

Output of a **make config**

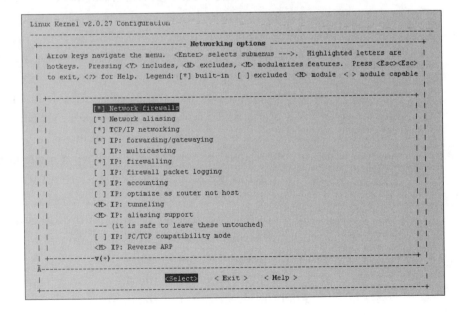

F I G U R E 9.8

Output of a **make config**

```
[root@toby linux]# make config
rm -f include/asm
( cd include ; ln -sf asm-i386 asm)
/bin/sh scripts/Configure arch/i386/config.in
#
# Using defaults found in arch/i386/defconfig
#
*
* Code maturity level options
*
Prompt for development and/or incomplete code/drivers (CONFIG_EXPERIMENTAL) [N/y/?]
*
* Loadable module support
*
Enable loadable module support (CONFIG_MODULES) [Y/n/?]
Set version information on all symbols for modules (CONFIG_MODVERSIONS) [Y/n/?]
Kernel daemon support (e.g. autoload of modules) (CONFIG_KERNELD) [Y/n/?]
*
* General setup
*
Kernel math emulation (CONFIG_MATH_EMULATION) [Y/n/?]
Networking support (CONFIG_NET) [Y/n/?]
```

F I G U R E 9.9

The menu-based kernel configuration screen

```
Linux Kernel v2.0.27 Configuration
-----------------------------------------------------------------------------------
+-------------------------------- Networking options -------------------------------+
| Arrow keys navigate the menu.  <Enter> selects submenus --->.  Highlighted letters are |
| hotkeys.  Pressing <Y> includes, <N> excludes, <M> modularizes features.  Press <Esc><Esc> |
| to exit, <?> for Help.  Legend: [*] built-in  [ ] excluded  <M> module  < > module capable |
|                                                                                    |
| +--------------------------------------------------------------------------------+ |
| |           [*] Network firewalls                                                | |
| |           [*] Network aliasing                                                 | |
| |           [*] TCP/IP networking                                                | |
| |           [*] IP: forwarding/gatewaying                                        | |
| |           [ ] IP: multicasting                                                 | |
| |           [*] IP: firewalling                                                  | |
| |           [ ] IP: firewall packet logging                                      | |
| |           [*] IP: accounting                                                   | |
| |           [ ] IP: optimize as router not host                                  | |
| |           <M> IP: tunneling                                                    | |
| |           <M> IP: aliasing support                                             | |
| |           --- (it is safe to leave these untouched)                            | |
| |           [ ] IP: PC/TCP compatibility mode                                     | |
| |           <M> IP: Reverse ARP                                                  | |
| +-----------v(+)------------------------------------------------------------------+ |
Ä------------------------------------------------------------------------------------
|                         <Select>    < Exit >    < Help >                           |
+-----------------------------------------------------------------------------------+
```

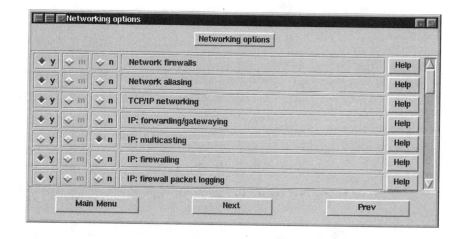

FIGURE 9.10

The X-Windows-based
kernel configuration
screen

Configuration Options Regardless of which method you choose, you will need to select which features you wish to enable or disable. A brief description of features related to networking are listed here. For a more complete list see the online help and how-to files.

Networking Support? This enables networking. If you do not answer yes to this prompt, you will not receive any of the other networking prompts. The default is yes.

Limit memory to low 16MB? Provided for older systems that have trouble addressing memory above 16MB. Most systems do not need this support. The default is no.

PCI BIOS support? Provides support for systems with one or more PCI bus slots. Most newer systems support PCI. The default is yes.

Network firewall? Allows the Linux system to act as a firewall. This option enables firewalling in general although firewalling for IP is the only protocol supported at this time. This option also needs to be enabled if you wish to do IP masquerading. The default is yes.

Network aliasing? Allows multiple network addresses to be assigned to the same interface. Currently, the only supported protocol is IP. This is useful if you need to route two logical networks on the same physical segment. This option should be enabled if you plan on using the Apache Web server in a multihomed capacity. Apache can use the different IP addresses assigned to the interface to direct HTTP requests to different Web sites running on the machine. The default is yes.

TCP/IP networking? This enables or disables IP networking. If you wish to use IP to communicate, then this option should be enabled. The default is yes.

IP: forwarding/gateway? This allows the Linux system to forward IP traffic from one interface to another acting as a router. This can be LAN to LAN or LAN to WAN. If the Linux box will be providing firewall services, this option should be disabled. If you will be using IP masquerading (even if the system will be a firewall as well), this option should be enabled. The default is yes.

IP: multicasting? If you will be using IP multicasting or transmitting routing updates using OSPF, this option should be enabled. The default is no.

IP: firewalling? This option enables the firewall support for the IP protocol. This option should also be enabled if you wish to do IP masquerading, traffic accounting, or use the transparent proxy. The default answer is yes.

IP: firewall packet logging? When the system is used as a firewall, this option creates a file which logs all passing traffic. It also records what the firewall did with each packet (accept, deny). Logging is a good way to keep an eye on who may be knocking at the front door. I usually enable this option. That way if you do not need the information you can simply clean it out from time to time. The default is no.

IP: accounting? When the system acts as a firewall or gateway, this option logs all passing traffic. If Linux will be routing on the internal network, you may want to disable this option as the log can get quite large. If Linux will be routing to or firewalling a WAN connection, you may want to enable this option if you wish to keep track of WAN utilization. The default is yes.

IP: optimize as router not host? If the Linux box will be acting strictly as a router, firewall, or proxy, you should enable this option. If the system will be hosting a HTTP, FTP, DNS, or any other type of services, this option should be disabled. The default is no.

IP: tunneling? This option enables support for IP encapsulation of IP packets. This is useful for amateur radio or mobile IP. The default is modular support which means you can load it while the system is active if you need it.

IP: aliasing support? This option allows you to assign two or more IP addresses to the same interface. Network Aliasing must also be enabled. The default is modular support.

IP: PC/TCP compatibility mode? PC/TCP is a DOS based IP protocol stack. There are some compatibility issues as older versions do not quite follow the same set of communication rules as everyone else. If you have trouble connecting to a Linux system from a host running PC/TCP, then enable this option. Otherwise, this option should be disabled. The default is no.

IP: Reverse ARP? Typically used by diskless workstations to discover their IP address. Enabling this option allows the Linux system to reply to these requests. If you plan on running bootp services, you may want to enable this option in case you need it (either now or later). If the Linux system will not be providing bootp or DHCP services, this option can be disabled. The default is modular support.

IP: Disable Path MTU Discovery? Maximum Transfer Unit (MTU) allows a system to discover the largest packet size it may use when communicating with a remote machine. When MTU is disabled the system assumes it must always use the smallest packet size for a given transmission. Because this option can greatly effect communication speed, MTU should be used unless you run into a compatibility problem. The default is no, which enables MTU discovery.

IP: Drop source routed frames? Source routing allows a transmitting station to specify the network path along which replies should be sent. This forces the system replying to the request to transmit along the specified path instead of the one defined by the local routing table.

There is a type of attack where a potential attacker can use source-routed frames to pretend to be communicating from a host inside your network when they are actually located out on the Internet. Source routing is used to direct the frame back out to the Internet instead of towards the network where the host claims to be located. When source routing is used for this purpose it is referred to as *IP spoofing*.

Some network topologies such as Token Ring and FDDI use source routing as part of their regular communications. If the Linux box is connected to one of these token based topologies, source routing should be left enabled. If you are not using these topologies to communicate, this option should be disabled to increase security. The default is yes, which will drop all source-routed frames.

IP: Allow large windows? This option increases the transmission buffer pool to allow a greater number of frames to be *in transit* without a reply. This is useful when the Linux box is directly connected to a high speed WAN link (multiple T1's or faster) which connect two sites that are separated by an extremely long distance (for example, from coast to coast). The additional buffer space does require additional memory, so this option should only be enabled on systems that meet the above criteria and have at least 16MB of physical memory. The default is yes.

The IPX Protocol? This option enables support for the IPX protocol. You must answer yes to this prompt in order to configure any IPX services. The default is modular support.

Full internal IPX network? NetWare servers use an internal IPX network in order to communicate between the core OS and different subsystems. This option takes this one step further by making the internal IPX network a regular network capable of supporting *virtual hosts*. This is more for development than anything else right now as it allows a single Linux system to appear to be multiple NetWare servers. Unless you are doing development work, this option should be disabled. The default is no.

AppleTalk DDP? This option enables support for the AppleTalk protocol. When used with the netalk package (Linux support for AppleTalk), the Linux system can provide file and printer services to Mac clients. The default is modular support.

Amateur Radio AX.25 Level 2? This option is used to support amateur radio communications. These communications can be either point-to-point, or through IP encapsulation of IP. The default is no.

Kernel/User network link driver? This option enables communications between the kernel and user processes designed to support it. As of this writing, the drive is still experimental and is not required on a production server. The default is no.

Network device support? This option enables driver level support for network communications. You must answer yes to this prompt in order to enable support for network cards and WAN communications. The default is yes.

Dummy net driver support? This option enables the use of a loop back address. Most IP systems understand that transmitting to the IP address 127.0.0.1 will direct the traffic flow back at the system itself. This option should be enabled because some applications do use it. The default is modular support.

EQL (serial line load balancing) support? This option allows Linux to use balance network load over two dial-up links. For example, you may be able to call your ISP on two separate lines, doubling your available bandwidth. The default is modular support.

PLIP (parallel port) support? This option enables support for communication between two systems using a null printer cable. Both systems must use bi-directional parallel ports in order for communications to be successful. This is similar to connecting two system via the serial ports with a null modem cable, except it supports faster communications. The default is modular support.

PPP (point-to-point) support? This option allows the Linux system to create or accept PPP WAN connections. This should be enabled if you plan on using your Linux system to create dial-up connections. The default is modular support.

SLIP (serial line) support? SLIP is the predecessor to PPP. It provides IP connectivity between two systems. Its most popular use is for transferring mail. Because of the additional features provided by PPP, SLIP is used very little. The default is to provide modular support.

Radio network interfaces? This option allows the Linux system to support spread spectrum communications. Spread spectrum is most commonly used for wireless LAN communications. You must answer yes to this prompt in order to receive prompts to configure the radio interface. The default is no.

Ethernet (10 or 100Mbit)? This option allows the Linux system to communicate using Ethernet network cards. You must answer yes to this prompt to later select an Ethernet driver. The default answer is yes.

3COM cards? This option allows the you to select from a list of supported 3COM network cards. If you answer no, you will not be prompted with any 3COM card options. If you select yes, you will receive further prompts allowing you to selectively enable support for each 3COM card that is supported by Linux.

Upon startup, Linux will attempt to find and auto-detect the setting used on each network card. The accuracy rate is pretty good, although it does sometimes miss on some ISA cards. When you reboot the system, watch the configuration parameters it selects for the card. If they are correct, you're all set. If they are wrong, you will need to change either the card settings or the configuration parameters. The card is set through the configuration utility that ships with it. The startup settings can be changed through the Red Hat control panel's Kernel Daemon Configuration option. The default answer for this prompt is yes.

AMD LANCE and PCnet (AT1500 and NE2100)? Similar to 3COM prompt, except this option will enable support for AMD and PCnet network cards. The default is yes.

Western Digital/SMC cards? Similar to 3COM prompt, except this option will enable support for Western Digital and SMC network cards. The default is yes.

Other ISA cards? Similar to 3COM prompt, except this option enables support for some of the more obscure network cards such as Cabletron's E21 series or HP's 100VG PCLAN. If you select yes, you will receive further prompts allowing you to selectively enable support for a variety of network cards that are supported by Linux. The default is yes.

NE2000/NE1000 support? This is the generic Ethernet network card support. If your card has not been specifically listed in any of the above prompts, then enable this option. Most Ethernet network cards are NE2000-compatible so this prompt is a bit of a catch-all. The default is modular support.

EISA, VLB, PCI and on board controllers? There are a number of network cards built directly into the motherboard. If you select yes, you will receive further prompts allowing you to selectively enable support for a variety of built-in network cards that are supported by Linux. The default answer is yes.

Pocket and portable adapters? Linux also supports parallel port network adapters. If you select yes, you will receive further prompts allowing you to selectively enable support for a variety of parallel port network adapters that are supported by Linux. The default answer is yes.

Token Ring driver support? Linux supports a collection of Token Ring network adapters. If you select yes, you will receive further prompts allowing you to selectively enable support for a variety of Token Ring network adapters that are supported by Linux. The default answer is yes.

FDDI driver support? Linux supports a few FDDI network adapters. If you select yes, you will receive further prompts allowing you to selectively enable support for different FDDI network cards that are supported by Linux. The default answer is no.

ARCnet support? ARCnet is an old token-based network topology that is used very little today. If you select yes, you will receive further prompts allowing you to selectively enable support for different FDDI network cards that are supported by Linux. The default support is modular.

ISDN support? This option enables support for ISDN WAN cards. If you plan on using ISDN, you should also enable the PPP support listed above. The default support is modular.

Support synchronous PPP? This option provides support for synchronous communications over an ISDN line. Some ISDN hardware require this to be enabled and will negotiate its use during connection. If you plan on using ISDN, you should enable this option in case you need it. The default is yes.

Use VJ-compression with synchronous PPP? This option enables header compression when synchronous PPP is used. The default is yes.

Support generic MP (RFC 1717)? When synchronous PPP is used, this options allows communications to take place over multiple ISDN lines. Because this is a new specification and not yet widely supported, the default answer is no.

Support audio via ISDN? When supported by the ISDN card, this option allows the Linux system to accept incoming voice calls and act as an answering machine. The default answer is no.

NFS filesystem support? This option enables support for mounting and exporting file systems using NFS. NFS is most frequently used when sharing files between Unix systems; however, it is supported by other platforms as well. The default answer is yes.

SMB filesystem support? This option enables support for NetBIOS/NetBEUI shares. This is most frequently used between Microsoft Windows systems for sharing files and printers. The default answer is yes.

SMB Win95 bug work-around? This option fixes some connectivity problems when the Linux system attempts to retrieve directory information from a Windows 95 system that is sharing files. If you use file sharing for Windows 95, you should enable this option. The default is no.

NCP filesystem support? This option allows the Linux system to connect to NetWare servers. Once connected, the Linux system can mount file systems located on the NetWare server. The default support is modular.

Dependencies Check

Once you have finished the configuration, it is time to run **make dep**. This command performs a dependencies check to ensure that all required files are present before compiling the kernel. Depending on your system speed, this command could take 1–15 minutes to run. While it is not quite as thrilling as watching grass grow, you should keep an eye on the dependency check to ensure that there are no errors. Errors are usually in the form of missing files. If you note what is missing, you can go back and see where you may have lost it.

Cleaning Up the Work Space

Next you can run **make clean** to ensure that any object files get removed. This is typically not required with the latest revision kernels, but it does not hurt to run it just in case. This command usually takes less than one minute to execute.

Compiling the Kernel

Up until now we have not changed the active system. All our changes have been to configuration files. Our next command, **make zImage** will create a kernel with the configuration parameters we selected and replace the one we are currently using. Notice the capital "I" in zImage. This is important because characters are case sensitive.

How long this command will take to run depends on your processor speed and the amount of physical memory that is installed in the system. A 133MHz Pentium with 32MB of RAM should take 10–15 minutes to create a new kernel. The first Linux kernel I ever configured was version .97 which was a bit smaller than the current release. The machine was a 16MHz 386sx with 4MB of memory. It took about 12 hours to create a new kernel. Your mileage may vary, but you can use these two configurations as a guide.

Configuring the Boot Manager

Our last step is to tell Linux's boot manager LILO that it needs to set pointers for a new image. This is done with the command **make zlilo**. The command should take a minute or less to execute. Once complete you can take a look in the root directory to compare your old and new kernels. If all went well, the time stamp for the new image should be more recent than the /vmlinuz.old file that we created. If we got real lucky, our new kernel should even be a little smaller. This is usually the case, but may not be true if you enabled support on many of the options.

We can now reboot the system and boot off of the new kernel. You should not notice any new errors during system startup. If you do, or if the system refuses to boot all together, you can use the original boot disk as an emergency recovery disk. This will let you onto the drive so you can copy back the original image until you can figure out what went wrong.

Changing the Network Driver Settings

As mentioned above, you may need to change the network driver setting if auto-probe fails to configure it properly. This can be done through the Red Hat control panel using the Kernel Daemon Configuration option. Figure 9.11 shows the Kernel Configurator window, in which you can add, remove, and change the settings of device drivers.

When you highlight a specific driver and select Edit, you will see the Set Module Options dialog box, shown in Figure 9.12. This allows you to change the configuration parameters that Linux uses to initialize your network card. Once the changes are complete, you can restart the kernel to have these changes take effect.

FIGURE 9.11

The Kernel Configurator

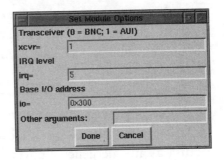

FIGURE 9.11

The Kernel Configurator

FIGURE 9.12

The Set Module Options window allows you to change the startup parameters for a specific driver.

Starting Network Services

The startup scripts for most of the networking services can be found in the /etc/rc.d/init.d directory. Most of these services are configured to initialize once their main configuration file has been created. Table 9.1 shows a list of services and the files that must exist in order for them to start.

If you need to temporarily disable one of the services from starting during boot up, simply rename its initialization file. For example, the initialization script for Sendmail is sendmail.init. If I rename this file sendmail.init.old, Sendmail will no longer initialize during system startup.

You can also use Red Hat's runtime editor, located on the control panel to load, unload, or prevent a service from initializing.

Service	Daemon	Main Configuration File
lpd	lpd	/etc/printcap
DNS	named	/etc/named.boot
news	innd	/etc/rc.d/news
NFS	rpc.nfsd & rpc.mountd	/etc/exports

TABLE 9.1 Networking services and the files they need in order to start

Configuring Routing

The Network Configurator option on the Red Hat control panel allows you to add and delete interfaces as well as setup aliasing. You can also configure routing.

Figure 9.13 shows the properties for a network interface alias. We can tell it is an alias because of the :0 designation in the interface name. Aliasing allows us to set up multiple IP addresses to the same interface.

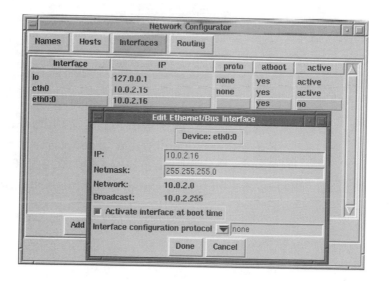

FIGURE 9.13 The Network Configurator window; this is where we can configure our alias options.

The Routing button allows us to configure static routing. Figure 9.14 shows an example of static routing configuration. The default gateway defines where to send traffic when the network address is not defined in the lower table. Selecting the Add button brings up the Edit Static Route window, shown in the foreground. This allows us to create entries for specific networks. We only need to do this if the IP address of the next hop router is different than the IP address of the default gateway.

FIGURE 9.14

Our static routing definitions

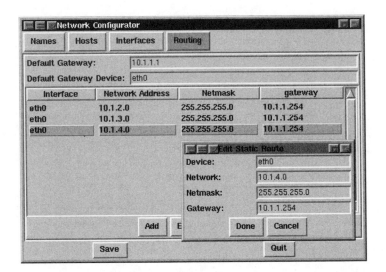

The specific entries in Figure 9.14 have been added because the next hop router is at a different IP address than the default gateway. Without these entries, traffic destined for 10.1.2.0–10.1.4.0 would first go to the default gateway address before being forwarded to 10.1.1.254.

Configuring IP Services

There are a number of wonderful resources available for configuring services on Linux and Unix in general. Some of these are:

The Linux How-To and FAQ guides (written by a wide range of authors) can be accessed at `HTTP://www.redhat.com/manual`.

TCP/IP Network Administration
by Craig Hunt
(O'Reilly and Associates, 1992)

Managing Internet Information Services
by Cricket Liu, Jerry Peek, Russ Jones, Bryan Buus, and Adrian Nye
(O'Reilly and Associates, 1994)

The Future of Linux

It is tough to predict the future of Linux or what additional features may be added in the future. Support for a given technology is added almost as quickly as it is released or discovered. While Linux is a solid production system, it is also a playground. Features are not added based upon market studies, or investment to sales ratios. There is no one attempting to control product cost, or worrying about target markets.

Features are added to Linux because its developers love the technology and think the innovations are cool. It's pretty amazing what can be accomplished when the money factor is removed from the questions, "Can we get it to work and will it sell?"

Of one thing there is no doubt, Linux will remain on the cutting edge of technology for many years to come.

Summary

This completes our discussion of the features and services provided by Linux. You should now have a good understanding of how to configure the kernel as well as enable protocols and services.

In Chapter 10, we will take a look Lotus Notes. While not a true NOS, it has a wide implementation and supports a number of network protocols.

Later in Chapter 12, we'll revisit Linux and look at options for optimizing network communications. In Chapter 14, we will again revisit this NOS to evaluate the network monitoring and connectivity tools it provides.

CHAPTER

10

Lotus Notes

Released in 1989, Lotus Notes set the standard for groupware and collaboration products before these terms even became buzzwords. In short, it revolutionized the way organizations can do business and share information.

At its core, Lotus Notes is a relational database. When multiple Lotus Notes servers are used, databases can be linked together and synchronized across multiple servers. This can be a powerful feature in a large networking environment. Linked databases allow users accessing information to retrieve all their data from a local Lotus Notes server. They do not need to tie up WAN links accessing information located on remote networks.

So why include Lotus Notes in a book dedicated to networks and operating systems? There are two reasons:

- the popularity of the product

- that it's a model for other client-server applications

Lotus Notes has enjoyed a wide deployment. As such, it is an application that is worth discussing because it is found on many networks. Lotus Notes is also a good example of the connectivity requirements of the typical client-server application. Many of the tuning and optimization tricks that we will use on Lotus Notes can be directly applied to other client-server applications.

Lotus Notes Features

Because Lotus Notes is not a true NOS, it requires that one be installed on the server prior to its installation. Lotus Notes server supports Windows 95, Windows NT, OS/2, NetWare (including Intranet-Ware), Solaris, HP-UX, and IBM's AIX. While OS/2 used to be the Notes platform of choice, as of the spring of 1997, Lotus announced that Windows NT is the preferred platform for running Notes—a strange announcement considering that IBM, who owns OS/2, also owns Lotus.

With this in mind, all examples for Lotus Notes assume an installation on a Windows NT server, version 4.0. Many of the configuration options, however, are applicable to every supported platform.

We will now cover some of the features of Lotus Notes in order to give you an overview of the product.

Lotus Notes Setup

As mentioned, Lotus Notes requires that an NOS be installed and operational prior to its installation. This includes enabling any protocols that Lotus Notes may require to conduct communications with clients and other servers.

The installation utility does little more than install the required files on the server. There is no prompt to name the Lotus Notes server, enable certain network protocols, or even create a server certification key. This lack of guidance can be a bit disheartening for the general network administrator who has not had the opportunity to receive formal Lotus Notes training.

The server is initially configured by running the Lotus Notes client on it. Once the client has been launched, you are prompted to name the server, assign an administrator, and select a default network protocol. The First Server Setup window is shown in Figure 10.1. Note that we can only configure one protocol and serial port. This initial configuration allows us to set up the bare minimums required to get our server communicating.

FIGURE 10.1

The First Server Setup
window

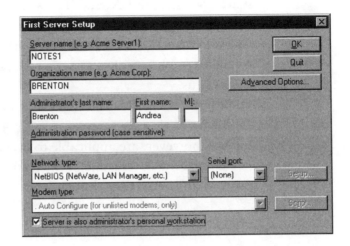

 If you are running the Lotus Notes client on the server for the first time and it does not prompt you to configure the server, check the settings in the NOTES.INI file. It should include the line KitType=2. This tells the system that a server has been installed on the machine. KitType=1 is used only for workstation installations.

Optimizing Windows NT for Lotus Notes

There are two Windows NT settings you will want to optimize when running Lotus Notes—both are accessible from the control panel.

The first is located through the System icon. Click on the Performance tab in the System Properties window and change the Boost in the Application Performance window to None. This ensures that if the

Lotus Notes server is not within the currently active window or is set up as a service, it will not suffer a performance degradation. This setting is shown in Figure 10.2.

FIGURE 10.2

Optimizing application boost for use with Lotus Notes

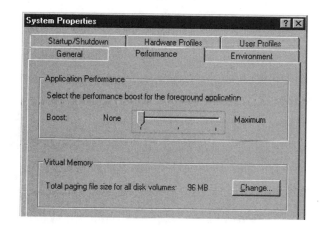

The second setting to optimize is located through the Network icon. Select the Services tab and select Properties for the Server service. You will want to ensure that Maximize Throughput for Network Applications is selected. This tunes the system to pay more attention to network communications instead of file or printer sharing. The Server window was shown in Chapter 8, Figure 6.

Once your settings are complete, you should reboot the NT server to make your changes take effect.

Core Features

As of the time of this writing, the latest release of Lotus Notes is version 4.6. As mentioned in the introduction to this Chapter, Lotus Notes is a relational database which can be linked across multiple servers.

Replication

With Lotus Notes, database information can be shared between servers using a process called *replication*. Replication allows two servers to synchronize the contents of one or more databases to ensure that each contains identical information. Replication can be performed on a predetermined schedule, or whenever an event takes place.

Lotus Notes servers can connect to each other over a LAN or WAN using a variety of networking protocols. They can also connect to each other directly via modem to exchange information.

As an example of this functionality, consider Figure 10.3. We have three networks which are connected by two 56 Kb leased line WAN connections. The fourth site has no network connection to the other three and is an isolated network. Let's assume we have corporate policies and procedures that apply to each of the four locations. We wish to provide access to a database system containing this information. There are employees at each of the four sites who will need to access this information.

If we where using a standard database program such as Access or dBase, all files would have to be located on a central server. Employees at each of the two remote sites connected by the leased line would need to access the database over the WAN. The more people accessing the database, the less bandwidth is available on the WAN for other services.

Also, our isolated network would have no way of accessing this central database. A modem pool would have to be created with enough modems to support the number of employees that may need to dial in simultaneously. Multiple modems would require multiple phone lines and software to connect to the network where the database is located.

If we were to replace the standard database model with one that uses Lotus Notes, the three Lotus Notes servers connected via WAN could exchange database updates over the WAN itself. Traffic is kept to a minimum, as only database changes need to traverse the WAN. Because each server contains the same information once replication is complete, employees can view the database directly from their local server. This

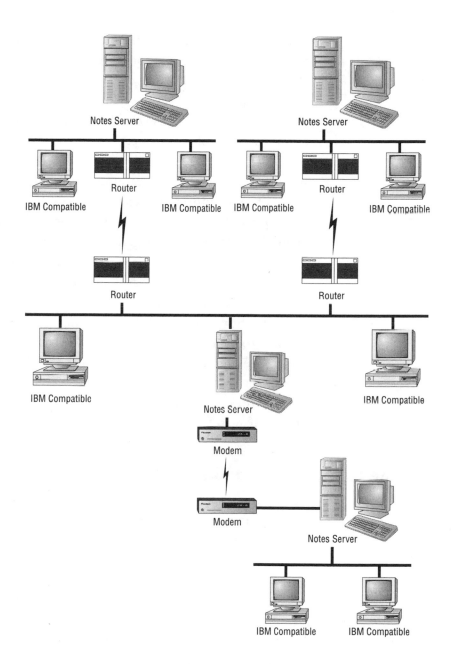

FIGURE 10.3

A geographically separated network which needs to share a database not only reduces WAN traffic, but it decreases the time required to view the database because the connection does not need to traverse the slower WAN link.

As for our isolated site, two Lotus Notes servers can be configured to connect via modem. This would require only one phone line at each site and no special software. Each Lotus Notes server can call the other whenever it needs to relay database changes. Once the changes have been sent, the dial-up link can then be terminated.

All of these information exchanges can be controlled on a per-server and a per-database level by adjusting the database properties. For example, we could configure replication so that our main server accepts document deletions from one server (and removes the appropriate documents from its own database), but rejects attempts at record deletions from the other two servers.

Replication is a powerful feature that made Lotus Notes a unique product for quite a few years. While there are currently other products hitting the market that can provide the same type of functionality, they do not yet have the maturity of Lotus Notes which makes it a stable product (of course "stable" is a relative term when you are talking about software).

The Client-Server Model

Lotus Notes is a true client-server application. By this I mean that some of the processing used to manipulate a database file is provided by the local workstation, while some of it is provided by the server itself.

For example, if I need to compress a database file (optimize it by removing unused space), I do not need to perform this function from my client. I can simply use my client to create the request and submit it to the server which will carry out the task. This frees up my desktop system to perform other functions.

The purpose of the client-server model is to isolate processes to the system that can best carry them out. In the above example it is more efficient to have the server perform the compression, as this is where the database is located. Performing the compression from my client would require that every byte of data contained within the database be transmitted over the network to my system. My client would then have to transmit this information back to the server as it optimizes the file. Clearly, this can dramatically increase the amount of traffic on the network. By having the server carry out the task, I create less of a traffic impact on my entire network.

Other OS Features

Along with text, Lotus Notes database entries, called *documents*, can contain embedded images, sound, video, applications, and even scripts. For example, a user can create a Java or ActiveX script which can be executed by simply clicking on an icon. This makes Lotus Notes a powerful tool for sharing any kind of information.

Along with Java and ActiveX, Lotus Notes supports Lotus Script, a scripting language similar to Basic that can be used for filtering information or carrying out certain tasks. While Lotus Script will only function with Lotus Notes, it is directly portable to any platform that Lotus Notes may be running on. For example, a Lotus Script created for Lotus Notes running on NT will operate unmodified on a Lotus Notes system running on Solaris.

Lotus Notes also supplies e-mail capability. Each user gets their own personal database file for storing their e-mail messages. When a message is received, it is stored in a user's database file. When servers replicate database information, they can exchange e-mail messages at the same time.

As of version 4.0, Lotus has integrated the interface of cc:Mail with Notes. This interface is simpler and yet more powerful than the original interface Lotus Notes used for e-mail. It supports advanced features, such as automatic message categorization through scripting as well as personal folders. Also included with 4.0, is a mail gateway which allows the Lotus Notes server to exchange messages with other mail systems using SMTP.

As part of Lotus Notes' e-mail security and management, a central address book of all users is maintained. As of the latest Lotus Notes version, this address book has been expanded to include contact management and scheduling information. Through Lotus Notes, you can now schedule other users and resources (such as conference rooms) for meetings. The user is allowed to see unscheduled time periods for the people they wish to invite. This helps to ensure that there are no scheduling conflicts. The potential attendee has the ability to accept or reject the meeting invitation, as well as attempt to schedule it for another time.

Lotus Notes also offers tight integration with most major office suites. For example, a user can choose to change the default mail editor to use their favorite word processor program. If a user has Office 97 installed, they can choose to use the Word interface when creating e-mail messages.

Account Administration

Lotus Notes maintains a tight integration with NT Server. User account information can be synchronized between the two such that account additions or deletions are propagated across both systems. Passwords can be synchronized between Lotus Notes and the NT domain so that only a single logon is required for access to both network resources. This is done by checking the Add NT User Account(s) box in the Register Person window, shown in Figure 10.4.

FIGURE 10.4

You can automatically add NT accounts when creating Lotus Notes accounts.

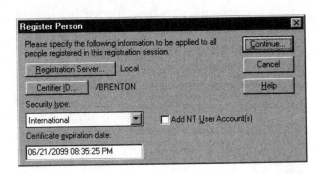

Lotus Notes can even use the NT server's event viewer for reporting operational events. The event viewer provides the administrator with a single point of reference to check the health of both Lotus Notes and the underlying operating system.

Security

Lotus Notes is arguably one of the most secure methods of exchanging information over a network. Its support for certifying user access and encrypting document information helps to ensure that the system remains secure.

When a user first logs on to a Lotus Notes server, they are challenged for a user name and password. This type of security is common with most networking systems. Lotus Notes takes this one step further, however, by requiring that the user have a valid User ID file.

The User ID File

A User ID is an encrypted identification number which uniquely identifies each user. This information is saved in a file format containing an *.id extension and must be made available during database access.

For example, let's assume you are away from your desk and realize that you need to access a particular Lotus Notes database. You sit down in front of the closest workstation and attempt to logon. While you have entered the correct user name and password, you find that the system will not allow you to access the required database.

This is because you also need to have your User ID file in order to prove you are actually who you say you are. While a snooping employee may be able to look over your shoulder and see your password as you type it in, if you protect your User ID file they will still be unable to access the Lotus Notes server using your account. How can you protect your User ID? One way would be to store it on a floppy and wear it around your neck as the latest fashion accessory.

The User ID file is made up of six components:

1. the user's name, as recorded in the server's address book

2. the Lotus Notes license number assigned to the User ID during creation

3. the user's public and private authentication keys

4. encryption keys used for encrypting fields within documents

5. certificates which grant the user access to specific servers

6. the user's password

The combination of these six items makes every User ID unique. If a user loses their User ID file and needs to have a new one created, any documents encrypted with the old key will be unreadable. This is because, even though the same user name and password may be assigned, the license and authentication keys would be different for the new ID file.

To ensure that a new key does not have to be generated when a user loses their User ID file, you should maintain a backup copy of every user's User ID file in a secure location.

WARNING   There is no way to remove or clear a password from a User ID file without knowing the existing password. Do not forget what you assign for a password or you will need to create a new ID file!

Lotus Notes servers also use ID files, except they are referred to as Server IDs. The files are identical except that a server name is used instead of a user name.

Certificates

Certificates are used on a Lotus Notes server to regulate who can gain access to it. This not only includes users, but also other Lotus Notes servers during replication. When a user or Lotus Notes server becomes certified, they are allowed access to the system. What kind of access is received is governed by the Access Control List (ACL) which we will discuss later in this section. A certificate simply regulates who is allowed through the front door. A server's certification file is named CERT.ID and is located in the Lotus Notes program directory.

When a user needs access to a Lotus Notes server, they must provide the Lotus Notes Administrator with a *safe copy* of their User ID file. A safe copy can be generated through the Lotus Notes client and produces a copy of the User ID that can be certified, but not used for Lotus Notes server access.

Once the Lotus Notes administrator receives the safe copy of the User ID, they can use the server's CERT.ID file to *stamp* it. This stamp becomes part of the User ID code and provides the authentication required to allow the user to access the Lotus Notes server.

Once the safe copy of the User ID has been stamped, the user must merge the copy back into their real ID file. Once the merge is complete, the user can gain access to the Lotus Notes server.

The process is nearly identical when certifying two Lotus Notes servers for replication. The differences are:

- A safe copy of the Server ID file is used instead of a User ID file.

- The process must be performed twice, once for each server. This is referred to as *cross certification* and allows either server to initiate a connection with the other.

Certification helps to ensure that users or servers attempting to access the Lotus Notes server are in fact who they claim to be. It adds an additional level of protection to ensure that the data remains secure.

Lotus Notes security can be configured to follow either a flat or hierarchical model. Hierarchical is the preferred method of configuration, as it increases the amount of control the Lotus Notes administrator has over the Lotus Notes domain.

Encryption

Lotus Notes uses RSA Corporation's Message Digest 2 (MD2) when performing encryption. Notes will encrypt:

- mail messages

- fields within a document

- communications with the server (either from a workstation or another server)

This is to help ensure that even when your information is being moved off of the server, it remains secure. Lotus Notes uses two separate encryption key lengths, a 40-bit key with the International version of their software and a 128-bit key for the US version. The larger the key, the harder it is for an attacker to break the encryption code and gain access to your data.

The International key is smaller due to US federal regulation. During WWII, encryption was designated as a type of munitions and a threat to national security. Because of this, it is heavily regulated. Messages sent across US borders are limited to an encryption key length of 40 bits. Despite the efforts of many individuals and organizations to increase the acceptable key length, no progress has been made in doing so.

The US government reserves the right to decrypt any message they feel may be illegal or a threat to national security. As the key length increases, the difficulty in breaking the key increases exponentially. The current record for decrypting a 40-bit encrypted message by a private citizen is eight days. With the computing power resources of the US government, they could probably do this in even less time.

If you are a global organization that requires encrypted connectivity from the US to any outside country, you should use the International version of Lotus Notes.

Access Control List (ACL)

The ACL controls the tasks users are allowed to perform on a specific database, as well as what information other servers are allowed to replicate. Each database has its own ACL to control access. The following sections cover the different levels of access.

Manager

Users with Manager access can modify ACL settings, encrypt a database for local security, modify replication settings, and delete a database. Managers can also perform all tasks allowed by each of the other access levels. Manager is the highest level of access that can be assigned to a user account. Lotus Notes requires each database to have at least one Manager. It's best to assign two people Manager access to a database in case one manager is absent.

Designer

Users with Designer access can modify all database design elements (fields, forms, views, and so on), as well as modify replication formulas, and create a full text index. Designers can also perform all tasks allowed by lower access levels. Assign Designer access to the original designer of a database or to a user responsible for updating the design.

Editor

Users assigned Editor access can create documents and edit all documents, including those created by other users. Editors can also perform all tasks allowed by lower access levels. Assign Editor access to a user responsible for maintaining all data in a database.

Author

Users assigned Author access can create documents and edit documents they create. They cannot, however, edit documents created by other users. Authors can also perform all tasks allowed lower access levels.

Reader

Users assigned Reader access can read documents in a database, but cannot create or edit documents. For example, you could create a Technical Support database describing helpful tips for resolving some of the more common problems your users encounter. You could then assign Reader access to all of your users so they can reference the information prior to calling you on the phone (hey, it could happen...).

Depositor

Users assigned Depositor access can create documents but are not allowed to view any documents, even the ones they create. Once a depositor saves a document, it is removed from their view and cannot be retrieved. This setting can also be applied to other servers during replication when you wish to accept additions but not changes or deletes.

No Access

The name says it all. Users assigned No Access cannot access the database.

The above ACLs allow the Lotus Notes Administrator to secure access to the databases as well as delegate tasks to other individuals. For example, we could assign Manager access to one of our Technical Support employees so they could maintain the support database mentioned above. This would allow the Lotus Notes Administrator to delegate the responsibility of this specific database to another individual, leaving the administrator free to perform other tasks (such as performing security audits by attempting to purse links to renegade internal Web sites which do not conform to the corporate security policy).

Networking

As mentioned, Lotus Notes requires that networking be enabled on the underlying NOS. Any protocols that you wish to use for Lotus

Notes communications must first be enabled and functioning correctly on the operating system itself. For example, if you wish to use IP for Lotus Notes communications, NT must be configured with a valid IP address, a default route when applicable, and have access to a DNS server or hosts file.

Once the underlying NOS is properly configured, Lotus Notes will support NetBIOS, NetBIOS encapsulated in IPX, IPX/SPX, VinesIP (Banyan Vine's communication protocol), AppleTalk, and IP. When IP is used, Lotus Notes uses the TCP transport and a destination port of 1352 for all communications. This includes all client-to-server and server-to-server communications.

If you will be connecting to your Lotus Notes server over the Internet for either client access or replication, you will want to make sure that TCP port 1352 is open on your firewall and/or packet filtering router.

Curiously, Lotus Notes must also be redundantly configured to use the same protocols configured on the NOS. It has no method of detecting which protocols the NOS is using in order to configure itself appropriately. While this is not a really big deal, as networking protocols are rarely changed once a server is in operation, it can be a bit of a hassle because Lotus Notes has its own unique way of configuring networking services. This method is very different than the configuration process used on any of the NOSes covered so far. We discuss the configuration of network protocols in the "Configuring Network Access" section of this chapter.

Lotus Notes also supports remote dial-up connections. As indicated in Figure 10.1, remote dial-up connections can be used to replicate information between servers. They can also be used to allow users to remotely access databases from home or on the road.

For example, let's assume I am a traveling salesperson who needs to periodically check in for e-mail. I would also like to keep my client database up to date with the latest contact information. Changes to the client database may originate back at the corporate office, or I may need to generate them while on site with a client.

With Lotus Notes, this is a fairly elementary process. I simply place a copy of my mail file and the client database on my laptop computer. If I am at a client site and need to update a record, I can edit the local copy located on my hard drive (I do not need to connect to the corporate network to perform this task). Then, when it is convenient, I can call the Lotus Notes server with my laptop and replicate the two databases (client and mail) with the originals located on the corporate Lotus Notes server. This keeps all the databases synchronized so they contain identical information.

Changes are not the only information replicated. For example, let's assume that while out on the road I receive a number of technical specifications on our product line from Engineering. Having no use for these documents, I delete them from the mail file located on my laptop's hard drive. The next time I replicate, these deletes are replicated as well and the documents are removed from my mail file located on the Lotus Notes server. This way I do not have to delete them again the next time I am in the office. The replication process ensures that my mail file remains identical on both the Lotus Notes server and my laptop.

As with networking protocols, the modem has to be properly installed within the NOS in order for Lotus Notes to utilize it.

Lotus Notes Client

The Lotus Notes client is designed to run on Windows 3.1, Windows 95, Windows NT, Mac System 7, Solaris, HP-UX, OS/2, and AIX. Along with allowing a client to remotely access the Lotus Notes server, the client is also typically run on the server as well in order to configure it. For example, if you need to add a protocol to a Lotus Notes server running on NT, you will need to launch the Lotus Notes client in order to configure it. With this in mind, configuring communications on either a client or a server is identical.

Care should be taken to secure the Lotus Notes server console. If a client is launched from the server and databases are accessed as "Local," all ACL security can be circumvented.

The Lotus Notes client also contains an integrated Web browser. This provides a single user interface for Web, mail, and database access. The Web browser has the ability to monitor specified pages to see if they have been changed. If a change is detected, the Web browser can retrieve a copy of the page for later offline viewing. This can be a real timesaver if you frequent Web sites that contain many graphic files, such as the comics page on the United Media Web site.

IP Applications

As of version 4.0, Notes includes Domino, Lotus's answer to Internet services. Domino includes some interesting features which make it an attractive fit for some networking environments.

Domino includes a Web server with support for CGI, Java, and ActiveX. While this type of functionality has become pretty common, Domino has the unique ability to directly integrate with one or more Lotus Notes databases.

One of the most difficult processes in developing a Web server is adding solid database support. It can be difficult at best for an administrator to link in basic services, such as document searches and retrieval. It can be an outright scripting nightmare if you need to link in real-time services such as a discussion database.

Because Domino directly integrates with Lotus Notes, it leverages the ability of Lotus Notes to provide this type of functionality and focuses on simply organizing the data when it is presented to the Web browser. Domino includes an easy-to-use question-and-answer configuration utility. Simply fill in the fields describing which database you wish to link to and what type of views you wish to present, and Domino does the rest. This can dramatically reduce the time required to develop a Web site with document search capability.

Domino also allows Lotus Notes users to access their mail using the POP-3 protocol. This is useful if you have users who need to occasionally check their mail from their ISP. Of course, by using POP-3 you lose all the replication and security benefits normally associated with Lotus Notes mail. Still, POP-3 can be an engaging solution given the right set of requirements.

Domino can even support news groups and allow users to connect to the system using a news reader. This is useful if you have a small number of actual Lotus Notes users but wish to create discussion forums that are accessible to all. News postings are saved to a database in the typical document format. Postings can then be viewed by either the Lotus Notes client or by any available news reader.

Configuring Network Access

To configure Networking on a Lotus Notes server, you must first shut down the server and launch the Lotus Notes client. From the client, select File ➤ Tools ➤ User Preferences. This will display the User Preferences dialog box. Select the Ports icon on the left-hand side of the screen. The User Preferences dialog box should appear as it does in Figure 10.5.

The Communications Ports list allows you to select which protocols and serial ports the server should use for communication. All active ports have a check mark next to them along with a check mark in the Port Enabled checkbox. The Reorder arrow buttons are only useful when configuring communications for the Lotus Notes client itself (not the server). This option sets up the order in which Lotus Notes

FIGURE 10.5

The Communication Ports
list of the User
Preferences window

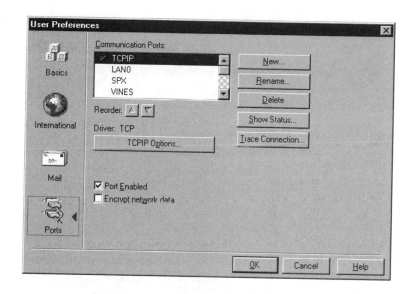

will utilize each protocol as it attempts to find a service. Because a server monitors each protocol equally, this setting has no effect.

The New button allows you to setup a new communications port. Because Lotus Notes comes with a configuration for each supported protocol, you usually do not need this button unless you accidentally delete a port.

The Rename button allows you to assign a new name to the selected communication port. For example, we could rename the port TCPIP to be IP_PORT if we found this name to be more descriptive.

The Delete button allows us to remove a port from the Communications Ports list. This button is usually not required, as Lotus Notes will ignore any port that is disabled. You do not need to remove them from the list.

The Show Status button displays the current state of the selected port. For example, our TCPIP port would show a status of being active and using TCP as a transport. Any of the deactivated ports would simply display "No Port information available."

TIP

If you activate a port, but the status states that port information is not available, remember to stop and restart the server.

If the server is running while the Show Status button is selected, the status display will indicate any active sessions with the server. Figure 10.6 shows a status of an IP port with one active session. Notes session 03730001 shows that a session is in progress from IP address 10.1.1.100. The status also indicates that the server is using port 1055 when sending replies. Notes session 03020002 is a session originating from the current client. This session is using a reply port of 1352.

FIGURE 10.6

The TCP/IP Port Status dialog box displaying session information regarding the IP port

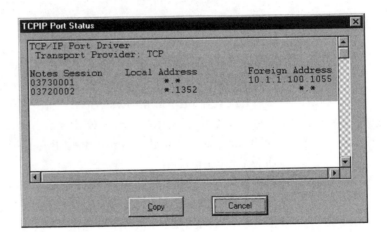

The Trace Connection button in the User Preferences window gives us a connectivity tool when diagnosing communication problems. We simply enter the name of the server we are looking for and the client will report diagnostic information as it attempts to contact the server. The following is an example of a successful trace of the IP port for a Lotus Notes server named Notes1:

```
Determining path to server notes1

Checking normal priority connection records only...
```

```
Checking for notes1 at last known address 'notes1' on
   TCPIP...

notes1 is available on TCPIP

Connecting to notes1 over TCPIP

Using address '10.1.1.232' on TCPIP

Connected to server notes1
```

The following is an example trace to a server that is currently offline. The line numbers have been added for annotation purposes only:

```
1 Determining path to server notes1

2 Checking normal priority connection records only...

3 Checking for notes1 at last known address 'notes1' on
   TCPIP...

4 No answer at last known address

5 Performing extended search... (CTRL+BREAK to cancel)

6 Allowing wild card connection records...

7 Enabling name service requests and probes...

8 Checking for notes1 on TCPIP using address 'notes1'

9 Checking low and normal priority connection records...

10 Allowing wild card connection records...

11 Enabling name service requests and probes...

12 No default passthru server defined

13 Unable to find any path to notes1

14 Local Error: Unable to find path to server
```

Lines 1–3 are the initial attempt to contact the server Notes1. At line 4 this connection fails. Lines 5–11 are two more subsequent attempts to contact the server using expanded pattern matching.

In line 12, the client attempts to look for another Lotus Notes server that may accept data destined for this system. For example, if Notes1 was located on a remote network, one of the servers on our network may be responsible for passing along requests to it. In lines 13 and 14, the trace gives up, determining that the server is unreachable.

Trace Connection can be used when verifying the connectivity between a workstation and the server or from one server to another.

The TCPIP Options button is protocol dependent and will change depending on the selected protocol. The available configuration options will change as well. For example, when TCPIP is selected, this option lets us change the communication time-out value. When SPX is selected, the name of this button changes to SPX Options and you can select whether Lotus Notes should look for NetWare servers using DNS, Bindery services, or both.

The Encrypt Network Data option specifies that any data sent through this port should be transmitted in an encrypted format. This is useful when data may be traversing an insecure network such as the Internet. The systems at both ends of the connection must have encryption enabled.

Once your changes are complete, you can exit the client and restart the Lotus Notes server. During Lotus Notes server initialization, you should watch the Lotus Notes server screen to ensure that it does not report any errors with the newly added protocols.

Summary

This completes our discussion of the server side of communications. It is now time to look at client operating systems to see how they can best be configured.

CHAPTER

11

Client Communications

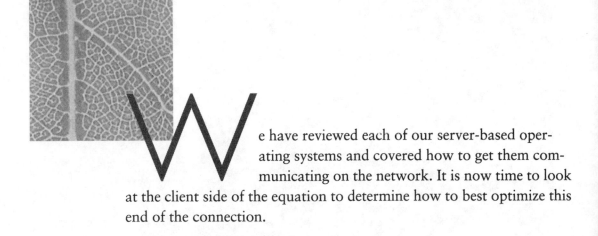

e have reviewed each of our server-based operating systems and covered how to get them communicating on the network. It is now time to look at the client side of the equation to determine how to best optimize this end of the connection.

Who Can Talk to Whom

First, we need to establish a baseline. We need to determine which client operating systems are capable of communicating with each server. If we look at native support or client support that is shipped with the server software, our connectivity matrix would appear, as shown in Table 11.1.

TABLE 11.1

The connectivity matrix

Client OS	NetWare	NT Server	Lotus Notes	Unix running NFS
DOS/Win 3.1x	X	X	Win 3.1x only	*
Win95	X	X	X	*
NT Workstation	X	X	X	*
Mac	X	**	X	*
Unix			X	X

*   Requires third party software
**   Requires that AppleTalk be enabled on the server

We now begin to see a few patterns. The first is that Lotus Notes supports all listed platforms. This is a bit misleading in terms of Unix because the only flavors of Unix Lotus Notes supports are Solaris, HP-UX, and AIX. Lotus Notes does not support Linux, FreeBSD, SGI, or a host of other Unix flavors.

After Lotus Notes, NetWare and NT provide the best connectivity support. NetWare has a bit of an edge, as it supplies both IPX and AppleTalk connectivity to Mac clients; this allows you to consolidate both PC and Mac clients on a single protocol (IPX). Windows NT provides support for the Mac only through the AppleTalk protocol. Because PC clients will use NetBEUI or NetBIOS over IP to connect to resources, a minimum of two protocols is required.

NFS appears to be the most difficult remote file system to support, as all operating systems except for Unix require additional third party tools in order to provide connectivity; this increases both the cost and complexity of our network configuration.

Now that we know which client operating systems can connect to each of our servers, it is time to look at the configuration process required to get each of our clients connected. In the interest of brevity, we will eliminate portions of the matrix with the poorest showing. Because NFS is only natively supported between Unix systems, we will discuss this configuration only. Also, because the Mac does not natively support half of our listed servers, we will eliminate it from further discussions.

Configuring Client Communications in a NetWare Environment

The client software used to connect to a NetWare server can come from one of two sources. The first is Novell, which supplies a set of client drivers when you purchase the IntranetWare operating system. Windows 95 and Windows NT Workstation ship with a set of NetWare client drivers, which are manufactured by Microsoft. If you are using Windows 95 or NT Workstation, you can choose which client (Novell's or Microsoft's) that you wish to use.

The Novell Client Drivers for NetWare

Novell's client drivers for NetWare, referred to as *client32*, have the greatest number of configurable options, and have been independently tested to provide the fastest connectivity. There are clients available supporting DOS, Windows 95, Windows NT, OS/2, and the Mac. Windows 3.1*x* is supported through the DOS client.

Legacy Clients

Novell's older clients directly supported the Open Datalink Interface (ODI). This is a fairly open programming interface (although Novell owns the trademark) that supports the use of multiple protocol stacks. For example, by using the ODI interface, a workstation can communicate using IPX and IP to access resources using both protocols.

There are two major drawbacks to the legacy drivers. First, they operated in 16-bit Real Mode which means that the software is capable of crashing the entire workstation if it fails. Because real mode does not afford any kind of memory protection between programs, crashing is a common problem with any real mode software. Also, ODI has not been as widely accepted as Novell hoped it would be. For example, Microsoft opted to focus on the Network Driver Interface Specification (NDIS) instead of ODI.

During a client32 install, you still have the option of installing the legacy 16-bit drivers which directly support ODI. You should use the new 32-bit drivers, unless you run into compatibility problems or you are using older NIC cards that do not support the new client software.

Client32

Since the advent of client32, Novell has incorporated the communication technology they have used on their servers for many years onto the workstation. Client32 drivers are very similar to the LAN and NLM modules used to enable networking on the server. While it still uses ODI technology, Novell has created a thin programming layer which allows LAN and NLM drivers to be used on other operating systems besides a NetWare server.

There are a few immediate benefits to using LAN and NLM drivers. The first is that the drivers operate in 32-bit protected mode. Along with being faster than their 16-bit counterparts, they are also more stable.

Client32 drivers are modular and dynamic. They are modular in that the driver software is not just one large program, but it is made up of many smaller pieces. Dynamic means that client32 can load and unload these pieces as required. This means that the memory footprint can be kept to a minimum by dynamically accessing support modules as required. The benefit is that while legacy 16-bit drivers may require 45KB–75KB to load, client32 only requires 4KB of conventional or upper memory. Memory management for all drivers is provided by the NetWare I/O Subsystem (NIOS).

Client32 even has benefits for NIC manufacturers. Because the workstation now uses similar LAN drivers to the server, the amount of effort required to develop NIC card drivers is reduced. The NIC manufacturer is only required to write code for one type of driver (LAN), they no longer need to develop a separate legacy ODI driver to support workstation communications.

Installing Clinet32 for DOS/Windows 3.1x

The client drivers for DOS/Windows 3.1x can be found in the SYS:\PUBLIC\CLIENT\DOSWIN32 directory. The latest version of the drivers can also be obtained from the Novell Web site.

To install the drivers, go to the client32 subdirectory. If you are installing from DOS, execute the file INST or INSTALL, depending on which version of the client32 for DOS you are using. If you are installing from Windows 3.1*x*, execute the file SETUP. Regardless of the method you choose, you can install support for both DOS and Windows 3.1*x*.

Curiously, there is no online help during the installation. While the prompts are very descriptive, it would be nice if some additional help was included in case the administrator is uncertain about some of the options.

Figure 11.1 shows the opening screen for the DOS-based installation utility. You can choose to install support for DOS or Windows 3.1*x*. By default, the installation program assumes you will be using IPX to communicate with the server. If you choose to install the NetWare IP stack, you can install NetWare IP as well. We will discuss NetWare IP later in this chapter.

FIGURE 11.1

The client32 DOS-based installation utility

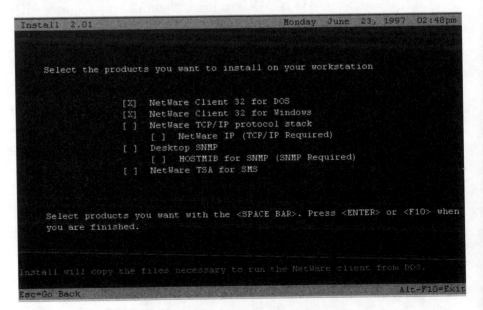

You are also allowed to install support for SNMP, which will allow the workstation to be polled and controlled from an SNMP management station. The final option, NetWare TSA for SMS, allows you to install the Target Service Agent (TSA) for Storage Management Services (SMS). SMS allows the NetWare backup utility to reach out from the server and back up files on the workstation. Once you have selected the options you wish to install, press the F10 key to continue the installation.

If you have opted for Windows support, you will be asked if you require support for multiple country codes. Usually, the answer to this question is no. Unless your workstation is on a global WAN and will need to access servers in multiple countries, single support should be fine. You will also be asked if you will be using a shared network copy of Windows. If you load Windows off of your local hard drive, the answer to this is no. If you access Windows through a shared directory out on the server, the answer is yes. When you have finished, press F10.

Next, you are asked if you wish to install support for 16-bit or 32-bit drivers. As mentioned above, you should install 32-bit support unless you know for sure that this will cause problems. Regardless of your choice, you are presented next with a list of available network drivers. If the NIC you are using is not listed, you will need to obtain the drivers from the manufacturer. Once you have the drivers you need, press the Insert key and enter the full path to the driver's location. Press F10 when you have finished.

You are next prompted to configure your NIC driver setting. You must enter the frame type you wish to use as well as any interrupt or I/O port settings you are prompted for. You can select support for multiple frame types by pressing Enter on the field and using the F5 key to select the ones you want. Once you have finished, press F10.

If you are upgrading your network drivers and have a NET.CFG file, the installation program will use the settings from this file to determine the correct frame type. The NET.CFG is described later in this chapter.

The next screen asks you if you want the installation utility to make the required changes to your CONFIG.SYS and AUTOEXEC.BAT files. The changes it will make are as follows:

16-Bit Drivers

■ Add the line lastdrive=z to the config.sys file.

■ Add the location of the network drivers to the path statement in autoexec.bat.

■ Add the command call startnet.bat to the end of autoexec.bat to initialize networking.

32-Bit Drivers

■ Remove the line lastdrive=z if it exists in the config.sys file.

■ Add the location of the network drivers to the path statement in autoexec.bat.

■ Add the command call startnet.bat to the end of autoexec.bat to initialize networking.

Startnet.bat contains different commands to initialize 16-bit and 32-bit networking. We will look at the contents of this file later in this section.

You are also prompted to input where you would like to have the network drivers installed. Unless you really need to put them elsewhere (such as on drive D instead of C due to space concerns), the default should be fine. The files to be installed take up 2.3MB of space for DOS only, and 5MB if Windows support is installed as well.

Finally, you are shown whether you selected to install 16-bit or 32-bit drivers and the name of the NIC driver you selected. This is your last chance to change these settings before the install utility begins copying files. If you are happy with your selection, press the F10 key to begin copying files.

If you are rerunning the setup utility because you have swapped in a new network card and need to install support for it, you will need to edit the `startnet.bat` file once the installation is complete. The install utility will not remove the load statement for the old network card driver; you will have to do this manually.

Once the installation is complete, you will be prompted to reboot your computer. This should initialize networking, and you should now be able to log on to a NetWare server.

The *startnet.bat* file   Depending on whether you choose a 16-bit or 32-bit install, the `startnet.bat` file will contain the commands shown in Table 11.2 and Table 11.3.

T A B L E 11.2 Commands for 16-bit install	Command	Description
	`set nwlanguage=english`	Sets the default language to English
	`lsl.com`	Loads Link Support Layer (LSL) support. This is the interface between the network card driver and the ODI driver.
	`nic_driver.com`	Network driver support. `nic_driver` is usually replaced with a descriptive name of the network card. For example, the driver name for an Eagle NE200 network card is `ne2000.com`.
	`ipxodi.com`	Loads legacy ODI support for the IPX protocol. There may be a TCPODI driver as well, if support for IP was installed.
	`vlm.exe`	Loads support for Novell's Virtual Loadable Modules (VLM). This is the legacy DOS requester which is responsible for monitoring application requests for file and print services and redirecting them to the network server when required.

TABLE 11.3	Command	Description
Commands for 32-bit install	`set nwlanguage=english`	Sets the default language to English.
	`nios.exe`	Loads the NetWare I/O Subsystem driver. This is the interface between DOS and the 32-bit LAN and NLM environment.
	`load lslc32.nlm`	Loads the Link Support Layer driver for client32
	`load cmsm.nlm`	The client32 media support module (CMSM). This driver acts as an interface between the LSLC32 driver and the LAN driver.
	`load ethertsm.nlm`	Loads Ethernet topology support. This driver will be replaced with `tokentsm.nlm` for Token Ring environments and `fdditsm.nlm` when the FDDI topology is used.
	`load nic_driver.lan`	Loads network driver support. nic_driver is usually replaced with a descriptive name of the network card. For example, the driver name for an Eagle NE200 network card is `NE2000.LAN`. There are also command-line switches for selecting the protocol and setting the correct port and interrupt. Refer to the "Configuring Networking from the Command Line" section of Chapter 7 for these parameters.
	`load ipx.nlm`	Loads support for the IPX protocol. `TCPIP.NLM` will also be installed if you selected support for that protocol.
	`load client32.nlm`	Loads the client32 requester. This driver is responsible for monitoring application requests for file and print services and redirecting them to the network server when required.

If you are using the 16-bit drivers, it may be beneficial to copy the listed drivers from the `startnet.bat` file and load them directly from the `autoexec.bat` file. This will allow your memory manager to include these files when it optimizes memory usage. Because the 32-bit drivers use very little memory, there is not much benefit to optimizing these files.

Note that the 32-bit `startnet.bat` file uses the `load` command when initializing support drivers. This is not a DOS-based command, but rather a command used on NetWare servers. The NIOS sets up the API interface which makes `load` a valid command.

Configuring Networking with the *NET.CFG* file   The `net.cfg` file is used by client32 to configure the networking environment. As each driver is loaded, the `net.cfg` file is referenced to see if the driver requires any special configuration parameters.

With client32, a basic `net.cfg` file would contain the following:

```
NetWare DOS Requester
   FIRST NETWORK DRIVE F
   NETWARE PROTOCOL NDS BIND

Protocol IPX
   IPX SOCKETS 40
```

The lines that are left justified are section titles that identify which driver is to be configured. For example, commands under the NetWare DOS Requester are commands used by either `vlm.exe` or `client32.nlm`. The lines that follow are commands used to configure that specific driver. These commands can be indented using the Tab key or spaces.

A `net.cfg` file used with 16-bit drivers would include an additional section title called `Link driver nic_driver`, with `nic_driver` being replaced with the actual name of the network card driver. Commands under this section are used to select the appropriate frame type and specify the correct interrupt and port number to use with the card.

Because the LAN driver used with client32 specifies these setting on the command line, this section is not required.

Because the available configuration options used in the net.cfg file are nearly identical to the setting used to configure client32 on Windows 95 and NT, we will cover all the valid settings at the end of this section.

Installing Client32 for Windows 95

Installing client32 for Windows95 is a straightforward process. The installation program is located in the sys:\public\client\win95 directory of the IntranetWare server. The latest version can also be downloaded from Novell's Web site. In either case, execute the file setup.exe.

Figure 11.2 shows the initial configuration screen for client32 for Windows 95. Thankfully, this installation has online help in case you need it. The utility also attempts to be helpful by replacing native NDIS drivers with ODI drivers. If you will only be running NetWare, this should not be a problem. If you need to support other protocol stacks such as NetBEUI or Microsoft's TCP/IP, replacing NDIS drivers with ODI drivers means that you will also need to install ODINSUP. ODINSUP is ODI's support driver which allows it to communicate with NDIS stacks. This just adds an additional layer of complexity if you later need to diagnose a communication problem. If you will be using other protocol stacks, you may wish to disable the replacement of your existing drivers. In either case, select Start to begin the installation.

Once you select Start, the utility will begin to install files and configure your system. It will display summary information to inform you of its progress. The first thing you will notice is that even if you tell it not to replace your NDIS drivers, it will display the message replacing existing drivers. Don't worry, if you instructed the utility not to replace the drivers, it will not. This is a generic prompt.

Once the file copy is complete, you are prompted to set a default tree or server. If your network is using NetWare Directory Services (NDS), set a default NDS tree. If your network consists of older bindery-based servers (version 3.12 and prior), set a default server. Once you are finished, select the OK button to continue.

F I G U R E I I.2

The initial banner screen
for the Client32
installation utility

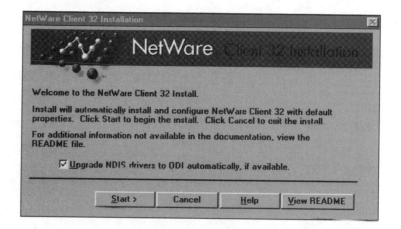

You are then asked if you wish to reboot the computer, return to Windows, or customize the settings. You should choose to reboot the computer unless there are other programs running in the background that you wish to shut down first. In this case, return to Windows, shut down the programs, and then reboot.

WARNING While it is tempting to customize the settings at this time, you should first restart the system to ensure that the new client is working properly. If you change the advanced setting now and then have a connectivity problem during startup, you cannot be sure if it is a driver problem or something you configured incorrectly.

During the installation process, client32 creates the log file:

`c:\Novell\client32\install\net2reg.log`

We also need the IPX/SPX protocol in order to communicate with a NetWare server. This protocol is automatically installed during client installation.

If you encounter problems with your newly installed client, you can check this log to see if the installation program had any difficulties while modifying the Windows 95 registry. For example, as part of the installation process, the registry is modified so that the Primary Network

Logon under Networking Properties is changed to Novell NetWare Client 32.

Configuring Client 32 for Windows 95

Once you are satisfied that your client software is working, you can proceed to the Network Configuration tab to customize the settings. Figure 11.3 shows this tab with the Novell NetWare Client 32 client highlighted. Select the Properties button to configure the client for Client32.

FIGURE 11.3

The Windows 95 Network Configuration tab

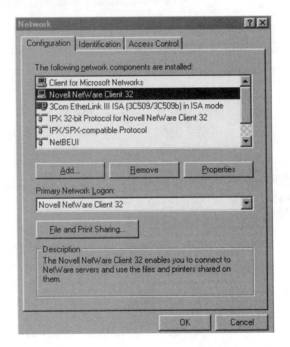

The Client 32 Tab   Figure 11.4 shows the Client 32 tab in the Novell NetWare Client 32 Properties window. This tab is used for setting a preferred server of NDS tree, just like you were prompted to do during the client installation. You should not need to use this tab unless you need to make changes because you have a new server or NDS tree.

FIGURE 11.4

The Client 32 tab of the Novell NetWare Client 32 Properties window

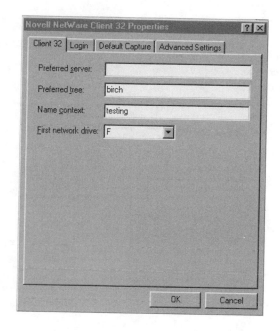

The Login Tab   Figure 11.5 shows the Login tab in the Novell NetWare Client 32 Properties window. The Display Connection Page prompt changes the banner screen during initial logon. When this setting is not checked, you are presented with the server or tree options selected under the Client 32 tab and cannot change them. When this setting is checked, the options are displayed in an editable format so that you can change them. This is useful for a network administrator who may be required to log on to different trees or servers.

Checking Display Connection Page sets up a second page to the logon banner that allows the user to switch between performing a logon to a tree and performing a logon to a server. If server is selected you have the option of choosing a bindery-based logon. The final option in this section, Clear Current Connections, is used if you are performing a logon from a system that is already authenticated to NetWare services.

FIGURE 11.5

The Login tab of
the Novell NetWare
Client 32 Properties
window

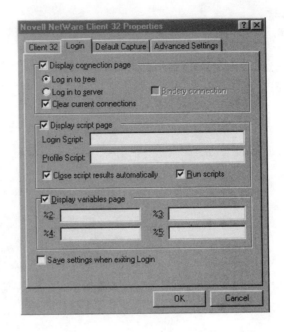

Enabling this setting logs you out of these services prior to performing
the new logon.

The Display Script Page prompt enables or disables the use of an
alternate logon script and profile during authentication. The logon
script is used to setup the workstation's network environment by mapping drives, capturing printers, and even launching applications. By
default, users authenticating to the NDS tree process the system logon
script in a bindery environment, and the container logon script in an
NDS environment. The Login Script field allows an alternate file to be
processed as the logon script.

Profiles are used to setup user access and even process additional
logon commands. With NetWare 3.1*x*, security access and the processing of additional script commands was typically accomplished
through the use of *groups*. A user would be assigned to a group and the
group would be given access to certain files and directories. The group
name may even be referenced, to process certain commands within the
logon script. By using profiles, trustee access and logon commands can

be maintained in a central place. The Profile Script prompt allows you to specify a profile to be used during network authentication.

The Display Variables Page checkbox is used to pass variable information on to login.exe during authentication. Under DOS, variables can be used during the logon process using the syntax: login %2 %3 %4 %5.

Because Windows 95 is graphical, you cannot access the login executable to specify variable information. The fields on the Display Variables Page allow you to pass along this information.

The Save Settings When Exiting Login box allows you to specify if your default settings can be changed during network logon. For example, let's assume you have defined the default tree, Birch. One day while performing a network logon, you realize that there is information you need to retrieve that is located on the tree, Oak. You change your preferred tree and perform authentication.

If Save Settings When Exiting Login is checked, the next time you perform a logon you will be asked to authenticate to the tree Oak. If the box is not checked, you will be asked to authenticate to the tree Birch. The setting Save Settings When Exiting Login determines if your defaults are absolute, or if they should be customizable from the logon banner screen.

The Default Capture Tab   Figure 11.6 shows the Default Capture tab. This tab is used to configure the printing environment. Number of Copies specifies how many copies of each print job should be sent to the printer. While it is usually easier to select the number of required copies from the application that is producing the print job, this setting is useful when you consistently need to print out a certain number of copies, regardless of what is being printed. For example, if you always print in triplicate, setting this field to three will keep you from having to select three copies from your application every time you print.

The Form Feed setting allows you to specify whether a form feed should be sent to the printer after every print job. This setting is useful if you have a dot matrix printer that you have to advance in order to remove your print job from the printer. It is also useful if you are using a laser printer with applications that do not send an end-of-job sequence.

FIGURE 11.6

The Default Capture tab
of the Novell NetWare
Client 32 Properties
window

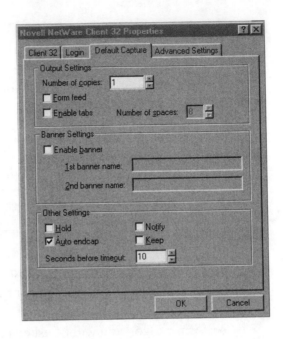

If you've noticed that your laser printer will not print the last page
unless you hit the form feed button or another print job comes through,
the application is probably not ending the print job properly. The
problem with this setting is that if you are using applications that will
send a correct end of job sequence, enabling form feed will print a blank
page after each job.

The Enable Tabs checkbox allows you to customize how tabs look
on your printed document. Enabling this setting replaces any tab characters with the number of specified spaces. This setting is somewhat of
a holdover from the old days when different DOS applications defined
tabs differently. Some defined a tab as 5 spaces, some as 8, and some as
many as 10. This setting allowed all these applications to produce
printed output that followed the same tab spacing format. You should
not need to use this setting if you are printing through Windows.

The Banner Settings allow you to produce a cover page at the beginning of each print job. On this page is printed the name of the file as
well as the name indicated in the banner name fields. This setting is
useful in a large environment when many people are using the same

printer. By enabling the banner page, it becomes easier to identify which print job belongs to whom.

Under Other Settings, the Hold checkbox allows you to send your print job to the print queue, but the job will not be passed along to the printer. This is useful if you typically send many print jobs to the printer, but do not want to spend the whole day walking back and forth retrieving print jobs. Hold allows you to queue up all these print jobs on the network queue. When you are ready to print, you can use the Pconsole utility to change the status on all the jobs from Hold to Ready. This will cause them all to be printed out at the same time.

Auto Endcap is used for controlling the printing on older DOS based applications. Enabling Auto Endcap causes all printing sent to the queue by an application to be printed when the application is exited. This setting has no effect on applications that send an end-of-job sequence at the end of every print job.

When the Notify box is checked, a dialog box pops up on the screen to notify you when your print job has been sent to the printer. This is useful in environments where many people share the same printer or when a printer usually receives large print jobs. Being notified when your print job is being processed prevents you from having to stand around and wait while other jobs are printing.

When the Keep box is checked, a print job will remain in the print queue even after it has been printed. This is useful if you wish to print a test copy of a document prior to printing many copies. Once you are satisfied that the test printout looks okay, you can then use Pconsole to increase the number of copies to print and release the job from the print queue.

The Seconds Before Timeout setting is useful for those pesky programs that will not send an end of job sequence. Once an application has stopped sending data to the print queue, the client will wait the specified amount of time and then send an end-of-job sequence. This method of dealing with these older applications is preferred over the form feed method as it will not produce an extra page on print jobs that are ended correctly.

The Advanced Settings Tab   Figure 11.7 shows the Advanced Settings tab of the Novell NetWare Client 32 Properties window. This tab is used to configure communication parameters for the network drivers. The Parameter Groups menu will display certain configuration parameters based upon the selected group. For example, selecting the group Printing displays the three advanced settings that deal with customizing printing. The default group is All, which is typically the easiest group to work with because all configuration parameters are listed in alphabetical order.

FIGURE 11.7

The Advanced Settings tab of the Novell NetWare Client 32 Properties window

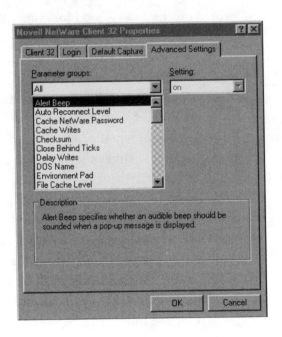

The Setting menu displays the available parameters for the highlighted configuration option. For example, the Alert Beep configuration option is highlighted—it has two available settings, On and Off.

The advanced settings are similar to the `net.cfg` settings used with client32 for DOS. For this reason, they are discussed together at the end of this section.

Installing the IntranetWare Client for Windows NT

The IntranetWare client (Client32) for NT may be used on an NT workstation or server. It is functionally identical to client32 for Windows 95 except in appearance and having less advanced settings to configure. The NT client does not ship with IntranetWare as of this writing. You must retrieve it from the Novell Web site. Once you have uncompressed the files, execute the setup.exe file to begin the installation utility.

Figure 11.8 shows the initial banner screen for the IntranetWare client for NT. You'll notice that it does not prompt you to upgrade any existing drivers. From this screen you can review the readme file for any last minute changes, and then continue with the installation by selecting the Continue button.

FIGURE 11.8

The Novell IntranetWare Client Installation window

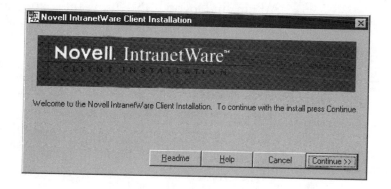

If you have the Microsoft Gateway (client) services for NetWare installed, the IntranetWare client will inform you that it must be removed in order to continue with the installation. While you can still share NetWare files through the NT system, you will not be able to manage account security like you can with the Microsoft client. This prohibits the use of the IntranetWare client in some networking situations where this type of file sharing is required. It is Novell's way of ensuring that only one user takes advantage of each NetWare connection—a point that is well justified in light of the license agreement. The dialog box for gateway removal is shown in Figure 11.9.

FIGURE 11.9

IntranetWare removes
Microsoft's gateway for
NetWare, if it is installed.

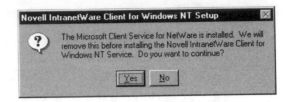

The installation utility will then begin to copy all required files and make modifications to the registry. Once complete, it will prompt you to reboot the system. During system logon, you will notice that the logon window has been changed to include the IntranetWare banner. This logon window is similar to the Windows 95 window except it allows a different name to be used for IntranetWare and NT authentication. For example, you can logon to NetWare with the user name Admin, and logon to NT using the logon name Administrator. If different logon names are used, different passwords may be used as well.

Configuring the IntranetWare Client for Windows NT

The IntranetWare client makes a few changes to the desktop. Along with a new IntranetWare program group, the dialog box produced by right-clicking the network neighborhood has two additional options, as shown in Figure 11.10. From this dialog box, we can log on to an NDS tree or bindery server, as well as check to see which system we are currently authenticated on.

The IntranetWare client can be configured by going to Network Properties and looking under the Services tab. The client is identified as Novell IntranetWare client for Windows NT. Highlight the entry and select the Properties button to configure it.

The Client Tab The Client tab is similar to the Client 32 tab under the client properties for Windows 95. As shown in Figure 11.11, the only real difference is that the NT client window allows you to configure multiple servers and NDS trees to authenticate to. By filling out

FIGURE 11.10

Additional properties have
been added to the
Network Neighborhood
dialog box.

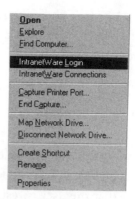

the Preferred server or Preferred tree fields and selecting the Add button, you can authenticate on multiple systems simultaneously. This assumes that you have the same user name and password on each NetWare system.

FIGURE 11.11

The Client tab for the
IntranetWare Client
Services Configuration
window

The Login Tab   The Login tab for the IntranetWare client is identical to the login tab under client32 properties for Windows 95. All the features are the same.

The Advanced Login Tab   The Advanced Login tab, as shown in Figure 11.12, is Novell's way of taking a Microsoft concept and making it even easier to administer. The Policy Path is used to define a path to the configuration file that defines which desktop resources will be available to users when they log on to the workstation. For example, the policy can state that the user is restricted to a specific program group and is not allowed to execute programs through the **run** command or through Explorer. What makes using Policies easier in an IntranetWare environment than in an NT environment is the hierarchical nature of NDS.

FIGURE 11.12

The Advanced Login tab for the IntranetWare Client Services Configuration window

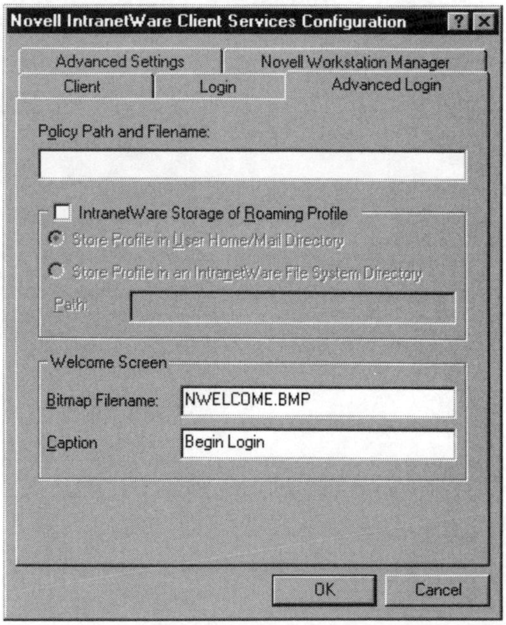

In an NT environment, policy files must be synchronized between the PDC and every single BDC. This is because the logon is server

specific. The policy file must be available on the server to which the user authenticates.

In an NDS environment, users log on to a tree, not a server. With this in mind, policy files do not need to be synchronized across every single NDS server. Once the user is authenticated to the tree, they can retrieve their policy file from any server they have access to. This allows the administrator to create a single point of management for policy files.

The profile field is similar to the policy file, except control is user specific. As with the policy files, IntranetWare allows a single point of management for policy files. They do not need to be synchronized across multiple servers.

The Welcome screen settings allow the administrator to customize how the logon banner appears to the user. The Bitmap field allows you to select a background while the Caption field allows you to add a text message to the welcome header.

The Novell Workstation Manager Tab   The Novell Workstation Manager tab, shown in Figure 11.13, allows NetWare administrators to manage the NT workstation through IntranetWare's NDS. This is a powerful tool that goes beyond the functionality provided in a pure NT domain.

In an NT domain, the network administrator is required to create both a domain account and a workstation account for each user. This is required because workstation security is maintained separately from domain security. This means that the administrator must configure every workstation that the user may need to use. This can be extremely time consuming in a large or shared workstation environment, as the administrator may be required to configure many systems.

By selecting the Enable Workstation Manager on these Trusted Trees, you can add NDS trees that are allowed to manage this NT workstation. As the NDS administrator uses the NWADMIN tool to manage the NDS tree, they can also manage this NT workstation. This means that user account information created on the NDS tree can be propagated out to the NT workstation. This propagation can be configured to

FIGURE 11.13

The Novell Workstation
Manager tab for the
IntranetWare Client
Services Configuration
window

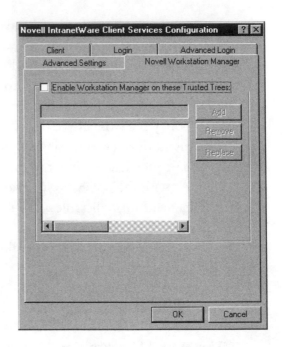

occur automatically, as soon as the user performs a logon at the system. These changes can even be configured to be permanent, becoming part of the NT security accounts manager, or deleted as soon as the user logs off the system. The benefit is that the network administrator is not required to manage the NT workstation as a separate system.

The Advanced Settings Tab   The Advanced Settings tab for the IntranetWare client is identical to the Advanced Settings tab under client32 properties for Windows 95. All the features are the same.

Advanced Settings and Configuring the *netcfg* file

As mentioned above, the available settings for each of the available clients are nearly identical. The differences are that settings under DOS are changed by adding lines to the net.cfg file, while Windows 95 and NT allow these settings to be changed through the advanced settings tab on the client's properties dialog box. Under DOS, if a parameter is not configured in the `net.cfg` file, the default setting is used.

Below is a list of available settings. Listed are the settings name, description, and default value. Also listed is the syntax to use when adding the setting to the `net.cfg` file. Unless otherwise specified, all commands should be added under the `NETWARE DOS REQUESTOR` heading within the `net.cfg` file.

Alert Beep   Alert beep enables a warning sound through the computer speaker when a pop-up message is displayed. The default is On. **Supported platforms:** DOS, Windows 95. This parameter is added under the NIOS heading within the `net.cfg` file. **Syntax:** `alert beep = on | off`.

Auto Reconnect Level   This setting determines which connection attributes are restored when a connection to the server is lost and then reestablished. The levels are:

- 0 = Do not reconnect to the server.

- 1 = Remap drive and reconnect to printers.

- 2 = Same as 1 but includes files opened for read access only

- 3 = Same as 1 and 2 but opens all files including those opened for write access and restores file locks

- 4 = Same as 1, 2, and 3, but adds file write data recovery guarantee

- 5 = Not yet used. If set to this level, the requester will revert to level 4.

The default level is 3. **Supported platforms:** DOS, Windows 95. **Syntax:** `auto reconnect level = number`.

Burst Mode   This is the Windows NT counterpart for the Packet Burst setting described below. It allows Packet Burst to be enabled or disabled. The default is On. **Supported platform:** Windows NT

Cache NetWare Password   This setting determines if the password entered during initial logon should be saved to memory and used to authenticate to additional NetWare resources. On is the default. **Supported platform:** Windows 95.

Cache Writes   This setting enables or disables the caching of information on the workstation that is destined to be written to the NetWare server. Caching improves performance, as many small blocks of information that need to be saved to the server can be transmitted simultaneously thus reducing traffic. The drawback is that if the workstation crashes before this transmission takes place, the data will be lost. On is the default. **Supported platforms:** DOS, Windows 95. **Syntax:** `cache writes = on | off`.

Checksum   Checksum determines if the checksum field within the NCP header should be used. This field can produce a redundant CRC check to the one included in the frame trailer. This produces a slight increase in data integrity at the cost of overall performance. This option should only be used if you know you are having data integrity problems. The options are:

- 0 = Disabled
- 1 = Only enable checksum if the server insists on it.
- 2 = Perform a checksum if the server is capable.
- 3 = Require a checksum. Do not communicate with servers that cannot perform a checksum.

Servers have a similar checksum setting which is why some servers may perform a checksum, while others will not. The default level is 1. **Supported platforms:** DOS, Windows 95. **Syntax:** `checksum = number`.

Close Behind Ticks   Close Behind Ticks determines how long a client should wait to close a network file when an application has requested that it do so. This is useful for applications that frequently open and close the same files. For example, let's say we set this setting to five seconds. Our desktop application then sends a request to close a file that it has been using. Because of our Close Behind Ticks setting, the client will wait five seconds before it actually sends the close request to the server. Now let's assume that the same client requests that the same file be opened three seconds later. Because the client has not yet closed the file on the server, it can access the file from local memory instead of having to create a network request. The benefits are faster application response time and less network traffic. The value for this field is set in ticks which are equal to 1/18 of a second. To change this value to five seconds, use a setting of 90. A tick is roughly the time it takes to traverse one hop on a 10 Mb Ethernet network. The default is 0 which closes files immediately upon request. **Supported platforms:** DOS, Windows 95. **Syntax:** `close behind ticks = number`.

Delay Writes   When Close Behind Ticks is set to some other value besides 0, Delay Writes determines if the close delay applies to read-only files, or files you have changed by writing to them as well. Enabling this feature improves application performance, because it does not have to wait for write acknowledgments. The drawback is that if the client crashes before the close is performed, any data changes may be lost. Off is the default. **Supported platforms:** DOS, Windows 95. **Syntax:** `delay writes = on | off`.

DOS Name   The DOS name setting defines the value to use for this system in the variable %OS. By correctly identifying this field, the system administrator can customize the logon script depending on the operating system in use. For example, the logon script could analyze the contents of this variable to determine which virus checker version should be used. The default name for DOS is DOS, the default name for Windows 95 is WIN95, and the default for Windows NT is WINNT. **Supported platforms:** DOS, Windows 95, Windows NT. **Syntax:** `DOS name = OS_name`.

Environment Pad   Environment Pad increases the available DOS environment space by the indicated amount whenever a DOS-based application is run. The DOS environment is a small portion of memory setup by command.com for storage of variables. Typing the command **set** at a DOS prompt yields some of the variables stored in environment memory. If a large enough environment space is not configured during system startup, some DOS-based applications will fail. This option allows an additional portion of memory to be set aside for each DOS program that is executed. The default is 24 bytes. **Supported platforms:** DOS, Windows 95. **Syntax:** environment pad = number.

File Cache Level   This setting determines what type of caching should be performed on network files. The available options are:

- 0 = Do not perform file caching.

- 1 = Use read-ahead and write-behind caching. With read-ahead caching, the client will read an entire block of information instead of reading only the information requested. This can increase performance during sequential file reads as the client can retrieve the data before it is even requested to do so by the application. Write-behind is similar except it applies when writing data to the server. The client will send write requests in blocks instead of smaller portions.

- 2 = Use short-lived caching as well as the features from option one. Short-lived caching allows the system to cache file information until the time the file is closed (closure time is set by close behind ticks).

- 3 = Use long-lived caching as well as the features from option one. Long-lived caching allows the client to continue caching a file even after it is closed. If another open request for the same file is received from an application, the client checks with the server to ensure that the file has not changed since the last time the file was opened. If the file has not changed, the file is read from local cache instead of from the server.

- 4 = Not currently in use

The default value is 2 (short-lived cache). This option is disabled if True Commit is set to On or if Cache Writes is set to Off. **Supported platforms:** DOS, Windows 95. **Syntax:** `file cache level = number`.

Force First Network Drive   When enabled, this setting sets the login directory to the first available network drive (usually F) once the user logs off of the server. When this setting is disabled, the login directory is set to whichever network drive was used last. This setting is more useful in a DOS environment because Windows hides the network drive used to authenticate with the network. The default is On. **Supported platforms:** DOS, Windows 95. **Syntax:** `force first network drive = on | off`.

Handle Net Error   This setting determines if the client software, or the application in use will handle network errors such as a server no longer responding. When set to On, the client software handles the error. When set to Off, the client generates an INT 24 and passes this along to the application. The default is On. **Supported platforms:** DOS, Windows 95. **Syntax:** `handle net errors = on | off`.

Hold Files   If a program opens a file using File Control Blocks (FCB_IO), this setting determines if the file is held open until the program exits. Some programs that are not network aware need this setting enabled. The default is Off. Supported platforms: DOS, Windows 95. Syntax: hold = on | off.

Ignore Below 16MB Memory Allocate Flag   When allocating additional memory for network drivers, this setting determines if additional memory should only be allocated from the first 16MB, or if all available memory should be used. When enabled, all memory is used.

When disabled, only memory from the first 16MB is allocated. If there is no memory free below 16MB, the request fails. Many LAN drivers have difficulties if they are moved above the 16MB area. You should leave this setting Off unless it is absolutely required. The default is Off. Supported platforms: DOS. This parameter is added under the NIOS heading within the `net.cfg` file. Syntax: ignore below 16meg memory allocate flag = on | off.

Large Internet Packets   This setting enables or disables the use of LIP for packet size negotiations across network routers. The default is On. **Supported platforms: DOS, Windows 95, Windows NT. Syntax:** `large internet packets = on | off`.

Large Internet Packet Start Size   When LIP is enabled, this setting sets the size in bytes to use when negotiating large Internet packets. The client and server will negotiate down from this size until a usable value is achieved. Setting this value to the largest packet size supported by your topology will reduce negotiation time. The default is 65535 bytes. **Supported platforms: DOS, Windows 95, Windows NT. Syntax:** `lip start size = number`.

Link Support Layer Max Buffer Size   Sets the buffer size, in bytes, that the client should use to queue inbound and outbound frames. This setting needs to be at least as large as the maximum frame size supported by the topology. Adjusting this setting to a value larger than the maximum frame size can waste memory because the difference will go unused. Adjusting this setting too low can cause communication problems because the workstation will be unable to receive frames larger than the specified size. The default is 4736. Supported platforms: DOS, Windows 95, Windows NT. This parameter is added under the Link Support heading within the NET.CFG file. Syntax: max buffer size = number.

Lock Delay   When an application receives a sharing error and is unable to achieve exclusive access to a file, the lock delay determines how long in ticks the client should wait before attempting to lock the file again. The default is 1 tick. **Supported platforms:** DOS, Windows 95. **Syntax:** `lock delay = number`.

Lock Retries   This setting determines the number of retries to be performed after a sharing error is received. Each retry is separated by the amount of time specified in the Lock Delay setting. The default is 5. **Supported platforms:** DOS, Windows 95. **Syntax:** `lock retries = number`.

Log File   This setting specifies the location and name of a log file to be created during initialization of the network drivers. The log is typically used for diagnostic purposes only. The default is blank which means a log file is not created. **Supported platforms:** DOS, Windows 95. This parameter is added under the NIOS heading within the `net.cfg` file. **Syntax:** `log file=c:\novell\client32\log.txt`.

Log File Size   When a log file is created, this setting specifies in bytes the maximum size the log file is allowed to grow to. The default is 64 Kb. **Supported platforms:** DOS, Windows 95. This parameter is added under the NIOS heading within the `NET.CFG` file. **Syntax:** `log file size = number`.

Long Machine Type   This setting defines the value to use for this system in the variable %MACHINE. By correctly identifying this field, the system administrator can customize the logon script dependent on the computer type or manufacturer. The default is `IBM_PC`. **Supported platforms:** DOS, Windows 95, Windows NT. **Syntax:** `long machine type = name`.

Max Cache Size   This setting determines the amount of memory in kilobytes to be used by NetWare for caching purposes. When this value is set to 0, the client, during initialization, sets aside 25% of the available free memory for NetWare caching. Any other value fixes the cache size to the value specified. This fixed setting cannot be larger than 75% of available memory. If it is, the client will adjust the cache size so that it is no larger than 75%. The default is 0. **Supported platforms:** DOS, Windows 95. **Syntax:** `max cache size = number`.

Max Cur Dir Length   This setting sets the maximum length of the DOS command line. The value specified is the maximum number of characters that can be entered at the DOS prompt. Any characters entered beyond this maximum are ignored. The default is 64 characters which is the default for DOS as well. **Supported platforms:** DOS, Windows 95. **Syntax:** `max cur dir length = number`.

Max Read Burst Size   This sets the maximum number of bytes the workstation can negotiate during a packet burst read. This setting is NT-specific and differs from the Packet Burst Read Window Size used on the DOS and Windows 95 client in that it specifies the number of bytes that can be read, not the number of packets that can be negotiated. The default is 36000 bytes. **Supported platforms:** Windows NT.

Max Write Burst Size   This sets the maximum number of bytes the workstation can negotiate during a packet burst write. This setting is NT-specific and differs from the Packet Burst Write Window Size used on the DOS and Windows 95 client in that it specifies the number of bytes that can be written, not the number of packets that can be negotiated. The default is 15000 bytes. **Supported platforms:** Windows NT.

Mem Pool Size   This setting specifies the amount of memory in kilobytes that client32 can allocate for special use. This pool is used when drivers are called from Windows or when no additional extended memory can be allocated to module loading. The memory pool is disabled if a value of 31KB or less is set. The default is 128KB. **Supported platforms:** DOS. This parameter is added under the NIOS heading within the `net.cfg` file. **Syntax:** `mem pool size = number`.

Message Timeout   If the client receives a network broadcast message, the message timeout value indicates how long in ticks the client should wait before automatically clearing the broadcast message from the screen. A value of 0 specifies that the messages should not automatically be cleared, but that the message should be displayed until it is cleared by the user. The default is 0. **Supported platforms:** DOS, Windows 95. **Syntax:** `message timeout = number`.

Minimum Time To Net   This value allows you to increase the amount of time in milliseconds that the system should wait for a response before deciding that the transmission failed. This setting is useful for large networks that span one or more WAN links in a bridged environment. If the client is having trouble connecting with a remote resource, try increasing this setting. The default is 0. **Supported platforms:** DOS, Windows 95, Windows NT. **Syntax:** `minimum time to net = number`.

Name Context   This setting specifies the context of the NDS tree where the user wishes to authenticate. This is usually the section of the tree which contains the user's user ID object. There is no default for this setting. **Supported platforms:** DOS (set elsewhere in Windows 95 and NT). **Syntax:** `name context = name_context`.

NCP Max Timeout   This setting specifies the amount of time (in seconds) that the client should continue retrying a failed resource before determining that the resource is no longer reachable. The default is 30. **Supported platforms:** DOS, Windows 95. **Syntax:** `ncp max timeout = number`.

NetWare Protocol   Determines the search order that the client should use when locating resources. If you have a pure NDS (NetWare 4.*x*) or bindery (NetWare 3.1*x*) environment, changing this setting can speed up the authentication process. The default is to use NDS first, and then bindery. **Supported platforms:** DOS, Windows 95. **Syntax:** `netware protocol=bind nds | nds bind | nds | bind`.

Net Status Busy Timeout   When a client receives a type 9999 reply (system busy, try again later) from a server, this setting determines how long in seconds the client should continue issuing the request while still receiving a busy response. After the specified amount of time, the transmission fails. A type 9999 response is indicative of a server that is overloaded. The default is 20 seconds. **Supported platforms:** DOS, Windows 95. **Syntax:** `net status busy timeout = number`.

Net Status Timeout This setting specifies the amount of time in seconds the client should wait without receiving a response before determining that a network error has occurred. The actual amount of time a client waits will be either the value set in this field, or four times the amount of time it takes for a packet to travel round trip between the client and the server, whichever is larger.

For example, if this value is set to five seconds, but the client determines that it takes two seconds for a packet to travel to the server and back, the client would wait eight seconds (2 X 4) before generating an error. If this setting was changed to 10 seconds, the client would wait 10 seconds before generating an error (10 > 2 X 4). The default is 10 seconds. **Supported platforms:** DOS, Windows 95. **Syntax:** `net status timeout = number`.

Network Printers When printing in a NetWare environment, print jobs sent to the local printer port (referred to as an LPT port) are redirected by the client out to a network printer. The number of network printers that a user can simultaneously access (access without changing their configuration) is determined by how many LPT ports are specified. This setting adjusts the number of LPT ports recognized by NetWare. The default is 3 which is the maximum number supported by DOS. **Supported platforms:** DOS, Windows 95. **Syntax:** `network printers = number`.

NWLanguage This setting determines which language should be used for NetWare help files and utilities. The default is English. **Supported platforms:** DOS, Windows 95, Windows NT. DOS does not have a `net.cfg` setting for this parameter. It is set through the use of the **SET** command in the `startnet.bat` file. **Syntax:** `set nwlanguage = english`.

Opportunistic Locking   Enabling opportunistic locking allows the client to auto-detect opportunities to gain exclusive access to files. This setting only affects access to files that may be in use by one or more users. The default for this setting is Off, as it has been known to cause problems in some database environments. **Supported platforms:** DOS, Windows NT. **Syntax:** `opportunistic locking = on | off`.

Packet Burst   This setting enables or disables the use of packet burst. In previous DOS-based NetWare clients, the PB Buffers parameter specified the number of Packet Burst buffers. Client32 uses the Packet Burst Read Window Size and Packet Burst Write Window Size to specify the number of buffers to use. To accommodate this change, client32 interprets a packet burst value of 0 to signify that Packet Burst is off. A value in this field numbering from 1 to 10 signifies that Packet Burst is on. The default is On. **Supported platforms:** DOS, Windows 95. **Syntax:** `pb buffers = number`.

Packet Burst Read Window Size   This specifies the maximum number of packets that can be buffered during a packet burst read. The number of packets specified, multiplied by the negotiated frame size, cannot exceed 65535 bytes. For example, let's say you are operating on an Ethernet network and your client has negotiated a packet size of 1500 bytes. You have also set the Packet Burst Read Window Size to a value of 100. The client will automatically adjust this setting to 43 during packet burst read negotiations because 43 * 1500 = 64500 bytes which is just below our maximum of 65535 bytes. The default is 24. Supported platforms: DOS, Windows 95. **Syntax:** `pburst read window size = number`.

Packet Burst Write Window Size   This specifies the maximum number of packets that can be buffered during a packet burst write. Like the Packet Burst Read Window, the buffer is limited to 65535 bytes worth of frames. The default is 10. **Supported platforms:** DOS, Windows 95. **Syntax:** `pburst write window size = number`.

Preferred Server   This setting specifies the name of the NetWare server the client attaches to for authentication purposes when `CLIENT32` `.NLM` loads. There is no default for this setting. **Supported platforms:** DOS (set elsewhere in Windows 95 and NT). **Syntax:** `preferred server = server_name`.

Preferred Tree   This setting specifies the name of the NetWare NDS tree the client wishes to authenticate to. There is no default for this setting. **Supported platforms:** DOS (set elsewhere in Windows 95 and NT). **Syntax:** `preferred tree = tree_name`.

Print Header   Print header sets the size of the print head buffer in bytes. This buffer is used to hold printer initialization information. This setting may need to be adjusted upward if you print complex print jobs or are using PostScript. The default is 64 bytes. **Supported platforms:** DOS, Windows 95. **Syntax:** `print header = number`.

Print Tail   This sets the size of the print tail buffer in bytes. This buffer is used to hold the necessary commands to reset the printer once your print job is complete. The default is 16 bytes. **Supported platforms:** DOS, Windows 95. **Syntax:** `print tail = number`.

Read-Only Compatibility   This setting determines whether a read/write call can be used to open a read-only file. Some applications, such as older versions of Microsoft Office, will attempt to open all files with read/write access. If this setting is set to Off, these applications will fail and be unable to open files to which you have been given read-only access. When this setting is set to On, the application opens the file using a read/write call. The application still receives read-only access, however, because file access security is still maintained. The default is Off. **Supported platforms:** DOS, Windows 95. **Syntax:** read only compatibility on | off.

Search Dirs First   Sets the display order when the DIR command is used. When this setting is Off, network files are listed before directories. When this setting is On, directories are listed first, then files. Note that the environment setting SET DIRCMD= will override the value set in this parameter. The default is Off. **Supported platforms:** DOS, Windows 95. **Syntax:** search dir first = on | off.

Search Mode   Search mode alters the method for finding support files when a program file is executed. The search mode is only referenced when the support file is not located in the same directory as the program file. This setting is useful when a program is set up to be shared over a network when it was not designed to do so. Available settings are:

- 0 = No search instructions. Default value for executable files.

- 1 = If a directory path is specified in the executable file, the executable file searches only that path. If a path is not specified, the executable file searches the default directory and network search drives.

- 2 = The executable file searches only the default directory or the path specified.

- 3 = If a directory path is specified in the executable file, the executable file searches only that path. If a path is not specified and the executable file opens data files flagged Read Only, the executable file searches the default directory and search drives.

- 4 = Reserved.

- 5 = The executable file searches the default directory and NetWare search drives, whether or not the path is specified. If a search mode is set, the shell allows searches for any files with .XXX extension; otherwise the executable file searches only for .EXE, .COM, and .BAT files.

- 6 = Reserved.

- 7 = If the executable file opens data files flagged Read Only, the executable file searches the default directory and search drives whether or not the path is specified in the executable file.

The default setting is 1. **Supported platforms:** DOS, Windows 95. Syntax: `search mode = number`.

Set Station Time   This setting determines whether the workstations time and date should be synchronized with the NetWare server. The default is On. **Supported platforms:** DOS, Windows 95. **Syntax:** `set station time = on | off`.

Short Machine Type   Similar to Long Machine Type except that the variable is %SMACHINE. The default is IBM. **Supported platforms:** DOS, Windows 95, Windows NT. **Syntax:** `short machine type = name`.

Show Dots   This setting allows . and .. to be displayed at the top of a directory listing when NetWare directories are viewed. Many DOS based programs use these entries when changing directories. The default is Off. **Supported platforms:** DOS, Windows 95. **Syntax:** `show dots = on | off`.

Signature Level   Signature level enables the use of a security token so that both systems can verify the source of a transmission. This token changes with each data exchange between a client and a server. Packet Signature helps to prevent a type of attack known as *connection hijacking*. For example, let's assume that Packet Signature is in use between a client and a server. Each time the two systems communicate, the token is changed. Next, let's assume that the server receives a packet of data which appears to be from the client because it has the correct source MAC address and session number. Let's also assume that the value of the signature token is not correct. In this case the server will assume that the transmission is in fact not from the client and ignores any data it contains. It will also display an error message on the server console.

Connection hijacking is a very real danger on a NetWare network. In the role of a security auditor, I have used connection hijacking to gain full server access in less than a minute of some very prestigious networks that where thought to be secure. If your account has administrator or supervisor access, you should ensure that Packet Signature is enabled.

The available settings for Signature Level are:

- 0 = Packet Signature disabled

- 1 = Only Enable Packet Signature if the server requires it.

- 2 = Use Packet Signature if the server supports it.

- 3 = Only communicate using Packet Signature. Do not communicate with servers that do not support it.

The default is 1. Supported platforms: DOS, Windows 95, Windows NT. Syntax: signature level = number.

True Commit   True Commit overrides all performance settings to insure that data is immediately written to disk. If any file write caching is enabled, this setting takes precedence. The default is Off. **Supported platforms:** DOS, Windows 95. **Syntax:** true commit = on | off.

Use Video BIOS   This setting specifies whether the client should use direct video memory access or video BIOS calls for displaying pop-up windows. Using video BIOS is slower but can add stability on some systems. The default is Off which uses direct video memory access. **Supported platforms:** DOS, Windows 95. This parameter is added under the NIOS heading within the `net.cfg` file. **Syntax:** `use video bios= on | off`.

The Microsoft Client Drivers for NetWare

Microsoft only supplies NetWare client drivers for the Windows 95 and NT platforms. The NT client only supports bindery services at the time of this writing. If you will be using Microsoft's NT client in an Intranet-Ware environment, you will need to enable bindery services on each of the servers the client will need access to.

The latest version of Windows 95 includes the Microsoft Service for NetWare Directory Services. This allows the Microsoft NetWare client for Windows 95 to become NDS aware. If you are running an older version of Windows 95 that does not include this service, you can retrieve it from the Microsoft Web site.

We covered NT's NetWare Client and Gateway Services in great detail back in Chapter 8, so reviewing it again here would be redundant. Instead, we will focus on the Windows 95 client and NDS service.

Installing the Microsoft Client for NetWare

To install the NetWare client that ships with Windows 95, enter the Network Properties screen through the Control Panel icon called Network, or by right-clicking the Network Neighborhood and selecting Properties. The Configuration tab of the Network window is shown in Figure 11.14. To begin installing the client, click the Add button.

The next dialog box is the Select Network Component Type dialog box. Highlight Client which is the first option and click the Add button.

The next window is the Select Network Client window, shown in Figure 11.15. Highlight Microsoft in the Manufacturers column, and select the Client for NetWare Networks in the Network Clients column. Now click the OK button.

FIGURE 11.14

The Windows 95
Configuration tab of the
Network window

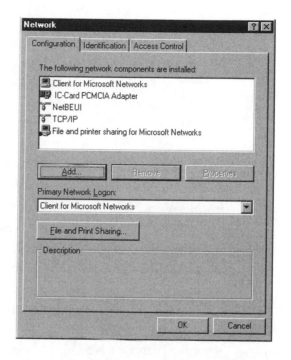

FIGURE 11.15

The Windows 95 Select
Network Client window

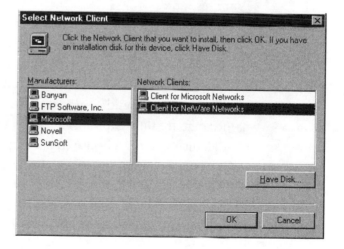

The installation will now begin to install the required software and
may request that you load the Windows 95 CD. Once this is complete,

you can configure the Microsoft NetWare Client for your specific environment. Simply highlight the client driver and click the Properties button.

We also need the IPX/SPX protocol in order to communicate with a NetWare server. This protocol is automatically installed during client installation.

Configuring the Microsoft Client for NetWare

Figure 11.16 shows the General properties tab of the Microsoft Client for NetWare Networks Properties window. The available options are pretty basic. You can configure which server you wish to log on to in the Preferred Server field. You can also select which drive letter you would like to use as your first network drive, and whether the logon script should be processed during authentication. If you do not process the logon script, you should set up permanent mapping to all required file systems and print queues. This will prevent you from having to navigate the Network Neighborhood every time you need to access a NetWare resource.

Unlike client32 with its plethora of configuration options, the Advanced tab of the Microsoft Client for NetWare Networks Properties window has only a single option. The Preserve Case setting can be set to a value of either yes or no. This determines if files saved to the NetWare server should conform to the DOS convention of creating file names that are fully capitalized. When this setting is set to Yes (which is the default), you can choose to use upper or lower case characters.

Once your configuration is complete, select the OK button on both the Client for NetWare dialog box, as well as the Network Properties dialog box. You will then be prompted to reboot your computer. After you do so, you will have access to NetWare bindery servers and services.

Installing the Microsoft NDS Service

To install the Microsoft NDS client, go to the Network Properties window as you did when installing the Microsoft client for NetWare.

FIGURE 11.16

The General tab of the
Microsoft Client for
NetWare Networks
Properties window

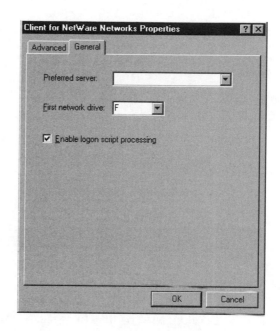

Click the Add button again but this time select that you wish to install a
service.

The Select Network Service window is shown in Figure 11.17. In the
Manufacturers column highlight Microsoft. You should now see the
Service for NetWare Directory Services. If you do not, you have an
older version of Windows 95 and will have to click the Have Disk
button and enter a path to the extracted NDS files that you retrieved
from the Microsoft Web site. Once you do this you will see the Service
for NetWare Directory Services. From here, the installation is identical
using either version.

Highlight the Service for NetWare Directory Services option and
click the OK button. All required services files will be copied to your
system. Once this is complete, you will be returned to the Configuration
tab of the Network window. The new service should be one of the last
network components listed. From here, you can click OK to complete
the installation and reboot your computer, or you can move on to configuring the service.

FIGURE 11.17

The Select Network
Service window

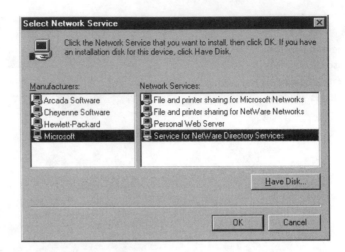

Configuring the Microsoft NDS Service

Like the Microsoft Client for NetWare, the Microsoft NDS service has very few configurable options. By highlighting the service from the Network Component list and clicking the Properties button, you can configure a preferred tree setting as well as a default context.

Once complete, select OK from the Service for NetWare Directory Services Properties dialog box as well as the Network Properties dialog box. This will initiate an additional file copy of required support files, as well as add statements to the autoexec.bat file to delete any older NetWare drivers you may have on your system. Once this process is complete, you will also be prompted to reboot your computer.

Comparing Client32 and the Microsoft Client

So how do client32 and the Microsoft client for Windows 95 compare? The results may surprise you.

Certainly client32 has more configuration options. This makes it far easier to customize the client for your specific networking needs. If the main concern is data integrity, you can tune client32 to commit files to disk immediately and even perform an additional CRC check. If raw throughput is your main goal, you can take advantage of file caching and increase the number of available packet burst buffers until your client is running like a 69 Boss Mustang bored .03 over.

There is something to be said for simplicity, however. While the Microsoft client may not have all the fancy buttons that are included with client32, this also means that your users have fewer settings to play with and ultimately less of a chance to incorrectly configure their system. By keeping it simple, the number of support calls incurred is kept to a minimum.

Of course, the big question is which client can move data while creating the lowest network utilization impact. As an unscientific test, we took three Windows 95 workstations and loaded up client32 so they could connect to our IntranetWare server. The clients were tested both at the default setting, and tuned many of the performance settings covered in the last section. These same workstations then had client32 removed and the Microsoft client installed. The identical NIC drivers were used on both configurations.

In both cases, we took a 5MB compressed file and measured the results as it was copied back and forth between the workstation and the IntranetWare server. During the test, we varied the amount of background traffic traveling on our 10 Mb Ethernet segment from 0 to 200 frames per second (fps). The background traffic did not contain any broadcast frames and we made sure that the destination MAC addresses used did not belong to any of our test systems. The idea was to simulate various levels of background traffic that the clients would normally have to contend with in a real-world environment. By ensuring that none of the background traffic was ever addressed to our test systems, we helped to ensure that all their processing was focused on the measured test.

A minimum of ten passes were made of each test. While this testing method is not precise, it will at least give us a ballpark idea of how these clients perform.

The result was that client32 averaged approximately 4500 frames to move the data, while the Microsoft client required only 4150. This makes the Microsoft client approximately 8% more efficient when transferring large files.

The difference is how the two clients react to delayed or missing frame retransmissions. Missing frame retransmissions occur when a recipient system either does not receive a frame of data, or receives it in an unusable format (such as with a bad CRC). When this happens the receiving system will request that the sender retransmit the data.

In Figure 11.18 you can see a normal client32 packet burst transaction. In frame number 223, the workstation Fenrus requests that the server Talsin send 26212 bytes of data. Talsin then transmits this data in frames 224 through 242. Because no errors occurred, Fenrus requests another 26576 bytes of data in frame 243, a quantity just slightly more than it had requested the last time.

F I G U R E   11.18

A normal packet burst
transaction

No.	Source	Destination	Layer	Summary	Error	Size	Interpacket Time	Absolute Time
223	FENRUS	TALSIN	ncp	Req Burst Read 26212 bytes		108	6 ms	3:00:20 PM
224	TALSIN	FENRUS	ncp	Burst Packet; 1428 bytes		1,512	2 ms	3:00:20 PM
225	TALSIN	FENRUS	ncp	Burst Packet; 628 bytes		712	577 μs	3:00:20 PM
226	TALSIN	FENRUS	ncp	Burst Packet; 1428 bytes		1,512	1 ms	3:00:20 PM
227	TALSIN	FENRUS	ncp	Burst Packet; 1428 bytes		1,512	1 ms	3:00:20 PM
228	TALSIN	FENRUS	ncp	Burst Packet; 1428 bytes		1,512	1 ms	3:00:20 PM
229	TALSIN	FENRUS	ncp	Burst Packet; 1428 bytes		1,512	1 ms	3:00:20 PM
230	TALSIN	FENRUS	ncp	Burst Packet; 1428 bytes		1,512	1 ms	3:00:20 PM
231	TALSIN	FENRUS	ncp	Burst Packet; 1428 bytes		1,512	1 ms	3:00:20 PM
232	TALSIN	FENRUS	ncp	Burst Packet; 1428 bytes		1,512	1 ms	3:00:20 PM
233	TALSIN	FENRUS	ncp	Burst Packet; 1428 bytes		1,512	1 ms	3:00:20 PM
234	TALSIN	FENRUS	ncp	Burst Packet; 1428 bytes		1,512	1 ms	3:00:20 PM
235	TALSIN	FENRUS	ncp	Burst Packet; 1428 bytes		1,512	1 ms	3:00:20 PM
236	TALSIN	FENRUS	ncp	Burst Packet; 1428 bytes		1,512	1 ms	3:00:20 PM
237	TALSIN	FENRUS	ncp	Burst Packet; 1428 bytes		1,512	1 ms	3:00:20 PM
238	TALSIN	FENRUS	ncp	Burst Packet; 1428 bytes		1,512	1 ms	3:00:20 PM
239	TALSIN	FENRUS	ncp	Burst Packet; 1428 bytes		1,512	1 ms	3:00:20 PM
240	TALSIN	FENRUS	ncp	Burst Packet; 1428 bytes		1,512	1 ms	3:00:20 PM
241	TALSIN	FENRUS	ncp	Burst Packet; 1428 bytes		1,512	1 ms	3:00:20 PM
242	TALSIN	FENRUS	ncp	Burst Packet; 1316 bytes		1,400	1 ms	3:00:20 PM
243	FENRUS	TALSIN	ncp	Req Burst Read 26576 bytes		108	568 μs	3:00:20 PM

C:\LZFW\CLIENT32.TR1

Figure 11.19 shows the results of the client32 packet burst transaction initiated in frame number 243. Talsin replies in frames 244 through 263 with the requested information. A curious thing happens, however—frame 245 shows that it was not transmitted to Fenrus for 2 ms. It is normal for there to be some delay in the first and last frame of a packet burst transfer. This is because the transmitting system needs to open and then close the requested information. It is abnormal, however, to experience a large delay during any of the middle packet burst transmissions. The transmitting system should already have the information sitting in queue and waiting to be pushed out onto the wire once the prior packet has been transmitted.

FIGURE 11.19

A delay in one of our frame transmissions

No.	Source	Destination	Layer	Summary	Error	Size	Interpacket Time	Absolute Time
243	FENRUS	TALSIN	ncp	Req Burst Read 26576 bytes		108	568 μs	3:00:20 PM
244	TALSIN	FENRUS	ncp	Burst Packet; 420 bytes		504	841 μs	3:00:20 PM
245	TALSIN	FENRUS	ncp	Burst Packet; 1428 bytes		1,512	2 ms	3:00:20 PM
246	TALSIN	FENRUS	ncp	Burst Packet; 1428 bytes		1,512	1 ms	3:00:20 PM
247	TALSIN	FENRUS	ncp	Burst Packet; 1240 bytes		1,324	1 ms	3:00:20 PM
248	TALSIN	FENRUS	ncp	Burst Packet; 1428 bytes		1,512	1 ms	3:00:20 PM
249	TALSIN	FENRUS	ncp	Burst Packet; 1428 bytes		1,512	1 ms	3:00:20 PM
250	TALSIN	FENRUS	ncp	Burst Packet; 1428 bytes		1,512	1 ms	3:00:20 PM
251	TALSIN	FENRUS	ncp	Burst Packet; 1428 bytes		1,512	1 ms	3:00:20 PM
252	TALSIN	FENRUS	ncp	Burst Packet; 1428 bytes		1,512	1 ms	3:00:20 PM
253	TALSIN	FENRUS	ncp	Burst Packet; 1428 bytes		1,512	1 ms	3:00:20 PM
254	TALSIN	FENRUS	ncp	Burst Packet; 1428 bytes		1,512	1 ms	3:00:20 PM
255	TALSIN	FENRUS	ncp	Burst Packet; 1428 bytes		1,512	1 ms	3:00:20 PM
256	TALSIN	FENRUS	ncp	Burst Packet; 1428 bytes		1,512	1 ms	3:00:20 PM
257	TALSIN	FENRUS	ncp	Burst Packet; 1428 bytes		1,512	1 ms	3:00:20 PM
258	TALSIN	FENRUS	ncp	Burst Packet; 1428 bytes		1,512	1 ms	3:00:20 PM
259	TALSIN	FENRUS	ncp	Burst Packet; 1428 bytes		1,512	1 ms	3:00:20 PM
260	TALSIN	FENRUS	ncp	Burst Packet; 1428 bytes		1,512	1 ms	3:00:20 PM
261	TALSIN	FENRUS	ncp	Burst Packet; 1428 bytes		1,512	1 ms	3:00:20 PM
262	TALSIN	FENRUS	ncp	Burst Packet; 1428 bytes		1,512	1 ms	3:00:20 PM
263	TALSIN	FENRUS	ncp	Burst Packet; 648 bytes		732	582 μs	3:00:20 PM
264	FENRUS	TALSIN	ncp	Req Burst Read 12236 bytes		108	336 μs	3:00:20 PM

The only logical explanation is that something occurred on the network that delayed delivery. This could have been an error or even a normal frame transmission by another station. Regardless of what caused it, what is interesting is how client32 deals with the increase in the interpacket gap. If you look at frame 264, you'll see that it is now requesting a packet burst transaction that is roughly half the size of the last one. The result is that less data will be moved before the next acknowledgment, thus increasing our total frame count. If the packet burst transaction initiated by frame 264 does not detect any further problems, it will respond in a similar manner to frame 243 by slightly increasing the quantity of information requested in the next packet burst negotiation.

Now let's look at how the Microsoft client deals with a similar problem. Figure 11.20 shows an initial packet burst request for 20992 bytes of data in frame number 184. The server Talsin then transmits this data in frames 185 through 199. If you look at the reply sent by

Fenrus in frame 200, you will see that all of the transmitted data was not received. Fenrus is stating that there where 4296 bytes that it either did not receive or could not process. Frame 200 is a request that this data be resent.

FIGURE 11.20

The Microsoft client recovering from an error

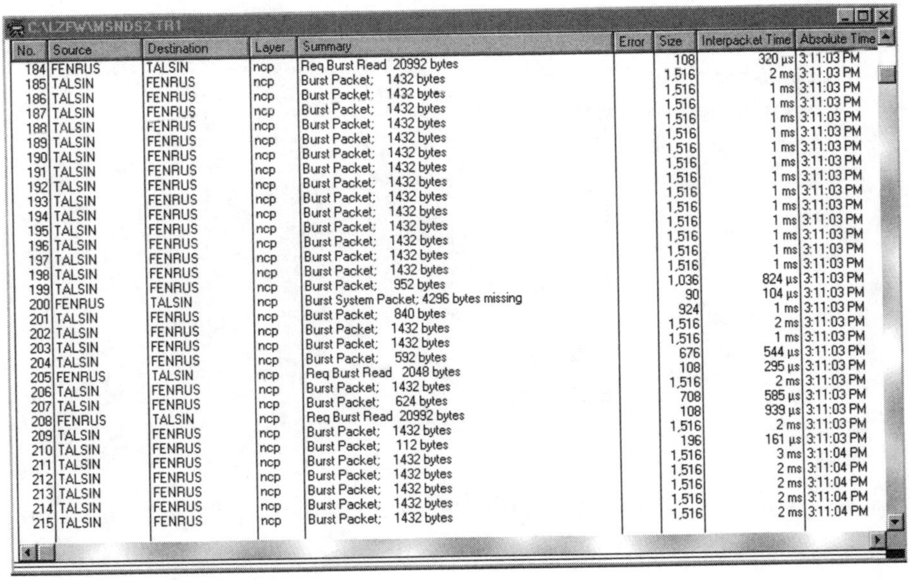

No.	Source	Destination	Layer	Summary	Error	Size	Interpacket Time	Absolute Time
184	FENRUS	TALSIN	ncp	Req Burst Read 20992 bytes		108	320 μs	3:11:03 PM
185	TALSIN	FENRUS	ncp	Burst Packet; 1432 bytes		1,516	2 ms	3:11:03 PM
186	TALSIN	FENRUS	ncp	Burst Packet; 1432 bytes		1,516	1 ms	3:11:03 PM
187	TALSIN	FENRUS	ncp	Burst Packet; 1432 bytes		1,516	1 ms	3:11:03 PM
188	TALSIN	FENRUS	ncp	Burst Packet; 1432 bytes		1,516	1 ms	3:11:03 PM
189	TALSIN	FENRUS	ncp	Burst Packet; 1432 bytes		1,516	1 ms	3:11:03 PM
190	TALSIN	FENRUS	ncp	Burst Packet; 1432 bytes		1,516	1 ms	3:11:03 PM
191	TALSIN	FENRUS	ncp	Burst Packet; 1432 bytes		1,516	1 ms	3:11:03 PM
192	TALSIN	FENRUS	ncp	Burst Packet; 1432 bytes		1,516	1 ms	3:11:03 PM
193	TALSIN	FENRUS	ncp	Burst Packet; 1432 bytes		1,516	1 ms	3:11:03 PM
194	TALSIN	FENRUS	ncp	Burst Packet; 1432 bytes		1,516	1 ms	3:11:03 PM
195	TALSIN	FENRUS	ncp	Burst Packet; 1432 bytes		1,516	1 ms	3:11:03 PM
196	TALSIN	FENRUS	ncp	Burst Packet; 1432 bytes		1,516	1 ms	3:11:03 PM
197	TALSIN	FENRUS	ncp	Burst Packet; 1432 bytes		1,516	1 ms	3:11:03 PM
198	TALSIN	FENRUS	ncp	Burst Packet; 952 bytes		1,036	824 μs	3:11:03 PM
199	TALSIN	FENRUS	ncp	Burst Packet; 952 bytes		90	104 μs	3:11:03 PM
200	FENRUS	TALSIN	ncp	Burst System Packet; 4296 bytes missing		924	1 ms	3:11:03 PM
201	TALSIN	FENRUS	ncp	Burst Packet; 840 bytes		1,516	2 ms	3:11:03 PM
202	TALSIN	FENRUS	ncp	Burst Packet; 1432 bytes		1,516	1 ms	3:11:03 PM
203	TALSIN	FENRUS	ncp	Burst Packet; 1432 bytes		676	544 μs	3:11:03 PM
204	TALSIN	FENRUS	ncp	Burst Packet; 592 bytes		108	295 μs	3:11:03 PM
205	FENRUS	TALSIN	ncp	Req Burst Read 2048 bytes		1,516	2 ms	3:11:03 PM
206	TALSIN	FENRUS	ncp	Burst Packet; 1432 bytes		708	585 μs	3:11:03 PM
207	TALSIN	FENRUS	ncp	Burst Packet; 624 bytes		108	939 μs	3:11:03 PM
208	FENRUS	TALSIN	ncp	Req Burst Read 20992 bytes		1,516	2 ms	3:11:03 PM
209	TALSIN	FENRUS	ncp	Burst Packet; 1432 bytes		196	161 μs	3:11:03 PM
210	TALSIN	FENRUS	ncp	Burst Packet; 112 bytes		1,516	3 ms	3:11:04 PM
211	TALSIN	FENRUS	ncp	Burst Packet; 1432 bytes		1,516	2 ms	3:11:04 PM
212	TALSIN	FENRUS	ncp	Burst Packet; 1432 bytes		1,516	2 ms	3:11:04 PM
213	TALSIN	FENRUS	ncp	Burst Packet; 1432 bytes		1,516	2 ms	3:11:04 PM
214	TALSIN	FENRUS	ncp	Burst Packet; 1432 bytes		1,516	2 ms	3:11:04 PM
215	TALSIN	FENRUS	ncp	Burst Packet; 1432 bytes		1,516	2 ms	3:11:04 PM

So Talsin resends the missing data in frames 201 through 204. Frame 205 is another burst request for a small amount of data, and frames 206 and 207 are the replies.

Frame 208 is where things get interesting. Despite the earlier errors, the Microsoft client is back to asking for 20992 bytes of data, the exact number it asked for when the error occurred! Unlike client32 which reduced the requested number of bytes to be read after an error and then slowly increases the value, the Microsoft client jumps right back in requesting the same amount of data.

This is why the Microsoft client was able to move our test file with a fewer number of frames. Because it did not negotiate a smaller packet burst read, it required fewer acknowledgments when moving data. The fewer the number of acknowledgments, the lower the overall frame count.

So the Microsoft client is more efficient than client32, right?

Not quite. Look at frames 208 through 215 in Figure 11.20. While the Microsoft client requested the same amount data during the packet burst read, it also increased the interpacket gap from 1 ms to 2 ms. The interpacket gap is the delay between frame transmission. The larger the gap, the longer a station waits before transmitting the next packet burst frame. If I increase my interpacket gap from 1 ms to 2 ms, it is going to take me twice as long to move my data from one system to another.

This gap becomes evident in the overall transfer times. While client32 was able to consistently move our 5MB file in roughly 10 seconds, the Microsoft client averaged 17 seconds. This is roughly a 70% increase in overall transfer time. So while the Microsoft client was using fewer frames, it was taking far longer to move the data from one system to another.

So client32 is more efficient than the Microsoft client, right?

Again, not quite. In order to measure network performance with the Microsoft client, we had to change the file name continually as it was moved back and forth between the workstation and the server. The reason? When the Microsoft client detected that it was working with a file that had been recently moved, it would generate just enough traffic to ensure that the version on the server matched the copy in memory. If this proved to be true, the file was pulled from memory instead of over the network.

This is referred to as a cache hit and when it occurs it can substantially reduce the number of frames generated, as well as the total transfer time because the file can be retrieved from local memory. How much of a difference? During a cache hit, the Microsoft client consistently generates less than 80 frames of data to verify the file and closes the transfer in under two seconds. This means that if a client consistently works with the same set of files, it can realize a dramatic performance increase by using the Microsoft client.

So the Microsoft client is more efficient than client32, right?

Do I have to say it? Our test file was 5MB, a bit on the large size for the average networking environment. While this large size helped to maximize the number of packet burst frames that would be negotiated, it does not present a real-world view of the number of packet burst frames that would be negotiated in the typical networking environment. The average would be somewhat smaller than we encountered during our testing.

So we need to take into account how efficiently each client reacts to many small file requests. With this in mind we took a look at how many frames where exchanged to both open and close a file for packet burst transfer.

Figure 11.21 shows the exchange required by client32 in order to find a file and initiate a packet burst transfer. In this case it took 16 frames to initiate the file transfer which was consistent through our testing. Client32 was also consistent in terminating the transfer using eight frames.

FIGURE 11.21

Client32 initiating a file transfer

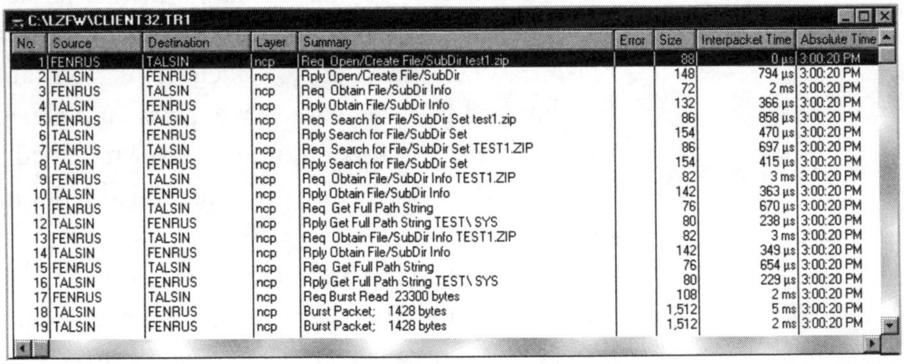

Figure 11.22 shows the exchange required by the Microsoft client in order to find a file and initiate a packet burst transfer. Notice that in this case we are using 26 frames in order to initiate a transfer. When closing the file, the Microsoft client used 10 frames.

FIGURE II.22

The Microsoft client initiating a file transfer

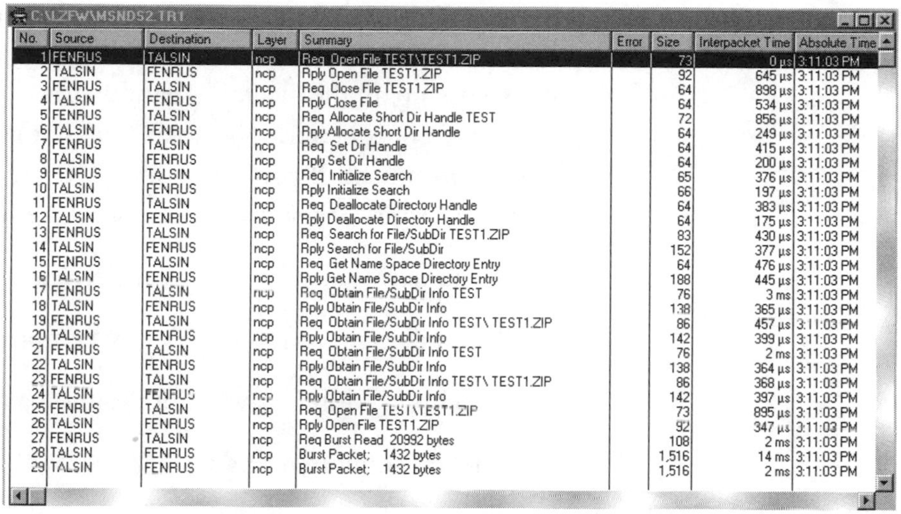

No.	Source	Destination	Layer	Summary	Error	Size	Interpacket Time	Absolute Time
1	FENRUS	TALSIN	ncp	Req Open File TEST\TEST1.ZIP		73	0 μs	3:11:03 PM
2	TALSIN	FENRUS	ncp	Rply Open File TEST1.ZIP		92	645 μs	3:11:03 PM
3	FENRUS	TALSIN	ncp	Req Close File TEST1.ZIP		64	898 μs	3:11:03 PM
4	TALSIN	FENRUS	ncp	Rply Close File		64	534 μs	3:11:03 PM
5	FENRUS	TALSIN	ncp	Req Allocate Short Dir Handle TEST		72	856 μs	3:11:03 PM
6	TALSIN	FENRUS	ncp	Rply Allocate Short Dir Handle		64	249 μs	3:11:03 PM
7	FENRUS	TALSIN	ncp	Req Set Dir Handle		64	415 μs	3:11:03 PM
8	TALSIN	FENRUS	ncp	Rply Set Dir Handle		64	200 μs	3:11:03 PM
9	FENRUS	TALSIN	ncp	Req Initialize Search		65	376 μs	3:11:03 PM
10	TALSIN	FENRUS	ncp	Rply Initialize Search		66	197 μs	3:11:03 PM
11	FENRUS	TALSIN	ncp	Req Deallocate Directory Handle		64	383 μs	3:11:03 PM
12	TALSIN	FENRUS	ncp	Rply Deallocate Directory Handle		64	175 μs	3:11:03 PM
13	FENRUS	TALSIN	ncp	Req Search for File/SubDir TEST1.ZIP		83	430 μs	3:11:03 PM
14	TALSIN	FENRUS	ncp	Rply Search for File/SubDir		152	377 μs	3:11:03 PM
15	FENRUS	TALSIN	ncp	Req Get Name Space Directory Entry		64	476 μs	3:11:03 PM
16	TALSIN	FENRUS	ncp	Rply Get Name Space Directory Entry		188	445 μs	3:11:03 PM
17	FENRUS	TALSIN	ncp	Req Obtain File/SubDir Info TEST		76	3 ms	3:11:03 PM
18	TALSIN	FENRUS	ncp	Rply Obtain File/SubDir Info		138	365 μs	3:11:03 PM
19	FENRUS	TALSIN	ncp	Req Obtain File/SubDir Info TEST\ TEST1.ZIP		86	457 μs	3:11:03 PM
20	TALSIN	FENRUS	ncp	Rply Obtain File/SubDir Info		142	399 μs	3:11:03 PM
21	FENRUS	TALSIN	ncp	Req Obtain File/SubDir Info TEST		76	2 ms	3:11:03 PM
22	TALSIN	FENRUS	ncp	Rply Obtain File/SubDir Info		138	364 μs	3:11:03 PM
23	FENRUS	TALSIN	ncp	Req Obtain File/SubDir Info TEST\ TEST1.ZIP		86	368 μs	3:11:03 PM
24	TALSIN	FENRUS	ncp	Rply Obtain File/SubDir Info		142	397 μs	3:11:03 PM
25	FENRUS	TALSIN	ncp	Req Open File TEST\TEST1.ZIP		73	895 μs	3:11:03 PM
26	TALSIN	FENRUS	ncp	Rply Open File TEST1.ZIP		92	347 μs	3:11:03 PM
27	FENRUS	TALSIN	ncp	Req Burst Read 20992 bytes		108	2 ms	3:11:03 PM
28	TALSIN	FENRUS	ncp	Burst Packet; 1432 bytes		1,516	14 ms	3:11:03 PM
29	TALSIN	FENRUS	ncp	Burst Packet; 1432 bytes		1,516	2 ms	3:11:03 PM

This means that each time a file transfer is initiated and closed (regardless of the file size), the Microsoft client uses 12 frames more than client32 as transfer overhead. While this difference is negligible during large file transfers (as we found out in our testing), it will begin to have an increasing effect on transmission efficiency as the size of the files we are using decreases.

One of the points we have yet to touch on is the bandwidth used by each client during the file transfer. During our testing, client32 achieved an average transfer rate of approximately 450 fps, slightly more than a 50% utilization level on our 10 Mb Ethernet network. The Microsoft client, on the other hand, only averaged 230 fps, roughly a 28% utilization level.

Deciding which transfer rate is preferable is like trying to decide how to best remove a band aid. You can rip it off quickly, which is very painful but is over almost immediately, or you can choose to peel it off slowly, which does not cause nearly as much pain but makes the pain it does cause last a whole lot longer.

With client32, file transfers can be performed much faster, but two workstations theoretically have the ability to use up all the available bandwidth. With the Microsoft client, the file transfers take place more slowly, but it would require more workstations performing a file transfer to use up all the available bandwidth.

So which client is better? The answer is that it depends on your networking environment. If your network fits neatly into one or more of the following criteria, then client32 may be the way to go:

- Predominantly small files are transferred.

- Collision domain contains very few computers.

- The Backbone utilizes switching technology.

- Servers are connected to a faster topology than the clients are.

- Users can access most of their resources locally (same logical network segment).

In short, if your network is well optimized for efficient communications, client32 will be an effective means of transferring data. Its ability to move data quickly in shorter bursts will have a positive impact on the above listed environments.

If one or more of the following criteria better describes your network, you may be better off using the Microsoft client for NetWare:

- There is heavy use of applications that frequently open the same files, such as databases.

- Collision domains consist of many computers (50 or more).

- Users frequently traverse routers to access network resources.

- Servers connect at the same topology speed as the clients.

- Clients do not need to connect to resources over a WAN.

Because the Microsoft client has a lower transfer rate, we can use this to our advantage by throttling the clients that connect to networks which may already be on the verge of overloading. By dropping the raw transfer rates of the clients, we help to limit the amount of data that can be pushed out onto the network at any given time.

Of course, the real test is to setup an analyzer and measure the average network utilization. If the average utilization is high (40% or more), go with the Microsoft client to help reduce the overall network traffic. If the average utilization is low (30% or less), then client32 will add some punch to your network access time by reducing the amount of time it takes to transfer files.

Sometimes you do not have a choice as to which client to use. For example, Novell's network analyzer, LANAlyzer, requires that client32 be used. This is also true for the administration utilities NWADMN95 and NWADMN3X. If you will be administrating IntranetWare servers, you need to use the client created by Novell (client32). This makes the choice of which client to use a bit more straightforward.

While this example applies specifically to IPX and the differences between client32 and the Microsoft NetWare client, the communication characteristics of these two clients and their effects on network utilization can be applied to any protocol.

NetWare IP

NetWare IP is a Novell client tool that allows you to connect to a NetWare server using the IP protocol. It does this by encapsulating a full IPX packet within an IP frame. Figure 11.23 shows a frame decode of a NetWare IP frame. As you can see in the figure, the frame contains the following headers:

- Ethernet

- IP

- UDP

- IPX

- NCP

All but the Ethernet header is located in the data field of the frame. The space used by these headers is no longer available for transferring data. This means that a NetWare IP frame that is exactly the same length as an IPX frame will not be able to carry as much data. This also means that it may require that more NetWare IP frames be transmitted in order to transfer all the required information from one system to another.

FIGURE 11.23

A decode of a NetWare IP frame

```
Packet Number : 227           1:55:17 PM
Length : 121 bytes
ether: ==================== Ethernet Datalink Layer ====================
       Station: AA-00-04-00-F5-07 ----> 00-80-5F-08-FA-CD
       Type: 0x0800 (IP)
   ip: ===================== Internet Protocol =====================
       Station:136.184.11.147 ---->136.184.2.48
       Protocol: UDP
       Version: 4
       Header Length (32 bit words): 5
       Precedence: Routine
              Normal Delay, Normal Throughput, Normal Reliability
       Total length: 103
       Identification: 44836
       Fragmentation allowed, Last fragment
       Fragment Offset: 0
       Time to Live: 31  seconds
       Checksum: 0xCD2E(Valid)
  udp: ===================== User Datagram Protocol ====================
       Source Port: 43981
       Destination Port: 43981
       Length = 83
       Checksum: 0x6B40(Valid)
  ipx: ================== Internetwork Packet Exchange ==================
       Checksum: 0xFFFF
       Length: 75
       Hop Count:  0
       Packet Type: 17(NCP)
       Network: 05 52 00 17       ---> 05 52 01 06
       Node:    7E-00-88-B8-0B-93  ---> 00-00-00-00-00-01
       Socket:  0x401C             ---> NCP
  ncp: ==================== NetWare Core Protocol ====================
       NCP Request: Open/Create File/SubDir
       Request Type: 0x2222 (Request)
       Sequence Number: 139
       Connection Number Low: 69
```

If you look at Figure 11.24 you'll see something else that is a bit strange—we are no longer using packet burst to communicate with the server! Each request for data is followed by an acknowledgment that the data was received. The result is that this transaction will require approximately twice as many frames to transfer the information than if IPX was used as the communication protocol.

This does not mean that NetWare IP cannot be an extremely valuable connectivity tool. For example, if I need to traverse a WAN link that only supports the IP protocol, NetWare IP is the perfect solution for filling this need.

FIGURE 11.24

A NetWare IP session transferring a file

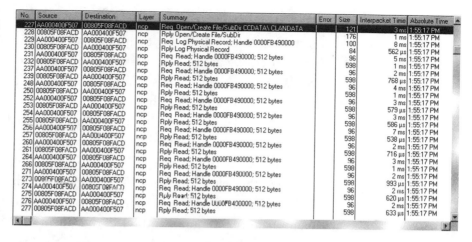

No.	Source	Destination	Layer	Summary	Error	Size	Interpacket Time	Absolute Time
227	AA000400F507	00805F08FACD	ncp	Req Open/Create File/SubDir CCDATA\ CLANDATA		121	3 ms	1:55:17 PM
228	00805F08FACD	AA000400F507	ncp	Rply Open/Create File/SubDir		176	1 ms	1:55:17 PM
229	AA000400F507	00805F08FACD	ncp	Req Log Physical Record; Handle 0000FB490000		100	8 ms	1:55:17 PM
230	00805F08FACD	AA000400F507	ncp	Rply Log Physical Record		84	562 µs	1:55:17 PM
231	AA000400F507	00805F08FACD	ncp	Req Read: Handle 0000FB490000; 512 bytes		96	5 ms	1:55:17 PM
232	00805F08FACD	AA000400F507	ncp	Rply Read; 512 bytes		598	1 ms	1:55:17 PM
237	AA000400F507	00805F08FACD	ncp	Req Read: Handle 0000FB490000; 512 bytes		96	2 ms	1:55:17 PM
239	00805F08FACD	AA000400F507	ncp	Rply Read; 512 bytes		598	768 µs	1:55:17 PM
248	AA000400F507	00805F08FACD	ncp	Req Read: Handle 0000FB490000; 512 bytes		96	4 ms	1:55:17 PM
250	00805F08FACD	AA000400F507	ncp	Rply Read; 512 bytes		598	1 ms	1:55:17 PM
252	AA000400F507	00805F08FACD	ncp	Req Read: Handle 0000FB490000; 512 bytes		96	3 ms	1:55:17 PM
253	00805F08FACD	AA000400F507	ncp	Rply Read; 512 bytes		598	579 µs	1:55:17 PM
254	AA000400F507	00805F08FACD	ncp	Req Read: Handle 0000FB490000; 512 bytes		96	3 ms	1:55:17 PM
255	00805F08FACD	AA000400F507	ncp	Rply Read; 512 bytes		598	586 µs	1:55:17 PM
256	AA000400F507	00805F08FACD	ncp	Req Read: Handle 0000FB490000; 512 bytes		96	7 ms	1:55:17 PM
257	00805F08FACD	AA000400F507	ncp	Rply Read; 512 bytes		598	538 µs	1:55:17 PM
260	AA000400F507	00805F08FACD	ncp	Req Read: Handle 0000FB490000; 512 bytes		96	2 ms	1:55:17 PM
261	00805F08FACD	AA000400F507	ncp	Rply Read; 512 bytes		598	716 µs	1:55:17 PM
264	AA000400F507	00805F08FACD	ncp	Req Read: Handle 0000FB490000; 512 bytes		96	3 ms	1:55:17 PM
266	00805F08FACD	AA000400F507	ncp	Rply Read; 512 bytes		598	1 ms	1:55:17 PM
271	AA000400F507	00805F08FACD	ncp	Req Read: Handle 0000FB490000; 512 bytes		96	2 ms	1:55:17 PM
273	00805F08FACD	AA000400F507	ncp	Rply Read; 512 bytes		598	993 µs	1:55:17 PM
274	AA000400F507	00805F08FACD	ncp	Req Read: Handle 0000FB490000; 512 bytes		96	2 ms	1:55:17 PM
275	00805F08FACD	AA000400F507	ncp	Rply Read; 512 bytes		598	620 µs	1:55:17 PM
276	AA000400F507	00805F08FACD	ncp	Req Read: Handle 0000FB490000; 512 bytes		96	2 ms	1:55:17 PM
277	00805F08FACD	AA000400F507	ncp	Rply Read; 512 bytes		598	633 µs	1:55:17 PM

It does mean that you need to analyze where and when to use Net-Ware IP. It is not designed to be a drop-in replacement for IPX communications, and can produce a reduction in performance if it is used in this manner.

The setup and configuration of NetWare IP is nearly identical to the client32 installation. The only real difference is that you must assign an IP address to the system or supply the address of a bootp server. When communicating, NetWare IP uses ports 43981 and 43982 as both the source and destination ports. RIP/SAP broadcasts are transmitted on port 396.

Configuring Client Communications in a Windows NT Environment

When selecting a client to communicate with an NT server, your options are a bit more limited than when you are setting up a NetWare client. Microsoft is the only supplier of client software when you are connecting Windows based clients. The required client software is installed by default, if the installation utility detects that a network card is installed.

Installing the Microsoft Client on Windows 95

Installing Microsoft's client support for Windows NT is very similar to the process we used when installing the Microsoft client support for NetWare. To begin the installation we must go to the Network Properties dialog box and click the Add button.

From the Select Network Component Type dialog box, highlight that you wish to add a client and click the Add button. This will bring up the Select Network Client dialog box.

When the Select Network Client window is displayed (you can refer back to Figure 11.15 to see this window), highlight Microsoft in the Manufacturers column, and select the Client for Microsoft Networks in the Network Clients column. Now click the OK button.

You will be returned to the Network window where you should now see the Microsoft client listed at the top of the list. The installation should also have installed the NetBEUI protocol. If all your NT communications will take place on the same logical network, you are finished with the installation. If you will be communicating over a router, you will want to install the IP protocol.

Installing IP Support

To install IP, again click the Add button in the Network window. This time, when the Select Network Component Type window appears, select Protocol and click the Add button. The Select Network Protocol window is shown in Figure 11.25. When this window appears, highlight Microsoft under Manufacturers and select TCP/IP under Network Protocols. Then click the OK button.

When IP is installed on Windows 95, the default is to obtain all required IP information from a DHCP server. If you are not using a DHCP server, you will need to manually configure each required IP parameter.

Once the installation process is complete, you can either configure each of these network components or select the OK button to copy any required files and to reboot the computer.

FIGURE 11.25

The Select Network
Protocol window

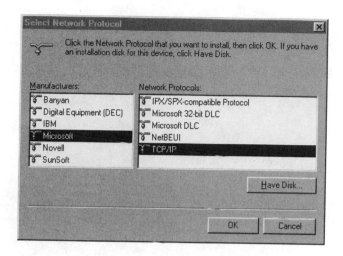

Configuring the Microsoft Client on Windows 95

To configure the client for Microsoft networks, highlight its entry in the Network Components field of the Configuration tab in the Network window, and click the Properties button.

This will bring up the General tab of the Client for Microsoft Networks Properties window, shown in Figure 11.26. We have only a few options that can be configured.

Our first configurable option under Logon Validation is to select whether we will be performing a logon to a Windows NT domain. If we select this box, our logon name will be authenticated on the domain as well as the local system. If we choose to authenticate to a domain, we should also specify which domain to authenticate to in the Windows NT domain field.

Under network logon options, we can choose between performing a quick logon, or a logon that verifies all network connections.

During a quick logon, you are authenticated to the domain and any permanent share mappings, or mappings that are set up as part of a logon script, are mapped and configured on your system. Access to each of these shares is not verified until you actually try to use the share resource.

FIGURE 11.26

The Client for Microsoft
Networks Properties
dialog box

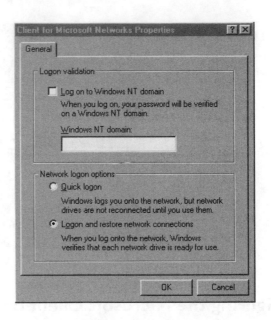

For example, let's say that you have found a share on your NT domain named Quake. You map a drive letter to it for easy reference, and access it during non-working hours (when your boss is in a meeting, for instance).

One day you log on to the NT domain and notice that all the shares are mapped as they normally are. When you go to access the Quake share, however, you are denied access to it. Security rights to this share have been changed so you no longer have access to the files.

This, in effect, is how a quick logon functions. It restores the potential path to resources without regard to whether you can actually reach those resources.

The Logon and Restore Network Connections option actually verifies each of the share connections. If you cannot access a mapped share during authentication, an error message is produced. This lets you know right away that one of your resources is not available.

Once the configuration is complete, select the OK button. You can now select OK from the Network Properties dialog box to reboot and implement your changes, or you can go on to configure another network component.

Configuring the TCP/IP Protocol

To configure Windows 95 to use the IP protocol, highlight TCP/IP in the Network Components field and click the Properties button. This will display the TCP/IP Properties dialog box.

The IP Address Tab   The IP Address tab of the TCP/IP Properties window is shown in Figure 11.27. The default is to obtain all required IP information from a DHCP server. If you are using DHCP, no additional IP configuration may be required. If you do not have a DHCP server, you will need to configure all required IP parameters manually.

FIGURE 11.27

The IP Address tab

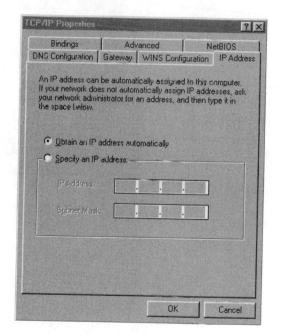

To set an IP address manually, click the Specify an IP Address button. This will activate the IP Address and Subnet Mask fields. Fill in appropriate values for each, depending on your network configuration.

The DNS Configuration Tab   The DNS Configuration tab of the TCP/IP Properties window, shown in Figure 11.28, is used to configure domain name information. If DNS is disabled, no other field on this tab requires configuration. By selecting the Enable DNS button, we can configure each of the displayed fields.

FIGURE 11.28

The DNS
Configuration tab

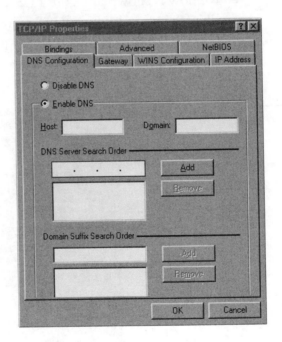

The Host field identifies the unique DNS name used to identify this system. Entering a host name in this field does not automatically register this name through DNS. The DNS administrator must do this manually from the DNS server. You should make sure that the host name you enter here matches the DNS entry for your system.

You should also make sure that this name matches the entry listed under the Machine Name field of the Identification tab. The identification tab can be accessed directly from the Network window (see Figure 11.14).

Our next configurable field is Domain. This field is used to identify the domain name where this system will be located. Only fill in the domain name, not the fully qualified domain name (FQDN) for this machine. For example, if my host name is Fenrus and I am located in the domain foobar.com, I would enter the domain as foobar.com, not Fenrus.foobar.com.

The DNS Server Search Order field is used to identify the IP address of the domain name servers that this system should use when resolving host addresses to IP address. For fault tolerance, the IP address of multiple servers may be entered. If the host is unable to contact the first server on the list, it will direct all DNS queries to the second listed IP address.

The Domain Suffix Search Order field is used to define other domain names to search, other than the one where this system is located, when only a host name is presented in a DNS query. For example, let's assume we have a system whose FQDN is fire.testing.foobar.com. From this system, we wish to access our local Web server located at www.foobar.com.

If we enter just the Web server's host name www, our DNS query will fail. This is because our system assumes that we are trying to access a system within the same domain. This means that our system thinks we are looking for the IP address of the system www.testing.foobar.com, which does not exist.

The Domain Suffix Search Order allows us to define additional domains to search when we enter just a host name for IP address resolution. If we were to add the domain foobar.com to the search order list, the address would now be resolved correctly. This is because once the DNS lookup on www.testing.foobar.com failed, the search order list would be referenced and a new query would be sent looking for the IP address for www.foobar.com.

The Gateway Tab   The Gateway tab has a single option, to configure the IP address of the local routers. The first address listed is considered the default router or gateway, and will be used for all non-local network communications. If we need to transmit information to a system that is not on our local network, we will forward it to the first listed IP address and let that system figure out how to best deliver the information.

If a second IP address is listed, traffic will be forwarded to the second address if the router located at the first IP address fails to respond. This provides some fault tolerance in case our first router should fail.

The NetBIOS Tab   The NetBIOS tab also has a single option. We can choose to enable or disable the use of NetBIOS over IP. When this box is checked, the system can take advantage of encapsulating Net-BIOS traffic within IP frames in order to communicate with systems that are not located on the same logical network.

The WINS Configuration Tab   The WINS Configuration tab, as shown in Figure 11.29, allows us to identify the IP address of the WINS servers located on our local network. WINS servers are used to propagate NetBIOS system names between logical networks. When our system needs to find another NetBIOS- or NetBEUI-based system, it references the WINS server to obtain the system's IP address. It can then use this address to communicate with the remote system by encapsulating the traffic within IP frames.

We are allowed to enter the IP address of two WINS servers. This provides some fault tolerance, in case one of them is not available. The Scope ID identifies the scope under which this system's name is considered unique. Scope IDs are similar to domain names and often share the same name or value. Unless you are part of an extremely large network, it is safe to leave the Scope ID blank.

There is an option at the bottom of the dialog box that we are not allowed to select—the Use DHCP for WINS Resolution button. This option is only active when you select Obtain an IP Address Automatically from the IP Address tab. When Use DHCP for WINS Resolution is

FIGURE 11.29

The WINS
Configuration tab

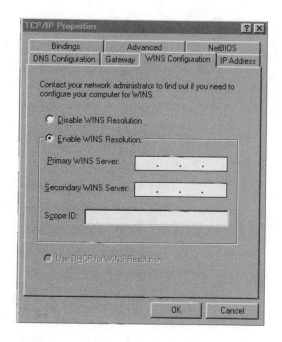

selected, it tells the system to retrieve WINS server information from the DHCP server when DHCP is queried for an IP address.

The Bindings Tab   The Bindings tab identifies which clients should use the IP protocol. If you want to enable IP, but you do not want to use IP when accessing network shares, deselect the option labeled Client for Microsoft Networks.

If you have file sharing enabled on your system, and you want to make sure that only local clients can access your file shares, make sure the option for File and printer sharing for Microsoft Networks is deselected.

Besides security, there are also performance gains to disabling services that do not require the IP protocol. Whenever you perform a search for a network resource, your system attempts to find it, using all available protocols. By deselecting protocols that do not provide a path to any network resources, you expedite the search process.

The Advanced Tab   The Advanced tab has a single option—you can choose to set IP as the default protocol. The default protocol is the first protocol used by the Microsoft client when searching for network resources. If the resource is not located using the default protocol, any other protocols the Microsoft client is bound to will be used.

If you deselect the binding of the Microsoft client to the IP protocol, you should not (even though you can) set IP as the default protocol.

Once you are satisfied with your changes, click the OK button to close the TCP/IP Properties window and click OK again to close the Network Properties dialog box. The system will now reboot so your changes will take effect.

Configuring NT Workstation

NT Workstation does not use a Microsoft client. Instead, it uses a service called Workstation when accessing NT resources. Configuring NT services, including the Workstation service, was covered at length in Chapter 8.

There is one additional step to using an NT workstation on a Microsoft domain, beyond configuring the proper services and protocols. You must also register the system with the domain controllers. The registration process ensures that users performing a logon from this system should be allowed access to domain resources. The user is still required to use a valid logon name and password, the registration process simply verifies that this system is acceptable to use for domain access.

Figure 8.3 showed the Identification Tab of the Network window. By clicking the Change button, we were able to rename our server or domain. When this same button is selected on an NT workstation, or an NT server which is not a domain controller, the Identification Changes dialog box, shown in Figure 11.30, appears.

From this dialog box, we can enter the name of the domain we wish to join in the domain field. If we select the Create a Computer Account in the Domain button, the two fields directly below it become active. These fields allow us to enter the logon name and password of a domain

FIGURE 11.30

The Identifications
Changes dialog box

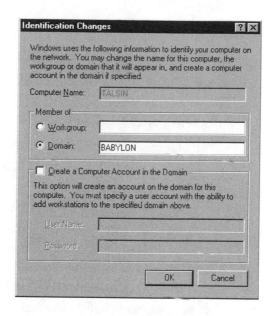

administrator (such as Administrator). When we click the OK button the name and password entered are verified by one of the domain controllers. If this combination is accepted, the NT workstation is allowed access to the domain.

Using NFS to Access File Services between Unix Systems

The Network File System (NFS) protocol can be used to share files and directories between Unix systems. It is functionally similar to the file shares or drive mappings, except that remote file systems are mounted to some point in the existing directory structure.

While the mainstay of NFS use is Unix, there are third party tools available for every major platform to support NFS. This allows other operating systems to access NFS servers and many of them, such as IntranetWare, are able to act as an NFS server as well.

There are two parts to configuring NFS:

▪ The server system must export the files to be shared.

▪ The client system must mount the shared files.

Configuring the NFS Server

The first step in configuring an NFS server is to decide which file systems to export and who should have access to them. File systems are exported at the directory level and are recursive, so if I export the directory /usr/games, I export all files within the games directory as well as the subdirectories located below this.

While Linux allows you to export a parent directory as well as one of its child directories, many Unix flavors such as Solaris will not allow you to do this. The second export attempt will fail. For example, if I wish to set up /usr/games and /usr/games/doom as two separate exports, Linux will allow me to do this while Solaris would fail on the second entry.

Exporting file systems can only be performed by the root user. This is to help ensure that someone does not accidentally make public a private section of the directory structure.

Who is allowed to access each exported file system is determined at the host level. You can set access permissions on a per system basis and have a small amount of control over file access once the connection is established.

NFS assumes that the user ID and group ID is synchronized between the two systems. It uses the IDs to determine file access rights instead of the logon name. For example, let's assume I am currently logged on to the Unix system Mars. My logon name is cbrenton and both my user ID and group ID is set to 150.

If I mount a file system on Mars that is being exported from the Unix system Venus, my user ID and group ID will be used to determine which files I have access to. If my account on Venus is also set to use a user ID and a group ID of 150, life is happy and I should have no problems accessing my files. If this ID number belongs to another user, or my ID is set to some other value, I will not have the same level of file access that I would normally receive when I Telnet directly to Venus.

Since the ID numbers do not match, the exporting system (Venus) cannot correctly identify who I am.

Configuring NFS Exports   To configure the file systems you wish to export, make sure you are logged on as the root user. You can use Red Hat's graphical Control Panel tool (accessed through XWindows) or you can directly edit the /etc/exports file. The Control Panel tool is by far the easiest method, and is self explanatory once you understand how the exports file is used. With this in mind, we will look at what is involved with editing the exports file directly.

Editing the Exports File   The exports file consists of two columns, separated by either tabs or spaces. In the first column is the name of the directory you wish to export. The second column lists the security criteria that must be passed in order to access the listed file system. Some valid security parameters are listed in Table 11.4.

T A B L E 11.4 Security parameters	**Parameter**	**Description**
	ro	Provide read-only access to the file system.
	rw	Provide read/write access to the file system.
	host	Only allow access from the specified host.
	domain	Only allow access from the specified domain.
	*	Only allow access from hosts which meet the wild card criteria.
	IP Subnet	Only allow access from hosts on the specified IP subnet.
	root_squash	File access requests that originate from the root user on the remote file system are handled as if they were anonymous users.
	all_squash	Handle all file access requests as if they originated from an anonymous user.

In Unix, the anonymous user is the equivalent of the guest user under NetWare or Windows NT. Typically, this account is provided with little to no file system access.

If you were to implement these parameters, an example export file could look something like this:

```
# Sample /etc/exports file

/home/cbrenton    fenrus(rw)

/home/ftp/pub     *.foobar.com(ro,root_squash)

/data/testing     sean(rw) test*.foobar.com(ro,all_squash)

/data/salary      10.5.7.0(r,w)
```

The first line is simply a comment to identify the file. Our second line exports the contents of /home/cbrenton for read/write access, but only to the system fenrus.

The third line exports the contents of /home/FTP/pub to everyone in the foobar.com domain. Access is restricted to read-only, and if a root user attempts to access files, they are given the same level of access as the anonymous user.

The fourth line exports the contents of /data/testing. Read/write access is provided to the system sean. Access is also provided to any host that meets the naming criteria test*.foobar.com. For example, if the systems test1, test2, and testing are part of the foobar.com domain, they are allowed access to this export. Access is at a read-only level and all user file access rights are handled as if they originated from an anonymous user.

Our final example exports the contents of /data/salary to every system on the IP subnet 10.5.7.0. All systems on this subnet are allowed read/write access.

Exporting our File Systems   Once we have finished editing our /etc/exports file, we must start up the services that will make these file systems available on the network. First we must ensure that the NFS daemon is running. This may be named nfsd, or rpc.nfsd, depending on the operating system you are using. You can see if one of these processes is running by typing the commands:

```
ps -ax|grep nfsd
ps -ax|grep rpc.nfsd
```

The command **ps -ax** generates a list of all running processes. We then take the output from this command and pipe it through grep which searches for the specified character string. You will see one instance of the command for the grep process itself (remember we are listing out all processes, including the process which is looking for other processes). If you see a second instance, then the NFS daemon is already running. If it is not running, you can start the daemon directly from the command line. Look in the /usr/sbin directory to see which version of the daemon you are using and simply type in its name at the command line.

Once the daemon is running, enter the command:

```
exportfs -a
```

This will cause the daemon to read the /etc/exports file and make all listed file systems available for network access.

Configuring the NFS Client

The NFS client configuration follows a similar process to the server configuration. We must edit the configuration file, start the required daemon, and execute the required command to initiate the process. The file we need to edit is /etc/fstab.

Configuring the *fstab* File   The fstab file is used by the operating system to identify each of the different file systems that it has to interact with. Figure 11.31 shows a sample `fstab` file from a system named Sean. In order for Sean to be able to mount the exported files from the system named Toby that we configured in the last section, Sean's `fstab` file needs to have an entry for these exported file systems.

FIGURE 11.31

Sean's *fstab* file

```
# /etc/fstab
#
# You should be using fstool (control-panel) to edit this!
#
# <device>      <mountpoint>    <filesystemtype> <options> <dump> <fsckorder>

/dev/hda1                      /                        ext2   defaults 1 1
/dev/fd0                       /mnt/floppy              msdos  noauto 0 0
sean:(pid226)                  /net                     ignore 0 0 0
sean:(pid225)                  /net                     ignore 0 0 0
toby:/data/testing             /mnt/toby                nfs    auto

none                           /proc                    proc   defaults
/dev/hda2                      none                     swap   sw
```

If you look down the first column you'll see an entry that begins `toby:/data/testing`. This tells Sean that the file system we wish to mount is located on the system Toby. This entry also tells the system that out of all the file systems being exported, the one we're interested in is /data/testing.

The second column indicates where Sean should locate Toby's exported file system. According to the entry, we asked that the file system be placed under the /mnt/toby directory. Once the mount is complete, a directory listing on Sean under /mnt/toby will produce the same information as a directory listing on Toby under /data/testing.

The third column identifies what type of file system will be attached to this mount point. Whenever we perform an NFS mount, we always identify the file system as being NFS, regardless of the source operating system.

The final column identifies how the operating system should handle this file system. The auto switch tells the operating system that it should try to restore this connection whenever the machine is rebooted. This way, Sean will automatically mount Toby during system startup. No user intervention will be required to restore this connection.

Mounting the Remote File System   Once we have finished editing our fstab file, we can start up the required services to mount the remote file system. To perform an NFS mount, the mountd daemon must be running on the system. We can check to see if it's running by typing the command: **ps -axlgrep mountd**

If two entries for mountd are printed, we know our service is running. If it is not currently running as a process, we can start it from the command line. Once mountd is running we can use the command **mount** to attach to the remote file system. We do this by typing: **mount /mnt/toby**

The switch tells **mount** to reference the fstab file and mount the file system associated with the mount point /mnt/toby. If we need to make multiple mounts, we can enter them one by one, specifying the mount point of each, or by entering the command: **mount -a**

The -a switch tells **mount** to initialize all mount points that have auto specified as one of their options. This is the command that is executed during system startup to restore the connections to our remote file systems.

Summary

This concludes our discussion on client software and how to connect our workstations to various network services. You should now have a good understanding of how to get a workstation communicating with some of the more popular NOSes.

In the next chapter, we will take a look at some of the less conventional methods of communicating with our servers. The focus will be on reducing the number of protocols in order to create a more homogenous networking environment.

CHAPTER

12

Connectivity Options

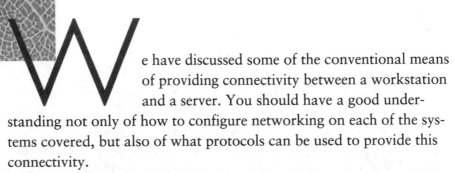

e have discussed some of the conventional means of providing connectivity between a workstation and a server. You should have a good understanding not only of how to configure networking on each of the systems covered, but also of what protocols can be used to provide this connectivity.

We will now look at trying to consolidate the number of protocols required to support all of our network servers. There are software packages available that can allow one type of system to emulate the services normally provided by another. When implemented correctly, this emulation can help to reduce the number of protocols needed to support communications on our network.

This is not to say that reducing the number of protocols is always a good thing. Other factors, such as bandwidth requirements and traffic patterns, must be taken into consideration. For example, in the last chapter we discussed that NetWare IP creates more traffic when moving data than its IPX counterpart. If we are administrating an environment that relies on heavy file access, we would not want to implement NetWare IP for the sole purpose of consolidating on the IP protocol. The additional traffic generated by using a less efficient means of communication could easily outweigh the bandwidth gains of removing the IPX protocol from the network.

If, however, we are administrating a network that relies on an NT or Unix application server, and the use of the NetWare server is occasional at best, then NetWare IP may be the perfect solution for eliminating the

IPX protocol as well as all the RIP and SAP frames that are generated to maintain it.

What Options Are Available?

Let's take a look at what options are available to allow our systems to consolidate on a single protocol. The three options we will look at are native IP support, Mars_nwe, and the SAMBA Suite.

We will also attempt to consolidate on a single type of file and print services. Even though our NOSes may support the same protocol, this does not automatically mean they can easily exchange information using the same type of services.

This discussion does not really pertain to Lotus Notes but rather the other operating systems we have covered so far. Lotus Notes is happy using a wide range of protocols which we discussed in the last two chapters. As long as we can get the underlying NOS to communicate, Lotus Notes will use this protocol to exchange information.

Also, Lotus Notes uses its own port numbers and thus runs as its own service. No matter which software we decide to use for file and printer services, Lotus Notes is going to do its own thing and establish communications using its default port numbers.

Native IP Support

Our first option is to try and provide support using IP through native services. Each of our servers provides support for the IP protocol as well as a number of IP services. The trick is to get all of our systems using the same set of services so that information can be exchanged easily.

Table 12.1 is a support matrix showing which IP services are supported by each of our platforms. Both server and workstations are included in this list.

TABLE 12.1		IntranetWare	Windows NT	Windows 95	Unix
IP services and the platforms they support	NFS	*	*	*	X
	NetWare IP	X	C	C	
	FTP	X	X	C	X
	HTTP	X	X	X	X
	lpd	X	X	X	X

X Provides full support for the service
C Provides client support only for the service
* Requires third party software

We discussed the problems with NFS in the last chapter. While it is capable of supporting all of our NOSes, it requires third party software for most of our platforms. If we have a mostly Unix environment, with only a few systems that are running other operating systems, then NFS may be a good fit. Otherwise it could be a costly solution.

NetWare IP uses its own set of unique port numbers and is specific to NetWare. Because it is based on IPX and NCP encapsulation, you cannot use NetWare IP to access services on a Windows NT or Unix system. If we are running a mixed NOS environment, we will still be required to run some other kind of file service in order to provide connectivity to our non-NetWare systems.

While FTP will provide connectivity services to all of our systems, it's not exactly practical. Users like to have a seamless integration between their local system and the server. FTP would add an additional step when trying to save or retrieve files. For example, instead of allowing a user to save their word processing document to drive I, they would have to save it locally, start their FTP client, transfer the file (did you remember to switch over to binary mode?), exit the client, and then delete the local copy. Wouldn't you just love to be a help desk person in *that* environment?

HTTP is no better than FTP except it requires the additional maintenance of constant administration of the Web server. If FTP is a bad choice, going with HTTP would be even worse.

LPD is our printing server and it is actually supported by each of our systems. If we settle on IP as our network protocol, LPD will provide printing services for all of our listed platforms.

We did not find a suitable file service, however. The closest we came was NFS which seemed most appropriate for environments that are predominately Unix based. Because most organizations have chosen to standardize on Windows for their desktop systems, we should continue exploring our options to see if we can find a more universally acceptable solution.

Mars_nwe

The mars_nwe tool kit is a set of client and server tools that allow a Linux or UnixWare system running IPX, to connect to, or emulate, a NetWare server. At the time of this writing, mars_nwe has only been ported to UnixWare and Linux. It is a fairly new tool kit, however, so you can expect to see it ported to other flavors of Unix in the future. The source code is covered under the GNU General Public License, so it is freely available to anyone.

Because mars_nwe comes pre-installed and minimally configured with Red Hat Linux, we will skip these procedures and go straight into using the tool kit to connect to a NetWare server. The tools are located in the directory /usr/bin.

The Mars_nwe Client Tools

The mars_nwe client tools allow us to access NetWare servers using the IPX protocol. There are a few caveats when using the client software. First, the software does not support logon scripts. This is just as well because the Unix system would not be able to process any of the logon script commands without running DOS emulation. Mars_nwe does not support NDS. It is a bindery-based set of tools which means any Intranet-Ware servers you need to access must be running bindery services. Finally, burst mode is not currently supported. This means that the system will require an acknowledgment for each frame of data sent or received.

ncpmount

ncpmount is used to authenticate to a NetWare server and mount the NetWare file system onto the Linux directory tree. A user and password switch is used to authenticate to the system. When the authentication is successful, all volumes on the NetWare server that the user has access to are mounted in the specified directory location. For example, review the following command string:

```
ncpmount -S Talsin -U cbrenton -P bovine /mnt/talsin
```

This command will authenticate to the server Talsin using the logon name of "cbrenton" and a password of "bovine." If the authentication process is successful, all available volumes would be mounted under the Linux directory/mnt/talsin. Our directory structure would resemble Figure 12.1. As you can see, the directory structure on the NetWare server will be mimicked under the directory /mnt/talsin.

F I G U R E   12.1

The directory structure
created when mounting a
NetWare server

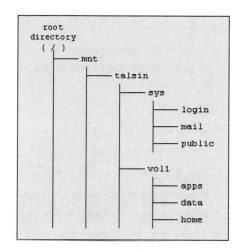

Available ncpmount switches:

-S *server*	specify the file server
-U *username*	specify the logon name to use
-P *password*	specify the password to use during authentication
-n	the account has no password, do not prompt me
-h	print out a brief help file
mount-point	the location in the Linux files system where the should be mounted

ncpmount can only be executed by the root user. If you wish to allow non-root users to execute the command, the root user will have to change the file permissions by entering:

```
chmod 4755 /usr/bin/ncpmount
```

Unix is case sensitive. When using these commands, make sure that you match the case exactly for all executables and switches.

ncpumount

ncpumount is used to disconnect a mounted NetWare file system. This is the equivalent of the **logout** command in the NetWare world. References to the file system are removed and the connection to the server is broken. ncpumount is also reserved for use by the root user only. You will need to change the permissions on this file as well, if you wish to allow non-root users to execute it.

Available ncpumount switches:

mount-point   the location in the Linux files system where theserver should be mounted

For example to remove the above mounted file system we would enter the command:

```
ncpumount /mnt/talsin
```

nprint

nprint allows Linux users to send print jobs to queues located on NetWare servers. Functionality is similar to the NetWare **nprint** command.

Available nprint switches:

-S *server*   specify the file server
-U *username*   specify the logon name to use
-P *password*   specify the password to use during authentication

-n   the specified account has no password, do not prompt me

-q *queue-name*	specify the queue name located on the NetWare server
-h	print out a brief help file including available switches
-b *banner-name*	use a banner page and identify it with the string specified in the place of *banner-name*
-N	do not send a form feed at the end of the job
file	the name of the file to be printed

For example, to print the file named `resume.txt` located in my home directory, to the print queue `mis` without form feeds, I would type:

```
nprint -S talsin -U cbrenton -P bovine -q mis -N /home/
cbrenton/resume.txt
```

nsend

nsend allows you to send a text message to another user on the NetWare server. This command is functionally similar to the NetWare command **send**.

Available nsend switches:

-S *server*	specify the file server
-U *username*	specify the logon name to use
-P *password*	specify the password to use during authentication
-n	the specified account has no password, do not prompt me
user	the name of the user to send the message to
'*message*'	the message to be sent. Single quotes are used, not double

For example, if I wish to send the user Sean a message I would enter the command:

```
nsend -S talsin -U cbrenton -P bovine sean 'Time to go
get some salad!'
```

nwfsinfo

nwfsinfo is used to collect information from a NetWare server. It can report what the server believes to be the current time, as well as version and connection information.

Available nwfsinfo switches:

-S *server*	specify the file server
-t	display the server's current data and time
-d	display the server's revision level
-i	display version and connection information

For example, the command:

```
nsend -S talsin -I
```

would produce the following output:

```
Version           4.11 Revision A
Max. Connections  9
currently in use  3
peak connections  3
Max. Volumes      255
SFTLevel          2
TTSLevel          1
Accountversion    1
Queueversion      1
```

```
Printversion      0
Virt.Consolvers.  1
RestrictionLevel  1
```

nwpasswd

nwpasswd allows a user on a Linux system to change their password on a NetWare server. It functions in an identical manner to the NetWare **setpass** command.

Available nwpasswd switches:

-S *server*	specify the file server
-U *username*	specify the logon name to use
-h	print out a brief help file including available switches

For example, the command string:

```
nwpasswd -S talsin -U cbrenton
```

would prompt me to enter the current password for the account cbrenton on Talsin. It will then prompt me twice for the new password I wish to use. If I have correctly entered the current password, it will be replaced by the new one. The utility does not warn me up front that I entered the original password incorrectly. This is to make password guessing more difficult.

nwuserlist

nwuserlist is used to produce a list of users that are currently logged on to the system. This utility is functionally equivalent to userlist on NetWare 3.*x* and nlist user /A /B on NetWare 4.*x*.

Available nwuserlist switches:

-S *server*	specify the file server
-U *username*	specify the logon name to use
-P *password*	specify the password to use during authentication
-n	the specified account has no password, do not prompt me
-a	displays the network and MAC address of the attached user

For example, the command:

```
nwuserlist -S talsin -U cbrenton -P bovine -a
```

would produce the following output:

```
Conn  User name          Station Address              Login time
--------------------------------------------------------------------------
  1: TALSIN.testing    32F478CB:000000000001:4007 Wed Jun 25 12:01:11 1997
  2: TALSIN.testing    32F478CB:000000000001:4040 Thu Jun 26 15:01:00 1997
  3: NOT_LOGGED_IN      32F478CB:000000000001:4043 Thu Jun 26 15:01:00 1997
  4: UNIX_SERVICE_HAN 32F478CB:000000000001:0000 Wed Jun 25 12:01:32 1997
  5: UNIX_SERVICE_HAN 32F478CB:000000000001:0000 Wed Jun 25 12:01:32 1997
  6: ADMIN              00008023:0080C885687C:400C Thu Jun 26 16:06:56 1997
  7: ADMIN              00008023:0020AF13D29A:4002 Thu Jun 26 16:06:33 1997
  8: NOT_LOGGED_IN      00008023:0080C885687C:4010 Thu Jun 26 16:06:55 1997
  9: CBRENTON           0A01010A:000000000001:4004 Thu Jun 26 11:10:00 1997
```

The *.nwclient* File

If you have decided to give non-root users on your Linux system access privileges to work with NetWare connections, you can use the .nwclient file to provide default server, logon name, and password information to most of the utilities.

The period (.) at the beginning of the file name makes this a hidden file. It should have permissions set so that only the owner has read-write access. If you create the file for the user, you will also need to ensure that the user owns the file. This can be accomplished with the following set of commands:

```
chmod 0600 .nwclient
chown username .nwclient
chgrp username .nwclient
```

The syntax of the file is pretty straightforward. Each server entry is entered as follows:

```
server/username password
```

If the account has no password you can simply enter a dash (-). If you do not want to have password information stored in a file (always a bad idea), you can omit password and the user will be prompted for it when they execute a utility. An example .nwclient file could look similar to the following. Any lines starting with the pound sign (#) are comments:

```
# This is a .nwclient for connecting to the server Talsin
talsin/cbrenton bovine
```

If my account had no password, the file would be changed to read:

```
# This is a .nwclient for connecting to the server Talsin
talsin/cbrenton -
```

If I did not want my password to be stored in the file, I would simply enter:

```
# This is a .nwclient for connecting to the server Talsin
talsin/cbrenton
```

Once this file has been created, and my permissions are set correctly, I can simply enter:

```
ncpmount /home/cbrenton/talsin
```

to mount my NetWare server (assuming the directory /home/cbrenton/ talsin exists), or

```
nwuserlist -a
```

to receive a list of connected users. I no longer require the switches for server name, user name, and password.

I can even create multiple entries in my .nwclient file. Each entry would be placed on its own line within the file. The only drawback is that the first entry is always used by default. In order to use any of the subsequent entries, I will need to use the server name switch (-S) with all commands executed at the command line.

For example, if I have the .nwclient file:

```
# This is a .nwclient for connecting to all NetWare servers
talsin/cbrenton bovine
zeus/cbrenton -
mars/cbrenton bovine
```

the **ncpmount** and **nwuserlist** commands will still produce the same results as they did in the last example. All commands will assume you are referring to the server Talsin. If I wish to mount the server Mars, however, I would need to type:

```
ncpmount -S mars /home/cbrenton/mars
```

Other Mars_nwe Client Tools

The above listed utilities have other switches besides the ones we reviewed. These switches are typically used when you are diagnosing a problem. There are also other utilities besides the ones we covered. We focused on the tools used for creating and administrating connections to a NetWare server. There are also other tools that allow you to search the bindery as well as add and delete user accounts. Check the *man pages* for additional information.

Most Unix systems have online manuals referred to as man pages. The manuals provide command descriptions as well as a listing of available switches and their usage. To access the man pages, use the syntax **man command**, where *command* is the tool or file you need help with.

The Mars_nwe Server Tools

Besides providing client connectivity, mars_nwe even has tools to allow the Linux or UnixWare system to emulate a NetWare 3.1*x* server. Users are allowed to authenticate, process logon scripts, and even print in the same fashion that they would with a regular NetWare server. Because the Unix system is only emulating a NetWare server, however, it can provide client connectivity but cannot execute NetWare Loadable Modules (NLMs).

The caveat with the server tools is that the server requires a full copy of NetWare files to populate login and public directories if you will be using DOS-based clients. These tools are owned by Novell and cannot be included with freely distributed software.

nwserv.conf

The /etc/nwserv.conf file is used to configure our NetWare server. This file contains the parameters used by nwserv during initialization. Most have defaults that will allow the server to startup without errors in most environments.

If you make changes to the nwserv.conf file, you will need to restart nwserv in order for these changes to take effect. Do not do this with NetWare users attached to the system or they will be logged off.

To restart a Unix daemon, log on as **root** and find the process ID the daemon is using with the **ps** command. Then, restart the daemon by typing **kill -HUP** *PID*, where *PID* is the process ID number the daemon is using. This is referred to as sending the daemon a *SIGHUP*.

A brief list of options that can be configured with the nwserv.conf file would be:

- Map Linux directories to NetWare volume names.

- Define the name of the server.

- Set an internal IPX network address.

- Set a frame type to use (802.3 is the default).

- Define IPX routing parameters.

- Set the NetWare server version to display when queried.

- Set user name mappings and password defaults.

- Set printer queue mappings.

- Decide how to deal with watchdogs and get nearest server requests.

The /etc/nwserv.conf file is well commented. You should review this file for a full description of each of these settings, as the available parameters may change with each new version.

nwserv

nwserv is the daemon responsible for allowing our Unix system to look like a NetWare server. During initialization, it looks to the /etc/nwserv.conf file for configuration information. In order to run the process in the background, you need to start it with the ampersand (&) option. The command would appear as follows:

nwserv &

If you are using Red Hat Linux, nwserv is automatically initialized during system startup. You will not need to start nwserv from the command line unless you kill it.

Figure 12.2 shows a portion of a Windows 95 Explorer screen. The system Toby.foobar.com is our Linux system emulating a NetWare server. Note that the fully qualified domain name is used by default for the server name. This can be changed in the nwserv.conf file to any other name you choose. The system is being listed under NetWare Servers, right along side Talsin which is a real IntranetWare system.

FIGURE 12.2

Toby.foobar.com is a Linux system emulating a NetWare server.

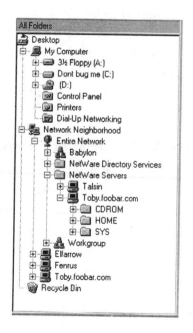

Other Support Files

In order to successfully emulate a NetWare server, there are other required support files besides nwserv. While these files must be loaded, they do not need to be configured. A brief description of each is listed below.

ncpserv   ncpserv is used to manage NCP requests. It is responsible for opening NCP sockets during communications as well as launching new instances of nwconn for each new connection.

nwconn   nwconn is the glue between the connected client and the ncpserv daemon. A single instance of nwconn is created for each user that authenticates to the emulated NetWare server. This daemon is responsible for managing the connection between the client and the ncpserv daemon.

nwbind   nwbind is the daemon responsible for maintaining the bindery files. In order to more closely emulate a NetWare server, mars_nwe uses a set of bindery files for managing account objects.

Appropriate Uses for Mars_nwe

So when can mars_nwe help with our connectivity problems? Mars_nwe is best suited for a mixed NetWare and Unix environment. It is most appropriate for environments that are predominately NetWare, but have a few Unix systems thrown into the mix.

For example, consider the network in Figure 12.3. We have a number of PC clients that are using an IntranetWare server for file and print access. This environment is also using the IntranetWare server as an IPX to IP gateway for Internet access.

Now, let's assume that we wish to create a Web and FTP server so we can provide these services to users on the Internet. Our company manufactures a network-based software product and we wish to use the

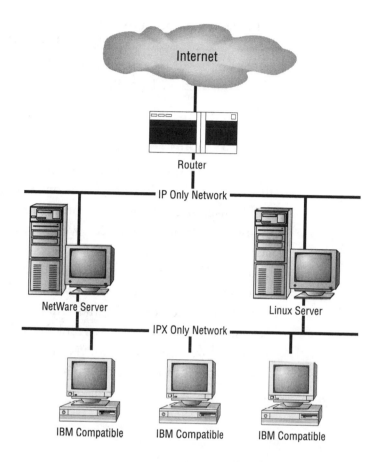

FIGURE 12.3

Using IPX to connect to our NetWare and Linux servers

Web and FTP server for publishing software patches and updates as well as technical documents. We also wish to provide inbound FTP access so that our clients can drop off trace files when they require technical support.

We do not want to add these services to the IntranetWare server as it is already overloaded with a number of other NLMs. Also, we compile our software over the network to a shared drive on the server, so the server must be able to respond to local file requests as quickly as possible. There are also some security concerns with providing any type of Internet access to our corporate server.

In this situation, Linux may be just the thing to fill all of our requirements. We can use the included Web and FTP server for servicing our Internet users. Mars_nwe can be used by local clients to save and retrieve files to this system. This allows us to maintain our internal network using only IPX.

What About Windows NT?

At the time of this writing, there is no port of mars_nwe available for the Windows NT platform, nor is one expected in the near future. If we will be using an NT server in our mixed network environment for providing file and printer services, we will need to add a second protocol to our network.

If the NT server will not be providing file services, but rather acting as an application server, we may still be okay. For example, if we were to add an NT server to the above described network for running Lotus Notes, we could use NT's NwLink IPX/SPX Compatible Transport Protocol for supporting Lotus Notes communications. It is the NT file system that cannot share information using IPX only (NETBIOS over IPX is required).

The SAMBA Suite

The SAMBA suite is a set of client and server tools for both accessing and advertising file and printer shares. Shares are used by Windows NT, Windows 95, LAN Manager, and OS/2 when exchanging information. Connectivity is supplied by the NetBIOS and NetBEUI protocols, including encapsulation of NetBIOS over IP.

The SAMBA suite is public domain and directly supports over a dozen different flavors of Unix. If you are using the Red Hat version of Linux, SAMBA is already loaded with a minimal configuration. If you do not have a pre-installed version of SAMBA, you can retrieve it from a number of different FTP and Web sites on the Internet. You will then have to tune the make file for your specific flavor of Unix and compile the source code.

There is even a version of SAMBA for IntranetWare. This was developed by Novell Consulting Services as a tool for migrating to IntranetWare from NT or LAN Manager. While it is still considered beta code at the time of this writing, it does allow a 4.1 or later NetWare server to advertise file and printer shares just like an NT server.

Through SAMBA, we can provide both file and printer sharing to all of our NOSes using a common protocol and service.

Using SAMBA to Access Shares from Unix

There are a number of SAMBA tools specifically designed to allow a Unix system to access file shares located on a remote server. The remote server can be Windows NT, Windows 95, or even another Unix system. If the remote server is advertising shares, the SAMBA client tools allow a Unix system to access them.

smbclient

The smbclient is used to access remote file shares. Once authenticated, the interface is very similar in appearance to FTP. A command line interface is provided for transferring files between the two systems. While not as elegant as the smbmount command, it is functional nonetheless.

Available smbclient switches:

sharename	complete share name path such as \\server\share
-U *username*	logon user name
password	logon password
-L	list all known servers and shares

You may need to play with the syntax for the share name in order to successfully connect to a remote system. For example, given the share name:

```
\\server\share
```

I found that in order to successfully access an NT system (workstation or server), I needed to enter the file share as:

\\\\\server\\share

Keep this difference in syntax in mind while using this utility. In this example, I will use the syntax that is normally associated with a share name (the first version). You may need to modify the examples accordingly.

If I am performing a logon to a system that configures share level passwords (such as Windows 95), I would use the **password** switch. If I am performing a logon to a system that uses logon accounts (such as Windows NT), I would use the -U switch.

For example, if I wanted to connect to the NT server Talsin to access the share notes, I would enter the command string:

smbclient \\talsin\\notes -U cbrenton

This command string will prompt me for a password and then present me with the **smb** command prompt. If I omit the **user name** switch, my user logon name for the Linux system is passed along in its place. If my password is "bovine," I can pass this along in the command string by typing:

smbclient \\talsin\\notes -U cbrenton%bovine

The percent sign after the logon name is required to let the system know that the remainder of the line is the password. There is no other switch to indicate this.

Some systems that are advertising shares require that the logon name, password, or both be entered in full capitalization. Play with these values to see what works best in your particular environment.

If I wanted to connect to the Windows 95 system ElfArrow and access the share named quake, which has a file system password of "tombstone," I would enter:

smbclient \\elfarrow\quake%tombstone

Our final switch, **-L**, will query a server as to what shares it has available. It will also query the system's browser to see what other shares the server has discovered out on the network. For example, the command string:

smbclient -L talsin

would produce the following output:

```
Domain=[BABYLON] OS=[Windows NT 4.0] Server=[NT LAN Manager 4.0]

Server=[TALSIN] User=[] Workgroup=[BABYLON] Domain=[]
```

Sharename	Type	Comment
ADMIN$	Disk	Remote Admin
C$	Disk	Default share
IPC$	IPC	Remote IPC
notes	Disk	
TEMP	Disk	

```
This machine has a browse list:
```

Server	Comment
ELFARROW	CHRIS BRENTON
FENRUS	CHRIS BRENTON
TANGNEY	TEST1
TALSIN	
THOTH	TEST2
TUTTLE	TEST3

```
This machine has a workgroup list:

    Workgroup              Master
    ---------              -------
    BABYLON                TALSIN
```

From this list, we can see what shares the server Talsin has available. We can also see what other servers are on the network advertising shares and could query each one of them directly.

NOTE The Comment field is the equivalent of the Computer Description on Windows 95.

smbmount

While the smbclient allows us to transfer files between the Unix system and systems offering file shares, it does not exactly provide transparent access to the file system. For this type of access we need to use the smbmount utility. The smbmount utility is functionally identical to the ncpmount utility, but the switches are slightly different.

Available smbmount switches:

share name	share entered in the format //server/share
mount point	the directory to which we wish to attach the fileshare
-I *server*	the server where the share is located
-U *username*	the user name to use during logon
-P *password*	the password to use during logon
-n	the logon name has no password, do not prompt for one
-h	print a simple help message listing available switches

For example, if I wish to mount the file share \\talsin\notes to the directory /mnt/talsin using a logon name of "cbrenton" and a password of "bovine," I would enter the command:

```
smbmount //talsin/notes /mnt/talsin -I talsin -U cbrenton
-P bovine
```

Notice that the command expects the share slashes to face in the opposite direction. The command also requires the -I switch, even though the server name is specified as part of the share.

smbumount

smbumount is used to remove file shares accessed with the utility smbmount. It is functionally identical to the ncpumount command. The only required switch is the mount point where the share is located. For example, to remove the mounted share created in the last example, I would type:

```
smbumount /mnt/talsin
```

Using SAMBA to Create Shares from Unix

In addition to client services, SAMBA can allow a Unix system to advertise both file and printer shares as well. There are three files that provide this connectivity. They are:

- nmbd

- smbd

- smb.conf

nmbd

nmbd controls the NetBIOS communication of the system. It is run as a daemon and is responsible for listening on the NetBIOS port for name service requests. When a name service request is received, nmbd responds with the system's IP address. It is also responsible for maintaining the browser informing which catalogs NetBIOS names within a given workgroup.

Available nmbd switches:

-D	tells nmbd to run as a daemon
-H *lmhost_file*	path and name of the NetBIOS host name file
-d *number*	run in the debug level specified by *number*. 0-5 are valid
-l *log_file_base*	specify the base name for the log file
-n *NetBIOS_name*	specify the NetBIOS name for this system if the host name should not be used
-p *port_number*	change the default port number to listen on
-s *config_file*	specify the location of smb.conf if it is not located in /etc

smbd

smbd is the daemon responsible for all file and printer share services. Once a client locates a SAMBA server through nmbd, it is smbd that takes care of servicing the clients file and printer requests.

While smbd will retrieve most of its configuration information from the file /etc/smbd.conf, it does have a few switches available to override the setting in that file.

Available **smbd** switches:

-D	tells nmbd to run as a daemon
-O *socket_option*	tune communication parameters
-a	overwrites the log files. The default is to append
-d *number*	run in the debug level specified by *number*. 0-5 are valid
-l *log_file_base*	specify the base name for the log file
-p *port_number*	change the default port number to listen on
-s *config_file*	specify the location of smb.conf if it is not located in /etc

smb.conf

The smb.conf file is used to configure nmbd and smbd during initialization. You should configure this file before loading the two daemons. If you makes changes to this file during server operation, you must send a sighup to both of the daemons. This will force them to reread the configuration file.

smb.conf supports too many switch options to list here. The man pages for this file is over 50 pages. Instead, we will look at only the most commonly used commands. Consult the man pages for a complete description. On a Red Hat Linux system, you can also review the documentation which is located in the directory /usr/doc/samba-revision, where *revision* is the revision number of the version of SAMBA you are using.

Global Settings Global settings are used to configure the overall SAMBA environment as opposed to configuring a specific share. Global settings are listed with the `smb.conf` file under the section heading [global].

`load printers = yes/no` Defines if the printcap files should be read, and printers available through lpd should be advertised as printer shares.

`guest account = username` Allows you to specify the valid guest account to use when browsing the shares. This must be a valid account name and should only have minimal system rights. Usually setting this to ftp will allow shares to be accessed.

`workgroup = Workgroup` Allows you to specify the name of the workgroup that this system should join. Workgroups are similar to domains in that they represent a collection of NetBIOS system. Workgroups differ from domains in that there is no central account administration—all logon names and passwords are managed by each individual system.

Home Directories   When a user authenticates to SAMBA, you have the option to allow them to access their home directory as a share. The directory location is retrieved from the `/etc/passwd` file which is used system-wide to define logon names and passwords. Home directory settings are listed with the `smb.conf` file under the section heading [homes].

Other Shares   You can create shares to any portion of the file system that you wish. When creating a share, begin the section with a share name enclosed in brackets, like this: [public]. After the share name, specify any parameters you wish to have applied to that share, with one command listed per line.

Share Settings   The following is a brief list of some of the commands that can be used to manipulate a share.

browseable = yes/no Identifies if this share is visible to a client which is browsing, or if the share can only be accessed by using the Universal Naming Convention (UNC). For example, to access the share named public which has browsing disabled, you must access it by entering UNC\\SERVER\public. It will not show up in a browse list.

create mode = number Allows you to assign default permissions to files when they are created on the SAMBA share. The value for this field uses the same numeric format as the chmod command. See the man pages for more information.

only guest = yes Users accessing this share will have guest level access only. If the file permissions are set correctly, this can be used so that users can see the files in a directory, but they do not have read or write access.

path = share directory path Defines the directory that will be accessed when a user accesses the advertised share name. For example, if I create a share named public, and I set the path statement equal to /usr/expenses/template, then accessing the share public will put me directly into the template directory. I am not allowed to navigate up the directory structure, only down.

public = yes/no Defines if a share is open to public access. When this value is set to yes, users who do not have an account on the system will receive access based on the attributes of the defined guest account.

valid users = username Only allow users with the specified logon name to access the share. Multiple logon names can be specified, separated by spaces.

writable = yes/no Defines if a share can be accessed with read/write permissions or if the file system should be considered read only. What defines the level of access a user receives is a combination of this setting and the permissions assigned to the user's Unix account, whichever is lower.

For example, if a user accesses a share marked as writable, but their Unix account has read-only permissions, the user will receive read-only access to the share.

Figure 12.4 shows an example `smb.conf` file with heading and settings put into place. This file sets some global settings, and advertises two shares—home and public. When a user sees their home directory in the browser list, it will be identified with their logon name. This is a minimal configuration. There are many other options available for configuring the system.

FIGURE 12.4

A sample *smb.conf* file

```
;A Sample smb.conf file with
;only a few configured options
[global]
    workgroup = Support
    guest account = ftp

[homes]
    browseable = yes
    writable = yes
    create mode = 0750

[public]
    path = /home/samba
    public = yes
    writable = yes
```

Using SAMBA to Create Shares on NetWare

Along with Unix, there is even a set of SAMBA tools available for NetWare versions 4.1 and above. These tools have been made available through Novell Consulting Services. While their original intent was to ease the migration path from LAN Manager or Windows NT to a NetWare environment, they can be used even if you do not plan on migrating services to a new platform.

At this writing, these tools are still considered beta code and can be a bit unstable. For example, the simple act of unloading `samba.nlm` will cause it to refuse to release some memory resources. Also, if you load `nbns.nlm` without the **-G** switch (even though it does not actually use it), `nbns.nlm` will cause a race condition and use up 100% of the processor's time.

If you are using IntranetWare, both of these conditions are recoverable. The garbage collection will eventually return the memory resources to the pool and the race condition will be stopped after a minute of hogging the processor. If you are still using 4.1, however, the race condition will bring the server to its knees.

Bearing in mind the above disclaimer, let's look at how to install and configure SAMBA for use with an IntranetWare system.

Retrieving the SAMBA Files for IntranetWare

The SAMBA files for IntranetWare are available from the Novell Web site. If you perform a search on the key word SAMBA, you will be linked to a document which will let you retrieve the archive. The archive should include:

- `samba.nlm` The equivalent of `smbd` for IntranetWare
- `nwglue.nlm` API layer to allow NetBIOS based access to the server
- `nbns.nlm` The equivalent of `nmbd` for IntranetWare
- `netbeui.nlm` Support for the NetBEUI protocol
- `tcpbeui.nlm` Support for NetBEUI over IP
- `smb.cfg` The equivalent of `smb.conf` for IntranetWare

Preparing the IntranetWare System

There are a number of steps to preparing an IntranetWare server for use with the `samba.nlm`. Do not simply load it and hope for the best. There is little (if any) documentation included with the above archive. With this in mind, we will step through the exact process required to install the files.

Preparing the Directory Structure   SAMBA for IntranetWare is hard coded to use a specific directory structure. If you do not duplicate this structure exactly, it can become very upset and retaliate by causing a server abend.

With this in mind, you will want to create a SAMBA directory named SAMBA directly off the root of sys. Within this new directory, create another directory called locks. You will also need to create a directory named tmp off of the root of sys.

Modifying Needed Support Files   In the sys:\etc directory, you will want to check your hosts file to ensure that it has an entry for the loopback address, as well as the system itself. The entries would appear similar to the following:

```
127.0.0.1      loopback localhost lb      #loopback address
10.1.1.10      hostname                    #IP address of
                                           this system
```

The format of the hosts file is to list IP addresses in the first column, host names in the second, and comments in the third. Columns should be separated by tabs, not spaces. The comment field should begin with the pound sign (#).

You should replace the entry 10.1.1.10 with the IP address of your server. Also, replace the hostname entry with the name of your server.

You will also need to create two empty files in the sys:\SAMBA directory. Name these files log.nmb and log.smb. These files will be used to record any run time messages or errors.

Placing the Files in Their Correct Locations   Copy the following files to the sys:\system directory:

- nwglue.nlm

- nbns.nlm

- netbeui.nlm

- tcpbeui.nlm

Copy the following two files to the sys:\SAMBA directory:

- samba.nlm

- smb.cfg

If your archive file did not contain a smb.cfg file (which mine did not), you can create one by using the parameters described above for the smb.conf file. In fact, the easiest way to create it would be to obtain a smb.conf file from a Unix system and modify the settings as you require.

Starting up SAMBA for IntranetWare

Load the support files in the exact order listed below:

- nwglue.nlm

- nbns.nlm G *workgroup*

- samba.nlm

- netbeui.nlm

- tcpbeui.nlm

nbns should be loaded with the workgroup switch, even though nbns appears not to use it. Setting this switch seemed to resolve race conditions with the NLM. This problem should be fixed in later releases. I still had to use the `workgroup=` switch under global settings in the `smb.cfg` file. nbns appears to support many of the same switches as `nmbd`.

Once the support files are loaded, you should now be able to advertise file and printer shares located on the IntranetWare server. Figure 12.5 shows the IntranetWare server Talsin advertising shares the same as an NT server, or a Unix system running SAMBA would do.

FIGURE 12.5

An IntranetWare server advertising file shares

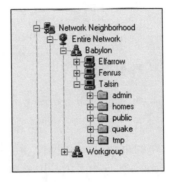

Appropriate Uses for SAMBA

SAMBA appears to be our best bet for supporting IntranetWare, Windows NT, and Unix, using a single protocol and a single set of services. Through SAMBA, we are able to gain access to file and print services on all of our NOSes, including many flavors of Unix.

This is not without its drawbacks, however. First, we standardized on IP for a networking protocol. While IP is extremely efficient, it is not nearly as efficient when providing file services as IPX and NCP. If our network relies on heavy NetWare use, we may actually increase traffic by losing the use of packet burst.

Also, SAMBA is still beta code on the NetWare platform and is not the most stable software available. There is a very real possibility that it would conflict with NLMs produced by third party manufacturers. For example, if you are running a server-based backup program and use it to back up workstations or other servers, SAMBA may not be able to use NetBEUI to communicate with these systems. SAMBA may expect to be able to use IPX because this is the default protocol on all NetWare servers.

So when would using SAMBA be a good idea? Clearly it would have to be an environment that does not rely heavily on NetWare servers. If you are running a mixed NT and Unix environment, or an environment that only has one or two NetWare systems that receive only a peripheral amount of traffic, SAMBA may be just the thing to standardize your network on a single protocol and service.

Summary

You should now have a much better idea of what connectivity options are available in a mixed server environment. By using the tools described in this chapter, you can help to reduce the number of protocols running on your network.

In the next chapter we will begin to take a look at how you can test the health of your network to isolate and resolve problems when they arise.

CHAPTER

13

Troubleshooting Tools

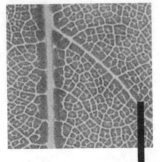

I n this chapter we will take a look at some of the testing tools available to ensure that our network remains healthy. We will start by looking at how to certify that our cabling is correct and work our way up to tools that can monitor and diagnose problems at the network and transport layers.

In an attempt to organize this information, we shall break devices up into five categories; they are:

- basic cable checkers

- cable testers

- handheld diagnostic tools

- network monitoring tools

- full network analyzers

We will also include a section on collecting diagnostic and performance information from network devices such as switches and routers. Finally, we will look at Novell's LANAlyzer program, a common network monitoring tool.

Each one of the listed tools is capable of supplying its own unique body of information regarding your network's health. A well-equipped tool kit will contain tools from more than one category. For example, a top of the line network analyzer will not report on the same information as a basic cable checker. There is some information you can collect from a $50 cable checker that a $4,000 analyzer cannot tell you.

Basic Cable Checker

Basic cable checkers are just that, they do little more than report on whether your cabling can provide basic connectivity. A small voltage is applied to each conductor in the cable. The checker then verifies if the voltage can be detected on the other end. Most checkers will also ensure that this voltage cannot be detected on any other conductors running through the same cable. When using a cable checker, you must disconnect the cable from the network prior to testing.

Figure 13.1 shows a basic cable checker. The LEDs provide a pass/fail condition on each of the tests performed. Performing a test requires little more than attaching the cable to the unit and pressing the test button. A good cable checker will have two separate components, one for each end of the cable. This is useful if you need to test cabling that runs through ceilings or walls.

Look for tests that do the following in a thinnet cable checker:

- verify connectivity on the center conductor

- verify connectivity along the shielding

- verify that the conductor and the shield are not shorted together

Look for tests that do the following in a twisted-pair cable checker:

- verify connectivity through each wire

- verify that wires are paired correctly

- verify that wires are not shorted together

- identify when the transmit and receive pairs are not crossed (cross cable)

Most cable checkers light up a series of either four or eight lights sequentially when performing these tests.

FIGURE 13.1

A basic cable checker

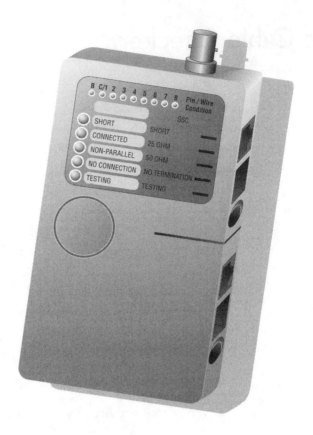

Topology Wiring Requirements

Each topology uses its own set of wire pair requirements. We covered the pairs used by 10 Mb Ethernet back in Chapter 2. In that chapter, we also mentioned that all pairs should be wired in case a new topology is introduced later. The twisted-pair wires used by other topologies is as follows:

- Ethernet 10Base-T uses pins 1–2, 3–6.

- Ethernet 100Base-Tx uses pins 1–2, 3–6.

- Ethernet 100Base-T4 uses pins 1–2, 3–6, 4–5, 7–8.

- Token-Ring uses pins 3–6, 4–5.

- 100VG-AnyLAN uses pins 1–2, 3–6, 4–5, 7–8.

- ATM uses pins 1–2, 7–8.

So long as all eight wires (four pairs) are connected, you should be able to operate any of the above topologies.

Because it uses light as a transmission medium, there are no basic cable checkers for fiber cable. If you have cables that have been previously certified with a tester and you need a simple tool for testing the path of wire runs, use a Mag flashlight. By shining a flashlight in one end of the cable, you should be able to see the light at the other end.

Cable checkers are fairly inexpensive, ranging in price from $50 to $100. In fact, if you are handy with a soldering iron, it is not all that difficult to build your own cable tester with a peg board and some batteries. While not as pretty as a professional tester, it will do in a pinch if you're tracing a wire fault at 2:00AM on a Sunday morning. Just say, "MacGyver."

Cable Testers

A cable tester will include all of the tests performed by a cable checker, but will also include performance testing to certify a cable's use at a specific topology speed.

Along with checking for shorts and opens, a cable tester will test:

- wire length to ensure that the conductor(s) are not too long

- attenuation or signal loss along the cable

- interference from other conductors known as Near-End Cross Talk (NEXT)

- the impedance (AC resistance) of thinnet terminators

- if there is active network traffic on the cable

A cable tester will usually have an LCD display for reporting the above information. Some are even capable of storing test results or powering off the unit if it is not used for a specified period of time. Figure 13.2 shows a typical cable tester. Like the cable checker, the better units are two separate components so that new and existing wiring may be tested.

FIGURE 13.2

A typical cable tester

What separates cable testers is how they check attenuation and NEXT. The Electronic Industry Association and Telecommunications Industry Association (EIA/TIA) are responsible for setting the category standards for cables. In order to certify a cable for CAT 3, the attenuation and NEXT test should be performed from 1MHz to 16MHz in 1 MHz steps. Because the level of signal loss or interference can change with frequency, a range of frequencies must be used to certify that the cable is acceptable over the entire range.

In order to certify a cable for CAT 5 use, the test frequency range must be extended up to 100MHz. A 1MHz frequency step should still be used. These parameters are important because there is a big difference in frequency range between a CAT 3 and a CAT 5 tester.

Just because you are using CAT 5 cables, connectors, and patch panels, it does not mean that your network will support 100 Mb operation per the CAT 5 specification. You must actually certify your network for use at this speed with a CAT 5 cable tester. Using CAT 5 hardware simply gives you the ability to create a 100 Mb network.

For example, NEXT is usually caused by crossed or crushed pairs at the connector end of the wire. Because you install most connectors on site while wiring the network, there is no way to detect this condition during the manufacturing process of each individual component. The only way to catch this condition is to perform a CAT 5 test on-site, after the wiring is installed.

Because NEXT is most likely to occur at the connector, both ends of the cable should be tested.

When selecting a twisted-pair cable tester, ensure that it performs attenuation and NEXT testing all the way up to 100MHz if you wish to certify at a CAT 5 level. While these units are more expensive than the 16MHz units, it is the only way to ensure that your network is fit for 100 Mb operation.

Faulty cables can cause some strange intermittent problems. For example, I have seen networks with faulty wiring function properly 85% of the time. During the other 15%, during heavy traffic loads, network users have experienced problems with connection drops or excessively slow data-transfer speeds. An administrator's first reaction, when attempting to diagnose connectivity, is to start checking server settings, driver revision levels, and network cards. It is not until all other options are exhausted that we think to check our cables. By certifying the cables beforehand, we can eliminate them as a potential problem area.

Most cable testing is performed with the cable disconnected from any active network devices. Despite this, a good cable tester should have a method of detecting network traffic. This can help when diagnosing a connectivity problem as it gives a quick indication as to whether a network drop is live.

Testing Fiber Cable

Because fiber uses light, not electricity to conduct network signals, it does not require the same testing parameters as twisted pair or thinnet. Fiber cable testers come in two varieties, one for checking multimode operation and one for testing single mode. The multimode version is the most popular as this is the communication method most widely implemented.

A fiber cable tester will check for signal loss along the length of the cable. This may be indicated with a pass/fail LED, an illuminated bar graph, or an LCD display that provides an absolute numerical value. The bar graph and numerical value are most useful as they give a quantitative reading.

For example, let's assume you have a fiber cable run that passes through a series of patch panels. When you test the circuit from end to end, you find out it fails. When you test each of the wire runs individually, you find that each one passes.

Obviously you have a connection along the run that is only marginally acceptable. If your tester has a pass/fail LED, you may not be able to isolate the problem. By using a unit that presents an absolute power level, you can determine which connection is causing an unusual amount of signal drop.

Because of the additional features, cable testers run a bit more in price than cable checkers. Expect to pay $200 to $500 for a CAT 3 cable tester. CAT 5 or fiber cable testers run in the $600–$1,200 range.

Handheld Diagnostic Tools

The handheld diagnostic tools can be viewed as a cross between a cable tester and a network analyzer. They not only include all the features normally associated with a cable tester, but can produce topology and even a minimal amount of protocol information as well.

Some tools that fall into this category are designed to troubleshoot a specific network environment. For example, one diagnostic tool may check dropped connections and get nearest server requests in a NetWare environment, while an IP diagnostic tool will be able to detect duplicate IP addresses and ping systems by IP address or host name. It is rare to find a tool that can combine these features.

At a minimum, a good handheld diagnostic tool should be able to:

- test connectivity to a remote host by MAC address
- detect transmission errors
- report frames per second and network utilization
- report on the number of collisions detected
- detect which protocols are in use on the network
- report on advertised routing information
- store test results for later retrieval

Figure 13.3 shows the display of a Fluke LANMeter. This unit has the unique ability to be placed in line between a network system and the hub so that communication between the two can be monitored.

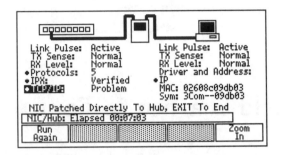

F I G U R E   13.3

A display from a Fluke LANMeter

Handheld diagnostic tools tend to be very expensive. A cheap unit will run around $800 while a top of the line model may run closer to $5,000, which is what you would pay for a full network analyzer.

Network Monitoring Tools

Network monitoring tools are used for the day-to-day monitoring of network performance. They are usually implemented as a software product that runs on a standard desktop machine or server. The packet captures which have been presented as figures throughout this book were generated with Novell's LANAlyzer product, which is a network monitoring tool.

The main focus of a network monitoring tool is the collection of network usage statistics. Unlike a handheld diagnostic tool or a network analyzer that is designed to be used when a problem has been detected, the network monitor is expected to be run continuously, gathering network data. This does not mean that a handheld tool cannot be left turned on to collect statistics or that a network monitor cannot be used to find and fix a problem, it simply means that each tool has its place in the grand scheme of keeping your network operational.

A good network monitor should be able to:

- report frames per second (fps) and network utilization

- graph overall network usage in fps and utilization

- export network usage statistics in a spreadsheet format

- report on network usage on a per station basis

- have some method of assigning station names to MAC addresses

- detect transmission errors

- report on single and multiple collisions

- detect which protocols are in use on the network

- perform and save frame captures

- allow frame captures to be filtered so that specific portions can be analyzed

In short, a network monitoring tool should be able to provide all the required information to plan short- and long-term network design changes.

Network monitors vary widely in price. For example, Microsoft's Network Monitor Tool is included with Windows NT Server. There are also many shareware or freeware monitoring tools available. In contrast to this, Novell's LANAlyzer product sells for a street price between $800 and $1,000.

When using a software-based network analyzer, be sure that your NIC card and driver is capable of passing all network frames up through the protocol stack. For example, part of the reason that a 3COM Etherlink III card can communicate so quickly is that it drops all error frames at the data link level. This prevents them from being passed up the communication stack and recorded by the network monitor. Your vendor should be able to tell you which NIC cards they have certified for use with their product.

Network Analyzers

Network analyzers are used for troubleshooting network problems that occur between the data link and transport layers. They will not diagnose physical layer problems. For example, a network analyzer will not tell you that your cable has an attenuation problem or swapped wire pairs. However, a good network analyzer will show you just about everything else that occurs on your network.

Network analyzers are usually implemented as both software and hardware. This is because a network analyzer may be required to capture every frame of data in an extremely busy networking environment, a task that the average NIC card was not specifically designed to do. By designing the network interface to be used for capturing data instead of conducting communications, a vendor can ensure that their analyzer can keep up with even the busiest of networks.

Along with the features provided by a good network monitor, network analyzers will also provide advanced diagnostic features. They will not only report on a problem when it is found, but they will tell you how to fix it.

Figure 13.4 shows the advanced diagnostic ability of the Network General Sniffer. The screen capture indicates that it has detected a delay in transmission between a server and a workstation. It describes what may be causing the problem, and possible remedies to resolve it. While most network monitors would be able to document this delayed transmission time, they would not have flagged it as a potential problem.

In addition to advanced diagnostics, some analyzers have advanced monitoring abilities as well. ExpertPharaoh from GN Nettest (formally Azure) has the ability to monitor up to eight separate network segments at the same time. These segments can all be the same topology or a mixture of different LAN and WAN topologies. Figure 13.5 shows a screen capture from the DuoTrack version, which is simultaneously monitoring two different LAN topologies.

FIGURE 13.4

The Network General
Sniffer

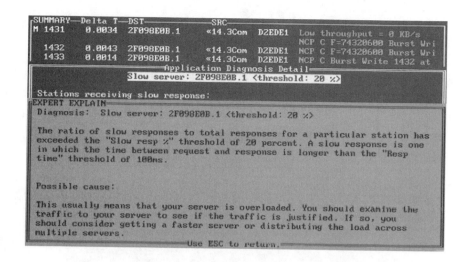

FIGURE 13.5

GN Nettest's
ExpertPharoah monitoring
two different topologies

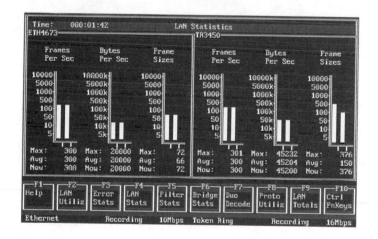

A good network analyzer is the most expensive piece of trouble-shooting hardware you can purchase. Depending on the unit's advanced diagnostic abilities, the number of protocols and services it can identify, and the number of segments it can simultaneously monitor, you can expect to pay between $2,000 and $18,000.

Monitoring through Network Hardware

When purchasing network hardware such as bridges, switches, and routers, one of the features to pay close attention to is the hardware's ability to collect statistics and record network errors. Consider the network design shown in Figure 13.6.

FIGURE 13.6

A switched network design

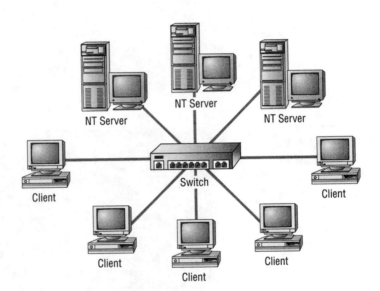

The figure shows a fully switched network. Each server and client has a dedicated connection to the switch. As we discussed in Chapter 4, this dedication creates a separate collision domain off of each port on the switch that only includes two systems—the switch itself and the attached system.

Now, let's assume we go out and spend $12,000 on a shiny new network analyzer. We plug it into the switch and proceed to see… nothing, or at least almost nothing. We can monitor network broadcast but cannot see any of the unicast communications. This is because a switch acts as a traffic cop and isolates unicast traffic to the ports that are actually carrying on a conversation. Our analyzer relies on the shared media properties of a

LAN topology in order to monitor communications. A switch segregates these communications, so, in effect, our media is no longer shared. We are unable to monitor network traffic with our analyzer.

To remedy this, we could purchase hubs and cascade them off of the switch. This would provide more than one connection to each switch port and give us a place to plug in our network analyzer. The problem with this configuration is that we can only monitor the traffic on the port we are attached to.

Referring back to Figure 13.6, if we plug each of our servers into a separate hub and then plug each of these hubs into the switch, we can now attach our analyzer to one of the hubs as well in order to monitor traffic. The problem with this configuration is that we can only monitor traffic to one server at a time. While we are monitoring communications to the first server, the second could be overloading from excessive traffic and we would never see it. Also, once we install a hub, we lose the ability to have the servers communicating in full-duplexed mode.

This is why having the switch report on network statistics is so important—it is the central communication point in the network and has the best chance of collecting the most statistics.

Monitoring Features to Look For

So what kind of monitoring ability should you look for in a switch? A switch should collect many of the same statistics that a network monitoring tool does. This will help you to isolate problem areas and determine which collision domains are in need of the most attention.

Figure 13.7 shows a screen capture from a Cisco Catalyst switch. Peak throughput levels are being reported on a daily basis. These statistics can help us to monitor traffic patterns to see if this portion of the network can be a potential performance gate for communications. This particular switch has 25 switched 10 Mb Ethernet ports and a switched connection to a 100 Mb FDDI ring for a theoretical maximum throughput of 350 Mb. As you can see, our daily utilization levels have been peaking out around 10 Mb. In other words, this switch is not even breaking a sweat.

A Cisco Catalyst switch
reporting daily
throughput peaks

```
            EtherSwitch 1400 - Bandwidth Usage Report
      --------------------Settings-----------------
      Current bandwidth usage                    0 Mbps
      [T] Capture time interval                  24 hour(s)

      ----------Last 12 Capture Intervals---------
      Start Capture Time      Peak Time           Peak Mbps
*  1. Mon Dec 16 00:00:00    Mon Dec 16 15:13:16    9
   2. Sun Dec 15 00:00:00    Sun Dec 15 17:53:28    8
   3. Sat Dec 14 00:00:00    Sat Dec 14 01:36:51    14
   4. Fri Dec 13 00:00:00    Fri Dec 13 00:29:50    12
   5. Thu Dec 12 00:00:00    Thu Dec 12 22:55:38    11
   6. Wed Dec 11 00:00:00    Wed Dec 11 22:48:04    15
   7. Tue Dec 10 00:00:00    Tue Dec 10 22:50:39    11
   8. Mon Dec 09 00:00:00    Mon Dec 09 15:55:22    13
   9. Sun Dec 08 00:00:00    Sun Dec 08 17:56:53    5
  10. Sat Dec 07 00:00:00    Sat Dec 07 00:28:15    18
  11. Fri Dec 06 00:00:00    Fri Dec 06 23:54:38    13
  12.
      --------------------Actions------------------
      [C] Clear table            [R] Reset current(*) entry
      [X] Exit to previous menu

Enter Selection:
```

Figure 13.8 shows the same switch reporting on the number of frames it has processed on a per port basis. The number of frames processed is from the last time the switch was restarted or this statistic screen was reset. This is valuable information that we can use to load balance the network and improve overall performance.

Per port statistics for the
number of frames
processed

```
       EtherSwitch 1400 - Utilization Statistics Report (Frame counts)

           Receive   Forward   Transmit        Receive   Forward   Transmit
          ------------------------------       ------------------------------
  1 :          0         0          0    13:  42256216  42256216   43731720
  2 :          0         0          0    14:   1863506   1863506    4531285
  3 :          0         0          0    15:         0         0          0
  4 :          0         0          0    16:         0         0          0
  5 :          0         0          0    17:    590049    590046    3486334
  6 :          0         0          0    18:  11512665  11512665   12877221
  7 :          0         0          0    19:   2352129   2352129    5439965
  8 :    5310680   5310677    8082272    20:   1588048   1582009    4591431
  9 :   10196001  10192530   13189976    21:         0         0          0
 10:    1088154   1088154    4099838    22:  48396860  48396851   49474427
 11:          0         0          0    23:   2126872   2126858    5019374
 12:   72322740  72322740   88197883    24:         0         0    3047675
                                        25:         0         0          0
  A :  235086729*  98289156   88745534*
  B :          0         0          0        *FDDI frame counts

Select [R] Reset all statistics, or [X] Exit to previous menu:
```

For example, let's assume that this switch is connected in the configuration shown in Figure 13.9. Our network servers are located on the FDDI ring, and each workstation is cascaded off of a hub which plugs into an Ethernet switch port.

FIGURE 13.9

Our switch installed in a potential network design

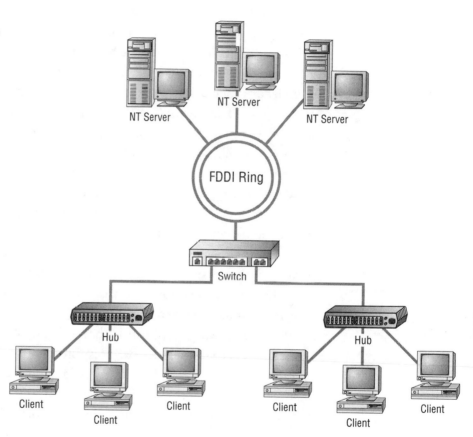

Now that we know what our network looks like, let's refer back to Figure 13.8 and look at the number of frames being processed on each of the Ethernet ports (ports 1–25). According to the report, ports 12, 22, and 13 (in that order) are processing the greatest number of frames. We obviously have some very busy users connected to the hubs off of these ports. Conversely, ports 17, 10, 20, and 14 (in that order) are seeing the least amount of traffic. The ports showing zero traffic are not yet connected to any workstations.

With these statistics in mind, we can now hook up a network monitor or analyzer to the busiest hubs to identify who the heaviest users are. Once these users have been identified, we can move their network connection to one of the quieter hubs.

For example, let's assume we hook up a network monitor to the hub off of port 12 for a few days and notice that the users Gretchen and Grendel are each responsible for 25% of the traffic being generated off of that port. If we move Gretchen to port 17 and Grendel to port 10, we will reduce the amount of traffic being processed by port 12 to half its current level. While still busy, this brings the amount of transmission down to a level that is more in line with the other ports.

While moving these users will increase the amount of traffic passing through ports 17 and 10, these ports are currently seeing very little traffic. Because users on these ports appear to be only occasional network users, they will probably not even notice the increase in traffic.

Why bother to even collect this information and balance the network load? Each collision domain consists of a shared medium; only one user can transmit at any given time. If you have an imbalance, where some ports are processing more traffic than others, you will have some users that experience sluggish network response while others underutilize the amount of available bandwidth. By balancing the network load, you ensure that all users receive the optimal amount of network bandwidth.

There are other clues as to how our network is performing on this screen. For example, look at the number of frames that the switch has received off of each port and compare this value to the number of frames it has forwarded. You will note that there is a discrepancy in quantity off of ports 20, 22, and 23. There are usually two situations which can cause this.

First, there may be stations accessing resources that are located on the same hub. For example, we may have one or more users who have enabled Windows 95 file sharing and have given other users access to their system. To see if this is the case, we could attach a network monitor or analyzer to the hub and see who is advertising services.

The other situation that can prevent a switch from forwarding frames is when it detects a transmission error. We may have a workstation off one of these ports that is generating frames with a bad FCS value. When these errors occur, it is good to have a switch that collects error information as well.

One last note before moving on—you will notice that port 24 has been receiving frames, but has not transmitted any. The Cisco Catalyst has the unique ability to allow one of the ports to operate as a monitoring port. You can configure any of the available Ethernet ports to monitor one or more of the other ports on the switch. This feature can be extremely useful because it allows you to change the port you are monitoring with a simple configuration change. It also allows you to monitor multiple ports simultaneously.

The monitoring port can also extend the capability of your network monitor. For example, we could choose to monitor the FDDI ring, something that LANAlyzer is normally incapable of doing because it does not have any supported FDDI drivers. While we will not be able to monitor topology-specific error conditions, we can at least monitor network utilization and capture frames.

Checking For Errors

Figure 13.10 shows a per port error report for our Cisco switch. If we compare this report to the one shown in Figure 13.8, we can see that the frames that were not forwarded on port 22 were in fact due to errors. This lets us know that out of the three ports that were potential problems, we only need to worry about port 22.

You may also notice that there is a discrepancy between the number of errors reported and the number of frames that were not forwarded by this port. This is because each of the statistic screens can be reset separately.

FIGURE 13.10

A per port error report

```
EtherSwitch 1400 - Exception Statistics Report (Frame counts)

      Receive  Transmit  Security        Receive  Transmit  Security
      Errors   Errors    Violations      Errors   Errors    Violations
     ------------------------------      ------------------------------
  1 :    0        0           0     13:     1        0           0
  2 :    0        0           0     14:     0        0           0
  3 :    0        0           0     15:     0        0           0
  4 :    0        0           0     16:     0        0           0
  5 :    0        0           0     17:     0        0           0
  6 :    0        0           0     18:     0        0           0
  7 :    0        0           0     19:     0        0           0
  8 :    0        0           0     20:     0        0           0
  9 :    0        0           0     21:     0        0           0
 10:     0        0           0     22:  3231        0           0
 11:     0        0           0     23:     0        0           0
 12:     0        0           0     24:     0        0           0
                                    25:     0        0           0

  A :    0*       0*          0
  B :    0        0           0      *FDDI frame counts

Select [R] Reset all statistics, or [X] Exit to previous menu:
```

The report in Figure 13.10 has been collecting information without being reset for a longer period of time than the report in Figure 13.8.

So we know we have a problem off of port 22. We now need to determine what that problem is. Fortunately, the switch will report on advanced statistics on a per port basis, as shown in Figure 13.11. According to this report, we have a workstation generating frames with a bad FCS. We now know we need to monitor the stations off of port 22 with our network analyzer and look for the culprit system. Once identified, we can test the NIC and cables to further isolate the problem.

There are some important lessons here. In a brief session we have learned the following about our network:

■ Three ports are seeing an excessive amount of traffic compared to the rest of the network.

■ Four ports are seeing a small amount of traffic compared to the rest of the network.

■ Users are capable of accessing a local resource from two of the ports.

■ We have a workstation generating frames with a bad CRC.

FIGURE 13.11

Detailed statistics on a
Cisco Catalyst port

```
            EtherSwitch 1400 - Port 22 Statistics Report
        Receive Statistics                     Transmit Statistics
-----------------------------------  ------------------------------------
Total good frames            48397911  Total frames                49474925
Total octets             >  483677286  Total octets              4030247614
Broadcast/multicast frames     116295  Broadcast/multicast frames   2883748
Broadcast/multicast octets   11874806  Broadcast/multicast octets 416724139
Good frames forwarded        48397902  Deferrals                     160762
Frames filtered                     9  Single collisions              22179
Runt frames                      3195  Multiple collisions            21018
No buffer discards                  0  Excessive collisions               0
                                       Queue full discards                0
Errors:                                Errors:
  FCS errors                     3231    Late collisions                  0
  Alignment errors                  0    Excessive deferrals              0
  Giant frames                      0    Jabber errors                    0
  Address violations                0    Other transmit errors            0

Select [A] Port addressing, [C] Configure port,
       [N] Next port, [P] Previous port, [G] Goto port,
       [R] Reset port statistics, or [X] Exit to Main Menu:
```

Because this switch supports telnet access, all this information could have been collected through a remote dial-in session while sitting home in our fuzzy slippers.

If this switch did not have any of the advanced capabilities described above, we would have been forced to move our network analyzer from port to port manually. Assuming we would want to monitor each port for a minimum of one full work day, what we learned in five minutes would have taken us nearly three weeks to determine.

Because a network device (such as a switch) should always be active while a network is in use, it makes the perfect device for gather statistics. It is possible that, when errors occur, your network analyzer may be turned off or monitoring another segment. By collecting error information from the network hardware itself you can be sure you will always be able to catch it.

Monitoring Features to Look For in a Switch

Besides the performance features covered in Chapter 4, a good switch should be able to provide you with the following statistical information and monitoring features:

- overall bandwidth utilization

- utilization on a per port basis

- the number of stations attached to each port

- error reporting on a per port basis, which includes collisions

- a diagnostic port for monitoring one or more switch ports

- remote access to the device through telnet or a Web browser

- a system's MAC address when only one station is attached

Network Monitoring with a Bridge

Because a bridge and a switch are functionally identical (the biggest difference being that a switch has more ports), it is good to look for the same features in a bridge that you do in a switch. The ability to collect meaningful statistics becomes a bit less important because a bridge tends to create larger collision domains. This produces less segmentation, and thus fewer points to be monitored.

The networks we have discussed so far in this chapter have been used to segment our network into many small collision domains. In fact, the first example used only two devices per collision domain. This gave us many different points that needed to be monitored separately in order to know the traffic patterns of our entire network.

A bridge, on the other hand, is used to segment the network into larger pieces. Instead of having one system located off of each port, there is more likely to be 25 or more. For example, a single switch installed into a network with 100 devices may create 16 or more collision domains. A bridge installed into the same network is likely to create only two or three. This gives us few points that need to be monitored with our analyzer.

At a minimum, you should be able to retrieve the following information from a bridge:

- the number of frames received per port

- the number of frames forwarded per port

- the number and type of errors detected on each port

- the number of collisions detected on each port

This information is a good starting point to determine which areas of the network require the most attention.

Network Monitoring with a Router

Like a bridge, a router creates large collision domains, which makes monitoring network activity with a network monitoring tool that much easier. There are some things that a router can detect, however, that a network monitor will miss.

Because the router's job is to route traffic, it is the perfect device for collecting this type of information. The report in Figure 13.12 shows general IP statistics for a Cisco 4000 router. From this screen we can pull some interesting information about the network it is attached to.

FIGURE 13.12

IP statistics for a Cisco 4000 router

```
IP statistics:
   Rcvd:  82361984 total, 1702782 local destination
          0 format errors, 0 checksum errors, 62 bad hop count
          0 unknown protocol, 6 not a gateway
          0 security failures, 0 bad options
   Frags: 0 reassembled, 0 timeouts, 0 couldn't reassemble
          0 fragmented, 0 couldn't fragment
   Bcast: 1685772 received, 325954 sent
   Mcast: 0 received, 0 sent
   Sent:  356328 generated, 80655134 forwarded
          3979 encapsulation failed, 22 no route
```

First, if we compare the number of frames received (Rcvd) to the number that were addressed to a local destination, we can see that an overwhelming majority of the traffic is being routed. This can be a bad thing as routers create an inherent delay in packet transmission as they are required to remove the frame header and trailer and then rebuild them upon transmission. Still, there are times when this type of design is desirable—for instance, in separating a slower topology with client systems from servers that are located on a faster backbone. We would need to collect more information to see if the large percentage of frames being routed is something we need to worry about or not.

If we look at the bad hop count value, we can see that we have had a few frames that have exceeded the hop count limit. 62 is not a large number compared to the received quantity, and it could have been caused by routing loops if another router had unexpectedly dropped offline recently. We will want to keep an eye on this statistic to ensure that it does not continue climbing. If it does, we need to review the configuration on each of our routers.

So our router has told us that it has encountered problems with routing frames on the network, something an active network analyzer would catch as well, but a fact that a network monitor may miss completely.

If we look at the broadcast field (Bcast), we see that this router has forwarded roughly 20% of the broadcasts it has received. Broadcasts that can traverse routers are referred to as *all network broadcasts* and can be a bad thing as they will be propagated throughout our network affecting every single attached system until the end of the network is reached or the maximum hop count is exceeded. Because they have such wide implications on network performance, we want to limit the number of all network broadcasts as much as possible.

Again, an active network analyzer attached to the network would be able to detect this type of traffic. A simple network monitor would have included them in the general category of "broadcast."

At a minimum, you should be able to collect the following statistical information from a router:

- the number of frames received per port

- the number of frames forwarded per port

- the number and type of errors detected on each port

- the number of collisions detected on each port

- the number frames with an excessively high hop count

- the number of frames with no route to host

- the number of broadcasts received and forwarded

If you are using a network monitor to maintain the health of your network, these statistics will help to fill in some of the deficiencies in the network monitor's abilities.

Collecting Statistics with SNMP and RMON

As we discussed in Chapter 6, SNMP provides the ability to monitor and control network devices. RMON (short for remote monitoring) is similar, except that it focuses on the ability to collect statistics from each device.

Using SNMP and RMON, you have the ability to configure a central management station to collect some or all of the statistics discussed in this chapter. From a central console, you can query devices about their health and measured performance levels. Without SNMP and RMON, you must attach to each device through a serial cable or through a telnet session.

How Important is SNMP and RMON Support?   How important SNMP and RMON should be to your organization depends on the size of your network. If your network is large, spanning many buildings or geographical regions, then the ability to simultaneously monitor multiple network devices should be considered a must. If the collision light is lighting up on a switch in the bowels of some remote basement, it will probably go undetected until it causes a major failure.

If your network is relatively small, consisting of only one or two floors of a single building, the additional money spent on devices that include SNMP and RMON support could probably be better spent elsewhere. If you are proactive with monitoring your network's heath, you can easily keep up with the statistics generated by a dozen or so devices. It does not take very long to sit down and telnet to each device to ensure that it functioning properly.

The money you save by refraining from purchasing devices that include SNMP and RMON can easily add up to the purchase price of a good analyzer that will tell you more about your network than SNMP and RMON ever could. I've seen many a network administrator talked into buying features that they will never use by a salesperson that knew all the right buzz words.

Novell's LANAlyzer

Novell's LANAlyzer is a network monitoring tool that is used by many network administrators to monitor the health of their networks. It has a simple interface that makes gathering statistical information about your network's traffic very easy. It even has some advanced filtering and capturing ability that makes diagnosing network problems that much easier.

LANAlyzer is a single product in a wide range of network monitors and analyzers. While each has its own unique screens and procedures for performing specific tasks, they all do relatively the same thing—monitor the traffic on your network. The difference is that some do it better than others.

Once you are familiar with one network monitor or analyzer, it is that much easier to sit down in front of another and figure out how to use it. With this in mind, we will focus our discussion on how to use a network monitor and what type of information it can give us.

Dashboard

The LANAlyzer dashboard, as shown in Figure 13.13, is the heart of the LANAlyzer program. From here we can view real-time statistics on frames and errors per second, as well as bandwidth utilization. The gauges give a visual representation of traffic on our network while the numeric value located below each gauge is an absolute value.

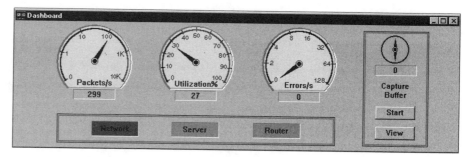

FIGURE 13.13

The LANAlyzer dashboard

Capture Buffer

The Capture Buffer on the right-hand side of the LANAlyzer dashboard allows us to capture frames as they are transmitted on the network. The packet decode figures we have used throughout this book were collected using the Capture Buffer. You have the option to capture all traffic on the network, capture only frames that originate from specific systems, or capture frames that are using certain protocols.

Once a capture session is complete, you can click the View button to observe the results. You can even select from filter criteria to further screen the frames that are presented. For example, you could choose to look only at SPX frames.

At the bottom of the dashboard are three buttons labeled Network, Server, and Router. Each of these buttons is normally colored green. When a problem in the appropriate category is detected, the button will flash and turn red. These are the alarm monitors, and they give a visual indication when a problem has been detected. We are allowed to set minimum thresholds for frame rate, utilization, and number of errors for the network alarm. Whenever one of these thresholds is crossed, it triggers the network alarm. The server and router alarms will go off on a per problem basis. You cannot set thresholds for these alarms.

Alarms

When an alarm light turns red, simply double-click on it to produce the alarm dialog box. Figure 13.14 shows the dialog box for Network

Alarms. On this screen we can see the date and time the error occurred, as well as which threshold was violated.

FIGURE 13.14

The Network Alarms
dialog box

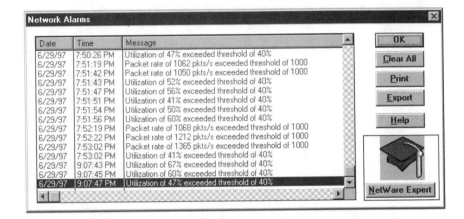

To the right of the screen are buttons which allow us to clear all of these errors from the Network Alarms dialog box, print out the error messages, or export them to a file. We also have a button called Net-Ware Expert. NetWare Expert allows you to access general information on the error message being highlighted. For example, in the case of high network utilization, the NetWare Expert would tell us that our network may be too busy.

Remember that the errors reported in the Network Alarms dialog box are instantaneous results. By this I mean a very short sample rate (typically one second) is used to determine if a problem has occurred. While this type of measurement is fine when recording errors, it can be an inaccurate picture of network performance. We are less concerned with a momentary spike in traffic than we are with a sustained level of high utilization. To see how our network is doing over a greater period of time, we need to look at detailed statistics and trends.

Detailed Statistics and Trends

The detailed statistics screens will plot frame rate, utilization, or error rate over time. Every five seconds a new data point will be plotted along a 15-minute window. This gives us a more accurate view of actual network utilization than simply looking for the peaks.

Figure 13.15 shows the Detailed - Utilization% graph. This graph shows an ideal trend in network utilization. While there are large spikes that show a large amount of data was being transferred on the network, there are also many quiet spots where network activity was at or near zero. The reason that this trend is ideal is that it shows that when a station needs to transmit data, it is doing so very quickly. The fact that there are quiet moments on the network tells us that there are plenty of opportunities for stations to transmit their data. If we look at the average utilization level at the bottom of the figure, it only reports 10%.

FIGURE 13.15

A graph of healthy
network utilization

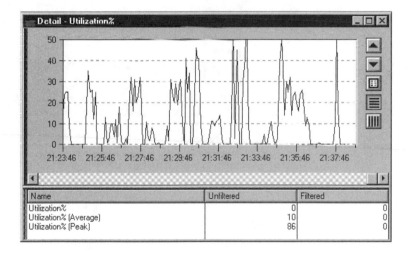

As average utilization levels rise, the chance that a station will need to transmit data while another station is already transmitting increases as well. For example, the network in Figure 13.15 was showing a 10% average utilization level. This means that there is a one in ten chance that when a station needs to transmit data, another station is already doing so.

As the average utilization level rises, it becomes more likely that a station will discover the network is busy and have to wait before transmitting data. Figure 13.16 shows a network segment that may soon need attention. The average utilization level is 21%. Thise means that our stations now have a one in five chance of discovering that the network is busy. More importantly, there are no quiet moments on our network. As soon as one station finishes transmitting, another one begins. This network is probably starting to feel a bit sluggish.

FIGURE 13.16

A network experiencing high utilization

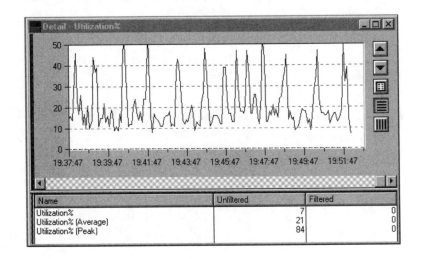

A 15-minute window is still a relatively short period of time. We could have simply had bad timing and measured this network at its all-time worst for the entire year. To get a more accurate picture, we need to monitor performance over a longer period of time.

In addition to detailed statistics, we can monitor long term trends. The trend graph is identical to the detailed statistics graph except it provides a 12-hour window and can gather statistics for up to six months. It also calculates the sample rate differently. The trend graph will average the results over a 15-minute period of time and then plot a data point. In other words, the average utilization level reported by the detailed statistics graph will create a single data point. This smoothes out all the peaks and valleys and gives us a better idea of the average usage.

If the trend graph shows this 20% utilization level to be a momentary spike, then we know or network is probably fine. If, however, it reports that the high utilization level is being maintained for the entire work data, it may be time to start performing some load balancing before it becomes a serious problem. To do this, we need to check out the station monitor to see who is generating the most traffic.

The Station Monitor

The station monitor, shown in Figure 13.17, allows us to monitor network activity on a per station basis. Normally, MAC addresses are displayed in the station column. This can make it a bit difficult to determine which stations are which. LANAlyzer has a feature that allows it to authenticate to one or more NetWare servers and find out which users are logged on from which stations. It will then use that user's logon name to identify each system in the station column.

FIGURE 13.17

The Station Monitor window

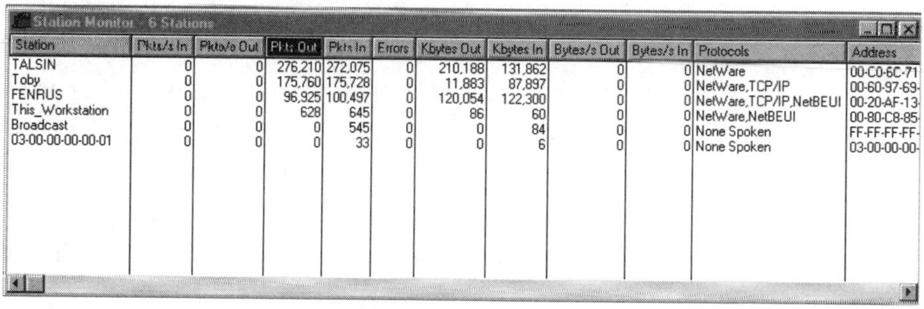

Station	Pkts/s In	Pkts/s Out	Pkts Out	Pkts In	Errors	Kbytes Out	Kbytes In	Bytes/s Out	Bytes/s In	Protocols	Address
TALSIN	0	0	276,210	272,075	0	210,188	131,862	0	0	NetWare	00-C0-6C-71
Toby	0	0	175,760	175,728	0	11,883	87,897	0	0	NetWare,TCP/IP	00-60-97-69-
FENRUS	0	0	96,925	100,497	0	120,054	122,300	0	0	NetWare,TCP/IP,NetBEUI	00-20-AF-13-
This_Workstation	0	0	628	645	0	86	60	0	0	NetWare,NetBEUI	00-80-C8-85-
Broadcast	0	0	0	545	0	0	84	0	0	None Spoken	FF-FF-FF-FF-
03-00-00-00-00-01	0	0	0	33	0	0	6	0	0	None Spoken	03-00-00-00-

This is a feature that is unique to LANAlyzer and is extremely useful in a NetWare environment. If LANAlyzer cannot identify the station, it allows you to edit a simple text file to add an entry for the system.

Most monitors and analyzers will at least identify the manufacturer associated with the MAC address. While this is helpful if the manufacturer is identified as being Cisco and you only have one Cisco device on your network, it is not very helpful, for example, to see 100 entries identified as 3COM. When choosing a network monitor or analyzer, make sure it has the ability to let you associate real names with MAC addresses.

Our next two columns report packets in and out on a per second basis. These will show us how many frames a station is sending or receiving at that exact instant in time. The next two columns report the total quantity of frames sent and received since the monitor was restarted. When making long term plans for network changes, the total quantity of frame transmissions is far more interesting and useful.

Our next column reports on the number of errors transmitted by each station. In an ideal world, this value will remain at zero. If you have a long station list and wish to quickly determine if there are any errors on the network, simply click the title at the top of the column. This will change the sort order so the station with the greatest number of errors is reported first.

Be very careful in interpreting the results of this column. Much of the information comes secondhand from the receiving station, not just the monitoring tool. For example, let's assume you sort this list and see that your server has generated 200 errors and you have a list of 30 stations that have error counts ranging from one error to 30 errors. These results do not mean that you may have 31 network cards that are malfunctioning. You may only have one.

If the NIC in the server is going bad, it is entirely possible that it is corrupting frames as they are received, not just when they are being transmitted. If this is the case, the data may be received intact, but will be corrupted before it is sent up through the communication layers. When the transport layer receives the information, it will determine that the data is unusable. The server will then send out a request for a retransmission.

When the network monitor sees the retransmission request, it assumes that the original transmitting system had sent a bad frame. The network monitor has no way of knowing that the information became corrupted after it was received by the server. The network monitor would then proceed to incorrectly indicate that the original transmitting station sent a bad frame.

The moral of the story is—be extremely lazy. Instead of running around trying to fix each station that was indicated as having transmitting errors, focus on the worst offending system and see if the other transmission problems do not go away as well.

After the Error column, there is the total KB transmitted and received as well as bytes per second transmitted and received. Like the frame count columns, these total quantities are the most useful.

If we compare the ratio of total KB transmitted to the total frames transmitted, we can get an idea of how efficiently each system is communicating. For example, look at the ratio difference between Toby and Fenrus.

Toby transmitted 175,760 frames to move 11,883KB of data. This means that Toby is communicating with an average frame size of 68 bytes, just barely over our minimum required Ethernet frame size of 64 bytes. Fenrus, on the other hand, transmitted only 96,925 frames while moving 120,054KB of data for an average frame size of 1,239 bytes. While not the maximum frame size of 1,518 bytes, it is still far more efficient than the transmissions being sent by Toby.

When monitoring average frame size, it is technically impossible to ever achieve an average size equal to the Ethernet maximum of 1,518 bytes. This is because workstations send out very small frames when requesting to read or write a file. It is not until data is actually being transferred that the frame size increases to the maximum allowable size. If you can keep the average frame size over 1,000 bytes, you are doing extremely well.

If I focus my attention on Toby and bring this system up to the same level of communication efficiency as Fenrus, I can reduce the number of frames this system generates while transferring data by nearly 94%.

Other Network Analyzers

We have been discussing the LANAlyzer product, but the tips and tricks we discussed can be applied to any network monitor or analyzer. For example, any monitoring device that displays frames and kilobytes transmitted can be used to calculate the efficiency of your clients.

Summary

This concludes our discussion of network monitoring tools. You should now have a good idea of what tools are available and how to use them to both prevent and diagnose problems on your network.

In the next section we will look at how to collect some of the same information when you do not have a network monitor or analyzer. If your budget is tight, you may still be able to collect statistics to determine your network's health.

CHAPTER

14

NOS-Supplied Network Tools

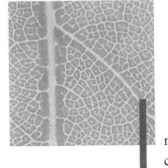

In addition to the commercial diagnostic and monitoring tools covered in the last chapter, most NOSes include a set of tools for network troubleshooting purposes.

None of the tools are capable of retrieving the sheer volume of information that can be recovered by a good network monitor or analyzer. When they are combined, however, they can be used to fill in some of the puzzle pieces as you evaluate how your network is performing.

IntranetWare

IntranetWare has both server console and workstation tools that can be used for diagnostic purposes. Each is capable of collecting its own unique pieces of information.

Console Tools

Console tools are designed to be run from the server itself. They can be run directly at the server console or from a remote Rconsole or telnet session. If you are checking network performance parameters, it's a good idea to work directly from the console. Remote sessions can generate additional traffic and skew diagnostic test results.

Command Line Tools

We will start by looking at tools that are executed directly from the server's command line. Unless otherwise noted, execute the command by typing its name at the server console prompt.

Config   The **config** command, as shown in Figure 14.1, displays output regarding the configuration on our network parameters. Most of this output should look familiar to you because the parameters were covered in Chapter 7. The only new information is the internal network address and the node address at the top of the screen.

FIGURE 14.1

Output from the **config** command

```
File server name: TALSIN
IPX internal network number: 32F478CB
    Node address: 000000000001
    Frame type: VIRTUAL_LAN
    LAN protocol: IPX network 32F478CB
Server Up Time:  1 Hour 29 Minutes 30 Seconds

16-Bit Ethernet Card v1.21 (931001)
    Version 3.21     October 19, 1993
    Hardware setting: I/O ports 300h to 31Fh, Interrupt 5h
    Node address: 00C06C712979
    Frame type: ETHERNET_802.3
    Board name: FD0490_E83
    LAN protocol: IPX network 00008023

16-Bit Ethernet Card v1.21 (931001)
    Version 3.21     October 19, 1993
    Hardware setting: I/O ports 300h to 31Fh, Interrupt 5h
    Node address: 00C06C712979
    Frame type: ETHERNET_II
    Board name: FD0490_EII
    LAN protocol: ARP
    LAN protocol: IP  address 10.1.1.232  mask FF.FF.FF.0  interfaces 1
<Press ESC to terminate or any other key to continue>
```

All NetWare servers use an internal IPX network address. This internal address is a communications *backbone* between the different modules that make up the server. For example, when a frame is received by a NIC, the NIC forwards the information onto the internal network just like a router sitting between two logical segments. Because the internal network is treated like any other network, it receives its own address.

The node address is the equivalent of a MAC address on a logical network.

694 Chapter 14 ■ NOS-Supplied Network Tools

The core OS of the server always has a node address of 1.

When reviewing this screen, pay close attention to the line titled LAN Protocol. Sometimes when manually loading and binding a driver you may misspell a word or use the wrong syntax. If you have a driver loaded but did not successfully execute a binding, this line will change to read "No LAN protocols are bound to this LAN board."

Display Networks The display networks command, shown in Figure 14.2, displays all known IPX networks and the metrics required to reach them from the local server. Our first value, 00008023, is the IPX network number. The values 0/1 mean that this network can be reached in zero hops and within one tick. The zero hop value means that this network is local to the network card. Frames transmitted by the card do not have to cross any routers to reach this network. This could be the network directly attached to the card, or this could be the internal IPX network number. We cannot tell which one it is by using this utility.

FIGURE 14.2

The display networks
command

```
TALSIN:display networks                              o
    00008023  0/1        0A01010A  1/2      32F478CB  0/1
There are 3 known networks.
TALSIN:
```

A tick is 1/18 of a second, or approximately the amount of time required to transmit a frame from one 10 Mb Ethernet segment to another.

Our next entry shows a network that is one hop and two ticks away. This means that it is either another IPX network located on the other side of a router, or the internal IPX network number of another server. We cannot tell which it is by using this utility.

Our final network is again zero hops and one tick. Again, this is either the internal IPX network number for this server or the network directly attached to the network card.

One thing to watch on the display networks screen is the ratio between hops and ticks. If you have a 10 Mb Ethernet network, the number of ticks should always be one more than the number of hops. For example, you should see 0/1, 4,5, or 7,8. If the number of ticks is greater than the number of hops plus one, you have a point of congestion somewhere on your network. This is only applicable if you are using NLSP, because RIP simply looks at the hop count and adds one. NLSP actually measures the delay.

Display Servers   The **display servers** command, shown in Figure 14.3, is similar to the display network command except it reports on known servers. The value listed after the server name is the number of hops that must be traversed to reach this server, measured from the network card.

FIGURE 14.3

The **display servers** command

```
TALSIN:display servers
   BIRCH_____    0   BIRCH_____   0   TALSIN      0   TALSIN
   TALSIN           0   TOBY.FOOBAR.    1   TALSIN      0   TALSIN
There are 6 known services.
TALSIN:
```

The first two entries, "BIRCH_____", is our server advertising the NDS tree name. We know this is the tree name because of the trailing underline. Novell identified trees this way on purpose so they would be easier to spot in a large server list.

So why are we even seeing the tree name in a server list? "Servers," in this case, does not identify the physical server itself, but rather the services being advertised on the network. For example, Talsin, which is the name of our physical server, is listed three times because it is offering file, print, and NDS services. If I was running a backup server on Talsin, it would appear in this list a fourth time.

All services advertised by the local server should have a hop count of zero. From our list, we see that there is only one server listed with a hop count greater than zero, TOBY.FOOBAR.COM (the COM is truncated on this list). Toby is listed as being one hop away.

Despite what this implies, the server Toby is not sitting on the other side of a physical router. The one hop is listed because NetWare server communications originate from their internal IPX network. The NIC in the server Talsin has to cross the NIC in Toby in order to reach this internal IPX network. Because we experience a network number change when moving from the physical network to the server's internal network, the network card installed in Talsin views Toby as being one hop away.

In short, Toby is actually connected to the same logical network segment as Talsin. If we compare the results of this utility with the results of the **display networks** command, we can deduce that the remote network listed by display networks must be the internal IPX network number for Toby.

Protocols   Typing the command **protocols** at the console screen generates a list of protocols loaded on the server. Also shown is the frame type each protocol is using. This command is not as useful as the **config** command because it does not show you network addresses. It simply gives you a quick list of which protocols are in use.

Packet Burst Statistics Screen   The packet burst statistics screen, shown in Figure 14.4, can look very cryptic indeed to the untrained eye. This screen is actually an excellent resource for monitoring the communication efficiency of each of your clients to ensure they are generating the least possible amount of traffic.

The full command for initializing the packet burst statistic screen is:

```
set enable packet burst statistics screen = on
```

F I G U R E 14.4

The packet burst
statistics screen

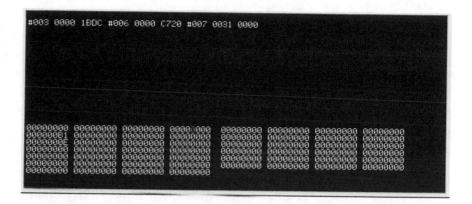

You will then have to change screens (Ctrl+Esc if you are at the console), as the console does not switch to it automatically.

The statistics are listed in groups of three, starting with the connection ID number. Any number that begins with a pound sign identifies the connection ID in a hexadecimal format (yes, a decimal would be much easier but that would take all the fun out of it). You can compare this number to the connections list on the Monitor screen to associate a logon name with a connection number. We talk about the Monitor screen later in this section.

So our figure is displaying information for only three connection numbers—3, 6, and 7. We know this because each one of these values starts with a pound sign. If this is a production server, the first thing we should do is refer back to the monitor screen and see if there are any connections that have not been listed. Only clients that support packet burst are listed on this screen. If a client is not listed, we should find out why and upgrade their client software if possible.

The number listed after the connection ID is the interpacket gap in hexadecimal format. This is not an absolute measurement, but a relative value, based on the negotiated gap time. This number represents the gap time that the client associated with this connection ID number has negotiated with the server for burst communications.

For example, connections 3 and 6 are Windows 95 machines using client32. Both of these clients have negotiated a gap time of zero (meaning "Send me data as fast as you can!"). Connection 7 is using the standard Microsoft client that ships with Windows 95. This client has negotiated a relative gap time of 31. This means that the client is unable to accept frames as fast as the server can dish them out. It has asked that the server pause in between transmissions.

The actual value of the gap time that was negotiated is not as important as how this number equates to other clients on the network. For example, I have two systems that were capable of negotiating a gap of zero while the third client has asked for extremely long pauses between transmissions. I now know I need to look at this third system to determine why it is unable to communicate efficiently.

Remember to keep your topology in mind when you review the negotiated gap time. Clients that are located one or more logical networks away will negotiate a longer gap time due to delays when crossing a router. When comparing these results, make sure you use the same yardstick for all systems.

The third number is a relative value in hexadecimal describing how many burst packets have been negotiated with the client. The higher the number, the more burst packets are transmitted between acknowledgments. For example, connection 3 has negotiated six burst packets per acknowledgment, while connection 6 is using 35.

Do not worry about what value equates to how many burst packets. Like the interpacket gap, use the displayed burst negotiation value as a yardstick to compare like stations. The idea is to identify stations that are unable to communicate as efficiently as others. For example, connection 7 has asked for an acknowledgment for every frame transmitted. I would obviously want to investigate this system first to find out what the problem is.

The bottom of the screen shows debug information and is not very useful for monitoring client communication efficiency. When you have finished your evaluation and wish to close the screen, switch back to the console prompt and type:

```
set enable packet burst statistics screen = off
```

The packet burst statistic screen uses a lot of CPU overhead. You should not leave this screen enabled all the time. Turn it on when you need to check it, but make sure you disable it when you are done.

Reset Router   Reset Router clears the router and server table on the server. Initiating a **reset router** command causes the server to send RIPs and SAPs in order to build a new table. This is useful if you suspect that there may be a routing loop and wish to clear it without downing the server. You can safely run this command with users logged on to the system.

Tping   Tping is short for *trivial ping*. If you have IP running on your server, this utility allows you to ping a remote host by name or IP address. The syntax is:

```
load tping host
```

where *host* is replaced with the host name or IP address of the remote system with which you wish to check connectivity. **Tping** has no configurable options and reports little more than "host is alive" or "host unreachable." It does not return transmission or round trip time like the **ping** command discussed below. The fact that you do not have a graphic interface to deal with makes this an easy tool to use if you need to ping multiple addresses.

Track On   The **track on** command is used for monitoring RIP and SAP packets on the network. When the command is executed, two separate console screens are started—one for monitoring RIP traffic, and the other for monitoring SAP. Figure 14.5 shows the SAP Tracking Screen.

F I G U R E   14.5

The SAP Tracking Screen

```
SAP Tracking Screen                                                      IN [000080
23:0080C885687C] 22:15:46   Get Nearest Server
OUT [00008023:0080C885687C] 22:15:46   Give Nearest Server
TALSIN
OUT [00008023:FFFFFFFFFFFF] 22:15:49    TALSIN_____1   TALSIN         1
    TALSIN_____1   BIRCH_____1
IN [00008023:0080C885687C] 22:16:37   Get Nearest Server
OUT [00008023:0080C885687C] 22:16:37   Give Nearest Server
TALSIN
IN [00008023:0080C885687C] 22:16:38   Get Nearest Server
OUT [00008023:0080C885687C] 22:16:38   Give Nearest Server
TALSIN
OUT [00008023:FFFFFFFFFFFF] 22:16:49    TALSIN_____1   TALSIN         1
    TALSIN_____1   BIRCH_____1
IN [00008023:0080C885687C] 22:16:58   Get Nearest Server
OUT [00008023:0080C885687C] 22:16:58   Give Nearest Server
TALSIN
OUT [00008023:FFFFFFFFFFFF] 22:17:49    TALSIN_____1   TALSIN         1
    TALSIN_____1   BIRCH_____1
<Display is paused; press any key to continue.>_
```

The first line actually starts way off to the right due to formatting problems with the utility. This line reads:

```
IN [00008023:0080C885687C] 22:15:46    Get Nearest Server
```

IN means that this is a SAP that the server received from the network, it was not generated internally. The numbers between the brackets list the network number from which the SAP was received, then a colon, then the MAC address of the station that transmitted the SAP. Then there is a time stamp followed by a description of the type of SAP. A Get Nearest Server request is typically sent by a workstation when it begins to initialize its network drivers.

If we look at the next line, it reads:

```
OUT [00008023:0080C885687C] 22:15:46    Give Nearest Server
  TALSIN
```

OUT means that this SAP was generated by the server. The address within the brackets identifies who the server transmitted the SAP to. We then have another time stamp followed by a description of the SAP. This time the SAP type is identified as being a Give Nearest Server request. The data transmitted was the server's name, TALSIN.

This get-and-give exchange is how a workstation first finds resources out on the network. Once a workstation receives a Give Nearest Server

SAP, it now has the resources it requires to find any server on the network. The give includes the source network and MAC address for the replying server, so the workstation can now carry on communications with this server directly. Also, because the server maintains a table of all other servers on the network, the workstation can query it for the address of the server it is looking for.

This can be an excellent aid in troubleshooting workstations that will not connect to the network. If the workstation's MAC address is not seen transmitting a Get Nearest Server request, you know the problem is with the workstations. If you see the workstation transmit a Get Nearest Server request but the server does not reply, it is the server that needs investigation.

As mentioned, **Track on** also starts a screen for monitoring RIP traffic. This screen follows the same "in/out" convention that the SAP screen uses. The only difference is that the information displayed deals with routing requests, not server requests.

To shut down the **track on** screens, switch back to a console prompt and enter the command **track off**.

Graphic Tools

NetWare includes a number of graphic-based utilities for monitoring network conditions. Each of these tools is started by using the **load** command. The syntax is:

```
load name
```

where *name* is replaced with the name of the tool you wish to use.

Many of these tools are console utilities for monitoring a specific type of connection or protocol. All of the console screens are functionally similar. The differences reflect the unique properties of the protocol or connection type it is designed to monitor. Rather than rewrite the network manual on these tools, we will focus on one and give a brief description of the rest.

ipxcon

ipxcon is used for monitoring IPX traffic. The main screen, shown in Figure 14.6, gives some general IPX statistics and has selections available to investigate more detail through the Available Options menu.

FIGURE 14.6

The main screen for the IPX console

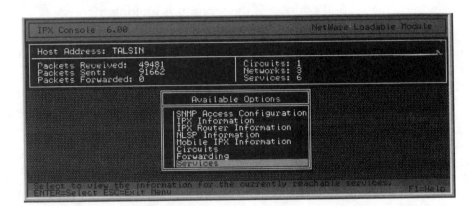

The Packets Received and Packets Sent fields show the total number of frames that this system has both sent and received with an IPX header. These fields are important; you can't obtain this information anywhere else. There is a LAN/WAN Information option on the Monitor utility which we discuss later in this section; however this it gives statistics for total traffic, not just a single protocol.

Packets Forwarded applies when we have two or more NICs in the server and we are routing traffic between two or more logical segments. Because this server is not performing any routing, the value is zero.

If you are routing with the server, you should pay close attention to the ratio between the Packets Received and the Packet Forwarded field. If the server is routing more than 15% of the packets it receives, it may be time to look at relocating users or resources. It is beneficial to do as little routing as possible because this improves server access time.

To the right of this information, we have statistics for circuits, networks, and services. Circuits are the paths the server has available for transferring information. For example, our NIC card is considered a circuit because it provides connectivity to the attached network.

The Networks field identifies how many IPX networks are known to this server. The Services field identifies how many services are available on the network. These two fields report the same information as the **display networks** and **display servers** commands covered earlier.

SNMP Access Configuration   The SNMP Access Configuration option allows us to view the SNMP setting if IPX is being used as the transfer protocol. The information displayed is identical to what is set using the INETCFG utility which we discussed in Chapter 7.

When we select the IPX Information menu option, the IPX Information dialog box appears. This dialog box is shown in Figure 14.7.

FIGURE 14.7

The IPX Information dialog box

The first set of statistics is Incoming Packets Received and Incoming Packets Delivered. The first is a count of how many IPX packets were received by the NIC that passed a CRC check. The second shows how many of those packets were forwarded along to the server. These numbers will not necessarily match, as the NIC does not forward every IPX packet it receives to the server. What is important to look for here is the ratio at which the two statistics are climbing.

When it appears that packets are being received faster than they are being forwarded to the server, there is a strong possibility that the server is becoming overwhelmed from the volume of traffic. The No ECB Available statistic within the Monitor utility would let us know for sure (described below).

The Outgoing Requests field indicates the number of frames that the server has attempted to deliver. The Outgoing Packets Sent field indicates how many were successfully transmitted. If you see a large discrepancy between these two numbers, you may have a faulty cable or excessive network traffic.

Detailed IPX Information   If we select the Detailed IPX Information field, the Detailed IPX Information box shown in Figure 14.8 appears. This gives us even more detail as to how our IPX communications are performing.

FIGURE 14.8

The Detailed IPX Information field

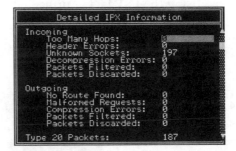

Too Many Hops records how many IPX packets were received which have traveled an excessive number of hops. Header Errors records the number of IPX packets received that had incorrect or unreadable information in the IPX, SPX, or NCP header section. Unknown Sockets describes the number of IPX frames received that referenced a socket number the server is not familiar with.

This is more common than you might think. For example, if a Doom game is taking place on the locally attached network, the server would be unfamiliar with the socket used by the Doom clients and would increment this field. Also, the Microsoft client frequently makes calls to socket numbers that are not used by the network server. If you are using the Microsoft client, you will see this number increment as well.

Decompression Errors occur when the server is unable to expand a compressed IPX header. Header compression can be used over a WAN link to reduce bandwidth utilization by reducing the space necessary to store the IPX header. If your server is not directly connected to a WAN, this value should remain at zero.

Packets Filtered identifies how many frames have been blocked due to a filter that has been configured with the FILTCFG utility. Filtering is useful in large environments when you wish to reduce broadcast traffic, or in environments where it is necessary to connect two logical segments but you wish to filter access from one direction. Whenever an IPX frame is blocked due to a filter setting, this value is incremented by one.

The Packets Discarded field is a catchall in that it records the number of frames not delivered for some other reason than the fields listed above. For example, if you are using packet signature and the server detects a spoofed packet, the information would be discarded and this field would be incremented by one.

The Outgoing fields are a mirror of the Incoming fields except that they record errors in transmission. The final field, Type 20 Packets, identifies the number of NetBIOS packets received by this system.

IPX Router Information   If we select IPX Router Information from the main menu, we are given a brief summary of the routing state of the system, including the following information:

- the IPX internal network number

- if RIP is enabled or disabled

- if SAP is enabled or disabled

- if NLSP is enabled or disabled

- if Mobile IPX is enabled or disabled

- the maximum paths that NLSP can load balance across

- the maximum hop count recognized by this server

While it may sound a bit strange to disable RIP or SAP on a server, it can actually be a good way to improve system performance.

Out of the box, NetWare will act as a router. If you install two NICs in the server, it will happily begin routing traffic between each segment. This may not always be necessary, however. For example, consider the network shown in Figure 14.9.

FIGURE 14.9

A multi-segment LAN that
does not require routing

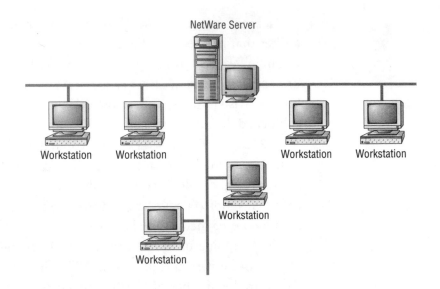

We have three logical segments with workstations attached to each. All workstations access all of their required network resources directly from the server. Each user can connect to the server directly from their own logical segment, so why bother broadcasting RIP information if nobody is going to use it? By removing routing support from the server (this is done with the INETCFG utility), we free up processor time to perform other tasks as well as reduce the number of broadcasts on our network.

NLSP Information   The NLSP Information screen offers detailed information of the NLSP configuration as well as route information it has discovered. This information was covered in detail in Chapters 5, 6, and 7.

Mobile IPX Information   The Mobile IPX Information option gives detailed information on WAN users using mobile IPX for communications. You can view statistics such as packets sent and received.

Circuits When the circuits option is selected, the user is allowed to choose from an available circuit (identified by the LAN or WAN card that creates the circuit) in order to view detailed information. Figure 14.10 shows the Circuit Information screen. Much of this information can be found under other options in this utility, or the Monitor utility. The Detailed Circuit Information option at the bottom of the screen provides information that we cannot find elsewhere.

FIGURE 14.10

The Circuit Information
dialog box

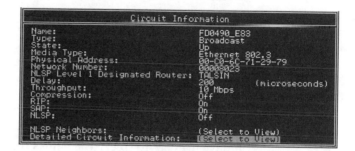

Figure 14.11 shows a portion of the Detailed Circuit Information screen. Here we can see where the server keeps track of how many RIP and SAP frames it is sending and receiving. Because both of these protocols are broadcast-based, we can use this number to get an idea of how many broadcasts are being transmitted onto the network.

FIGURE 14.11

The Detailed Circuit
Information screen

For example, we could record the IPX packet totals shown on the main screen as well as the quantity of RIP and SAP packets from this screen. We can then record these values again a few hours later. We can now calculate:

- average IPX frames per second

- average RIP and SAP frames per second

- thc percentage of total IPX traffic that is broadcast based

While not quite a network analyzer, this record will at least get you in the ballpark as to how your network is performing. In fact, we could also record the quantity for total frames sent and received from the Monitor screen and add this information into our calculations.

Make sure you use a fairly long period of time between measurements when using this method, at least an hour should be fine. Because you have no way to freeze the values recorded at a certain time, the data will become skewed as you navigate the menus. Still, this method will at least give you an idea of how much traffic your network is seeing if you do not have a proper network monitor or analyzer.

Forwarding and Services   Our last two options, forwarding and services, report the same information as the **display networks** and **display servers** commands. These menu options simply give you a graphical way of viewing the information.

Aiocon
Aiocon can be used to monitor asynchronous communications across a serial port connection. From this utility you can view the amount of data sent and received.

Atcon
Atcon is the utility for monitoring AppleTalk communications. It is very similar to the ipxcon utility in that it allows you to monitor packet statistics as well as view network and zone information.

Atmcon

Atmcon is the utility for monitoring ATM connections to your server. From this utility you can view virtual circuit configuration information, send queues, and bytes transmitted and received.

Ipxping

Ipxping is identical to the IP ping utility except it uses IPX as a transport. This utility allows you to enter the network and node address of a remote host in order to test connectivity.

A useful feature of this utility is that it records the time it takes a packet of data to contact a remote system and then return back to the transmitting station. This is a quick way to be able to check link speed if you suspect that a WAN link may be overloaded. By using this utility during peak and off peak hours, you can get a good feel for the responsiveness of the connection. It can also help identify trends in bandwidth utilization.

For example, let's assume that every work day you perform a few test pings over a WAN link and record the average results. Over time, you will be able to determine the following:

- what round trip time correlates to a slow WAN response for users

- if your bandwidth requirements over the WAN link are increasing, decreasing, or staying the same

This method is by no means as accurate as using an analyzer. If you do not have an analyzer however, this will at least create some general numbers for you to gauge WAN performance.

Monitor

Monitor, as the name implies, is the main utility for overseeing the health of your server. It reports on a lot of information regarding every aspect of server performance. For the purpose of this discussion, however, we will focus on the statistics that pertain to network performance. The Monitor General Information screen is shown in Figure 14.12.

FIGURE 14.12

The Monitor General
Information screen

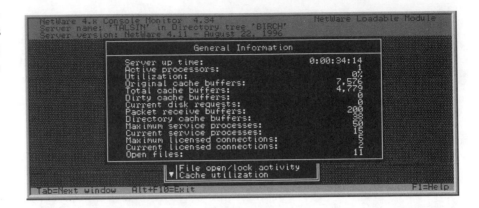

The first statistic of interest on the General Information screen is Packet Receive Buffers. Packet receive Buffers is the queue available to the server to store inbound frames. As the NIC receives the frame, it stores it in a packet receive buffer to await processing by the server.

Packet receive buffers have minimum and maximum settings that can be configured directly through Monitor under the Server Parameters menu option. The minimum setting is the number of buffers allocated during system startup. If the server requires more buffers than the minimum value, it is allowed to allocate additional buffers until the maximum is reached.

As frames are stored in the packet receive buffers, the server will begin processing them. If frames are coming in faster than the server can remove them from the packet receive buffer pool, the server may eventually reach a point where the buffer becomes full. It will first try to slow down incoming traffic by transmitting a false collision warning. This gives the server a moment to try and catch up with the contents of the queue. If it continues to have trouble keeping up, it will allocate additional packet receive buffers to queue inbound traffic.

The Service Processes, also shown on the General Information screen, are responsible for processing the queue. As the NIC places frames into the queue, the service processes are responsible for removing them. If the above described condition occurs where the server is having trouble keeping up with inbound traffic, it will not only allocate additional packet buffers, but service process as well. The more service processes allocated, the faster the packet receive buffer pool can be processed.

Once your server has been in operation for at least a few weeks, record the reported values for the packet receive buffers and the current service processes. Compare these values to the minimum values under the server parameters option. If the values match, you are all set. If the server parameters value is less than the number you recorded from the General Information screen, you should increase the configured minimum value to match the current levels being used.

What you are doing is tuning the server for the next time it is rebooted. By increasing the minimums so that they match current usage levels, the server will not have to reallocate these resources after it is rebooted next time.

Using Figure 14.12 as an example, let's assume our server has already been in use for a month and we wish to tune these parameters. We record the number of packet receive buffers to be 200 and the current service processes to be 15.

Now let's assume that we look under the server parameters option for the minimum settings for these two pools. We note that the minimum packet receive buffers is set at 150 and the minimum service processes is set to 10. This means that over the last month our server has had to allocate 50 new packet receive buffers (for a total of 200) and five service processes (for a total of 15).

Unless the last month was exceptionally busy, we can assume that if we need to power down our server again, and it is restored to the original values for these two settings, that the server will again have to allocate 50 new packet receive buffers and five service processes. By increasing the minimums to the current usage levels we can prevent the server from having to go through this a second time.

The reason we wish to avoid having the server allocate its own resources is that it does not do it immediately. It will wait until it is absolutely sure it needs additional resources before it will allocate them.

During this time our server performance may appear sluggish. By increasing these values ahead of time, we eliminate this problem.

TIP

These memory resources are normally allocated very slowly. If you ever notice the packet receive buffers climbing rapidly, it may be because of a bad NIC or a buggy NIC driver.

You also want to ensure that these values are not approaching their maximum settings. If the maximums are reached, the server will begin to ignore data requests.

If we press the Tab key we can view the Available Options menu. Besides Server Parameters, the option we are interested in is LAN/WAN Information. Highlight this entry and press Enter.

You will be presented with the Available LAN Driver dialog box as shown in Figure 14.13. This dialog box is a bit misleading, as it appears you can view different information on a per binding basis. For example, Figure 14.13 shows two options within the box. The truth is, information is presented on a per LAN driver basis. Because our figure shows two protocols bound to the same card, the statistics under each will be identical (except for the report protocol and network address). We can select either driver to view this information.

FIGURE 14.13

The LAN Driver screen

Figure 14.14 shows the LAN Driver statistics screen. At the top of the screen is the driver version we are using, the node or MAC address of the card, and the protocol and network address for this particular selection. The important information is the Generic Statistics section.

F I G U R E 14.14

The LAN Driver statistics
screen

The first three statistics—Total packets sent, Total packets received, and No ECB available count—will be present for any network card. The statistics that follow vary depending on the card's manufacturer.

The values in the Total Packets Sent and Total Packets Received fields include all protocols, not just the protocol listed at the top of the screen. These are the statistics to check if we wish to quantify the amount of traffic on a network segment. If you record these values and measure them over a period of time, you can get a general idea of how much traffic is on your network.

The No ECB Available Count records the number of times the NIC has tried to place a frame into the packet receive buffer pool but there were no buffers available. A high number here is indicative of a server that does not have a high enough minimum setting for the packet receive buffers and the server processes.

Below is a brief description of some of the other statistics that may be listed:

- Send Packet Too Big Count—server transmitted a packet that was too large for the NIC to process

- Overflow Count—indicates an overflow in the adapter's receive buffers

- Receive Packet Too Big Count—receive a frame that exceeds topology maximum size

- Receive Packet Too Small Count—receive a frame that exceeds topology minimum size

- Send Packet Retry Count—number of transmission failures due to a hardware error

- Checksum Errors—checksum does not match FCS value

- Hardware Receive Mismatch count—specified packet length does not match actual size

- Total Send OK Byte Count Low—number of bytes transmitted

- Total Send OK Byte Count High—increments by one every time the Total Send OK Byte Count Low reaches 4 Gb

- Total Receive OK Byte Count Low—number of bytes received

- Total Receive OK Byte Count High—increments by one every time the Total Receive OK Byte Count Low reaches 4 Gb

- Adapter Reset Count—the number of times the adapter was reset due to an internal failure

- Adapter Queue Depth—indicates an overflow in the adapter's transmit buffers

- Send OK Single Collision Count—single collision with data being sent after recovery

- Send OK Multiple Collision Count—multiple collisions with data being sent after recovery

- Send OK But Deferred—number of delayed transmissions due to heavy network usage

- Send Abort From Late Collision—collision that may be due to excessive cable length

- Send Abort From Excess Collisions—too many collisions detected to transmit

- Send Abort From Carrier Sense—lost contact with the network during transmission

- Send Abort From Excessive Deferral—network too busy for station to transmit

May of these statistics can give us some great clues as to how our network is performing. For example, if we see the Send OK Multiple Collision Count or Send OK But Deferred values starting to increment, there is a very good chance that the segment is seeing too much traffic.

Ping

Ping uses the IP protocol to send out a test message to a remote system in order to test connectivity. The settings and uses for ping are identical to IPXPING except they apply to the IP protocol.

Tcpcon

Tcpcon is the utility for monitoring IP communications. It is very similar to the IPXCON utility in that it allows you to monitor packet statistics as well as view network and routing information.

Workstation Commands

NetWare has only a few workstation commands that are useful for documenting your network and troubleshooting connectivity.

NLIST SERVER /A/B

The **nlist server /a/b** command produces a list of known NetWare servers. This command is the equivalent of the command that was available on NetWare 3.1*x*. If the **/b** is omitted, only NDS servers are listed.

NLIST USER /A/B

The **nlist user /a/b** command produces a list of users who are currently authenticated to the NDS tree. The output also lists the network and MAC address that the user has logged in from.

If you have a network monitor or analyzer that is not capable of collecting NetWare logon names, but the device does allow you to input names from a file, you can use the output from this command to create your list. This is far quicker than having to enter each one manually.

NWD2

NWD2 is a diagnostic utility that is included with the client32 workstation drivers. While this tool does not document or troubleshoot your network, it will identify all the client drivers installed on the workstation.

NWD2 is useful if you are trying to track down a connectivity problem that is related to only one or two workstations. NWD2 documents which drivers and modules are loaded and reports on the revision and date/time stamp of each. This is useful because you can compare the results to a similar workstation that is functioning properly. If you note any variations, you can take steps to upgrade the appropriate drivers.

Windows NT Server

Windows NT does not have a separate console interface as does IntranetWare. This means that all utilities can be accessed from the server console. We have again broken up our utilities into command line and GUI based categories.

Command Line Networking Tools

The command line tools should be run from within a Command Prompt box. While they can be executed using Run or Explorer, the utility will close before the results can be reviewed.

Arp

The **arp** command is used to display the entries of the ARP (Address Resolution Protocol) cache. The ARP cache contains a map of IP addresses to MAC addresses for the local segment. In order for the system to communicate with a host on the same logical network, it must create an ARP entry for it first.

This is a useful tool for troubleshooting problems such as duplicate IP addresses. If you know that an IP address is being used that shouldn't be, you can ping the address and check the contents of the ARP cache to find out the MAC address of the machine using the address.

Available switches are:

-a	list all entries in the ARP cache
-d *ADDR*	delete the entry with the IP address *ADDR*
-s *ADDR ETH*	add an entry for the system with IP address *ADDR* and the MAC address of *ETH*.

Ipconfig

Ipconfig is used to report on the systems current IP configuration. When used with the **/all** switch as shown in Figure 14.15, ipconfig reports on all aspects of the IP configuration including which IP services have been configured.

Available switches are:

(none)	when no switches are used, IP address, mask and default gateway are reported
/all	report on the above as well as available name services

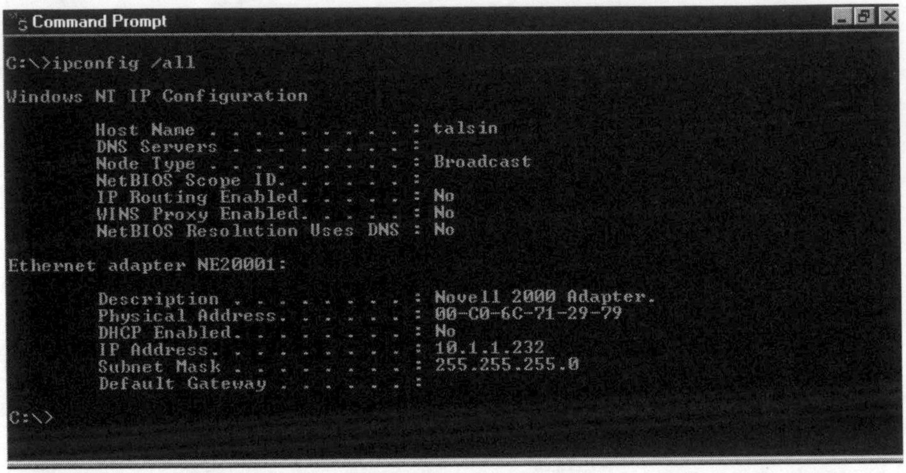

FIGURE 14.15

The ipconfig utility using the **/all** switch

```
Command Prompt                                              _ 8 X
C:\>ipconfig /all

Windows NT IP Configuration

        Host Name . . . . . . . . . : talsin
        DNS Servers . . . . . . . . :
        Node Type . . . . . . . . . : Broadcast
        NetBIOS Scope ID. . . . . . :
        IP Routing Enabled. . . . . : No
        WINS Proxy Enabled. . . . . : No
        NetBIOS Resolution Uses DNS : No

Ethernet adapter NE20001:

        Description . . . . . . . . : Novell 2000 Adapter.
        Physical Address. . . . . . : 00-C0-6C-71-29-79
        DHCP Enabled. . . . . . . . : No
        IP Address. . . . . . . . . : 10.1.1.232
        Subnet Mask . . . . . . . . : 255.255.255.0
        Default Gateway . . . . . . :

C:\>
```

Ipxroute

Ipxroute is used to collect IPX related information from the network. In order for this command to collect information, RIP for NWLink and the SAP agent must be loaded.

This command is useful for ensuring that the NT system has connectivity to NetWare servers or remote IPX networks.

Available switches are:

servers	list known NetWare servers
stats	identify the number of IPX packets sent and received
table	display the IPX routing table

Nbtstat

Nbtstat is used for reporting the NetBIOS names known to this system, or to a remote host. It will also report which systems have been located through network broadcasts or through WINS.

Figure 14.16 shows the **nbtstat** command using the **-r** switch. Reported here is a list of each system discovered from broadcast packets, and a list of each system discovered through the WINS server. There is no WINS server list in our example because a WINS server is not configured.

FIGURE 14.16

The nbtstat command using the **-r** switch

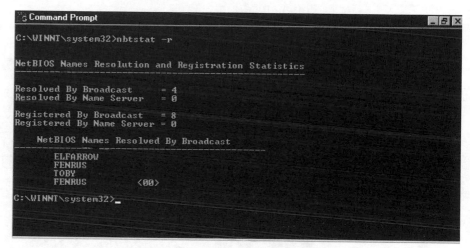

If you have a WINS server configured, you can use the names listed in the "NetBIOS Names Resolved by Broadcast" section to determine which systems may need to be reconfigured to use the WINS server.

Available switches are:

-a *host*	print the name table for the host named *host*
-c	print the contents of the local name cache
-n	print the name table for the local system
-r	report systems discovered through broadcasts and WINS
-s	display the connect connection table

Netstat

Netstat reports on IP connection information and LAN card statistics. This utility is useful when you will be offering other IP services besides NetBIOS over IP, as all IP sessions are recorded.

As shown in Figure 14.17, this is also a good place to look for general Ethernet statistics. Displayed here are total bytes sent and received as well as how much of this traffic was due to broadcast and unicast communications.

FIGURE 14.17

The netstat command using the **-e** switch

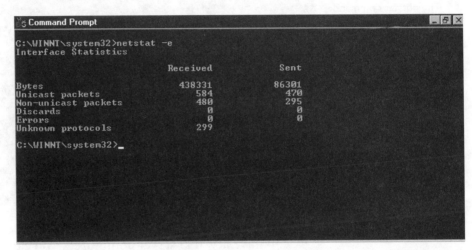

If we compare the ratio of broadcast transmissions to unicast, we see that there are almost as many broadcasts being used to transmit information as there are unicasts. Because broadcasts affect all local systems, this is a bad thing. If we were to see a statistic like this in a production environment, we would know it is time to dust off the old network monitor to see who is generating all these broadcasts.

Available switches are:

-a   list all active connections and ports

-e   list Ethernet statistics

-n	same as "a" except systems are listed by address, not name
-r	print the IP routing table
-s	list statistics on a per port basis
NUM	when a switch is followed by a number, the command is executed at a time interval equal to the numeric value in seconds

Nslookup

Nslookup is a powerful tool for troubleshooting connectivity problems to determine if they are DNS related. The nslookup tool can be pointed at a specific name server to determine if names are being resolved to an IP address correctly. The best way to understand nslookup is to walk through situations when you may need to use it.

Let's say you are cruising the Web and decide to stop by the Sun Web site to check out their latest product line. You enter the address:

```
http://www.sun.com
```

and attempt to connect to the site. The connection fails, and your browser states that the server could not be contacted. At that moment a friend calls who is all excited about the latest SuperSPARC line. When you complain that you are unable to connect to the Web site, your buddy states that they are on the site as you speak and server response is zippy.

This looks like a job for nslookup. When you launch the utility, the following screen appears:

```
C:\nslookup
Default Server: clover.sover.net
Address: 204.71.16.10
>
```

Not very exciting, is it? What nslookup is displaying is that it will use the DNS server `clover.sover.net` to resolve all name queries. The IP address of this system is `204.71.16.10`. Your starting server and IP address may vary. This is actually some pretty useful information as we now know exactly who will be responding to our DNS requests. We can also point at other DNS servers on the fly without having to change our system's primary DNS server (What's that you say? A network change on NT that does not require the system to be rebooted? It's true!).

Our next step would be to enter the host name we wish to resolve. When we do, nslookup will produce the following information:

```
> www.sun.com

Server:  clover.sover.net
Address:  204.71.16.10

Non-authoritative answer:
Name:   www.sun.com
Addresses:  192.9.9.100, 192.9.48.5
```

The first line is the address we entered, `www.sun.com`. The rest of the output is produced by nslookup in response to that query. The first thing nslookup does is remind us which name server we are using. It then proceeds to respond with the requested information.

"Non-authoritative answer" means that `clover.sover.net` is not a DNS server for the host in our query. This lets us know that the information listed was received secondhand from another DNS server.

You will note that the query returned two different IP addresses for this host. Sun is using a DNS feature called "round robin." As users attempt to connect to `www.sun.com`, a different address is handed out each time. This helps to load balance traffic across two identical systems. Because we are using nslookup, however, we were able to retrieve both addresses.

The next step would be to exit the nslookup utility and try pinging each of the two sites. For the purpose of our example we will assume that one server responds while the other one does not.

We now know why our friend was able to connect to Sun's Web site while we were not. They had connected to the functioning system while we happened to connect to the one that was offline.

NSLOOKUP accepts the following commands, once launched:

NAME	print info about the host/domain NAME using default server
NAME1 NAME2	as above, but use NAME2 as server
help or ?	print info on common commands; see nslookup(1) for details
set OPTION	set an option
all	print options, current server and host
[no]debug	print debugging information
[no]d2	print exhaustive debugging information
[no]defname	append domain name to each query
[no]recurse	ask for recursive answer to query
[no]vc	always use a virtual circuit
domain=NAME	set default domain name to NAME
srchlist=N1[/N2/.../N6]	set domain to N1 and search list to N1,N2, etc.
root=NAME	set root server to NAME
retry=X	set number of retries to X

timeout=X	set initial time-out interval to X seconds
querytype=X	set query type, e.g., A,ANY, CNAME,HINFO,MX,PX,NS,PTR,SOA,TXT,WKS,SRV,NAPTR
port=X	set port number to send query on
type=X	synonym for querytype
class=X	set query class to one of IN (Internet), CHAOS, HESIOD or ANY
server NAME	set default server to NAME, using current default server
lserver NAME	set default server to NAME, using initial server
finger [USER]	finger the optional USER at the current default host
root	set current default server to the root
ls [opt] DOMAIN [> FILE]	list addresses in DOMAIN (optional: output to FILE)
-a	list canonical names and aliases
-h	list HINFO (CPU type and operating system)
-s	list well-known services
-d	list all records
-t TYPE	list records of the given type (e.g., A, CNAME, MX, etc.)
view FILE	sort an 'ls' output file and view it with more
exit	exit the program, ^D also exits

Ping

Ping on Windows NT is functionally identical to ping on every other platform. Ping is used to verify connectivity between two IP hosts and will report the travel time required to echo out the remote host and back again.

Available switches are:

-n *NUM*	echo the number of times specified by *NUM*
-l *NUM*	specify the size of the echo packet
-r *NUM*	record the route traveled for the number of hops specified by *NUM*. If more hops are required than the specified value, do not record the remainder of the route.

Route

The **route** command was discussed in detail in Chapter 6. Use it to define and display static IP routes to remote networks segments.

Tracert

The **tracert** command is the Windows NT equivalent to Unix's traceroute. It was explained in detail in Chapter 5 (see Figure 5.5).

GUI Networking Tools

The following utilities can be launched directly from the NT desktop or by using the **run** command off of the Start menu.

Network Monitoring Tool

While we discussed the Network Monitoring Tool in Chapter 8, its functionality is great enough to warrant another mention here. The Network Monitoring Tool provides a similar level of functionality to Novell's LANAlyzer. The tool is capable of capturing traffic and performing frame decodes. While the format is different than LANAlyzer, the quantity of frame information is the same.

The only real drawback with the Network Monitoring Tool is that it only runs on NT Server. This means that you can only monitor the network segments that the server is directly attached to. Also, in a switched environment where multiple collision domains are created, you are limited to only being able to capture traffic statistics that directly affect the server.

Unlike LANAlyzer, that will create trends as well as capture traffic, the Network Monitoring Tool relies on Performance Monitor to create any required trends.

Performance Monitor

The Performance Monitor, as shown in Figure 14.18, allows us to graph multiple performance parameters at the same time. The three listed traces are all network-related. However we could have chosen to monitor disk or processor utilization as well. This makes it extremely easy to look at the cause and effect relationship between different parameters. For example, we can see there is a direct correlation between network utilization and total bytes received while the total frames received remains relatively unaffected.

There are some drawbacks to this tool, however. The most significant is that I must preset my sample rate to a specific value. Unlike LANAlyzer, which collects both trend and detailed statistics at the same time, I can only choose one or the other with Performance Monitor.

Also, my collection of trend data is accomplished by extending the time between which samples are measured. Performance Monitor does not measure a block of results and then average them out like LAN-Alyzer does for long term trends. Performance Monitor simply takes an instantaneous reading at longer intervals. This means that if the sample rate happens to hit a few bumps or valleys in my measurement, the entire trend can become skewed. The result is that you lose accuracy as you try to extend the monitoring period.

F I G U R E   14.18

Performance Monitor

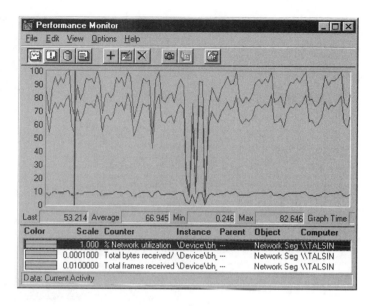

Winmsd

Like the NWD2 utility for NetWare, winmsd can report on driver data and revision information. The difference is that while NWD2 is designed to be run on a workstation, winmsd is used when diagnosing the server.

Figure 14.19 shows the Network tab of the winmsd utility. Reported here is not only driver information, but similar statistics to what can be found under the LAN/WAN Driver menu on IntranetWare. While total bytes sent and received is not shown, these statistics are available on this screen if you scroll down to the bottom.

Unix

All of the Unix troubleshooting tools we will cover are command line utilities. When a tool has been covered in a previous section of this chapter, we will refer you back to the appropriate section.

FIGURE 14.19

The Network tab of the winmsd utility

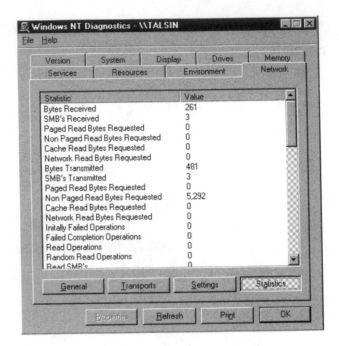

arp

This command is identical to the **arp** command under Windows NT. It is used for viewing and modifying the contents of the ARP cache.

ifconfig

ifconfig is normally used to configure a network interface. When used without any switches, it can also be used to report communication information for each network interface.

Figure 14.20 shows the output of the ifconfig utility. The figure shows the IP address as well as transmit and receive errors. If your Unix system is suffering from poor network performance, this is the first place to look to see if any errors are being generated.

FIGURE 14.20

The ifconfig utility

```
[root@toby /root]# ifconfig
lo        Link encap:Local Loopback
          inet addr:127.0.0.1  Bcast:127.255.255.255  Mask:255.0.0.0
          UP BROADCAST LOOPBACK RUNNING  MTU:3584  Metric:1
          RX packets:88 errors:0 dropped:0 overruns:0
          TX packets:88 errors:0 dropped:0 overruns:0

eth0      Link encap:10Mbps Ethernet  HWaddr 00:60:97:69:18:C3
          inet addr:10.1.1.10  Bcast:10.1.1.255  Mask:255.255.255.0
          UP BROADCAST RUNNING MULTICAST  MTU:1500  Metric:1
          RX packets:565 errors:0 dropped:0 overruns:0
          TX packets:370 errors:0 dropped:0 overruns:0
          Interrupt:10 Base address:0x300
```

netstat

The netstat utility is identical to the netstat utility under Windows NT. Netstat is used to monitor the routing table as well as connection and session information.

nslookup

The nslookup utility is used to diagnose problems related to DNS. It is functionally identical to the nslookup utility supplied with Windows NT.

ping

The ping utility is used to test connectivity between two network hosts. This utility is identical to the ping utility supplied with Windows NT.

route

The route utility is used to both view and modify the static routing table. It is functionally identical to the Windows NT utility with the same name.

statnet

When statnet is executed, it enables the screen shown in Figure 14.21. This utility gives us a snapshot picture as to what type of traffic conditions exist on the network at any given time. All values are dynamic, meaning they will adjust up and down as traffic conditions change. There is no way to produce cumulative or trend data.

F I G U R E   14.21

The statnet network
statistic screen

```
                              NETWORK STATISTICS


       GENERAL                    TYPES     2934 FRAMES


       KB/sec:       45.94        IP:       2934 100.0%
       Frames/sec:     733        ARP+RARP:    0   0.0%
       Av. frame len:   64        ICMP:        0   0.0%
                                  IPX:         0   0.0%
                                  Vines:       0   0.0%
       ETHERNET: eth0             NetB 802:    0   0.0%
                                  SNAether:    0   0.0%
       KB/sec:       45.94        Other:       0   0.0%
       Frames/sec:     733
       802.3 Fr/sec:     0        TCP/IP    2934 100.0%
       Av. frame len:   64        FTP:         0   0.0%
       Load:         3.76%        NNTP:        0   0.0%
                                  RPC/NFS:     0   0.0%
       PLIP/PPP/SLIP             WWW:          0   0.0%
                                  SMTP:        7   0.2%
       KB/sec:        0.00        DNS:         0   0.0%
       Frames/sec:       0        NETB NS:     0   0.0%
       Av. frame len:    0        NETB Dg:     0   0.0%
                                  NETBIOS:  2925  99.7%
```

Because we cannot generate long term trends, the usefulness of this utility is severely limited. We would need to keep an eagle eye on this screen in order to catch anything out of the ordinary. While this is fine if we know we are currently experiencing a problem, it limits our ability to generate long term statistics.

Still, the ability to break down network traffic by protocol and service as well as view it in a format that presents this value as a percentage of total bandwidth in use is an alluring feature. Considering that the utility is free, we cannot complain too loudly.

tcpdump

tcpdump is a frame capture utility that allows you to view the header information of IP frames. A sample of its output is presented in Figure 14.22. From left to right, this utility identifies:

- the time stamp

- the source host and port number

- the destination host and port number

- the flag setting (P=PUSH, S=SYN, F=FIN, R=RST, .=none)

- the start byte:stop byte for packet sequencing

- the amount of data transferred (the number in parenthesis)

- the ack means this is an acknowledgment to a data request

- the acknowledgment number (1)

- the data window size (31744)

FIGURE 14.22

tcpdump recording a
telnet session

```
15:05:46.692522 toby.foobar.com.telnet > ElfArrow.foobar.com.1040: P 8370:8476(106) ack 1 win 31744 (DF)
15:05:46.792522 toby.foobar.com.telnet > ElfArrow.foobar.com.1040: P 8476:8675(199) ack 1 win 31744 (DF)
15:05:46.792522 ElfArrow.foobar.com.1040 > toby.foobar.com.telnet: . ack 8675 win 7845 (DF)
15:05:46.792522 toby.foobar.com.telnet > ElfArrow.foobar.com.1040: P 8675:8781(106) ack 1 win 31744 (DF)
15:05:46.892522 toby.foobar.com.telnet > ElfArrow.foobar.com.1040: P 8781:8980(199) ack 1 win 31744 (DF)
15:05:46.892522 ElfArrow.foobar.com.1040 > toby.foobar.com.telnet: . ack 8980 win 7540 (DF)
15:05:46.892522 toby.foobar.com.telnet > ElfArrow.foobar.com.1040: P 8980:9086(106) ack 1 win 31744 (DF)
15:05:46.992522 toby.foobar.com.telnet > ElfArrow.foobar.com.1040: P 9086:9285(199) ack 1 win 31744 (DF)
15:05:46.992522 ElfArrow.foobar.com.1040 > toby.foobar.com.telnet: . ack 9285 win 8760 (DF)
15:05:46.992522 toby.foobar.com.telnet > ElfArrow.foobar.com.1040: P 9285:9391(106) ack 1 win 31744 (DF)

94 packets received by filter
0 packets dropped by kernel
[root@toby /root]#
```

While not a graphical utility, we do have all the information required to track communications between systems. tcpdump has many available command line switches. Some of the most useful are:

-e	print Ethernet header information
-i *INT*	monitor interface *INT*
-n	do not convert host and port numbers to names
-q	reduce the amount if information recorded
-S	absolute instead of relative sequence numbers
-t	do not print the time stamp
-v	more verbose output
-vv	maximum output
-w `file`	Capture the frames to a file named `file`
host `hostname`	record traffic to and from `hostname`
net `network`	record traffic to and from `network`
type	record traffic of only a certain type. Valid type options are ether, ip, arp, tcp, and udp
qualifiers	src (source), dst (destination)

Table 14.1 lists some examples of how these switches can be used.

TABLE 14.1 Switch examples	**Command**	**Effect**
	tcpdump -v	capture all traffic and report verbose information
	tcpdump -i eth0	only monitor the interface Ethernet 0
	tcpdump udp host talsin	capture all UDP traffic involving Talsin
	tcpdump dst host talsin port 23	capture all traffic headed for port 23 on talsin
	tcpdump tcp net 10.1.1.0	capture all TCP traffic going to and coming from network 10.1.1.0

Telnet

Telnet as a troubleshooting tool? It is when you use it correctly. Telnet can be used to verify that a particular server is accepting connections for a particular service.

For example, let's assume that we wish to set up a Lotus Notes server-to-Lotus Notes server replication over the Internet. We believe that we have configured the Notes servers correctly and we ensure that each system can ping the other across the Internet. However, when we initiate the replication, the process fails, stating that the remote server could not be reached.

What went wrong? Most likely we have a firewall or router blocking the port that Notes is attempting to communicate on. This is the most likely candidate when one service can reach a remote system (ping), but another one cannot (Notes).

To test this theory, enter the following command:

```
telnet notes.foobar.com 1352
```

where "notes.foobar.com" is the name of the remote Notes server we are trying to reach, and 1352 is the TCP port number that Notes uses to communicate.

If we see:

```
trying notes.foobar.com...
telnet: Unable to connect to remote host: Connection
refused
```

we know that either port 1352 is blocked between here and the remote Notes system or that the remote system is not configured to accept services on that port.

If we see:

```
trying notes.foobar.com...
Connected to notes.foobar.com.
Escape character is '^]'.
```

we know we have a clear path between here and that the remote server on port 1352 and that the remote server is accepting services on that port.

While ping is fine for testing general connectivity, it does not take into account firewalls or packet filters. These devices are configured to restrict services on certain ports, which will allow some services through but not others.

Telnet was not listed under NT because the version included with the operating system has trouble echoing back characters during this type of communication. If you want to be able to use Telnet for testing general connectivity under Windows NT, replace the supplied version with one that has a slightly better VT100 emulation.

traceroute

The **traceroute** command is identical to the Windows NT **tracert** command. This tool is used to record the routers or hops that must be crossed in order to communicate with a remote host.

Summary

Now that we know what tools we have to work with when diagnosing a network problem, it's now time to look at some real issues and learn how to apply these tools.

CHAPTER

15

Diagnosing Real-World Problems

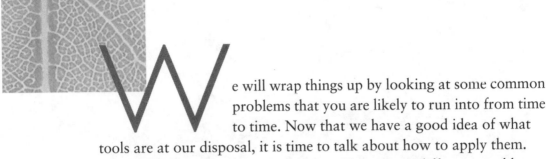

We will wrap things up by looking at some common problems that you are likely to run into from time to time. Now that we have a good idea of what tools are at our disposal, it is time to talk about how to apply them.

Each case outlined in this chapter will require a different trouble-shooting process for resolution because a network administrator of a multiprotocol environment can be called on to solve a wide range of problems.

Ping Strangeness

Our first case involves tracking down unknown traffic on our network. While performing a packet capture with our network monitor, we note the packet exchange recorded in Figure 15.1. We have seven separate hosts that are continually pinging an eighth host which is our Cisco router. No matter what time of day we perform a capture, this exchange is taking place.

There are two very good reasons why it is worth our time to investigate why this event is taking place.

Security

The excessive pings could be an attempt to probe available network resources, or perform a denial of service. Ping is one of those utilities that everyone takes for granted. Because ping is viewed as a simple tool for testing connectivity, most network administrators have no policy in place to control it.

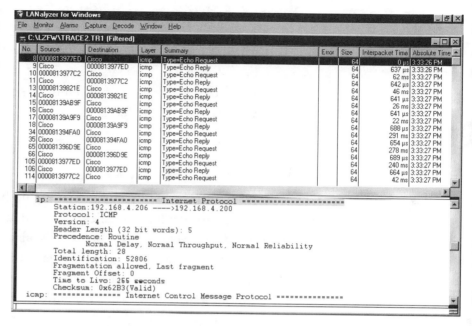

FIGURE 15.1

Excessive pings on the
network

It is for this reason that ping is a very good tool to use when you want to verify the existence of network resources inside a firewall. While an administrator may block telnet or FTP access to their network, you can usually pass right through a firewall using ping. This is not to say a firewall cannot block ICMP traffic, it simply means that many administrators do not configure it to do so.

It is unlikely, however, that this trace is an attacker's probe. A would-be attacker would not be foolish enough to continually check your resources. They would be in and out as quickly as possible.

The other trouble that ping can cause is when it is used with the -f switch. If I use this switch when pinging a host, I tell the ping utility "ping the remote host as fast as you possibly can and do not bother waiting for a reply." This causes a flood of ping packets to be sent to the remote system.

Ping is normally used as a means of measuring travel time to a remote host and back again. Because the ability of the remote host to respond to these echo requests can greatly effect the final results, most systems will attempt to reply to a ping echo as quickly as possible.

This is where the trouble starts. If I am sending a flood of ping traffic to a host, it may become so busy trying to respond to the echo requests that performance for other services slows to a crawl. This is referred to as a *denial of service*.

It is unlikely that this trace is an attempt to perform a denial of service because each host is only pinging the destination system once per second.

Bandwidth

If nothing else, this constant pinging is eating up bandwidth. While it is true that 14 fps is not a lot of traffic, it still reduces our potential bandwidth by 20KB. This effect is somewhat cumulative in that the 14 frames are occurring every second of the day. This is not simply a one-time event.

Also, without knowing why this exchange is taking place, we have no way of knowing if the effect will spread to other systems. There could be an error in a configuration file or a script that is causing this to occur.

Looking For Clues

Let's make this interesting and say we do not know who the source IP addresses belong to. We'll assume this is a wild and free environment that allows people to choose IP address by counting on their toes or by using Tarot cards.

Our first clue is that the destination system is a router. This implies that the continual pinging may have something to do with the routing table or gateway settings.

Our next clue is that all the systems that are generating the ping requests have the same Ethernet vendor address (000081). This implies that whatever is causing this to occur may be vendor specific. We could then use LANAlyzer's Station Monitor to sort on known MAC addresses and verify that every system with this vendor address is generating ping requests.

Let's assume we have verified this. We have seven devices that are using this Ethernet vendor address and each one of them is generating ping requests.

Our next step is to find out which vendor is using that code. By referencing the list in Appendix B, we see that these devices were all manufactured by Synoptic. A quick inventory check verifies that our network is using seven Synoptic manageable hubs for connecting users to network resources.

Our next step is to see if the vendor maintains an online support database, and if so, does it contain any resolutions to this problem. A search of the technical database at Bay Networks (Bay owns Synoptic) reveals that pinging the router is not a bug, but a feature.

The seven hubs support the use of ICMP for dynamically discovering IP routers. The Synoptic Network Management Module (NMM) attempts to discover available routers in order to establish communications with a management stations. Because our network does not use a management station, the hubs are still looking for one.

The document states that the NMM will ping the router if:

- It has not detected an ICMP redirect message (pointing it to another router).

- It has not detected an ICMP router advertisement (which are not used in a static route environment).

- It has not received a packet from the router for a specified period of time.

In other words, we have three choices:

- Purchase a management station so the hub will stop looking for it.

- Begin broadcasting ICMP router advertisements on our network.

- Disable IP on the hub.

Our first option is expensive and hardly worth the investment to simply reduce this small amount of traffic on our network. Our second would replace 840 unicast frames per minute (total number of ping requests and replies) with a single broadcast frame. Implementing this option would be contingent on what other IP devices are on the network and how this routing information would effect them.

Our third option is clearly the easiest—simply disable IP on each of the hubs. Without an IP address, the hubs have no way to issue ping requests to other IP hosts. One word of caution about removing the IP address. If you do not assign an IP address to some network devices, they will automatically begin issuing bootp requests to try and get one on their own.

If this occurs, you have to decide which is the worst of two evils—a unicast ping echo once per second, or a bootp broadcast once per minute.

Duplicate IP Addresses

A common problem in many networking environments occurs when two machines try to use the same IP address; this can result in intermittent communications. The following series of events is what causes the intermittent communications to occur. Let's assume that host2 and host3 have both been assigned the IP address 10.1.1.10.

- Host1 needs to transmit data to the IP address 10.1.1.10.

- Host1 determines that this is a local address and issues an ARP request.

- Host2 responds to the ARP request with its own MAC address.

- Host1 makes an ARP entry associating the IP address 10.1.1.10 with host2's MAC address.

- Host1 delivers data to host2.

- Host3 responds to the ARP request with its own MAC address.

- Host1 removes the ARP entry for host2 and replaces it by associating the IP address 10.1.1.10 with host3's MAC address.

- Host2 requests more data.

- Host1 delivers host2's data to host3 per the ARP table entry.

Host2 will eventually time out the data request because it is no longer able to communicate with host1. Every time host2 issues a request, the data will be sent to host3. When the entry *ages out* of the ARP cache, the whole process starts over.

Information is only cached for a limited period of time. When this time expires and the entry is removed, it is referred to as being aged out.

It's possible that the second time host1 issues an ARP request that host3 will reply first. This will restore connectivity to host2 but interrupt communications with host3. This ping pong effect will continue until one of the systems powers down or changes its IP address.

So now that we know why duplicate IP addresses are a bad thing, all we need to know is how to identify the offending systems. If you are using a Mac or Windows 95, the machine will send an ARP request during startup to ensure the address it wishes to use is free. If it's not, the console displays a warning message. While this process will identify one of the two systems, we still have to find the other.

Our best bet is to power down the system we know about and go to a system that does not have an address conflict. From this system, we ping the IP address in question and display the associated MAC address by typing:

```
ping ADDR
arp -a ADDR
```

Where ADDR is the IP address that is in question. You must be on the same logical subnet as the IP address in order for this to work.

We now know the MAC address as well as the illegal IP address the system in question is using. Where we go from here depends on what kind of network environment we are using.

- NetWare—Generate a userlist and match the MAC address to a logon name.

- NT—Run NBTSTAT to associate the IP address with a machine name.

- Unix—Run **who** to associate a logon name with the IP address.

All of these options assume that the user on the system is logged on to one or more network resources. If they are not accessing network resources, it may be difficult at best to determine who they are. While we could check the Ethernet vendor address to see who made the NIC card for the system, this is not as useful when tracking down a workstation because organizations tend to standardize on only a few network card vendors.

If we have a network monitor or analyzer, we could set the device to capture all traffic exchanged with the system's MAC address. This would let us know exactly what network resources the user is using, and help to simplify the process of tracking them down.

We could also view the decode of the data field in each frame. This may yield even more clues as to who this mystery user may be. For example, if while viewing the data we notice that the user in question is accessing the sales database, we can assume that the user works in sales.

Once we have identified the offending system, we can flog the user and assign them a legitimate IP address.

Undeliverable Mail

As mail interfaces become more user friendly, they tend to hide much of the information that can be used for debugging purposes. Most modern mail clients remove the mail header before the message is delivered to the client's mailbox. This "cleans up" the message for the user so that when they open the message it only contains pertinent information.

Error messages have also become more generic. When a user receives a bounced mail message that simply states "message could not be delivered," what exactly does that mean? There are a number of reasons why a message delivery may fail:

- The post office to SMTP gateway process does not pick up the message.

- The SMTP gateway is unable to resolve the domain name portion of the destination e-mail address.

- The SMTP gateway is unable to find a mail system for the destination domain.

- The SMTP gateway can find a mail system, but cannot find a route to get there or the connection is down.

- The SMTP gateway connects to the remote mail system but times out due to lack of response.

- The SMTP gateway connects to the remote mail system but the user name portion of the e-mail address is rejected.

Each of these issues has a different failure mode and a different method of resolving the problem. As we walk through the process of determining the cause of failure, we will assume that the bounced message contained no useable errors.

Our first step should be to check the error log generated by the SMTP gateway. The gateway should generate a running log of all messages sent and received. It should also indicate when a message delivery failed and why this failure occurred.

But what happens when our error logs do not indicate where the problem lies? When this is the case, we need to emulate a mail system and see what happens during the process of trying to deliver the mail message.

In order to test manual delivery, we will need to perform the following steps:

1. Test local connectivity.

2. Verify the SMTP mail gateway is working.

3. Find the name server for the remote domain.

4. Find the mail system for the remote domain.

5. Test connectivity to the remote mail system.

6. Verify the recipient's e-mail address.

Our first step is to ensure that we still have a valid connection to the Internet. To do this we can simply try to ping a known host outside of our network. A company's Web server is usually a good bet.

Once we know we still have an Internet connection, we should ensure that the SMTP gateway is still working. We can do this by sending an e-mail to ourselves. If the gateway is capable of processing the address and returning it correctly, it should also be able to perform a delivery outside of the domain.

This assumes that we are dealing with an existing gateway that has been working up until now. If this system has just been configured this test is not valid because the IP parameters may be set up incorrectly. If this is a new installation, or if we suspect the IP setup, we will need to deliver an e-mail message outside of the domain to verify correct operation of the mail gateway.

Now that we are sure that the mail gateway is working correctly, we can begin the process of emulating mail delivery to see where the problem lies.

Our next step is to find the name server for the remote domain. This can be done by using the **whois** command or through a search in **nslookup**. Because the **nslookup** process is a closer match to the process the mail gateway uses, we will use that method.

So we fire up **nslookup** and receive our greater than prompt. The output looks something like the following:

```
Server:   clover.sover.net
Address:   204.71.16.10
>
```

where `clover.sover.net` would be replaced with the name of your local DNS server. We next configure nslookup to only show us name servers by typing:

```
>set type = ns
```

Next, we will need to get a list of name servers for the remote domain our e-mail message is failing to reach. We do this by typing in the name of the domain. This causes nslookup to respond with the following output:

```
> foobar.com

Server:   clover.sover.net
Address:   204.71.16.10

Non-authoritative answer:
foobar.com     nameserver = NS1.FOOBAR.COM
foobar.com     nameserver = NS.FOOBAR.COM
foobar.com     nameserver = NS2.FOOBAR.COM
```

```
Authoritative answers can be found from:
NS1.FOOBAR.COM   internet address = 10.50.5.10
NS.FOOBAR.COM    internet address = 10.50.5.5
NS2.FOOBAR.COM   internet address = 10.50.5.20


>
```

We have received a non-authoritative answer. As we discussed in the last chapter, this simply means that this is secondhand information received from another DNS server. To ensure that we receive authoritative answers, we must point nslookup at one of the listed name servers by typing:

```
> server ns1.foobar.com


Default Server:  ns1.foobar.com
Address:  10.50.5.10
>
```

We will now receive authoritative answers for any queries regarding foobar.com. Next, we need to configure nslookup to only look for mail servers. We do this by typing:

```
> set type = mx
```

This tells nslookup to only return mail servers in response to all of our queries. Now we simply enter the domain name that we are trying to send mail to in order to find out which systems it uses to send and receive mail.

```
> foobar.com


Server:  ns1.foobar.com
Address:  10.50.5.10
```

```
foobar.com          preference = 10, mail exchanger =
                    ns2.foobar.com
foobar.com          preference = 0, mail exchanger =
                    mail.foobar.com
foobar.com          nameserver = ns1.foobar.com
foobar.com          nameserver = ns2.foobar.com
foobar.com          nameserver = ns.foobar.com
ns2.foobar.com      internet address = 10.50.5.20
mail.foobar.com     internet address = 10.50.5.30
ns1.foobar.com      internet address = 10.50.5.10
ns.foobar.com       internet address = 10.50.5.5
>
```

The mail system with the lowest preference is the preferred mail server. This means all mail should be delivered to mail.foobar.com. If that system is unavailable, mail should be sent to ns2.foobar.com. It's a common practice to use one of the name servers as a backup mail system.

We can now record the address information and exit the nslookup utility. Next, we need to determine if the mail system is online and accepting e-mail messages. We do this by typing:

telnet mail.foobar.com 25

This allows us to use Telnet to attempt to deliver a mail message to the remote system. If all goes well, we should see a message similar to the following:

```
$ telnet mail.foobar.com 25
Trying 10.50.5.30...
Connected to mail.foobar.com.
Escape character is '^]'.
220 mail.foobar.com ESMTP Sendmail 8.8.4/8.8.4; Wed, 2
Jul 1997 10:34:02 -0400
```

The first thing to note is the IP address Telnet is *trying*. This should match the IP address we found through nslookup. If it does not, the remote mail system may have been moved to a new IP address and our current DNS information is out of date. This can occur when the remote host has a long time to live set. When the IP address changes, DNS servers on the Internet will not attempt to reread the IP address (thus finding the new one) until the TTL has expired.

If this is the case, we can force our DNS server to discover the correct IP address by stopping and starting the DNS service.

If we receive a "connection refused" message instead of the rest of the listed output, we were unable to access mail services on the remote machine. There are four possible causes for not being able connect to the mail system:

- The Internet connection for the remote domain is down.

- There is a firewall blocking the service.

- The remote mail system is down.

- Mail services are not running on the remote system.

To see what the root cause may be, we could try pinging the remote mail system. If this is successful, we know the remote mail system is online, it is just not accepting any mail messages. If the ping fails, any one of the first three failure modes could be the problem. We could then try pinging other hosts in the domain. If this is successful we know the remote mail system is down. If we cannot ping any other hosts in the domain, we are left with the possibility that the connection may be down or we have an improperly configured firewall. In either case, there is no way to reach the remote mail system at this time.

Let's assume that we where able to connect to the remote mail system and received the above listed output. Our next step would be to verify the e-mail address that we were attempting to send the message to. We do this by using the **vrfy** command. When we attempt to verify the e-mail address, we should receive the following output:

```
vrfy somebody@foobar.com
250 Mary Somebody <somebody@foobar.com>
```

where somebody@foobar.com is replaced with the e-mail address we are testing. If this e-mail address is known to the mail server, it should reply with the second line shown above indicating the user's full address including proper name.

If the mail server reports back:

```
vrfy somebody@foobar.com
550 somebody@foobar.com... User unknown
```

we know that the e-mail address is incorrect. This could be due to a spelling error or the user may no longer have a mail account on the system. We can verify which problem is the case by sending mail to postmaster@foobar.com. This is a generic mail account that should be (operative word being "should") set up on every mail system for reporting e-mail problems. We could send the Postmaster an e-mail indicating the e-mail address we are trying to send mail to. The Postmaster should know if this is an address that was recently removed or if the spelling is incorrect.

Some mail administrators disable the **vrfy** command because a would-be attackers may try to use it to discover logon names. Some mail systems like Microsoft Exchange do not even support this command. If the mail system comes back with:

```
vrfy somebody@foobar.com
500 Command unrecognized
```

then **vrfy** has been disabled or is not supported. You are left with contacting the Postmaster on the remote mail system to verify the address.

As shown, there are may places in the e-mail delivery process where the transfer can fail. The trick to resolving e-mail problems is to isolate the failure mode and take appropriate steps to fix it. This is not always possible. For example, if the failure was due to the destination domain's Internet connection being down, there is not a whole lot you can do to help them get back online. At least now you can tell the user who was attempting to send the e-mail message exactly why it did not go through.

Connectivity Problems after a Server Upgrade

In our next case, we upgrade a NetWare file server from version 3.12 to 4.11 and immediately experience a connectivity problem with one of our network devices. Consider the network drawing shown in Figure 15.2. We have two routed segments separated by a network file server. On one of our networks is a Shiva LANRover E, a device which provides dial-in and dial-out connectivity for our network.

FIGURE 15.2

Our simple two segment network

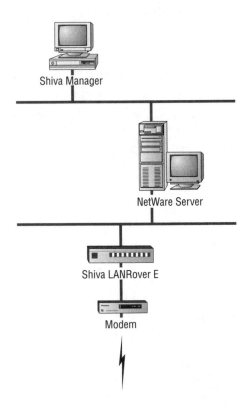

Shiva Manager

NetWare Server

Shiva LANRover E

Modem

Our network has been functioning just fine, but we have decided to upgrade the NetWare 3.12 server to version 4.11 in order to take advantage of some of the features the NOS can provide. We upgrade the server and verify that workstations located on both segments can log on to the file server and see their files.

All is going well until we power up the LANRover and attempt to connect to it with the management software in order to verify its operation. The management software finds the LANRover, but after a brief period of time it disappears from the selection screen of the management utility. If we power cycle the device again, it will show up in the management window for about a minute and then disappear.

Figure 15.3 shows a trace of what is occurring. We have set our capture utility to monitor all inbound and outbound communications with the LANRover, and it shows what information is being exchanged just prior to the LANRover dropping offline.

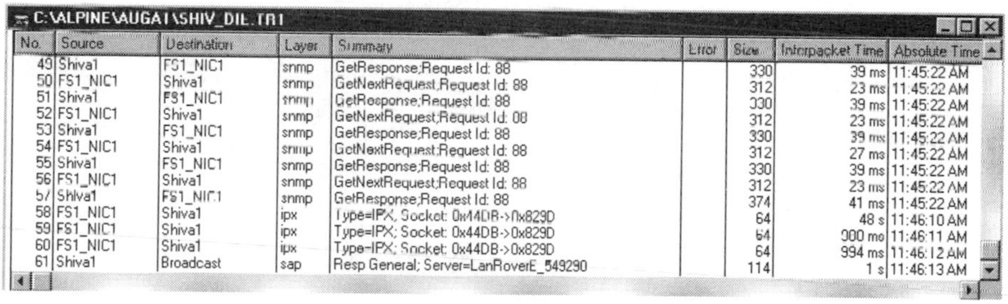

FIGURE 15.3

A trace of our LANRover dropping offline

No.	Source	Destination	Layer	Summary	Error	Size	Interpacket Time	Absolute Time
49	Shiva1	FS1_NIC1	snmp	GetResponse;Request Id: 88		330	39 ms	11:45:22 AM
50	FS1_NIC1	Shiva1	snmp	GetNextRequest;Request Id: 88		312	23 ms	11:45:22 AM
51	Shiva1	FS1_NIC1	snmp	GetResponse;Request Id: 88		330	39 ms	11:45:22 AM
52	FS1_NIC1	Shiva1	snmp	GetNextRequest;Request Id: 88		312	23 ms	11:45:22 AM
53	Shiva1	FS1_NIC1	snmp	GetResponse;Request Id: 88		330	39 ms	11:45:22 AM
54	FS1_NIC1	Shiva1	snmp	GetNextRequest;Request Id: 88		312	27 ms	11:45:22 AM
55	Shiva1	FS1_NIC1	snmp	GetResponse;Request Id: 88		330	39 ms	11:45:22 AM
56	FS1_NIC1	Shiva1	snmp	GetNextRequest;Request Id: 88		312	23 ms	11:45:22 AM
57	Shiva1	FS1_NIC1	snmp	GetResponse;Request Id: 88		374	41 ms	11:45:22 AM
58	FS1_NIC1	Shiva1	ipx	Type=IPX; Socket: 0x44DB->0x829D		64	48 s	11:46:10 AM
59	FS1_NIC1	Shiva1	ipx	Type=IPX; Socket: 0x44DB->0x829D		64	900 ms	11:46:11 AM
60	FS1_NIC1	Shiva1	ipx	Type=IPX; Socket: 0x44DB->0x829D		64	994 ms	11:46:12 AM
61	Shiva1	Broadcast	sap	Resp General; Server=LanRoverE_549290		114	1 s	11:46:13 AM

We can see that the LANRover (identified as Shiva1) has been communicating with its management station on the other network, through the NetWare file server (identified as FS1_NIC1). The management station is performing a series of SNMP **get next** commands in order to retrieve the LANRover's configuration information. In this particular case, it is SNMP over IPX (identified in the frame decode, which is not shown). In frame 57 the connection switches over to pure IPX. The management station makes three attempts at an IPX connection after which the LANRover broadcasts a SAP. It is at this point that the connection dies and no further communication is possible. So what happened to our connection?

First, let's collect our clues and see what we know for sure:

■ Workstations connect to the server and never drop offline.

■ The management station can initially connect to the LANRover.

■ At some point the connection between the LANRover and the management station falls apart.

■ The condition is resolved when the LANRover gets rebooted.

■ This condition is repeatable as the connection always drops after a short amount of time.

■ This configuration worked when the server was NetWare 3.12.

We can rule out a cabling problem because the LANRover and the management station can actually connect to each other. Also, if it was a cabling problem, rebooting the LANRover would have no effect.

To analyze this complex situation, we need to consider the changes that were made to the way a server communicates from NetWare 3.12 to NetWare 4.11. One of the biggest changes was the introduction of the NLSP routing protocol which is enabled by default with backwards compatibility to RIP/SAP.

Examine Figure 15.4. This is a RIP/SAP server advertising the networks and services that are known to it. Notice that it is sending a RIP and a SAP once per minute which is being delivered to the broadcast address.

Now examine Figure 15.5. This is an NLSP server looking for other NLSP devices. Notice that we are no longer blindly advertising route and service information to anyone who happens to be around. We are specifically looking for other NLSP devices with whom to exchange information.

Capture Buffer (Filtered)

No.	Source	Destination	Layer	Summary	Error	Size	Interpacket Time	Absolute Time
12	TALSIN	Broadcast	sap	Resp General; Server=TALSIN		370	29 s	2:51:45 PM
13	TALSIN	Broadcast	rip	Resp network=32 F4 78 CB; 1 hop		64	29 s	2:52:14 PM
14	TALSIN	Broadcast	sap	Resp General; Server=TALSIN		370	29 s	2:52:43 PM
15	TALSIN	Broadcast	rip	Resp network=32 F4 78 CB; 1 hop		64	29 s	2:53:12 PM
16	TALSIN	Broadcast	sap	Resp General; Server=TALSIN		370	29 s	2:53:41 PM
19	TALSIN	Broadcast	rip	Resp network=32 F4 78 CB; 1 hop		64	29 s	2:54:10 PM
20	TALSIN	Broadcast	sap	Resp General; Server=TALSIN		370	29 s	2:54:39 PM
21	TALSIN	Broadcast	rip	Resp network=32 F4 78 CB; 1 hop		64	29 s	2:55:08 PM
22	TALSIN	Broadcast	sap	Resp General; Server=TALSIN		370	29 s	2:55:37 PM
23	TALSIN	Broadcast	rip	Resp network=32 F4 78 CB; 1 hop		64	29 s	2:56:06 PM
24	TALSIN	Broadcast	sap	Resp General; Server=TALSIN		370	29 s	2:56:35 PM
25	TALSIN	Broadcast	rip	Resp network=32 F4 78 CB; 1 hop		64	29 s	2:57:04 PM
26	TALSIN	Broadcast	sap	Resp General; Server=TALSIN		370	29 s	2:57:33 PM
27	TALSIN	Broadcast	rip	Resp network=32 F4 78 CB; 1 hop		64	29 s	2:58:02 PM
28	TALSIN	Broadcast	sap	Resp General; Server=TALSIN		370	29 s	2:58:32 PM
31	TALSIN	Broadcast	rip	Resp network=32 F4 78 CB; 1 hop		64	29 s	2:59:01 PM
32	TALSIN	Broadcast	sap	Resp General; Server=TALSIN		370	29 s	2:59:30 PM
33	TALSIN	Broadcast	rip	Resp network=32 F4 78 CB; 1 hop		64	29 s	2:59:59 PM

Capture Buffer

No.	Source	Destination	Layer	Summary	Error	Size	Interpacket Time	Absolute Time
217	TALSIN	Broadcast	nlsp	LAN Level 1 NLSP Hello Packet		92	3 s	2:19:09 PM
218	TALSIN	Broadcast	nlsp	LAN Level 1 NLSP Hello Packet		92	8 s	2:19:17 PM
219	TALSIN	Broadcast	nlsp	LAN Level 1 NLSP Hello Packet		92	8 s	2:19:25 PM
220	TALSIN	Broadcast	nlsp	Level 1 Complete Sequence Numbers Packet		116	7 s	2:19:32 PM
221	TALSIN	Broadcast	nlsp	LAN Level 1 NLSP Hello Packet		92	1 s	2:19:33 PM
222	TALSIN	Broadcast	nlsp	LAN Level 1 NLSP Hello Packet		92	8 s	2:19:41 PM
223	TALSIN	Broadcast	nlsp	LAN Level 1 NLSP Hello Packet		92	8 s	2:19:49 PM
224	TALSIN	Broadcast	nlsp	LAN Level 1 NLSP Hello Packet		32	8 s	2:19:57 PM
225	TALSIN	Broadcast	nlsp	Level 1 Complete Sequence Numbers Packet		116	692 ms	2:19:57 PM
226	TALSIN	Broadcast	nlsp	LAN Level 1 NLSP Hello Packet		92	7 s	2:20:05 PM
227	TALSIN	Broadcast	nlsp	LAN Level 1 NLSP Hello Packet		92	8 s	2:20:13 PM
228	TALSIN	Broadcast	nlsp	LAN Level 1 NLSP Hello Packet		92	8 s	2:20:21 PM
229	TALSIN	Broadcast	nlsp	Level 1 Complete Sequence Numbers Packet		116	2 s	2:20:23 PM
230	TALSIN	Broadcast	nlsp	LAN Level 1 NLSP Hello Packet		92	6 s	2:20:29 PM
231	TALSIN	Broadcast	nlsp	LAN Level 1 NLSP Hello Packet		92	8 s	2:20:37 PM
232	TALSIN	Broadcast	nlsp	LAN Level 1 NLSP Hello Packet		92	0 s	2:20:45 PM
233	TALSIN	Broadcast	nlsp	Level 1 Complete Sequence Numbers Packet		116	5 s	2:20:49 PM
234	TALSIN	Broadcast	nlsp	LAN Level 1 NLSP Hello Packet		92	3 s	2:20:52 PM
235	TALSIN	Broadcast	nlsp	LAN Level 1 NLSP Hello Packet		92	8 s	2:21:00 PM
236	TALSIN	Broadcast	nlsp	LAN Level 1 NLSP Hello Packet		92	8 s	2:21:08 PM
237	TALSIN	Broadcast	nlsp	Level 1 Complete Sequence Numbers Packet		116	7 s	2:21:15 PM
238	TALSIN	Broadcast	nlsp	LAN Level 1 NLSP Hello Packet		92	2 s	2:21:17 PM

So what happens when you combine RIP/SAP and NLSP devices on the same network? Examine Figure 15.6. Frame number 410 is Toby sending out a SAP broadcast. In return, Talsin sends out a SAP as well. In frames 412 - 415 Talsin has returned to sending out NLSP Hello packets.

In frame 416, Toby then sends out a RIP broadcast. At this point, Talsin realizes that there is a RIP/SAP device on the network and that it must switch into RIP/SAP compatibility mode to ensure that information can be exchanged with this system. Once the server sees the RIP packet, it knows that backwards compatibility is required.

FIGURE 15.6

A mixed RIP/SAP, NLSP network

No.	Source	Destination	Layer	Summary	Error	Size	Interpacket Time	Absolute Time
410	Toby	Broadcast	sap	Resp General; Server=TOBY.FOOBAR.COM		114	3 ms	5:35:21 PM
411	TALSIN	Broadcast	sap	Resp General; Server=TALSIN		370	157 ms	5:35:21 PM
412	TALSIN	Broadcast	nlsp	LAN Level 1 NLSP Hello Packet		92	7 s	5:35:28 PM
413	TALSIN	Broadcast	nlsp	LAN Level 1 NLSP Hello Packet		92	8 s	5:35:36 PM
414	TALSIN	Broadcast	nlsp	Packet sliced		148	160 ms	5:35:36 PM
415	TALSIN	Broadcast	nlsp	LAN Level 1 NLSP Hello Packet		92	8 s	5:35:44 PM
416	Toby	Broadcast	rip	Resp network=0A 01 01 0A; 1 hop		64	6 s	5:35:50 PM
417	TALSIN	Broadcast	nlsp	LAN Level 1 NLSP Hello Packet		92	2 s	5:35:52 PM
418	TALSIN	Broadcast	nlsp	LAN Level 1 NLSP Hello Packet		92	8 s	5:36:00 PM
419	TALSIN	Broadcast	nlsp	Packet sliced		148	2 s	5:36:02 PM
420	TALSIN	Broadcast	nlsp	LAN Level 1 NLSP Hello Packet		92	5 s	5:36:08 PM
421	TALSIN	Broadcast	nlsp	LAN Level 1 NLSP Hello Packet		92	8 s	5:36:16 PM
422	TALSIN	Broadcast	rip	Resp network=32 F4 78 CB; 1 hop		64	3 s	5:36:19 PM
423	TALSIN	Broadcast	sap	Resp General; Server=TALSIN		370	160 ms	5:36:19 PM
424	TALSIN	Broadcast	nlsp	LAN Level 1 NLSP Hello Packet		92	4 s	5:36:24 PM
428	TALSIN	Broadcast	nlsp	Packet sliced		148	5 s	5:36:29 PM
429	TALSIN	Broadcast	nlsp	LAN Level 1 NLSP Hello Packet		92	3 s	5:36:32 PM
431	TALSIN	Broadcast	nlsp	LAN Level 1 NLSP Hello Packet		92	8 s	5:36:40 PM
432	TALSIN	Broadcast	nlsp	LAN Level 1 NLSP Hello Packet		92	8 s	5:36:48 PM
433	Toby	Broadcast	sap	Resp General; Server=TOBY.FOOBAR.COM		114	336 ms	5:36:49 PM
434	TALSIN	Broadcast	nlsp	Packet sliced		148	6 s	5:36:54 PM
435	TALSIN	Broadcast	nlsp	LAN Level 1 NLSP Hello Packet		92	2 s	5:36:56 PM
436	TALSIN	Broadcast	nlsp	LAN Level 1 NLSP Hello Packet		92	8 s	5:37:04 PM
437	TALSIN	Broadcast	nlsp	LAN Level 1 NLSP Hello Packet		92	8 s	5:37:13 PM
438	TALSIN	Broadcast	rip	Resp network=32 F4 78 CB; 1 hop		64	5 s	5:37:17 PM
439	TALSIN	Broadcast	sap	Resp General; Server=TALSIN		370	160 ms	5:37:18 PM

So the next time Talsin sends our route and service broadcasts (417 - 423), it includes a RIP and a SAP broadcast as well. This will continue as long as Talsin thinks there is a device on the network that requires this information.

So what went wrong with our LANRover? If NetWare 4.11 is backwards compatible, why is it dropping offline? To find out why, examine Figure 15.7.

FIGURE 15.7

Shiva modem pool with a NetWare 4.11 server

C:\LZFW\SHIV2DIE.TR1

No.	Source	Destination	Layer	Summary	Error	Size	Interpacket Time	Absolute Time
31	Shiva1	Broadcast	sap	Query General All		64	5 s	5:15:33 PM
32	TALSIN	Shiva1	sap	Resp General; Server=TALSIN		370	780 µs	5:15:33 PM
33	TALSIN	Broadcast	nlsp	LAN Level 1 NLSP Hello Packet		92	3 s	5:15:37 PM
34	TALSIN	Broadcast	nlsp	LAN Level 1 NLSP Hello Packet		92	8 s	5:15:45 PM
35	TALSIN	Broadcast	nlsp	Level 1 Complete Sequence Numbers Packet		116	6 s	5:15:51 PM
36	TALSIN	Broadcast	nlsp	LAN Level 1 NLSP Hello Packet		92	2 s	5:15:53 PM
37	TALSIN	Broadcast	nlsp	LAN Level 1 NLSP Hello Packet		92	8 s	5:16:01 PM
38	TALSIN	Broadcast	nlsp	LAN Level 1 NLSP Hello Packet		92	8 s	5:16:09 PM
39	TALSIN	Broadcast	nlsp	Level 1 Complete Sequence Numbers Packet		116	8 s	5:16:17 PM
40	TALSIN	Broadcast	nlsp	LAN Level 1 NLSP Hello Packet		92	692 ms	5:16:17 PM
41	TALSIN	Broadcast	nlsp	LAN Level 1 NLSP Hello Packet		92	8 s	5:16:26 PM
42	Shiva1	Broadcast	sap	Resp General; Server=NM230A47		114	3 s	5:16:29 PM
43	TALSIN	Broadcast	nlsp	Level 1 Link State Packet		100	964 ms	5:16:30 PM
44	TALSIN	Broadcast	nlsp	LAN Level 1 NLSP Hello Packet		92	4 s	5:16:34 PM
45	TALSIN	Broadcast	nlsp	LAN Level 1 NLSP Hello Packet		92	8 s	5:16:42 PM
46	TALSIN	Broadcast	nlsp	Level 1 Complete Sequence Numbers Packet		132	852 ms	5:16:42 PM
47	TALSIN	Broadcast	nlsp	LAN Level 1 NLSP Hello Packet		92	7 s	5:16:50 PM
48	TALSIN	Broadcast	nlsp	LAN Level 1 NLSP Hello Packet		92	8 s	5:16:58 PM
49	TALSIN	Broadcast	nlsp	LAN Level 1 NLSP Hello Packet		92	8 s	5:17:06 PM
50	TALSIN	Broadcast	nlsp	Level 1 Complete Sequence Numbers Packet		132	2 s	5:17:08 PM
51	TALSIN	Broadcast	nlsp	LAN Level 1 NLSP Hello Packet		92	6 s	5:17:14 PM
52	TALSIN	Broadcast	nlsp	LAN Level 1 NLSP Hello Packet		92	8 s	5:17:22 PM
53	Shiva1	Broadcast	sap	Resp General; Server=NM230A47		114	5 s	5:17:27 PM
54	TALSIN	Broadcast	nlsp	LAN Level 1 NLSP Hello Packet		92	2 s	5:17:30 PM
55	TALSIN	Broadcast	nlsp	Level 1 Complete Sequence Numbers Packet		132	4 s	5:17:34 PM
56	TALSIN	Broadcast	nlsp	LAN Level 1 NLSP Hello Packet		92	4 s	5:17:38 PM
57	TALSIN	Broadcast	nlsp	LAN Level 1 NLSP Hello Packet		92	8 s	5:17:46 PM
58	TALSIN	Broadcast	nlsp	LAN Level 1 NLSP Hello Packet		92	8 s	5:17:54 PM

Our Shiva device (this one is a NetModem E) broadcasts a SAP looking for all local service information. Talsin then responds directly to the NetModem with a unicast reply. Talsin then goes on to transmit NLSP Hello packets as it did before.

Now, look at frames 42 and 53. Our Shiva device sends out a SAP but Talsin never replies. There is something else missing from this trace. Our NetModem never sends out a RIP broadcast. It will SAP until the cows come home, but it does not broadcast any RIP information.

This was also evident on the initial trace in Figure 15.3. The last thing our LANRover did was send a SAP to which it never received a reply.

As we mentioned in previous chapters, NetWare servers use an internal IPX network number for internal communications. This means that by default, any NetWare server will send both RIP and SAP information. The Shiva devices are not real NetWare servers, and do not have an internal IPX address to broadcast. Because these devices do not RIP, the NetWare server assumes that it does not need to switch to RIP/ SAP compatibility mode.

But if the server is not switching to RIP/SAP compatibility mode, how can we communicate at all? The answer lies in the aging time that is used by RIP and NLSP.

If we refer back to Figure 15.7, Talsin responded to the NetModem's initial SAP request. When it did this, the NetModem realized that there was a NetWare server on the wire and created a server and router entry for it. This would allow the device to carry on communications with the server. As we also noted from that figure, the NetModem started sending out SAP broadcasts to which Talsin never replied. Because the NetModem never received a SAP from Talsin, it assumed that the server must have died a firey death and removed it from its server and router tables.

So how does this apply to our initial problem? When Shiva1 was first powered up, it would send a SAP query, receive a reply, and create an entry for FS1. If we launch the Shiva Manager just after this occurs, we will be able to connect to the device and exchange information.

Once Shiva1 started sending SAP broadcasts and did not receive a reply from FS1, it assumed that the server was down and that the remote network (where the Shiva Manager was located) was no longer reachable. This interrupted the SNMP transfer in our trace as Shiva1 would not know how to reach the Shiva Manager to reply to queries. This caused the Shiva Manager to send a few final IPX queries in order to reestablish the connection. Because the device was unable to reply, the manager would eventually give up trying.

We have three possible ways of rectifying this problem:

■ Upgrade the Shiva device to support NLSP routing.

■ Have the Shiva device send RIPs as well as SAPs.

■ Switch the NetWare server into RIP/SAP only mode.

Our first option is out of the question. While the vendor may eventually be able to have their devices support NLSP, it is doubtful they can do this by throwing together a patch for you to download. Changing the way a device handles routing information cannot be done as a quick fix.

Our second option has possibilities. As mentioned, the LANRover allows users to dial-in and dial-out of the network. When a user dials-in to the network, they must appear to have a valid network and MAC address in order to communicate.

There are two ways the device could handle the inbound connection. The first would be to have the dial-in connection appear to be directly attached to the network by spoofing a MAC address. When traffic is sent to this spoofed address, the LANRover could act as a proxy and forward the information to the dialed-in user. This would make the user appear to be attached to the existing network.

If the LANRover has the ability to create a virtual IPX network—it can make the user appear to be on this phony network instead of the local network. The LANRover could then act as a router between these two segments forwarding data to the user as required.

It is this option we are most interested in because if the device sets up a virtual IPX network, it must advertise it to the rest of the network by sending RIP broadcasts. This would trigger RIP/SAP compatibility mode on our server, which would keep the device from dropping off-line.

In order to determine if this latter configuration is possible, we would need to review the device's documentation.

Our third option is probably the easiest to implement. Simply run the INETCFG utility and modify the IPX protocol to use RIP/SAP only. The only drawback with this option is that we would be unable to perform load balancing on the server. NLSP allows us to install two or more NICs per logical network segment in the server. The benefit of having two or more NICs per segment is that the server will use both cards to transmit data. This doubles the bandwidth potential while the server is transmitting. If we use RIP as our routing protocol, however, we cannot use this feature.

Excessive Network Collisions

Our next case involves a small network with slow connectivity. A diagram of this network is shown in Figure 15.8.

As you can see our network configuration is not very large. It consists of a single NT server and hub. There are only seven or eight users on the network and all equipment is one year old or less. The topology is 10 Mb Ethernet. All cabling is CAT 5 twisted-pair which was certified after installation.

The problem is that users are experiencing very slow network response. This occurs when communicating with the server, and occasionally when communicating on a peer-to-peer basis with another Windows 95 workstation.

FIGURE 15.8

A network with slow
connectivity

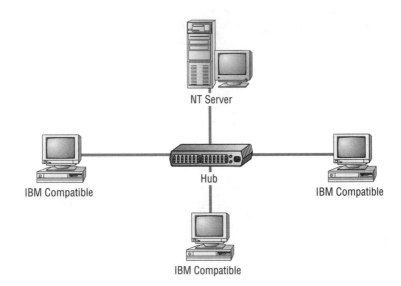

Diagnosing the Problem

Our first step should be to check the activity lights on the hub. This is
the quickest way to check if our network is seeing an excessive amount
of traffic. If the hub has a separate transmit light for each port, we may
even be able to isolate the system generating all the traffic.

If we notice a system transmitting frequently, we can trace the drop
back to the system to determine if the user is transferring a lot of information or if this failure is due to a jabbering network card.

A jabbering network card is a NIC that is stuck in a transmit mode.
This will be evident because the transmit light will remain on constantly, indicating that the NIC is always transmitting. This problem
can also be caught with a network monitor or analyzer as the frames
the jabbering NIC transmits will produce size errors. If our hub only
has a single transmit light—we will need to use a network monitor or
analyzer to isolate the offending system.

Let's assume this is not the case. The transmit light(s) is relatively
quiet, but the collision light is going off like a strobe light. We now have
a very interesting problem—we are seeing a large number of collisions
on our network but there is a relatively small amount of traffic. How
can this be?

Working Through the Problem Logically

Let's review what we know about collisions. A collision occurs when two or more NICs try to transmit data at the same time. When this happens, the transmissions collide with each other on the wire making each transmission unusable. If a system detects that it was involved with a collision, it signals a collision warning to tell all network systems to back off and stop transmitting for a moment.

So in theory, a workstation should never signal a collision unless it has first attempted to transmit data. We already noticed that the collision light is going off far more often than the transmit light(s). This means that one or more of our stations appears to be signaling collisions without first trying to transmit data. The question is, how can this occur? What would cause a NIC to send a collision signal without first trying to transmit data?

The cabling we are using is twisted-pair. You may remember from our discussion on 10 Mb Ethernet that it uses one pair of twisted-pair wires to send and receive data, and another pair to send and receive collision warning. This creates two separate circuits for our NIC cards to exchange information.

You may also remember that in a full duplexed environment, the collision pair can be used to transmit data. When only two systems exist on a collision domain, we can configure one of the systems to use the collision pair of wires when sending information and the data pair when receiving. The other system is conversely configured to receive data on the collision pair and to transmit on the data pair. The result is that both systems can transmit simultaneously without fear of causing a collision.

If one of our systems has been incorrectly configured to operate in full duplex mode, it could be attempting to transmit on the collision pair. While this is fine when we only have two systems and both are configured to operate in full duplex mode, this can be detrimental to a shared hub environment. Every time the full duplex system tries to transmit data on the collision pair, every other system will interpret this to be a collision warning and back off. The more data the offending system transmits, the slower our network response becomes, because each NIC believes that multiple collisions are taking place.

So it is possible that we have a NIC that is configured to use full duplex mode. This would explain why the collision light is going off but the transmit light is not. The problem with this theory is that the offending system would never be able to locate network resources. We would undoubtedly have a user complaining that they cannot connect to the network.

The reason we do not have a single user who is unable to access the network is that NICs can also be configured to auto-detect when they can use full duplex mode. When the NIC is initialized, it will attempt to negotiate a full duplex connection. If only one other system is detected, and both are capable of full duplex operation, the operational mode is switched from half duplex to full duplex communications.

Because this is a small environment, there is the potential that there may only be two systems active at the same time. If this is the case, what happens then? Unfortunately, many of the earlier NIC cards that were capable of negotiating a full duplex connection, were not able to detect when a hub was between them and the other NIC. The result was that the two systems would successfully negotiate a full duplex connection. As other systems would power up, the system transmitting on the collision pair would interfere with the communications of these systems.

This problem would be viewed as intermittent as all that would be required to fix the situation would be to power cycle the two systems that negotiated full duplex communications. This problem would cause network performance to be perceived as sometimes being normal, while other times being slow, even under the same traffic load.

To resolve this issue, we need to use the manufacturer's configuration utility that shipped with the NIC cards. By running the utility, you can hard set each NIC to communicate in half duplex mode only. This will ensure that full duplex mode is never negotiated between two systems.

Summary

One interesting detail to note with the last case was that the main tools we used to resolve this problem were brain power and deduction. The only other aids we used to diagnose the problem were a few blinking lights on the hub. Even a network monitor such as LANAlyzer would have been useless, because it does not monitor collisions. While some other utilities will monitor collisions, they usually represent them as a cumulative number for the entire network. They have no way of indicating which station is actually generating the collisions. In short, even our most expensive of tools would have been of little help in solving this problem.

The point here is that there is no replacement for understanding how all the pieces of a network fit together in order to communicate. There is no magick or voodoo here, only an intricate web of hardware and software that allows us to send information from point A to point B. A network administrator in a multiprotocol environment must be able to don their detective's cap, and analyze this web in order to find the root cause of any given problem.

APPENDIX

A

Resource List

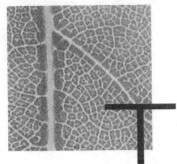

The following are resources I have found on the Internet; they not only helped me find the information I needed for this book, but have generally been wonderful aids for finding information on a variety of subjects.

HTTP://www.iol.unh.edu/training/

Located at the University of New Hampshire, this is online course material covering topologies, protocols, and even programming. It's one of the best online resources around.

HTTP://www.iftech.com/oltc

Online course material from Interface Technologies. This site covers everything from Web development to NT.

HTTP://www.ots.utexas.edu:8080/Ethernet

Charles Spurgeon's Ethernet Page. All you wanted to know about Ethernet but were afraid to ask. There is also a link page that connects to many networking vendors.

HTTP://www.access.digex.net/~ikind/babel.html

A glossary of computer related acronyms maintained by Irving Kind.

HTTP://wfn-shop.princeton.edu/foldoc/

The Free Online Dictionary of Computing, which is maintained by Dennis Howe.

`HTTP://www.nexor.com/public/rfc/index/rfc.HTML`

An online search engine of Request For Comment (RFC) documents.

`HTTP://lake.canberra.edu.au/pub/samba/`

The SAMBA Web pages. Full of information about the SAMBA suite, including online documentation and FAQs.

`HTTP://www.Linux.org`

Where to go to find out more about Linux.

`HTTP://www.windows95.com`

Contains shareware and freeware for Windows 95 and NT.

`HTTP://www.feist.com/~thrasher/bofh/`

Sometimes the best way to resolve a problem is to step back and have a good laugh. If part of your job description is Help Desk, it is easy to relate to the antics of this individual.

APPENDIX

B

Manufacturer's Ethernet Identifiers

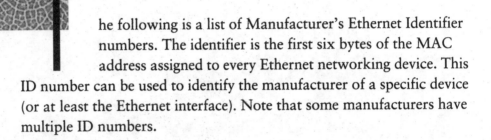

The following is a list of Manufacturer's Ethernet Identifier numbers. The identifier is the first six bytes of the MAC address assigned to every Ethernet networking device. This ID number can be used to identify the manufacturer of a specific device (or at least the Ethernet interface). Note that some manufacturers have multiple ID numbers.

00000C	Cisco
00000E	Fujitsu
00000F	NeXT
000011	Tektronix
000015	Datapoint Corp.
00001B	Eagle Technology
000022	Visual Technology
000044	Castelle
00004C	NEC Corp.
00005E	U.S. Department of Defense (IANA)
000061	Gateway Communications
000062	Honeywell
000065	Network General
00006B	MIPS
00006E	Artisoft, Inc.
00006F	Madge Networks, Ltd.

000073	DuPont
000075	Bell Northern Research (BNR)
00007D	Cray Research Superservers, Inc.
000080	Cray Communications
000081	Synoptics
000083	Optical Data Systems
000083	Tadpole Technology
000086	Gateway Communications, Inc.
000089	Cayman Systems
00008A	Datahouse Information Systems
000093	Proteon
000094	Asante
000098	Cross Com (now owned by 3COM)
0000A2	Wellfleet (now owned by Bay Networks)
0000A8	Stratus Computer, Inc.
0000AA	Xerox
0000AC	Apollo
0000B1	Alpha Microsystems, Inc.
0000C0	Western Digital (now SMC)
0000C6	HP Intelligent Networks Operation (formerly Eon Systems)
0000D1	Adaptec, Inc.
0000D3	Wang Labs
0000D7	Dartmouth College
0000E2	Acer Counterpoint
0000E3	Integrated Micro Products, Ltd.
0000EF	Alantec

0000F0	Samsung
0000F6	A.M.C. (Applied Microsystems Corp.)
0000F8	DEC
000163	NDC (National Datacomm Corporation)
0001C8	Thomas Conrad Corp.
0001FA	Compaq (PageMarq printers)
000204	Novell NE3200
000205	Hamilton (Sparc Clones)
000502	Apple (PCI bus Macs)
000701	Racal-Datacom
002048	Fore Systems, Inc.
002061	Dynatech Communications, Inc.
002067	Node Runner, Inc.
002094	Cubix Corp.
0020A6	Proxim, Inc.
0020AF	3COM
0020D2	RAD Data Communications, Ltd.
0020F8	Carrera Computers, Inc.
00400C	General Micro Systems, Inc.
00400D	LANNET Data Communications
004023	Logic Corp.
004025	Molecular Dynamics
004028	Netcomm
004032	Digital Communications
004033	Addtron Technology Co., Ltd.
004054	Thinking Machines Corporation

004057	Lockheed-Sanders
004068	Extended Systems
00406F	Sync Research, Inc.
004074	Cable and Wireless
004076	AMP Incorporated
004088	Mobuis
00408C	Axis Communications AB
004095	Eagle Technologies
00409A	Network Express, Inc.
00409D	DigiBoard
00409E	Concurrent Technologies, Ltd.
00409F	Lancast/Casat Technology, Inc.
0040A6	Cray Research, Inc.
0040B4	3COM K.K.
0040C2	Applied Computing Devices
0040C5	Micom Communications Corp.
0040C6	Fibernet Research, Inc.
0040C8	Milan Technology Corp.
0040CC	Silcom Manufacturing Technology, Inc.
0040DF	Digalog Systems, Inc.
0040E5	Sybus Corporation, Inc.
0040EA	PlainTree Systems Inc
0040ED	Network Controls International, Inc.
0040F0	Micro Systems, Inc.
0040FB	Cascade Communications Corp.
0040FF	Telebit

00608C	3Com
008000	Multitech Systems, Inc.
008006	Compuadd
00800F	SMC (Standard Microsystem Corp.)
008010	Commodore
008013	Thomas Conrad Corp.
008019	Dayna Communications
00801A	Bell Atlantic
00801B	Kodiak Technology
008021	Newbridge Networks Corp.
008023	Integrated Business Networks
008024	Kalpana
008026	Network Products Corp.
008029	Microdyne
00802A	Test Systems & Simulations, Inc.
00802C	The Sage Group PLC
00802E	Plexcom, Inc.
008038	Data Research & Applications
00803E	Synernetics
00803F	Hyundai Electronics
008043	Networld, Inc.
008048	Commodore
008057	Adsoft, Ltd.
00805B	Condor Systems, Inc.
00805F	Compaq
008060	Network Interface Corp.

008072	Microplex Systems, Ltd.
008079	Microbus Designs, Ltd.
00807B	Artel Communications Corp.
00807C	FiberCom
008087	Okidata
008090	Microtek International, Inc.
00809A	Novus Networks, Ltd.
0080A1	Microtest
0080A3	Lantronix
0080AD	Telebit
0080AE	Hughes Network Systems
0080B1	Softcom A/S
0080C7	Xircom, Inc.
0080C8	D-Link
0080D3	Shiva
0080D8	Network Peripherals
0080F3	Sun Electronics Corp.
0080FE	Azure Technologies, Inc.
00AA00	Intel
00B0D0	Computer Products International
00C007	Pinnacle Data Systems, Inc.
00C00D	Advanced Logic Research, Inc.
00C013	Netrix
00C017	Fluke
00C01B	Socket Communications
00C01C	Interlink Communications, Ltd.

00C01D	Grand Junction Networks, Inc. (now owned by Cisco)
00C021	Netexpress
00C025	Dataproducts Corporation
00C027	Cipher Systems, Inc.
00C02E	Netwiz
00C031	Design Research Systems, Inc.
00C033	Telebit
00C036	Raytech Electronic, Corp.
00C039	Silicon Systems
00C04D	Mitec, Ltd.
00C051	Advanced Integration Research
00C055	Modular Computing Technologies
00C058	Dataexpert Corp.
00C064	General Datacomm Ind, Inc.
00C065	Scope Communications, Inc.
00C06D	Boca Research, Inc.
00C080	Netstar, Inc.
00C081	Metrodata, Ltd.
00C084	Data Link Corp, Ltd.
00C087	UUNET Technologies, Inc.
00C08E	Network Information Technology
00C09F	Quanta Computer, Inc.
00C0A0	Advance Micro Research, Inc.
00C0AA	Silicon Valley Computer
00C0AB	Jupiter Technology, Inc.
00C0B0	GCC Technologies, Inc.

00C0B3	Comstat Datacomm
00C0B5	Corporate Network Systems, Inc.
00C0B6	Meridian Data, Inc.
00C0B7	American Power Conversion Corp.
00C0B9	Funk Software, Inc.
00C0BA	Netvantage
00C0C2	Infinite Networks, Ltd.
00C0CB	Control Technology Corporation
00C0ED	US Army Electronic Proving Ground
00C0F3	Network Communications Corp.
00C0F4	Interlink System Co., Ltd.
00C0FA	Canary Communications, Inc.
020701	Racal-Datacom
026060	3Com
02608C	3Com
080001	Computer Vision
080002	3Com
080007	Apple
080009	Hewlett-Packard
08000A	Nestar Systems
08000B	Unisys
08000F	SMC (Standard Microsystems Corp.)
080011	Tektronix, Inc.
08001B	Data General
08001E	Apollo
08001F	Sharp

080020	Sun
08002B	DEC
08002F	Prime Computer
080030	CERN
08003E	Motorola
080046	Sony
08005A	IBM
080069	Silicon Graphics
080079	Silicon Graphics
080087	Xyplex
080089	Kinetics
08008F	Chipcom (now owned by 3COM)
09006A	AT&T
10005A	IBM
1000D4	DEC

Index

Note to the Reader: Throughout this index **bold** page numbers indicate primary discussions of a topic. *Italicized* page numbers indicate illustrations.

NOW AVAILABLE WHEREVER COMPUTER BOOKS ARE SOLD.

GURU MARK MINASI PROVIDES UNDOCUMENTED & EXCLUSIVE SOLUTIONS.

If you use NT Server — as a system administrator, help-desk person, MIS professional, or corporate programmer — you absolutely need this high-level, irreverent, readable discussion of essential operations, undocumented featrues, secrets, and walkarounds of the new Windows NT Server. This newest edition of the world's #1 NT Server classic is heavily revised to reflect changes and enhancements to the product since its release in August.

Mark Minasi, Christa Anderson,
Elizabeth Creegan
ISBN 0-7821-2067-9
$54.99

SYBEX Inc. • 1151 Marina Village Parkway • Alameda, CA 94501 • 510-523-8233